This sketch, entitled "The Route across the Pacific Discovered by the Augustinian, Andrés de Urdaneta", shows the route followed by the Manila galleons on their annual trek from New Spain, today Mexico, to the Philippines. Note the return eastward journey that led north from the Philippines, east of Japan, and south along the west coast of North America. The westward trip, out of Acapulco, followed a southerly route, at approximately 10° N, until it reached the vicinity of the Micronesian islands, then it veered north toward Guam and Rota, and from there on to the Philippines. By permission of the Museo Oriental de los Padres Agustinos Filipinos, Valladolid.

# THE LIFE AND MARTYRDOM OF
# DIEGO LUIS
# DE SAN VITORES, S.J.

FRANCISCO GARCÍA

MARC MONOGRAPH SERIES No. 3

Copy Editor: Marjorie G. Driver
Design and Technical Editors:
Melissa G. Taitano
Mary M. Castro
Brian Bell
Ron J. Castro

Copyright © 2004, 2024, Univresity of Guam Press.
All rights reserved.

Delete the ISBN that is currently at the bottom of the copyright page
and the statement about the book being manufactured in the US and
instead put the following ISBNs below "All rights reserved.":
ISBN: 978-1-878453-55-6 (hardback)
ISBN: 978-1-935198-99-4 (paperback)
ISBN: 978-1-961058-00-2 (library ebook)
ISBN: 978-1-961058-01-9 (trade ebook)

Francisco García, S.J.

*The Life and Martyrdom
of the Venerable Father*
# Diego Luis de San Vitores
*of the Society of Jesus
First Apostle of the Mariana Islands
and
Events of These Islands
From the Year Sixteen Hundred and Sixty-Eight
the Year Sixteen Hundred and Eighty-One*

*Translated by*
Margaret M. Higgins
Felicia Plaza, M.M.B.
Juan M.H. Ledesma, S.J.

*Edited by*
James A. McDonough, S.J.

Richard Flores Taitano
Micronesian Area Research Center
University of Guam

Originally published as *Vida y martyrio de el Venerable Padre Diego Luis de Sanvitores, de la Compañía de Jesús, primer apóstol de las Islas Marianas y sucesos de estas islas desde el año de mil seiscientos y sesenta y ocho asta el de mil seiscientos y ochenta y uno.* Madrid: Ivan García Infanzón. 1683.

## MARC MONOGRAPH SERIES
## NO.3

*Spanish Documents Collection
Richard F. Taitano Micronesian Area Research Center,
University of Guam*

This publication was supported by funds granted to
MARC's Spanish Documents Collection by
*The Twenty-Third Guam Legislature*

by grants from

*The Guam Humanities Council*
funded, in part, by the National Endowment for the Humanities

*The Guam Historic Resources Division of the
Department of Parks and Recreation*

*The N.M.I. Division of Historic Preservation*

The publication was assisted by grants provided by the Historic Preservation Fund grant, from the U.S. Department of the Interior, National Park Service. Any opinions, findings, and conclusions or recommendations expressed in this material are those of the author(s) and do not necessarily reflect the views of the U.S. Department of the Interior. The Guam Historic Resources Division of the Department of Parks and Recreation and the N.M.I. Division of Historic Preservation receive federal financial assistance for identification and protection of historic properties. Under Title VI of the Civil Rights Act of 1964, Section 504 of the Rehabilitation Act of 1973, and the Age Discrimination Act of 1975, as amended, the U.S. Department of the Interior prohibits discrimination on the basis of race, color, national origin, age, sex, sexual orientation, or disability in its federally assisted programs. If you believe you have been discriminated against in any program, activity, or facility as described above, or if you desire further information, please write to the Office of Equal Opportunity, National Park Service, 1849 C Street, N.W., Washington, D.C. 20240.

*TO THE PEOPLE OF THE MARIANA ISLANDS*

# ILLUSTRATIONS

**Frontispiece.** Sketch showing the route of the galleons across the Pacific from the Philippines to Mexico, returning via the Mariana Islands. From the poster *"Agustinos en America y Filipinas,"* International Conference, Valladolid, 16–21 April 1990. Courtesy of the Museo Oriental.

**Fig. 1.** García, Francisco, S.J. *La vida y martyrio del venerable padre Diego Luis de Sanvitores...* Ivan García Infanzón, Madrid. 1683. ................................................................................................ xx

**Fig. 2.** Father Diego Luis de San Vitores, S.J., before departing for the Indies. An image preserved in the archives of the Marqueses de la Rambla, heirs to the brother of the martyred priest. From: Ledesma, Juan M.H. S.J. *The Cause for Beatification of Ven. Diego Luis de San Vitores, Apostle of the Marianas.* Manila and Agaña: Sacred Congregation for the Causes of Saints Historical Section 94. Deposition (*Positio Historica*) on the life and martyrdom officially presented. Rome. Translated from the Spanish by Juan M.H.Ledesma, S.J. Tamuning: Guam Atlas Publications. c.1986. ................................................................ 2

**Fig. 3.** "A true likeness of the Venerable Father Diego Luis de Sanvitores." Engraving by Gregorio Fosman. Source unknown. ......... 82

**Fig. 4.** Map of the Archipelago of St. Lazarus, or the Mariana Islands, by Jacobo Nicolás Bellin, 1752, based on the charts of Father Alonso López and the *Memoria* of Father Luis Morales, Spanish Jesuit missionaries in these islands. From *The General History of the Voyages,* by Jacobo Nicolás Bellin, naval engineer, 1752. ....... 164

**Fig. 5.** A painting of Father Diego Luis de San Vitores. At one time it was in the Catholic Church, at Garapan, Saipan. From: *The South Sea Islands, Geography and Customs of Japan.* Vol. 1. Shinkosha, Tokyo, 1931. Microfilm (MARC Collection). ................... 258

**Fig. 6.** "The Reigning Queen." *Doña* Mariana de Austria, 1635-1696. Source unknown. ......................................................................... 328

**Fig. 7.** Map of the Island of Guam, by Alonso López, S.J. From: Charles Le Gobien, S.J., *Histoire des Isles Marianes nouvellement converties à la Religion Chrestienne; et de la mort glorieuse des premiers Missionnaires qui y ont prêche la Foy.* Chez Nicolas Pepie, Paris. 1700. ................................................................ 330

# CONTENTS

Illustrations . . . . . . . . . . . . . . . . . . . . . . . . . . . . . . . . . . . . . . . . . . . . . . vi

Contents . . . . . . . . . . . . . . . . . . . . . . . . . . . . . . . . . . . . . . . . . . . . . . . . vii

Editor's Preface to the Translation, by James A. McDonough, S.J. . . . . . . . . xii
Introduction to the Translation, by Francis X. Hezel, S.J. . . . . . . . . . . . . . xv
Addendum to the Translation, by Marjorie G. Driver . . . . . . . . . . . . . . . . xix

*The Life and Martyrdom of the Venerable Father Diego Luis de San Vitores*
      Dedication to María Guadalupe, Duquesa de Aveyro y
           Maqueda, Duquesa de Arcos . . . . . . . . . . . . . . . . . . . . . . xxii
      Authorization by the Order . . . . . . . . . . . . . . . . . . . . . . . . . . . . . . xxiii
      Approval of Dr. Simón Fernández de Molinillo. Madrid.
           Synodal Examiner . . . . . . . . . . . . . . . . . . . . . . . . . . . . . . xxiv
      Authorization by the Ordinary . . . . . . . . . . . . . . . . . . . . . . . . . . . . xxv
      Approval of the most Reverend Father Dr. Agustín de Herrera.
           Alcalá. Synodal Examiner . . . . . . . . . . . . . . . . . . . . . . . xxvi
      License to Publish . . . . . . . . . . . . . . . . . . . . . . . . . . . . . . . . . . . . xxvii
      Tariff . . . . . . . . . . . . . . . . . . . . . . . . . . . . . . . . . . . . . . . . . . . . . xxvii
      To Mary Most Holy . . . . . . . . . . . . . . . . . . . . . . . . . . . . . . . . . . xxviii
      Author's Prologue and Disclaimer . . . . . . . . . . . . . . . . . . . . . . . . . xxvix

## Book One

### Of the Life and Martyrdom of the Venerable Father Diego Luis de San Vitores, of the Society of Jesus, First Apostle to the Mariana Islands

| | | |
|---|---|---|
| Chapter I. | The Birth of the Venerable Father Diego Luis de San Vitores | 3 |
| Chapter II. | The Childhood and First Studies of the Servant of God | 7 |
| Chapter III. | His Miraculous Vocation to the Society of Jesus | 12 |
| Chapter IV. | The Great Obstacles to His Entering the Society of Jesus | 16 |
| Chapter V. | The New Obstacles That Diego Overcomes and the First Omens of His Martyrdom | 22 |
| Chapter VI. | Having Overcome New Obstacles, Diego Enters the Society and God Makes Known His Pleasure | 28 |
| Chapter VII. | His Novitiate and Studies | 36 |
| Chapter VIII. | His Ordination and First Assignments | 42 |
| Chapter IX. | As A Professor of Philosophy at the Colegio de Alcalá | 47 |
| Chapter X. | His Mission of the *Acto de Contrición*; Other Successful Missions in Spain | 52 |
| Chapter XI. | His Vocation to the Indies and the Supernatural Signs by Which God Manifests His Will | 58 |
| Chapter XII. | He Obtains Permission to Go to the Indies | 68 |
| Chapter XIII. | His Departure for Cádiz for Embarkation; Prophesies and Happenings Along the Way | 73 |
| Chapter XIV. | He Embarks for New Spain; the Good Works He Performs on the Voyage | 78 |

[contents cont.]

## Book Two

### Of the Life and Martyrdom of the Venerable Father Diego Luis de San Vitores, of the Society of Jesus, First Apostle to the Mariana Islands

| | | |
|---|---|---|
| Chapter I. | The Venerable Father Diego Luis de San Vitores's Many Good Works in the City of Mexico; Extraordinary Happenings | 83 |
| Chapter II. | He Restores a Sodality of Saint Francis Xavier and Tries to Establish a Shelter for Women | 91 |
| Chapter III. | Father San Vitores's Departure for the Philippines and His First Calling to the Islands of the Ladrones | 95 |
| Chapter IV. | He Goes From Manila to Taytay to Learn the Tagalog Language; the Wonders He Performs Among These People | 98 |
| Chapter V. | The Good Works Father San Vitores Performs in Manila | 102 |
| Chapter VI. | The Missions of the Servant of God in the District of Manila | 106 |
| Chapter VII. | His Mission in the Mountains of Santa Inés and Maralaya | 110 |
| Chapter VIII. | Father San Vitores's Mission on the Island of Mindoro and the Hardships He Suffered | 113 |
| Chapter IX. | The Means the Servant of God Used to Convert the Infidels; the Obstacles Imposed by the Devil | 118 |
| Chapter X. | Extraordinary Happenings and Divine Providence in the Mission of Mindoro | 123 |
| Chapter XI. | The Miracles With Which God Confirms the Preaching of His Servant on the Island of Mindoro | 131 |
| Chapter XII. | In Manila, He Applies for the Mission to the Ladrones | 136 |
| Chapter XIII. | He Appeals to the King for His Desired Mission | 140 |
| Chapter XIV. | How He Obtains Permission to Go to the Islands of the Ladrones; the Signs Whereby the Lord Manifests His Pleasure With This Mission | 144 |
| Chapter XV. | Father San Vitores Sails for Mexico in order to Go to the Marianas; the Wonders of the Voyage | 148 |
| Chapter XVI. | The Great Obstacles He Overcomes in Mexico With the Aid of Heaven, in Order to Continue the Voyage to His Longed-for Mission | 151 |
| Chapter XVII. | The Voyage of the Servant of God to the Marianas | 156 |

[contents cont.]

## Book Three

### Of the Life and Martyrdom of the Venerable Father Diego Luis de San Vitores, of the Society of Jesus, First Apostle to the Mariana Islands

Chapter I. The Nature of the Mariana Islands; the
Temperament and Customs of Their People ................. 165

Chapter II. Their Religion and Government ........................................... 172

Chapter III. The Venerable Father Diego Luis de San Vitores's
First Entry into the Mariana Islands and the
Premonition of Evil ............................................................. 176

Chapter IV. How He Began the Church and Residence in
Agadña, and the Method He Used to Catechize
the Infidels ............................................................................ 181

Chapter V. He Distributes His Companions Throughout the
Islands, and the Baptism of Adults Begins ...................... 186

Chapter VI. The Persecution That an Idolatrous Chinese
Instigates Against the Faith, and How the
Servant of God Converts Him ........................................... 190

Chapter VII. The State of the Church in the Marianas After the
Victory Over Choco ............................................................. 196

Chapter VIII. The Servant of God Goes to the Island of Tinian
and the Neighboring Ones; How He Dresses and
Conducts Himself When Visiting the Villages ................. 200

Chapter IX. He Establishes a Seminary for Boys on the Island of
Guam, and He Dedicates the Church in Agadña ........... 205

Chapter X. Father San Vitores Visits the Islands Already
Discovered and Discovers Those of Assonson and
Maug; the Beginning of the War on Tinian ................... 212

Chapter XI. The Pacification of the Island of Tinian and Some
Miraculous Happenings ...................................................... 218

Chapter XII. He Returns to the Island of Guam and Sets
Admirable Examples ........................................................... 225

Chapter XIII. New Companions Arrive to Join Father San Vitores;
How He Sends Three *Marianos* to Manila ...................... 229

Chapter XIV. The Origin of the Great War on Guam; How it Is
Prophesied in Mexico by the Beads of Sweat on a
Statue of Saint Francis Xavier .......................................... 234

Chapter XV. The War of the *Marianos* and the Victory of the
Spaniards Due to the Prayers of the Servant of God ..... 238

Chapter XVI. The Last Missions of the Servant of God and the
Death of Several Lay Companions .................................... 245

Chapter XVII. Father San Vitores's Glorious Death for Christ ................. 251

[contents cont.]

## Book Four

### Of the Life and Martyrdom of the Venerable Father Diego Luis de San Vitores, of the Society of Jesus, First Apostle to the Mariana Islands

| | | |
|---|---|---|
| Chapter I. | Father San Vitores's Reputation for Sanctity Among His Own and Among Strangers | 259 |
| Chapter II. | The Greatness of His Sanctity and His Perfection | 264 |
| Chapter III. | His Faith, Hope, and Charity | 268 |
| Chapter IV. | His Charity Toward His Neighbor | 273 |
| Chapter V. | His Admirable Prudence | 281 |
| Chapter VI. | His Justice in Regard to God | 285 |
| Chapter VII. | His Justice in Regard to Other Persons | 294 |
| Chapter VIII. | His Invincible Fortitude | 298 |
| Chapter IX. | His Rare Temperance | 302 |
| Chapter X. | With What Excellence the Gifts of the Holy Spirit Were Found in the Venerable Father San Vitores | 307 |
| Chapter XI. | Of the Graces *Gratis Datae* With Which God Adorned His Great Servant | 310 |
| Chapter XII. | How Father San Vitores Was Endowed With the Three Halos of Martyr, Doctor, and Virgin | 318 |
| Chapter XIII. | The Miracles and Apparitions of the Venerable Father San Vitores After His Martyrdom | 321 |

## Book Five

### Of the Lives of Some Companions of Father Diego Luis de San Vitores and Events in the Marianas After His Martyrdom, Until the Year 1681

| | | |
|---|---|---|
| Chapter I. | The Birth and Manners of the Venerable Father Luis de Medina Before He Enters the Society of Jesus | 331 |
| Chapter II. | His Entrance Into the Society and His Life in it Until He Departs for the Indies | 336 |
| Chapter III. | Father Luis Departs for the Indies; What He Does on the Voyage | 347 |
| Chapter IV. | The Achievements of the Venerable Luis de Medina in the Mariana Islands and the Hardships He Suffered | 353 |
| Chapter V. | Father Luis de Medina's Death for Christ With His Companion Hipólito de la Cruz and the Discovery of Their Blessed Remains | 365 |
| Chapter VI. | The Virtues and Miracles of Father Luis de Medina | 374 |
| Chapter VII. | The State of the Christian Community in the Mariana Islands After the Martyrdom of Father San Vitores, and the Death of Several Spanish Soldiers for a Good Cause | 385 |
| Chapter VIII. | A Brief Account of the Virtues of Father Francisco Solano, Companion of Father San Vitores | 395 |
| Chapter IX. | Happenings in the Mariana Islands After the Death of Father Francisco Solano | 401 |

[contents cont.]

| | | |
|---|---|---|
| Chapter X. | The Happy Death of Father Francisco Ezguerra and Five Lay Companions | 408 |
| Chapter XI. | The Life of the Angelic Martyr, Francisco Ezguerra | 414 |
| Chapter XII. | Several Uprisings of the Natives Are Quieted and the State of the Christian Community Is Improved After the Martyrdom of Father Ezguerra | 424 |
| Chapter XIII. | New Disturbances Are Quieted and Greater Progress for the Faith Is Made; Several Miracles That God Worked for His Soldiers | 431 |
| Chapter XIV. | Brother Pedro Díaz and Two Lay Companions Die in Defense of Chastity; the Virtues of This Venerable Brother | 438 |
| Chapter XV. | The Very Religious Life of Father Antonio María de San Basilio, Killed at the Hands of the Barbarians | 445 |
| Chapter XVI. | Miracles That God Worked in Honor of His Most Holy Mother; Several Happenings at This Mission | 452 |
| Chapter XVII. | The Great Treachery of the Barbarians Against the Jesuits and the Spaniards; the Precious Death of the Venerable Father Sebastián de Monroy and Seven Military Companions | 457 |
| Chapter XVIII. | A Brief Eulogy of the Venerable Father Sebastián de Monroy | 463 |
| Chapter XIX. | New Wars of the Barbarians Against the Jesuits and the Spaniards | 470 |
| Chapter XX. | Gains for the Christian Community With the Success of the Spanish Arms | 479 |
| Chapter XXI. | The New Gains of the Christian Community in the Marianas Following the Punishment of Several Rebels and Malefactors | 488 |
| Chapter XXII. | Christianity in the Marianas Progresses Rapidly With the Establishment of New Villages and Churches | 497 |
| Chapter XXIII. | The Present State of the Mariana Islands; Success That Has Been Attained These Past Years and What Is Hoped for in the Future | 504 |

Appendix ........................................................................................... 511

Glossary ............................................................................................ 512

Acknowledgments ............................................................................ 514

Index ................................................................................................. 525

# EDITOR'S PREFACE

The title of this work, *The Life and Martyrdom of the Venerable Father Diego Luis de San Vitores, of the Society of Jesus, First Apostle of the Mariana Islands, and Events of These Islands, from the Year Sixteen Hundred and Sixty-Eight, through the Year Sixteen Hundred and Eighty-One*, by Fr. Francisco García, S.J., informs us that this book is both a life of Diego Luis de San Vitores, S.J., and a narrative of events in the Mariana Islands from the death of Fr. San Vitores in 1672, until the year 1681. It is fortunate that Father García (1641-1685) undertook this work when he did, because he was able to use many contemporary letters and documents, personal and official, and to consult with persons involved in that history. Of particular importance were the account of Fr. Diego Ramírez, S.J., and the testimonies collected in Mexico and the Philippines shortly after the death of Fr. San Vitores, in view of possible beatification and canonization. Many of these testimonies García quotes verbatim. Others he wove into the narrative. In all this he was conscious, as he tells us, of an obligation to write true history, so that even the limitations of García's point of view are instructive to us.

García's *Life and Martyrdom of San Vitores* appeared in Madrid in 1683. The title of the original work was *Vida y martyrio del Venerable Padre Diego Luis de Sanvitores de la Compañía de Jesús, primer apóstol de las Islas Marianas y sucesos de estas islas desde el año de mil seiscientos y sesenta y ocho, hasta el de mil seiscientos y ochenta y uno*. The printer was Juan García Infanzón. Although either García or the printer ran San Vitores together as one work (i.e., as "Sanvitores"), the Blessed Diego Luis always wrote his patronymic as two words.

The first published English translation of García's biography of the Blessed Diego Luis de San Vitores, S.J., was a partial translation that appeared serially in the *Guam Recorder* from September 1936 to July 1939. That translation was the work of Margaret M. Higgins, and she entitled it *The First History of Guam*. Higgins included just those parts of the original work that she considered to be of general historical interest, omitting the first two Books and much else. The reader who reads the whole work – 616 pages in the original Spanish – may wish at times that the other translators had followed her example. Yet in all the varied content of this *Life and Martyrdom*, one will find significant facts that were lost in the process of abridgement and important insights into the history and ethnology of the Philippines, the Marianas, and even Spain.

The remaining portions of García's book were subsequently translated by the late Sr. Felicia Plaza, M.M.B., and the Reverend Juan M.H.Ledesma, S.J. The following list specifies the translators of the five books and multiple chapters into which García divided his life of San Vitores:

| | | |
|---|---|---|
| Book One | Chapters I–XIV | Plaza |
| Book Two | Chapters I–XVII | Plaza |
| Book Three | Chapters I–IV | Plaza |
| | Chapters V–XVII | Higgins |
| Book Four | Chapters I–XIII | Ledesma |
| Book Five | Chapters I–IV | Ledesma |
| | Chapter VII | Higgins |
| | Chapter VIII | Ledesma |

| Chapter IX | Higgins |
| Chapters X–XI | Ledesma |
| Chapters XII–XXIII | Higgins |

Notes marked (M.H.) are the work of Higgins. The rest of the notes are mine. The glossary and the index are the work of myself and of Dr. Michael T. Hamerly. Words found in the *American Heritage Dictionary of the English Language* (3$^{rd}$ ed.) are not explained in the glossary or the notes. Terms requiring explanation that appear frequently, such as *colegio* or *acto de contrición*, are defined in the glossary, but terms requiring explanation that appear only once or a few times at best are defined in notes. As the editor, I am responsible for all deficiencies in the translation.

García's *Vida y martyrio* of San Vitores is a special book, a work of its own time and place, with its own objectives and point of view. These define its choice of materials and its message. Thus this book has a twofold purpose: as the life of a saintly man and his companions it was intended to inspire the reader to a deeper religious life, while, as the story of the mission, it was supposed to publicize the mission enterprise and to provide a permanent record of it. Letters and publications about the mission are a tradition of the Society of Jesus, begun by Saint Ignatius Loyola and continuing until the present day.

It was a book of its time, an age that looked for miracles in ordinary coincidences, in which religious experience was often expressed in sentimental language and in the social forms of his day, and yet it was an age that produced classics of religious literature. In García's book we see the "new lands" of the Philippines and the Marianas through the eyes of scholarly men of the last years of the Renaissance, of Spain's Siglo de Oro, of the Golden Age of Cervantes, Calderón de la Barca, and Velázquez. Their background gave them both vision and blindness. They were not cultural anthropologists. Yet the opening chapters of Book Three are a unique source of information about Chamorro culture in the mid-seventeenth century.

Like their fellow Jesuits in the missions of South America, Father San Vitores and his companions dreamed of creating a utopia, a Christian utopia (they called it a *Cristiandad*), free of the vices of the Old World, cleansed of its own vices, living in peace and in health, blending the best of its own culture with that of Spain. The lack of minerals and other sources of wealth would discourage European adventurers from settling in the Marianas. The few soldiers needed for protection and police work could easily be kept under control. That was the dream. What happened was different. Most of the islands' people did not want a Christian utopia. They preferred their pleasant vices and their feuding, and they resented the incessant churchgoing to which baptism bound them. They saw no reason why foreigners should change their customs and control their lives. And when the Chamorros declared war on the Spaniards to drive them out or to exterminate them altogether, the colonial authorities finally sent enough soldiers to conquer the islands. What percentage of the villages freely joined in these wars and how many abstained is not clear.

Worst of all, the epidemics that were devastating the cities of Europe struck these islands with equal or even deadlier effect. Two of the first priests in the Marianas arrived mortally ill with tuberculosis, exposing a virgin population to this always debilitating, then usually fatal, disease. If we compare what statistics for battle casualties are available for those thirteen years (1668-1681) of the history of the Marianas with what we know of the history of epidemics in the islands from other sources, we will see that it was disease– not war– that wiped out most of the original population of these islands.

Father San Vitores and his companions came to bring new life to the islands. Instead, they brought death, swift and terrible. It was a tragic price to pay for the richness and diversity of the present island culture, with its echoes of pre-Spanish society and the contributions of Spanish, Western Pacific, and contemporary international cultures.

JAMES A. McDONOUGH, S.J.

Agaña, Guam
October 1994

# INTRODUCTION

Francisco García's book is of a genre that has no modern equivalent. Although its title would seem to stamp it as a biography, the book might better be described as part history, part hagiography, part travel adventure, and part devotional literature. It is easy to understand why García's biography was translated into English piecemeal. Three different translators extracted from the volume what corresponded to their own interests, Margaret M. Higgins selecting what touched on the local history and culture of the Chamorro people, Sr. Felicia Plaza excerpting those parts that touched directly on the life of San Vitores, and Fr. Juan Ledesma translating the remainder.

The idiom of García's volume is as foreign to us today as is the genre. His confident recounting of miracles attributed to San Vitores and some of his Jesuit companions strains the credulity of the modern reader. We are chagrined to find that every little event in San Vitores's life is presented as a moral parable. Will we never be spared the sermonizing that comes through on page after page? The book is cast in a style that was as familiar to the seventeenth century Spanish readers as it is alien to most of us today. We must consider that García's readers lived in a world of sharp contrasts, a milieu in which reminders of the universally accepted religious truths were to be found everywhere. The struggle between good and evil was reflected ceaselessly in everyday life, with the opposing powers often taking the forms of devils and angels. There are few accidents of life in this seventeenth century Spanish Catholic view of the world: the purposeful intervention of God, one of the dominant themes in García's work, emerges on every page.

García's original was intended as a testimony to the saintliness of Diego Luis de San Vitores, the man who introduced the Christian faith to the Marianas. It was written as a tale of personal heroism, its hero the Jesuit missionary priest whose virtues were not allowed to speak for themselves but were authenticated by numerous instances of divine intervention. Miracles, those extraordinary instances of God's action in the world, were regarded as rather common occurrences in the day in which García wrote, and the volume offers many examples. But such excesses, as we would regard them today, and the simplistic world view that inspired this style of writing should not blind us to the fact that the book rests on a solid historical base. We should recall that García drew upon the missionaries' own letters an annual reports to fashion his biography. Although some of his sources have been preserved and can be found among the rich Spanish Collection at the Micronesian Area Research Center, many are no longer extant and have only been preserved in the secondary form in which they appear in García's book.

While drawing a portrait of the life and virtues of his subject, García also intended to present to his readers a history of the first Jesuit missionary enterprise in the Mariana Islands.

All this would seem, a dubious distinction in the judgment of many today. If San Vitores was venerated by García and his European contemporaries as the bearer of the message of salvation, there are many of our own day who regard him as sowing the seeds of cultural destruction. The message of peace that San Vitores intended to convey was somehow perverted into a violent force that all but swept away the people and their ways. San Vitores, the hero of García's volume, is the villain of many a modern day revisionist history. Even if the so-

xv

called Spanish-Chamorro wars were never the bloodbath they were often depicted as being by authors who were no less ingenuous than García, albeit in a very different way, the Chamorro population was incontestably reduced to a mere fraction of what it had been just before the arrival of the first missionaries. Mounting evidence shows that it was the scourge of disease and epidemic rather than the notoriously inaccurate arquebuses of the small rag-tag company of Spanish and Filipino troops that led to depopulation. Although this mitigates the charges of deliberate genocide, it does nothing to reduce the death toll. Even worse in the eyes of nineteenth and twentieth century critics, the survivors were herded into towns and forced to live as colonized subjects of a foreign king.

Then why this publication? García's book offers us a *text*, to use the term of which post-modernists are so fond. As Margaret Higgins recognized, it offers an almost first-hand, if biased, chronicle of the first lasting contact between the people of the Marianas society and Europeans. However filtered the vision of these events, García's work offers a far more primitive text than the derivative French narrative of Fr. Charles LeGobien, *Histoire des Isles Marianes*, which had been preferred for generations. The popularity of LeGobien's account over the decades is in large part due to the greater availability of this work, which was translated into English years ago. With this translation of García, we may hope that this oversight will be corrected. In the future those with historical interests in Marianas history and San Vitores's personal religious journey may consult one of the oldest primary sources on both.

Francisco García, the author of this work, died just two years after his life of San Vitores was first published in 1683. García, a Jesuit priest who spent years working in Madrid, was an ardent publicist for the overseas missions even though he himself had never served in one. García corresponded directly with some of the Jesuit missionaries in the Marianas and related news of their achievements to the Duchess d'Aveiro and to Mariana, the queen mother of Spain and generous benefactor of the missions. His published works included the lives of three Jesuits who labored and died in the Marianas: Luis de Medina, the first of the missionaries to be martyred, and Carolus Borango, another martyr, in addition to San Vitores. García's devotion to the work of his fellow Jesuits led to his appointment as assistant postulator for the causes of several Spanish Jesuits. García also penned several biographies of Jesuits who had already been raised to the altar, among them Ignatius Loyola, Francis Xavier, and Francis Borgia.

The scope of the book includes not just the four brief years of San Vitores's life on Guam, but another ten years of missionary work following his death. The volume offers a detailed narrative of the early critical years of mission activity between 1668 and 1682 in this earliest of mission fields in Oceania. As a historical source for this period García's book is indispensable.

García's main purpose, of course, was to promote the advancement of San Vitores, a fellow Jesuit, toward beatification and canonization – that is, official church recognition of his sanctity and formal confirmation of his status as a model for others of his faith. A few years after his death, his brothers in the Jesuit order recognized the heroic virtues of San Vitores's life and proposed his as a candidate for beatification, the first step toward sainthood. As time passed, San Vitores's process became dormant. Only about twenty-five years ago was it revived, thanks to the interest of Guam's late Bishop Felixberto Flores, and San Vitores was finally beatified more than three centuries after his death on Guam. In a ceremony that took place in Rome in October 1985, Fr. Diego Luis de San Vitores was elevated to the status of Blessed Diego Luis.

García portrays San Vitores as the bearer of religious and cultural treasures to the islands he sought to convert. San Vitores was not only charged with the task of bringing the people of the Marianas to the faith; the *patronato* system that dispatched missionaries to the most remote parts of the Spanish realm required him to lead the Chamorro people to submission before Spanish law and civilization. By the terms of this *patronato* system, San Vitores was to be a harbinger of both the gospel and colonial rule, the latter seen not only as a prerequisite of the former but as a value in its own right. He could rightly be called, then, not only the proto-missionary of the Marianas but its proto-colonizer. The "blessings" that endued, although envisioned as aiding the people of those islands, were in reality mixed. From the perspective of our own day, they may appear tragic. Yet, we do the man and his work an injustice unless we attempt to see his program through the lens of the beliefs of his day rather than our own.

From an historical point of view, San Vitores was much more than the man who led both priests and troops into the Marianas to usher in a period of Spanish rule that lasted for two centuries and brought a Catholicism that has endured to the present day. He was the first missionary in the entire area between the Americas and the east Asian coast that goes by the name of Oceania. The christianization of the Pacific islands followed in time, but San Vitores was the vanguard of a force that, in its various denominational forms, swept the Pacific within the next two centuries and won enthusiastic acceptance throughout the area. Christianity may have entered the Pacific as yet another innovation, but it has not remained such. The church, adapted into and reshaped by local cultures, has been absorbed into the very bloodstream of these island societies. Today the church everywhere in the Pacific wears distinctive island garb.

The life of San Vitores was widely acclaimed in the religious circles for which it was written. An Italian translation of García's work on San Vitores came out in 1686, and the German version appeared in 1732. LeGobien incorporated much of García's original material in his own chronicle of Jesuit work in the Marianas, which was published in 1700.

An English translation of García's volume was not attempted until the twentieth century, and even then only in parts. Margaret Higgins, a Guam resident with a passion for local history, translated most of Book Five and published it serially in the *Guam Recorder* between 1936 and 1939. Years later, in 1985, the portion she translated was published as a monograph by the Flores Memorial Library under the same title as this present volume.

The next major contributor to the translation process was Sr. Felicia Plaza, a Mercedarian sister who had taught on Saipan for many years before she began working for the Micronesian Area Research Center of the University of Guam. More than any other single person, Sr. Felicia was responsible for the rapid growth of MARC's prized collection of Spanish documents. From 1968 she traveled widely in Europe and Mexico to gather copies of key materials on the early missionization and colonization of the Marianas. In 1972, Sr. Felicia completed the translation of Books One and Two, and the first four chapters of Book Three. In 1980 her English version of the first part of Book Three appeared as a monograph (No. 22) of the MARC Working Papers.

Fr. Juan Ledesma, S.J., was the third person to contribute to the English translation. Ledesma is a Filipino Jesuit who, like García himself, has had a lifelong interest in the achievements of his religious brothers. After assisting the postulator for Fr. San Vitores's cause for beatification, between 1985 and 1989, Ledesma translated the remainder of García's book: Book Four (on the miracles of San Vitores) and the later chapters of Book Five. Even before this, he rendered Alberto Risco's book on San Vitores into English. This was published in 1970 under the title *The Apostle of the Marianas*.

xvii

It was left to Fr. James McDonough, S.J., a priest who has served on Guam for over thirty years, to pull together and polish these partial translations, shaping them into this present volume, the first full English translation of García's biography of San Vitores. During the three decades he has worked on the island on which San Vitores shed his blood, Fr. McDonough has assumed many different roles. At times Fr. Jim has been a teacher, at times an administrator at the University of Guam, but always a dedicated Jesuit priest whose life and labors have proclaimed the same ideals that San Vitores lived and died for. Let this translation of a memorial to the man who inaugurated the evangelization of Oceania also stand as a testimony to the good works and devotion of Fr. Jim McDonough, one of his spiritual offspring.

This volume, the first full English translation of García's life of San Vitores, is fittingly published on the 350th anniversary of the ordination of the man who instituted the evangelization of Oceania.

Francis X. Hezel, S.J.
December 23, 2001

# ADDENDUM

During the fall of 2001 members of the faculty and staff of the Richard F. Taitano Micronesian Area Research Center and several others made a Herculean effort to prepare a memorial volume of *The Life and Martyrdom of the Venerable Diego Luis de San Vitores* to commemorate the 350th anniversary of the martyred missionary's ordination. On December 23, 2001, the anniversary date, a beautifully encased commemorative volume was presented to His Excellency the Reverend Archbishop of the Diocese of Agaña, Anthony Sablan Apuron, O.F.M. Cap., D.D., at the Dulce Nombre de María Cathedral in Agaña.

Yet, copyediting remained to be done to ready the lengthy manuscript for publication. Once that work was finished, electronic manuscript specialist Mary M.Castro prepared the camera-ready copy for printing.

An attempt has been made to standardize the work of the three translators and, with few exceptions, the guidelines set forth in *The Chicago Manual of Style*, Fourteenth Edition, have been followed.

Marjorie G. Driver
February 25, 2003

Fig. 1. A copy of the title page of Father Francisco García's original Spanish volume, published in 1683, in Madrid.

*The Life and Martyrdom*

*of the*

*Venerable Father*

# Diego Luis de San Vitores

*of the Society of Jesus*

*First Apostle of the Mariana Islands*

*and*

*Events of These Islands*

*From the Year Sixteen Hundred and Sixty-Eight*

*Through the Year Sixteen Hundred and Eighty-One*


**By Father Francisco García**

*of the Same Society of Jesus*


*Dedicated*

*To the Most Excellent Señora*

*Doña María de Guadalupe,*

*Duquesa de Aveyro y Maqueda,*

*Duquesa de Arcos*


*With Privilege*

*In Madrid: By Ivan García Infanzón*

*In the Year MDCLXXXIII*

*(1683)*

# TO THE MOST EXCELLENT
## Señora Doña MARIA de GUADALUPE,
### Duquesa de Aveyro y Maqueda,
### Duquesa de Arcos
### S.G.

When I was asked to write the biography of the life of the Venerable Father Diego Luis de San Vitores and the history of the Mariana Islands, there was no question as to whom I would dedicate the book, which by any criterion is Your Excellency's. Without speaking of Your Excellency's greatness, to whom everyone owes veneration, or of the many obligations that our Society of Jesus ascribes to your Excellency, of which we, all her sons, are consummate debtors, especially myself, for the special honors that I receive from Your Excellency. Because of the topic and the individual, it would be criminal and an outrage were it to be dedicated to anyone other than Your Excellency.

The book exists because of Your Excellency, since it is the life of the Venerable Father Diego Luis de San Vitores, whose insatiable zeal is clearly reflected in that of Your Excellency–a peerless example among those of your sex and station in life–who so strongly yearns to spread the Faith to the four corners of the earth, sending apostolic missionaries to Asia, Africa, and America–not forgetting Europe–as the result of your concern, your tireless energy, and your wealth; nourishing compassion as religion becomes a reality, as Your Excellency is the missionary of all missionaries, consequently of all missions; preaching through the words of so many preachers, who can only preach by example: yearning to imitate what is permissible between what is human and what is so divine, for the glory of Jesus, the glory of Mary, celebrated by the Holy Church that stilled the world's heresies, thereby achieving the praise that Christ showered on another Mary: *Ubicumque praedicatum fuerit evangelium istud in universo mundo, quod fecit hec narrabitur in memoriam eius.*

In regard to the Mariana Islands, they owe no less to you than to Father San Vitores. Although he planted the Faith there, Your Excellency's zeal, authority, and concern have saved this apostolic mission from great and powerful enemies. Your Excellency has been the shield that defended it from so many afflictions, the safe harbor in so many storms, the support for its growth. Thanks to their Majesties' royal Catholic compassion, the mission today has strong support: a *Presidio* of soldiers to defend it, a zealous governor to rule, and a boat to communicate [with its neighbors]. Your Excellency's charitable gifts have adorned the churches, vested the altars, and clothed the living temples of Christ, the nude *Marianos.* You make it seems as though what you do and what you give is not much, but only because it is less than your zeal and generosity.

Your Excellency's modesty does not permit such heroic actions to be celebrated, nor does their greatness allow them to be properly praised, but the Lord will reward them eternally in heaven. On earth, he rewards them with the prize given to those who serve him in the salvation of souls, wanting those who accomplish much to suffer much, so that they will be great in the kingdom of heaven, accomplishing and enduring, achieving and teaching. And as Your Excellency is so Marian because of your love and zeal, God will reward you as he does the Mariana mission, causing it to suffer as he seeks to exalt it, proving that he is pleased with your gifts by sending you travails, like the maxim Rafael directed to Saint Tobias, who was always occupied in doing good to everyone: *Quia acceptus eras Deo, necesse fuit ut probatio tentaret te,* which a famous historian of our times says more humanly, though with great elegance and discretion in his native French: "This has always been the destiny of great men, to do great things while suffering great persecutions, so that their virtue, which is above praise and recompense may expect a reward only from God."

I shall not speak of Your Excellency's perseverance and magnanimity, as Seneca and Caton both said: *Ecce espectaculum dignum ad quod respiciat intentus operi suo Deus. Ecce par Deo dignus vir, fortis cum mala fortuna compositus, utique si provocavit. No video inquani quid habeat in terris Jupiter pulchrius, si convertere animun velit, quam ut spectet Catonem iam partibus non semel fractis, stantem nihilominus inter ruinas publicas erectum.*

I shall not mention the other excellent qualities of character and charm with which God has generously endowed Your Excellency: so much prudence, so much discretion, such a knowledge of languages, such a knowledge of sciences, so many examples of compassion, so many testimonies of religion, together with an abundance of perfections, so superior that fortune itself might be envious and knows only to do battle with those it should please. In sum, *Señora*, Your Excellency is a phenomenon worthy of the gods, which the most discrete philosopher paints for us, and which, with the Great Apostle, even Your Excellency might add, if your modesty did not embarrass you, *Spectaculum facti sumus mundo, et angelis et hominibus*.

May God keep Your Excellency's most excellent person many years, as the Marianas and all the missions need you, and as all sons of our Society wish and implore of the Lord, of which I am the least worthy one and Your Excellency's most indebted chaplain who kisses your hand.

Francisco García

## AUTHORIZATION BY THE ORDER

I, Diego Jacinto de Tevar, Provincial of the Society of Jesus, in the Province of Toledo, by the authority vested in me by our Very Reverend Father Carlos Noyelle, Provost General of the Society, hereby grant permission to print the book on the life and martyrdom of the Venerable Father Diego Luis de San Vitores, a priest of the Society of Jesus, and of the events in the Marianas following his martyrdom, until the year 1681, written by Father Francisco García, a priest of our Society. It has been seen and examined by serious and learned persons of the Society to whom we submitted it. In testimony of which we submit this document, signed with our name and sealed with the stamp of our office, in this our Colegio Imperial of Madrid, on the twentieth day of the month of May, of the year one thousand six hundred eighty-three.

Diego Jacinto Tevar

# THE APPROVAL OF DOCTOR DON SIMON FERNANDEZ DE MOLINILLO, FORMER COLLEGIATE OF THE COLEGIO MAYOR de SAN ILDEFONSO, PRESENTLY THE CURATE OF MADRID'S PARISH OF SANTA CRUZ AND THE SYNODAL EXAMINER OF THIS ARCHBISHOPRIC OF TOLEDO

In compliance with Your Majesty's order, I have seen the book entitled *The Life and Martyrdom of the Venerable Father Diego Luis de San Vitores, of the Society of Jesus, First Apostle to the Mariana Islands*. Its author is the Reverend Father Francisco García, a priest of the Society of Jesus. God has rewarded the special affection that I had for this outstanding man by placing in my hands the book that recounts his life, before the public is able to enjoy it. In this book, I have read with amazement what I have seen and venerated with admiration and tenderness. In order to give credence to the written word, it is necessary to see with one's eyes and feel with one's hands the greatness of his work, so that the author's pen may not be suspected of exaggerating his accomplishments by placing him in a more exalted position than that which his merits deserve.

Fate takes some men under her wing and from birth, or when the light of reason is born in them, leads them with sure steps along roads so holy on the way to perfection, that as they proceed on the road of life, their steps take them closer to ordination. They were born to be saints, and as the goal is arduous and difficult, Fate disposes that they start on the road at an early age. Prominent among these was Father Diego Luis de San Vitores, in whom perfections matured in such a manner that it appears he had no childhood, for the fruit and maturity of age were already noticeable during his tender years. Growth and new interests characterized his life; and no pause is known to have interrupted his goodness, the gold of his life increasing its carats, until finally, upon his death, steel provided its most precious gloss to the saintliness of his life: the crown of martyrdom.

I was fortunate to see him and communicate with him at the University of Alcalá, where he taught natural philosophy to the men of his order. He taught the highest Christian philosophy to everyone at the university, providing such magnificent examples of saintliness, and his zeal was so discreetly religious, that even the licentious youth, finding themselves led where they did not want to go, could not find it in themselves to stop caring or fail to comply with the advise that Father Diego Luis de San Vitores, with his gentle force, persuaded them to follow. Most of those at the university chose him as their confessor, although they were among the least interested in the blessings of salvation. I was one among others, and what happened to me happened to many: we did not want to change our confessor, because, although the blame was the penitent's, Diego assumed the pain and the repentance. When the penitents found that the most difficult part was already finished, they came to his feet without resistence, because from his pain came the repression of their sins. In order to reprove the penitents, Diego imposed contrition on them, which they did not have. I have read and meditated over this story several times and the same will happen to those who read it, because the examples make goodness so gratifying, and his zeal provides so much fire to the most lukewarm spirits that they urge meditation, his example soothing the harshness, because, without doubt, it is possible to do what he did.

All the books submitted by the author for the stamp of approval have received the applause of the learned, the veneration of the virtuous, and at the same time, recognition of his work, because everyone seeks them out for their enlightenment. Consequently, he has established his credibility among all those at Court. There is no one in Madrid who cannot report on the Apostle of the

Indies, Saint Francis Xavier, a natural result of people who want to see the object of their adoration.

This blissful circumstance was denied people in the past century, when Xavier, the new Paul, flourished. And now, the author, bringing to light the life of Father San Vitores, whom we all knew, the new apostle of the Mariana Islands, gives them the Xavier that they so desire, and he is so vividly portrayed that they will not miss seeing Xavier, when they see Luis. If the Pythagoreans reached Xavier and Luis, then, by using them, they will uphold such a transfer of souls from one body to another, and they would believe that the soul of Xavier had passed to the soul of our Luis. He who saw Luis, saw Xavier; he saw a heart so expansive that he needed new worlds in which to placate himself; he saw a new Apostle of the Indies in regions unknown; he saw how ardent and embracing was his zeal, one that the ice of many seas could not chill. He saw the insatiable thirst for winning souls for God, a thirst that caused the thirst to convert by converting. He saw those tricks, so saintly human, to do everything with everyone to win all, without forgiving actions at odds with his modesty, in order to make peace between God and the course barbaric souls of the *Marianos* and of other more savage nations, who even renounced their men's clothing, so as not to demean the boorishness of their customs. He saw an Xavier, who like the phoenix, rose a century later in Luis. Everyone wants to see Xavier. Your Majesty should satisfy these justifiable desires, by ordering that this book be sent to the printer as soon as possible, because there is nothing in it that is not favorable to the Faith, to religion, or to Christian perfections. This is my opinion: *Salvo meliori*. Basing myself on what is instructed in the decrees of Urbano VIII, of holy memory, concerning the printing of books about those who die with a reputation for saintliness.

In Santa Cruz de Madrid, 20 May 1683
Doctor *don* Simón Molinillo


## AUTHORIZATION BY THE ORDINARY

I, Doctor *don* Antonio Pascual, Archdeacon of Las Selvas, Dignidad, and Canon of the holy church of Girona, and Vicar of this *Villa* of Madrid and its ecclesiastical district,by the authority of the Most Eminent *señor* Cardinal Archbishop of Toledo, etc., my lord. With this, we hereby make it possible to print and do authorize the printing of the book entitled *The Life and Martyrdom of the Venerable Father Diego Luis de San Vitores, of the Society of Jesus, First Apostle of the Mariana Islands*, written by Father Francisco García, of the Society of Jesus, mindful of the censorship of Doctor *don* Simón Fernández Molinillo, curate of the parish church of Santa Cruz, of this *villa*, since there is nothing in it contrary to our Holy Catholic Faith and its good customs.

Given in Madrid on 20 May in the year 1683.

Doctor *don* Antonio Pasqual

By his order,
Juan Alvarez de Llamas
Notary.

# THE APPROVAL OF
## THE MOST REVEREND FATHER DOCTOR
## AGUSTIN DE HERRERA,
## PROFESSOR *de PRIMA* OF THEOLOGY AT THE
## UNIVERSITY OF ALCALA,
## HIS MAJESTY'S *PREDICADOR*,
## AND THE SYNODAL EXAMINER
## FOR THIS ARCHBISHOPRIC OF TOLEDO, etc.
## M.P.S.

I have read the biography of the Venerable Father Diego Luis de San Vitores, written by Father Francisco García, of our Society. And, as I had the pleasure of knowing and dealing with him, from the time he entered the Society until he left for the Indies to follow the apostolic calling of the conversion of souls–as well as the glory and crown of martyrdom–the memory of him touches me. I was close to him during his novitiate and studies, and later as a priest, a teacher of philosophy and theology, and an apostolic missionary. At all times and in all his pursuits, everyone who knew him admired and venerated him because of his great virtues. From the time he crossed the threshold into religious life, he was looked upon as a saint, and as he grew in age, he grew in virtue and perfection, and at this point, when we all dealt with him, our concept of his virtue and saintliness grew beyond doubt. Although he was very young when he entered religious life–he was only twelve years old–he went about his affairs with such valiant zeal, prudence, and maturity, that it seemed as though the perfection of youth and the white hair of age were intertwined. He was never known to act as a child or to invoke his age as an excuse, rather, it seemed that as one especially chosen, God had gifted him with uncommon grace and prudence, so that all his actions would be admirable and miraculous.

At such a tender age, with such pure innocence, his austere penance was astonishing, as though his life was among the most scandalous. He continued his studies with the same enthusiasm he showed during his novitiate, and he began at that time to reveal his consuming zeal for the salvation of souls, which he later continued in various missions in Spain. Still later, he perfected his zealous activities, suffering great hardships, converting innumerable infidels in New Spain, in the Philippines, and finally in the Mariana Islands, of which he became the apostle. There, after immense travails, unnumerable conversions, and amazing miracles, a savage cutlass (*catana*) stained his glorious crown of martyrdom–as our glorious father, Saint Ignatius had foretold him– and which his fervent and ardent zeal had sought beyond the immense oceans and into the far corners of the world.

What is written about this life is so extensive and so glorious, yet it does not exaggerate in any way the concept that we all had in Spain of his prodigious virtue. His humble discreet charm made him our beloved brother and amiable companion, but our respect for his great virtues already venerated him as one of the saints of the Church. If his preaching in the Indies had been less prodigious, and if the news of his glorious martyrdom had not reached us with the accounts of so many examples of his fervent zeal and unconquerable patience, we would have been most surprised, because the firm concept of his saintliness and the assurance of his martyrdom was so strong in those of us who knew him, that we did not expect news, doubt, or suspicion, but rather the certainty of the greatest and the most glorious of all that was worthy of an apostolic spirit. In sum, I believe this book deserves to be brought to public light and to be printed many times in the press, for all to enjoy. This is my opinion, *salvo meliori*.

From this Colegio Imperial of the Society of Jesus
27 May 1683

Agustín de Herrera

## LICENSE TO PUBLISH

His Majesty has granted The Very Reverend Father Francisco García, of the Society of Jesus, the license to publish, during a period of ten years, the book that he has authored, entitled *The Life and Martyrdom of the Venerable Father Diego Luis de San Vitores, of the Society of Jesus, and Events in the Mariana Islands*. No other person may print it without his consent, as the license implies.

Authorized in the *oficio* of Manuel de Moxica,
Escribano de Cámara del Consejo Real

20 June 1683

## TARIFF

The gentlemen of the Consejo Real have taxed this book entitled *The Life and Martyrdom of the Venerable Father Diego Luis de San Vitores and Events in the Mariana Islands*, at six *maravedís* per sheet, as noted in said tariff.

Authorized in the *oficio* of Manuel de Moxica,
Escribano de Cámara del Consejo Real.

Madrid, 6 September 1683.

# TO MARY MOST HOLY

Mother of heaven and earth, Mother of the Redeemer of men,
Protector of the human race, Mistress of the apostles, Queen of the martyrs,
Special patron of the Mariana Islands, honored with her name,
So as to merit her protection, assuring the protection of her name
and that of Mary's great servants, Saint Ignatius of Loyola
and Saint Francis Xavier,
Two lights of the world, two luminaries of heaven,
The first, the founder of the Society of Jesus, the second,
the glory of the same Society,
Xavier, the apostle of the Indies, Loyola, the apostle of Xavier,
both apostles of Luis,
Whom the latter wanted in his house to be a martyr,
Whom the former wanted in the Indies to be an apostle,
Ignatius seeking his mother's permission, Francisco snatching him from illness,
And Mary, more of an apostle than both of them, called him to
the Society of Jesus,
Where he was to become an apostle and a martyr.

O.D.G.

The praises, examples, and virtues of the
Venerable Father Diego Luis de San Vitores.
Father Francisco García, of the Society of Jesus,
so that Mary with her powerful intercession,
Loyola and Xavier with their effective pleas,
may bring to life the lifeless words, energize the written examples,
so that those who read the admirable life may imitate the virtues,
may repeat the examples,
and may deserve the praises of such a divine man,
so that many saints may be born of one saint; of one apostle, many apostles,
and who may with his life and evangelic preaching,
converting Gentiles, heretics, Moors, Jews,
and sinners, may fill the world with the faithful,
fill the Church with those perfect ones,
fill the heavens with the blessed
for the greater glory of God,
to honor Mary,
the praise of Saint Ignatius of Loyola and Saint Francis Xavier,
with all the angels and saints
of the Heavenly Court.

# AUTHOR'S PROLOGUE and DISCLAIMER

Everything written in this work on the life, martyrdom, virtues, and miracles of the Venerable Father Diego Luis de San Vitores is based on the information gathered by the ecclesiastical authorities of Mexico, the Philippines, and the Marianas in view of his beatification, and also on his own letters and those of his companions and of other persons who communicated with and dealt with him. All these papers I have seen and read and have at my disposition.

That which is recounted in the second, third, fourth, and fifth chapters [of Book One] is based on an [unpublished] account entitled "The Childhood of *don* Diego San Vitores and His Efforts to Enter the Society of Jesus." This was written by Father Diego Ramírez, a man of exceptional learning in every branch of letters, human and divine, of exemplary life and apostolic zeal that he exercised for many years in missions throughout Spain and in other forms of preaching. [Father Ramírez, S.J., (1589-1647). His *"Niñez, pretensión, y entrada en la Compañía de don Diego San Vitores"* has been authenticated. It includes San Vitores's letters of 12 June 1640, and of 10, 17, 27 July 1640 to his father.] When age and illness put an end to his mission journeys, Father Ramírez became Prefect of Studies in the grammar division of the Colegio Imperial [in Madrid] at the time when *don* Diego chose him as his confessor and made several general confessions to him. Father Ramírez also received Diego's account of conscience, the story of his soul up until he entered the Society. The prudent counselor marveled at the action of God's grace, saying with those people in the hill country of Judea long ago: "What then shall this child be, for the hand of the Lord is with him." [Luke 1:66. The version of the Bible used by the author was the Vulgate. All translations from Latin are by the editor.] Father Ramírez has left us a written account of what he saw and experienced so that it might not be forgotten, so certain was he, as he said, that one who entered the course with such giant steps toward perfection would one day be a great saint. These papers were found by chance, or rather by the Providence of God, when the news of *don* Diego's martyrdom came, in the Colegio of Murcia, where Father Ramírez had died. He had left orders that they be kept till the proper time, without being shown to any person, a prudent measure, because no one should be so praised before his death. The authenticity of the document was tested and proved, inasmuch as acquaintances of Father Diego Ramírez recognized his handwriting, lest anyone should suppose his account to be exaggerated or incredible.

Obeying the decrees of His Holiness Urban VIII regarding the printing of books that treat persons who are not yet canonized or beatified, as a priest and as a religious I promise to tell all the truth, which is the soul of history. Nonetheless, I must protest that when I call Father Diego Luis de San Vitores or any of his companions saint, apostle, or martyr, or refer to any miracle or prophecy, it is not my intention to anticipate the judgment of the Apostolic See, whose office it is to verify such claims, all of which I leave to the determination of the Church.

xxix

# BOOK I

*Of the Life and Martyrdom of the Venerable Father Diego Luis de San Vitores, of the Society of Jesus, First Apostle of the Mariana Islands*

Fig. 2. At the request of his father, Diego Luis de San Vitores reluctantly sat for this portrait before he left Madrid on his way to the mission field in the Philippines. (See page 74).

# CHAPTER I

*The Birth of the Venerable Father Diego Luis de San Vitores*

The all-powerful and all-merciful Lord whose hand is not too short to save, as Isaiah says,[1] sends into the world in every age apostolic men, imitators of the first apostles, whose sanctity edifies the Church, whose example inspires the faithful, and whose zeal and preaching enlighten the Gentiles and convert sinners. In this century God has given one of these to the Society of Jesus, fruitful mother of such children, namely the Venerable Father Diego Luis de San Vitores. In the innocence of his ways, in his vocation to the religious life, and in his observance of the rules of his order, he was a second Aloysius Gonzaga; and in the fire of his zeal, in the fervor of his preaching, and in the extension of his conquests for the gospel, he was a second Francis Xavier, truly a new apostle to the barbarians, a glorious martyr, a learned professor, a delicate soul whom the Lord adorned with so many graces and privileges that he might be a worthy vessel of election who would carry forth God's name to new islands and peoples where the trumpet of truth had never been heard before.

It is my intention to record his life and death, his virtues and miracles, basing my account on all the information gathered by the bishops of Mexico, the Philippines, and the Marianas in view of his beatification; also on his own letters and those of his companions and of other persons who communicated with and dealt with him. All these papers I have seen and read and have at my disposition. And although as priest and religious I promise to tell all the truth, which is the soul of history, still, when I call Father Diego Luis de San Vitores, or any of his companions, saint, apostle, or martyr, or refer to any miracle or prophecy, it is not my intention to anticipate the judgment of the Apostolic See whose office it is to verify such claims, and I submit all this to the determination of the Church.[2]

The Venerable Father Diego Luis de San Vitores was a citizen of the noble City of Burgos, ancient capital of the kings of Castille, a city famed for its beauty, its history, its countryside, and above all for its sons renowned in letters, in arms, and in sanctity. And among these Father San Vitores was outstanding. From his considerable learning he forged a weapon to conquer new kingdoms for Christ, and with his sanctity he brought a new glory to his native land. His parents were *don* Jerónimo San Vitores de la Portilla, Knight of the Order of Santiago, and *doña* María Alonso Maluenda. Noble ancestry, of course, adds nothing to the greatness of a saint, since, as the satirist says, what we ourselves have not done we cannot claim as our own.[3] Yet, although our Diego Luis gave up

---

[1] Isa. 50:2; 59:1.

[2] The preceding paragraph was transferred to this place in the text by Sister Felicia Plaza. It originally formed the first and last paragraph of García's Prologue.

[3] Juvenal, *Satires*, VIII. This is the subject of Satire VIII; see especially 8:1-2, 68-70.

*Book One, Chapter 1*

titles of nobility for the love of Christ, I must mention that the family tree was planted from time immemorial in the mountain country of Burgos, in the Merindad of Transmiera, in the place from which the family takes its name, and was transplanted to Burgos by the ancestors of *don* Jerónimo over two hundred and fifty years ago. Aside from its links with the most illustrious families of the city, this family has produced men outstanding in arms and in the sciences, men who have held positions worthy of their genius.

Not to mention *don* Francisco de San Vitores who in the time of the Duke of Parma defended the castle of Louvain besieged by the king of France,[4] as well as others who shed their blood for king and country. *Don* Jerónimo de San Vitores, father of our Diego Luis, had a distinguished career. He was twice procurator to the Court (at Madrid) for the City of Burgos. His second term, in 1647, was under special circumstances, since he was elected while absent. This had never happened before, but it did happen later to his son, *don* Joseph de San Vitores, *Marqués* de la Rambla and *Visconde* de Cabra, *Gentil hombre de la boca*,[5] and member of the Council of the Treasury of His Majesty.

After *don* Jerónimo had served His Majesty in offices of great honor, he died as councilor to the Royal Treasury and as major auditor. But all this is unnecessary in the evaluation of this gentleman, since his piety is enough to do honor to his name, as his son so often said.

I should mention another distinguished member of the San Vitores family, the Most Reverend *don* Alonso de San Vitores, Superior General of the Order of Saint Benedict, and later bishop of Orense, Almería, and Zamorra, and author of *El Sol del Occidente*, a learned two-volume commentary on the *Rule of Saint Benedict*.

The noble tradition of the family of *doña* María Alonso Maluenda is famous in Spain. I will merely mention one well-known example of outstanding devotion, that of her ancestor Fernán Alonso Antolínez, son of Martín Alonso Antolínez, cousin of the Cid. Thus it will be seen how the piety of this Servant of God was inherited both from his father's side and his mother's.

As Almanzor, King of Córdoba, with a powerful army made his way to besiege the Count of Castille, Fernán González, in the town of Santisteban de Gormaz, the count determined to sally forth and meet him in the open field.[6] All his knights armed themselves for battle. Fully armed, Fernán Alonso entered the church of Nuestra Señora del Rivero to hear Mass. He left his servant at the door with his horse, to be readily available.

The trumpet sounded for battle, but Fernán Alonso, out of devotion to the Mass, stayed till the end of the one he was attending and of another which had begun. Such was his usual practice. When he left the church he realized that the count had already defeated the Moors, and he felt embarrassed because he himself had not taken part in the battle along with the other knights. But God wished to prove through a

---

[4] Alessandro Farnese, Duke of Parma (1545-1592), commander of the Spanish Forces in the Low Countries, 1569-1592.

[5] *Gentil hombre de la boca*, a courtier whose function was to accompany the king on certain public functions.

[6] The tradition apparently refers to Muhammad Almanzor (939-1002), Muslim general.

*The Birth of the Venerable Father Diego Luis de San Vitores*

miracle how much he had appreciated Fernán Alonso's devotion, that Fernán Alonzo had won the victory with his prayer as much as the others had with their lances. The guardian angel of Fernán Alonso had appeared dressed as Fernán Alonso and performed such heroic feats that the count and others gave credit for the success of the day to Fernán Alonso. Apparently all the marks of the blows received by that knight (the angel) on the field of battle had been transferred to Fernán Alonso's armor and horse. The count thanked him and made reference to Easter *(Pascua)*, the day on which it had happened, saying, "Because of you, we have such a happy Easter *(Por ti hemos tenido tan alegre día pascual. Vivas)*. With the final words, in memory of the event, Fernán Alonso was henceforth called by the name of *Pascual Vivas*. Everyone used this name, never his real one, so that *Pascual Vivas* was carved on his tomb, which stands by the doorway of Nuestra Señora del Rivero. His epitaph was proper to the simplicity of those days, days when swords were sharpened to cut off the heads of the enemy, not for trimming pens. It read: "Here lies *Vivas Pascual*, whose weapons were fighting on the field of battle, while he was hearing Mass, and this is so."

Notable though *doña* María Alonso was for her ancestors, she was much more so for her sons, as she had two martyrs, one for the faith, the other for charity, both members of the Society of Jesus. This noblewoman, in a previous marriage to *don* Juan de Quintanadueñas, had among other children a certain Juan de Quintanadueñas, Knight of the Order of Saint John of Jerusalem and of Malta. When he was young, he was prevented by his parents from entering the Society of Jesus. And so, on an expedition from Malta, he disembarked in Sicily, where he insisted so persistently that the Jesuits could not refuse to accept him. From Sicily he transferred to the Province of Castille, in which he completed his studies and was ordained priest. Then he joined the Japanese mission with the desire of converting many souls to Christ and of shedding his blood for the love of God. And God changed the martyrdom that he desired and gave him a shorter one instead. He embarked at Lisbon in 1637, where the plague struck the fleet, and he died serving the plague-stricken on board. He ministered to them in body and soul, and thus received the sickness that charity offered, instead of the fire and the sword that awaited his zeal in Japan.

We cannot disregard amid this well-ripened fruit another flower gathered for heaven, namely *don* Miguel de San Vitores, a blood brother to Diego Luis. *Don* Miguel died when he was seven. Though so young, his kindness was so great that if he encountered a beggar, his heart was moved to compassion and he would give him his breakfast or afternoon snack, and often enough he would give him his clothes, too. The promise of sanctity in both these brothers pleased God. He willed that the desire of the one for sanctity and the other for martyrdom after converting many pagans would bear fruit in Father Diego Luis de San Vitores, who grew to great holiness and won over to the Lord innumerable souls. He would deserve the crown of martyrdom, as we will see in the course of this history.

This glorious martyr was born on November 12, 1627. From birth he was marked by our Father Saint Ignatius as his own. His mother, when in labor, was in danger of death and of losing her child. She applied to her body a signature of Saint Ignatius, commending herself with full confidence. And so after brief pain, on a platform, without any assistance, she delivered her child with full confidence in the saint to whom she commended herself. The child was baptized on November 19 in the parish of San Gil, in Burgos, and they gave him as special patrons our Lady and Saint Martin, Pope and Martyr. They gave him as first name "Diego" and as his second "Jerónimo" after his father, but this he changed to "Luis" when he entered the Society. He did this as a sign of separating himself from the ties of the flesh as well as in the hope of resembling Saint Aloysius (Luis) Gonzaga, his model and patron. Diego's father, who wrote in a notebook the births and baptisms of his children, would add these words to the names of all the others: "May God bring you up for his service." But he changed his style in the case of Diego, and his pen, governed as by a superior hand, wrote: "May God make you a saint."

Not only Saint Ignatius but also Saint Dominic wished to have a part in the life of this blessed boy, who was to imitate these two apostolic patriarchs in their zeal. When he was four or five-years old, he was seized by three illnesses, all at the same time. Any one of these would have been enough to overcome even a more robust constitution. A very bad case of smallpox with a high fever was followed by diptheria and a severe pain in the side. The weak patient struggled against these three powerful enemies. Neither nature nor medicine were able to counteract them, and Diego found himself one day without any feeling. All thought him dead. He remained so for some hours. They applied a relic of Saint Dominic to him, sprinkling him with water in which they had bathed it. At once he rose from the bed, hail and hearty, uttering broken cries throughout the house, "Saint Dominic of Soria has cured me."[7] Diego remained very devoted and indebted to Saint Dominic. When he was in the Marianas, every year on August 4 he celebrated his feast. When asked by his companions why he did so, he answered, smiling as at a boyhood memory, that he owed him his life, that as a small boy he seemed to see in a dream an image of Saint Dominic of Soria that said to him, "Get up, Saint Dominic of Soria has healed you."

---

[7]Saint Dominic de Guzmán lived for many years in the province of Soria, hence Soriano.

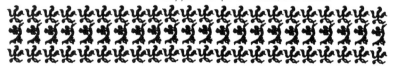

# CHAPTER II

*The Childhood and First Studies of the Servant of God*

In this chapter and the four following ones I will base my narrative on an account called *Childhood of Don Diego San Vitores and His Efforts to Enter the Society of Jesus*. This was written by Father Diego Ramírez, a man of exceptional learning in every branch of letters, human and divine, of exemplary life and apostolic zeal, which he exercised for many years in missions throughout Spain and in other forms of preaching.[8] When age and illness put an end to his mission journeys, he became prefect of studies in the grammar division of the Colegio Imperial (in Madrid) at the time when *don* Diego studied there. *Don* Diego chose him as his confessor and made several general confessions to him. He also received Diego's account of conscience, the story of his soul up until he entered the Society. This prudent counselor marveled at the action of God's grace, saying with those people in the hill country of Judea long ago: "What then shall this child be, for the hand of the Lord is with him."[9] He has left us a written account of what he saw and experienced, so that it might not be forgotten, so certain was he, as he said, that one who entered the course with such giant steps toward perfection would one day be a great saint. These papers were found by chance (or rather by the providence of God when the news of his martyrdom came) in the archives of the *colegio* of Murcia, where Father Ramírez had died. He had left orders that they be kept till the proper time without being shown to any person, a prudent measure, since no one should be so praised before his death. The authenticity of the document was tested and proved, since acquaintances of Father Diego Ramírez recognized his handwriting, lest anyone should suppose the account to be exaggerated or lightly credulous.[10]

In childhood and in his first studies *don* Diego de San Vitores was called "the holy angel." He deserved this name because of his gentleness and the kind disposition with which he won all. They were impressed by the purity of his ways, which seemed not those of a sinful child of Adam, and by the greatness of his virtues, so much beyond those of a child. His practical wisdom and unusual maturity, his innate discretion and outstanding prudence, his insight and contempt for mere worldly values, and his knowledge and appreciation of the eternal ones were rarely seen in one of his age. Never did anyone hear him tell a lie or swear, or gossip, or use improper words that children learn, however innocently. Thus did the Lord keep that vessel of his Word forever undefiled.

When *don* Diego made a general confession of his whole life at the age of thirteen, his confessor, Father Diego Ramírez, a man of learn-

---

[8]Diego Ramírez, S.J. (1589-1647).
[9]Luke 1:66.
[10]The preceding paragraph makes up the rest of Garcia's Prologue.

ing, spirituality, and experience, could find neither any mortal sin nor any deliberate venial sin in his whole life—surely a miracle of grace seen only in persons chosen by God for his highest service! And yet he made his confession with sobs and tears, as if he were a Magdalene or publican[11] sinful tax collector in Luke 18:11 ss., and his major scruple was that he had not done much more for the service of God.

Those works which seemed to him so small and insignificant would have seemed quite adequate to much older people, if humility could be content with what it does, or if our debt to God did not make our greatest services seem all too small. He did not like childish games; all his amusements were serious and devout. This was an indication of his future actions. From the time he learned to read his most enjoyable recreation was to read the lives of the saints and to imitate what he read. He learned to fast almost as quickly as he learned to eat. At first he surreptitiously deprived himself of the food he liked best. Later on, fasting twice a week became a regular habit with him. He did this over and above the church's regular fasting days of precept or the fasts of devotion customary in certain localities. We might say that he fasted every day since he seldom took breakfast. He ate dinner about 2:00 p.m. when he lived in Madrid, and many times he did not have supper because in his home supper was served at midnight or later, and he would miss the meal in order to fast or to receive Holy Communion the next day. He never asked to have supper earlier, and God permitted that in his home they would overlook this, in order that he might bestow this merit on the boy whom he had chosen for spiritual perfection.

This innocent child, not content with fasting alone, added many other penances, as if he had committed many faults. He would retire to a small room after midnight, and there he would take the discipline for more than a half hour until he bled. He allowed himself no respite other than that dictated by his fervor and the desire of imitating the saints. At first he had no hair shirt to wear. But the same spirit that moved Blessed Aloysius Gonzaga[12] prompted Diego to adopt the following plan, even before reading his life. When Diego's home was being carpeted with mats for the winter, he kept a piece of plaited fiber and pressed it onto his flesh with the prickly part downward. This caused him irritation for a long time. He used this invention until he found a still more prickly hair shirt. He usually slept very little, not enough to satisfy his needs, and often he slept in his clothes, so he could rise more easily for his pious exercises.

Still more admirable than his penance was his patience. It is so much more difficult to suffer what we have not chosen of our free will than to suffer what we ourselves have chosen. While still young he was punished for another's mischief, and he calmly suffered the punishment, saying only: "It is not my fault, but let it be for the love of God." He never became angry nor showed discontent with his parents, teachers, classmates, or servants when they hurt him. His mother was not affectionate toward him, either by temperament or because she had more love for

---

[11]Mary Magdalene, the sinful woman in Luke 8:2; the publican, the sinful tax collector in Luke 18:11 ss.
[12]Blessed Aloysius, since he was not canonized until 1726.

*The Childhood and First Studies of the Servant of God*

her other children. The servants of his household neglected him, because he never complained of their carelessness. With his usual perceptiveness he was well aware of all this, yet he behaved toward his mother and the rest of his household as if he were their favorite. While in Madrid, his mother would go out in winter to visit people until late at night. Local custom imposed these visits upon people of her social position. She had to leave the house locked during these hours, so that when Diego returned home from study hall, the servants could not open the door for him. He did not wish to bother the neighbors, so he would wait in the vestibule until after ten o'clock at night, cold and hungry. Nevertheless, when his mother arrived, he would smile at her and utter no complaint. But this is not too remarkable, because he had employed the time in devout meditation, and the warmth of his spirit had overcome the cold. God favored him with heavenly consolations, and thus Diego would tell his confessor that he did not feel sorry because of being left alone for a long time, even with little comfort, because he always had things to keep him entertained and good ideas to contemplate.

The attention, devotion, and reverence with which he heard Mass daily, said the rosary and the Little Office of Our Lady,[13] as well as other devotions, was admirable. Almost without understanding what he was doing, he engaged in long periods of mental prayer, contemplating the divine mysteries and the greatness of God and his Blessed Mother. God was his only teacher, speaking to his heart of the disdain for passing things and the esteem for things eternal, God who takes delight in the children of men[14] and converses with the simple and pure of heart. He knew well that God was pleased with his prayer, because of the liberality with which God granted his petitions, especially through the intercession of the sovereign Queen of the Angels. Once Diego frankly told his confessor in all sincerity that he never in all his life had asked for anything from the Mother of God that she did not completely grant him. After that his confessor asked him to obtain from the Blessed Virgin the remedy to certain problems. Diego returned soon to tell him that he had made the petition and to rest assured he would receive an answer. The very same confessor says he experienced the truth of the youngster's words and the compassion of the Mother of Mercy.

Diego received these favors from the Virgin of Virgins because of his modesty and caution, what I would call "scrupulosity", if there could be such a thing as excessive diligence in such an important and even dangerous matter. He was never alone with women, even if it was his mother or one of his sisters. If his sister or a maid servant came to the door of his room, as soon as he heard the sound, he would meet them pleasantly and courteously, following the example of Blessed Aloysius Gonzaga, and in an open place would speak briefly with them, with his eyes lowered. To excuse the maids from entering his room in his absence, he learned to sweep his room and make his bed. Thus he removed the occasion for their entering the room to perform their tasks. Another

---

[13] The Little Office: a set of prayers arranged like the Divine Office, in honor of the Blessed Virgin Mary.
[14] Prov. 8:31.

reason for taking on these chores was because they were customary practices of the members of the Society of Jesus, to which he felt that God was calling him. And so he also learned to wash the dishes. He went and watched the black kitchen maid wash them, while he held a spiritual conversation. Then feigning curiosity, he would take the dish brush and help her until he was able to perform this menial task more cleanly and gracefully than his teacher.

He grew in these and other virtues and advanced with giant steps. He reached a height of spiritual perfection before leaving puberty and joined to it the virtue proper to a student: assiduity in studies.

After some early and rudimentary instruction he started taking the course in grammar at our Colegio Imperial in Madrid. That was in 1638. He soon showed such exceptional ability and made such progress in a short time that he was promoted to the second class and was listed in the catalog as "*don* Diego de San Vitores, emperor more than graduate," an honor given to no other student, since even the best students were only called "graduate emperor."

The fact that the members of the Sodality of Our Lady elected him prefect of the sodality at the age of eleven and only four months after entering the school is clear proof of the esteem they had for his character. A special feature of that election was that the school administration did not propose three names as candidates (the usual procedure). Rather the election was left open so the students might elect whomever they thought was best. *Don* Diego de San Vitores received the majority of votes. He performed his charge for a half year with so much prudence and good example that he was the admiration of all, and he ended his term by giving a generous donation for the Feast of the Annunciation, the patron feast of the Sodality, which they celebrated on the first Sunday after Easter.

I would never end if I attempted to tell of all the virtues of the childhood of this Servant of God, but so that you may understand that I have not said all that I might, I will cite a brief statement from his confessor's account. I have disregarded many other ones, some even more exaggerated. "I confess," he says, "that I have formed such a high concept of this angel and I have such a high esteem for his purity, virtue, and sanctity, and of his power before our Lord and his Holy Mother that I do not know how to express it, since whatever I say is bound to be inadequate. I consider myself most fortunate to have known Diego, to have dealt with him and to have had some small part in his training and vocation. And to awaken my conscience and repent of my tepidity and sins and inspire a reformation of life, I have only to remember what I have seen and known in this angel. And even if I did not have so many splendid patrons and advocates before the face of God, each and all the gift of his Divine Majesty, I would have full confidence that through the intercession of this child alone, so pleasing to the Lord, God would pardon my sins and grant me his eternal grace, if only I were not so rebellious to his divine inspiration. To me one of the great signs of how much God values this angel is to realize what has gone through my heart because of my conversation with and knowledge of him. I could never, even when I first met him, bring myself to love him as one loves other children. For him I have had and still have a respectful and appreciative love far greater than I can express. I never caressed him nor made any show of affection that was not perfectly serious and deliberate. I never dared to joke or say anything in his presence that I would not say before a man of highest respect and veneration. Though I loved him and had such high regard for him, more in fact than anyone can imagine, I never missed him very much when he was absent. On the contrary, now that he is in the novitiate, I feel a special satisfaction in his absence and remembering him gives me a certain vigor to serve God and conform my life to the rules and institute of the Society. I could write at length on this point, if I allowed myself to be carried away by my feelings and by the high esteem for this child, who is great in my eyes and very great in those of the Lord."

# CHAPTER III

### *His Miraculous Vocation to the Society of Jesus*

Our Diego could not remember when or where his thoughts and desires first turned to the Society of Jesus. He knew that in 1631, when his father came with all his family to the king's court in Madrid as Procurator at Court for Burgos, at a time when he was only four years old, Diego already was fond of the Society. Since God had chosen him to serve in this order and thereby to save many souls, he gave him a love for the Society before he had reached the age of reason, if, indeed, God had not anticipated the time in one so destined to his service.

Around 1635, when he was eight years old, he went with his parents to Guadix, where his father had been appointed *corregidor*. In Guadix, Diego almost never left our college during the day, conversing with the porter, the sacristan, and other fathers and brothers. To be with them longer he would rise very early in the morning, and many nights he did not undress in order to go to our house sooner, though it was close to his. As our religious considered the child's conversation prudent and holy, they found it most attractive.

Diego returned to Madrid with his parents in 1638 and was enrolled in the grammar division of our *colegio*. His love for the Society grew steadily and with it the desire to be a member. He was greatly pleased by what he heard and saw among the Jesuits, their modesty, their religious observance, and fraternal charity. He admired the variety and multitude of their works in behalf of others, their zeal for the conversion of souls, the disinterestedness of their works, their teaching of children, especially in catechism, the comfort they brought to people in prison and to the sick in hospitals, their retreats and parish missions, and in particular he admired the vow they took not to seek or accept positions of honor, unless required to do so by the Holy Father. Along with the desire to be a Jesuit was the determination to question and examine everything concerning them. Then he weighed all of it with his considerable judgment and prudence. The truth is, as his confessor tells us, that many times Diego placed himself before God to ponder these and other reasons for joining the Society. Although all these were powerful reasons, one reason seemed most important to him: God seemed to draw him with a sweet violence and a powerful sweetness to carry away his will, free yet captive, content though a prisoner.

Diego was already a member of the Society in his zeal and desire for the good of souls. He talked to everyone about things spiritual, taught catechism to his household, and advised people to avoid evil and practice virtue, to each according to his ability and capacity. But he wished to be a Jesuit in reality, to take the vows and wear the habit. He was not deterred by the promise of worldly success based on the noble birth and services to the crown of his parents, nor by the esteem of ministers of

*His Miraculous Vocation to the Society of Jesus*

high rank, with whom he had dealt when sent by his mother on important family business, nor by the habit of a Knight of Santiago offered him
by His Majesty, which he never wore and which his own father deferred.
Father and son both realized that Diego must be excused since he was to
be a religious, something the son desired his whole life long and something his father dreaded. The only thing at that time that blocked the
attainment of his desires was that when he began to speak of it to his
confessor, the latter answered, "Even if there were no other reasons,
such as regard for your parents, you would not be received into the
Society until you are fourteen years old." At this time he was only twelve
and two more years seemed like two centuries. The thought of the delay
tormented his soul and afflicted him tremendously. Yet he was neither
bitter nor distrustful but rather hopeful and devout, trusting that he would
obtain what he so ardently desired and that God would shorten the postponement of his joy.

To be worthy of so great a grace he had recourse to our Lord
and to his Holy Mother through long hours of prayer and continual visits
to our church, especially on days when he received Communion, that is
on every Sunday and on many feast days. The way he prepared to receive the great sacrament and the devotion with which he gave thanks
afterward is worthy of mention. But this is evident already from his other
virtues. To obtain from God the favors he desired he made use of the
intercession of the saints, especially of our father, Saint Ignatius, of Saint
Francis Xavier, and of Blessed Aloysius Gonzaga, whom he had taken as
a model. When he did so I cannot say, but it must have been at a very
early age, because all his childhood, as we have seen, was a vivid re-living
of the early life of Blessed Aloysius. There is another even greater resem-
blance in the fact that the Queen of Heaven bestowed the same type of
favor on these her two sons.

In this time of anxiety and intense devotion the Feast of the
Annunciation of Our Lady, March 25, 1640, arrived, and he received
Holy Communion in our Colegio Imperial with greater devotion than
usual. He went to make his thanksgiving close to the altar of Our Lady of
Good Counsel, so called because of the good counsel she had given Blessed
Aloysius Gonzaga regarding his vocation. At that time the statue was in
the old church opposite the pulpit. So Diego knelt before the blessed
statue and started to pray with extraordinary fervor, begging the Blessed
Mother time and again to open a path to the accomplishment of his
desires. Then the sacred statue spoke to him once, twice, and three times,
and told him clearly that he should no longer delay putting his desire
into practice, but he should try to enter the Society of Jesus at once. He
was overwhelmed with consolation when the Mother of God granted
him this favor. He felt unworthy, but very happy for the compassion
shown him by the Blessed Mother. To think that she had deigned to
speak to him and counsel him! He was happy with the hope of obtaining
very soon what she had commanded, she who could overcome all obstacles. As he reflected upon his poor self and reflected upon the Mother
of Mercy, his heart was ready to burst. Now there was no restraining his

*Book One, Chapter 3*

desire to carry out the command of our Lady. Then and there Diego made a strong resolution to overcome all the obstacles that the whole world and the powers of evil might try to use in stopping him. He was confident that they would not be able to do so. He would push forward resolutely following the voice that was calling him.

He was sorry that his confessor was away on a mission at the time, since his confessor would have been able to iron out the difficulties. But even as he waited he prayed all the more for the grace he so desired. Again by means of a statue the Lord reassured him in the same way as his Mother had done. One day Diego was praying at the foot of the altar of the Santo Cristo de la Caridad (which was then located toward the center of our old church and is now located in the new church opposite the altar of Our Lady of Good Counsel).

With great fervor and confidence he began to speak familiarly with the Lord saying: "You see, Lord, that you are not going to deny what I ask of you. You will grant it, Lord, won't you? Lord, what do you say? Grant me this favor." While insisting time and again in these and similar words with his eyes fixed on Christ crucified, he suddenly felt that his eyesight (he had always been nearsighted) was fully restored.[15] At the same time he saw the statue of our crucified Lord open its eyes kindly and look at him. Its head nodded twice, showing him that the Lord would grant him what he so insistently asked of him. How did Diego react to this favor of Christ, after being so favored by his Mother? Let whoever knows tell us, since I do not know. Would it be right to say that there was competition between the Mother and Son to bring Diego into their company?

He carried out what Raphael said to Tobit, namely that it is good to keep the secret of the king, and it is honorable to make known the works of God.[16] And so for a time he did not reveal these favors until there was need, or rather until God compelled him to speak. When Diego's confessor arrived, without disclosing what had happened, Diego reminded his confessor that he knew how long he (Diego) had desired to belong to the Society of Jesus, and that it was high time to put this desire into practice, and so would he (the confessor) request this with all his influence, since Diego's conscience compelled him to request it? The confessor did not know his new reason for speaking, but he saw Diego's resolute firmness. In the past he had considered this desire impractical because of Diego's youth. But now he was moved to ask for it without delay. Now it seemed that he would offend God if he did not foster with all his might a purpose which was God's. But to perform his duty faithfully the confessor first proposed for his consideration the many difficulties and burdens entailed in the religious life, and especially the aspects that might seem strange. Diego did not consider them as such. Prudently and clearly he would respond when this point or that was mentioned, that for years now he had not only looked into the matter, but that after serious consideration, he was pleased with all of it.

---

[15] In after years he had extremely poor eyesight. Was this occurrence only a momentary cure, or a permanent gift of close-up vision?

[16] Tobit 12:7, 11.

Diego easily came to an agreement with his confessor on the matter of making many novenas, of masses, of saying prayers, of doing penance, of fasting, and of other devotions to the Blessed Sacrament and to our Blessed Mother, to our father, Saint Ignatius, Saint Francis Xavier, Blessed Aloysius Gonzaga, and the other saints, praying that he might carry out the will of God in all things. At the same time Diego conferred with his confessor about the obstacles and the means to overcome them. After these conferences and novenas the confessor was convinced that this was our Lord's business, and it should be put into effect without fear of any difficulties, however many or great they might be. Diego did not fear the battle he might have to fight with his parents and relatives, but rather he expected a victory from God through Christ. Father Ramírez writes: "I don't know how to explain it. But I had this confidence or rather certitude, and from then on I began to feel in my heart that all would be accomplished in a short time. And I am not able to express the great appreciation and the unbelievable esteem that I have had for the virtue and talents of this child almost from the beginning, and which at this time increased almost beyond my power to express it. I can only say this, that it is more like the esteem we have for persons in heaven than for those on earth. Then I would add that in the midst of the greatest difficulties and impossible obstacles that arose later on in his attempt to join the Society of Jesus, never did I entertain the smallest doubt that he would succeed in entering religion, and very soon, nor do I doubt that if the boy (Diego) lives, he will be an outstanding example of virtue and observance in the Society."

# CHAPTER IV

*The Great Obstacles to His Entering the Society of Jesus*

The first step taken by Diego in his attempt to enter the Society was made easy by an error. It seemed the work of Divine Providence, since God knows how to bring success out of error. The major objection on the part of the Society was his age, since he was only twelve and a half years old. So a letter was sent to Burgos asking for his baptismal certificate, to determine his exact age and thus find out if he were eligible. It so happened that the person who transcribed the baptismal record, so it seems, made a mistake. He added a year to his age and thus Diego appeared as thirteen and a half years old. Now, if the other difficulties were overcome, the lack of a few months seemed of little importance. What remained was that all cooperate to convince his father and relatives.

Diego then had recourse to the father provincial and to the rector of the Colegio Imperial, who later became provincial. He made manifest his desire to enter the Society (of which they were already aware) and the reasons he had for choosing this order. His reasons were unworldly and full of zeal for the glory of God and the salvation of souls. Diego asked them, if he obtained permission from his father (they had always told him that without this permission he would not be accepted), would they overlook those few months that were lacking until he should become fourteen. If they did not promise this, Diego did not want to take any further action or discuss it with his family before the time. The provincial realized that Diego's prudence and virtue would amply make up for his lack of sufficient age. He promised him that if all other obstacles were overcome, this one of age would not count.

Happy with this answer, Diego resolved to ask permission of his father, who was in Seville at that time, involved in the administration of the great wealth of that province. Diego now commended his intention to the Queen of Heaven and to his holy patrons and prepared himself by a whole night of prayer before the Blessed Sacrament, which was exposed in the Royal Convent of the Discalced Nuns because it was the octave. In the morning he went home and wrote the following letter to his father:

> My lord and father, I have much assurance of the great love that you have, as a good father, for me. Your steadfast observance of the Law of Christ provides me with unfailing confidence that you will grant my desires; they are just, and so I feel that now is the time to reveal them to you in order to fulfill my duty. I am certain you will support me in carrying out my plans in the immediate future, since I have made this resolution long ago and I cannot delay any longer. This is the story, my father

## The Great Obstacles to His Entering the Society of Jesus

and lord, as you must have realized: for a long time now I have wanted to follow Christ in some religious community. I believe that the religious state is the surest way to attain life eternal and the most orderly one for our brief life upon this earth, where there are so many dangers and occasions in the world, and so many snares set by our common enemy. Here, too, there are a number of cares that necessarily involve men of duty. The community that I have chosen to enter is the Society of Jesus. Its Institute, besides being so holy, so prudent, and dedicated to the salvation of souls (which is the most pleasing work in the eyes of the Lord), fits me more than any other for the reasons I have already stated, including my health, station, and natural disposition. In addition there are many other reasons I feel excused from mentioning. Do not suppose that I have made my decision under the influence of any other person. It is something I have from no one else. And do not explain it as the passing whim of a very young person, because it has always been so rooted in my mind that I cannot remember when it began. And I feel that God is calling me so explicitly to his service in this holy order that it is not possible to resist his divine will. I would be afraid that some misfortune would happen to me if I did not carry it out promptly. Although when God calls, we should not be stopped by any hindrance, yet I say, for your benefit, as to my brother, although you have no other son in this world, his achievements and success will be more complete and his life longer if I enter religion. The greater happiness of our home is linked to our obedience to God in this matter. You, like Abraham, will be generously offering a son to God,[17] not for the knife but for the gentle yoke of the Law of God, which is kept with perfection in the religious life protected by the wall of the evangelical counsels.[18] You will offer your son not for death but for life, so that His Divine Majesty will give you numerous descendants and all happiness as he did to this patriarch. And if I were not to join the Jesuits (as our Lord intimates is his wish), you might lose your two sons at an earlier age because I did not fulfill my vocation. This is all the more true of my brother, should he go to war. Obeying the Lord we would be more fortunate. And if you should judge that my entrance should be delayed for a while, I would say that besides the fact that God inspires me in an obvious, special, and constant way (there has not been a day in which I did not experience these desires which grow greater every day) one should obey God with all speed. I am at the best age to carry out my intentions, since my baptismal certificate, which I persistently asked for, says that I will be fourteen on the twelfth of November. I am in good health, my studies are good, and finally God, who is favorably disposed, has answered my prayers and

---

[17]Genesis, chapter 22.
[18]Matt. 11:29-30.

granted me this favor. There is but one point left for me to make: to implore your blessing, which, as a loyal son, means much to me. Thus I will be able to add your blessing to the happiness I will experience in this state of life. God wants this, and so it has to be. You are aware, because you are so prudent, that God has to be obeyed before men and that in matters of religion the parents do not have the last word, as I have read in Saint Jerome and in the teaching of other saints. He whom God calls must readily obey without further consideration. Please give me your blessing, so that I may immediately do what I have always wanted to do so earnestly. My desire is now so intense that I can find no peace until I attain it. To my mother (although she cannot be entirely unaware of my wishes, since without seeming to, she has tried to dissuade me) I have said nothing so far, because I wanted you to be the first person to know my wishes. You are the only one who controls this decision, which is God's own. I will talk clearly to my mother about it as soon as I have your answer, which I hope is soon. May the Lord keep you many years, as your humble son asks and wishes. Madrid, June 12, 1640. Your most humble son who kisses your feet.

Diego Jerónimo de San Vitores

When Diego's father received this letter, the very prudent and holy reasons of a person undeceived by the world and taught by heaven should have influenced him. But he could not, or would not see these compelling truths, blinded as he was by love for his own flesh and blood.

Up to this time he considered his son as a man and had entrusted to him important business to be transacted with the highest ministers of state. On this occasion alone he considered him merely a boy and thus persuaded himself that the letter was not written by the boy but rather had been dictated by some Jesuit. Thus the contents were not seen as a vocation from God but rather the connivance of men or the childishness of a boy. So the father wrote a letter to Diego's mother telling her to send Diego immediately to Seville, and if this were not possible to confine him in the house of one of his relatives who was very hostile to the Jesuits, or in the house of a certain friend and confidant to whom he was also sending instructions. In any case she should not allow Diego to enter the Society or deal with any member of it.

The son had revealed his plans to his mother before the letter written by his father had arrived. Of all the orders from Seville, she only carried out the last one withdrawing Diego from the Jesuits. She kept him secure at home during the night and during the day in the monastery of Saint Martin, which was close by. The abbot was the Very Reverend *don* Alonso de San Vitores (brother to *don* Jerónimo), whom we have already mentioned and who at that time was absent from Madrid. Diego's mother then went to talk to the father provincial and other fathers of the Colegio Imperial, to explain to them her reasons for withdrawing Diego from the Society. The Jesuits all answered that she should do with her

*The Great Obstacles to His Entering the Society of Jesus*

son as she pleased. They assured her that Diego would not be admitted into the Society without his parents' consent, not only because Diego was their student but also because of the courtesy due to his family.

Diego answered his father's letter and continued writing more letters to him urging the same reasons. He wrote them in the presence of his mother to convince his father that the first letter was his own, or rather the Lord's, who was speaking through him. Because of the sameness of the words with which he kept on expressing himself, it was evident that they were dictated by the same Spirit. He continued to prove how real his vocation was by the constancy with which he persevered, in spite of assaults that would have overcome a man of mature fortitude.

The attacks that he weathered both from his own and from outsiders, from seculars, and even from religious cannot be told. They proposed a variety of reasons, some offering gratifications or threats, others playing on hope or fear, and all with that eloquence that the world uses to detain those who would leave it. Diego's mother, quite out of character, showered him with love and affection, gentle fetters that only grace could break. At times some of his relatives would promise him, as the saying is, mountains of gold, beyond all reasonable expectation. At other times they would try to frighten him with threats of life-time imprisonment. There were those who would argue on the basis of his obligation not to displease his parents. Others would speak with little respect for the community of his choice. But those who thought they were dealing with a boy, found that they were answered by a man who despised both fear and promises, and who countered the displeasure of his parents with the will of God himself. Diego would keep silent if the offense was personal, but would speak up if the insults were directed at the Society. He would prove with manifest truth the deceit and the calumnies of the crowd who did not believe those very things they stood up for. Diego would thus put to shame those who without shame had dared to offend what Diego esteemed above all things in this life. The full fury of the battle lasted twenty days until all were persuaded by his answers and constancy either that Diego's vocation was from God or that it would be useless at any rate to oppose it. Although not everyone admitted defeat, all lost hope of victory and for the last days did not try to dissuade Diego, but only asked him not to carry out his plans until his uncle, the abbot, returned. Diego was to wait for the abbot's blessing. The relatives insisted on this in the hope that time might open another avenue for them, or that at least Diego might change his mind regarding the order and might enter another where some high office might bring honor to his lineage and favor to his parents.

His mother, who had masked her usual frown with affection, returned to her natural disposition. She examined him, as she thought necessary to satisfy her husband, who insisted in each of his letters that she send their son to Seville, since he mistrusted the proceedings in Madrid. The son, to come off victorious in all these battles, armed himself with more prayer, fasting, and the sacraments, besides having many masses said for this intention. In addition he sought salutary counsel. He not only stole out of the house to visit his confessor, despite the watch set up, but the Lord also gave him as neighbor and friend a young gentleman with a truly religious spirit. His name was *don* Antonio de Huerta. In the flower of youth he had the wisdom of age and principles more monastic than worldly. This Raphael was Diego's guide and master.[19] Because his mother tried to keep Diego away from this gentleman also, he made use of a thousand tricks to see him and talk to him.

The mother observed that the usual conclusion to all arguments with her son was that Diego would ask her not to tire herself needlessly, because the Lord and his Holy Mother had called him to the Society. From this she took occasion to ask him at different times how he knew that God and his Mother were calling him. Diego answered giving general reasons. But the more the boy was evasive, the more anxious she became to understand the mystery, since she judged that his answers did not reflect the strong conviction with which he assured her that God and his Mother had called him to the Society. On a certain occasion she pressed him excessively and commanded him strictly that he tell her the truth. Either because of obedience or because he was caught off guard, or by some divine impulse, he revealed to his mother the favors bestowed upon him by Christ and his Mother, something he had never revealed to anyone up to that time. When he reflected on this confession he was extremely confused, fearing he had acted wrongly. He earnestly begged his mother not to reveal it to anyone in the world. The same day he went to his confessor and told him all that had happened, in fear and doubt whether he had acted rightly or wrongly in revealing such secrets, although he added that he had been moved so strongly to speak of them that it was not in his power to remain silent.

It was in these circumstances, then, that the Lord disposed that these extraordinary favors should no longer remain hidden, but that he should confide to his confessor the mercies that Christ and his Mother had shown him.

The confessor then examined them in detail and had them examined by Father Luis de la Palma, a man well known to all for his writings and to us of the Society because of his piety, his prudence, his governing of this province, and the spiritual direction of souls.[20] They could not doubt that these were favors from heaven, since Diego became still more humble and more devout, more depreciative of self, more appreciative of heavenly things, and a great lover of the Lord. They were the more impressed by the effect his words had on his mother.

The change that the simple, humble words of the boy made in that lady of the court is hard to believe, since she was not the credulous type, and she had made up her mind. From this point on she was convinced that this was God's doing and to resist it would be to oppose his will, and so she sided with her son. She wrote letters on Diego's behalf to his father, and she satisfied the relatives. Some considered her not

---

[19]Cf. Tobit, chapters 5–14.

[20]Father Luis de la Palma, S.J.(1559-1644) was rector and later provincial for many years until 1727. Astraín considered him the finest Jesuit spiritual writer of his generation. *Historia de la Compañía de Jesús en la Asistencia de España*, vol. 5: 94-96.

much of a mother, though she really was more of a mother now than ever before.

The mother had been won over, but the father, who was far away, could be approached only by letters, which Diego wrote frequently. *Don* Jerónimo stood firm in his resolution that his son be sent to Seville. His excuse was to further examine his vocation. The reason which he made known in several letters was the need to delay Diego's entrance because he was too young, and because he, the father, believed that this was a connivance of men, not a vocation from God.

The boy, whose longing made the delays seem so long, wrote a letter to his father complaining lovingly because he did not send him his blessing and permission. Among other clauses that show much discretion and detachment, Diego writes: "You wish me the best of life, health, honor, and wealth. I am sure I will find all of these in religion in the highest degree. I cannot then persuade myself that you prefer the perishable and earthly to the heavenly and eternal things (which are the only ones we should seek), so that you would not accept with the greatest pleasure the unfailing promise that God makes to me of goods that are so lasting and so precious. If some earthly lord would make such an offering of some temporal treasure, would you not consider this great good fortune? How much greater fortune it is to enjoy the incomparable and infinite treasure in the following of Christ."

The father replied, and among other reasons for forgetting about or delaying his entrance into the Society was that he had no other sons but *don* José and Diego who might carry on the family name. Diego replied (as *don* Ioseph de San Vitores himself told me) that if he would grant permission to join the Society, he assured him numerous offspring. At the time *don* Jerónimo paid no attention to the promise, which seemed to be a desire rather than real knowledge on the part of his son. From what happened later and because of the many prophecies uttered by the boy, we are convinced that at the time the Spirit of God spoke through his mouth. *Don* Jerónimo, who married his son *don* Ioseph to the daughter of the Count de Priego, lived to see nine children from this marriage. The oldest of these married a daughter of the Count de Garcies. And he also saw a son of this couple and became his godfather. Today this great-grandson has six children, so that the offspring of *don* Jerónimo have indeed increased. God has given him many grandchildren and great-grandchildren for the one son that he gave to the Lord, although so much opposition had first to be overcome on the part of Diego's father and relatives.

# CHAPTER V

*The New Obstacles That Diego Overcomes and
the First Omens of His Martyrdom*

Things seemed to move smoothly but suddenly became worse than ever. The boy who thought he was safe in port found himself on the high seas in the midst of a tempest. He would have perished if the *Star of the Sea*[21] who had called him and led him onward had not brought him to safety.

As the relatives of *don* Diego and some religious saw that his mother was determined to help Diego, they turned their weapons against her, touching her to the quick. They claimed that she showed little love for her son or for her husband in disposing of Diego so hastily against the express wish of his father, who had repeatedly asked that Diego be sent to Seville to be examined. They claimed, too, that she should not be scrupulous about resisting a call from God, or rather what seemed to be such to the piety of a child, which is like some flower that withers as the plant grows. Rather she should be more scrupulous about her disobedience to her husband's just command. If she sent Diego to his father, she would perform her duty both before God and the world. God would not call her to account for what the father had resolved for his son, nor would the world be able to say that she did not love her son. They would no longer say that she was driving him out of the house while still so young, and this, too, in the absence and against the will of the one who was the son's master more than she. She should consider how she would answer her husband's just complaint. There was not one excuse in her favor.

It was not easy for a woman who had regard for the respect of society and her good name in the world to resist these specious arguments. Moreover there was at this moment a good opportunity to send the boy to Seville with a very good friend who was leaving by carriage. So she determined to send the boy to his father. Her conscience bothered her because of the express will of the Blessed Virgin Mary and because of her friendship with the Jesuits. So she tried to please all parties. With this in mind she brought her son to our church on Saturday, July 14, so that he could say farewell to the Jesuits and Our Lady of Good Counsel. He could also go to confession and Communion as preparation for the journey. She talked to Diego's confessor, letting him know of her decision. She asked him to order Diego, as his confessor, to undertake the journey. The confessor tried to dissuade her, asking her to consider the boy's frail constitution, the season's heat, and the needlessness of the journey, since the Jesuits would not receive the boy without her consent. She left the church displeased and had her servants lead the boy out by

---

[21] *Star of the Sea*, a title of the Blessed Virgin Mary.

The arms, because some religious had warned her to be on her guard lest he be kidnapped by the Jesuits. Although his confessor was not able to persuade her, God spoke in her heart and in time dictated the counsel which the Jesuits did not supply.

The mother returned home and confined her son until the following morning when the journey to Seville would begin. She kept the keys of the house, becoming in effect the doorkeeper or jailer. But if God calls with a strong voice there is no locked door or wall that will block the escape.

The boy was convinced that this journey was a trick of the devil to frustrate his vocation, so he determined not to make the journey. At the very first chance he would run away either from his home or afterward on the journey. And he was resolved further, that in case the Jesuits would not admit him to the Society, at least they would protect his person from the violence of his relatives, so that he might have a chance to speak to the nuncios of His Holiness, to the *Conde duque*,[22] to the President of Castille, and to the king himsel, if it were necessary. He would give reasons for his desire and then would have his vocation examined by the persons they might think fit. Then, if they found it was from God, they would defend Diego from those who sought by violence to hinder his vocation, and they would arrange for the Jesuits to receive him into the Society.

Having made this resolution, all that day and night Diego was wide awake, a veritable Argo, searching this way and that for some means to escape from his place of confinement by breaking some door or window. But all his efforts were in vain, because guards had eyes as sharp as his. In the morning when the time for departure was close at hand, Diego was dressed for the journey, and everybody was giving him messages for his father, when one of his sisters, a very good child about eleven or twelve years old, stood there saying nothing. They asked her why she gave no message for her father. She answered (I know not by what spirit she was led, since Diego was hiding his reluctance) that she wasn't giving any message, because she was quite certain that her brother would not go to Seville.

It turned out to be a prophecy because that Sunday morning, July 15, between 9:00 a.m. and 10:00 a.m., someone came to talk to Diego's mother and forgot to close the door.

Diego decided this was his chance, although humanly speaking he had none, because his mother was in the next room accompanied by her maids, with a huge mirror placed so that he could be seen from all sides either by the maids, or by his mother directly, or in the mirror. The next doorway and the room through which he must pass in order to escape were full of serving men, but Diego, heartened by God and the Virgin (to whom he said a *Salve Regina*[23] and commended himself fervently), made the sign of the cross, and walked through, without anyone noticing that he had left. I know not if God made him invisible or not.

---

[22] Gaspar de Guzmán, *Conde-duque* de Olivares (1587-1645), head of the government under Philip IV, deposed by Queen Mariana de Austria in 1643.

[23] *Salve Regina*, a prayer to the Blessed Virgin Mary.

Otherwise I cannot understand how it could have happened, since everyone was in the house and was deeply concerned. They did not miss him until it was time to leave. Having left his house dressed as he was, he came to our college running through the Calle de las Hileras, the Plazuela de los Herradores, and the Calle de Toledo. No one stopped him, although the streets were crowded and it would have been natural to stop a boy of such elegant dress and bearing.

He walked into our *colegio* as if he were walking into paradise, thanking God who had broken the snares that had kept him in prison. He then went to the room of his confessor, which was close to the main entrance. They brought him to a more interior part of the house to await what the father provincial, who was at the Professed House, should determine.[24]

The grief and anger of Diego's mother, when the time came for Diego to depart for Seville, is beyond telling, as she looked for him in his place of confinement and did not find him anywhere in the house.

She sent servants to look for Diego, and without waiting for them to return, took her carriage and came in hot haste to our *colegio*. She asked for the father provincial and was told that he was at the Professed House. She then went to the Professed House, but the provincial told her that he knew nothing about her son. So she returned to the *colegio*. Still more irritated and suspicious of some deceit, she rushed like a lioness to the front door (which was then in the Calle de la Merced, next to what is today the regular door). Then something marvelous happened, which she repeated to several of the older fathers and to Father Diego Ramírez, the boy's confessor, who left us a written account of it.

First she asked for the age of our father, Saint Ignatius, at the time of his death. Did he have gray hair? What were his features? They answered her questions according to our traditions. She heard all this with obvious pleasure and then asked if, at the spot where a small window stands close to the door, there was space or possibility of setting up some stage machinery. We told her that this was not possible because inside that window there was only a narrow, visible stairs leading to the porter's room. She then said:

> Father, I realize that these are nonsensical questions and will seem very odd to you. I know that what I have seen was no stage trick nor any invention of men, but rather something from heaven. My heart dictates this to me very clearly, but to forestall any doubts, I have desired to ask these questions. I want Your Reverence to know that when I returned for the second time to the *colegio* after midday, with orders from the provincial that my son be returned to me, if he were in the *colegio*, I was waiting for the superior with feelings I cannot explain. I rehearsed the rights and wrongs that I would express so that he would return my son to me. All at once I saw through that little window facing my carriage a flash of lightning or some extraordi-

---

[24] Professed House (*casa profesa*): Jesuit Residence not attached to a school, expected to live on alms.

nary ray of light and in the midst of it an elderly person of superior authority or majesty, dressed in the habit of the Society, who at this point was revealed to me as the glorious patriarch Saint Ignatius, since he had the figure and form that you have described. He led by the hand a boy whom I at once recognized as my son, who was dressed in the same habit. My son seemed to have been slashed, his head covered with blood, wearing a crown, and bearing other symbols of martyrdom. The holy father spoke these words, which I will never forget because he left them printed in my heart: "Do not try to take your son with you, because I want him in my house as a saint." All this was very brief, but it remained fixed in my soul as if I had seen it or heard it for many hours. At that very moment I found myself so changed that I could not recognize myself, because my heart was touched, my anger had subsided, my intentions were altered, my words were softened, and I spoke to you and the superiors with a calmness and moderation that Your Reverence must have noticed.

And thus it is, says Father Ramírez, that whoever had seen her before and saw her now could not doubt that that change was wrought by the right hand of the Most High.

Now was fulfilled a prophecy that the boy had spoken on different occasions to his mother when she was most obstinate in opposing him. He said he knew that soon she would change and take sides with him to help him attain his goal. At the time she detested this prediction, but now she published it as her son's prophecy. And it was fulfilled in such a way that from then on the mother was the agent for her son's entry into religion. She took it upon herself to win over his father and to hinder Diego's uncle, the abbot, from freeing him from his destiny.

He stayed in our *colegio* for eleven days, from July 15, the day on which he ran away from home, until July 25, the day he was received into the Society. He was already a religious in his ways before he received the religious habit. His life was very orderly. His hours were divided between his devotions, which were many, and the duties which he faithfully performed, never wasting a moment of the time, spending it for God or with God. Thus he merited to dwell forever in the house of God, where he had only been a guest.

During these days people spoke with him in our church, not only his mother, who was now his counselor, but many other relatives and religious, eager to renew the battle that they had lost the first time. Although each day they tried different means to overcome Diego's steadfastness, they found him always the same. He subdued them all with his arguments and convinced many of them in such a way that they could not doubt that God was speaking through the boy, and so they were not ashamed to surrender to him whom they had failed to conquer. Among others there, it was delightful to see his younger sister, who had been on Diego's side all the time and was now very happy to see her brother so

*Book One, Chapter 5*

close to attaining his desires. She said that if she could, she too would join the Society, but instead she would leave the world and become a sister.

Diego still waited to obtain his father's consent, although his father had written to the mother that he, the father, would approve whatever she might decide, with the approval of the father abbot, his brother. Hence *don* Diego wrote the following letter which I will transcribe word for word because it is a testimony to his maturity at the age of thirteen.

My father and lord, I cannot deny that it would be a great consolation to me to be able to go and kiss your feet and receive your blessing close at hand, but God who knows what is fitting has made other arrangements, perhaps to give me and maybe you as well some occasion to merit, and perhaps because he wishes that his designs be carried out punctually, without delay or exposure to greater risks. His Divine Majesty knows full well that for no cause but for the one which is his and also for the good of my soul, would I oppose, in any way, your least pleasure. I know well that I owe you ever so much in a thousand different ways. I am sure you know the experiences my mother has gone through these days, and I must confess that I am indebted to her more than any son can be indebted to his mother. It is true that on this point of testing and delaying my vocation she has shown more diligence than even a very firm and affectionate father would have had in following the dictates of nature. What I can praise most is the good intention that she had, and I forgive her excessive diligence. Certainly you may be satisfied with that. Here I can see God's great providence because you have written to her (as I heard my mother say) that in regard to this point you approve whatever my mother and my uncle together decide. In that you show both your Christian spirit as well as your prudence, since both of them here have seen my vocation more closely and have realized that it is a true vocation and the express will of God (as my mother has already fully realized) and have made their submission in obedience to that will. Whereas you, free from the painstaking details of the scrutiny, will enjoy the reward of giving me to the Lord. Thus you will be able to ask not only His Divine Majesty but also the Society of Jesus for whatever you may choose in this world or in the other for yourself or for yours. Not until this moment have I been so aware of the sanctity and the gracious courtesy of the Society. After so many trials and after having tested my vocation for so long and even having me now in their house, they have been unwilling to accept me until my parents granted their permission. Otherwise they would not have accepted me. But since you have entrusted this to my mother and she has surrendered to God, only the permission of my uncle is lacking (although his is not indispensable). Since his Reverence will be here either today or tomorrow, I am confident that I will soon don the habit of the Society and be able to send you the good news, perhaps in the very next letter. I beg you, indeed I do, that you thank the Lord for the great favor he has shown to you and to me and that you write a letter of thanks to Father Provincial and to the other fathers to whom I owe infinite thanks, as well as you do. They are praying to God for you with much love because they have learned that you are a little bit displeased. May the Lord keep you and may I see you here in his good time very content with God's will and filled with his divine gifts. Madrid, July 17, 1640.

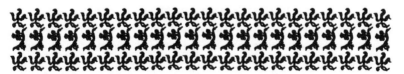

# CHAPTER VI

*Having Overcome New Obstacles, Diego Enters the Society and God Makes Known His Pleasure*

Two days after Diego wrote this letter, the abbot arrived, so eagerly awaited by our candidate. Immediately Diego wrote a letter of welcome, courteously excusing himself from going personally to visit him in view of present difficulties. He only asked for the abbot's blessing and hoped he would receive it. But the abbot sent word by a monk that Diego should come and visit him at the monastery. He wished to discuss the matter at length and to make all the arrangements.

The Jesuits tried to persuade Diego to go and brought up many arguments, but Diego obstinately refused. He would not leave the Society. He felt it was neither necessary, nor safe, nor proper, since if they wished to examine him further after so many other tests, he would give an account of himself to whomever his uncle deemed fit, but in the Jesuits' house. Among other reasons it did not seem right that one who had fled from his parents' house to come to that of the Society should now leave this house to go to his uncle's. Diego finished by saying that he would not go, even if they cut him into bits.

The mother saw the considerable displeasure that the abbot manifested when the boy refused to go to his monastery. The abbot believed that his resolution came through another's influence, so the mother feared that new difficulties might arise. Consequently, she insisted that the Jesuits receive her son and that they make all preliminary arrangements. With this in mind she came to our church on Thursday, July 19, took her son by the hand and led him to the altar of our father, Saint Ignatius. With tears of devotion she prayed to him, "Holy Father Ignatius, I give you this son of mine so that you obtain for me salvation." The Lord deigned to show how pleasing the sacrifice of this woman, rival of Abraham, was to him.[25] Our holy patriarch heard the prayers that accompanied a gift so pleasing to him. Besides other pledges of salvation that she left at her death (based on a good Christian life), there is a remarkable correspondence between the day of her death and the one on which she made this offering to God.

Thus seventeen years later, in the midst of many acts of the love of God, acts of conformity and hope, in 1657, also on a Thursday, July 19, after having received all the sacraments, she surrendered her soul to the Creator to whom she had given her son with so much joy and goodwill.

Nevertheless, the fathers of the Society, excessively prudent and desirous of satisfying everybody (which cannot be done when the will is to be pleased rather than the understanding), talked to the abbot, giving him an account of everything. He replied with much courtesy that he could not but praise and esteem his nephew's choice and the kindness

---

[25] Genesis, chapter 22.

*Diego Enters the Society and God Makes Known His Pleasure*

shown to him by the Society. Nevertheless, to unburden his conscience he must say that it was neither right on the part of Diego nor on the part of the Jesuits to receive Diego into the Society. Diego would be a burden to them, since he was a very frail boy and very nearsighted. Diego would be in perpetual desolation in the religious life, since he would end up blind by the end of his studies. He would find himself useless, and by the same token, forgotten and disregarded. The abbot wanted this to be considered by everyone, and then the Jesuits could do as they thought best. Although the Jesuits were well pleased with Diego, they wanted to please the abbot, so the best doctors of the king's court were called together. The doctors declared that Diego had no eye disease but rather a special quality of vision. For within a certain area, which was not wide, he could see the most minute letters even better than people with extremely good eyesight. He had nothing to fear from a weakening or loss of his sight. Indeed, he had vision enough for more years than he would have life. Incidentally, Dr. Matamoros, who was chairman of the committee, after examining the boy carefully said that his physique and constitution were about the best he had seen in his life and of a kind which indicates great talent and prudence and other excellent qualities. He marveled that the Jesuits would hesitate to receive such a promising boy.

The uncle was informed about the findings of the doctors' committee and he seemed to be satisfied. He would personally attend Diego's reception of the habit, which was planned for July 25, the Feast of Saint James. But the effect of this was that on the vigil of the feast a petition was addressed to the royal council in the name of Diego's mother but without her knowledge. This complaint said that Diego was being kept in the *colegio* of the Jesuits by violent means and by deceit, and it petitioned His Majesty that Diego be set free. The council wished to send an officer of the court to examine the boy. Later, however, at the instigation of someone (using another's name) who requested that there be a more extensive examination and who based his hopes on delay, they decreed that the action be carried out by the bishop.

That very afternoon the bishop sent a minister to our *colegio* to give notice under threat of severe ecclesiastical penalties that within an hour *don* Diego de San Vitores be handed over to him to be set at liberty. It so happened that the father rector was not at home. He was at the house of the nuncio, so the father left in charge declared himself incompetent, since his jurisdiction covered only things ordinary and commonplace. He would give the superior a complete account when he returned, and meanwhile the boy would be safe, neither hidden nor smuggled away.

His confessor told the boy what had happened and could not hide his sorrow. But the boy only smiled and said, "Don't worry, Father, the orders cannot be legitimate. They did not originate with my father, since he is far away nor with my mother who has so sincerely offered me up to God and to Saint Ignatius. And if it did not originate with one of them, with whom did it originate? And even if it is legal, I will not set a foot outside the Society. If the mandate addresses the father provincial, I have no obligation to obey the vicar, because it is not addressed to me.

Nor do I have to obey the provincial, since I still have not joined the Society and therefore the provincial is not my superior. In case the mandate is addressed to me, I will appeal to the judge, since he is misinformed. If necessary I will complain to His Majesty, and only if they guarantee me sufficient security will I leave the Society." The confessor admired the fortitude and discretion of the boy, but he admired him all the more that evening when the boy affirmed, "These people are wearing themselves out in vain, because tomorrow I shall be received into the Society." The confessor asked him how he knew this, when the vicar had told him (the confessor) that Diego without any doubt would be set free. Diego answered, "What I have said will happen, as you will see for yourself, because here within me he who often tells me other things which are for my good has told me this." As he said this he tapped his heart gently with the palm of his hand, with an expression of wonderful happiness.

Diego's mother learned that night what was happening and was distressed that her name had been used in an intrigue so contrary to her desires and contrary to what she had promised a short time ago. She wrote a note to our fathers and came to the *colegio* at nine o'clock at night to see how the mandate could be stopped. In the morning of Saint James' Day, July 25, the fathers held a meeting to deliberate whether it would be better to receive the candidate into the Society. That way they would bind him more closely and increase his fortitude, and thus decrease the expectancy of the adversaries. On the other hand, would it be better to await the final outcome of these maneuvers so that everybody could see the sincerity and truthfulness with which the Society was proceeding in this matter. While the Jesuits were still at the meeting and had not come to a conclusion, a monk arrived from Saint Martin's with a message for the provincial from the abbot. The latter asked the provincial to wait for him, since he was at a meeting and wanted to see the provincial because the business was urgent, and once they had discussed it, the Jesuits' meeting would not be necessary. The abbot's message turned out to be an apology for his previous course of action. He had wished to test the boy and thus to please his father. The abbot had given this much thought during the night. He had come to realize that Diego's calling was from God and that it would cause him (the abbot) serious scruples should he hinder it; and so would the Very Reverend Father give the habit to his nephew that very evening. He himself with his monks and relatives would come to assist at the ceremony. The message as well as the change of attitude aroused their admiration. Those who knew what Diego had said the night before had no doubt that he had prophesied, and that by his prayers he had drawn everyone to his will or rather to the will of God, even when they were most adverse to it.

The evening of Saint James Day arrived, so long desired by *don* Diego, and in the presence of the father abbot, who spoke with him at length beforehand, and of many monks from Saint Martin's, and of relatives, and our community, Diego was received into the Society in the lower church of Santo Cristo of this Colegio Imperial. The relatives now felt much pleasure since they had sacrificed their human love to the

*Diego Enters the Society and God Makes Known His Pleasure*

divine will. Still happier were the Jesuits, who visualized in that small boy the liniments of a future saint.

Diego was happiest of all. He was not only safe in port after many storms, but the desires and hopes of so many years had been fulfilled. Ready to burst with sheer happiness, Diego's face shone like that of an angel. Invested in the new livery of Jesus he left for the church where his mother awaited him. But first he went to the main altar to give thanks before the Blessed Sacrament and then thank Our Lady of Good Counsel. He then went to the altar of Saint Ignatius, where his mother sought him, impatient at the delay caused by her son's devotion, and at the feet of our holy father she joined in the thanksgiving and again offered him up with many tears. She considered herself fortunate in making this offering, all the more so because Saint Ignatius had asked her to do so. His father also offered the sacrifice just as generously when he learned the news. He wrote the following to Diego, words that he never forgot: "My son Diego, I have learned that you have entered the Society. Be assured that if you do not go forward in virtue and become very holy, you are no son of mine!" In all the letters that he wrote at this time *don* Jerónimo insisted that nothing afforded him greater consolation and confidence before God than to have his son in the Society. Thus the Lord who consoled Abraham and Isaac in their sacrifice, rewarding both Isaac, the victim, and Abraham in like manner, granted Diego the blessing of his father, the one thing Diego desired and had not yet obtained.[26]

The day after the investiture, Brother Diego asked that they complete his reception into the Society. He said this because they had put on the habit over his secular clothes, and it seemed to him that he was not sufficiently stripped of the world as long as he kept vestiges of it. Nor was he satisfied until he dressed in the simple and poor way of the religious. To celebrate this day in a fitting manner he arranged that some of his jewels be given to the poor as well as all the money given him for his journey to Seville. He also requested that a good number of masses be said in thanksgiving and for the souls in purgatory, especially for the ones whose prayers had helped him to reach his goal. Diego began to fulfill his promises of prayers, penances, and other good works, promises made to God, the Blessed Virgin Mary, our father, Saint Ignatius, Saint Francis Xavier, and other patron saints.

During the time of his struggle to enter the Society, Diego had found Blessed Aloysius (Luis) Gonzaga most favorable to him. Hence he wanted to resemble him in every way, including his name. Perhaps he thought this would oblige him to imitate Aloysius in religious observance now that both were Jesuits. So Diego had determined from the day of his investiture he would change his second name "Jerónimo," which was his father's name to that of "Luis". He did so until his father noticed the signature "Diego Luis". The father complained and wrote to the provincial asking him not to allow Diego to drop "Jerónimo". The provincial gave orders accordingly and Diego obeyed, sacrificing devotion to obedience. Diego wrote of this to his confessor: "I have received

---

[26]Ibid.

a letter from my father with his blessing, which makes me very happy. But my father complains about my taking the name Luis, he says not to drop Jerónimo. Father Provincial wants me to please my father in this respect and as an obedient son I am happy to do so. But I keep the name of Luis in my heart, because he is my advocate on all occasions." For all that, the son's devotion won the battle, because the father forgot about his demand (if you want to call it forgetting) that Diego call himself Jerónimo, although Diego was now signing all his letters Diego Jerónimo, the father addressed all his answering letters to Diego Luis. Brother Luis made use of this fact to request permission of the provincial to continue his pious custom and, that received, he henceforth signed his name Diego Luis de San Vitores.

During these days the happiness which God imparted to Diego was manifest in his words and actions. It brimmed over in his face and permeated his whole being, body and soul. In a letter written to his father the day after the investiture, Diego begins:

> I am writing to you wearing the habit of the Society of Jesus. I assure you that I value this more than if I had been granted the archbishopric of Burgos or of Seville. I will be most sincere with you and believe me, I would take an oath to this effect, if it were necessary. This is the one thing I have wanted all of my life. The desire is from God alone and his Blessed Mother. I have been influenced by no one. It comes from such a profound knowledge of things that those who have heard of it find that this knowledge is greater and more deeply rooted than my age would warrant. My mother, my uncle, the monks of San Martin, and even the Jesuits very diligently tested me and tried to delay my entrance and change my mind, but when it is God's work, nothing can stop it. I am exceedingly happy, and my only regret is that you were not here that you might see and test my vocation. I have always felt and still feel that you would have been the very first person to approve of it. You would have confirmed me in it and would have helped me carry it out as I have done. I trust in God that you will soon see me for yourself and be satisfied. Meanwhile I beg of you that you conform to God's holy will or rather that you rejoice in it and send me your blessing. Please thank Father Provincial and all the fathers here, since with much courtesy and holiness they have done us so great a favor.

The same day that Diego wrote this letter, July 27, he left for the novitiate at Villarejo de Fuentes, having bid farewell to mother and all those close to him.[27] There was no sign of sentimentality on Diego's part, rather joy and happiness. Diego's younger sister, who was always, so to speak, his sibyl or prophetess of good news, said: "Be happy, Brother, as I am, though I am crying, because you are going where you will

---

[27]Villarejo de Fuentes, about 75 miles south-east of Madrid.

## Diego Enters the Society and God Makes Known His Pleasure

become a great saint." As Diego left Madrid he started singing the psalm *In Exitu Israel de Egypto*[28] and then the *Te Deum*, as if in leaving Madrid, he were leaving oppressive slavery and captivity behind. All along the way he gave thanks and sang praises to God, to his Mother, and to the angels and saints for the extraordinary favor of bringing him to the Society of Jesus.

As the sun begins to shine at its very first rising, so Brother Diego Luis from the first moment he joined the Society manifested the apostolic spirit which shone all his life. Thus this first road to Villarejo was a symbol of all the roads of his life, those that he walked in Spain and in the Indies, because he never entered any path save for the good of souls. At Arganda the first stage of the journey,[29] his confessor, who was to accompany him as far as Villarejo, lay down for a nap since they had continued their journey during the night. But Diego saw some children at the door of our house and he began to teach them their prayers. Passersby began to join the group until there was a goodly congregation drawn by the charm of that twelve year-old missionary. He taught them their catechism with so much tact, spirit, and fervor, that a father who lived in that house said to Father Diego Ramírez in all admiration, "Neither you nor any other experienced teachers could teach religion with more charm or discretion." Diego ended the class by giving as prizes to the best pupils a good number of medals which had been given to him in Madrid. Let us pass over other incidents of the journey, though all breathe a similar religious spirit. No sailor was ever happier at the sight of land after a difficult voyage at sea than Diego when he arrived at the novitiate of Villarejo. In the words of his confessor, With "a mad wisdom and a wise madness"[30] he began to chant the *Te Deum*, the *Ave Maria Stella*, and similar hymns. As he entered the novitiate it seemed, as he said later, that there could be no greater happiness unless it were in heaven.

Diego arrived on the eve of the Feast of Saint Ignatius, July 31. One of our customs in the practice of mortification is to kiss the feet of some of the brethren seated at table. When the religious came to Brother Diego Luis to kiss his feet they noticed a very fragrant odor. They were astonished and could not but look at him time and again. They mentioned it to his confessor, who went to the dormitory at bed-time and, unnoticed, took one of the shoes. He affirms that it smelled extraordinarily good, that he had never in his life smelled tanned leather with this comforting fragrance. This happened in spite of the heat and the exercise of that day and the preceding ones. Whether this was natural to the boy, as they say it was to Alexander the Great, because of his excellent constitution or for some higher reason, God alone knows, said the confessor, regretting that he did not carry away one shoe as evidence of the fact. I add that God wished to testify to the good odor of virtue and sanctity that those feet were to spread in preaching the gospel of peace, drawn by the unguents of the spouse.[31]

---

[28]Psalm One hundred fourteen.
[29]Arganda is about twenty miles from Madrid. Presumably they made the journey on foot.
[30]A traditional description of Don Quixote.
[31]Sg (Song) 1:3-4.

*Book One, Chapter 6*

The day after the Feast of Saint Ignatius, the superiors ordered Diego to recite in the refectory a Latin and Spanish prayer in prose and verse. He had composed and recited it in our refectory in Madrid on the Feast of Saint Anne, July 26. It was based on a distich by Ausonius[32] and dealt with offering gifts to God without delay and dwelt on the great mercy of God in drawing him to the Society so early and of the Society in receiving him at that early age. He added to the poet's distich his own verses and those of others, blending them into his own. Besides the talent seen in the composition they admired the sweetness with which he spoke as well as the deep feeling with which he acknowledged the greatness of the divine gift, never ceasing to thank God for such a unique favor.

When the moment came for Father Diego to return to Madrid, everyone was impressed by the quiet fortitude with which Brother Diego, still a young child and still a newcomer, took leave of his confessor. Some even tried to play on his emotions, and when they did not succeed, someone asked him where were the love and gratitude that were due to Father Ramírez? Brother Diego pronounced these noteworthy words, "I recognize, Father, that I am indebted to Father Ramírez more than to anyone else in this world, and so I love him more than any other person, but now that I am in the Society, I feel sure that love and gratitude do not depend on times and places." And he added, "Some other day I will be sent to the Indies, and Father Ramírez will be happy to see me leave." It seems that Brother Diego prophesied his mission to the Indies, which came about in time for the greater glory of God.

Brother Diego wrote letters to his mother and to other persons to whom he was indebted, letters marked by discretion and detachment. Although they are pleasant and edifying, I will only transcribe the first part of the one he wrote to his mother telling of the consolation the Lord bestowed on him in his house. "I arrived at this holy novitiate on Monday morning very well and happier than ever before in my life. I was received by all the fathers and brothers with as much affection and kindness as if they had known me all my life. Everything about the house and the life here has seemed to me a sheer heaven on earth, so that I am happier than if I had been made a king. To you I am most grateful for your great part (after God made it manifest to you) in this benefit. May the Lord reward you in his own way always. I shall ask him for this in my prayers. Please do the same for me."

I will conclude this chapter, as he now enters upon his life as a religious, with these words of his confessor: "I left him extraordinarily happy in the house of the Lord, and I returned to my *colegio* very much consoled. I trust in the goodness of God that Diego will conduct himself in the novitiate and in future years as a Jesuit, so that he will bring great glory to God, good example to men, and much spiritual joy to those of us who played a part in his entrance into the Society. And I have no doubt that if there are any who observe his life, they will see much that is worthy to note and to record." Later on he added something that I wish to include here, since I want it to reaffirm what has been said so far and

---

[32]Ausonius (c.310–c.395), distinguished Latin poet and man of letters.

also to serve as a preface to what will be said later on. This may forestall a charge of exaggeration in any future statements. The confessor says: "I have come to hold him in the highest esteem for his rare virtue, and I have a firm hope that God has chosen him for heroic sanctity in order to make of him an outstanding luminary in the Society, so that, speaking with due submission and restraint, I affirm that I look on him now and have looked on him for a long time with a kind of reverence and with a veneration superior to what we pay to the most eminent men of this world. This has moved me to speak as strongly as I have, though I always feel that it was not enough. I wish that when someone reads this paper, he will have known Brother Diego as well as I have. Then I am sure that his esteem for Brother Diego would be as great or even greater than mine and he would speak of him in greater detail and with higher praise than I have done. Finally, in all this I submit my statements to God and to the Church and to the judgment of wise and pious men."

# CHAPTER VII

### *His Novitiate and Studies*

The life of a novice of the Society of Jesus who follows the rule and the daily order is like a perfect clock that strikes every hour of the day and night, signaling new acts of virtue. These acts are regulated by obedience, which is the mainspring that moves the instrument as well as the clock hand that points out the duties to be performed. Brother Diego adapted himself to the duties of his new state of life, so that from the beginning, he was a model to inspire the fervent and an embarrassment to the tepid.

What we know of Brother Diego's novitiate comes from an eyewitness, a Jesuit classmate who died this very year and left the account in writing. It is a pity that we cannot consult his master of novices who might tell us of more interior gifts and heavenly favors which Brother Diego would only reveal in the prescribed account of conscience.

A deep and profound humility, which is the basis for all sanctity, was the foundation of perfection for Brother Diego. Humility made him blind to his virtues and all too conscious of faults in himself which really were not there. Thus he had no high opinion of himself and expected others to see him in the same way, as if there were anyone who did not see the holiness that made him loved and venerated by everyone.

His joy was to sweep, to wash dishes, and to perform the other humble tasks of the house. He applied himself to prayer, meditation, and spiritual reading, asking permission of superiors for more prayer, whenever his other duties permitted. Whenever he was not in solitary prayer, he was in the presence of God. God and the rule of seeking greater perfection became the measure of all his actions. Thus he put into every act and word as many good motives as possible so as to practice in each one many different virtues. His love of God was the driving force behind all his efforts. The fire in his heart burned in his words, so that during recreation periods—the only time speech was permitted—they kindled the fire of his fellow novices and had a noticeable influence on the whole novitiate.

His two principal maxims were to please God and to make things unpleasant for himself. His actions were born of the former and his corporal afflictions from the latter, since he mortified himself as if he had many faults to expiate and many perverse inclinations to overcome. He allowed himself no pleasures; anything he wanted he denied himself, even if it was not bad, only that he wanted it. If he had to make a choice between two things equally good, he would choose the one he liked least. If a very striking remark or a very prudent observation occurred to his naturally clever mind, even if it were in matters spiritual, he abstained from making the remark, so that he would not be considered clever. There were some things from which he could not abstain such as eating, drinking, sleeping, standing, or being seated. Hence he still found a thousand ways to mortify himself. Brother Diego sought denial of self in all things possible according to our rule, with more diligence than those who seek pleasure. He would hold one foot a little above the ground; he would never lean back in a chair or against a wall. He knelt on the prickly seams of mats or on rough surfaces. To the worldly these may seem minute details and to pleasure seekers nonsense, but just as tiny stitches show finer workmanship in needlework, so these minute details show the texture of his sanctity. I say this now, once and for all, since his fervor never did decrease through the years but rather increased everyday. He never rejected any afflictions that came his way.

He mistreated his body with fasts, hair shirts, and the discipline; he slept either clothed or without clothing on a board or a mat. Such austerities would be termed folly if they were not the common practice of the saints in their novitiate or if the discretion pertained only to the novice and not to the master as well. The master of novices granted Brother Diego ample permissions, without regard for his youth, frailty, or for an austerity which would be severe in a robust man, until the director of the clothes room reported that every week Diego's shirts were bloody and infected. Then it was discovered that he was covered with sores from the blows inflicted on himself. Only his face and hands were free from the chastisement, so that no one could realize the mortification inflicted on the rest of his body. He confidentially told another novice that his whole body trembled when he was about to take the discipline. Nevertheless, his resolution was so firm that he never did omit it or lessen the blows, until the master of novices, after the above incident, ordered him to curb his severity from then on. The master had Diego's sores taken care of and told Diego the number of times he could take the discipline and the number of blows at each one.

God began to test Diego, who was still a novice, as if he were already advanced in spiritual perfection, since he placed upon the shoulders of a boy a cross which is given only to giants. God submitted him to the test that is the most difficult for those whom he loves. God withdraws himself and seems to be, so to speak, absent. He denied Diego the comfort of prayer. He took away the pleasure of spiritual exercises; he left him totally alone and as if in the dark, without even an open window in heaven through which a ray of light might shine to which he could turn his eyes, because God seemed deaf to his cries. The Mother of God, who he had always felt was his mother, now seemed not to listen to his lamentations. The saints abandoned him. This aridity in devotion lasted for seven or eight months. It would have exhausted anyone with less virtue than his, but Diego did not slacken one bit in his usual devotions, acting now on principle and not on feelings.

He was so diligent and attentive now that he seemed more devout than at any time when he had consolation. The thought that he was to blame for this abandonment and separation from God oppressed Diego exceedingly. He examined himself many times, but could not find the cause; he did not know how to appease God or avoid his displeasure. Diego later told a friend confidentially that although he had not committed a deliberate venial sin and had tried to seek what was best in all things, he nevertheless felt in all these months that he belonged to the Society only externally, since he did not have a bit of its spirit.

The Lord who gives death and gives life, who buries in the depths and brings forth to life, as Saint Hannah says,[33] now wished to console the one he had afflicted by revealing to him his happy destiny. One day three novices were conversing during noon recreation. The subject of their talk was the last judgment. One of the novices said, "Lucky Brother Diego, if my dream last night about the last judgment comes true. My lot was not as good as yours, but I'm satisfied with it." "Well, I dreamt about the Judgment Day, too," added the third novice. "I dreamt that the community bell rang. It was for judgment, so all the novices gathered here in this room where we are. Christ, our Lord, was dressed in a red tunic, very majestic and accompanied by numberless angels. In an instant, without a word, we were all assigned our sentences. I only remember those of the three of us here and that of Brother N.," (whose name he mentioned).

At this Brother Luis said, "It seems instead of your dream you are referring to mine. So far yours was no different from mine. But now I can see the foolishness of believing in dreams. Brother N. who is so virtuous and observant of the rule, is condemned to hell, while I who am so tepid and bad am sent straight to heaven." Meanwhile, the first novice, who had brought up this subject, was astonished, since the others were giving such an accurate account of their dreams. So, to unravel what he thought was a mystery, he asked them to mention the sentence imposed on each of the three present. Each of the three without hesitation said that Brother San Vitores had been sent to heaven and the other two to purgatory. "That's how it was," said the first novice, "And I must confess that I was so happy with my purgatory, compared with his sentence to hell, that I started to embrace you and ask you to congratulate me and help me to celebrate the good news."

Natural dreams, of course, have their origin in the dispositions of the body and simply repeat in images the activities of the day. These are futile and worthless. But it cannot be denied that there are divine dreams through which God tells the future to men, as he promises he will do in the Book of Numbers and the Prophecy of Joel.[34] God spoke in dreams before and after this to the patriarch Jacob, to Joseph, to Pharaoh, to Nebechadnezzar, and to many others, as we see in Scripture.[35] The dream of the two eunuchs in Genesis 40 is very much to the point: to one it announced death and to the other freedom.

Similar to these dreams was the dream of which we have been speaking, as the following circumstances prove. The person who was condemned to damnation was tempted in his vocation and two months later left the novitiate, although the master of novices tried to stop him. Of the three who had the dream, Brother San Vitores had the happy end that we know, while the other two, after serving devotedly in many

---

[33] 1 Sam. 2:6.
[34] Num. 12:6; Joel 2:28.
[35] Gen. 28:10-17; 37:5-11; 40:5-23; 41:1-32; Daniel, chapters 2-4.

*His Novitiate and Studies*

works of the Society, died leaving us many pledges of their predestination to heaven.

Diego finished his novitiate when he was a little more than fourteen years old, so he could not take his vows for nearly two years, when he was a student at the University of Alcalá. Yet he never ceased to be a novice in the fervor, punctuality, and exactness in his spiritual exercises, his prayer, spiritual reading, obedience, mortification, and observance of the rule. He now added the study of the sciences to that of the virtues. He gave himself to both pursuits as though each was the only one, as a perfect model for scholastics of the Society and, as it were, a fresh portrait of Blessed Aloysius Gonzaga. God seemed now to have transferred the holiness of Blessed Aloysius to the new Aloysius in order that those who had not learned it from the first might imitate it in the second. Thus in the course of their studies they might see that studies and godliness went together, as good brothers who lovingly help one another.

Diego spent one year in the seminary at Huete reviewing his studies in grammar and the humanities. From Huete he went to Alcalá for philosophy and theology. Thanks to his great intelligence and unremitting application, he came out first in his studies and was awarded the highest honors, the public *acto* in philosophy at the completion of his arts program and again at the end of theology.[36] A special feature of Father San Vitores's *acto* in theology was this: the man who was to do the *acto* the previous year, 1650, was not ready then and so was to do it in 1651, Father San Vitores's final year. When they both made their presentations, Father San Vitores was awarded the highest honors and his senior came in second.

In order not to waste any time he prepared materials beforehand which he reviewed on his way to and from school and whenever he left the house. He even stole from the time allotted to rest to spend it in study. Thus he himself confessed that all the materials for the book which he afterward wrote in Mexico on the miracles and patronage of Saint Francis Xavier (which he published under the name of the Sodality of Saint Francis Xavier) were culled from notes he made in Alcalá during siesta time.

Two motives drove him on in his continual labors. The first was the will of God, since obedience had placed him in this position. The other was that his studies would enable him to be a more competent minister for the salvation of souls. In accordance with our rule, he let no occasion pass when he might help his neighbor, as far as his current status permitted. His superiors ordered him (as they do with outstanding students) to repeat with lay students the lectures he had heard from his professors. This he did with no less profit to their characters than to their minds, since he gave them examples and ideals and reasons to avoid evil and to love an infinitely lovable God, and he found all this in the very material of their studies. Since his students regarded him as a saint, and since he spoke with such kindness and love, his words had a special power.

---

[36]The grand *acto* was a ceremonial public examination either in the whole field of scholastic philosophy or in theology, or in both. One student out of the graduating class would be designated to be examined by a panel of visiting professors. The examination topics would be presented in form of theses which the examinee would defend.

Everyone admired his modesty, and his self-control impressed his fellow Jesuits in the disputes that occurred in the philosophical and theological discussions which often were more heated than reasoned. He neither departed from the form or matter of the argument nor made personal remarks, however much others did to him. He only feared that his quiet reception of such barbs might encourage the faults of others. He showed the same quiet joy whenever someone hurt him, whether deliberately or not. Once he was caring for a patient suffering from a form of sleeping sickness (*modorra-pléthora*) who was in a frenzied state. Diego's task was to keep the patient awake. Suddenly the patient struck his hand with a stick. It was sudden and very painful, yet he did not move from the bed nor even take his hand away, happy to suffer what was no fault on the part of the patient.

During most of his student years he received permission from his superiors to feed the poor who came to our door each day. In the person of the poor he recognized Christ. This was evident in his loving concern for them, since he was careful to season the food and increase the supply of it. First he would give a spiritual talk and then would bless the food. After the meal he would lead a thanksgiving prayer which he had taught them.

He also begged alms from the cardinal of Toledo and others for the support of certain poor students at the university. From these funds he also provided small gifts to the poor on certain feast days. There was at this time an old man, blind and poor, who lived in a small room in our house, where he had worked in previous years. He was the object of Diego's loving care and humble service. He fed him and during his free time would talk to him about the things of God, opening the eyes of his soul, giving him a new and deeper vision. He made his bed, disposed of his waste, and with motherly care rid him of the vermin that a blind man might not easily control. No one knew of this charity until the old man died. He began to call for Brother Diego and learned he was absent. Then he told what he had concealed till then to please his benefactor.

Before ordination Diego had asked permission of his superiors to leave with a companion on feast days to preach in the country side, especially in the region of Jesús del Monte, where our scholastics spend their summer vacation. Sometimes he would go for a whole week, thus preparing himself by these encounters for greater battles later on with the devil. In his divine providence, the Lord permitted one encounter in which Diego's chastity won the laurels of victory, like another Joseph in Egypt.[37] It so happened that he was giving a mission in a certain town together with a companion who left this account in writing. They were staying in a house not only respected and decent, but generally regarded as religious. A rumor suddenly began to spread that there was a hobgoblin in that house, because footsteps had been heard at late hours in the night and imagination had added further details, the invention of superstitious fears. Everyone was afraid; only Brother San Vitores had no fears, not realizing that he had good reason to fear that devilish hobgoblin

---

[37] Gen. 39:7-20.

who was planning to rob him of the precious jewel of his virginity. The hobgoblin, in short, was someone they least expected because of her duties in the house. She was in fact madly in love with the holy youth and had tried to enter his bedroom on previous nights, but had withdrawn because someone must have heard her footsteps or she simply lost her nerve. Finally she took courage, trusting in the general fear of the hobgoblin, and entered his bedroom and laid her head on his pillow. He awoke with a fright, which this Circe tried to charm away with loving words and caresses. But without uttering a word, he leaped from his bed and fled— the sensible way of winning that kind of battle. He entered his companion's bedroom which was across from his. He remained there for a quarter of an hour sitting on the bed without pronouncing one word, so fearful of the risk of falling that he had incurred. This victory did not give him the confidence which is a pitfall for others. Instead, he became more cautious of even lesser dangers.

# CHAPTER VIII

## *His Ordination and First Assignments*

Father San Vitores finished his studies in 1650. He was ordained subdeacon on March 12 and deacon on April 2, the Saturday be fore Passion Sunday, a date that corresponds to that of his martyrdom, April 2, also the eve of Passion Sunday.[38] He was killed preaching the gospel on the day he was given the power to preach it. He had yet one year to wait before he was old enough to be ordained a priest, and he spent it preparing himself with more prayer, fasting, disciplines, hair shirts, and other good works. He chose as intercessors, the Blessed Mother, Saint Joseph, her spouse, and the aged Simeon, that they might obtain for him from the Lord some portion of the purity and worthiness with which they held Jesus in their hands, that he might more confidently take into his the One whom the thrones and dominations are not worthy to approach.

This feeling was especially evident on the day of his ordination, December 23, 1651. As he was waiting in church for the bishop who was to ordain them, he noticed that other ordinands were talking and laughing in a very loud voice. Filled with that divine zeal of which the prophet speaks in the name of Christ, "The zeal for your house consumed me,"[39] he asked for silence and gave them a talk on the sublimity of the priesthood, a talk based on sound reasons and the words of Scripture and of the saints, a talk quite to the point. For as the Lord said to his disciples, "It will be given to you what you are to say,"[40] he could not have spoken more to the point, had he studied it and written it beforehand. His hearers knew that it was not Diego who spoke, but God who spoke with his voice, and so they remained silent and full of compunction.

This was not the only time that Diego preached extemporaneously, if it can be said that one who stored up so much learning, especially in the sacred sciences, preached extempore. It often happened later on, as on a certain occasion at the University of Alcalá. He went to the Church of Saints Justus and Pastor to attend a sermon on the translation of the bodies of the boy saints. When the preacher did not appear, he mounted the pulpit and preached a sermon which astounded the university. Returning to our point: he led a life of holiness in proportion to his esteem for the priesthood. As he advanced in holy orders he strove to advance in personal holiness. He said Mass with deep devotion and spent much time in preparation for Mass and in thanksgiving. He faithfully observed all the rules and rubrics of the Mass and Divine Office. For him nothing was trivial that belonged to divine worship.

Obedience assigned him some very different tasks. We can say in general that in all the positions he held in the Society, he was a model

---

[38]Now called the Fifth Sunday of Lent.
[39]Ps. 69:9; John 2:17.
[40]Matt. 10:19.

*His Ordination and First Assignments*

worthy of everyone's imitation. It would be wonderful if those who admired him had recorded more examples of his actions. He read and meditated on the rules for each office and obeyed them, performing his duties down to the last detail.

Diego made his third probation at Villarejo. This third year of novitiate was instituted by Saint Ignatius so his sons, as mature men, as scholarly men, would become novices in practice and children in submission, in order to revitalize the virtues that the years of study might have weakened. But Diego had remained a novice in his fervor throughout the years, and he had only to remain himself. But out of humility he tried to become a new man, as though he were only taking the first steps in the way of perfection.

In Oropesa he taught grammar, to the great benefit of his pupils in letters and in virtues. Then for a few months he was minister of the *colegio* at Oropesa, where he showed much prudence by being "gently efficient" and "efficiently gentle" in promoting religious observance by example rather than by word. He had learned from the words and the example of Christ that the superior is the servant of all and should be the least of all.[41] Consequently he chose for himself the menial tasks in the house, those in which charity is practiced most, those of a father rather than of a judge. He prepared the rooms for guests and would humbly wash their feet. He did the same for boarders in the *colegio*, depending on circumstances. Father Gregorio de Obeso, who was preacher there, later testified under oath that Father San Vitores made his bed for him, swept his room, and performed other more menial services for him. Father de Obeso found this a bit overwhelming, but had to accept the charity and authority of Father San Vitores. He had even greater care for the sick, since their need was greater. He saw that the *colegio* could not provide much for the sick because of its poverty at that time. He then wrote to his father for a generous donation, so that none of the sick in the house of the Lord should lack the comforts they might have had in their homes. He would stay at their bedside all the hours of the day when he was free from his other duties and the greater part of the night, or all of it, if it was necessary. He would say the Divine Office there and perform his other spiritual exercises so as to be at hand if the sick needed him. He was a father to all his subjects, but to the sick he was a loving mother.

At this time Father Juan de Guadarrama was living at the *colegio* in Oropesa. Everyone felt that he was a most observant and religious man, so much so that he seemed a "living rule" of Saint Ignatius. A learned and religious father who lived with Father Guadarrama at Oropesa once said to me that God who sees with other eyes than ours may know a higher spiritual perfection than Father Guadarrama's, but we cannot see how there could be a greater perfection. Father San Vitores became a close friend of Father Guadarrama since they were so alike in their aims. He would say the Office with him to warm his tepidity and lack of devotion, as he felt, at the fire of this man's faith. When Father Guadarrama realized that Father San Vitores had sought his company out of admira-

---

[41] Mark 9:35.

43

*Book One, Chapter 8*

tion, in his humility he sought Father San Vitores one day and said, "Dear Father, I am good for nothing, so please look for someone else to pray with." Father San Vitores sensed the reason for this excuse and decided not to disturb the modesty of Father Guadarrama any further, admiring his holiness all the more.

He next came to Madrid where he served as tutor in theology. During the year and half that he was there, without neglecting his academic work, he missed no occasion of helping his neighbor. Not to mention other pious works, he spent long hours in prayer to Our Lady of Good Counsel, who once had spoken to him in words but now spoke to his heart, setting him afire for the service of her Son. He took delight in tender colloquies with El Santo Cristo de la Caridad, who in the past had given visible aid to Diego's vocation and now blessed his prayers for the good of his soul and that of his neighbors.

Every day he would empty the bedpans of the sick in the house and if the infirmarian objected, he always found reasons to carry out an office so much to his liking. Two days a week, at the cost of much walking about, he would collect a number of small gifts and would gather the employees in the house, the sacristy, the stables, and the other work places, as well as those who came in from Torrejón or Arganda, and would teach them their catechism and how to make an Act of Contrition and prepare for Communion. He urged them most effectively to avoid cursing and swearing and all mortal sin. He also preached and taught in the streets and squares of the capital and with words filled with the Spirit of God moved many sinners to repentance.

During this time as tutor in theology, he accompanied and helped preach "street corner missions" given by Venerable Father Jerónimo López, a truly apostolic Jesuit.[42] Father López was a missionary not only to the missions but to the missionaries themselves. He deserved this title because he not only covered all the provinces of Spain for forty years converting countless souls but also won over many vocations for the missions. But the one whom we might call the Elisha of his Elijah, to whom he left "a double portion of his spirit"[43] was Father San Vitores who added to the missions in Spain those of the Indies and to the souls converted by his master those of the Gentiles, or infidels. Father Jerónimo López himself prophesied this, saying that he would introduce the *Acto de Contrición*[44] expressing sorrow for sin. He gave Diego instruction in this and then asked him to give a public reading from his notes. He did this in the presence of his father, who shed tears of joy, moved by the zeal and fervor of his son. Father Jerónimo López later wrote concerning Father San Vitores: "This father has been my greatest consolation while in Madrid, because he is so religious, prudent, zealous, and loved by all for his many good qualities. He works hard to gain missionary vocations and devotees of the *Acto de Contrición*." Diego also assisted Father Manuel de Ortigas, whose fervent preaching in the streets and squares of the

---

[42] Jerónimo López, S.J. (1590-1658).

[43] 2 Kings 2:9.

[44] *Acto de Contrición:* a public procession held at night in the streets of the city, with torches, sermons, hymns, and other devotional actions, whose purpose was to inspire penitence and lead people to confession; whereas by Act of Contrition, I mean the traditional short prayer expressing sorrow for sin. See Book 1, chap. 10.

## His Ordination and First Assignments

capital brought such great profit to souls. Once Father San Vitores, accompanied by one of the fathers, was preaching in the street. He suddenly looked at a man in the crowd and told him he must fear God's punishment and it would come upon him that very night. And that night the man he had warned summoned him. He had been in a fatal accident and he said, "Father, you said this afternoon that I would die a sudden death." He confessed his sins with deep repentance and died with every sign of predestination.

At this time Father San Vitores wrote most of his book, *Casos Raros de la Confesión*, which was reprinted many times and was very useful.[45] The first four or five pages were written by Father Cristóbal de Vega. Father San Vitores wrote the rest of the book and prepared the text for the printer. But because Father Vega wrote the beginning, Father San Vitores listed Father Vega as author. But some people insist that Father San Vitores wrote the book. He also assisted the Venerable Father Juan Eusebio Nieremberg in writing his *Festi Conceptionis*, a book of lasting value.[46] Once when he had a bad headache he was thinking of the Immaculate Conception and desiring ardently that it be defined, when he began to compose an anagram of the given name and surname of the pope, who was then Alexander VII.[47] This seemed to be prophetic since this pope later so strongly favored this mystery. The moment the anagram was complete, the headache disappeared. He felt it was a singular favor from our Lady, as though pleased with his devotion. He mentioned the incident to a friend in order that the latter might join him in thanking our Lady, and his friend in turn told me about it. He afterwards regretted telling about it, lest he be praised and he asked the friend for secrecy. He refused to put his signature to the anagram, although it was so good that they presented it to the Holy Father with someone else's signature. I will not mention many other small works Diego wrote to promote piety in every way.

But I cannot keep silent about an instance of zeal and humility which many people witnessed and admired. Diego was preaching in our church on the Feast of Saint Lawrence in the presence of his father, mother, and a large group of relatives and distinguished persons. He praised the virtues of the martyr with eloquence and devotion, brilliantly weaving in facts and reasons. In his presentation he summarized the points he had made, focusing all on the love of God and the hatred of sin. At this point the congregation was so moved that he chose this moment to end up with an Act of Contrition that drew tears from all in the church. But sure enough, there was a Jesuit there, a man of some distinction, who thought this fervor all too indiscreet in a new preacher. Presuming on his own experience to reprehend Diego, he went to his room and in the presence of many persons gathered there to praise Diego, gave him a scolding in loud and intemperate words. Even a very strict superior, in a

---

[45] The authorship of this work is disputed. Blessed Diego at least contributed to it and saw several editions of it through the press.

[46] Juan Eusebio Nieremburg y Otín (1595-1658), professor of natural history for fourteen years, one of the two best Jesuit spiritual writers of his generation in the opinion of Father Astraín. *Historia de la Compañía de Jesús en la Asistencia de España*, vol. 5: 96-98.

[47] Fabio Chigi (1599-1667).

serious case, would have been more moderate in his speech. Diego listened meekly and without a word or sign of displeasure. Those present admired his patience more than his previous eloquence and fervor. Actions and suffering speak louder than words. It so happened that later, on the Feast of Saint Ignatius, when the happy news arrived of Diego's martyrdom, this same preacher, who had mortified Diego, commended and praised him from the pulpit.

# CHAPTER IX

### *As A Professor of Philosophy at the Colegio de Alcalá*

Father Diego Luis de San Vitores left Madrid in 1655 to teach philosophy in our *colegio* in Alcalá, to the great benefit of that *colegio* and of the whole university and town. Regarding his intelligence and success in academic affairs it can be said that he became a consummate master. Yet he was so humble that he never gave an opinion as his own, but as that of Father Francisco Suárez, whenever he treated the subject, or else of Father Gabriel Vázquez or of some other author. When he had to preside at the defense of a thesis, he would first go with the defender before the Blessed Mother. He said he had learned this from Father Francisco Alonso, who had been a professor at the *colegio* and who was esteemed for his scholarly writings and much more for his heroic virtues. Thus Alcalá inherited from both Father Francisco Alonso and Father San Vitores this beautiful custom. He was not content to study only in books the matter that he taught. He learned in prayer that wisdom of which Saint James speaks: "If any one of you lacks wisdom, let him ask it of God who gives abundantly."[48]

Though he taught philosophy, he did not neglect the training of the spirit. No student ever went to his classes or repetitions without receiving a counsel regarding religious observance. He served as admonitory of faults, but he corrected with so much tact and love that no one was hurt and no one considered it a continual nuisance. If he heard them talking in the corridor, he would leave his room and take a turn in the hallway without saying a word. At most he would just call the name of one of them, and this was enough of a correction.

His very presence was an incentive to religious perfection for the scholastics as well as the professors. Since they never saw him break the least rule, his life was an exhortation, silent but eloquent, and his conversation, discreet and spiritual, was supremely persuasive. He would make his meditation and examinations of conscience in the community chapel, so that even the ones who were not obliged to be there joined those who were.

He was the first to set an example for public penances in the refectory, an example which all followed. Thus the *colegio* was ablaze with a fervor that still burns. The sparks of that fire are seen throughout the province, because many spiritual and apostolic men who have been of great help to souls started and developed in the Colegio of Alcalá.

The one who most shared in this flowering was Father Juan Guillén who lived for more than two years with Father San Vitores[49] and was a distinguished preacher of parish missions. The close friendship that they shared at that time was maintained by a life-time corre-

---

[48]James 1:5.

[49]Juan Gabriel Guillén, S.J. (1627-1675).

spondence. Father Guillén, who was already very zealous and fervent, increased in both virtues in such a way that he became a second San Vitores and a new apostle for Spain as San Vitores was for the Indies. People would come to Father San Vitores for prayers and for counsel for their spiritual problems. Father Manuel Chacón, a distinguished professor who held the chair of Moral Theology, in his last and very painful illness, asked Father San Vitores to be his spiritual director. He placed himself completely in his hands to prepare him for the judgment of God. Father San Vitores assumed this task with such charity that he did not abandon his sickbed day or night. He even invented a kind of sign language to prompt Father Chacón to make acts of faith and of other virtues proper and easy for the dying man to make. On one occasion the sick man said, "Of all the cares that trouble me in facing death, the one I fear most is my restless, vivid imagination. I fear that it may be a tool in the hands of the devil, with which he may carry me away in those all-important moments. I beg Your Reverence to ask our Lord that as soon as I am prepared, I may lose the use of reason so that I may be unable to offend him." The Servant of God promised to do so, and as soon as the patient received Viaticum, much to everyone's astonishment, he began to rave. It was a gift of God's mercy and providence that he lost his sense and awareness of everything, save what brought him closer to God. This was seen when some of the community entered the sickroom and expressed pity at his insanity. But Father San Vitores would answer with a smile, "Just talk to him about God and he will no longer be insane." This proved to be true. When they did so, the patient answered with such good sense and piety that when they left they were filled with devotion and admiration. But if they talked of something else, then the sick man's mind would wander. This state of affairs continued until the death of the patient, who was reconciled many times by the Servant of God and died in his arms, leaving many of the bystanders envious of his happiness.

Outsiders also sought his aid at the moment of death. Those who died in his arms were happy. His words had power because of his prayers. He moved people to sorrow and repentance for their sins and to such conformity with the divine will that they willingly embraced sickness, pain, and even death.

He assisted a lad at the *colegio* of Lugo, who had lived in hopes of prospering in the world because of his studies. Father San Vitores showed him how contemptible is our life on earth in comparison to eternal life. He ministered to him in all his bodily needs with great charity and made death a joy, since he died in Diego's arms with the happiness of one who will go from here to the glory of the blessed. As Diego was highly esteemed for his sanctity, he possessed authority among his own and among outsiders because they listened to his words as to the words of God, so that they did not easily reject what he said. It happened that certain decisions made by serious and learned persons had annoyed some people, and these complained about the men whom they thought responsible. But when they learned that it was Father San Vitores, they said, "That holy San Vitores has really mortified us, but who can complain about him? He has only stopped us where we were in the wrong."

In addition to his post as professor, Father San Vitores was prefect of the Sodality of Our Lady for the university students. The Sodality meets in our *colegio* and there they go to confession and Communion. Every Saturday and on the eve of feast days he would recruit "customers" throughout the patios and *colegios*, speaking to them one by one with an irresistible charm. They admitted that he was "selling" them something, but they liked it anyhow. His argument was, "Does going to confession and Communion for the love of God seem too much for you, when he descended from heaven to give his life and shed his blood for us? If we give less than our life and our blood for him, we give nothing." He said this with such conviction and force that learned and sensible people said, "There is no doubt that this priest will be a martyr and will shed his blood for Christ." Some afraid to go to confession or Communion, would try to hide, taking advantage of his poor eyesight. Then Father San Vitores would raise his voice and say, "Even if you try to run away, this banquet has been sufficiently advertised. Anyone who plays deaf will answer for it before the throne of God." He may have spoken thus at times to persons of authority, but there were no hurt feelings, only a change of heart. A priest who used to accompany him at this time says that he often heard the senior boarders say, "The day we have Sodality, we must either leave Alcalá or else receive Holy Communion at the Sodality, because Father San Vitores will get us out of our garret and make saints of us before we realize it."

Getting to confession became a kind of contest, since so many students from the university and the colleges as well as professors tried to reach him for confession. They wanted him and no other. Whoever went to him once wanted no one else, because of the spiritual progress they felt in their souls. The afternoons the Sodality met, although they were spent in exercises of devotion, the time passed quickly, so well were they planned. Each month he would assign each member a saint and a pious quotation, so that all would be moved to Acts of Contrition and the love of God. Because of his concern that all should attend our Lady's Sodality and become devoted to her, he was called "the page of our Lady."

Not content with these two offices, either of which would tire out a much more robust individual, charity urged Diego to visit the prisons and hospitals frequently and console the sick and the prisoners with the word of God. He made the beds for the sick, lifting them in his arms to help them in and out of bed. He swept the rooms, cleaned the vessels, and performed all the offices a careful servant could do with the solicitude of a kind nurse or a loving mother. Afterwards he would try to persuade them to go to confession or at least make an Act of Contrition and dispose themselves for confession on the following day or the closest feast day.

To induce his companion to imitate him in helping the poor, he would throw aside his long black cape and say with a smile, "Has Your

Reverence never seen me without my cape? Well, now you do." Whereupon his companion followed suit and the poor were taken care of. To the sick he brought as many gifts as he could. While attending Doctor Buendía, a professor at the University of Alcalá who was ill, Father San Vitores contracted a violent fever. He wrote to his father for certain things that he needed, because the doctors told him to ask for them. Later on he said, "I can't understand what led me to ask for those things. I already have too much." Then he distributed among the poor everything that his father had sent him.

During Diego's convalescence his father and a councilor for Aragón came to visit him loaded with sweets and other boxes that the father rector ordered him to accept and thus please his father. He obeyed, but as soon as he was up and around he obtained permission from the rector to go to the hospitals at Altozana and San Lucas and distribute the gifts among the poor. Then he said to his companion, "No wonder I could not convalesce until I had made this visit to the poor and cleared the house of what belongs with the poor in the hospital and in the houses of the rich."

He always tried to have some gifts to distribute on his rounds. He would beg alms from the university students and the boarders. With this he would buy cookies and other gifts. On a certain occasion a boarder from whom he was asking a donation replied roughly, "You are wasting your time asking alms from the students. They need to receive alms, not to give them." But Father San Vitores answered, "Doctor, I never waste my time, because I always receive a donation. If they give, it's for the poor. If they refuse, that's for me." He personally distributed what he collected according to people's needs. He did not leave it to the judgment of those in charge, though he did oblige them by gifts to take good care of their charges, reminding them that they were serving Christ, our Lord, by whatever they did for his little ones.[50]

The Hospital of Altozana was continually under his care. Our father, Saint Ignatius, while in Alcalá, attended the sick here, so Father San Vitores never missed an occasion to do likewise and to visit the room where Saint Ignatius had lived. There was an altar in the room and the walls were painted, although rather roughly. Out of love for Saint Ignatius he wished to perpetuate the cult of the saint in this place. He collected about a thousand ducats for a painting which he hung above the high altar of the hospital. It was a painting of Saint Ignatius at the moment when our Lord appeared to him carrying the cross. At the rear of the church he placed another painting of the struggles that Saint Ignatius had with the demons at this hospital. The balance of the money was used to decorate the room where Saint Ignatius had lived. Later on, after many endeavors, he had the church lengthened so that the entrance area of the hospital where the door of Saint Ignatius' room was located would fall within the church. Some years later the Venerable Father Juan de Almarca, who died at the *colegio* of Alcalá in the odor of sanctity, turned the room into a remarkable chapel. He was an imitator of Father

---

[50]Matt. 25:40.

San Vitores in his devotion to Saint Ignatius and in his veneration for the walls blessed by his presence.

He was deeply concerned to prevent any offense to God that came to his notice, and God on his part saw to it that he would be given notice when he could not find out in a natural way, as appeared on many occasions. The following is just one remarkable case. The devil, who is a sower of discord, sowed jealousy in the heart of a certain inhabitant of Alcalá in order to reap the usual harvest of that evil seed. It happened one evening as this man was returning home to his wife that he saw a well-dressed stranger leaving his house. The stranger actually had called at his house to ask directions to another house which he was trying to find. Thanks to the darkness he escaped the husband who sought him everywhere. With no more information than that, he determined to kill his wife. Blind with rage he returned home. He locked the street door of his house. He saw that his wife was alone in her room and he locked the door of that. He seized his dagger to carry out his mad purpose, when he saw Father San Vitores before him calming his anger and restoring him to a reasonable state of mind. The man started to accompany Father San Vitores to the *colegio*, but when he reached the door of the house, the father had disappeared. The man realized that this was all miraculous, and so he believed it all the more. The next day he went to thank Father San Vitores, who out of humility begged him and his wife for secrecy in this extraordinary matter. But neither the admiration of the husband nor the gratitude of the wife could leave this a secret for long.

# CHAPTER X

### *His Mission of the Acto de Contrición;*
### *Other Successful Missions in Spain*

To all his other occupations Father San Vitores added the apostolate of the parish mission. Since God had chosen him to be an apostle, this was the sauce without which all his other tasks would seem insipid. At night, in Alcalá, he would leave the *colegio* to make, as he called it, "a general attack upon sinners." This was a street mission that sought out and took by surprise in their homes people who avoided sermons in churches. Here is how it was done: Towards evening he would leave the *colegio* accompanied by four or six priests or brothers and some devout lay people. The procession was preceded by a cross, two torches, and a bell. All marched in deep silence, broken from time to time, as the priests took turns chanting in a loud, devout voice some brief, striking phrase about death, judgment, hell or a similar telling lesson, generally in verse so it would be impressed upon the memory. At this voice that suddenly sounded in the darkness of night like the trumpet of judgment, people would run to the doors and windows, and the father would invite them to come and follow their Redeemer who as their Grand Shepherd came looking for his sheep. No one could resist these voices or the deep impression made by the *saetillas* (the darts, or couplets) as he called his flying quotations. So the people kept joining the procession, as his words and the sting of conscience imposed a great silence on the crowd, who meditated on the lessons they learned as they walked along. From time to time he bade them say an Our Father or a Hail Mary for those who were in mortal sin or for the souls in purgatory or for some other intention.

As soon as they arrived at one of the city squares or some other convenient place, he would stand on a table and would deliver a brief but striking talk, moving his hearers to a sincere Act of Contrition, with which he always ended. And usually the audience was in tears. He had couplets and brief exhortations printed, and although he knew them by heart, he would use the leaflets himself to save from embarrassment those who did not know the words.

When they finished the Act of Contrition, the procession would resume in the same manner as before: the couplets, the brief exhortations, and Acts of Contrition until they all reached our church. Although the church was large, at times the crowd that assembled from all walks of life was so great that the church could not hold them all. The evening ended with a fervent talk on the seriousness of mortal sin, or the danger involved in putting off penance, or something similar. The following day the number of those who would return for confession was in direct proportion to the crowd on the previous night, although some out of fear of the judgment of God did not dare leave till they had confessed. The

*His Mission of the Acto de Contrición; Other Successful Missions in Spain*

harvest reaped at Alcalá through this means and the variety of fish caught in this net is not easy to tell. A very trustworthy person, who was a student at the university at this time and was in a position to know, bore witness to the fact that some of the conversions obtained by Father San Vitores were truly remarkable, those of persons of a worldly life, who sought him out to change their lives, and of those whom he sought out and revealed to them their secret weaknesses. Who could have told him, they thought, save the holy angels, to whom he was so devoted? Father San Vitores mentioned in his book *Casos Raros de la Confesión* the valuable results reaped everywhere by the *Acto de Contrición* and in particular he mentions in Chapter 25 of the Spanish edition many remarkable cases he handled. Later on he added many similar cases that occurred in New Spain.

He learned of this powerful instrument of conversion from Venerable Father Jerónimo López (who used it in imitation of the early fathers of the Society, as Father San Vitores states in one of his letters). At first he valued it because of his esteem for Father López. Later he praised it from his own experience and tried to have it practiced in the streets of Alcalá by the most distinguished men of our college. Even to this day it is practiced with the same fruitful results as in the beginning. Diego began his missions with the *Acto de Contrición*. It substituted for the missions he could not give. In towns where he stopped on journeys it was his evening practice. He never missed an occasion to use this weapon against the devil and in favor of sinners. In conversation and in letters he praised and recommended it. He called it his weapon for battle, a sword to strike the heart, and many other titles of honor, recommending it to all the missionaries of the Society, so that they would all be missionaries of the *Acto de Contrición*. Later on he introduced it to Mexico, the Philippines, and the Marianas, as Father Jerónimo López had foretold. He took care that the procession of the *Acto de Contrición* might be perpetuated in Spain when he left for the Indies by leaving many disciples who took delight in this, so to say, "bait for sinners." Not content with this, when setting out for the Indies, he wrote from Seville to Cardinal Sandoval, a very zealous prelate, begging His Eminence earnestly that he introduce in his archdiocese the *Acto de Contrición* procession four times a year. He assured the cardinal that to preserve his flock in the grace of God, there was no means more effective or easy than the procession of the *Acto de Contrición*. He tried to attain the same from other prelates in Spain.

In the summer the scholastics and faculty go to Jesús del Monte, a house of the *colegio* of the Society of Jesus located above Loranca de Tajuña. Not satisfied with the fruit of his apostolate in Alcalá, his zeal reached out as far as it could. With another father on the road to the villa house and also on his return, he would preach missions in all the towns along the way or at least would hold the procession of the *Acto de Contrición*. One night the whole town of Antorcaz followed him to Jesús del Monte two leagues distant. So struck were they by his words that they kept the confessors busy all the next morning. This was the beginning of a practice still carried on in our day. On the eve of the monthly feast day,

53

the scholastics in twos leave for the little towns around Jesús del Monte and lead an *Acto de Contrición* procession to invite the people of the countryside to come next day to our church for confession and Communion. He asked his father to set up a fund of thirty ducats whose income would supply souvenirs of these missions.

Whenever he was free of school work he asked permission of his superiors to preach a more complete mission in those towns. On one such occasion the Lord taught him and all religious the lesson that obedience is better than sacrifice.[51] The Servant of God came from Alcalá to Jesús del Monte to recuperate from an illness. His zeal was greater than his strength, and he asked the vice-rector (there was no rector at the time) for permission to go out on a mission. Permission was denied because of his weakness. A letter arrived announcing that a new rector had been appointed and installed at Alcalá. Father San Vitores took advantage of the opportunity to write, sending his congratulations and asking for the permission which he admitted the vice-rector had denied, since, he said, he now was strong enough to carry out the ministry. Permission was granted, but within six days he had to return, having accomplished little or nothing. He had a dangerous relapse, a reminder that for a religious the better thing is not better unless obedience tells us that it is the will of God.

I am not surprised that he should be so eager, even so anxious, for missions, with his experience of success wherever he went, confessions of secret sins, banishment of swear words, and other faults and scandals, as well as the introduction of good habits, frequent reception of the sacraments, devotion to our Lady's rosary, the pardon of wrongs, and the reconciliation of enemies. During one of these mission trips a strange incident occurred which he tells of in his book *Casos Raros de la Confesión*. Someone attributed it mistakenly to Father Jerónimo López, though he says it happened to himself. He and a companion had arrived at a certain place to give a mission. In the course of a conversation, they spoke of the indulgences that the Jesuits' mission offered for the living and the dead. A rather carefree young man who was all too unconcerned for his salvation remarked, "The Jesuits are putting on a nice show, but as far as I'm concerned, they will not catch me with their indulgences for after death. I'm not worried about dying. Living is trouble enough." Father San Vitores set out that night with the crucifix to begin the mission, and among other couplets, he sang this one, "Awake, sinner, and hear! Awake, death is near. Confess your hidden sins. You end when day begins." These words pierced the heart of the lad, and the more he tried to flee from them, the less he could escape the call of the Good Shepherd, who was seeking him to lead him back to the fold of his chosen ones. The heart that seemed unconquerable yielded at the first assault. He felt that those words spoke of him. Walking along with the others who followed the crucifix, he stood out for his tears of penitence. Nevertheless, he could not bring himself to go to the priests, but as he returned to his home, his thoughts were vastly different from before. His wife recognized his anguish and tried to soothe

---

[51] 1 Sam. 15:22.

*His Mission of the Acto de Contrición; Other Successful Missions in Spain*

him and have him sleep. But hardly had he quieted down and fallen asleep, when he started up awake and awakened his wife. "Don't you hear, don't you hear?" he said. "I don't hear anything," she answered. "Go back to sleep. Stop fretting." "How can I be quiet? Don't you hear the priests chanting: "Confess your hidden sins. You end when day begins?" It was midnight and there were certainly no voices to be heard in the street. The fathers had retired, but the Holy Spirit had so impressed those words in his soul that they still echoed in his ears. Unable to resist any longer, the young man leaped from his bed, dressed, and deaf to his wife's assurances, went in search of the fathers. He found no one in the street. He went to the inn, but the innkeeper said the fathers were sleeping and must not be disturbed. But the Lord, who had awakened the patient, now awoke the doctor, who desired no other rest but the health of that sinner. Father San Vitores heard the noise, came out and heard the young man's confession (he had concealed a sin for eleven years). Who can tell the peace of mind that was his, eased of a burden that had oppressed him for so long? He was filled with gratitude to God who had lovingly waited for him till that hour. In fact, he had been close to death in a previous illness, and even then could not bring himself to confess that mortal sin for very shame. He did not return home until morning. Reconciled at last, he received the Bread of Life with great longing and a joy born of a feeling of peace and consolation, such as he had not known in his past communions, received in mortal sin.

Not in vain did God's inspiration move him to repent, because ten hours later, stricken by a fatal accident, he surrendered his soul into the hands of his Creator, peacefully and with joy in his heart. He asked his confessor to tell his story as an example of the goodness of God and the care of our Lady, whom he thanked for this blessing, since in all the years of error when his soul was frozen in sin, he had kept alive a spark of devotion to her.

All those missions and other missions were made on foot, if his companion agreed to it. He offered the fatigue and mortification for the souls of those to whom he was going to preach. Besides, that way he could more easily talk to the poor and those who needed instruction when he met them on the road.

Once when he had to go from Madrid to Alcorcón for a mission, his father sent him a carriage, which would take him as far as the Segovia Bridge, and two horses to take him and his companion the rest of the way to Alcorcón. But Father San Vitores dismissed the carriage at the door of the *colegio* and the horses at the bridge and went all the way on foot in company with some charcoal burners. He spoke to them of the importance of salvation and did not let them go until he had heard their confessions.

On these missions he offered up to God not only the weariness of the road and of his preaching—a burden he did nothing to lighten—but he did not even change his shirt, ending up bathed in perspiration and covered with vermin, which served as an extra painful hairshirt added to his ordinary one. After taking a severe discipline he lay down to sleep on the floor or on a board, giving the bed, when there was one, to his companion, even commanding him to accept it, if he was unwilling. Not to mention all the many missions he preached in Spain, I will only point out some of the most outstanding. When he was preaching in Siguenza with another father, the bishop, *don* Bartolomé Santos, was so moved by the success of the mission and the holiness of Father San Vitores that he decided to found a *colegio* for missions of the Society. To this effect he donated a house that he had built for boarders of San Jerónimo in Siguenza and of the university. This donation was not carried out for reasons I need not mention. The zealous prelate then insisted on arranging for the foundation in some other way, but death cut short his pious desires for which the Lord has surely rewarded him.

There were two leading families in Casarrubios del Monte, an important town in the Archdiocese of Toledo. They were at odds over the right to carry the canopy poles in the Corpus Christi procession, and since both had many relatives, the whole area was divided into two camps and each day the danger of an open quarrel was greater. Both the cardinal Archbishop of Toledo and the President of Castille tried to reconcile the two parties, but to no effect. The cardinal had seen the happy outcome in such crises and in others of the missions of the Society in the archdiocese, and he knew the zeal and sanctity of Father San Vitores. As a last resort, therefore, the cardinal sent him to preach a mission in that town. He arrived as an angel of peace and he brought peace to those who needed it. In a sermon on the union and harmony that the members of Christ—all Christians—should have among themselves and with Christ, their Head, he moved the congregation to tears and contrition. Suddenly the heads of the two factions and all the others stood up and embraced each other and asked for pardon. Then something marvellous happened: when the former enemies were embracing each other, Father San Vitores suddenly appeared in the midst of them strengthening the bonds of friendship. No one had seen him come down from the pulpit (as his companion bore witness) and with his poor eyesight he would have needed time and help to climb down. He proved himself an angel of peace in the act of flying as well as in the favor granted. Although it was September they held a Corpus Christi procession. All were content to share the canopy poles in the order suggested by the Venerable Father.

At certain intervals the procession would stop and Father San Vitores would recite Acts of Contrition in place of the usual hymns and Christmas carols, prayers which rose in harmony with the weeping of the congregation to join with the hymns of the angels to the glory of God in the highest and on earth peace to men of good will.[52]

It would be unfair to Father San Vitores if I passed over what happened on the road to Barajas. It was late afternoon as he arrived in a certain town and made his visit to the Blessed Sacrament, always his first stop in any town. He then sought out the pastor to ask his permission for a procession of the *Acto de Contrición*. They told him that the pastor and the whole town were in the plaza watching a comedy put on by a com-

---

[52]Luke 2:14.

pany from Madrid. It seemed to Father San Vitores' companion that they had missed their chance, since you do not sow the word of God among the thorns of profanities. But the servant of the Lord was governed by a prudence higher than that of man. He waited till the comedy was over and spoke to the pastor on the very bench where he had watched the play. The pastor objected that this was the wrong moment, but he gave him permission to do as he pleased. Then Father San Vitores mounted the improvised stage and gave a moving exhortation. He persuaded them to follow Christ crucified, who in the drama of the Passion presents the mysteries of our redemption, a drama that reminds us of the gratitude we owe for what he suffered for us, that awakens our will to love of him who loved us so much. The whole town followed him to the church and then marched through the streets in the *Acto de Contrición*. And so the fiesta of the afternoon ended in tears and cries of repentance for their sins. Although he was on a journey and pressed for time he was obliged to remain all the following day to hear confessions. The fisherman of Christ netted a great and varied catch for penitence.

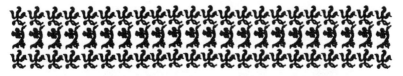

# CHAPTER XI

### *His Vocation to the Indies and the Supernatural Signs by Which God Manifests His Will*

We can best learn of his vocation to the Indies and of the signs by which the Lord showed his will to the superiors of Father San Vitores from a letter that he wrote to Father Goswin Nickel, of happy memory, Superior General of the Society. As it is so difficult to leave what we have and give away what we cherish, even after his superiors were convinced of his vocation to the Indies, they were reluctant to give up a subject in whom they saw a saintly teacher, one whose teaching and example would be an inspiration to our schools, an apostle whose zeal would inspire many others here in Spain. Hence, they found many reasons and excuses to keep him here. After convincing superiors, he still had to overcome his father's will. It would not be just to break with him, and yet it was so difficult to win his consent. His father was most reluctant to surrender, since the love of flesh less easily yields to sacrifice than that of the spirit. It is all in the letter written in Latin to our father general.[53] I translated it later into Spanish at the request of superiors to give it to his father. It reads as follows:

> Reverend Father: the Peace of Christ, etc.
>
> Up to now my confessors have told me to communicate the matters in this letter only to the father provincial. But now they have seriously advised me that for the greater glory of God, I should give an account of all, as I do, by transcribing the first copy, which I started on another sheet of paper and by the addition that I will make later.
>
> From the time I can remember, as a child everything in me was a desire for the conversion of souls, especially those of unbelievers, and a desire of martyrdom, according to my age or perhaps beyond it. At the age of twelve, by the great mercy of God and of his most Holy Mother, I was called to the Society with so much intensity and persistence, that although at first there was an error about my age in the records, even when they finally discovered that I was not yet thirteen years old, I was still received when a dispensation arrived from Father Mucio.[54] He was perhaps moved to do so by an incident that happened to my mother.
>
> My mother wanted to send me to Seville where my father was. He had sent for me to examine my vocation. I was afraid this meant, at best, a postponement of my goal. So I decided that the safest thing was to escape to my refuge, the Colegio

---

[53]Goswin Nickel, Superior General of the Society of Jesus (1652-1664).
[54]Musio Vitelleschi, Superior General of the Society of Jesus (1615-1645).

Imperial of the Society. As soon as my mother discovered this, she drove in a rage to the Jesuits to find me and the provincial, as well, Father Francisco Aguado, because he had given his word not to receive me without her consent. Well, she was waiting, seated in her coach in the old entrance way of our *colegio* just opposite the small window of the porter's lodge. Suddenly it seemed to her that she saw me so vividly that she sent the servants flying to seize me, crying out, "There's my son!" But while the servants looked through the window and neither saw nor heard anything, she stared at me all the more and seemed to see me dressed in the cassock of the Society (though I had not yet received it and was far inside that large building). She seemed to see me covered with blood and with evident signs of martyrdom. Leading me by the hand was our father, Saint Ignatius, who with a clear voice spoke to her, "Let him be, for he is to be a martyr." This changed her completely. She had been so vexed, so opposed to my entering the Society (at least until I should see my father and obtain his consent) that she had begged this of me on bended knees. Now she suddenly became calm, ceased looking for me and went directly to see Father Provincial, who happened to be visiting the Professed House. She told him, as though in confession, what she had seen and heard and promised not to impede my entrance into the Society but rather to help me with all her might. She told the same story and made the same promise in confession to my dear spiritual father, Father Diego Ramírez, and she told it to Father Luis de la Palma and other trustworthy priests.

My mother kept her word in such sort that, although my uncle had got letters from the nuncio ordering that I be set free, she came personally to Father Provincial, though it was late at night, and informed him that the letters were not according to her wish and requesting that he state the fact before a notary public, and that he receive me at once into the Society. Finally when all that had been settled, my mother arranged everything for my reception into the Society and the journey to the novitiate at Villarejo, without considering the absence of my father or what feelings he might have. She did not even wait for his answer, much less his consent. Here in Madrid another remarkable thing occurred. After that vision she spoke with me at the church of the Society, and taking me to the Chapel of Saint Ignatius and standing me in front of his altar (this before I was received into the Society), she said, "Holy Father Ignatius, I give you this son of mine that you obtain salvation from God for me." She said this on Thursday, July 19, 1640, and she died on July 19, 1657, which also fell on Thursday. She passed from this life with every sign of salvation, as we hope, by the mercy of God and the intercession of our Holy Father. I am going to omit several dreams to which I

*Book One, Chapter 11*

give no importance, because it is not strange that I dreamed about what I continually thought and desired. This is the reason why I omitted these dreams from the original draft of my letter to our father general.

With all that and the impulse of God's grace and the vocation rooted in my heart and recognized as sound by many spiritual men who studied my conscience, I have not been able to banish this desire from my mind. Rather there grew in me every day more and more that innate desire to lead souls to Christ, especially those of unbelievers, and to pour out my blood for this cause. I have never been able to turn my mind from this thought nor could I do more than resign myself, in patience and obedience, to the long delay which in the meantime I have offered up to God these last nineteen years as a sacrifice of my will and inclination. Several times I made my desires manifest to the fathers provincial, although I do not recall telling any of them, except those that already knew, the incident about my mother. This because of the embarrassment and confusion I felt because my conduct was so unlike what you would expect of one who had received so great a grace from God. Also I thought that the divine calling in my heart already approved by superiors would attain the object that I so much desired. Then as I found myself rejected many times and sorry for the delay, I confess that I desired and asked of our Lord that he would give to superiors some sign of his will, for instance, that I would contract a serious illness that would cause me to make a vow and that this would be approved by superiors. This through the mercy of God I did obtain.

First, last year, in November of 1657, the Lord sent me a malignant fever, which for me was most benign. The day and the hour that the doctors, both spiritual and corporal, told me to prepare myself for the reception of the last sacraments and for my last hour, I was almost persuaded that because of my sins God was rejecting me for that other more precious kind of death. So I began to prepare myself with heart and soul for the death that was so near. Then they read to me a letter written by the cardinal of Toledo on the very day when I fell ill. In this letter the cardinal urged me, apropos of a mission that I had given, to dedicate myself entirely to the missions. With holy and serious words he pointed out that God was calling me to this, etc. This letter wrought such a change in me that from then on I spoke no more of the death that I had so desired and was so near. Instead, turning my whole being to the missions, I asked that they bring me a signature of Saint Francis Xavier and another that I had of the Venerable Martyr Marcello Mastrilli.[55] After consulting with my confessor and with Father Rector, I obtained permission to make a vow. Father Rector gladly granted the

---

[55]Marcello Mastrilli de Sammarsan, S.J. (1603-1637), missionary to the Philippines and then to Japan, where he died after two days of continuous torture.

*His Vocation to the Indies and the Supernatural Signs by Which God Manifests His Will*

permission, as he later told the community, because he now was confident that I would live. Finally, to the greater glory of God, to the honor of the Blessed Virgin and of our father, Saint Ignatius, and (because of the matter of the vow) under the patronage of Saint Francis Xavier and the Venerable Father Marcello, I made this vow: "From this day forward I will spend all my life and strength in the ministry of the missions, principally among unbelievers and, if this be not permitted, among the faithful, according to the disposition of superiors and the Institute of the Society of Jesus." I made this offering on the day I completed thirty years since my birth in Christ by holy baptism. The result of this vow and of the intercession of Saint Francis Xavier was that I immediately began to get well and without any intermittence I convalesced quickly and perfectly, so that on the very feast day of Saint Francis Xavier the doctors gave orders that I get up. This is the reason why the community as well as others piously attributed all this to the vow for the missions and the merits of Saint Francis Xavier.

As soon as Father Provincial heard about my vow he approved of it in a letter that he wrote to me and he assigned me to a mission. This and other similar ministries have been prevented up to now by my assignment to lecture on the liberal arts, which has been my status for the past five years. I accepted that teaching assignment willingly but not without sorrow, since only during vacation time could I exercise the ministry of missions. Also I am a bit afraid of what was told me by that holy man, Father Jerónimo López, who died recently in Valencia in repute of sanctity. He said that I would lose the health God had restored to me on condition that I go to the missions. In another letter he wrote shortly before his happy death, he told me I was destined to go to the Indies.

Our Lord seems to have confirmed this by the following events. For seventeen years prior to that serious illness I had never run a fever. Then last year, in September 1658, I suffered from a severe tertian fever. Yet here again I saw proofs of the divine mercy. For a whole month I had these attacks of malaria and had been bled five times and all to no avail. Then I received a letter from Father Alonso de Andrade inviting me to the missions, and in particular to a new mission in the Kingdom of Arda.[56] With the letter came a great confidence that I would skip the next bout of fever. To reinforce this hope, as I noticed that the date for the next attack was the feast day of Saint Francis Borgia, I asked of this saint (since he was the special patron for these tertian fevers and since as Superior General of the Society he had founded so many missions and offered to God the blood

---

[56]Alonso de Andrade, S.J. (1590-1672), a popular spiritual writer. In 1658 the King of Arda, in present day Nigeria, sent an embassy to Philip IV to negotiate a commercial treaty with Spain. He hoped that contact with the powerful Spanish Empire would give him access to the sea, since Arda was cut off from it by the Lagos River and a coastal kingdom. The mission was assigned to the Capuchins at this time and seventy years later to the Jesuits. Cf. Henri Le Bouret and Paul River, *Le Royaume d'Arda Et Son Evangelisation au XVII<sup>e</sup> Siècle*, Paris. 1929.

of so many of his sons) that he would now obtain from God that on his day and from there on I would be rid of the malaria, if God had chosen me for the missions. I was moved to do this by a sudden impulse, but on reflection, I rejected whatever in it might be less pleasing to our Lord. While asking for this grace I venerated a signature of the Blessed Francis Borgia, and as a special act of devotion to him, I renewed the vow of the missions, and in particular, I promised to offer myself for the mission of Arda. Besides, in honor of Saint Francis Borgia and for the help of the sick, I promised to have the signature of the saint mounted in a beautiful reliquary. I did not hope in vain. Without any medical intervention on the Feast of Saint Francis Borgia the fever did not recur, nor did any of its symptoms. The previous time it had attacked with all its painful symptoms. So the tertian fevers never recurred except for the sporadic fevers, which as an epidemic afflicted the whole community as well as others during the autumn and winter in Alcalá. Consequently, much to my consolation, I was confirmed in the obligation to carry out my vow by Father Andrés Junio, my local superior, and by the professors of the *colegio*, who had studied the question carefully.

Your Paternity can imagine what courage and ardor were kindled in me as I saw my vow and desires approved by those three saints: Ignatius, Xavier, and Borgia, as well as Father Marcello. (I shall later add what God added through them.) What vigilance to pin-point and correct my negligence, etc! What hope of conquering every difficulty! There was only one real difficulty in my case. The objection that I am useful for certain occupations here in this province is one that is common to all whom they send, and which is without substance in my case in view of my uselessness. Besides, there is the possibility of my dying of one or other of those diseases of which I was freed by the vow of the missions and the intercession of Saint Francis Xavier, as we piously believe, and even by the hand of God, as that holy man Jerónimo López solemnly assured me. There is only one difficulty, one special to me, the objection of my father to any missions outside of Spain. I have heard this excuse several times when superiors refused to send me far from my father against his will. I asked Your Paternity about this in another draft of this letter which I began to write before the incident occurred which I will later relate. What I asked was this: "If per chance this difficulty should be overcome either because God called my father to himself, or if God should give me the words or should give my father and me the grace that would move my father to sacrifice his will and the supposed consolation of my presence, then would you see to it that from no other source would anything impede the sacrifice of this victim?" There is nothing that I would not face nor anything I would not dare to do with the help of God, since I have seen much greater difficulties overcome at the time of my entrance into the Society. Could not and would not our merciful Lord, who changed my mother's disposition which was one of anger and opposition into a tranquil favorable one at the time of my entrance, change my father's resolution in the same way? Thus I hoped, thus I wrote, and I had not yet finished the letter, when the Lord willed—as one may conjecture of his goodness—to put his own hand to the work and bring it to perfection.

At that time my father called me to Madrid to visit a sick brother, when the Lord sent me a malignant fever (to me no less benign than the two already mentioned). The doctors had lost hope and I was about to receive Viaticum, when inspired by God, as I believe, I spoke to my father who was very afflicted and concerned. I told him that if he wanted me to live, he should consecrate my life entirely to the service of God and of souls in whatever part of the world God might want me through the disposition of my superiors in the Society. My father at once agreed and promised that by no means would he resist any disposition of my superiors in my regard.

I was absolutely delighted at these words of my father. I now hoped to escape from the present danger for the sake of greater dangers for the glory of God and the benefit of souls. Of this, our Lord seemed to be assuring me with special kindness, since after I had received the Blessed Sacrament and fervently renewed the vows of the missions, someone brought me the signature of Saint Francis Xavier and one of the martyr Marcello—quite by chance, since I knew of no one in Madrid who had these. Marcello's signature was part of a document in his own hand containing the vow and the prayers dictated to him by Saint Francis Xavier. By this vow he had consecrated his life to the missions of India and renounced his native land and his family. It was read to me to my great consolation and remained deeply impressed in my heart. Finally, about five hours after receiving Holy Viaticum, in a dream—different from others of those days—that came upon me very gently, I seemed to see my two patrons, Saint Francis Xavier and Father Marcello who came to my aid and ministered to me in a way I could not well perceive. It also seemed to me that I heard the voice of a third person whom I did not recognize, but who was sent by the two others. It seemed that he walked between my bed and the wall where the signatures of my patrons were hung. And that voice seemed to say, "Now you are cured." I suddenly awoke at the sound of it and felt my pulse to see if the words were true, words that kept repeating within me, "Now you are cured, now you are cured." At first I was filled with wonder and doubt until I realized through my pulse and the good disposition of my body and my heart that the fever was completely gone. I was bathed in perspiration, which had come so copiously and opportunely in my dream. A brother heard me say that I was cured and that he should bring me a fresh shirt since the one I had on was soaked with perspiration. The brother and several priests came and found me without a trace of fever or any of its symptoms, so that I convalesced perfectly in a very short time.

This seemed an opportunity from the hand of God to talk to Father Provincial and give him an account of all my experiences and of my mother's vision. This time I was not ashamed to talk on account of my poor conformity to the ideals of the Society. I told him that I had a profound conviction that those illnesses, recurring so often within a short time after years of excellent health, seemed clear signs from God that I should move quickly to fulfill my vow. I said that I felt that this last illness was sent precisely in Madrid, before my father's eyes, in order that I might more easily obtain permission to absent myself from Spain. Father Provincial listened to me kindly and said that I might confidently hope, since at the moment there were representatives of the Indies in Europe, that I might be appointed, etc. Finally I have told all of this to Father Rodrigo Deza, who heard my general confession as a preparation for Viaticum; to Father Alonzo Andrade; and here in Alcalá to Father Tomás de Rueda, my former confessor; and to Father Andrés Junio, my immediate superior at present, since he is vice-rector, and all have seriously urged me to relate everything to Your Paternity. I therefore humbly ask of you, for the love and blood of Jesus Christ, that if you see it would be for the greater glory of God, you would command that this very small holocaust be offered to the Lord who offered himself on the cross for all men. This offering is for the souls, especially of those most destitute of the means to enjoy Redemption. This is a small holocaust that the Lord, having overcome my malice through his infinite goodness, has deigned to show is acceptable to him, as by the above signs at least could be inferred. And beyond that, there is this desire in me which for so long, so constantly, so urgently ever burning, could only have been kindled by God, our Lord, in this heart of mine which is of stone or iron, or, what is worse, of flesh. Here I am, most loving Father, send me to any region of barbarians. They too were redeemed by the Precious Blood of Christ. I place myself in the hands of Your Paternity, completely indifferent regarding any kind of missions and in any nation, because I would wish nothing to be by my choice and decision, from which I would expect nothing good. Thus I will feel safe in embracing any assignment of obedience with no fear whatsoever, since I know it is the will of God. But as I wish to reveal to Your Paternity quite sincerely all the movements of my soul, I confess that as long as our fathers are not permitted to enter the mission of Arda (to which mission I especially bound myself by vow and in this letter I offer myself again),

I confess that I feel deeply attracted by the Japanese. This, in the first place, because of Saint Francis Xavier. Many times it causes me pain that the conversion of that nation seems so hopeless, since the preaching and labors of its holy apostle Xavier entitled us to hope for and promote great numbers of conversions. In this regard Xavier says in the first letter of the collection of Father Masseo: "Unless our sins are an impediment, I have high hopes that God will favor what has already begun, and a great multitude of the souls of the Japanese will be added to the fold of the Church." Then below, as if he foresaw and wished to disarm the fears and reasonings of our century, he says: "Many times the fear assails me that the most learned men of our Society, if by chance they were sent to these places, would judge this as an imprudent enterprise and as tempting God by exposing ourselves to obvious dangers." Then I free them of this suspicion because I trust that the indwelling Spirit of the Lord presides over the teachings and writings of our Society. Very often I recall what I heard from our blessed Father Ignatius: "That all who live in the Society should try with great effort and zeal to rid themselves of all vain fears and of everything else that can be an impediment to placing all our confidence in God!" This the saint said when he was on earth; now that he is in heaven, he has well proved his point through Father Marcello promoting this confidence and the Japanese cause. Watered by the blood of martyrs, the seed of the gospel was planted and has sprouted, even though it has withered because of the arid soil. The Chinese, too, are touched and are calling to us for the same reason. It was with deep longing and pity that I heard from Father Magino Sola (who is in Madrid, having arrived from the Philippines recently) that the Chinese have a great desire to become Christians and cannot do so for lack of missionaries. They asked for priests from the Province of the Philippines, but were refused because the Philippines suffer from the same lack of priests.

While we see no shorter way, because of my sins, to the happy goal which in reality or in appearance or at least in my desires has been proposed to me, namely to shed my blood for the name of Christ and the salvation of the most abandoned souls (concerning which, I must make clear that my feelings in this matter are not of such sort that I desire the missions for the sake of martyrdom, but only that for the sake of the missions I would fear no labor or manner of death for one soul that I might win for Christ or for one only additional degree of love for God or my neighbor) if I were to be of some use to the Japanese or the Chinese, or even adding to the number of those who labor in the Philippines, ready as they are to help the neighboring nations. If God should offer an occasion for this special mission of the Philippines, I would offer myself to Your Pater-

*Book One, Chapter 11*

nity, for which perhaps there is now occasion, if the procurator of the Philippines is asking Your Paternity for volunteers.

I beg of Your Paternity to receive all that I have said not as a petition but rather as an account of conscience given in a very serious matter to the common father of all Jesuits. For I fear to be the one to put myself into such arduous circumstances, in view of my unworthiness and general uselessness. Moreover, my spiritual directors here, whom I have mentioned above, have warned me of the danger of an imprudent silence and negligence of duty which would be displeasing to God. So, obedient to them, I am writing to you. And in that same spirit of obedience, I hope to hear the voice of Your Paternity, as I would the voice of my Lord Jesus Christ. His honor and glory and the victory of his Precious Blood in all the redeemed is my only desire as far as this letter, my wishes, and my petitions are concerned. Would that I might obtain this grace with a heart directed to God alone and all my deeds pleasing to His Divine Majesty, through our Blessed Mother and our father, Saint Ignatius, and the patrons of my mission vows, Xavier with Marcello and Borgia and all the saints. Through them may the Lord guide and direct Your Paternity and keep you for us for many years as is our wish and our need for the good of the Society and of so many souls!

Alcalá, July 2, 1659

Someone may have noticed a discrepancy between the words of Saint Ignatius to the mother of Father San Vitores as reported by Father San Vitores and the same speech as reported by his confessor. The confessor says that the words of the holy patriarch were: "Do not try to take your son with you, because I want him in my house to be a saint," whereas Father San Vitores reports that he said: "Let him be, for he is to be a martyr." My answer to this is that the difference is accidental and therefore the substance does not vary. Furthermore, there is no difference if you consider the intention of the confessor and that of Father San Vitores. The confessor wanted to stress the formal words of Saint Ignatius, since he affirms that he heard them several times from the mother and she insisted that they remained printed on her memory so that she could never forget them. The Venerable Father, on the other hand, wished only to give us the substance, joining what Saint Ignatius said with what he showed the mother. Father San Vitores spoke with as much precision as his humility would permit. The words said: "Leave him here to become a saint," while the symbols said that he was to be a martyr. San Vitores suppresses the word "saint" out of modesty and speaks those that could not be suppressed, what the picture proclaimed all too clearly: "Leave him here, for he is to be a martyr."[57]

I wish to point out something else, lest in this *colegio* the memory of such a memorable event be lost, and in order that the very walls may

---

[57] This will motivate the rest of his life.

enjoy the respect and reverence that they deserve. The room where Saint Francis Xavier and the Venerable Marcello appeared to Father San Vitores and miraculously restored him to health so that he might go to the Indies where he was to be an apostle and martyr is the last room but one in the infirmary on the north side, going from the main stairway towards the *merced*, the room which at present has the number VI over the door.

# CHAPTER XII

*He Obtains Permission to Go to the Indies*

Father General, having read the letter from Father San Vitores, had no doubt that it was God who called him to his service for the conversion of the Gentiles. Consequently, he gave him permission to go to the Indies and wrote the following letter to the provincial.

> *Pax Christi*, et. I have just received a letter from Father Diego Luis de San Vitores which has caused me no less admiration than consolation. In it he tells of his vocation and reception into our Society, of the desires he has always had of going to the Indies to labor in the conversion of unbelievers, of the vow he made with permission, of the many times his health has been restored, all of which he says you know because he has told you and which I therefore will not repeat. I have considered this with particular attention before the Lord, both his vocation to the Society as well as all that has happened since then. I have decided that I would offend gravely against the obligation of my office and against my conscience if I did not grant to the said Father San Vitores the mission to the Indies that he desires and requests quite justly, yet with perfect detachment. God wishes him there, and it seems to me there is no doubt that this is the express will of His Divine Majesty. And so in any case Your Reverence is to send him to the Philippines. I am not ordering you with greater urgency since I am persuaded that it is not necessary. I am writing to him that I am granting him this favor, and I am informing Your Reverence that you send him with the first group that sets sail for the Philippines, and I am resolved not to change my mind or to rest till it is accomplished. Yes, I know that he is a gifted person and could be very useful to this province. But so were Saint Francis Xavier and others who have gone. If God wants it so, we cannot resist his will. I beg Your Reverence not to place any difficulties in his way, because it has to be, and I cannot fail to put it into execution.

The provincial did not dare to decide by himself something which was to cause so much distress in the province: to send away a son who was the apple of their eye and on whom they had set their highest hopes. He called a meeting of the most prudent fathers in Madrid and read them the letter of our father general. He asked their opinion as to what he should do, although Father General's letter left him no choice in the matter or any opening for an answering letter, unless there were some reasons so powerful and clear-cut that they would excuse him from obeying His Paternity's very determined mandate.

*He Obtains Permission to Go to the Indies*

The opinions of the priests were divided. One group of priests spoke out (and they were a minority) against their own personal feelings, guided only by the force of reason. They said you would have to be deaf and blind not to see and not to hear that God was calling Father San Vitores to the Indies. The insatiable hunger and thirst that he had always had for the salvation of souls and particularly of the souls of the Gentiles had persuaded all of them that the Lord had chosen him for this enterprise. And now there could no longer be any doubt since our superior had spoken clearly. He is our oracle who governs us in the place of God. They could not understand how anyone could cut off Father San Vitores from his passage to India without a sense of guilt at cheating God of the glory of that mission, cheating heaven of souls and souls of heaven. No one surely could doubt what a blaze his zeal would kindle in that vast and barren field. We have laid a foundation there; now we must build and preserve. The provinces of Spain should keep alive the pristine spirit, and that demands men like those earlier missionaries. It was only just to offer to God with cheerful hearts what he had given to us, to give to our Lord and Master what he was asking of us. It was dangerous to cheat America of a priest whom the Lord had destined for its conversion and the spread of the Faith, a priest whom superiors had clearly marked out for that work.

The other group agreed that God was calling Father San Vitores to the Indies. But God does not always call, they said, in order that the call be carried out. He wants the will but not the actual sacrifice. He accepts the obedience, but refuses the victim. Not all who desire to preach and save souls become preachers. Not all who desire to suffer for Christ suffer martyrdom. God called Saint Francis of Assisi to Syria desiring to be a martyr, but there he was honored and feted by the man who was supposed to kill him. God called Saint Francis Xavier to China, but he died at the very doors, unable to enter in. Let us bring to mind just one more example, the first of all, in fact: God commanded Abraham to sacrifice his son Isaac, but as soon as the holy patriarch had offered up his will and the love of his son, God prevented the sacrifice by a message from the very angel who had brought the command. How do we know if God is calling San Vitores to the Indies as he called Isaac to die and in asking "the mother" (if we may so describe the province) to sacrifice her son, as once he had asked it of a father? God wants him to prepare his will to embrace the immense labors and the death that threaten him in those far-off regions, but we do not believe the actual performance is God's will, because Father San Vitores' weak health could never bear such great fatigue. To expose him to these conditions is to shorten his life and deprive the souls in Spain of that which he will not be able to give to those in America. His success in Spain is great and certain. Who then would snatch from his hands this great and certain harvest in exchange for doubtful hopes and certain fears? We know the spiritual harvest he reaps among those in every college where he lives, and they are our first obligation, as well as on his missions to the people in other places. This harvest is a clear vocation from God, and by it God shows that he wants him for this work. It is surely a special favor of God that the harvest is so abundant, that everything is blessed to which he turns his hands.

Some fathers added that the Indies had no need of priests so highly qualified as Father San Vitores. To convert barbarians or idolaters there is no need for great learning and great talent. Great virtue and moderate wisdom is enough. On the other hand Spain needs such superior persons to be a credit to religion and an inspiration to piety. After all, no one is obliged to give away what he needs and has too little of. Charity begins at home. Hence, the province should not and the superior could not give away a subject who was needed so badly, especially since it was better for the Indies if he remained in Spain. Out there he would be of little use, what with his poor health. At most in the Indies he could do the job of one man, while in Spain he could do the job of many, by inspiring others to sail to the Indies and by preparing men for that work. Experience had shown how many his words and example had won for the missions.

They added other reasons and concluded that the whole matter be brought up to Father General again. He would thus judge what was to the greater service of God, when he had more knowledge of the case.

The other group of priests responded that Father General already had too many replies concerning this point and there was no reason for repetition, since His Paternity had considered them all and had definitively decided that Father San Vitores should sail for India. There can be no doubt that sometimes God calls when he wants only the good will. Then he blocks the execution of the call. But in this case God's will is absolute. He showed this by giving Father San Vitores serious illnesses and then curing them in virtue of a vow to go to the Indies. Granted that he is frail and that his health and strength are poor. Everyone knows this. But what if God wants this because he is pleased to defeat the strong by the weak and to give spiritual strength to the one who lacks corporal strength. If they fear that by going to the Indies he may die and be of no use either to the Indies or to Spain, they should fear still more that by remaining in Spain he may die with no advantage to either Spain or the Indies because God would take away from Spain what Spain had taken away from God. On the contrary, they should have confidence that he who can make sons of Abraham out of stones[58] would give them many men for the one whom they had offered voluntarily as a sacrifice. They admitted that not so many gifted men were necessary in the Indies as in Spain, but who can deny that some are needed. Nowhere, in fact, are they more necessary than where universities are few and far apart, where some highly talented men who are, so to speak, abridged universities, are available to people who have doubts and difficulties that are serious and recurrent and liable to have grave consequences for good or ill. This well known fact is most evident in the case of the many first-class men whom the Society has had in the missions in every generation and has always sent to the East Indies, since Saint Francis Xavier, who was in nothing inferior to any of the first companions of Saint Ignatius. If we want to trace this to earlier days, do you believe that Saint Thomas, who

---

[58]Matt. 3:9; Luke 3:8.

*He Obtains Permission to Go to the Indies*

was destined by the Lord to be the Apostle of India, had less wisdom than the other apostles who were sent to more civilized nations?

Others insisted, emphasizing the great advantage of having here in Spain a saintly professor, himself an apostle who would form the young men of the province in piety and letters and would inflame them with love for the missions, which are the prime work of our Institute.

Finally, someone suggested: "Why don't we call in Father San Vitores himself (who happened at the moment to be in Madrid) and hear his reasons so that we may make an informed choice." Father San Vitores was called in and Father Provincial had him read to them the letter he had written to our father general. Not another word was necessary. All said with one voice, "This is God's business. To oppose it is clear opposition to the will of God."

Of all the marvelous ways in which God called Father San Vitores, what seemed to all most admirable and most surely a sign of God's calling was the utter indifference with which he placed himself in the hands of superiors as though he were completely blind and deaf to the clear signs with which God called him. He was willing to leave God for God, to turn from the message spoken in his heart to the one spoken by superiors, which is, as he used to say, the certain rule for religious; following this, they cannot err or miss their road.

Once the permission of the superiors had been obtained, there still remained for Father San Vitores the very difficult task of consoling his father so that he would willingly accept his going away. The father had given his consent to his son's vow and his permission, if the superiors gave theirs, but he wished that the superior would not consent or that some other obstacle would arise. Love and scruple contended in his heart, or rather human love and divine love, love for his son and love for God, wanting what he did not want, not wanting what he wanted, lest he offend God, lest he lose his son, especially in the hour of death. Here he saw a double loss: to be without the assistance of his son, the assistance of a saint. He was after all, advanced in years and his death could not be far off. It would only be a short delay. It could not be against God's will to hope to have his wish.

Father San Vitores consoled him saying that if a father leaves his son at the moment of death, that is not sacrifice, that's necessity. That is to lose him, not to give him. It is a wise precaution to give freely what will later be taken by force, to give willingly what you will have to lose. For the very reason that his life is so short, he should make haste to offer his son to God, lest he lose the chance of a generous gift and the merit of so great a sacrifice. He recalled the example of Abraham and discussed the debt his father owed the Lord for this opportunity of imitating that great patriarch, of offering the son he loved to the knife of separation and of the long absence and even, if God wished, of death. He, too, would become in some sense, a father of many believers, like Abraham, since he would engender in Christ by his willing gift those whom God would lead to the Faith by the preaching of his son.[59] He added not to

---

[59]Gen. 22:17-18.

*Book One, Chapter 12*

lose heart at the thought of being left alone; it would be up to God to console him in his desolation for the love of God. God would show himself all the more a father to one who for God's glory had given up his son. He should not fear his absence at his deathbed, since "nothing is impossible to God,"[60] and His Divine Majesty could dispose that this comfort would be his.

But his father was not convinced. Human love cannot or will not understand purely spiritual reasons. So he continued more explicitly: "If you allow me to go to the Indies I will assist you at your deathbed. I give you my word and I will keep it. I have a deep interior feeling that this must come to pass. But if you delay my departure, I will not assist you." With this threat and this promise his father was both frightened and consoled. Specifically he was consoled by the letter that Father San Vitores had written to our father general. He translated the letter into Spanish and gave it to his father by order of his superiors. There he read some marvels he had not known before and others of which he was aware. He understood still more clearly that to oppose this enterprise was to oppose the will of God, his son's happiness and his own honor, depriving his son of the glory of a martyr and apostle and depriving himself of the glory of having such a son as he could never deserve.

Father San Vitores added the following to the letter he had translated into Spanish for his father:

> I wrote this letter in the hands of the Blessed Virgin on the Feast of the Visitation (July 2) and I received the very happy answer on the Feast of the Expectation of the same Holy Mother, December 18, the year 1659. This answer and the letter of Father General to Father Provincial were written on October 12, a day when I was making the spiritual exercises of our father, Saint Ignatius, and asking our Lord most earnestly that he give an answer that would be to his greater glory and the greater good of my soul and of the most abandoned souls. Finally, through the great goodness of God and the mercy of the Blessed Virgin, I was told of the very happy resolution of the province and of the blessing of my father and lord, both on January 2, Friday, the octave day of the protomartyr Saint Stephen, in the year 1660.
>
> May God and his Blessed Mother grant that I may not ruin it all by my sins. To which end I ask my father and lord, *don* Jerónimo, to whom in obedience to my superiors I entrust these papers, that he intercede for me before our Lord Jesus Christ crucified and his Blessed Mother, that their holy purpose may be accomplished in me to his greater glory and the good of our souls and of our neighbors.

---

[60] Luke 1:37.

# CHAPTER XIII

*His Departure for Cádiz for Embarkation;*
*Prophecies and Happenings Along the Way*

Father San Vitores had now broken so many chains that bound him to Spain. The time had arrived to leave for the Indies. In Alcalá, where he was at the time, everyone tried to obtain some object or signature of his, as a relic of the saint that he was and the martyr he was to be. And indeed he left many relics of his zeal and memories of his holiness in his great and wonderful works in the service of God. He bade farewell to the town and the university in a sermon about Saint Sebastián. He preached it in a field outside the hermitage of San Sebastián on the saint's feast day, January 20. There is a traditional custom of the college of Alcalá (a sign, I believe, of the mortified spirit of our forefathers) that some of the students and perhaps of the masters go in procession to the hermitage of the holy martyr dressed in ridiculous clothing, which inspires veneration for the humility of those who wear it. This year the sermon with which the ceremonies end was preached by Father San Vitores. That day the field by the hermitage seemed small, partly because these festivities always attract a crowd (there is always something new, even for those who have seen them before), partly because the weather was pleasant and inviting, and partly because of the preacher, always venerated, but now about to depart on a glorious enterprise in distant lands.

He talked about the tortures suffered by the martyrs and of the pains of hell, comparing what is suffered for the love of God with what is suffered for having offended God, and he spoke most eloquently about martyrdom. He could not conceal his own longing to suffer and die for Christ, so that those who heard his fiery words still kindle at their memory.

He took leave of many, but especially of those to whom he owed special respect or other obligation. They asked to be remembered in his prayers. Humbly he promised and then asked for theirs, saying he had greater need than they. When he bade farewell to the prioress and nuns of the Magdalene, where he used to give spiritual conferences, a novice, Sister Angela of the Presentation, was present. She was deeply distressed because her father, Francisco Bravo, had suffered serious financial losses and had little chance of providing the dowry required for her profession. Sister Isabel of the Holy Spirit told the Servant of God of the novice's problem and asked him to give her his blessing and to pray to the Lord for a favorable solution. He did as he was asked and said to the novice, "Come now, don't be sad. Within six months you will be professed." And it happened just as the man of God had predicted. On another occasion the prioress, Sister Catalina de San Francisco, asked him to beg the Lord that he move someone's heart to build a church for the sisters, because they did not have one. He answered, "Perhaps the one who is to build it is already born and brought up." This was his usual way of talking about future things to hide his certain foreknowledge, for fear people would consider him a prophet. A little later, the daughter of the secretary, *don* Andrés de Villarán, knight of the Order of Santiago, now of His Majesty's Council for the Royal Treasury, built the church and the beautiful convent which now houses the sisters.

At the last farewell, his father asked that he might have—and keep as some comfort—a portrait of his son. Well, it required a stern command of obedience for this humble man to allow it. And during the sittings he remained so confused and embarrassed, with his eyes cast down, that they had to give the painter the authority of a superior to command him to raise his face and open his eyes so that he could get a good likeness.

He left Madrid for Cádiz about the middle of February 1660, and the whole journey was a continual mission, a replica of what Saint Peter said of Christ: "He went about doing good and healing those oppressed by the devil."[61]

On the road he inspired his companions to a love of God by his burning words. He exhorted the travelers he met on the road and the peasants working in the fields to an entire and perfect confession and to devotion to our Lady and to other devotions. He also taught Christian doctrine to those he found ignorant of it. When he arrived in the evening he would walk the streets with a crucifix and lead a procession of the *Acto de Contrición*. Then he would hear confessions almost until dawn, when he would set out again on his journey. For sleep and for rest from his journey, he would take the same one that Christ took when "tired from his journey" by the well in Samaria: the conversion of sinners.[62]

He wanted to put on the *Acto de Contrición* in Toledo, but the fathers in our house there objected, alleging that it was a novelty liable to cause serious difficulties and improprieties in a populous city with a packed crowd of men and women parading at night. To these reasons, which were by no means trivial from a purely human point of view, Father San Vitores answered citing his experience of the modesty, silence, and compunction they had encountered everywhere. But he could not convince the fathers. Finally, His Eminence, Cardinal Sandoval, fell on his knees before Father Francisco de Cepeda, his confessor, and begged him to ask the priests in behalf of the cardinal not to hinder such a holy exercise, to bid them place their trust in God who works wonders beyond all expectations of human prudence. A request from one who can command is a double command and cannot be opposed. So Father San Vitores conducted the *Acto de Contrición,* and God filled him with such inspiration that those who were against it changed their minds, and all the more so on the following morning when they reaped the harvest of so many necessary general confessions. They kept the Venerable Father all that day even though he hurried. There were so many persons who wanted him to hear their confession. Just one of the conversions that day would

---

[61] Acts 10:38.
[62] John 4:6.

*His Departure for Cádiz for Embarkation; Prophecies and Happenings Along the Way*

have been a rich harvest: the case of a certain sinner obstinate in his vices. Twice he had been at the point of death, had closed his eyes to the fires of hell, and had delivered himself to Satan rather than make his confession. Now, full of sadness and melancholy, he longed to escape this temporal life at the cost of his eternal life, to end this life with a noose. But he was stopped by the blazing words he heard from the lips of the Servant of God. They changed his heart. He made a sincere confession. He changed his vicious life for a Christian one and despair of God's mercy for the hope of salvation.

Then there is what happened to a distinguished woman of this city at the time of the *Acto de Contrición*. Father San Vitores needed a crucifix that was large but not heavy. He heard that there was such a crucifix in one of the finest homes in the city. It had been brought from the Indies and was made of fennel. He went to the house and asked the lady of the house to lend him the crucifix. She excused herself saying that it had been set up in the family oratory, and that they would have to take it apart to remove it, and that in any case she was not going to lend it. At that he raised his eyes and his heart to heaven and said to her, "You won't lend me the crucifix? Well, then you will give an account to God on the day of judgment for the souls who would have received the grace of God this night through this crucifix in the *Acto de Contrición*. His words struck her like a verdict of condemnation, and immediately she not only lent the crucifix for the *Acto de Contrición* but made a donation of it to the Professed House so that it might always be carried in the procession of the *Acto de Contrición*. It had been her most precious possession. It is now kept in the Sodality chapel of the Professed House and every year is carried with much solemnity before the great procession at the beginning of the missions preached in that church.

At the order of superiors, he traveled by way of the town of Cabra del Santo Cristo, formerly called Cabrilla, to take leave of his brother, the Viscount of Cabra. He did so with less repugnance than he usually had for visiting his relatives, because here he could visit a certain crucifix that was an object of devotion to himself and his family. It was a true-to-life copy of the Santo Cristo of Burgos, which his father had had made in spite of considerable difficulties, yet with the help of providential interventions. *Don* Jerónimo sent it to Guadix, of which he had been made corregidor. En route the crucifix occasioned such miracles that the people of Cabra, a neighboring town, stole it, or rather it stole itself and later, by way of restitution, as it were, gave the same town, by royal grant, to *don* Joseph de San Vitores, brother of our martyr, with the title of Viscount of Cabra.

Here, the Servant of God left a hundred pesos, which the cardinal of Toledo had given him for a picture of Saint Ignatius and another of Saint Francis Xavier, pictures that are still there. In the same church he preached a fervent mission with the help of the father rector of Jaén and obtained from his brother a foundation of fifty ducats per year. Before he left, he established a jubilee of Christian doctrine for May 3, Feast of the Finding of the Holy Cross and the jubilee of General Communion for the third Sunday of each month. As he wrote to his father, in the eight days he was there, he did not waste much time, by the goodness of God.

Passing through Córdoba, he met Father Luis de Medina in the *colegio* of the Society of Jesus, where he was studying philosophy.[63] He had the same desire to sail to the Indies. Although Father de Medina did not mention this the first time they met, Father San Vitores said to him with special affection, "See, we are going to be very great friends." These words puzzled him, and as he pondered them in his heart as the words of a saint, which concealed some mystery, he heard an interior voice that said to him, "You are to go with him." These words puzzled him even more because he had no permission to sail to the Indies nor could he obtain it so soon. But time and events proved that it was God who spoke to him by Father San Vitores and who spoke to him directly. Nine years later, Father Medina, on his way to the Indies, met Father San Vitores in Mexico. The latter had come from the Philippines on his way to the Marianas. Later they had the good fortune to enter the Marianas together to harvest the first fruits of martyrdom.

He was detained for some time in Seville, waiting for the departure of the fleet and for the arrival of his companions in religion who were to go with him. He worked hard for the good of souls and held the *Acto de Contrición* in various churches. Because of continual rains he was not able to do so in the streets, which was what he most wanted. But God consoled him in his zeal by revealing to him, as it seems, how much this holy exercise would give glory to God in Seville and in all Andalucia, because of the letters he wrote from this place to Father Tirso González and to Father Juan Gabriel.[64] The former was teaching theology in Salamanca, in his Province of Castille, the latter in Toledo. He urged each of them to communicate with the other. He also wrote to Father Guillén telling him what he had written to Father Tirso, and he added: "Your Reverence should write to him about this matter and be assured that this correspondence is of the highest importance."

The two priests did not understand at the time the significance of these words, but the one who put the words on the tongue and the pen of this prophetic man did. Later it was understood, when the two left their chairs of theology and dedicated themselves to the missions. At times as a team and at times separately, they traveled throughout Spain, though principally through the province of Andalucia, with a splendid harvest of missions due in great part to the example of their lives.

The matter becomes clearer in a letter he wrote from Cádiz concerning the success of the *Acto de Contrición* in that city, in which he adds these words: "All this is nothing but a small preparation for the time when Your Reverence comes to establish it. And don't think now that this is a prophecy of the missions of the Indies. It might well be something else." This was all fulfilled in due time. Some time later, contrary to the reasonable expectations of an academic career and contrary to the ordinary practice of the Society of going to give missions in different

---

[63]Luis de Medina, S.J. (1637-1671) was the first Jesuit martyr in the Marianas.

[64]Juan Gabriel Guillén, S.J. and Tirso Gonzáles, S.J.(1624-1705), became notable preachers of the mission in Spain. Father Gonzáles was Superior General of the Society of Jesus from 1687 to 1705.

provinces, he established the *Acto de Contrición* in the streets at night, not only in Cádiz and Seville but in all of Andalucia.

Of the mission in Cádiz we could write at length, but that would be a repetition of previous successes. Let it suffice to say that in addition to the innumerable confessions of hidden sins, many made restitution, many scandalous situations came to an end, many enemies became friends, many concubinages were resolved in marriage, and with the alms that were collected, women whom poverty had forced into prostitution were given a decent way of living. And so, this apostolic man left Spain in such a way that they felt an even greater sense of sacrifice in offering to the Indies a man that Spain needed so much.

# CHAPTER XIV

*He Embarks for New Spain;*
*The Good Works He Performs on the Voyage*

On Friday, May 14, 1660, the Venerable Diego Luis and other companions of the Society embarked for Mexico. They looked forward to a happy voyage and were pleased to be traveling in distinguished company. Among others were the *Conde* de Baños and his lady, the former as viceroy of Mexico. They had a high regard for the Servant of God. The following day, May 15, the Feast of San Isidro and the Vigil of the Feast of the Holy Spirit, they set sail with favorable winds. Imagine the joy of the Servant of God, seeing himself at last on the high seas that would take him to the land of his desires. How thankful he was to the Lord and how he praised him! How many times he offered the holocaust to the Redeemer for the salvation of the redeemed! The works he performed on board, and the people he helped, and how he multiplied himself to be of use to all are beyond description. It could well be said that this voyage was an abridged and summarized example of all the different tasks of his life or rather of our Institute, which combined zeal with forces beyond the natural.

The Jesuit community on board was made up of many priests, scholastics, and novices. The passengers were thus religious and seculars from many walks of life. He was master of novices and superior of the scholastics, preacher, missionary, and counselor, as well as father and mother of all in need. The Jesuits observed the same daily order as in all our houses, dividing the time between spiritual exercises and study. For lessons and conferences, the community was divided in three: students of theology, philosophy, and humanities. Father San Vitores taught the theology with such dedication that the classes were conducted as if at the university. He wanted them to make real progress in their studies, and he succeeded. In fact some of his students assert that they made more progress on that voyage than in a whole term at the university. To this end he had to study the subject matter of his classes and of the disputations as if he had to defend the theses publicly at the University of Alcalá or of Salamanca. As master of novices he taught them by interviews and spiritual conferences. He received their account of conscience and saw to it that all points of training were as well taken care of as in the most observant novitiate, and the brilliance of the master was seen in the swift progress of the disciples. They admired the punctuality with which the master was first at all community exercises, whether it was the rosary (each mystery being said by alternating groups) or the points for the meditations of the next morning, which were read aloud to the community, or the litanies and other night prayers. Those who did not wish to retire could remain on deck after night prayers to enjoy the cool air. He never did. He always retired to his cot, not to sleep but rather to pray and

*He Embarks for New Spain; The Good Works He Performs on the Voyage*

to suffer, since many nights the heat was so unbearable that he could not have endured it, if the fire of the Spirit had not exceeded the smothering heat of that cabin.

Father San Vitores served the needs of the lay people as if he were completely free from domestic occupations. He did not miss a single occasion to help them, caring for them in body and soul. It was as if Saint Francis Xavier were sailing for Mexico, as he once sailed for Goa.

At least two days a week the Jesuits took turns teaching Christian doctrine to the people on board, ending the lesson with an example and the Act of Contrition. When it was his turn, his extraordinary fervor was paralleled by the tears and devotions of his hearers. Because of these instructions, as well as private conversations, the pamphlets he distributed, and other means dictated by charity, the number of confessions and communions increased, especially on feast days. The greatest burden of hearing confessions fell on his shoulders since all wished to confess to him, attracted as they were by his affability and understanding. He made confession easy and moved the penitents to sorrow for their sins by speaking of the infinite goodness and mercy of God. Since charity is no acceptor of persons unless they be the poor and the humble, the Venerable Father went among the cabin boys showing them special kindness and giving them little gifts to oblige them each evening at the sound of the Angelus to make the Act of Contrition. Several times he climbed up where the bell was and rang it as a reminder and even a motivation. By his zeal and perseverance he made this a custom on board. He would go to the bow of the ship and minister to the sick, taking advantage of the occasion to console them and lead them to repentance and a good confession. If they thanked him for his good services, he would ask them as repayment to practice some devotion to our Lady or to the saints.

Those who sailed with him to New Spain testify in the official documents to a miracle of grace: the peaceful, harmonious life of all on board, both passengers and crew. There were no disturbances, and there had been plenty of occasions for them, were it not for the prudence and zeal of the Servant of God, nor was there any swearing or other bad language, as is usual on such voyages. Rather, there was the frequent reception of the sacraments, repentance, devotion, and good works, so that someone said the ship was like a house of religious, or as another said, a place of great austerity where only the praise of God was heard.

The captain of the ship had provided insufficient supplies for the sick and even for the healthy. So with the permission of the superior, Father San Vitores supplied the sick with what they needed. He also came to the aid of those who were well, and for many days the Jesuits fed all on board. Nevertheless, the Jesuits did not suffer from need, either as a special reward for their charity or through the prayers of the Servant of God. To these everyone attributed the happy course of the voyage, one of the most prosperous of all the crossings to the Indies. Apropos of this, they noted that Father San Vitores was saying Mass when they sighted Puerto Rico and again when they sighted New Spain. While everyone was happy that the voyage was so pleasant, he complained lovingly to the Lord because the Lord had not treated him as he does his friends: with sufferings and hardships. So Diego writes to a friend: "God has treated me as a weakling, as one he has forgotten, sending me no hardships. Pray that our Lord may give me great ones, with the patience to bear them for his love." For his words and deeds he won the name of *Santo Padre*, as he was called by one and all aboard ship. They entered the port of Vera Cruz on July 28, 1660.

After six days the missionaries set out in six groups for Puebla de Los Angeles. Father Diego Luis went with the group of novices. The superior of the mission, Father Magino Sola, appointed a brother to assist him, but he insisted so strongly to the contrary that the superior deferred to his wishes. But the Venerable Father treated himself so poorly, that is, he rode on the worst mule, took off the cushion, and performed other mortifications, that afterwards when the novices left Puebla for the novitiate at Tepozotlan, the superior ignored his protests and appointed a novice to take care of him on the road, substituting obedience for mortification.

From the novitiate, he traveled to Mexico, visiting the miraculous picture of Our Lady of Guadalupe en route. His consolation was great and in a letter that he wrote to his father on September 22, he says: "I am very consoled. Not over a hundred years ago this country was, so to speak, a wilderness of pagans and idolaters. Now, I see how our holy Faith has spread and is manifest in the remarkable temples and other proofs of religion. Yesterday I was particularly consoled as I visited the miraculous picture of Our Lady of Guadalupe, which is a league distant from Mexico. The picture is a support of and a heavenly portrait of the mystery of the Immaculate Conception.

"There, before the Blessed Mother, I remained for a while meditating on my obligations and consoling myself with the thought that there might be someone who would remember me, a sinner, on the Feast of Our Lady of Good Counsel or of Our Lady of Almudena. The thought that it is the very same Blessed Mother to whom we present our duties and works before such different images is no small consolation to those of us who are far away."

# BOOK II

*Of the Life and Martyrdom of the
Venerable Father Diego Luis de San Vitores,
of the Society of Jesus, First Apostle of the
Mariana Islands*

Fig. 3. "A true likeness of the Venerable Father Diego Luis de Sanvitores". An engraving by Gregorio Fosman. Source unknown. Father San Vitores's poor eyesight was to plague him all his life. (See pages 29; 156; 202).

# CHAPTER I

*The Venerable Father Diego Luis de San Vitores's*
*Many Good Works in the City of Mexico;*
*Extraordinary Happenings*

Never did the City of Mexico, foremost of the New World, receive a greater recompense for the tribute of silver and gold paid to Spain than with the arrival of the new apostle with the fleet of 1660. He remained less than two years but reaped a harvest of many more. His reputation had preceded him and had filled them with desire to see him and kindled the highest expectations, but his activities soon exceeded all expectations and were greater than they could possibly have desired. Father Francisco Solano, who had accompanied him on the voyage to Mexico and in later years was his successor in the Marianas, wrote as follows: "I am convinced from what I see that the esteem in which Father San Vitores is held in Mexico is no less than that of Saint Francis Xavier in Goa."

There is no need to say more than that to give some idea of his activities, of their sheer number and of the admiration that they deserved. Day and night he thought of nothing but the salvation of souls and of the means to serve his neighbor. He was continuously on the go to hospitals and jails, attracting others by his example to concern for the sick and the imprisoned, collecting alms to relieve their needs, and serving in body and soul people who were in need of everything. He was tireless in preaching missions and blessed in their outcome. His whole stay in the city might be called one long mission. He spent his mornings in the confessional for any who might come, and the number was more than his strength could have withstood, were it not for the power of his charity. He would forget to eat and sleep, so caught up was he in bringing peace to souls. There were persons who went to him in confession on five or six consecutive days. He heard them with the greatest patience and was repaid by the thought that he had freed them from the oppression of the devil. This charity attracted many and smoothed away the embarrassment of confessing their faults. The very gentleness with which he received them moved them to sorrow for their sins. One day a penitent knelt before him and burst out laughing. Father Diego Luis asked him why he was laughing. The man answered that he had come in a spirit of true penitence for his sins, but right there came the temptation to laugh. "Well," said the Servant of God, "Let's both laugh." And so they did, and when the man began his confession, sorrow for sin so moved him to tears that Father Diego Luis wept along with him, to the great edification of several priests present who saw the confession end in tears that had begun in a burst of laughter.

On all Sundays and feast days, in the evening, following the example of Saint Francis Xavier, Diego went through the streets ringing a little bell and inviting everyone to attend religious instruction with the words: "For the love of God, come to religious instruction and gain indulgences!" At this street cry many gathered around. He took his stand at a street corner and explained an area of Christian doctrine and ended with an Act of Contrition. Then he would go elsewhere and do the same. In this way he covered the whole city, neighborhood by neighborhood. If few people lived there, he used to begin with one child and teach him the sign of the cross. Eventually a crowd would collect. One Sunday close to Carnival time, Diego left with a companion and his little bell. They came to a main square of the city where they found a large crowd attending a cock fight. But as soon as the people saw him, they left the cocks, gathered round him, and listened in perfect quiet. He realized that he had an ideal congregation, so he organized an *Acto de Contrición*, with its hymns, rhymes, and Hail Marys for people with unconfessed sins and all who were in mortal sin. At the end he led them to the church singing and saying prayers. Just then two other fathers arrived with a large following that they had gathered in other streets. The church could not hold all those people. So Father Diego Luis organized another religious instruction and an *Acto de Contrición*. The result was a great many necessary confessions. The one that most consoled him was that of a person who had not assisted at the religious instruction. He began by saying he had heard that the fathers had led a Hail Mary for a person who had not been to confession for a long time, and he was that person. Another time while Father San Vitores was giving religious instruction in the street, the vicereine, the *Condesa* de Baños, was passing by in her carriage. She stopped the carriage and all were edified because she remained listening to the end.

Father Diego Luis established these instructions in Mexico every Sunday and feast day. Some fathers would go to one neighborhood and others to another. The fact that he had learned from the history of Mexico that this had been done by the first priests who came to this province from the *colegio* of Alcalá helped to re-establish the practice.

He was anxious to have this way of teaching religion established in all the provinces of Spain, especially in places where teaching in the city square is not enough, so that those who need it may get it. Since they did not seek out the instruction, the instruction should seek them out. He strongly insisted on this. The teaching should be presented simply and without display (except three or four times a year) in order to facilitate this necessary ministry. Following the example of Saint Francis Xavier, he would go out every night through the streets with a little bell, asking the faithful to pray for the souls in purgatory and people who were in mortal sin.

Several times he led the *Acto de Contrición* through the streets in the early evening rather than at night, to please those who feared that problems might arise in such a large city. These of course, had not yet experienced the efficacy of this devotion. On one occasion the procession made a station at the cathedral at the request of the dean and the chapter. Father San Vitores writes to Father Juan Gabriel Guillén that

*His Many Good Works in the City of Mexico; Extraordinary Happenings*

this mission has been incredibly successful. As elsewhere, there have been innumerable cases of confessions that had been neglected for years, of lifelong enmities turned into cordial friendships. Of each of these he gives an example. A rather distinguished gentleman approached him in the street and asked him, "Father, I am married now, so when are you coming out with the Santo Cristo?" Then he explained: He had been living five years in concubinage until by chance he came upon the crowd following the Santo Cristo in the *Acto de Contrición*. He followed the crowd and was so impressed that he said: "This is finished," and went and got married. He was so happy that he never failed to follow the Santo Cristo afterwards. He mentioned marvelous effects he had seen in other persons and the fact that the whole city wanted the procession to be held as often as possible. There was a certain citizen who had gone around looking for his enemy in order to kill him. After the *Acto de Contrición* he went looking for him to throw his arms around him and so they became friends. "And so on—the list would never end," said Father Diego Luis. "Thanks to the Lord who does it all through his Holy Mother and Saint Ignatius and Xavier and Father López with his Hail Marys."

To these cases which the Servant of God relates, I will add another no less extraordinary. It is the testimony of a certain captain contained in the beatification documents collected in Mexico. This young man had led a life well satisfied with his worldly ideas, avoiding the physician of his soul whom he so badly needed. Unexpectedly he came upon Father San Vitores who was conducting the *Acto de Contrición*. It would have been noticeable to turn back, so he stopped to hear one of those short talks that Father San Vitores gave to move the crowd to sorrow for their sins. His words pierced the heart of the young man. In tears, he could hardly wait to go to confession the next morning. He changed his life and gave up the occasion that would have led him to hell. But a few months later he had a quarrel with a priest. He decided to kill him. Gun in hand, he waited in the darkness, when it started to drizzle. There was no storm, yet suddenly a bolt of lightning struck like a blazing torch and passed between his legs without any injury to him. But he was struck by the thought of the resolutions he had made when he listened to the words of Father San Vitores, words that now reproached him. At once he went straight to the priest, fell at his feet, and begged pardon for his evil purpose. A few days later he went to hear Father San Vitores who was preaching at the Professed House, and in the whole sermon it seemed that the Venerable Father was giving thanks for the Christian action of that young man. The second time it took place, a certain father of that province had shown himself more fervent and zealous because of it. When they returned home, even before they could take off their capes, Father San Vitores knelt down before him and thanked God for the father's enthusiasm for it and asked him to put it into practice. He praised the father for his fervor and assured them that he would reap an abundant harvest of souls by this means.

At the moment of Father Diego Luis' departure for the Philippines, this same priest said he would miss his advice and example. He answered, "Don't say that. It is good for you that I leave. There are many things that you do not do now because I do them. When I go you will be on your own and will do it all." And so it was. This priest became his substitute in apostolic zeal.

He appealed to Father Hernando Cabero, who was Father General's visitor to the Mexican Province, to impose the practice of the *Acto de Contrición* several times a year as an order of his visitation, although that very religious province already knew its value from experience. He also tried to have the practice extended to all the *colegios* and residences of the province. The father minister of the novitiate of Tepozotlan was so fond of it that he had the novices practice it one day a week, and at times, he would have the novices go to the surrounding towns and conduct the *Acto de Contrición*. God spoke with force and made strong the words of these little ones. One novice led the exercise at a religious exercise given by the fathers of Saint Francis and did it with such fervor that all the fathers embraced him in admiration at the effectiveness of it.

Generally the *Indios* avoid sermons and religious instruction classes unless forced to attend. But when they saw the Santo Cristo in the street, they came running in all haste, forced this time by the love of him who promised that when he was lifted up above the earth he would draw all things to himself. In view of this, the Act of Contrition and the verses were translated into the Mexican language.

The conversion of a certain Jew was a miracle either of Father San Vitores or of the Act of Contrition or of both. At a certain public *auto-de-fe*, where the Jew was to be burned at the stake, no reasons or arguments of learned men or of Father San Vitores could change his mind. Seeing the time grow short and eternal damnation so near, the father made a brief exhortation and said the Act of Contrition, and his words awakened the man and opened his eyes to see and recognize his Redeemer, so that at the end he died a Christian, repenting his sins, kissing the feet of the crucifix, and invoking the name of his Redeemer.[65]

Father San Vitores gave the spiritual exercises of Saint Ignatius personally and had other fathers give them. Through them he led people from an evil life to one of Christian habits. To make this method available to persons who could not go into seclusion entirely, since he felt that through the exercises people in all walks of life could be drawn to spiritual perfection, he arranged that the exercises be given in such a way that some people could return to their homes for necessary business, while spending the rest of the time in our house making the exercises. In this fashion, twenty or thirty of the most distinguished persons in Mexico used to come to our *colegio* to hear the points for meditation and for hours of prayer and spiritual reading, with great benefit to their souls and an effective change in their lives.

Doctor José de la Llana, lawyer of the Royal Audiencia of Mexico, made the exercises under the direction of Father Pedro Juan Castini at

---

[65]John 12:32.

the suggestion of the Servant of God. Doctor de la Llana testified in the process for beatification to the spiritual progress and consolation bestowed on him by the Lord during the retreat. But sometime later he fell into great distress of mind, doubting whether in one of his confessions he had been completely honest. Unable to find peace of mind, he went to our *colegio* of Saint Peter and Paul in search of Father Diego Luis. He had just finished celebrating Mass. Before Doctor de la Llana could explain his scruples, Father Diego Luis addressed him pleasantly and quietly in his usual manner, "Go and kneel before our Blessed Mother (the statue was at the altar where Mass was offered on Saturdays for the students) and say to her, ' "Blessed Mother, I'm crazy!" ' He went to the altar to carry out the Venerable Father's orders. There, on his knees, before he could say a word, a sudden impulse to laugh struck him, as well as feelings of deep interior happiness and joy and consolation in his heart, with such effect that he could hardly pronounce the words. But pronounce them he did, and from that moment he never again suffered from those vain scruples. He attributed this favor and the peace of soul and the consolation to the holiness of the Servant of God. He added that he thought so highly of the sanctity of Father Diego Luis, of his prudence and integrity, of his admirable life, his example and reputation, that even if he had not heard of Father Diego Luis' martyrdom, he would judge that every effort should be made to advance his canonization.

He had *Casos Raros de la Confesión*, his book, printed again in Mexico, to which he added many other examples that had occurred later. He distributed it very cheaply or without cost, as long as people would read it. He thought it would make a clean sweep among sinners. People esteemed it highly for the good it did them. People more than three hundred leagues away were looking for it. He wrote this to Father Guillén and urged him to find a way to have it reprinted in Spain in such a way that it could be given away free or very cheaply or at least that copies be lent, even though some were lost, saying that people pay for it simply by reading it.

There was, of course, someone who despised the book, but it cost him dearly. Father Diego Luis offered the book to a certain loose-living gentleman. He hoped the man would find in it the remedy that many others had found. The gentleman glanced through the book, then and there, but found it not to his way of thinking. He handed it back and said, "What's this all about? The gloom of people full of guilt or of someone who died without confession. Well, Your Reverence can keep your book, because right now I don't intend to die." The Servant of God took the book, hoping for a better occasion to approach that sinner. Unfortunately, a few days later the man died without confession, to the grief of Father Diego Luis, who was deeply concerned for him.

With another case of one in dire need he had more success. Father San Vitores invited this man to make the Ignatian Retreat under his direction. The man excused himself saying he was very busy, so Father Diego Luis gave him the book *Casos Raros* and asked him to read it. The man promised and three or four days later returned to make his general confession with the Servant of God. People who had known him in the past were much edified with the change of life that followed.

Juan Isidro, a merchant of the City of Mexico, who was very fond of Father San Vitores, paid for the printing of *Casos Raros de la Confesión*. His generosity was well rewarded by Father Diego Luis. His wife had suffered from an attack of liver disease for three days. The doctors had prescribed several medicines, but nothing helped. Finally, Juan Isidro, desperate, went to Father Diego Luis, told him of his trouble and begged for his prayers. Would she still be alive when he returned home? The father answered with a smiling face, "Don't worry. Let's just kneel and say an Our Father and a Hail Mary." When they finished Father Diego Luis dismissed Juan Isidro saying, "Go with God, Juan Isidro. The sickness will not progress." So it happened: on his return home he found his wife cured. Both thanked God for this great favor.

It came to the knowledge of this zealous priest that there lived in Mexico City a gentleman whose life was utterly scandalous. He was not only deaf to all entreaties but he had closed the door to remorse, saying, "Don't waste your time. It's too late for my salvation." After consulting with the Lord in prayer, Father San Vitores asked some learned and spiritual men what would be the best way to lead this soul back to God. All brought up so many difficulties that he said he would go to the man's house and take him by surprise and talk to him very earnestly in the name of God. They all tried to dissuade him. He was endangering his life. The man was desperate. Fears and threats would not detain him. He wanted to offer his life for the salvation of souls. He answered intrepidly, "For the service of God, I am not put off by fear." He went to the man's house. The servants could not stop him, as he entered the innermost quarters where the man was with his mistress. He fell on his knees before them. At times, with loving words, he appealed to them with the mercy of God; at other times, with menacing words, he threatened them with the divine justice. Finally the woman burst into tears. She promised then and there to break with this sinful situation and amend her life. The fury of the man is not easy to describe in the face of what he called contemptuous and gross disrespect to his privacy and person. Beside himself with passion, he drew his dagger and twice came close to stabbing the Servant of God, who awaited death motionless as a reward for the life he had gained for that soul and still hoped to gain for the man. But God stopped the man, so that more because of a sudden confusion of mind than for any reason, as he afterwards admitted, he changed his intent.

Diego took the woman with him to a safe place where she amended her life and did penance for her sins. Powerful, O Lord, are your words! That very night, as the man went over the words pronounced by Father Diego Luis, God so changed his heart that, bathed in tears, he sought his godfather to go with him to the Servant of God and, on his knees, he asked forgiveness of him for his mad attempt.

As the father received the prodigal son in his arms, so did Father Diego Luis receive this sinner whose tears intermingled with those of

Diego. Two days later, after making a good confession, he returned to his true wife from whom he had separated many years before because of this mistress. Completely converted, he began a new Christian life of prayer, penance, frequent confession and Communion, and all sorts of good works, much to the amazement of the city, which saw in this change a miracle of divine mercy.

The medicine was different but the cure the same for a certain ecclesiastic. He was highly respected but his life was quite contrary to his obligations. How Father San Vitores knew the true story of worldliness behind a veil of artful concealment is hard to say, unless it was by a special enlightenment of the Lord, as this person ultimately believed. Father San Vitores at different times visited the ecclesiastic. The man was surprised at this because the father was a stranger who had never had any dealings with him. Father Diego Luis put him at his ease, never giving the least hint that he knew the man's real way of life—until one day. Apropos of something in the conversation, the Servant of God quoted some words of Scripture. He said them emphatically and he said them twice, and he never returned to see that man again. The words remained impressed on his memory. He could not get them out of his mind until they brought him back to the Lord and separated him from his vice. He conceived an admiration for the Servant of God, because His Divine Majesty had revealed material so secret and had given the father words that had turned his life around without any preaching.

Another priest was in deep distress, his mind unbalanced, so that he feared to receive the sacraments. Although several learned and pious men had come to his assistance, they had no success. Finally, a pious woman cried out, "Let's go and bring the Angel of the Society. He will free us from this!" Many people in Mexico called Father San Vitores that. They did call him, and as soon as he talked to the sick priest, all his dark fears were dispelled, and as if his words were rays of light, peace returned to his soul, his mind was enlightened, and with outward signs of repentance, after receiving the sacraments, he died a holy death. To those present he seemed to be entering eternal happiness.

A certain father who was close to him at this time said that many people who approached Father San Vitores with problems of conscience found that he had given them the solution and the desired peace of soul as if he had divined their need even before they expressed it in words. This was the case with *doña* Agustina Picazo, a penitent of the Servant of God, as she testified in the Process for Beatification. One day he was visiting with her along with Father José Vidal and the *bachiller don* Agustín de Medina. While they were conversing about the spiritual life, she remained lost in thought about something else that was troubling her deeply. Suddenly, he turned to her and spoke comforting words that spoke to her thoughts and promised a happy issue in the matter of her fears. She was astonished that he read her thoughts and even more so when his prediction came true. She had such regard for his sanctity that to this day she keeps, as a relic, a spoon that he had used. On another occasion this same woman was terribly worried and wished to speak to

Father San Vitores. But he was leaving that day at Acapulco for the Philippines. But although she did not see him nor was able to bid him farewell, he sent her a message through the *bachiller* Cristóbal Vidal, easing her troubled spirit with a complete answer to her problem.

I was forgetting the conversion of a heretic that took place in the city, a memorable occasion. A word said off-guard gave Father San Vitores a clue that the heretic was one. With zeal, he investigated and diagnosed until he found the wound he was desirous to cure. Then he used reasonings until the intellect was convinced and the will moved by Father Diego Luis' God-given words. He abjured his heresy and was reconciled to the Church. He remained thankful to the master through whom God had enlightened his blindness and brought him to the true light of the Catholic religion.

# CHAPTER II

### *He Restores a Sodality of Saint Francis Xavier and Tries to Establish a Shelter for Women*

In the City of Mexico, in the parish of La Santa Vera Cruz, there was a Sodality of Saint Francis Xavier, which was such in name only. Father San Vitores had a profound devotion to the saint. So he set out zealously to restore the sodality that bore Xavier's name and was created in his honor. His success surpassed all his hopes. The sodality reached a height it had never seen before. To be a sodalist was to imitate Saint Francis Xavier in his zeal for souls, and soon they were all devoted sodalists. He set rules for them adapted to the age and status of each. Thus, each might grow and help others grow in the life of the spirit. Anyone who may be interested more particularly in the origin, purpose, rules, and exercises of this congregation should consult the book *The Apostle of the Indies*, Division 3, FF. 11, 12, and 13, which was written by Father San Vitores.[66] Reading it, one sees his zeal and his prudence. Here, I will limit myself to a brief summary of the activities of this extraordinary sodality. Indeed, in the testimonies of the *Processus*, all the witnesses call this the foremost of the apostolic works of Father Diego Luis in the City of Mexico. Pope Alexander VII had approved the Sodality in his apostolic brief of October 12, 1657. He granted many indulgences for the activities of the sodality, naming each expressly. But none of these activities had been put unto action, according to a letter of the Servant of God. They were more like a prophecy of what would be established by Father San Vitores after he came in 1660.

The number of sodalists was fixed as follows: 33 priests, 33 seculars (men) and 33 women. This was in memory of the 33 years of Christ and the 33 years since Francis Xavier was declared Apostle of the Indies. Besides the regular practices of penances, prayer, the frequent reception of the sacraments, and spiritual conferences that are intended for the spiritual perfection of the members themselves, they used to visit jails and hospitals to serve and bring comfort to the ill and the imprisoned. They gave alms to the poor, especially to the secretly needy, and performed all the works of mercy, both spiritual and corporal. The priests taught Christian doctrine every week in their parishes. They accompanied the fathers of the Society when they taught religion in the streets. They, too, preached in the streets and always ended with an Act of Contrition. These priests were the most highly regarded in Mexico, and so they were the first to attend Father San Vitores in the solemn processions of the *Acto de Contrición*. Here, they had to overcome a reluctance born of fear that the procession would be marred by their inexperience. Later they became his constant companions and assistants. They remained inseparable from this field of endeavor. Every group participated in the

---

[66] *El Apóstol de las Indias y Nuevas Gentes*, México, 1661, 1664.

91

apostolate. The women helped in their way, lending *mantillas* on feast days to women who needed them for Mass. There were witnesses enough who testified for the *Processus*, that these good works were so many and so fervent that they exceeded those of the sodalities of Europe. The soul of it all was Father San Vitores, who set everyone moving and inspired them all in the service of God and neighbor. He was venerated as an oracle of wisdom and holiness. So nothing was too difficult if the Servant of God wanted it done.

They took particular pains in their devotion to the holy Apostle of the Indies. In his honor they built a lovely chapel in the parish of La Vera Cruz. To promote devotion to and imitation of his holy patron in the whole city and throughout the province, he wrote the above-mentioned book, *Apóstol de las Indias y Nuevas Gentes*, a summary of his great virtues and miracles. Before the book was printed, he convinced the archbishop and chapter to keep Saint Francis Xavier's Day [then, December 2] as a holy day of obligation in accord with the desire of the people of the City of Mexico and to fulfill a vow that he had made in this regard. The archbishop had ordered him to proofread the book before an imprimatur would be granted. Father San Vitores was so impressed as he read again the extraordinary miracles of the holy apostle and the names of the many cities that had chosen him as their patron saint, that he determined then and there to fulfill the vow he had not yet acted on. The City of Mexico had submitted a petition to the archbishop, dean, and chapter. One of the motives for it, they said, was and would remain their devotion to the apostle, because, by his intercession, their city had been freed from epidemics rampant in Mexico. As soon as some people heard that some new holy day of obligation was to be imposed on the city, they were much displeased and protested. But when they heard that it was in honor of Saint Francis Xavier, they accepted it with pleasure. One of them, in fact, in reparation for the offense to the saint, vowed to assist at five masses on the feast each year as his contribution to the solemnity of the feast.

December 2, 1660, was the first day they celebrated the feast as a holy day of obligation. The city solemnly and under oath took Saint Francis Xavier as their patron at our Professed House. A special feature was that Father Diego Luis, the great imitator of the saint, made his solemn profession of four vows on that day. Diego writes to his father saying: "I am writing to you again today, on the very feast of our glorious patron and my father, Saint Francis Xavier, on this very special day when our Lord has deigned to admit me despite my unworthiness to the profession of four vows in the Society of Jesus. I bring this to your knowledge so that you may help me to thank the Lord and his Blessed Mother and our fathers, Saint Ignatius and Saint Francis Xavier, asking them through the merits of the Passion and cross of our Lord that I may carry out what I have professed and become through my deeds a true child of the holy Society of Jesus. In this fashion I will be a true son of him who is my father for a double reason, since he has offered me to God a second time. You will be my father again and again, as often as you are willing to sacrifice me to the divine will and to obtain for me the grace to carry out that will lovingly with all my strength, body, and soul, in all the works it may please God to send me."

When he returned on his second voyage to Mexico,[67] he brought with him as a gift to the sodality so close to his heart: the chalice with which Saint Francis celebrated Mass while in Japan. Though it is only made of tin, it is more precious than all the treasures of the Indies. The sodality had acquired through the Jesuits some other valuable relics: a portion of Xavier's flesh and the envelope of a letter written to Saint Ignatius. Nowadays the sodality's most cherished relic is the memory of its father founder, the saintly man who deserved to be a martyr of Jesus Christ, a living portrait of the soul of Saint Francis Xavier.

I cannot mention all the admirable work performed by members in the City of Mexico and in all New Spain where branches were organized in the principal cities, but I must say something about the *bachiller* Cristóbal Javier Vidal, a priest, who was a member of the sodality. Father San Vitores called him "my hands." He was Father Diego Luis' principal instrument in all the activities of the main sodality and all the others undertaken by Father San Vitores in Mexico and later in the Mariana Islands. Although he died some years later (I don't know the date) I mention him here as the finest example of a sodalist.

The *bachiller* Cristóbal Javier Vidal was born in Mexico. His parents were distinguished people, God-fearing, living like religious in the state of matrimony. His mother especially was devoted to prayer, mortification, and works of mercy. The son inherited these virtues, plus a love of purity such that, if anyone uttered an indecent word in his presence, he would blush and leave abruptly. From childhood he was very devoted to Saint Francis Xavier, through whose intercession he was able to pursue his studies. His eyesight was so poor that for days he could not open his eyes if the sunlight was bright. He commended himself to the saint, and on the day he started school, was freed of his malady. Ordained a priest, his reputation for sanctity was such that Father San Vitores said he was kneaded by the grace of God. Saint Francis Xavier seemed to be his business partner in all things pertaining to the salvation of souls and the cult of the apostle. The zeal for Xavier's honor came from his close association with Father San Vitores whose least wish was a law to him. When Father San Vitores was away, his letters were received as though from Saint Francis Xavier. He procured doctors and medicines for all the needy of the city and was available to every need. The Lord manifested his good pleasure by a kind of special providence that came to his aid when he was short of money for materials or workers. It would be some project for the greater glory of God, one which Father Diego Luis had entrusted to him, and then all channels seemed to have closed. Then a letter would arrive with a draft for the exact amount needed. In some letters he foretells events that actually took place. He died after being received as a Jesuit. At the time of his death, Saint Francis Xavier appeared to him, bringing him a sense of

---

[67]January 1668.

peace and joy, as if to make up for Father San Vitores, who was absent in the Marianas.

With the sodality solidly established and at work, Father San Vitores turned to a new apostolate for the glory of God, with the help of the sodality. He saw that in the City of Mexico there were many women whom poverty forced to sell themselves as a way of living, and this at the cost of their souls. He collected alms through his sodalists to redeem these souls from the captivity of the devil and the fetters of poverty. He desired to place the work on a more universal and enduring basis. For this he founded a refuge for women that would offer, as it were, a harbor for those who wished to escape that tragic shipwreck. He proposed the project to the Sodality of Saint Francis Xavier, with many forceful arguments. Then he wrote a very scholarly paper giving solid reasons, examples of the saints[68] and of Christian governments, and of the authority of the popes, proofs of the necessity and the importance of this work. He says that one can offer no other work more pleasing to God, because it is at once a corporal work of mercy as well as a spiritual one, a work that redeems the body from need and the soul from guilt. In the measure that a person works to keep his neighbors from sin, his own sins will be forgiven. Furthermore, he will be less likely to fall into sin for having helped others because he has done this for the love of God, whom we should serve and love with all our soul, with all our heart, and all our strength.

Mexico City was afire with this document of Father San Vitores. Many copies were made and distributed. People responded from all classes according to their means, all desirous to cooperate in this work for the glory of God. They then bought some large buildings for 7,000 pesos, buildings that were worth much more but were given for this price, because of so worthy a cause. The foundation grew through the zeal of Father San Vitores who continued to solicit for it from the Philippines and the Marianas, as well as through the efforts of the Sodality of Saint Francis Xavier and especially the work of the *bachiller* Cristóbal Javier Vidal. Finally, it attained a foundation of 100,000 pesos and buildings that could house 600 women. But when the *bachiller* Cristóbal Vidal died, this pious project did not materialize, because the Lord Archbishop Viceroy gave the foundation to the Bethlemite Brothers who take care of the convalescent sick. Oh, that some day the Lord would move someone to establish such a necessary foundation in Mexico! As the Venerable Father writes in his document, citing the words of Clement VII: "The work with these women surpasses the works of the hospitals and similar works of mercy, even as the soul surpasses the body, the eternal the temporal, the heavenly the earthly, and the spiritual the corporal."

---

[68] In this apostolate to women, San Vitores was following the example of his patron, Saint Ignatius Loyola, who founded the House of Saint Martha in Rome for this purpose.

# CHAPTER III

*Father San Vitores's Departure for the Philippines and
His First Calling to the Islands of the Ladrones*

With all his success in Mexico, Father San Vitores was not satisfied. He thought he was doing nothing as long as he was not among the *Indios* and the abandoned Gentiles. To him these were the poorest and the blindest. These he wished to help, to give them the light and the vision of the gospel. Through his unceasing prayers, he obtained that a ship that had left Guatemala would sail for the Philippines, and this at the moment when all had lost hope that any would set sail for the Philippines that year. Father San Vitores gives full credit to Saint Francis Xavier, through whose intercession and merits this was obtained. The ship was spotted, strangely enough, on the same day that a solemn Mass had been sung to start the novena in honor of Saint Francis Xavier, which the blessed martyr Marcello had initiated for obtaining graces and favors from God.[69]

With the news of the arrival of the ship, Father San Vitores hastened to the viceroy, who was then His Excellency, the *Conde* de Baños. With telling reasons, he persuaded him to arrange transportation, although they were pressed for time. There were other difficulties also, the greatest one that Mexico should let Father San Vitores go to the Philippines, when so many had high hopes that through his ministry a complete reformation of the city and the whole province would take place. One of the Jesuits, a master of theology, told Father Francisco Solano that the Mexican Province would happily exchange four priests for one Father San Vitores. But what were four, even four of the most fervent, in exchange for a man who did the work of ten or twenty, to say the least?

The Servant of God left the City of Mexico, a city that would gladly have followed him, as his friends and sodalists wept, thinking they would never see him again. Sadder still were fourteen Jesuits, half of his group, who had to stay behind because the ship was so small. These waited to sail to the Philippines the following year. Father Diego Luis sailed from Acapulco on April 5, 1662 in the *San Damián*, a small *patache*,[70] with fourteen Jesuit companions of whom he was superior. There is much to tell about this voyage, but it would be repetitious, since the same things happened as on the voyage from Cádiz to Vera Cruz. Quarters on this ship were very tight, especially for a novitiate. But regular observance and the practice of all the ministries of confessions, communion, the teaching of Christian doctrine, the *Acto de Contrición* for all on board, and the care of the sick were carried out as if in a town.

---

[69]The Novena of Grace in honor of Saint Francis Xavier was instituted by Marcello Mastrilli, S.J., in 1635 in Lisbon, and has been very popular until recent days.

[70]*Patache*, a small sailing ship, generally used as a tender.

With his persuasion and affability he led those on board to abstain from the gambling, cursing and swearing, and blasphemy that are the ordinary custom on ships. And so the Lord granted to all, through the prayers and merits of his servant, a safe and prosperous voyage, although for himself he would have preferred one full of hardships and dangers, provided, of course, that no one died on the whole voyage. I read in a letter that Father San Vitores not only assisted everyone in spiritual matters, but also that there was not a single person aboard who did not receive some assistance in his bodily needs as well.

Upon passing the Ladrones, which are 300 leagues this side of the Philippines, the islanders sailed out, as usual, to obtain iron, knives, and similar small objects in exchange for fruits of their land.

It is impossible to express the feelings of the zealous Father San Vitores when he saw the poor, naked natives, who although living in the path of the Spanish galleons, had never enjoyed the light of the gospel. But when he realized that their poverty and that of their islands was the cause of this abandonment, he could not restrain his tears. "Why," he lamented, "are there so few men who are greedy for the richest mines in the world, namely the souls redeemed by the Precious Blood of Christ?" And he prayed to God that the light might be sent to those islands so that the souls might not be lost that were redeemed at such a cost. As the ship was surrounded by the natives' canoes, he fell into an ecstasy in which he now understood the words he had heard spoken so clearly (by the lips of Christ, it seemed) in the last illness in Madrid, of which he was cured miraculously: *Evangelizare pauperibus misi te.*[71] Along with these words had come a vision of many dilapidated huts, which he thought were in the kingdom of Japan, but now he was more convinced than ever that these naked islanders were the poor people the Lord was sending him to evangelize. The account of his ecstasy is based on the testimony under oath for the *Processus* given in Iloilo by the Licentiate *don* Mateo de Cuenca, pastor with temporary benefice of the village of Arévalo and vicar forane of the Province of Otem. He was formerly a member of the Society and had sailed to the Philippines with the Servant of God. He was then his secretary. He died in the Society as Father Diego Luis had foretold. We will mention him later.[72] Let it now suffice to say that he knew many secrets.

From this spark, or rather volcano, that God set burning in his heart, flowed the longing to come to the islands he afterwards named the Marianas. He would gladly have remained here in spite of his ignorance of the language and the lack of resources in these islands. But obedience was his star guiding him now to the Philippines.

On July 10, 1662, the *San Damián* put into port at Lampong, in the Philippines. A few days later the Jesuit procurator for the Philippines came to welcome them at the port. From there the party of missionaries had to go on foot to Manila, over mire and cliff. He began the novitiate of hardships he was to endure in the Philippines, yet with joy in

---

[71] Cf. Matt. 11:5. I have sent you to evangelize the poor. All translations from the Latin are by the editor.
[72] See Book 4, chap. 13:322.

his heart, because, he writes: "I have heard the *Indios* singing the *Salve* in their own language. It reminded me of the prophecy of the Blessed Mother: *Ecce enim beatam me dicent omnes generationes.*"[73] All fifteen arrived safe and sound in Manila, where they sang a glad *Te Deum Laudamus* in thanksgiving for a happy voyage. The ship *San Damián*, as if refusing to serve any other purpose than bringing so many apostolic men to the Philippines, was lost in a storm between the port of Lampong and that of Cavite, among the islands near Cavite.

There was now great rejoicing among the Jesuits of the Province of the Philippines with the arrival of the new European co-workers. These would now draw in the nets in that great archipelago ready for the harvest, but in dire need of harvesters. They rejoiced especially because of Father San Vitores, whom his companions praised so highly, but whose work promised so much more. In the Philippines, rich soil and a tropical sun produced crops abundant in quantity and variety. As a crossroads of East-West it enjoyed prosperous commerce. But vice was as abundant as wealth, and Father San Vitores found a sharp spur for his zeal and even more for his sorrow.

Upon arrival he went into retreat with his companions to arm themselves to battle the enemy of souls, strong in that land.

The younger Jesuits still in training resumed their studies, while those who had completed them left for different towns or teaching centers to study the native language and to begin instructing the *Indios*.

Of the four Jesuits who went to Pintados, or the Province of Visayas, the Moros of Tolo took captive Father Andrés Ventura de Bárcena, a Jesuit of theProvince of Castille. Father San Vitores was distressed at his suffering. "There is no lack of those who envy him. Of the fifteen of us, he has been the first one chosen to taste the sweetness of prison for preaching the faith of our Lord Jesus Christ." His holy envy increased when he heard that Father Andrés had died in prison, a victim of the ill treatment inflicted by the Moros because of his witness to Christ. They put a dagger to his breast to force him to become a Moro. But he scorned all fears with the courage of Christ who rewarded him with the crown of martyrdom.

---

[73]Luke 1:48. Behold, all generations will call me blessed.

# CHAPTER IV

*He Goes From Manila to Taytay to Learn the*
*Tagalog Language; the Wonders He Performs*
*Among These People*

Father San Vitores started his apostolate in Manila among the Spaniards, as he had done in Mexico (more about this when we talk about the City of Taytay). But very soon his zeal led him to learn the Tagalog language, which is the vernacular of that province. He wanted to help the natives, both Christians and pagans. That was his main reason for coming to the islands, otherwise it seemed he was doing nothing if he were doing the same things as he did in Spain.

Everyone thought he would be teaching theology as soon as he arrived in Manila, but as he himself wrote, God had other plans and he was given permission to learn Tagalog and prepare himself at once for ministries among the *Indios*.

Taytay is a town of the *Indios*, at six or seven leagues from Manila. Father Miguel Solano, former provincial of the Philippines, was minister there at that time. Former provincials in the Philippines, as Father San Vitores wrote, had no other relaxation after their years of strain than the work of teaching the natives.

Father Solano, then in Taytay, asked his superiors to send Father San Vitores to learn Tagalog. He in turn would learn from the recently arrived Father San Vitores, whom he regarded as theApostle of the Philippines. Although Tagalog is a very difficult language, the Servant of God learned it with such facility and in such a short time, that when some of his companions considered themselves as rather advanced, since they knew the first elements, he was hearing confessions and preaching with elegance and facility. They thought it miraculous and believed his teacher was the Holy Spirit, who had descended on the apostles in tongues of fire.[74] They were not deceived, since he himself attributed it to the *Acto de Contrición*, which we could call "tongue of fire of the Holy Spirit," the Spirit which is divine love. Father Diego Luis writes that he had some clever *Indios* translate the *Acto de Contrición* into Tagalog, in the format of Father Jerónimo López, with its slogans and Hail Marys. He then memorized it and put it in practice in the town with all its chants; and so, the *Acto de Contrición* made easy what previously had been difficult. Soon he was able to hear confessions and preach fluently in all matters concerning the mission and teaching.

In his daily talk with the *Indios*, he says, God gave him the knowledge in the measure he needed it, and if at any time he was at a loss, he would go to the *Acto de Contrición*, which he knew by heart. More marvelous still was the way he learned the Tagalog lan-

---

[74]Acts 2:3-4.

guage, of which the Venerable Father gives us an account in his humble way.

He preached his first sermon in that language only three months after his arrival at Taytay, on the occasion of the visit of the provincial, Ignacio Zapata. Upon arrival everyone seemed to want Father Zapata to know how quickly Father San Vitores had obtained a perfect command of the Tagalog language. Father Zapata asked him to preach in Tagalog the following day, which was the Feast of the Circumcision (January 1). At first Father San Vitores excused himself because of the very short notice, but he had to obey. He preached to the admiration of all who heard him, as much at ease as if it were his native tongue. This is so much the more admirable, since Tagalog is elegant, but artful. Father Colín puts it this way in his *History of the Philippines*: It has the four qualities of the four best languages in the world: Hebrew, Greek, Latin, and Spanish.[75]

Much more surprised were those who later on learned all the circumstances of the case. The *donado*, Marcos de la Cruz,was Father San Vitores' language teacher and later on would be his disciple in the mission. The night before, he heard some noise in the father's room. He stopped at the door and listened. He noticed that the father was repeating his sermon while a sweet melodious voice corrected every one of his mistakes. After a short while he entered the room, wanting to know who was Father Diego Luis' teacher. He found no one but the father. He was persuaded it was his guardian angel, to whom he had much devotion, and as we shall see later, dealt with quite familiarly. No wonder he mastered Tagalog in so short a time under the direction of such a teacher!

Almost all the time he was in Taytay, he lived in the room once occupied by the Venerable Father Marcello Mastrilli. In the shelter of those very same walls, which silently revealed to him the secrets of this apostolic martyr, he was set afire in zeal for the salvation of souls and the desire for martyrdom. He writes to his father that this blessed martyr is the model always set before his eyes, yet much to his confusion since he fell so short in imitating his example. Then he adds: "Oh, that I may live and die with the very same spirit and love of God and zeal for the souls redeemed through the Blood of our Lord Jesus Christ. Amen, Amen, Amen."

From this fire, set aflame in his heart, flame forth the letters written to his father and other zealous persons, asking that they intercede with His Majesty to put an end to many disorders that hinder the spread of the Kingdom of God in the Philippines, and to obtain a *cédula* commanding the governor of the Philippine Islands to provide a ship and the necessary things for him to embark for Japan or some other mission (the Ladrones), provided this latter assignment comes first, in accord with the orders and disposition of his superiors, since this mission of the Marianas was always his foremost desire from the time he landed in the Philippines.

---

[75]Francisco Colín, S.J. (1592-1660), *Labor Evangélica*, Madrid, 1663: Barcelona, 1900, p. 56. Colín compared the structure of Tagalog to that of Hebrew and Greek and its richness and civility to those of Latin and Spanish.

*Book Two, Chapter 4*

The Servant of God did many good things in general, but especially for the *Indios* of this village at the time he was among them and even in his absence on some mission. He was always present to his beloved children in their need. The province suffered a plague of locusts. The *Indios* of the village, distressed at the inevitable ruin that menaced their crops, came to him in tears and begged some remedy of him. He exhorted them to sorrow for their sins and to a great trust in God, since punishments come from God for our sins and the way to avoid punishment is penance. Then he accompanied the *Indios* to the fields and commanded the locusts with the words of the Church and blessed the fields and the crops. God in his goodness willed that on the third day all the locusts died, and the crops were entirely unharmed.

The lack of foresight on the part of the *Indios*, who did not bother to pick up the dead locusts, caused a repetition of this marvel on a wider scale. After a few months the locusts reproduced in still greater numbers and covered all the fields and crops. There was not a green leaf free from the plague. The *Indios* came to Father San Vitores in greater affliction and distress, but with more confidence now, because they had experience of his powerful charity. He blessed the fields and God protected them so that not a leaf was lost in all the crops. The *Indios* marveled to see that his blessing covered not only the boundaries of their town, but the rest of the province as well, as though the blessing were not to be narrower than the charity behind it.

*Don* Juan Auij, a leading *Indio* of the place, had assisted him in learning the Tagalog language and in translating the *Acto de Contrición* as well as other pious papers. He was more than liberally repaid for his labors. At the time of his death he was in deep distress, not because he was dying, but because Father San Vitores was absent on a mission and could not assist him. As *don* Juan prayed and lovingly complained that Father Diego Luis had abandoned him in his hour of need, all at once he saw Father San Vitores before him, talking to him of the mercy of God and preparing him with prayers and ejaculations for the moment of departure. Death came to him in deep peace and serenity, after he had confided to those present the visit of the Servant of God.

Another *Indio*, named Francisco Amagsali, was on his deathbed terribly afflicted by the devil. A group of *Indios*, following instructions given by Father San Vitores, remained by his bedside reciting the Act of Contrition to prepare him for a happy death, when all at once a boy ran into the room in great excitement. He said that a man in the street had told him that the town was on fire and they had better come and help put it out. They all ran out leaving the dying man alone. Then the devil, who had planned the trick, appeared to him in a horrible figure and tried to drive him to despair. After a while the people returned from the false alarm and found the dying man utterly desolate and in mortal anguish. When they asked him about it, he said he had been attacked by the devil ever since they left him alone and was still under attack. He asked them to pray for him. All those present began to pray to God and to call the saints to aid him, and they soon saw the sick man pass from anguish to serenity and from sadness to joy. They asked him the reason and he said, "Because the devil fled from the moment Father San Vitores entered the room to help me to die in peace." No one present saw Father San Vitores, but they believed the man, since the fervor with which he pronounced the acts of faith, hope, and charity as he gave up his soul to the Lord were sure tokens of his predestination.

# CHAPTER V

*The Good Works Father San Vitores Performs in Manila*

Having mastered the Tagalog language, he returned to Manila by order of his superiors and was able to do much for the Spaniards and Filipinos. He was appointed master of novices, prefect of studies for both houses, prefect of studies of our university, prefect of the sodality of the Spaniards, prefect and minister of the *Indios*. Each one of these charges would have been a full-time job for anyone, and previously they had been handled by four men. He managed each as though it were the only one. He had time for everything except rest. Rest for him was helping his neighbor. He felt great consolation being with the *Indios* and being in the midst of God's little ones to whom the Lord made himself known more than to the wise and prudent of this world.

Besides the novices, who were a credit to their master and guide, almost everyone in the *colegio* went to confession to him. This, with all its counseling, took most of the evening; yet he never complained of people who came at an inconvenient hour or with senseless scruples. All went away at peace and inspired by his gentle charity.

He frequently gave conferences to his sodalists, both Spaniards and Filipinos. He taught them various devotions, principally the frequent reception of the sacraments and purity of conscience through the Act of Contrition. So that the *Indios* would not forget what he had taught them, he had various leaflets printed in the Tagalog language. These leaflets were distributed free of charge, as were the monthly leaflets for the sodalists, which he had printed in quantity and distributed in all the towns and catechism centers. He taught the *Indios* who were capable the way to administer baptism in case of an emergency in the hill country and the farms and how to help make the Act of Contrition at the moment of death. He paid special attention to the instruction of the Filipinos. He felt that they cooperated with grace, because they apply themselves to the things of our holy Faith and to Christian practices. They generally do better than the small towns of Castile, and in their good will and devotion they do best when they have the regular assistance of the priests. However, he warned that it is important to take care of the Spaniards, lest their bad example destroy the work done with the *Indios*.

He continually visited the hospitals, which were his paradise, since he delighted in works of charity and humility. Very often he would leave the *colegio*, broom in hand, and would walk through the main streets, as if it were a palm of victory, a victory over the world and its vanities. He swept the rooms of the hospital, picking up the waste with his hands and doing the rest of the hospital chores. With the same charity he visited the prisons. With equal fervor he preached to Filipinos and Spaniards. There was no heart that could resist the gentle power of his words, kindled as they were by the fire of the Holy Spirit. The sinners that he wounded in the pulpit were healed by his unfailing charity in the confessional, where he was found morning and evening, whenever his other obligations left him free, since so very many sought his confessional. As if this was not enough, on all feast days he would go out to the country villages to teach Christian doctrine.

When the Chinese pirate Pumpuan menaced Manila with a fleet of nearly a thousand vessels and a large army ready to put ashore, the people were terrified. At this time, however, Father San Vitores urged the archbishop and the governor that the first battle should be against sin, which is our worst enemy and betrays us to our foes. If we conquer sin, we can conquer any army of men or devils. God will be on our side and if God is with us, who can stand against us?[76] He proposed that the general assault be an *Acto de Contrición* at night. There were some prudent men who objected to this in such a large city where it could cause trouble. Their fears were in contradiction to all that his experience had proven. But finally his zeal won out. He took Saint Michael as his patron for this war and organized an octave in his honor and set out on the first night of the *Acto de Contrición*. One of the generals carried the Santo Cristo and all the soldiers attended as well as the governor. Father San Vitores called his *saetillas* the artillery of Saint Michael and he chanted the words of the Prince of the Heavenly Host: "Who is like God, that we fear? Who is like God, that we love?"[77] The priests in the procession imitated him in his fervor, intoning the couplets and making Acts of Contrition, so that the people were moved to tears and penance. Those who had been opposed to the procession for one night now asked that the procession proceed every night of the octave. Finally, it was decided to go though the streets on three nights only and for the rest of the octave to congregate in our church in the following way: there would be an exemplary story and they would end with an Act of Contrition, and there would be a discipline. The governor would assist at all services. On three other days there would be an *Acto de Contrición* for the *Indios* in their language in the surrounding towns. The *Indios* took great pleasure in this type of procession with the *saetillas* and chants. They were deeply moved to repentance.

When he finished his mission of the *Acto de Contrición* in Manila, by order of the archbishop and the governor, he left for Cavite, the main port of the island and the only Spanish city outside of Manila, to preach the mission there. This mission was equally or even more successful because all the religious orders joined the Jesuits in the practice of the *Acto de Contrición*: the Dominicans, Franciscans, Augustinian Recollects, and the religious of Saint John of God. Everyone took turns and chanted and gave the sermons. Father San Vitores says the Dominicans distinguished themselves in fervor and enthusiasm for the practice and that the father vicar provincial, who was present and had a beautiful voice, was one of the most enthusiastic and he inspired the people with his *saetas*. Then he and another devoted priest, who was regent of stud-

---

[76] Rom. 8:31.

[77] A play on the name Michael, a word meaning, "Who is like God."

## Book Two, Chapter 5

ies there, led the *Acto de Contrición*. The processions were held for three nights within the walls and another time for the *Indios* outside the walls.

Father Diego Luis took great spiritual joy in the rich harvest in Manila and Cavite. The *Acto de Contrición* was the bait. Not only did he catch the fish, but also the fishermen; not only the sinners, but the preachers, since not only the Jesuits but also some of the Dominicans and Augustinians would end their Lenten sermons with the *Acto de Contrición*. They also added it to their religious instruction. An Augustinian called *fray* Luis de Amezquita, a very holy man, after overcoming great difficulties, established it in his parish on all the Fridays in Lent. He said its effects had to be seen to be believed.

Father San Vitores has written an account of all this,[78] telling of his joy because the *Signum cui contradicetur*,[79] as he called the *Acto de Contrición*, remained the ordinary refuge in time of need or calamity throughout the country. When the great earthquake of July 19, 1665 rocked Manila, nine persons died and buildings were badly damaged. The archbishop ordered that the fathers should organize the *Acto de Contrición* that very night. They did so and the next night as well. Father San Vitores took advantage of this warning from heaven to move the living to penitence through the misfortune of the dead.

He did so much for the people, both Spaniards and Filipinos, that we would never finish, if I were to recount all the cases. Among the very many were the dubious attachments that were either broken off or ended in marriage; unhappiness in marriage that found reconciliations; enmities changed to friendship; and so many scandals and other evils done away with. If he knew that someone was in mortal sin, he would not rest until he freed him from that evil state. He would pray earnestly to God and use the means dictated by prudence and charity. An example of this is seen in the testimony for the process of canonization given by *maestro fray* Juan de la Paz, O.P., a man of great prudence and piety. He tells of a certain ecclesiastic who was at the point of death, after a life most unworthy of his vocation. When no one could persuade him to go to confession, as a last resort they summoned Father Diego Luis, knowing the power of his word and of his prayers. He came full of grief and fear that the man would die unrepentant. He spoke to him many times with the force that this crisis demanded, using every motive his fervor could dictate. But the sick man was adamant. Father Diego Luis wept bitterly seeing the man on the way to perdition. He cried out in his heart to the Lord Jesus, but feeling himself unworthy of such a difficult victory, in his humility he sought out the Reverend Father *maestro fray* Juan de Paz to use his charity and zeal to win back this soul in its great peril. Both went to the house of the sick man, but he persisted in rejecting the spiritual medicine of his soul. Finally, our Lord in his mercy rewarded the labors of his servant and opened the eyes of the dying man to see his sin. He surrendered to the words of Father San Vitores, made a good confession, and with his soul at peace died two or three days later.

---

[78]San Vitores wrote this account in a letter to Father Juan Gabriel Guillén, S.J., letter no. 2 of the Nagasaki College collection of San Vitores letters.

[79]Luke 2:34. The sign that will be contradicted.

It was a wonderful thing, said Father *fray* Juan de Paz to see the anguish of Father San Vitores, as if the trouble were his. Like the apostle Paul he was sick with the sick and consumed himself for his brothers.[80]

I omit many other such cases. I will relate one which the same *fray* Juan de Paz tells and which is similar to one in Mexico that we have already mentioned.[81] A priest was seriously tempted and close to giving in. He said nothing about it to Father San Vitores, but the latter spoke to him some words from Sacred Scripture, which described his state of soul. He believed that God was speaking to him through Father San Vitores and he gave up his sin. This case was referred to *fray* Juan de Paz by the person to whom it refers.

There was a poor man (I omit the details to protect his identity) who went out to the country and drew his dagger to stab himself in the breast. He was about to strike when he heard a voice say clearly and distinctly: "Don't do that. Go to the *colegio* and ask for Father San Vitores. He will tell you what to do." The name was repeated three times so he would not forget it. The man obeyed the voice and went to Father San Vitores who heard his confession and comforted him. Diego took care of the financial need that had brought the man to despair. Diego urged him to thank God for that extraordinary favor and to practice devotion to his guardian angel whose voice must have spoken those words.

Of the wonders he worked in the City of Manila I will relate only one here. *Doña* Isabel Díaz had been suffering severe pains of childbirth for three days. Her husband and all the family were in terrible distress because of the danger to the mother and the child. Father Diego Luis happened to be passing along the street when he saw some people at the door of that house. They were excited and seemed terribly anxious. He asked the reason for it, and they told him that there was a woman there in labor for three days and now on the point of death. He entered the house and recited a gospel passage with his hand upon the patient. At once she happily gave birth to a healthy baby. The godfather was *don* Francisco Ponte. He himself told us the story and he heard *doña* Isabel tell of the great comfort she felt when she saw Father San Vitores enter her house.

---

[80]1 Cor. 9:22.
[81]See Book 2, chap. 1:85.

# CHAPTER VI

*The Missions of the Servant of God in the District of Manila*

Although the whole time Father San Vitores was in Manila could be called one continuous mission, held sometimes in the city, sometimes in the outskirts, in 1664 he left the city with another father to preach missions in the villages of the surrounding countryside. He did so at the request of the archbishop, of whom he writes to his father humorously: "The Blessed Mother has decided that I am not to ruin the good work of other men by my tepidity and incompetence, especially the good work of the excellent prelate to whom God has entrusted this metropolitan see. I have already written to you how he persecutes us in the same manner as the cardinal of Toledo. He leaves us no rest from preaching the *Acto de Contrición* and missions, on the occasion of earthquakes, of anniversaries, of the continuous celebration of his zeal, etc., etc."

This zealous prelate gave our priests all the faculties for absolution, for marriage and other cases, as well as a great quantity of rosaries, medals, and other religious articles. After receiving his blessing, the priests left at the end of Lent. When word got round that the priests had come to preach and that they had faculties to absolve all kinds of sins, a great multitude came down from the hill country, as if they had abandoned their towns, homes, and fields to hear the word of God and go to confession. The priests would stop in the middle of the fields at a place where they could be heard by all. At the bell of the Angelus, so that the farm hands, slaves, and other workers could attend, the rosary would begin, recited in two alternating choirs, Spaniards and *Indios*, each in their own language. Then came the procession of the *Acto de Contrición*, parading through the fields while the priests chanted the phrases alternately in Spanish and Tagalog. This was followed by instruction in some mystery of our Faith, how to go to confession, or other necessary and important matters. There was always an example of someone who had willingly concealed a mortal sin, and with crucifix in hand, the priests would severely reprove the terrible sacrilege, ending with the Act of Contrition and some Hail Marys for those who make bad confessions and for other needs, spiritual or corporal. They ended at ten or eleven o'clock at night, but the time never seemed long to the congregation.

The fruit of their labors was beyond counting. The confessions of sins hidden for ten, twenty, thirty, forty, fifty, sixty or more years were innumerable. Couples in concubinage were married, with dispensations when needed. Other scandals were ended and vices corrected—all the fruit of these confessions. Two Muslims were attracted by the fame of the Servant of God, and struck by his words, they abandoned Mohammed for Christ. One of these was the Prince of Tidore, in the Moluccas Islands, who abandoned his riches and a prospective marriage to the daughter of the Malayan king, and went with Father San Vitores to Manila. He received religious instruction and was solemnly baptized. There were also baptisms of Calvinists and Lutherans.

So that the effect of the mission would be lasting, he first gave a general instruction to all on how to baptize in case of emergency, how to prepare a person for death by Acts of Contrition in the absence of a priest, and then in each town or ranch, he left a chart giving the basic religious instruction. When he found a more capable person, he instructed him with greater care and entrusted him with reading the above-mentioned chart of religious instruction and of leading the rosary. And he gave out large numbers of rosaries.

He encountered many noteworthy cases, but for fear the individuals may be identified, we will relate only a few where there is no danger. A certain person told two others what he had heard in an instruction on bad confessions, and the two persons who had not heard the instructions were so impressed that they went to confession the following day with great sorrow and repentance, although one of them had been making sacrilegious confessions for many years and the other had not been to confession at all for years.

On one occasion the Venerable Father was already in the pulpit, the subject matter of his sermon well prepared, when after making the sign of the cross, he felt an interior motion to speak against lewdness, saying that one of the effects of this vice is to close the mouth through embarrassment, so as not to confess the sins. He said one must resolve to overcome our shame and confess any sin, regardless of how ugly it might be. He showed how the confessors know well our human weakness, accustomed to hearing all sorts of sins, and are never shocked by any. It was clear that it was God who had moved his preacher to speak of that matter for the benefit of a certain sinner in the congregation. He went to confession to Father San Vitores that very day and confessed the very ugliest sins. He had never dared confess them before out of shame, though they had driven him to the point of hanging himself.

On another occasion he went to confess a sick man who had led a scandalous life. In his despair the man would hear nothing of confession or the mercy of God. As the sinner lent deaf ears, he turned to the Mother of Sinners, who is never deaf to our prayers, and entrusted that soul to her care. He then told the man a story from the book *Casos Raros*. He spoke with so much love and earnestness that the sick man, trembling, took his hand and said, "Father, don't be put off by my embarrassment. I have so seldom gone to confession. In fact, I wish I hadn't gone at all, they were such bad confessions." Father San Vitores embraced him lovingly and spoke to encourage him of the mercy of God and the great gift of time to repent. The man made a sincere confession, received the other sacraments, and died a happy death, thanking God for sending him a sure guide to heaven.

Another very old man had made bad confessions almost all his life, but his troubled conscience warned him that he must prepare for death, which could not be far off. But he said, "If only Father San Vitores would come to my town! I would surely confess to him. He is so holy and has such faculties to absolve sins." God did send him Father San Vitores. The old man's words had been an excuse rather than a sincere desire. When he saw the father his resolution cooled. But that night he heard the *Acto de Contrición* and the talk on hidden sins. The old man could no longer resist the ardent words pronounced by that zealous apostle. Bathed in tears, he made a confession of his whole life.

More noteworthy is the following case: One morning a soldier came to Father Savitores' lodging, fleeing, it seemed, from the wrath of God and his justice. The father tried to calm him down asking him what was troubling him so very much. His speech broken by sighs, the man said: "Since I heard that example you gave during religious instruction about those who conceal sins in confession, I cannot rest day or night, I resolved to confess to you and I came different times to look for you at your lodging. But as soon as I arrived here, something held me back with a secret violence. An invisible hand seemed to be pulling my clothes to turn me away. And, in fact I made little resistance, though I could not rest day or night. I begged God for a remedy, praying for it every night until God gave me the grace to kneel before you for my confesison." Father San Vitores asked him how he had managed to get in. Did no one stand in his way? He answered: "Last night between eleven and twelve, as I knelt at my prayers, asking God's mercy, you entered my room and stayed for a quarter of an hour, persuading me gently to come for confession. You assured me there would be no obstacle." The Servant of God, realizing that his guardian angel—who is always solicitous for our good—must have taken his form, showed no surprise and heard the man's confession.

I will here add the mission that he preached at Cavite, which belongs to the district of Manila, although this took place the following year. Because the archbishop attended the mission, the crowd, attracted by this holy and apostolic man, was enormous. The archbishop preached by his example. He visited the prisons and the galleys. He helped the needy with alms, was a father to the poor and a truly humble shepherd to his sheep. He had Father San Vitores preach the *Acto de Contrición* three times. The other members of the team were Dominicans and Augustinians, in a new format that originated in this port. Not satisfied with the work of the day, which was spent in preaching and hearing confessions, Father San Vitores would go through the *ribera*, where the work-places of the dockyards, the sailors, and the galley men are located. He would give these poor fellows religious instruction during the evening because they could not attend during the day. One evening as he left the house where the archbishop lodged, His Eminence ordered Father Diego Luis's companion not to let him go anywhere but to his *colegio* so that he might rest a little from such an exhausting experience. Hardly had they reached the street but Father Diego Luis said, "Let's go to the galleys, Angel, and we'll see if we can organize an *Acto de Contrición*." They went, and the Venerable Father gave the instruction such charm and the *Acto de Contrición* afterwards, that they all listened with great pleasure and devotion, little as such people are inclined to pious practices. Not the least fruit of this mission was the more than fifty marriages of the poor soldiers and sailors. The archbishop's generous purse provided for the fees, which might have been a difficulty.

# CHAPTER VII

*His Mission in the Mountains of Santa Inés and Maralaya*

I n the Philippine Islands there are mountains inhabited by infidels who have not received the yoke of Christ, and Christians who have thrown off this yoke in their close contact with the Gentiles, people who for debt or crime had sought refuge in these cliffs whose inaccessibility promises impunity and liberty. Father San Vitores set out in 1665 in search of these lost sheep to restore them to their Divine Pastor and of the fugitive wild ones to make them Christ's sheep. The roads were steep and perilous, the valleys full of danger and hardship, but his heart was full of joy as he entered the Lord's "hunting grounds."

He first went to the mountains of Santa Inés evangelized long ago by the Jesuits from Antipolo. In those days the Jesuits had converted about three hundred native Etas living in those mountains. They could only visit them twice a year for one or two weeks, since the laborers were few and the roads impassable in the rainy season.

As Father Diego Luis approached Santa Inés, one of his main objectives was a ninety-year old man, a Gentile notorious for his obstinacy, since he always refused to give a hearing to the Law of God. It was the Feast of the Visitation of the Blessed Virgin Mary, suited to the occasion since on that day our Lord, carried by his Mother, accomplished his first mission in the hill country of Judea, that of sanctifying the child John the Baptist.[82] On this same feast in the afternoon, Father San Vitores sent the *Indio* a picture of the Blessed Virgin with the message: "The Mother of the Lord of heaven, the Lord who has come to visit these mountains (in the Sacrifice of the Mass), would like to take you to his home if you would be baptized." A wonderful thing happened through the power of God and the intercession of his Mother. With no hesitation or discussion, that obstinate heart was moved and wished to be baptized. As he was old and feeble, he was carried in someone's arms down to the town and the church for instructions. But as soon as he was baptized the old man exclaimed, "Now, Father, I am a Christian. As soon as you poured the water on me, my body changed. It felt like the body of a child. My aches and pains were gone, and I could feel the strength of my youth." He proved this. From that moment the *Indio* began to walk, to go up and down the mountain and work at whatever was offered. By this miracle God showed the spiritual power that this water of life gives to the soul, since it gave so much strength to the body, a proof of the miracle that puzzled Nicodemus: how an old man could be born again and become a child by the waters of baptism.[83]

As this "message" from the Mother of God worked out so well (he says in a letter), from then on he gave and would continue to give all

---

[82]Luke 1:39.
[83]John 3:4-5.

his missions with this magic, with this title of "Embassy of the Mother of the Lord of Heaven." And indeed this embassy comes from there in spite of the devil and his own sins. After talking of this and other missions that were carried out successfully because of the conversions of infidels and sinners, he says in conclusion: "I did not convert them. By the time they came to me the embassy of our Lady had done its good work."

This old man, whose name was John, came to his baptism with a girl ten years old. At her baptism Father San Vitores gave her the name of Mary Elizabeth, because this was the Feast of the Visitation. She had fled down the mountain, leaving the infidels who were raising her in place of her parents who were dead. On her own she had asked to be baptized.

In the short seven days that obedience had allowed the Servant of God for this mission because of the pressure of other tasks, he converted twenty-four persons besides the two already mentioned. These were children and adults who were baptized, in addition to many Christians who had fled into hiding from several towns. Some had not been to confession in the previous thirty years. Among these was an old woman more than ninety years old who was very ill. She had been baptized as a child, but had never gone to confession because the devil had convinced her that, if she did, she would surely die. Finally the Servant of God persuaded her to confess her sins and receive the sacrament of the sick. But she did not die then nor for long after.

Another poor woman arrived with three children whom she wanted baptized. The embassy of the Blessed Virgin had persuaded her to break with the infidel who had her ensnared for many years. The man had not wanted to be converted, so he had fled into the mountains with their other three children, as it is their custom to divide the children when they separate. This division of the family caused the mother and Father San Vitores much sorrow, seeing them and so many other souls abandoned without baptism. But the next time the rector of our residence visited this mission, some were found, and others, too, through the ordinary diligence of the fathers, and especially of a leading Tagalog layman. He is well instructed and zealous and he helps in the mountains with the prayers and the administration of baptism in case of emergency, in the manner of the Canacapolas of Saint Francis Xavier, although on this occasion he wondered at the harvest of good works reaped in so short a time. The visit was successful because it was the right kind of mission (said Father San Vitores), a mission of the Blessed Virgin, and included in the form planned by Father Jerónimo López, which seems to be the most efficient means for both Spaniards and *Indios*. It is preached in the native language in the towns as well as in the mountains, to Christians and to unbelievers, and is followed by many conversions, friendships between former enemies, evil friendships broken off, and the many cases of wonderful confessions, such as the ones we mentioned at Santa Inés and others best not described further to preserve due secrecy.

Before leaving, Father San Vitores asked the new converts, as well as the old ones, to take advantage of the visits of Jesuit fathers to go to confession. And they were to try to attract unbelievers to receive baptism. He then returned to Manila well pleased with the bounty taken from the devil, yet still hungering for more souls to save. Soon he left for the mountains of Maralaya in search of the fugitives and criminals who fled from human justice to invite them to divine mercy.

The sufferings of this mission were intense not only because of the ruggedness of the mountains and the lack of all necessities, but much more so because of the barbarous nature of the inhabitants. They were not accustomed to see priests, and they thought the visit was a stratagem to catch them off guard. They were so afraid that to reassure them Father San Vitores had to leave his companion with them as a hostage. They had led him away into the mountains for several days until the charm of Father Diego Luis's company persuaded them that he had not come to seize their bodies, but to give their hearts true freedom. They became so attached to him that he was able to do as he wished among them. He heard their confessions and instructed them in the essential truths of religion. Because of past crimes they dared not return to the cities, and so they asked that fathers of the Society of Jesus come from time to time to assist them. Father San Vitores requested permission for this, but in vain. The mountains belong to other jurisdictions.

The victories won at Maralaya were to the credit of the *Acto de Contrición*; according to Father San Vitores the bows and arrows with which the *Indios* had come out to meet him had been overcome by the *saetas* (arrows) of the fear and the love of God that precede the Act of Contrition. It was to these arms alone and to the holy cross and to the standards of Saint Ignatius and Saint Francis Xavier that the fortress of Satan surrendered. Yet all these missions in the mountains and valleys of Manila or Luzon were only skirmishes compared to the battles on the Island of Mindoro.

# CHAPTER VIII

*Father San Vitores's Mission on the Island of Mindoro
and the Hardships He Suffered*

The most famous mission preached by the Servant of God while in the Philippines was that of Mindoro, which he later called a try out for the Mariana Islands. The Mangyans who inhabit Mindoro are very similar to the natives of the Marianas in their nakedness and ignorance, as well as in the hardships he experienced living there. From this mission Father San Vitores wrote a report by order of his superiors, without keeping any chronological order. He does this to observe greater secrecy about the place and his activities there. From his narrative we select events without establishing any order of travels.

Mindoro is located at a distance of six or eight leagues from the coast of Manila. It is one of the larger islands of the archipelago and measures some sixteen leagues in length, eight in width, and seventy in circumference. The island is mostly made up of highlands, craggy ridges, and wide woodlands with abundant palms and crops of all kinds including rice. It is covered by mountains and rivers and is inhabited by pagan unbelievers who speak different languages, but in general are called Mangyans. Scattered here and there throughout the mountains are some Christians from different nations. As on other islands they wander through the mountains having fled the burdens and obligations they suffered in the towns: debts, or slavery, or other oppression, or the excessive fees for marriage licenses have made them flee with bad companions to the mountains. Those who wander through the mountains and wilderness are more numerous than those who live in the settlements, of which there are some twenty on the island.

The island is administered today by three holders of benefices for the districts of Naujan, Calavite, and Baco. Naujan, which comprises one half of the island, has one other priest, but the harvest is so great and the laborers only two, that most often in Naujan the Christians die without the sacraments, and the infidels who are much more numerous than the Christians, live and die without baptism or any religious instruction. For the lack of instruction somehow they have come to fear baptism in such a way that they flee from it and from the true life more than from death itself.

For a short time the district of Naujan was given to the Jesuits who, through the zeal and hard work of four or five dedicated missionaries, accomplished much in softening and attracting the Gentiles. Over six hundred received baptism and the rest would have been baptized (according to native Tagalogs who were there in those days), if at the critical moment the seed of the gospel had not been trampled upon or pulled up by the enemy. Orders came in a *cédula real* bidding the Jesuits return the district to the diocesan clergy, who themselves

113

had asked the Jesuits to administer it, since it was too extensive for their resources.

The unbelievers here go naked. Using the bark of trees they cover only what nature bids us to conceal. Their lives are even more "naked" of the vices to be expected from nudity and barbarian customs. In general they are strangers to the vices most common in other nations: drunkenness, theft, deceit, cruelty. They have no arms to defend themselves and they respect other men's wives. They marry only one wife when very young and are scandalized at the vices of unfaithfulness in other nations. At times they live twelve to twenty in one relatively small house, related or not, all in complete security. They do not marry within the second degree of kindred. Their diet, which is simple and frugal, is a help to this continence, but one cannot deny that it is a great grace of the Lord and a natural disposition for our holy Faith. What a pity if these good customs are lost!

The majority believe only in what they can see, or little more than that. But it seems that some of them reason that there is a superior being, the cause of the sky and of the earth, but few consider whether the Creator is one or many. They worship no being; they only fear the demon they call *Bucao* because he sometimes frightens them. They believe that the soul lives after death, but they are not concerned where it goes, or what it does or suffers. Some, and these are the most civilized, in sickness or when their relatives are ill, offer food and drink to the souls of their parents, in the belief that the sickness is the result of their parents' hunger or thirst. The Servant of God found this superstition on one or other of the mountains. On one of the mountains he came across some idolaters who had come from some other island, because these islanders do not practice idolatry or Mohammedanism or the more ordinary forms of superstition found in the archipelago.

Concerning the creation of the world, they believe in some fables similar to that of Deucalion and Pyrrha, which more civilized nations also believe. They claim that their land (they are not concerned with that of others) was created by one of their grandparents and the rivers by his wife, who being a woman did not make her lines very straight, so that the rivers twist and turn in curving lines. On one of these mountains where a *visita* of Saint Francis Xavier was organized, the people believed in something like the Blessed Trinity, although with many errors, as would be expected of infidels and barbarians. They believed that the Creator is one, but also three, and so had three names Ulaon, Ubai, Caloni. The Servant of God suspected that these were traces of former preaching of the gospel. He pursued this further and was told that Ubai was a woman, the mother of Caloni. Ulaon was the father, and from the three who are one, all things precede. They were so imbued with the idea of father, mother, and son that when they learned the sign of the cross they would invariably say: God the Father, God the Mother, and God the Son, although they would at once correct themselves, showing no stubbornness, because as soon as they started taking instructions they were quite ready to accept whatever the priest taught as the teaching of the Lord of

*Father San Vitores's Mission on the Island of Mindoro and the Hardships He Suffered*

Heaven. Here, their former belief or error served as a step up, so that they might more easily enter our holy Faith; that they might feel the sweetness of devotion to the Blessed Virgin, whom they embraced tenderly, whom they now recognized as the true Mother of the Creator of all things. They transferred to her the affection they once had for Ubai, as if we should say, says Father Diego Luis, *Ignotae Matri Dei*.[84] He told them that she was not God and that God was something much higher than that trinity of theirs. All this they believed without any difficulty.

Father San Vitores left Manila with another Jesuit priest and an *hermano donado*[85] of the Society of Jesus, of whom Father says there was no one who labored more fruitfully than he in the mission. The difficulties of this journey would have been unbearable had it not been for the valiant spirit of Father Diego Luis and the encouragement he gave his companions. Lost on the trail and going in circles with no idea of direction, they trekked one whole day from one mountain to another. Night overtook them among precipices. They could go no further. They tied themselves to trees so as not to plunge over the cliff, if they fell asleep, exhausted as they were by the day's climbing. Father San Vitores' companions state that his joy was so great among these hardships that it simply burst out and filled his companions with a feeling that there was no happiness like this anywhere, that they were ready for even greater labors if the Lord should send them for the sake of souls to be saved.

They overcame all these difficulties, obviously the work of the devil, the enemy of their mission, and so came to a stretch of sea, where they crossed and entered the town of Naujan. Here the natives met them carrying twenty-five sticks, which stand for the number of enemy sails, since many do infest these regions. It seems as if it were a trick of Satan to scare him away from the innermost parts of the island that were so much in need of religious instruction. But it was useless to try to frighten men who embraced danger in the pursuit of souls. From Naujan he traversed the whole island, at times alone, at times with a companion, exposed to every sort of hardship, a victim of the burning sun, waters, winds, hunger, thirst, weariness, every sort of hardship, in perils by land and perils by sea.[86] He offered it all to the Lord for the souls he had redeemed by his Passion and Death. He made his way on foot through the wilderness, opening a way with bare feet because his shoes had worn out, his feet bloody from leeches and thorns, regretting that the suffering touched only his feet, when the thorns had covered the head of his Lord. Perhaps his wish was granted, but never entirely. As he was walking across a mountain, he slipped and fell down a ravine full of thorns which pierced his hands till they were unrecognizable. His companions asked if he was in much pain. He smiled and said, "It's just a little gift from God." In his own report he tells the story in the third person: "It was funny. He thought he was grabbing a tree, but it was fistful of thorns." He often slept in the forest at night with no regard for weather or other dangers. I should not say he slept, because the whole night was spent in

---

[84]To an unknown mother of God. Cf. Acts 17:23.

[85]The *donado* was Marcos de la Cruz. See Book 2, chap. 4:99.

[86]2 Cor. 11:25-26.

prayer, asking God for the salvation of these poor people, until fatigue would overcome him, and he would fall asleep. He would go without food or drink for long stretches at a time. At these and other hardships he would only say, "Thanks to my good God." On one journey, to relieve his thirst, some *Indios* there with him brought him some stagnant water from a muddy pool, which they, no epicures, would not dare to drink. He, out of a spirit of mortification, added to the torment of thirst by drinking a whole glass of the thin mud so that it smeared his lips. The *Indios* wondered at this and asked him if it was good. He answered, "The water was a real treat."

He suffered all these difficulties and dangers, plus many others, but considered it all very worthwhile in return for the small harvest reaped in so sterile a land. Any small conquest among these lost sheep gladdened his heart for a long time. During this mission there were seven who died shortly after being baptized. Four of these were adults. There was another adult over eighty years old who had led such a good innocent life that Father Diego Luis did not hesitate to say that he was one of those of whom the theologians say that if they observe the natural law, God finds a way of salvation for them, even by miracle. The other three baptized were infants less than a year old. In all, the results would have compensated for even greater difficulties, sicknesses, and perils suffered to serve the Lord in his dearest enterprise.

If we tried to relate all the fruits of this mission, words would fail us: the harvest was in proportion to the sowing and the sower through whose merits God gave increment to the seed. This is quite obvious, if the thorns and thistles are taken into consideration. Speaking of the results in general, Father San Vitores says in his report that some five hundred Gentiles were converted. This number is far more than can be expected in an ordinary mission. Many of these converts, because of difficulties of distance or communication, could not be incorporated into the existing *visitas* and churches of Tagalogs and Visayas, so three new *visitas* with their churches were established for the Mangyans. One was dedicated to our Blessed Mother, close to the old town of Bungabun, the other to our father, Saint Ignatius, close to the lake and mountains of Pula (Pola), the third to Saint Francis Xavier in La Ilaya de Naujan. There were no parish priests available to care for these chapels, so he entrusted them to the care of certain old Christians as sacristans and leaders chosen among the Mangyans. Another church was established close to the river Angsalin for the Christian runaway slaves whom government soldiers had not been able to subject for many years. Nevertheless the priests persuaded them to come down from the mountains, come to confession, and live as Christians subject to the king. The governor lightened the burden of the king's tribute by means of a four-year exemption to give them a better chance to reestablish themselves as Christians. This victory we owe to the lay volunteer who through his simple style and words convinced the runaways. Father San Vitores sent him with other reliable Christians who served as guides with the embassy of the Blessed Virgin, while he himself and his companions attended to the

*Father San Vitores's Mission on the Island of Mindoro and the Hardships He Suffered*

instruction and care of the new converts. This shows, says Father San Vitores, the power of our Lady's intercession and the grace of a missionary vocation, even in a lay volunteer, who would have had difficulty following the daily prayers in a Jesuit house.[87] The number of runaway slaves converted publicly was more than 200, not counting the secret ones. Those that were free of impediments had their marriages blessed and their children baptized. Some of these were over twenty-four years old. Their parents were old Christians, either Tagalogs or Visayas.

---

[87] The prayers were said in Latin.

# CHAPTER IX

### *The Means the Servant of God Used to Convert the Infidels; the Obstacles Imposed by the Devil*

The method followed by Father in instructing new converts followed the natural order suggested by God: "The invisible things of God are known by the visible ones he has made."[88] Thus we use the things of the earth as a stepping stone to rise to the things of heaven, and creatures to rise to the Creator. He first used as images the things they saw with their eyes to prepare them to hear the message of Faith. This is the method he was always to use in the Marianas, as we shall see. Also, the festive celebration of the baptisms in the *visitas* and churches, whenever possible, helped the Gentiles appreciate the beauty and meaning of the sacrament. The feasts of Saint Francis Xavier, of the Immaculate Conception, of Christmas, and of the Magi were celebrated with all the solemnity possible in those mountains, though with more devotion than solemnity, and yet the angels must have celebrated it with all solemnity, seeing the multitude of baptisms.

But the best means by far, according to Father Diego Luis, to attract the Gentiles were deeds of charity, friendliness, and kindness. This was necessary to banish the fear that the *Castillas*, as the Spaniards were called, would deceive them and reduce them to slavery. Only if nothing were asked of them, only if they were not commanded to do anything, unless it were to their advantage, would they believe in the sincerity of the preaching and the unselfishness of the preachers. It was very difficult to convince these people who had learned so well to fear deception.

Finally, when they saw that the fathers asked nothing of them, and during instructions even fed and clothed them, as the first missionaries did when they began the evangelization of these Mangyans, they said to the Tagalogs: "The truth, you told us the truth, that the fathers want nothing but to teach us the way to heaven."

They were also deeply moved by the simple and coherent narration of the things of our Faith, which the fathers called the Story of God: creation, sin of angels, and fall of man, the devil's (*Bucao*) envy, the birth, passion, and death of our Lord to expiate the sins of men. The Venerable Father would explain that man had offended the Lord of Heaven by rejecting the light given to do good; how could man who is so low offer expiation to the Lord of Heaven who is so high, unless a man should come who is as high as God, being both God and man? When the *Indios* were moved to the love of this Lord who had done so much for them, he would show them the crucifix and have them make the Act of Contrition. When he recited the Commandments of God, they

---

[88] Rom. 1:19-20.

*The Means He Used to Convert the Infidels; the Obstacles Imposed by the Devil*

at once approved of them. But they embraced them when they heard that they were the same for all people, like the light of the sun. They did have their difficulties with baptism; some were trivial, but the devil's resistance was there. An old man, who Father San Vitores tried to persuade to accept baptism, excused himself saying, "Our elders were not baptized. It isn't right to introduce this new custom in our country." In spite of the excuse, as he observed that Father San Vitores was kind and generous, he asked him for a blanket because he was cold. Father San Vitores answered, "Is the use of blankets your custom of your elders?" He confessed it was not, but said he had seen the Tagalogs use blankets and the use of them seemed good. Then said Father Diego Luis, "If baptism is good for your soul, even if it were not received by your elders, you should receive it as the Tagalogs and *Castillas* have. Their elders did not receive it either, but God sent his ambassadors as he is now sending us to your people." No further persuasion was necessary, with the help of divine grace. Others were convinced because of a comet that had appeared the year before, because he pointed out that its appearance was unusual in the heavens, so they could do things their elders had not done.

One of the most stubborn arguments on this point was the one held with an old Mangyan whom Father Diego Luis sought out because of the news of "cruel mercy and barbarian compassion." His wife had given birth to twins. He killed one so that the mother could more easily feed the other. Such is the darkness of those who live without the light of faith, and this is the charity taught in the devil's school. Father Diego Luis entered the house, saw the mother and five children and urged them to believe in Jesus Christ. The *Indio* was cunning. He had had many contacts with the Tagalogs and had a considerable knowledge of the mysteries of our Faith, so he affirmed that he believed all the things that the father mentioned. "Then," said the father, "let's get on with the baptism." "That I will not do, even though you kill me. It is not the custom of this country." "If you know all the mysteries of the Faith," said the father, "then you know that he who rejects baptism will burn forever." "I know," he answered, "but I am too old to be baptized. Here is my son," he said, pointing out the oldest of his children. "I will give him to you to be baptized. I love him and I would be sorry to see him lost." "Why don't you feel sorry for yourself?" said Father Diego Luis. "Because I am already old," he answered, "and I cannot work to earn money for clothes and for the tribute." "They won't ask tribute of you," he said, "because you are old. And you will have clothes. And if you do not, you get along without them now. Why wouldn't you, if you were baptized?" "No," he said. "It's very ugly for a Christian to go around naked." "It is much uglier," said the Father, "if your soul goes naked and is clothed with fire." With all these discussions Father Diego Luis achieved nothing more than the baptism of the oldest son. When Father San Vitores urged him to have compassion on his wife and children, he would answer that he could not work to supply clothes for all and to comply with the other duties of a Christian. The *Indios* who accompa-

*Book Two, Chapter 9*

nied Father Diego Luis offered their own clothes to the old man, both for him and his family, even though they would go naked. But he always answered the same thing, so the father left the matter in the hands of God and went on his way. The Lord heard his prayers, because when he returned two days later, the old man met him and said he wanted to be baptized and that he would summon relatives from the mountain. So he and his wife and children and some others of the family were baptized. The surviving twin was named Matthias because "the choice fell to Matthias," not, in this case, to his twin brother.[89]

Although fettered by lesser shackles or only by threads, the devil nonetheless held two other old men captive on the mountain. These men sent Father San Vitores a message saying, that if he did not oblige them to pray and make the big cross, they would be baptized. The message sounded strange, but he suspected what might be the cause. He sent a message to the old men, bidding them come and all would be done as they wished. When they came down, he learned that the difficulty lay in the fact that they thought the prayers would have to be memorized in Tagalog, which for them was a difficult foreign language. The second difficulty was that they could not make the three crosses plus the one that embraced all three, which they called the big cross, but only wanted to make the simple sign of the cross. He instructed them very kindly in their own tongue and was satisfied with the simple sign of the cross.[90] So they were baptized. Later as they attended the prayers, which were said in Tagalog, they memorized them in Tagalog. The same happened with the crosses; as they saw the other Christians making the "big cross," they likewise mastered the procedure. With such prudent kindness he attracted to baptism others whom strictness would have frightened away.

The obstacle raised by the people of Naujan, both Christian runaway slaves and Gentiles, was not so easily overcome. It happened at the beginning of the mission that these people asked as a necessary condition that only the Jesuits administer confession and baptism to them. They did this either because they had seen the charity of Father San Vitores and expected the same from all the Jesuits, or, as he himself said, because the Jesuits had not demanded fees for marriage, baptisms, or funerals. In their simplicity they did not understand or would not understand that there was good reason for charging those fees, and so they wanted ministers who would not be an expense to them. The Servant of God was very distressed since he had no authorization to grant their wish nor could he persuade the *Indios* to abandon their stand. He now had about a hundred catechumens ready for baptism and not one wanted to give in. He offered prayers and penances for this intention, and then on December 2, the former Feast of Saint Francis Xavier, he asked the saint's intercession and led the *Acto de Contrición* through the countryside in the form planned by Father Jerónimo López. With crucifix in hand he exhorted them to seek baptism purely for the love

---

[89]Acts 1:26.

[90]Three crosses: one each on the forehead, lips, and breast.

of God and for the good of their souls without distinction of persons as to who was their spiritual father. God would provide them with the ministers most suitable for their salvation. He then continued with other reasons, insisting they seek baptism for God alone. Then they began to cry out: "For God alone! For God alone!" Convinced by Father San Vitores, they said they wished to be baptized and subject to any minister appointed by their bishop. So the following day, December 3, the present Feast of Saint Francis Xavier, those who were prepared received baptism and opened the door to many who later entered the church through baptism.

A similar or even greater resistance was offered by another group of tributary Mangyans who live in the mountains called Mansalay, Dangay, and Balansay. These Mangyans pay tribute even though they are not Christians. But if they become Christians they must pay double besides what they pay for the priests and the Church. So they are very stubborn about not receiving baptism. Before the Servant of God reached their mountains, the report of his many baptisms had preceded him. So, before he arrived, they took counsel as to what they should answer. Among them were two older men, venerable gray-beards, whose advice they agreed to follow. These men agreed there was no reason to change; they would follow their old customs. Why should they insult their old customs by adopting new ones? Their taxes were high enough, without having them doubled by becoming Christians. The priests who were coming were good and wished their welfare. There should be no danger in taking them for teachers, if later these priests were to be their spiritual fathers. They would look on them as their children and make every effort to relieve their burdens. But these priests were going to leave and then into whose hands would they fall? This was the answer Father San Vitores received on his arrival: the door was closed. These were now the last days of the mission. He could stay no longer. But through continual embassies back and forth and the warm welcome he gave them and his little gifts, they finally softened and some sixty agreed to take instructions. They were baptized and joined the *visita* of Nuestra Señora de Bungabun.

The devil not satisfied with the resistance to baptism by the Mangyans, decided to wage war personally by appearing to these poor people and deceiving them. Father San Vitores had sent his usual embassy of the Mother of the Lord of Heaven to a hamlet of Mangyans, bidding them descend and receive baptism. Some did come down and promised to bring the others later. But when the baptized returned and urged their comrades to come down and keep their promise, they were unwilling. They said another ambassador had come to them in the meantime as the true ambassador of the Lord of Heaven and had ordered them to make no change and not be baptized. What the priests said were lies and their God false. They wished only to make them slaves of the *Castillas*. Although at the moment they did not wish to come, finally through the prayers and the love of the Servant of God, the devil was defeated. His friendliness and warmth and that of his companions and the fact that the captain of the *Castillas* had been the godfather of several of the baptized, persuaded sixteen to be baptized in the *visita* of Saint Francis Xavier, although others persevered in their obstinacy.

# CHAPTER X

*Extraordinary Happenings and Divine Providence
in the Mission of Mindoro*

Father San Vitores speaks about certain notable happenings on this mission journey. He says that there was not a step taken the whole time without tokens of God's special providence. First there was the good health the Lord gave him and his priest companion in areas and under weather conditions where not only Spaniards but the *Indios* themselves suffered continually from sickness. The one who fell ill was the lay volunteer who asked our Lord to give him the sicknesses that were meant for the priests, so that the latter might do their work in spite of the tremendous hardships of the mission. Notable, too, was God's protection from enemies the whole time they were on the island, particularly from the pirates who continually infest the surrounding seas and raid the coasts. It was as if God sent his swift angels to proclaim in peace the peace they brought from him. Father San Vitores passes over in silence many of the dangers on land and sea from which God delivered them. He does mention some of the sufferings God sent them as well as other gifts of his providence. For these, he thanks God. I will only mention a few of the great works of the Lord whereby he brought to his servant souls who would seek and find their Redeemer.

To show his divine providence and infinite goodness, the Lord provided Father San Vitores in those mountains with some Christians who were to be his helpers in his apostolate to the Gentiles. But there was also an infamous group of Christian *Indios* who were not native to the island but had migrated from neighboring islands of Tagalogs and Visayas. These contrived to block the conversion of the Mangyans for their own profit. As long as the Mangyans remain unbelievers, they are free of taxes and other charges incurred by Christians and so can work for the old Christians, for whom they labor almost as slaves in their fields and to whom they sell very cheaply the wax and other products from the mountains. They could not do this, say the *Indios* and others, perhaps, if they incur the expenses of becoming a Christian. This is how they discourage the Gentiles, exaggerating the heavy yoke they would impose upon themselves by receiving baptism. And so they wage a war more fatal to the Faith than the tortures of the persecutors of old.

This is why Father San Vitores began the missions in every town with the Christian *Indios*, and why God kept him there by the floods that came longer than he had planned to stay. In his talks and teaching he scourged that loathsome greed, that hellish impiety that was as deadly to their own souls as to their neighbors', besides destroying their own good name and making them devils on earth for base profit. Moved by Father's words and ashamed of themselves, they now desired to erase their bad reputation for such criminal conduct. They reversed tactics and now their campaign for bringing infidels to baptisms far exceeded their former antagonism. They would set out and "hunt" the Mangyans. Weather and road conditions as well as other hardships were disregarded. Sometimes they were away fifteen or twenty days without returning to their homes, until they had a catch of some twenty or thirty Gentiles. They brought them in for instruction and during the many days of instruction they fed them, depriving themselves of food to feed their guests. Charity went further. Not only did they lend their clothing to cover their nakedness on the day of baptism, but following the example of Saint Martin, after the baptism these barbarians shared the little they had with the newly baptized.[91] There was a chief who took off his shirt and trousers to give them to a Mangyan who was to be baptized, while he remained in his scanty underclothes. Father San Vitores adopted the necessary measures to compensate these Christian *Indios* for their solicitude toward the newly baptized. He collected alms in the houses of the Society for the Christian *Indios* so that they and the infidels might realize the power of Christian charity that obliges us to clothe the needy for the love of God, but then sees to the needs of those who have stripped themselves for the love of God. Charity will feed the hungry who are hungry because they fed the needy ones.

With the help of these good Christians who accompanied our missionary on his journeys and who at other times were missionaries sent by the fathers to bring the Gentiles to the missionary, the Servant of God won many souls whose position was desperate. From the *visita* of Saint Francis Xavier near the town of Naujan, he sent messengers to call in some Mangyans who lived some three leagues away and would have to cross two rivers to come. Although the messengers tried three times to get through, they could not because the land between the rivers was flooded and impossible to wade. God took matters into his own hands: the flood increased to the point of converting the whole region into a lake, so that sixteen Mangyans and six runaway Christian slaves came in canoes, the former for baptism, the latter for confession.

Because of his kindness and the word of the many who came to the *visita* for baptism, even distant peoples came to see the priests at this post. Some came from the opposite side of the island. It took them ten or more days of the most wretched roads through swamps, underbrush, and rugged terrain in the worst weather. Father Diego Luis praised the divine goodness and power that calls those whom he wills, when he wills, and as he wills, wounding with his voice the most distant heart, drawing with his grace the most far off.

When the waters subsided and his isolation was broken, he set out again on the mission. He felt once again, as he confesses, that every overnight stay, every storm, all winds favorable and contrary, all are the plan and loving work of the Lord who uses every means for the salvation of his chosen ones.

After sailing most of the day with favorable winds, he wished to pass by a town where he had already given a mission. Thus he could take

---

[91]Saint Martin of Tours (316-397), as a Roman officer he is said to have cut his cloak in half and to have given half to a beggar.

*Extraordinary Happenings and Divine Providence in the Mission of Mindoro*

advantage of the tide to round a particularly tricky point of land. But just as he was rounding the point, the wind turned to the opposite quarter and the sea became so rough that they thanked God that they could retrace their course and safely enter the port they had passed. His gratitude increased the more when he realized that the winds had been those of the Holy Spirit which had carried them there so that certain souls could obtain the grace of a good confession which they had missed on his first visit. It was a special grace for a woman over seventy years old who had been in the mountains away from instructions for twenty years. She had come to that post in search of the fathers and not having found them, she decided to wait. Anxiously she felt that death was near. So she prayed and had other pious Christians pray that God would send a contrary wind, since they were unable to signal to them as they passed by. So what had seemed bad weather was Divine Providence at work. The woman went to confession and received Extreme Unction and died a happy death. All those present felt that her soul would go from the arms of the Servant of God to the arms of the merciful Lord who had brought about that unexpected encounter.

On another occasion they had to travel by land because of unfavorable winds. Toward the middle of the long journey, they found perfect relief for their tiredness. They came upon a hamlet of runaway Christian slaves. If he had been traveling by sea, these would have remained lost. Some fled from him as soon as they saw him. But the bolder ones were soon won by his friendliness and charity, and they brought back their companions. About forty-three persons went to confession. God sent the unfavorable winds so that these Christians could go to confession. Now the winds changed again and ships came in sight. One was coming for the priests and the other ship brought Christian *Indios* who wanted to go to confession to Father San Vitores. These asked him to come in their ship so they could make their confessions more fittingly in their own town. He agreed, although it was well out of his way, feeling that the shortest road is the one that leads to the salvation of souls. A lay volunteer left in the ship originally intended for the priests. A great storm came up and the ship that carried Father San Vitores hit the sand banks. Everyone believed they owed their lives to his presence on board. After their escape he offered three masses in honor of the Blessed Trinity through Saint Francis Xavier. The other ship was wrecked, too. Those on board did not know to which apostle (Xavier or San Vitores) they owed their lives, because after three days the volunteer and the rest of the *Indios* arrived at the time when the third Mass was being offered. Their ship had sunk, but all were alive. They praised God, who had saved them from death. A bell was saved from the wreck, which the lay volunteer was bringing for one of the churches. He had escaped, carrying a crucifix given him by Father San Vitores. The outsiders were much impressed by the mercy of God obtained through the prayers of Father Diego Luis. They went to confession with all the greater devotion. At this point in his narrative he writes of a mission journey, one of the most important phases of the mission to Mindoro, whose location he kept secret. One day he

125

and a companion were traveling on foot. He was walking not for any lack of a boat or of favorable winds. Typically he was seeking the unexpected chance encounters with the souls along the way. Someone met him and told him about two women, a mother and a daughter. Their husband and father had been a Christian, and they wanted to be baptized. But they could not come down from the mountain, because they were very ill. So he changed his plans and made a difficult two-day climb up the mountain to their home. There he suffered his greatest hardship. They had changed their minds, either from natural flightiness or because the mother's new husband, a Mangyan, was now present and had dissuaded them. Father Diego Luis tried to convince them, but all in vain. The *Indios* who had brought him there were terribly embarrassed and disappointed. But he consoled them by telling them that at times God permits bad results, to teach us that the good ones are his free gift, not our human achievement, and also that success is its own reward not a reward directly from God. Moreover this way we learn not to mix self-satisfaction with what we offer to God.

Very soon God consoled everyone by proving that he had brought them all that way not for the two women, but for someone else. As they set out to resume their original plan, they saw a man who fled. One of the *Indios* followed him and calmed him down with the news of the kindness and understanding of Father San Vitores. So the *Indio* came to him and went to confession. He was a Christian Tagalog, a runaway slave for many years. If God and the fathers would forgive him, he said, he would lead a Christian life. Not he alone, but thirty of his friends who were hiding would do the same. The Servant of God pardoned him and assured him of the pardon of God. Then the *Indio* guided him to the place where the thirty were. Again with his new guide, Father Diego Luis and the others climbed three mountains, uphill and downhill, that now seemed so much less rugged, so very easy of access, and came to the town. There twelve of the Tagalogs, Christian runaway slaves, went to confession and twenty pagan Mangyans received baptism. They all went to live on a farm, part of the new *visita* just dedicated to the Blessed Virgin in the mountains of Bungabun.

The Venerable Father was looking for a Christian *Indio* from Baco, one of those who roam through the mountains, who might serve as a guide and a scout to look for Christians and Gentiles. He found a Mangyan called Andrés. He went to confession and Father Diego Luis gave him a rosary, a crucifix, and a picture of the Blessed Virgin, with which, said the father, he was invested as ambassador of our Lady. More than thirty received baptism through his good guidance and embassy. Among others was a little girl, twelve years old, a Christian. Three years before she had been attracted to our Faith and to devotion to the Blessed Virgin through conversation with a Christian woman, a Tagalog. As this orphan girl was learning her prayers at the woman's house, her own brothers kidnapped her one night and carried her off to the mountains. When Father San Vitores heard of this, he went to find the little girl. After several searches he found her with ten other people who fled. They

*Extraordinary Happenings and Divine Providence in the Mission of Mindoro*

caught up with one and assured him that he had nothing to fear. When the latter said the girl and her kidnapper were there, Father Diego Luis sent her a cape so that she might come to him decently clad. When the little girl and her companion came in sight, the father appeared under a paper parasol with a crucifix at his breast and a very ornate statue of Our Lady of Good Counsel in his hands. With him were the volunteer who was a good musician and a boy soprano (in order to expel with music the spirit of fear that had overcome these poor people). Accompanied by the guitar, they sang a tender melody in the Tagalog language, which the Mangyans understood. The words of the song invited them to recognize and adore the Lord of Heaven in the arms of his Mother, whom the statue represented. Calmed by the harmony of song, they listened to the words of the Venerable Father, words chanted in the tones of the *Acto de Contrición*. At once the little girl burst into tears and her kidnappers were moved by the father's words, which condemned their evil deed in stealing from God his little lamb. He then asked her to repeat the prayers she had not yet forgotten and all the rest repeated them. So the kidnapped catechumen turned into an apostle to the kidnappers who were now entrusted to her care. As a reward and as a token of her good faith and her new charge, he gave her a rosary.

Then all the rest asked him for one, and he answered that if they asked for the rosary with a sincere desire of becoming Christians and of hearing the Christian doctrine and if they would repeat the Creed and the Act of Contrition with faith, he would give them one, although usually it was given only at baptism. As they did so, Father passed out the rosaries, and they remained prisoners, so to speak, of the Blessed Virgin with strong perseverance, as we see from what followed. The fathers were suddenly called away to Naujan because the pastor there had had a serious accident. Now the devil had his chance to prevent their baptism. Their pagan relatives came, won over the majority of them, and led them back to the mountain. But all those who had received the rosaries were baptized before the missions ended. There was one man who had been there from the beginning, but had left to bring his wife, he said, to the instruction. He thus missed the instruction and did not receive a rosary. Though he had seemed the most receptive, at the end he was the most obstinate and was never baptized.

There were two little girls about ten or eleven years old who lived with pagan relatives. When the ambassadors of the Blessed Mother arrived, all the relatives fled. But the girls received the ambassadors and showed their loving devotion to the statue of the Blessed Virgin. They went down with the ambassadors, learned the Christian doctrine with great facility and were baptized on the Feast of the Immaculate Conception, taking the names María and Catalina. They became the priests' catechists and in this capacity taught the catechumens the prayers. We would never finish if we were to relate all the happenings similar to these which the good Lord brought about through the mission. But it would not be fair to omit the incident of *la Buena Samaritana*, as Father San Vitores called a certain pagan Mangyan woman who after her baptism was called María. While Father San Vitores was speaking to her about the Faith, she mentioned to him that her husband was a Christian. He asked her to guide the ambassadors through the mountains of Naujan and bring her husband down. She obeyed him, sought out her husband, but could not persuade him by any pleading to come down. He would not listen to the ambassadors or accept the rosary they offered him. So she simply took the rosary and forcefully threw it around his neck, as though it were a chain or necklace of the Blessed Virgin. Then something wonderful happened. The man's heart at once changed so radically, as if he were a captive in chains of the Blessed Mother, that he now prayed fervently to her and her Son. Then he came down with the ambassadors to the place where Father Diego Luis was, to be instructed and go to confession. But *la Buena Samaritana* was not content with this conquest. She traveled through the mountains from one hamlet to another, spreading the good news. She brought back twenty-three pagan Mangyans who received baptism with her.

Other souls came to the Servant of God through a merciful punishment. God sometimes inflicts a wound only to heal, mortifies only to give life. There was a boy who stubbornly resisted being baptized. No reasoning would convince him until one day he had an attack of pain as he was walking along a road. He fell to the ground. But the blow that hurt his body softened his obstinacy to the degree that he asked a Christian who had come to his aid to take him to the priests for pardon and baptism. He realized, he said, that this was a just punishment from God for rejecting Christianity. Although the Christian did as he was asked, the priests were at the point of leaving for Manila and the boy was still too ill to go to them. So Father San Vitores sent a capable *Indio* who instructed and baptized him. With the waters of baptism health was restored, as if to show that his resistance to baptism had been the cause of his misfortune.

There was an old woman who could not be persuaded to receive baptism. She was struck by high fevers. She recognized the just and merciful hand of God in this and begged insistently to be taken to the Venerable Father, who after brief instruction (because she was so ill) administered baptism. Four days later the Lord in his infinite mercy called her home.

It is not right to pass over in silence the piety of the newly baptized, especially those of the *visita* of Saint Francis Xavier, where Father San Vitores stayed the longest. One saw in them a great fear of the Lord. Even the elderly were as docile as children. They agreed to whatever the fathers proposed for the good of their souls. In case of disputes among themselves, the fathers were called upon to be arbitrators and the parties abided by their decision. Two chiefs in the mountains and their followers were so at odds that if one came to instructions, the other walked out. But as soon as they were baptized they embraced each other publicly in the church and pardoned one another for past grievances.

To these virtues observed in the new converts we must add a great zeal for bringing many others to the Faith they had received. Such

*Extraordinary Happenings and Divine Providence in the Mission of Mindoro*

was the case of Ignacio who traveled twenty days through bad roads and continuous rain to bring more than forty Mangyans to the Venerable Father, who had promised him a knife as a reward and an encouragement. He often offered such rewards, although there were those who for no reward whatsoever, not even a medal, traveled for ten days at a time over punishing roads to a distant mountain in order to persuade a few pagans to come down and attend the catechism classes. Twice they were rejected and told harshly that the priests had deceived them with practices contrary to the custom of their ancestors. They had lost their reputation and their liberty as well. Finally zeal and patience won the battle, because at the third try, seventeen persons asked for baptism, among them a ninety year-old man. Afire with the same zeal as the *Indios* who had brought them to the Faith, they promised to bring in over a hundred who still remained in the mountains. As the fathers were about to leave, the pastor of the *visita* of Saint Francis Xavier would instruct and baptize them.

During the time Father San Vitores was at Saint Francis Xavier, he established a school for children who said the rosary and other prayers most of the day and part of the night, except for the time they dedicated to the catechism, which was taught in question and answer form either by him or his companion. These children learned the prayers in Tagalog because he was not sure of the exact meaning of Mangyan words, and he wished to have the approval of the ordinary. Still these Mangyan children learned the prayers so well that two of the little girls led the prayers when Tagalogs and Mangyans congregated in church to pray alternately in two choirs. The old people also came to the school, though they did not have to recite the prayers. Both in the school and in the church, Father Diego Luis taught the Act of Contrition because he felt it was most necessary in these regions where often there was no one to hear a confession at the time of death. Likewise he taught the method of baptism and had all, men, women, and children, recite the formula of baptism for cases of need.

Before the mission ended, he reaped the fruit of this concern. A chief of the Mangyans, who had been made sacristan of Saint Francis Xavier Church, was sent on an embassy to the mountains. He came upon a woman in childbirth who was in great pain without being able to deliver the child. He encouraged her, built up her confidence, and as he kept speaking the sweet names of Jesus and Mary, he applied a medal of Saint Ignatius and Saint Francis Xavier. Whereupon she delivered the child. But it was in such bad condition that it died two days later after the *fiscal* had baptized it. The companions of the *fiscal* told the grandmother of the child what had happened. Since then they were all encouraged to learn more carefully the method of baptism for such emergencies, and their devotion to Saint Ignatius and Saint Francis Xavier increased. Another baby was baptized by its own father, although he was a new convert. There was no one else there who could do it and he saw that his child was in danger of death. It died eight days later, and the father came and told the story to the priests, so consoled was he at the thought that his child was in heaven.

I cannot adequately describe the devotion of the new converts for all sacred things, but especially for the holy cross. The older generation of Christians said it was wonderful to wander through those mountains, where at every turn you came upon a cross because the newly converted Mangyans would place one at the door of their homes following the advice of the Servant of God. Inside the house they placed a smaller one together with a pious picture of Christ or the Blessed Mother. There they said their prayers. They loved rosaries and medals, which they treasured and hung around their necks as if they were a priceless necklace. Holy water as well as Saint Paul's Earth (*Tierra de San Pablo*) were among their favorites, too. The Lord desired to accept their veneration and devotion by working some marvelous things among them.

# CHAPTER XI

*Miracles With Which God Confirms the Preaching
of His Servant on the Island of Mindoro*

God performed many miracles on the island of Mindoro through the Venerable Father. Thus he gives greater strength to the father's words, as he usually does in a mission to the Gentiles, so that convinced through what their eyes see, they may accept what they have heard and not understood. The Servant of God says little in his report to avoid the honor that might come to him even when he reports in the third person when relating such matters.

He says that from time immemorial the Mangyans felt a horror for baptism because the devil had persuaded them that baptism caused the death of those who received it. To prove this false, the Lord permitted that at the beginning of the mission, some persons who were ill and then were baptized recovered through this water of life.

He adds that the converts became very devoted to *Tierra de San Pablo*, which the priests would apply to the sick. Marvelous effects followed. This was also true of holy water and of the water in which the cross of Saint Turibius had been immersed. All these objects of devotion had been sent from Spain by *don* Jerónimo San Vitores. He told this about *Tierra de San Pablo*: a poisonous animal had bitten a boy whom his parents had brought to be baptized. The child's arm was swollen, but as soon as he was given a drink of water mixed with a little bit of Saint Paul's Earth, he recovered completely. But Father San Vitores says very little about these miracles or writes about them only in general terms. So I will add only the striking examples that I found in a report made in the Philippines. Note that many cures effected by Father San Vitores are not recorded, because at times he was alone and was careful to hide the marvels the Lord worked through him. He was able to veil by discretion or evasive remarks what even the sharpest eyes might have discovered. Thus we know only the most public or striking cases, those which his humility could not conceal.

First and foremost, something happened in Naujan. He had asked the pastor, the captain, and the *fiscal* of the town for a boat to sail up the river to the interior of the island where there were pagan Mangyans. They answered that the river was not navigable, that no one had ever sailed it. The current was too swift, fed by streams rushing down from the mountains. Yet in some places it was so shallow that no boat could float on it. But he insisted so much that finally they gave him a boat, protesting that it was a vain attempt of which he would repent when he was beyond help. But the Lord who opened the Red Sea so that the Israelites might cross it dryshod and freed from captivity, now increased the waters of this little river, so that he who was to set souls free from the captivity of the devil might navigate it unharmed. The wonder of it all was that from then on the river remained navigable, to the amazement and joy of the natives.

On another occasion, in this same town, he was embarking to sail to some Christians who were much in need of instruction. He tried to jump into the boat, but being nearsighted, he missed and fell and went under the water. His companions, the *Indios*, rushed to save him from drowning but discovered to their amazement that his clothing was perfectly dry. The incident caused still greater veneration for the Servant of God who was now considered as a man from heaven rather than a mere earthly human.

At times, he walked over rough mountain country and marshy valleys with such speed that his *Indio* companions thought it miraculous. No one could explain how a weak and emaciated man, nearsighted as he was, could walk so rapidly over those mountains, unless his guardian angel bore him in his arms. Once, in particular, some Mangyans were looking for him for catechism instructions, but he sped along so quickly that the *Indios*, accustomed to climbing those hillsides like deer, could not catch up with him. They arrived at the post long after, exhausted, and found him quietly instructing the pagans.

It is true that he did become tired at times, but this was all the more to his credit or glory. Once, he could not cross a stream or descend a certain steep slope because of his weakness, a soldier named Juan de las Casas met him and carried him over and down. The Servant of God thanked Juan and promised that in a few hours he would repay him. After leaving San Vitores he embarked for the island of Luban. A storm came up and cast him on a nearby islet where he remained half dead nearly nine days without food or drink. He saw no one except Father San Vitores, who was at his side all this time giving him a liquor which kept him alive. The Licentiate *don* Mateo de la Cuenca testified to this in the *Processus* from Manila and said he learned the story from the soldier himself.

Although all the Mangyans held him in high esteem because of his wonderful deeds and because he healed them of sickness, those Mangyans called *Bungabun*, who live in the mountains, proclaimed that when they looked at him, he did not seem a human person, but more than human in the beauty and light that gladdened their hearts as they looked at him. They felt that same sweetness fill their hearts as they listened to his words. Almost everyone agreed, whether Spaniards or *Indios*, that those who came in contact with him never tired of his words, but would be so entranced that they were reluctant to leave him. This was perhaps the reason why the *Indios* so readily obeyed him in whatever concerned the good of their souls. For them, his words were the word of God, and they considered it dangerous to disobey in the least.

We see in Father San Vitores an example of that gift of tongues with which at times God favors his apostles for the teaching of the Gentiles. It is obvious that Father San Vitores was amazingly gifted in this respect, although in his report he tries to conceal this marvel. The more he denies it, the more evident it becomes. The languages spoken in

*God Confirms the Preaching of His Servant on the Island of Mindoro*

Mindoro were at least six in number, as different from one another as Latin from Spanish. Yet he taught the Mangyans in all six, speaking to each group in their own language for hours at a time. He did this to the amazement of the Tagalogs, who were aware of the difficulty involved and could not explain how he had learned all of them in so short a time. They considered this a miracle, and they were right, because in the five months the mission lasted, he was busy day and night, with absolutely no time to learn new languages. The fact is that he was able to hear confessions and preach fluently and precisely in all.

What shall we say concerning the spirit of prophecy in which he so much resembled Saint Francis Xavier? Here is an example quite similar to a prophecy of the Apostle of the Indies. When the Venerable Father was at Baco, the pastor, *don* Pedro Ruiz de Valderas, sent word to him to come to Naujan and hear his confession because he was very ill. He came and heard his confession. The pastor set sail for Manila to seek medical aid, while Father San Vitores remained in Naujan giving a mission. Meanwhile a storm forced the pastor to land at Baco, where he died four days later. At that moment, Father San Vitores was in church instructing the *Indios*. Suddenly, he stopped and asked the *Indios* to pray for the soul of their pastor, because he had died at Baco. Everyone wondered how the news had reached Father Diego Luis, because no one had come from Baco. But on the third day news arrived that the pastor had died on the day and the hour the Servant of God had given the news.

Father San Vitores had sent Brother Marcos de la Cruz to a town called Vallete to bring to the Faith the non-Christian Mangyans who lived there. On the return trip their *caracoa* was lost in a storm at sea that swamped the *caracoa* and capsized it. At the same hour of the morning, Father San Vitores said to the *Indios*, "My children, let us now hear Mass and offer it for our companions who went to Valette and are in great danger of drowning." A few days later Brother Marcos returned to prove the truth of what the father had seen with prophetic spirit.

Father San Vitores was in Naujan when Brother Marcos de la Cruz arrived in Baco to instruct the Mangyans. Brother Marcos suddenly fell ill of a violent fever. One night Father San Vitores appeared to him, consoled him, recited a gospel and placed his hand on his head, and then disappeared. The next morning the fever was gone and Brother Marcos felt so well that, entirely cured and with a good appetite, he was up and around. Two or three days later, he went to Naujan to thank the Venerable Father for the visit and the recovery, but he only answered, "Little Angel, thank God, who did this favor."

On his return from a town called Pola, Diego came across a group of very unhappy Christians who had been trying to leave port for three months but could not leave because of contrary winds. Was it a punishment for their sins, or was it really a merciful providence, since they had now found the Venerable Father who could restore them to the friendship of God? Diego exhorted them to prepare for confession. That evening they prepared themselves. The next morning they went to confession and Communion. Wonderful to tell, at the moment when the

*Book Two, Chapter 11*

father finished Mass, a gentle flowing wind began to blow and the *Indios* made a happy voyage, praising God and his servant.

The following case is not known from particular eyewitnesses. But it was widely publicized throughout the island, because the Mangyans heard of it from the Visayans to whom it happened. Father San Vitores had sent his companion priest to some mountain area where there was a large pagan population to instruct and baptize them. And he had sent Brother Marcos to another post to baptize children in danger of death and to instruct adults so that as soon as the father arrived he could baptize them. Father San Vitores was now alone, so he decided to seek out certain pagan Mangyans. He did not have a boat available, so he asked some Visayans, who happened to be there, to take him. They did so very willingly, but they had just set sail when a strong contrary wind arose. For a day and a half they were driven one way and another in constant danger of drowning until finally they came to a shore where they landed to rest and eat. They were tormented by thirst because, as strangers, they had no idea where there were rivers or streams of fresh water. In desperation one of them drank sea water and realized that the water that had come in contact with Father San Vitores's feet was potable. Then they all drank from that spot. Admirable is the power of God, who works such wonders by his faithful servants!

Finally, the time came that his superiors had appointed for his return to Manila, where he was badly needed. So as not to completely abandon the mission in Mindoro, he had his companion priest and Brother Marcos de la Cruz remain at least for a few days. He gave the latter two holy cards, one of the Santo Cristo of Burgos and the other of Saint Francis Xavier, so that he might apply them to the sick for their consolation. Through these holy cards, Father San Vitores, even though absent, performed many miracles, driving away demons and curing the sick. This was the way Saint Francis Xavier acted when he sent children to the sick with some little item of his and they would be cured. I will give an example or two of this.

For five years, a certain Christian *India* had been suffering from a painful illness that did not permit her to leave her bed. Brother Marcos visited her and tried to console her with encouraging words. She told him that many times some horrible, frightening men appeared to her whom she did not recognize. Brother Marcos left her the picture of Saint Francis Xavier, bidding her have confidence in the intercession of the holy apostle and the merits of Father San Vitores, who had given the holy card to him for the consolation of the sick, the afflicted, and the needy. Two days later, the brother returned and found the woman very happy. During the days when the picture was in her house, those fierce and frightening men had not dared to enter her house, and as if for good measure, her health improved and in a few days she had completely recovered. Brother Marcos applied the picture of the Santo Cristo to a pagan woman who was so swollen that she could not move. Her husband had to carry her on his back. First the brother urged the pair to have confidence in God and to show a desire to follow God's Law. Immediately the *India* recovered and started to walk. She and her husband received instructions and were baptized.

Almost the same thing happened to another pagan woman who had the same disease. She was crying out day and night at the violence of the pain. Brother Marcos urged her to become a Christian and then applied the holy card of the Santo Cristo and a bit of Saint Paul's Earth. At once the pain disappeared and she was cured. She thanked the Lord for his mercy and then asked to be instructed in the mysteries of the Faith, so she could be baptized as soon as possible.

A woman in Bungabun was dying. Her relatives were waiting for the moment of death to enshroud the corpse. Brother Marcos happened to pass by. They asked him if he had any remedy for the swelling (a common disease in those regions) that was killing the woman. He replied that he had only the picture of Saint Francis Xavier that Father San Vitores had given him for the sick. He had them all kneel down and say an Our Father and a Hail Mary in honor of the holy apostle and he applied the picture to the dying woman. This happened late at night as the woman lay there without the power of speech. In the morning she started calling everyone in the house to tell them that God had restored her to life and health through the intercession of Saint Francis Xavier, to whom she remained ever thankful and devoted.

Another Mangyan had been consumptive for two years. Brother Marcos talked to him about Saint Francis Xavier's life to move him to love and confidence. Then he applied the holy card, and the Mangyan was cured.

I will pass over other similar cases to get back to the story of Father San Vitores who, at this time, was in Manila engaged in his usual apostolic labors.

# CHAPTER XII

*In Manila, He Applies for the Mission to the Ladrones*

From the time when Father San Vitores had passed through the Ladrones Islands en route to the Philippines and had seen how those poor souls were abandoned and blind to the light of the gospel, whose messengers had passed them by so many times, his spirit could not rest.[92] The idea of evangelizing these poor people became more and more his obsession. God gives his light gratis, and there they were without it. And so from the moment he now arrived back in Manila, he never stopped taking vigorous measures to be given this mission. Neither his fruitful apostolate in Manila nor the conversion of sinners and of unbelievers in the missions that he preached in the towns and hill country of Mindoro could quench his longing nor silence his anxiety for the mission of the Marianas, which he thought had the first right to hear the gospel, even as it was the first of all those islands to fall under the survey of the King of Spain. The very poverty of the islands was another reason for his hunger for their souls. He was the more eager to clothe them with the grace of Christ, as they were the more stripped of the goods of this earth. Above all, he was driven by the words spoken years before when he first sailed past the Ladrones, words that spoke the will of God to him: *Evangelizare pauperibus misi te.*[93]

This desire was the constant occupation of his mind, the goal of his plans, the matter of his conversations, even the theme of his sermons. He was preaching one day at the dedication of the Church of Blessed John of God.[94] He presented dramatically a dialogue in which the Ladrones Islands pleaded their abandonment, their blindness, and their extreme need to the Lord. Taking as intercessors the Blessed Virgin and Saint Ignatius Loyola, they begged the Lord for the light of the gospel and the missionaries to teach his holy Law. The Servant of God would then answer in the role of the divine mercy promising a remedy, since God is the Creator who does not abandon the work of his hands, the souls he destines for eternal salvation.

Yes, God would provide the means to his end. The dramatization was so effective that the audience was moved to tears and so undoubtedly was the Lord by their prayers.

He had spoken to the superiors of the Society. At first they saw only the difficulty: the number of Jesuits was too few to open new missions. But then, trusting that the Lord would send new workers, they yielded to his instances and bade him make his requests to the ministers of His Majesty of Spain. He set forth in speech and in writing many reasons to undertake this new spiritual conquest. The desire of our Catholic Kings has always been to widen the frontiers of the Kingdom of Christ

---

[92]See Book 2, chap. 3:96.
[93]Isa. 61:1; Luke 4:18.
[94]Saint John of God was canonized in 1690.

*In Manila, He Applies for the Mission to the Ladrones*

more than those of their own empires without concern for the expense involved. What they expend in material things, they gain in souls which Christ has purchased with his blood. They could give no better evidence of this than in caring for these poor, naked natives, who have neither gold nor silver nor any other wealth in their country, thus closing the mouths of heretics, who judging by their own yardstick, like to say that the lust for gold rather than religious zeal is what caused the Spaniards to seek the riches of the Indies, not the riches of their souls. And although His Majesty seeks souls and not the riches, that is why God gives him the riches along with the souls he saves, thus rewarding his piety on earth and in heaven with rewards both eternal and temporal. These riches are best assured where there are no riches, since there is nothing that so much moves the Lord as disinterestedness; in this way the Lord will preserve the Indies for His Majesty and grant him other conquests besides.

He adds that the LadronesIslands are in the path of our ships. The islands are many and well populated with a people of docile character, without idolatry, and with fewer vices than most other peoples. They are friendly to the Spaniards. They have received and treated them well when they were shipwrecked in past years. Every day they have been welcoming travelers. They are unwilling to admit the Dutch to their islands, since they are enemies of the Spaniards. This entitles them, in all justice, to what has been given to other peoples free of charge and at times with much bloodshed and always at much cost to the Treasury. Moreover, they have had this right for more than a century, since *don* Miguel López de Legazpi took possession in the name of the king in 1565, before the Philippines were taken. We then promised to send them priests to teach the Law of God. We took possession of them by the Sacrifice of the Mass, which was said on one of the islands, as well as by *cédulas* that His Majesty sent on several occasions, giving orders that the gospel be preached to these peoples. All this proves that His Majesty recognized his duty toward them and wished to pay the debt. Precedence is to be given to payment of this debt, which does not concern a subject or another king like himself, but the King of Kings. Moreover, it should be expedited in the measure that the spiritual exceeds the temporal and souls are to be preferred to money.

These were his words in his letter stating the reasons for his project, and he continued by mentioning the extreme spiritual need of the adults and the children who died in infancy, the ease with which they could be converted because they had no idolatrous practices, their docility and gentleness, excellent qualities that would provide good soil for the propagation of the Christian religion. Undoubtedly these people are anxious for the spiritual nourishment they lack for their salvation. According to what Admiral Esteban Ramos has said, as well as the others who have come from there, provided ministers are sent there who will teach them more by their example than by their preaching, they will do what they see us do and will embrace our holy Faith, and will gladly be baptized. After all, the zeal of His Majesty has gained so much glory in the conversion of these islands [the Philippines], corrupted as they were by idolatry and the sect of Mohammed. That demanded so much effort, so much bloodshed, and an enormous drain on the public treasury. But here the way is free and open to conversion. If we neglect this opportunity, we would appear to forget past glories and spurn an even greater success. Having achieved the most difficult, we would neglect what is easiest. Moreover, to create and preserve this new Christian community, no great expense would be incurred. Fifteen or twenty Christian *Indios* from this island, God-fearing Filipinos, plus a few men who have been there before and know the language would be enough. No military escort would be needed. We would need wheat and wine for masses and a supply of clothing and other things until we could produce them there. We could be put ashore there by any of the ships that pass each year between New Spain and the Philippines. And whenever a *patache* would be sent from Manila to these islands with supplies for the missionaries, after its stopover there, it could set sail for Acapulco, taking advantage of the first *colla* winds and using the monsoon for the voyage. This might eliminate the two and three year periods of abandonment that occur when no ship visits the islands. This inconvenience is so great that when it does happen, these islands are so profoundly affected and are so weakened that almost no hope of recuperating remains. Experience has shown how delightful the voyage can be from New Spain to the Ladrones, and from there to New Spain, and how difficult is the remainder of the way to Manila. The cause of the difficulty may be the timing of the voyage or even the devil, who masters those regions and brings up the storms for fear the seed of Faith may be planted and take root in his dominions, while he would be uprooted and we might sail those seas with a better knowledge of storms and seasons. Furthermore, the fact that our ships are delayed so long in such a short passage—and in a region infested with typhoons—may mean that God does not want us to bypass those poor souls who are in the path of our ships without leaving them a ray of the light of the gospel. The Ladrones, being the first islands that the Faith could have conquered, the first islands where the missionaries were received in a friendly manner,[95] the first to be taken possession of for the crown by *Adelantado* Legazpi, the first to whom a promise was made to return and Christianize them, and the first land on which Mass was celebrated, they above all deserve immediate attention. Moreover, being in the path of our ships, shiploads of missionaries have passed them by, even though many natives have visited our ships. These latter, in their forlorn condition, tacitly charge us with having neglected them, as we have passed that way for a hundred years without noticing the rich harvest that could be reaped there, leaving the devil in quiet and peaceful possession before the consenting eyes of all Christendom and its ministers. This is the reason why God punishes us with the ill-success of our voyages, with the late arrival of our ships.

The king's ministers praised the zeal of Father San Vitores, saying they would like to cooperate with him, but to everything they raised difficulties. There were no missionaries, there was no ship to carry them,

---

[95]See Marjorie G. Driver, *Fray Juan Pobre in the Marianas*, Guam 1989, pp. 1-2, and passim.

there was no money. There were no missionaries for Guam because there were not enough to take care of all the work in the Philippines. It would be criminal extravagance and ill-ordered charity to give away what they needed, leaving them in greater want. There was no ship, because a ship en route to Mexico could not put in at the Ladrones without being caught in a zone of contrary winds, while sailing to Mexico first meant sailing five thousand leagues to travel three hundred, and the cost would be in proportion to the distance sailed. There was no money for this, because the Royal Treasury could not finance a ship to service this mission only, and still less could it support a mission in islands that could contribute nothing to its support. What seemed so easy at a distance was very difficult seen close up, and a strong enough desire can make anything look easy. The ministers offered other reasons and concluded, expressing surprise, that such zeal needed to look for new fields, long forgotten fields of such difficulty and such a financial burden, when the Philippines presented so many pagans to convert—why could they not be content with the rich harvest to be reaped among the Christians who had already embraced the Faith?

Father San Vitores answered these somewhat specious reasons with his own solid and true ones. But the ministers of state remained firm in their decision, whether prompted by reason or by invincible stubbornness. It is not surprising that lay persons should argue thus where self-interest weighs so heavily. But even some religious who do not value a land merely for its mineral wealth, rejected the plan, judging it impracticable. Many good men had desired that mission, but had given it up as too difficult and not because they lacked zeal. Only the Venerable Father, whom God had chosen for the task, undismayed by opposition, grew more confident because of it, remembering the words of the Angel Gabriel to Mary: *Non erit impossibile apud Deum omne verbum* (Nothing is impossible with God).[96] And so, with his confidence placed in God, he increased his fasts and penances. At night he took as little sleep as possible, spending much of the night in prayer and writing letters to persuade those who opposed him. With this intent, he chose a room that by all standards was uncomfortable to live in but most suitable for prayer and thought without disturbing or being disturbed, facing the main altar of the church with the statue of Our Lady of the Immaculate Conception above the tabernacle of the most Blessed Sacrament. Oh, if the walls might speak, what secrets they might tell of his colloquies with Jesus and Mary and of the gifts from the Mother and Son! At this time the Servant of God was granted one that we will only mention later, which concerns the fulfillment of his desire.

---

[96]Luke 1:37.

# CHAPTER XIII

### *He Appeals to the King for His Desired Mission*

Since he could not obtain a satisfactory hearing in Manila, Father San Vitores sent a statement to His Majesty, Philip IV (now in heaven), presenting the arguments that we have presented above, accompanied by a letter from the Archbishop of Manila, His Excellency *don* Manual Poblete, who in his zeal wished to share in all the apostolic enterprises of Father San Vitores and whose letter affirmed the usefulness and even the necessity of this mission.

Together with these papers Father San Vitores sent a memorial to his father, *don* Jerónimo, in the name of Saint Francis Xavier, for the poor *Marianos*, to make sure that it would be read by His Majesty. I wish to include it here, but not for the reason some have alleged, namely because it contains a prophetic warning of the approaching death of His Majesty, which took place within a few months. This could have been a prudent guess, given the ill health of His Majesty. Rather, I cite it because it shows the extraordinary zeal and the extraordinary care with which he attended to every possible detail that could further the glory of God and the salvation of souls.

The memorial reads as follows:

The Apostle of the Indies, Saint Francis Xavier, writing to Father Simón Rodríguez, one of the first companions of Saint Ignatius, who governed the Society of Jesus in Portugal, says: "The time has now arrived, dear brother, Master Simón, to undeceive the king, because the time is closer than he thinks when God, our Lord, will call him to give an account of his stewardship, saying *Redde rationem villicationis tuae.*[97] For this reason, try to have the king lay solid spiritual foundations in India, because it seems to me (and God grant that I am mistaken) that at the hour of his death the good prince may find himself much in debt. I fear that in heaven, God, our Lord, looks down on him together with his saints and says: 'The king shows good desires of promoting my honor by his letters to India, and rightly so, because it is for my honor that he possesses India, but he does not punish those who disobey those letters, arresting and punishing only those in charge of his treasury, if they do not procure and increase the revenues.'

'I see only one way, from the experience I have in these matters, to propagate our Holy Faith in India and that is for you to tell the king and his ministers that none serve so well in India as those who with all their might work for the extension of the Faith in Christ. For that reason, order them to seek the

---

[97]Luke 16:2: Give an account of your stewardship.

140

conversion of Ceylon and the increase of converts at Cape Comorin. For this, let them search everywhere for religious persons and make use of the work and ministry of our Society and of all others who may seem suitable for the increase of the service of God.'

'And if by chance the ministers should be negligent in this, threaten them with an oath (and it would be a great service to God to take this oath and a greater one to carry it out) that if they do not thus assist the royal conscience, helping in every way possible the Christianization of India, recall them immediately to Portugal, where they must be punished by long imprisonment and confiscation of their property.'

'I have said what I feel [Xavier continues] and will say no more, simply adding that if this be done, and I propose and greatly desire its accomplishment, then the poor *Indios* recently converted to our Faith and others who will easily be converted, will be freed of many injuries and oppressions which they suffer. If in this matter the authority of the king and the governor is lacking, much time will be lost. Believe me. I speak with more experience than may be apparent, but so it is and I know it all too well.'

'This I write to you, Simón, for the relief of the king's conscience, to whom our Society owes so much. If I were certain that the king knows the great love I have for him, I would ask of him a great favor, and that is that every day he would spend a quarter of an hour asking God to make him understand or rather to embrace with his soul those words of Christ: *Quid prodest homini si universum mundum lucretur, animae vero suae detrimentum patiatur.*[98]'

Thus far Saint Francis Xavier is intent on arranging beforehand the total remedy so badly needed for the affairs of Christianity in the Indies in those days. Saint Francis is particularly concerned about Ternate and Zamboanga (Your Majesty's only garrisons in Mindanao), which are places where Saint Francis Xavier is known to have preached in the Philippines. Both of these forts have been abandoned, to the great detriment of Christianity, especially because of the fort at Zamboanga.

The propagation of the Faith that the saint requests for those islands where it had not yet been preached, as we have said of the great island of Burley,[99] is exactly what is needed for the Ladrones. For many years these have been within sight of our ships. Yet they have not received the light of the gospel, which God our Lord has sent to the farthest corners of the earth, thanks to the zeal of our Catholic Kings. Their royal *cédula*, for the conversion of the Ladrones is totally forgotten, to the great disadvantage of their souls. They are in greater need than the

---

[98]Matt. 16:26, What does it profit a man if he gain the whole world and suffer the loss of his own soul?
[99]Burley, Buru, or Boeros, one of the Moluccas Islands, in Indonesia.

*Book Two, Chapter 13*

souls in purgatory, since they are in want of the essentials for their salvation. And they can be given this aid without much difficulty and with no small hope of spiritual returns before they are infected with the infernal sect of Mohammed, which is a great embarrassment to us and no small bar to the spread of the gospel, and which has arrived before us in most of the islands of the archipelago.

For these poor souls Saint Francis Xavier pleads, and what is more important, so also does the Blood of our Lord Jesus Christ and in his name ought all his ministers likewise, even the least of all Diego Luis de San Vitores.

And in order to leave nothing untried, or because he knew that the queen, *doña* Mariana de Austria (whom God save), was soon to be the one patroness and protector of the Mariana Islands, he wrote to Father Johann Eberhard Nidhard, confessor of the queen and later a cardinal of the holy Church of Rome, urging that the matter be taken up with the queen, in an attempt to obtain her favor and assistance for the mission.[100]

He presented in a general way other reasons for soliciting the support of the queen and then dealt with the excuses of people who were more interested in gold than in the salvation of souls, people who did not wish to cultivate land where the evangelical plow does not open furrows of precious metals. He said:

Who can doubt that if the queen could procure the conversion of all the heretics and infidels in the world, she would do so at whatever cost! And if some were unwilling to come, at least she would do anything within her ability for the conversion of those who did not resist, and especially for the salvation of the souls of multitudes of children who are perishing every day. They could be rescued, were priests at hand and the parents offering no opposition to baptism, and thus their salvation would be obtained.

If there were even one child within the palace who was close to death and with no one to baptize it, if the queen heard of it, she would rise from her throne and rush to baptize it, if the case being such, you told her it was her obligation. Then how much greater evidence of her piety would it be, were she, who is known for her piety and gentleness and charity, were she, I say, without even rising from her throne, to procure the salvation of thousands of children by insisting on the execution of existing royal *cédulas*.

For every year's delay in the dispatch of these orders from the court or their execution in the islands, for lack of the breath of life from the lips of Her Majesty, there will perish infallibly and irremediably all those who die that year and the following

---

[100] Johann Eberhard Nidthard, S.J. (1661-1700), Prime Minister of Spain (1666-1669).

*He Appeals to the King for His Desired Mission*

ones in those islands and lands, where for lack of requisite action, the only remedy for such spiritual need was lost in delay.

Any woman, of any social position, if she heard a child was dying without baptism, would cry out for someone to act quickly; will not the knowledge that many children die and will die every day move us to act quickly and find a remedy?"

Then he adds with considerable discretion: "Finally, I must insist that the thousands of little angels who will owe the blessedness of heaven to the devotion and care of Her Majesty will be the best intercessors for the prosperity of Their Majesties and the happy education and life of the prince and the blessing of more children.[101]

Imagine what will happen in heaven when those children know their great debt to Her Majesty, who came to their rescue with the salvation which, had it not arrived in time, would not have provided the happiness they now enjoy.

And if the *niños* of silver or of wax, which the parents offer to God and the Blessed Mother as votive offerings and petitions for the health and life of their children and for successful childbirth and an heir to their name, if these *niños* are pleasing in the sight of God, how much more acceptable will be the souls of those infants not of silver or gold, souls redeemed and purified in the Blood of the Lamb of God, whom they will praise and follow throughout eternity?

The first thing the Heavenly Father did for the Prince of Glory, when he became a child, was to surround him with an army of children, giving them to him as soldiers of his guard, who would receive the wounds and blows aimed at the life of the Child Jesus by the fury of Herod, whose wicked plans the Heavenly Father converted into the greater glory of his only begotten Son and the honor of his childhood.[102]

And this is why he was so happy when the children came to him and he said: "Of such is the kingdom of heaven."[103] How much joy will this army now give him, and what a beautiful guard and protection will they be for our own prince, because of the alms and devotion that will create this army of children: a guard for the prince while they live on earth in the grace of baptism, and a joy to the Lord in heaven. No longer the work of a cruel Herod, but now that of the gentle heart of our queen as she happily turns to the conversion of these islands.

---

[101] The Prince, Charles II (1661-1700), a rachitic child, would succeed his father in 1665. Then Queen Mariana ruled as regent until 1677.

[102] Matt. 2:13-18.

[103] Matt. 19:14; Mark 10:14; Luke 18:16.

# CHAPTER XIV

*How He Obtains Permission to Go to the Islands of the Ladrones, and the Signs Whereby the Lord Manifests How Pleased He is With This Mission*

While the king's reply was awaited, opposition increased in the City of Manila, and many another man would have yielded to the difficulties but not this great Servant of God, who always kept these words in his heart and on his lips: *Non est impossible apud Deum omne verbum* (Nothing is impossible for God).[104] The superiors of the Society feared greater evils, that a violent storm would arise against the Society. They could see the waves rising higher and higher, and so they ordered Father San Vitores not to speak about the matter to the governor, and if the latter spoke of it, to divert the conversation to other matters. Father San Vitores, as an obedient son of the Society, agreed to do so, but he said with the greatest assurance, "Now there is no doubt. It certainly will happen."

At this point, His Majesty Philip IV intervened with that incomparable zeal that made him say that for only one soul saved, he would give his whole income from the Indies. Preferring the salvation of the poor islanders to his own temporal advantages, he issued orders by royal *cédula*, signed June 24, 1665 (which was the last day of his reign), to the Governor of the Philippines to give to Father San Vitores a ship and all necessary provisions for that holy mission.

He sent a second *cédula* to Father San Vitores so that he could pressure the governor, if he were remiss in complying. And God anticipated the arrival of this message as a special consolation to his servant. The *cédula* had been dispatched on June 24, 1665, the Feast of Saint John the Baptist. On the same day in 1666, before it was known in Manila, as he was completing his morning meditation, the Venerable Father heard a knock at the door of his room. He said, "Come in," and a voice outside said, "A ship is on its way bringing the royal *cédula* for you to go to the Marianas." He left his room, overjoyed to find out who was responsible for the good news, but he found no one. But later on, in secret, he told Father Lorenzo Bustillos it had been his guardian angel sent by the Blessed Mother. It should be noted that the Blessed Virgin sent the news at the same time, hour and day, that the ship *Concepción*, which brought the royal *cédula*, sailed past the island of Guam, which he afterwards called San Juan and which is the main island of the Ladrones.

Alluding to the fact that the royal *cédula* was signed on the Feast of Saint John and arrived in the Marianas on the Feast of the Holy Precursor, he cited the text: *A diebus Joannis Baptistae regnum coelorum vim patitur, et violenti rapiunt illud* (From the days of John the Baptist

---

[104] Luke 1:37.

## How He Obtains Permission to Go to the Islands of the Ladrones

the kingdom of heaven suffers violence and the violent [the Ladrones, he said] carry it away).[105]

Father Bustillos asked Father San Vitores what his guardian angel looked like when he gave him the news, but Father San Vitores would give no information about this or other favors granted by the Lord and his Blessed Mother during the time when he was applying for this mission that was so much to the glory of God. He suffered both mortifications and humiliations, and the Lord repaid him generously.

Father San Vitores was Father Bustillos's spiritual director, as well as his fellow missionary. Often Father Bustillos acted as secretary for his letters and papers, so that he came to know the treasure hidden by the Father's humility. "Oh, who could guess the things he hid from me, so unwilling to speak of them, although I did come to know of the many visits from heaven that he received from the Blessed Virgin, Saint Ignatius, Saint Francis Xavier, the Venerable Father Marcello Mastrilli, and other saints to whom he was devoted, in the seven years of tears and petitions, penances and prayers, that he spent in an out-of-the-way room of the Colegio de Manila, which had a small balcony above the main altar. Although the room was uncomfortable, he would have taken nothing in exchange for the chance to be there alone, undisturbed, and disturbing no one else, as he watched through the hours of the night, writing letters and papers for his mission. All those heavenly visits and all the other divine favors he kept secret, because he was shrewd enough and humble enough to know the talk that would go around. So he went his way with great caution so that nothing was known." Thus far Father Bustillos.

After the *cédula* from His Majesty arrived at Manila, there was an apparent change of heart, or at least a change of words and behavior on the part of those who had most firmly opposed the mission. In obedience to the *cédula*, the governor, *don* Diego Salcedo, ordered that a ship be constructed in Cavite and that the ship be called *San Diego* after his own name and that of Father San Vitores.

About the same time, God showed to one of his servants of the Order of Saint Augustine, *fray* Luis de Mezquita, friar of the *convento* at Taniguan, how great was his pleasure in the mission. One day the friar was in deep contemplation, when he saw in a vision a golden statue high above the tower of the Jesuit church in Manila. Rays of light from the statue shone up to heaven, and then the statue seemed to descend and bless or dispatch a beautiful ship setting out from the tower in full sail, its main mast crowned with the name of Jesus surrounded with splendor. It sailed happily through the air to Cavite, where it disappeared. He did not know at the time what the vision might mean until he heard that the Venerable Father San Vitores was making ready to set sail for the Ladrones Islands. He understood then that the ship that was to bring the light of the gospel to those poor Gentiles was the ship he had seen in his vision. He came to Manila and begged his superiors to allow him to sail with Father San Vitores, but his request was refused. The Lord accepted the sacrifice of his desires in lieu of the sacrifices of the mission. There

---

[105]Matt. 11:12.

*Book Two, Chapter 14*

remained for our speculation the question: Whose statue was it that was blessing the ship, Saint Ignatius Loyola, the father of so many missionaries of the Society, or Saint Francis Xavier, his son, protector of the missions?

Although matters had progressed satisfactorily so far, the devil did not cease to put obstacles in the way of an enterprise so much to the greater glory of God. When the ship was ready and about to set sail from the harbor at Cavite, adverse interests were brought to bear and suddenly there was a public announcement in Manila, ordering it to head directly for Peru with a cargo of merchandise. This was a hard blow for Father San Vitores. Now he must either abandon the voyage or sail all the way to Peru and spend two years getting to Guam, with the loss of innumerable souls.

Fired as he was with religious fervor for the glory of God, he threatened Manila with calamities and misfortunes of every kind, if the will of God, so plainly set forth, was ignored. The ship *San Diego*, as if she realized the offense to God and his servant, at the moment when the announcement about Peru was read in Manila, began to capsize and settled onto her side, in such a way that no human means could right her. The Servant of God said that unless orders were reversed, regardless of all their efforts, the ship would stay that way. As he was venerated by all and believed by many to be a saint and a prophet, his words were believed and the governor ordered a proclamation to be read that the ship should go to Acapulco with Father San Vitores and from there should carry him and his companions to the Marianas. Wonderful to relate! At that very moment the ship righted itself, all by itself. This incident was told by Father Bustillos who heard it many times from Father San Vitores in the Marianas. Father San Vitores would then praise and admire the works of God and the means he provides for the salvation of his chosen ones. Then Father Bustillos asked him if there had been other wonders, prophetic of his voyage to the Marianas. He answered that if he were to tell them all, he would never end; he had only mentioned this instance for his consolation. Then, when pressed for other examples, he was reluctant, saying that if it were the will of God that these wonderful events should be known, the Lord would find a way. After all, it was not important, since the mission of the Marianas was now a reality.

I pass over in silence many of the miracles that God worked through his servant at the time when he was preparing for his departure to the Marianas, thus showing his divine pleasure in the enterprise. It is enough to mention here what is written in a report from the Philippines: "Father San Vitores cured so many sick people that those who accompanied him said that he never left the house without working miracles by the dozen, that sheer abundance of them made them less noticeable. His diligence in hiding his cures was no less than in working them. To obscure his part in the cure, he would recite a gospel over the patient or would apply a relic of Saint Francis Xavier or some other object of devotion. In the *Annua* of the Province of the Philippines, among the many marvels they tell of him, there is one that practically all those relate who served as his companions: he was continually going out at night to visit the sick and dying; yet in the rainy season when the streets of Manila were flooded, even though his sight was so poor that he could not recognize people unless they were very close, he was never seen to stumble or to get mud on himself, or to wet the bottom of his cassock or cloak, although his companion would return home splashed with mud and water up to the knees. The same happened in the mission to Mindoro where he walked through mountains and swamps in continual rainy weather.

I will pass over his remarkable prophecies for a better occasion, since we should catch up with Father San Vitores as he begins his voyage to the Marianas. They have already stolen his heart. And he will have no rest till he returns to the Redeemer those now caught by the devil.

# CHAPTER XV

*Father San Vitores Sails for Mexico in order to Go to the Marianas; the Wonders of the Voyage*

The Venerable Father Diego Luis de San Vitores embarked at the port of Cavite with Father Tomás de Cardeñoso on the seventh day of August 1667, the octave day of the Feast of Saint Ignatius. One may well imagine his joy, since the devil, who had placed so many difficulties and obstacles in the way of this glorious enterprise, was finally overcome. His departure from Manila was the cause of much sadness among his friends and followers. They had never cared so much for him as at the moment when they were about to lose him. Many sought his autograph as a memento. The person who was most deeply touched by his departure was Archbishop Poblete, who loved him as a son and venerated him as his spiritual father. He made this clear in a letter he wrote to *don* Jerónimo San Vitores, in which he said: "I weep for his absence with tears of blood both for the loss to my spirit and to the universal good of these islands, where he has accomplished so very much. But as the judgments of God are inscrutable and deep, so it is better to leave him to his vocation, for it will carry him to higher things such as the conversion of so many infidels who live in the Ladrones." Even the island of Manila expressed great sorrow in the fearful earthquakes that caused so much consternation among the inhabitants. Yet it may have been the trembling fear of the evil one in dread of the many souls he would now lose in the Marianas, since similar earthquakes took place in New Spain when he arrived in Acapulco.

On this voyage he did as he was accustomed to do on others, and yet these same deeds always seemed new and unprecedented, so extraordinary were they. With his gentleness, his Christ-like charity, and his words, he won the hearts of those on board, so that they did willingly whatever he asked of them. They listened to his word as to the word of God. They spoke openly of him as a saint, a prophet, and a father to all. Hence, many practices, such as gambling, cursing, swearing, and other vices were banished from the ship, while the reception of the sacraments, the Act of Contrition, and devotion to the saints and the Blessed Mother were practiced as never before. All made a vow to defend her Immaculate Conception. No wonder God granted them the most fortunate voyage known to that route—and the most Christian. They were free from the dangers of disembarking and many others. It was a miracle that no one died in the zones where a majority perish from the climatic changes and the extreme cold of the northern latitudes. Also, the passage was a fortunate one in that it took only five months, whereas it usually took eight months or even a year. None of those who sailed had any serious misfortune. All arrived at Acapulco safe and well. A number of the company later reported that they were all so happy in the companionship of

*He Sails for Mexico in order to Go to the Marianas; the Wonders of the Voyage*

Father San Vitores, so charmed by his gentle and holy conversation, that the voyage of five months seemed less than one month to all on board. In Manila the following has remained a proverb among his former companions: "Never sail on the *San Diego* because she no longer carries Father Diego," since those who traveled so happily with him found subsequent voyages on the same ship a hardship.

But there were several illnesses on board and storms as well to show how much they owed their health and safety to Father San Vitores, to his prayer, at which he spent a great part of the night and day, and above all to the Holy Sacrifice of the Mass, which he offered every day, even in the worst weather. The ship encountered one severe storm in which the winds and the sea conspired against the ship. It rolled and tossed, now on the crest of a great wave, now plunging to the bottom of an abyss. The members of the crew thought that each plunge would bury them forever. Father San Vitores saw that they were about to cut down the main mast. He counseled them not to do it. "These are but demons in the air, and all will soon be calm again." And within two hours the weather was fair again.

Captain *don* Juan de Santa Cruz had accompanied him from Manila and was to continue with him to the Marianas. There, he rendered much service as a faithful companion of Father Diego Luis. He testified in the *Processus* that when two sailors fell from the topsail, he called out to them and they landed unharmed. They considered this a special favor from God, granted to them through the merits of Father San Vitores. When Captain *don* Juan de Santa Cruz embarked, he did not dare take along his grandson, then six or eight months old, because the child was ill and had no nurse. Yet he was distressed at the prospect of leaving the child in Manila almost alone. The Venerable Father saw his sorrow and spoke to him sympathetically: "Son, take the child on board. He has no mother, but the Blessed Mother will take care of him, and he will live many years." He brought him on board and God not only preserved the life and health of that delicate young child, though he had neither mother nor nurse to provide milk, but he is still living, as his grandfather testified nine years later.

The general of the ship, *don* Antonio Nieto, testifies that he cared for the sick with great devotion. He would apply a bit of ginger and would recite a gospel, whatever the sickness might be, and they were cured very soon. It seems also that he had the gift of tongues, because he not only taught the Tagalogs in their own language, but also when he heard persons of other foreign nations reciting prayers, he corrected their errors, although he did not know the language.

The ship arrived at Acapulco at the beginning of January in 1668. Father San Vitores leaped ashore, and barefoot led his companions in procession to the hermitage of San Nicolás. He carried a statue of the Blessed Virgin, his patroness in all his undertakings. They held services for several days, and the guard of honor included the general and the officers of the ship. Father San Vitores continued, in part, the same services and ministries as on the ship and so the life of the crew and passengers was much the same as on board. In the morning they all heard Mass and in the afternoon they all gathered for the rosary, which was followed by instructions. His manner was so charming that they were all happy to follow his suggestions. General Antonio Nieto testifies that the good example of the sailors and other personnel was the more noticeable as it was unexpected.

Unfortunately, the conversion was not a total one. It was due to the person and influence of Father San Vitores. All the time they were in Acapulco there was no trouble. But as soon as the father left the port city, many ran to their former vices with the speed of wild horses.

# CHAPTER XVI

*The Great Obstacles He Overcomes in Mexico With the Aid of Heaven, in order to Continue the Voyage to His Longed-for Mission*

Father San Vitores had not intended to go to Mexico City. He wrote to the viceroy and other persons, informing him of his plans and asking their assistance for the mission. They replied promptly, stating that since the Royal Treasury was heavily encumbered, his plans presented many difficulties that could be resolved only by his presence in the capital and expressing their eagerness to see him and talk with him.

Upon receipt of these messages, he departed for Mexico City, accomplishing in a week a journey that usually took twice the time, traversing eighty leagues over rough and difficult roads. On the last day, having walked eleven leagues, he arrived at the capital at eleven o'clock. Instead of entering the *colegio*, he went straight to the parish church of Vera Cruz and to its chapel of Saint Francis Xavier, where he celebrated Mass, commending to God through the intercession of Saint Francis Xavier the problems of this mission, which was so close to the heart of the holy apostle.

Great was the joy of the City of Mexico when his arrival was known, as one of our Jesuit fathers wrote: "Our Lord deigned to bring to this city, all unexpectedly, my holy Father Diego Luis de San Vitores for the joy of all this kingdom of New Spain. Those who saw him thought themselves most fortunate, and those who talked to him felt themselves blessed."

The Mass finished after midnight. He went to the *colegio* of the Society without stopping to eat or to rest, because his zeal for his Marianas would not let him rest. He took a picture of Our Lady of the Immaculate Conception and hastened to the palace of the viceroy, who was then His Excellency the *Marqués* de Mancera. The *marqués* could not receive him at that hour, so he sent the picture of the *Señora Ladrona* with the message that she was going to rob the palace for the benefit of her *Ladrones* children, that she would speak for them, and that he would return for an answer.

He returned many times to talk to His Excellency. He explained the reasons for his enterprise, namely the salvation of many souls, the expressed wish of His Majesty (which was his obligation), and the need of ten thousand pesos.

Although the viceroy, in his religious zeal and his faithful service of the king, wished to comply with Father San Vitores's request, he stated that grave difficulties lay in his path because of lack of funds in the Royal Treasury. And since he had no orders for the distribution of funds, Her Majesty might not be pleased.

*Book Two, Chapter 16*

The members of the *Audiencia* gave the same answer, especially one member who was especially obstinate in his opposition. Filled with the Spirit of God, the Venerable Father addressed this man:

> Señor, consider how precious are the souls redeemed by the Blood of Jesus Christ, and what ought to be given for those for whom Christ gave so much. All the treasures of the Indies would be small price to pay for one soul, and the queen (who was then governing the empire) would give all, emulating the piety of the king, our lord, now in heaven, who said on many occasions that for one redeemed soul he would give all the wealth of the Indies. Such expenditures cannot impair the Royal Treasury, because if our Lord promises a return of one hundred for the gift of one to feed the body of a beggar, how much will he return for one given to redeem many souls from the sufferings of hell?[106] If we allow souls to be lost to save the treasury, the treasury will be lost with the souls. Your Excellency, remember that this was why God gave the Indies to our kings, saying what the other king said to Abraham: "Give me the souls, and take the rest for yourself."[107] Your Excellency, remember that this is the desire of our Catholic Kings, who try more to extend the frontiers of the kingdom of Jesus Christ than their own, who are more eager to win vassals for the Redeemer than money for their treasury. Your Excellency, remember that on your decision may depend the salvation or condemnation of innumerable souls, and remember that you will have to answer to the supreme Judge of the living and the dead, who will take as strict an account of small things as of large ones, and will demand an eye for an eye and a tooth for a tooth, when he asks an account of the souls who were lost through your fault.

With these words, Father San Vitores made the minister tremble, and God so changed his heart that he agreed with the others to grant what was requested. To this end a certain event contributed, which seemed the work of Divine Providence.

One day the Venerable Father was conferring with the viceroy and his wife in her apartments at the palace, soliciting the dispatch of his enterprise. The viceroy offered some resistance, alleging various reasons, but the vicereine who had conceived a great esteem for the Venerable Father and wished to assist this work for the glory of God, made the gesture of kneeling before her husband to plead with him, when the palace and the whole city began to shake in a terrifying earthquake. The vicereine grasped the cloak of the Servant of God, as though it were a sanctuary from the wrath of heaven.

When people learned the circumstances in which the earthquake had occurred, they were convinced that God was trying to hasten the success of Father San Vitores's efforts in behalf of the Ladrones. And

---

[106] She was not pleased. See n. 108.

[107] Gen. 14:21, a common and literal, but mistaken, translation of the Vulgate text: *Da mihi animas, cetera tolle.*

## The Great Obstacles He Overcomes in Mexico With the Aid of Heaven

so it happened that on the next day, although it was the Sunday in Carnival time, the viceroy summoned his Council, and all the members, reversing their previous vote, voted that ten thousand pesos be given to Father San Vitores for his mission.

Some concern was still expressed as to how news of the matter would be received by Her Majesty, since it had been done without her express permission. But the Lord provided in his emergency, as eighteen wealthy men came forward as guarantors of the Servant of God. They promised to repay, from their own property, to the Royal Treasury the full amount, if Her Majesty did not accord her full approval.[108] One of the guarantors said, "Not only ten thousand, but sixty thousand pesos could be guaranteed." So great was the love they had for the Venerable Father, who had more than enough friends who came to his assistance. So anxious were they to have a part in a work so pleasing in the sight of God and so greatly desired by his servant.

His credit secured, there remained one more difficulty in his path, usually the greatest one: that of obtaining the money promptly. But the Lord sped this process, too, as all the officials in the chain of command bent every effort towards procuring the funds quickly, as if they were laboring for their private interests. They saw it as their private interest because of their love for him and because it was such a service to God. The Lord gave some proof of this, as in the case of Ventura de Ugarte, who was an official copyist and testified to this for the *Processus*. Father San Vitores paid sixteen pesos to Ventura for copies of the bonds and other documents that he had transcribed for the mission. The father added that he wished he could give him everything that he needed. God heard the wish of his servant. From then on, as Ventura testified ten years later, he was never in need, although previously, no matter how hard he worked, he sometimes went hungry; this with no extra work on his part, but only through the merits of Father Diego Luis.

Something very different happened to a certain royal minister whose name I will not mention. Repeatedly, he had opposed the Servant of God, who had visited him three or four times and urged his cause forcefully. The man was deaf to all his reasons. After one of the visits Father Diego Luis's companion, who had been present at the interview, said, "Very stubborn, *don* So-and-So!" "Let it be," said Father San Vitores. "He is an unfortunate man. Before long, you will see where he ends." And before a year had passed he was arrested for crimes against the Treasury, suffered a most painful imprisonment, died in prison, and was buried in a pauper's grave.

One can only wonder at the ways of Divine Providence, which consistently aided in obtaining those ten thousand pesos from the Royal Treasury, and yet the actual money never could be received, because the admiral of the ship that was bringing it, *don* Bartolomé Muñoz, died. Then, as there were so many recommendations for the money, it was finally allotted to Manila. Thus the Lord rewarded and tested his servant.

---

[108]The queen gave her official approval of the gift, but was most displeased at this procedure and strictly forbade any repetition of it. The Royal Order (*real cédula*) of May 20, 1670, quoted in Alberto Risco, *The Apostle of the Marianas*, 1627-1672, Agaña, Guam, 1970, pp. 102-103, n.3.

The esteem and appreciation shown for the project in Mexico was a reward, while the actual lack of resources in the Marianas was a test. And so the donation, which had the approval of Her Majesty, had no effect save in her merit before God.

There was nevertheless much assistance from other sources. Many devout persons in Mexico City contributed money or jewels for the churches that must be built and furnished with crosses, statues, paintings, altars, chalices, vestments, and all the other things needed in the establishment of the Christian community.

What he particularly wanted and asked of the piety of his supporters was cloth, of any variety or quality, to cover those who began to be the living temples of God at their baptism, the naked islanders. He intended to evangelize and in the meanwhile to provide this necessity of Christian decency.

The most liberal contribution of all came from his beloved Sodality of Saint Francis Xavier. The sodality gave him ten thousand pesos, showing on this occasion, as in all others, the apostolic zeal inherited from their patron and from their founder or restorer.

He remained three months in Mexico, busy with his affairs until the last hour arrived for his embarkation to the Marianas, which he called his Promised Land of Mary. But as he could not limit his zeal to only one employment, he occupied himself with all the ministries of the Society of Jesus. He visited prisons and hospitals, heard confessions, gave lectures, and carried out the *Acto de Contrición* and all the activities of his first stay in Mexico. Morning and afternoon he was on the go. He replaced his exhausted companion of the morning with a fresh one in the afternoon, and wore him out. No one could understand how he could keep up with all this activity, weakened as he was by penance, fasts, and hard work. In all this he was as punctual as if he had only the one task to perform. He walked the streets a living portrait of modesty and recollection, his heart in God and in his beloved Marianas, of which he talked constantly. With downcast eyes, he was yet aware of and embarrassed at the respect and reverence with which all regarded him, looking on him as if he were a saint descended from heaven, eager to have some relic of the father, feeling themselves blessed if they acquired one.

The Sodality of Saint Francis Xavier, not content with keeping the letters and jewels that he had donated to them as precious relics, had a portrait painted of him by detaining him, all unaware, in the chapel of the saint. Then this portrait was hung with that of other holy men including that of the Apostle of the Indies to be a consolation to them when they missed him. Some of his friends wanted a better portrait, one with a better likeness, so they lured him to the room of a friend of his, Father José Vidal, where a very good painter was hidden. Although the *bachiller* Cristóbal Javier Vidal called Father San Vitores to the room under the pretext of taking a close look at some important business, he must have received some special light regarding their intentions, because at first he excused himself. They insisted, and he went as far as the door of the room, but was unwilling to enter the room. When they dragged him in, he covered his face with some papers as though he had to read them. The painter could hardly see his face, but somehow the portrait turned out to be a very good one.

The very day Father San Vitores was to leave Mexico, his dear friend Miguel Damián Morillo played a pious trick on him. He exchanged the father's old hat for a new one, so that both might be winners in the exchange, especially *don* Miguel, who considered that old hat a precious relic. And so it was for him, since it saved his little son's life. An animal kicked the boy in the forehead and fractured the bone. They carried the unconscious child to his mother, and she, in desperation, commended him to Saint Michael, his namesake, and then placed the Venerable Father's hat on his head. He revived immediately and recovered so quickly that the surgeons considered the cure miraculous. On a later occasion, the mother was sick, her face swollen with erysipelas. The doctors tried many medicines to no avail. Then she put on the father's hat, at once she began to get well and was cured in a few days.

# CHAPTER XVII

*The Voyage of the Servant of God to the Marianas*

After he had brought his affairs in Mexico City to a happy conclusion, as we have stated, Father San Vitores set out for the port of Acapulco toward the middle of February 1668, accompanied by another father (Tomás de Cardeñoso) and a scholastic (Lorenzo Bastillos).

Many of his friends wished to follow him even unto death, and some begged him urgently not to go without them but to allow them to serve God always in the Christianization of the Gentiles. But as this was not possible, they set out, meaning to accompany him as far as the town of San Agustín de las Cuevas, which was more than three leagues distant from Mexico City. But when the Venerable Father arrived at the village of Coyoacán, he saw the church and asked to whom it was dedicated. They answered, "To Saint John the Baptist." He said that it was not fair to pass by without paying a visit to a friend. There he remained for more than four hours in prayer. It was too late then for them to go on to San Agustín, so in tears they took leave of him there. His beloved friend, the *bachiller* Cristóbal Javier Vidal fell to his knees, begging his blessing. Father Diego Luis said, "Go with God, till we meet again at the feet of Saint Francis Xavier." Many took this as a prophecy, for within a short time the *bachiller* Javier died (1668) and Father San Vitores followed him on the second of April 1672.

During the journey Father Diego Luis wrote to *bachiller* Vidal and answered two questions known only to the *bachiller* and God, as he himself testified.

The first concerned the name Xavier, which he wished to take (it was not his name). He had told no one at all about it. In the letter Father San Vitores told him to call himself Xavier.

The second question was: What were the colloquies he held with Saint John the Baptist and the gifts he received during those four hours of prayer? This we do not deserve to know. It may well be that he asked the holy precursor that he too might be a forerunner in his preaching in those islands, preparing their souls to receive Christ, that as John had baptized Christ, so John might help him to baptize and Christianize these Gentiles. It would seem that the holy precursor promised him this, since he opened the door of the gospel on the island of Guam, which the father named, with a slight change, San Juan, in honor of the Baptist. The saint had already shown his desire to share in this conquest, since two years earlier on Saint John's Day, Father Diego Luis had had a revelation that the royal *cédula* had been signed granting him permission to go to the Marianas, and this at a time when the ship bearing the news was sailing past the island of San Juan. And now the Lord willed that the first one he met en route to his mission was San Juan. Surely this was no accident but a special providence of him who

*The Voyage of the Servant of God to the Marianas*

governed every step of the Apostle of the Marianas. The daily order that he observed on this journey, his usual pattern, is worthy of imitation by all apostolic missionaries. He spent most of the night, or practically all of it, in prayer. He celebrated Mass very early, made a devout thanksgiving, and began the day's journey reciting the *Itinerarium* as he walked along. He recited it in a loud voice, and his companions said the responses. He added many other prayers, especially the one that Saint Francis Xavier composed for the conversion of unbelievers, the one that begins *Aeterne Deus*, etc.[109] He used to say it with special feeling for his Ladrones. He also introduced the custom of saying it on all his voyages at the end of each rosary.

On the road he would talk to God or about God. There was not a passerby to whom he did not try to do some good, either instructing him in some mystery of the Faith or giving him some solid advice. As soon as the group approached a town he would ring the little bell he always carried to gather the inhabitants for a talk or some other pious exercise. He would put a crucifix before the door of his inn and recite the rosary and other devotions before it. He would say the Act of Contrition, inviting all present to go to confession and many of them did.

The amount of work done by Father San Vitores during his short stay in Acapulco is almost unbelievable. He completed arrangements for the voyage, spending entire nights without sleep, consoling those who came to him for confession or spiritual counseling. In prayer and contemplation he presented to God his concerns for his soul and for his Marianas.

He chose as most suitable for his business (he said), the most unsuitable room in the house of Admiral Bartolomé Muñoz. The room was fit for cabin boys or slaves, though really it was well suited for his purpose, a maximum of mortification. There he spent the night sweating in mortal misery, in what we might call purgatory, but he would call a paradise of delights. And were they not moments of paradise when he was visited again and again by the Lord and the Lady of the Islands where he was going to proclaim the glory of the Son and the Mother? Father Lorenzo Bustillo, who was his companion at this time, said that he had here many visits and apparitions of the Blessed Virgin. He could not very well conceal them because of the many people who lived in the house. A young Spaniard, who was very devoted to Father San Vitores, asked him if it were true that the Blessed Mother talked to him every night. He blushed and answered, "Don't be so curious. It's no concern of yours." For him, in his humility, not to deny it was tantamount to an admission.

A few days after his arrival in Acapulco a group of Jesuits arrived en route to the Philippines. These were waiting in Mexico for passage thither. In this group was the Venerable Father Luis de Medina, whom God had promised him as a companion when he passed through Córdova in 1660.[110] We will have more to say about him in

---

[109]See Appendix for tanslation of this prayer. San Vitores translated it into Spanish and urged people to say the prayer at least once a week.
[110]See Book 1, chap.13:76; Book 5, chapters 1-6.

its proper place. He was the first to win the palm of martyrdom in the Mariana Islands.

Father San Vitores had brought from Manila an order from the father provincial, Domingo Ezquerra, giving him the right to choose two priests from among those who came from Spain, and he had chosen Father Medina and another one. But when they arrived in the Marianas, the captain of the ship, in the name of Her Majesty, ordered that additional missionaries should remain in the islands because of the extreme need of these souls. And so, those who were to remain with Father San Vitores, besides Father Tomás Cardeñoso, who had come from Manila for that purpose, and Father Luis de Medina, were two other priests and a scholastic, namely Father Pedro de Casanova, Father Luis de Morales, and the scholastic Lorenzo Bustillos, who was not yet ordained a priest. There was much rejoicing among those who were chosen and no less envy on the part of those continuing to the Philippines.

But we have gotten ahead of ourselves. From Acapulco they set sail on March 13, 1668. The ship also carried an image of the Virgin called *La Misionera Nuestra Señora de Buen Viaje*, which was carried in procession from the Hermitage of San Nicolás to the ship.

New Spain, or rather the heavens, bade farewell to the Servant of God with the apparition of a blood-red comet running north to south, a subject of much discussion. He wrote to his friends that heaven was declaring war against the tyranny of the demons, which had oppressed those islands for so many years. Others said that it meant many missionaries would shed their blood in that place. But let us forget these conjectures, although there was another earthquake at this time, which might well seem to be the fear of the devil at the war Father San Vitores was soon to wage against him.

He chose as his living quarters the most uncomfortable place on the ship, a small space behind a small window or door in the pilot's quarters. This was his room and oratory. Here he placed a picture of the Santo Cristo de Burgos, to which he raised his eyes frequently when reading or writing, besides making his prayer in front of it. I do not speak of his bed, because on all his voyages it was no more than a chair or a stool. A bed was unnecessary for one who slept so little. If anyone sought him out at any hour whatever of the night, they found him awake. I do not speak of his fasts and penances, which knew no remission, but only an increasing rigor, nor of the observance and religious regularity of his companions. His example alone was enough for all to behave like fervent novices.

Charity—both spiritual and corporal—to teach and preach, this alone drew him out of his retreat, especially in service to the sick. It aroused the admiration of all to see him going along in his near blindness, leaning on the cabin walls and cables of the ship, seeking out the sick and spending time with them, helping and comforting them. He would share his poor rations with them, keeping the worst for himself in order to give the best to Christ. Moreover, he gave alms and assisted all who were in need.

*The Voyage of the Servant of God to the Marianas*

Admiral Bartolomé Muñoz fell deathly ill, and Father Diego Luis remained at his bedside until he expired, full of confidence in the hope of salvation, repaid by the prayers and sacrifices of the father for his own many acts of kindness and generosity.

The ceremonies and processions of Holy Week, as well as the fiestas of the principal saints, were celebrated with all the solemnity the cramped condition of the vessel permitted. He composed hymns in the Mariana language, so that they might be helpful in the conversion of the natives. In this way he practiced the language with the help of an interpreter, whom he himself corrected when he made a mistake. He learned the language so thoroughly that on the Feast of Saint John the Baptist of the same year (1668), eight days after arriving in the Marianas, while celebrating the Feast of the Blessed Sacrament, which had been postponed till that date, he preached in that language with such elegance and propriety that the natives marveled.

When they knew from the ship's position that they were drawing near the Mariana Islands, his anxiety grew as he neared the object of his desires. He increased the number of his devotions and asked everyone to pray for the successful preaching of the gospel. But he feared that sins (his own, he said, in his humility) might steal this glory from the Lord. So in the beginning of the month, he distributed the patron saints and then promised a very beautiful reliquary to the one whose patron feast fell on the day land was sighted, but on condition that he had confessed and received Communion. After this they began to pray more fervently, asking God and their saint that they might have luck. They wished to possess a remembrance prized for itself as well as for the hand of the holy father, whom they venerated and whose prayers they sought in those storm-infested seas, as though he were no longer living, but already a saint in heaven.

Lastly, he offered a novena of masses in honor of the family of the Blessed Virgin, *la familia Mariana,* and the second day of the novena, Friday, June 15, was the one dedicated to the glorious Saint Anne. This happened to be the day on which they began in Mexico City the ten Fridays in honor of the ten years of the apostolate of Saint Francis Xavier. It was a devotion created by Father San Vitores and fervently practiced by the Sodality of Saint Francis Xavier for the intention that God would prosper the voyage of the imitator of the great Apostle of the Indies. It was on this day, then, that while Father Casanova was saying Mass, a cabin boy sighted the island of Zarpana (Rota), which already Father San Vitores was calling Santa Ana. He cried out, *"Tierra, Tierra."* To the Father it was as if he heard "Heaven, heaven," so great was his joy, a joy beyond words. A little later they saw the island of Guam, as the Spaniards call it, or Guahan, as the natives say.[111]

---

[111]Higgins found the chronological sequence of events confusing at this point. On Friday, June 15, the Feast of Saints Vitus, Modestus, and Crescentia, being the second day of San Vitores's novena to the Holy Family, land was sighted for the first time, namely the island of Rota. Apparently each day of the novena was dedicated to a different member of the Holy Family. The second day of the novena, June 15, on which land was sighted, was dedicated to Saint Anne, and he named Rota Santa Ana in her honor. That evening they reached Guam and remained on board the ship overnight. The next day, Saturday, June 16, San Vitores sent two fathers ashore. They stayed that day and the succeeding night in Agaña with Quipuha. The next day, Sunday 17, Father San Vitores came ashore for the first time and Mass was celebrated on the beach.

*Book Two, Chapter 17*

The ship arrived at nightfall at this island. Up to fifty canoes of the islanders, each carrying four to six persons, men and women, surrounded the ship. They kept repeating in their language *mauri, mauri,* which means, "friends, friends." But because the ship had come closer inshore than was usual, they did not dare to come on board. They feared it might be a stratagem to seize them. It was nothing but the devil, fearful of losing his dominion over those islands, who instilled his fear in the islanders.

The Servant of God regretted this very much. He asked the general to have them chant the litanies of our Lady at the very side of the ship. He did so, and as the father said, *Santa Maria, ora pro nobis,*[112] they began to come on board without any fear at all. At the end of the litany, the father writes: "We could not see ourselves free of those who wanted to come aboard, and they remained with us all night." With what a show of affection he received his beloved *Marianos!* He could not have enough of embracing them, of touring the ship with them, showing them everything, giving them presents, though of little value in themselves, yet appreciated by them.

He asked them, in their own language, who were their chiefs. These he placed at his side in a place of honor and gave them a little talk and explained why he had come. He explained the principal mysteries of our Faith with so much fervor and spirit (writes one of his companions) that it seemed as if the Lord had given us another Francis Xavier in his zeal for souls and his gift of tongues.

The islanders heard him with pleasure, especially when he said the fathers would remain. The islanders remained on board all night, unwilling to part from one who showed them so much love.

The following morning was a Saturday, the day consecrated to the Blessed Mother. And so that all might begin in her name, and that all would be due to her protection, a Christian named Pedro brought his daughter, a child of two years, for baptism. He was one of those who had remained on Guam in 1638 after the wreck of the *Concepción* near these islands. He was a man highly regarded by the leading people of the island of Guam. Happy was Father Diego Luis to see the first fruit of the land for so many centuries sterile, but which now offered him its fruit without any cultivation. He gave thanks to the Lord for his mercies. Not wanting the primacy in anything, though owed to him in everything, he had Father Luis de Morales baptize her. He named the child Mariana, as the first fruit of the Mariana Islands, because of his devotion to the Queen of Heaven, Mary most Holy, as well as from regard for the queen of Spain, *doña* Mariana de Austria, even as he had named this group of islands *Las Islas Marianas* for the same reasons. The Christian, Pedro, assured him that they would be well received in the islands. His experience that same day proved it. He sent out two explorers, the Venerable Father Luis de Medina and Father Pedro de Casanova. At this point, we will enter the land with these two fathers and examine its characteristics and customs in order to give some information to the

---

[112]Holy Mary, pray for us.

160

curious, leaving the Servant of God with his longing to enter the islands and occupied in conversation with the islanders who came to visit him on the ship.

# BOOK III

*Of the Life and Martyrdom of the
Venerable Father Diego Luis de San Vitores,
of the Society of Jesus, First Apostle of the
Mariana Islands*

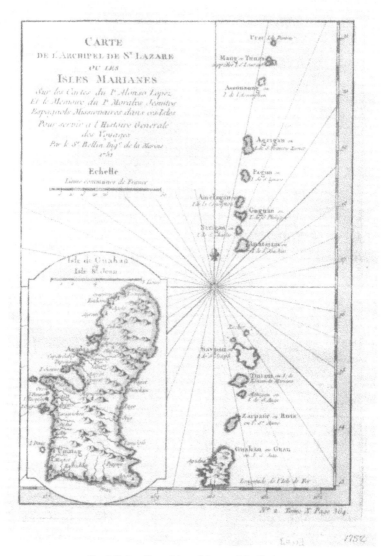

Fig. 4. Father Alonso López, S.J., served the Marianas mission from 1673 to 1675. During that short time, he charted the islands of the archipelago-identifying them by their indigenous names as well as by those given by Father San Vitores. Father Alonso also prepared a detailed map of the island of Guam. (See Figure 7). His maps were first published in Paris in 1700 by Father Charles Le Gobien, S.J., in *Histoire des Isles Marianes Nouvellement converties a la Religion Chrestienne...* . Later, in 1752, they were published by the French naval engineer, Jacobo Nicolás Bellin.

# CHAPTER I

### The Nature of the Mariana Islands; the Temperament and Customs of Their People

The islands formerly called *de los Ladrones* or *de las Velas Latinas* have now happily been changed through the influence of religion to *Las Marianas*. They are simply innumerable and run from north to south from Japan to Peru. The thirteen discovered and illumined by the gospel are the only ones of which I wish to speak, on the basis of information provided by the ministers of the gospel. They have traveled over them many times and have corrected the accounts of the older voyagers who saw them only from a distance or in great haste. These islands are situated in longitude 164 degrees, more or less, from Palma, in the Canary Islands, and are three hundred leagues nearer than Manila on the voyage from New Spain to the Philippines. They extend from 13 degrees north latitude [Guam] to 22 degrees north, which is at Maug, the island nearest to Japan of all those that the missionaries have reached in the small boats available to them. According to the letters and charts of voyagers, it is a matter of six days journey from Japan. This group of thirteen islands is so "marian" in configuration that, starting from south-southwest and ending in the north-northeast, they form a crescent, a very appropriate throne for the feet of Mary and a symbol of the protection of this sovereign Queen, in spite of Mohammed, who has united to his crescent many of the islands of this archipelago.[113]

Their names, not as they are confused in some historical accounts, but as they were written by Father San Vitores, who changed the names into sacred ones, since he wished to make the land Christian, are in order, from south to north, as follows: Guam, which he called San Juan; Zarpana (Rota),[114] which he called Santa Ana; Aguigan, renamed Santo Angel; Tinian, Buenavista Mariana; Saipan, San José; Anatajan, San Joaquín; Sarigan, San Carlos; Guguan, San Phelipe; Alamagan, La Concepción; Pagon, San Ignacio; Agrigan, San Francisco Javier; Asonzón, La Asunción; and Maug, San Lorenzo. The largest are Guam, which is 35 square leagues, and Agrigan, which is fifty.[115] The latter is more fertile and pleasant than the others. The islands are not far apart, the farthest only a day's journey from another. They have commerce and use the same language, a rare thing among Gentiles who are not subject to one dominion.

The climate is healthful and benign, although the last (northern) islands are cooler than the first and in none is the cold or heat excessive. They do not suffer the terrible earthquakes that are known in

---

[113]The woman robed with the sun of Rev. 12:1 is often attributed to the Virgin Mary, so is represented by Velázquez and other painters as standing on a crescent moon. By "this archipelago", García seems to refer to all or most of the islands of the Western Pacific. See Book 1, chap. 5:22 n. 21.

[114]Zarpana, the name given by early Spanish navigators to Rota. The indigenous name is thought to be a form closely related to Rota. (M.H.)

[115]Agrigan is actually smaller than either Guam or Saipan. Moreover, the location of Agrigan is not correctly given by García. (M.H.)

Book Three, Chapter 1

other islands of this archipelago.[116] The land is mountainous and has great marshes, always covered with thorny sorbs and with many other trees, none of European type. The most notable tree is the one they call in their language *María* (*Palo María*),[117] with which they construct their houses and boats. It was an omen of the name of Mary, a harbinger of the happiness that must come through this name. The islands have full flowing rivers of fresh water. On the island of Guam alone there are more than thirty. No crocodiles are found, or snakes, or other poisonous animals. There are fish in the rivers, especially eels, but on account of some superstition they do not catch them. On land one finds no animals but cats and dogs, and these are believed to have remained here after the wreck of the *Concepción* (1638). The only birds seen here resemble doves. The islanders do not eat them, but keep them in cages and teach them to speak. There are no gold or silver mines or other precious articles. What is most valuable to them is iron, for which they trade their produce and tortoise shells with the Spanish ships, and the one who has the most iron is the most powerful. Nature is so parsimonious with these islanders and yet they are content with so little. It is a lesson to those who exhaust all nature to satisfy a pathological hunger and thirst; it shows how little suffices for one who seeks no surplus, while nothing is surplus for one dissatisfied with what is enough.

The islands have many harbors where ships can anchor, some of them very suitable for the ships that come from New Spain as well as those that come from the Philippines, if only the contrary winds did not prevent the latter from taking this route. The Servant of God attributes this largely to the dominion the devil had won over these islands. His ambition was to prevent the Faith from coming from nearby countries. But now we are confident that these winds will be tamed by the Star of the Sea, who keeps the *Marianos* under her protection as well as under her name.

On the Island of San Juan there are seven harbors. One is called San Antonio and is in the western part, across from a town the natives call Hati.[118] Here there are two good rivers from which to obtain water. There is another harbor where the Dutch stayed years ago for three months careening three ships. This is half a league from a headland, the south side of which faces a town called in their language Humatag. It has a very fine river where the Dutch got their water. Continuing along this southern side, you come to a third harbor three leagues distant, opposite a town called Habadian. It has some shelter from the west and more from the north, but lacks a river. Walking three more leagues toward the east, you find two inlets separated by a point of land with two rivers. The first inlet faces a village called Pigpug, and the second inlet more to the east faces a village called Irig (Ilig). They provide good shelter from the east and enough protection from other winds.

---

[116]It cannot be said in the present day that the island is free from quakes. Among others, violent earthquakes occurred on January 25, 1849 and on September 22, 1902. (M.H.) The earthquake on August 8, 1993 measured 8.1 on the Richter scale.

[117]*Palo María: daok; Calophyllum inophyllum.* (M.H.)

[118]San Antonio here seems to refer to Cetti Bay. There is confusion surrounding the term "San Antonio". It seems to have been used generally for Umatac Bay. It is also used in connection with Agaña Bay. (M.H.)

The Nature of the Mariana Islands; the Temperament and Customs of Their People

Leaving the port of San Antonio, which we mentioned before, and proceeding along the coast to the north, a musket-shot away, there is another harbor at a village called Taragrichan with good water from the two rivers which it has beside it. It has the same shelter from the winds as San Antonio. Continuing to the north, near the town of San Ignacio de Agadña (Agaña), where are now located the principal church and house of the fathers of the Society, in front of a reef that faces west-northwest, at a distance of an arquebus-shot from the said reef, there is found a very good anchorage with a bottom of sand and earth to a depth of 18 fathoms; and at two musket-shots from the reef, a ten-fathom bottom, and going in further, at an arquebus-shot from land, the depth of the water is 22 fathoms. It has a very good river that flows into the center of the bay. It is protected from all winds and appears to be the best harbor and the most useful of the island of San Juan. On the island of Zarpana, or Santa Ana, which the natives call Rota, there is a harbor in which the Dutchman anchored the three ships mentioned above. It faces a settlement called both Socanrago (now Sasanlago) and San Pedro and looks toward the northeast. One league to the south there is another harbor with good depth and shelter from all winds. On the island of Saipan there is a good harbor, whose entrance faces the east and is protected from all winds by the principal point of land of the island, which looks to the southeast. This harbor faces the village they call Raurau (Laulau). In the islands further north, called Pani and Los Volcanes, it is said that there are good harbors, especially one on the west side of Agrigan, a distance of fifteen leagues beyond Los Volcanes, which is said to be a suitable anchorage for ships when they come from Manila. Nature has opened all these parts as portals for the Faith to enter these islands, if men only knew how to enter any other portal than that of greed.

Where the people of these islands came from originally is a matter of conjecture, not of knowledge. Father Colín, in his *India Sacra*, believes they came from Japan, arguing from the nearness to Japan of the northern islands and from the similarity of the people's preferences, especially their esteem for the nobility in the midst of their nakedness.[119] They preserve their history in their memories, if you can call this mixture of fables history, and this contains the belief that they came from the south and west. The similarity of their skins and language, their color, the custom of blackening their teeth, and their mode of governing, or the lack of it, suggest that they have the same origin as the Visayas and the Tagalogs. Some people trace their origin to the Egyptians, as Gomara claims in his *Historia General de las Indias*, stating that Magellan discovered this when he came to these islands in 1521. When or how the first settlers came is still unknown. It must have been a storm that spared their lives but drove them to a sterile land. The number of inhabitants is large. On Guam alone there are fifty thousand, on others forty thousand, and less on others, scattered in villages along the beach,

---

[119]Francisco Colín, S.J. (1592-1660), *Labor Evangélica*, Madrid, 1663; *India Sacra*, Madrid, 1663. Francisco López de Gomara (1512-1562), *Historia General de las Indias*, Saragossa, 1522; Antwerp, 1554.

*Book Three, Chapter 1*

usually in groups of fifty, sixty, or even a hundred houses. On the mountains there are from six to ten to twenty in a group. The houses are the cleanest that have yet been found among *Indios*. They build them of the wood of the coconut and *palo maría*. The walls and roofs, made in the form of a vault, are curiously woven of coconut leaves. They have four rooms with doors or curtains made of the same matting. One serves as a sleeping room, another for storing produce, another as a kitchen, and a fourth is large enough to hold and store boats.

The *Marianos* have a yellowish brown skin color, a somewhat lighter shade than that of the Filipinos, and are larger in stature, more corpulent and robust than Europeans, pleasant and with agreeable faces. They are so fat they appear swollen. The women wear very long hair and in various ways; they bleach it white. They color their teeth black, believing this is the greatest adornment of their beauty. The men do not wear long hair but shave their head, leaving only a small top-knot on the crown, about the length of a finger. They remain in good health until an advanced age, and it is quite common to live ninety or a hundred years. Among those who were baptized the first year of the mission, there were more than one hundred and twenty persons who were more than a hundred years old. It may be due to their natural strength, being accustomed to certain illnesses from the cradle, which later on do not affect them, or to the uniformity and natural condition of their food, without the artificiality that comes of gluttony and destroys while it nourishes, or to their occupations, which give them sufficient exercise, without strain, or to the lack of vices and worries, which are roses with thorns, which flatter and stab and finish men off. Or perhaps all of these contribute to the long life of these islanders. Since they have few ailments, they know few medicines, and they treat themselves with a few herbs that experience and necessity have proved helpful. Their costume is that of the state of innocence, but not without the vices Adam's fault has brought, yet fewer than their nakedness and barbarity would promise. Only the women cover what modesty requires with an apron called *tifis*. They live for four months of the year on the fruits of the earth: coconuts, of which there is a great abundance, bananas, sugar cane, and fish. The rest of the year they make up for the lack of fruits with certain roots similar to sweet potatoes. The little rice they grow, they save for feasts. They practice no excess in eating. They have no wine or other intoxicating liquor, which is a great impediment for the Faith in other countries. Their drink is water and their commonest ailment is dropsy. Their occupation is to cultivate the coconut groves, banana trees, and fields; and they fish in the sea. They are brought up from childhood in this skill, so that they seem more like fish than men. Their boats are very light, small and pretty, painted with a kind of pitch that they make of the colored earth of the island of Guam, mixed with lime, and kneaded with coconut oil. This makes the boats very beautiful.

Their language is easy to pronounce and to learn, especially for those who know Tagalog and Visayan. It has many features in common with them. It may be reduced to a few rules, and much liberty is allowed in the variety of vowels and consonants in one and the same word. This variation occurs in the same island and within the same village. It causes difficulties for beginners, since the difference in tense is small. It is an elegance of style to place the adjective before the noun. Thus they called Father San Vitores from the time he arrived in the islands *Maagas Padre*, which means Great Padre.

They practice many courtesies, and an ordinary usage on meeting and passing in front of one another is to say *Ati arinmo*, which means, "Allow me to kiss your feet." And if you pass by a house, they ask if you will remain to eat; and they bring out *buyo* (betel nut), which is a plant they like very much and keep in their mouths, like a tobacco leaf. To pass the hand over the breast of the person they visit is a great courtesy. They rarely expectorate, never near another person's house and never in the morning. This seems to involve some superstition, I don't know what. No need to ask if they know anything of letters, science, or the arts, when they do not know even the elements of them and did not even know that there was fire in the world until they saw it lighted by Spaniards who survived the shipwreck of 1638.[120] For all that, they admire poetry, and consider poets men who work wonders. We wonder, at times, how such great ignorance goes hand in hand with their great conceitedness, through which they think themselves men of the greatest genius and wisdom in the world and despise all other nations in comparison to themselves.

Their barbarity is contradicted by the rare esteem they have for the aristocracy and their perception of distinctions of lineage, high, middle, and low, which seem to point to an origin in some civilized nation. And so we see how pride banished from heaven lives in all parts of the earth, among clothed people and unclad alike. For nothing in the world would one of their upper class people, called *chamorris*, marry the daughter of a commoner, even if she were rich and he poor (as people say of the Japanese). In times past parents of the nobility killed sons who married daughters of plebeian families, whether for love or greed.

In order to maintain their noble status with splendor, the eldest son inherits large estates of coconuts and bananas, as well as other choice properties, and it is not the son of the deceased who inherits his father's estate, but rather the brother or the nephew of the deceased. The heir now changes his name and takes the name of the founder or chief ancestor of the family. Those of low estate are not permitted to eat or drink in the houses of the nobles or even to go near them. If they need anything, they ask for it from a distance. This pride obtains principally in the village of Agadña. Here, for the goodness of the water and other natural endowments of the place, the nobles, who came from Japan or elsewhere, gathered. All the people of the island fear and respect the chiefs of Agadña. There are in this settlement fifty-three upper class houses, and for the rest about one hundred and fifty. Since these belong to the low people, they are in a separate quarter, and these people have no part in the affairs of Agadña, either as village or as capital.

---

[120]People living within sailing distance of volcanoes know fire. Archeological remains also indicate the use of fire. (M.H.)

*Book Three, Chapter 1*

Their nature and temperament, at first, seemed simple and as lacking in deceit as they were of clothing, and so they were highly praised in Europe by the fathers of the Society and the first Spaniards who dealt with them and allowed themselves to be persuaded by the demonstrations of kindness and hospitality they saw in them. But afterwards, they were found to be deceitful, double-dealing, and treacherous, because for a year or two their words and manners conceal their hidden resentment, until they find a chance for vengeance. They pay no attention to promises, but act only to their own advantage.

They are warriors of a barbarous kind, easily aroused and easily appeased, hesitant to attack and prompt to flee. One town gets ready to go against another with much shouting but without any leader or order or any discipline. They are usually two or three days on campaign without attacking, observing one another's movements. When they finally join battle, they very quickly make peace, because when one or two are killed on one side, that side gives up and sends ambassadors to the other carrying tortoise shells in token of surrender. The victors celebrate the triumph with satiric songs, exalt their valor, and make fun of the conquered. The arms they use are stones and lances, not tipped with iron but with long human bones. These are sharpened to three or four points. They easily pierce the flesh, and then some of the points break off, and remaining in the wound, inevitably cause death. No remedy for this poison has ever been found, although a team of doctors in Mexico later sought one. They use these arms from childhood and are very skillful in handling and throwing them; and they can throw stones from a sling with such dexterity and strength that they are able to drive them into the trunk of a tree. They do not use the bow, the arrow, or the sword; they have only some cutlasses and knives acquired from our ships in exchange for their fruits. They have never used the shield or other defensive arm, but only the swiftness of their movements to escape the blows and wounds of the enemy.[121]

They are by nature comedians, lovers of fun and *fiesta*. The men get together to dance, to play with lances, to run, leap, wrestle, and to test their strength in various ways, and amid these entertainments they retell with great laughter their stories or fables, and they generously share rice cakes, fish, fruit, and a beverage composed of *atole*,[122] rice, and grated coconut. The women have their own *fiestas*, in which they adorn themselves with pendants on their foreheads, sometimes with flowers like jasmine, or beads of glass, or tortoise shell, pendants made of strings of small colored shells, esteemed among them as pearls are by us. They also make belts of them with which they gird themselves, adding pendants all around made of small coconuts, beautifully arranged over a skirt of hanging roots of trees, with which they complement their regalia and finery, and which looks more like a cage than a dress.

---

[121]Their ceremonial manner of warfare, their swiftness of foot, the adoption of shields, and the inaccurcy of the Spanish weapons make it unlikely that they suffered very many casualties in battle with the Spaniards. Their terrible enemy was disease introduced by the Spaniards.

[122]*Atole*, a porridge of maize meal. The Chamorro adaptation is a mixture of ground corn boiled and seasoned with coconut milk. (M.H.)

*The Nature of the Mariana Islands; the Temperament and Customs of Their People*

Twelve or thirteen women get together in a circle, without moving from one spot, and sing in verse their stories and ancient lore with measured time and three-part harmony, soprano, contralto, and falsetto, with the occasional tenor assistance of one of the nobles who assist at these *fiestas*. Movements of the hands accompany the voices, so that with the right they go on forming half moons, and in the left they have small boxes full of little shells that serve as castanets. This is all done in such perfect time and swaying movement, with actions that interpret what they say, that it arouses no little admiration to see the liveliness with which they perform what they have learned.

Of their customs I must say, that although they were given the name of thieves (*ladrones*) because of some small thefts of iron they must have done on our ships, they do not deserve the name, since, for all the houses standing open, rarely is anything missing from them.

The young men, who are called *urritaos*, are very indecent. They live in the public houses with the unmarried women, whom they buy or rent from their parents for two or three hoops of iron and a few tortoise shells. This does not hinder them from marrying later. The married men are usually content with one woman and do not bother the others. They abhor murderers, and for this reason they do not pay the customary respect to certain villages of the island of Saipan, because for several years they found them to be cruel and much given to making lances. They are liberal and kind to guests, as our ships have found when passing through these islands, especially the men who landed there at the wreck of the *Concepción*. In conclusion, although their customs are generally those of an unenlightened people, these customs are not so barbarous as their barbarous state [would suggest], or as those of other nations.

# CHAPTER II

## *Their Religion and Government*

I do not know what to say about their religion and government. At least I can say that they are a people without God, without king, without law, and without any kind of civil policy. Neither the islands taken all together nor the individual villages have a head who governs the others. Only the nobles live as sovereign princes, forming in each village a kind of republic in which opinions are heard, but each one does as he pleases, if no one stronger with weapons does not interfere. In each family the head is the father or elder relative, but with limited influence. Thus, a son as he grows up neither fears nor respects his father. As with brute animals, the father has this advantage: he has the place where he gives them their food. In the home it is the mother who rules, and the husband does not dare give an order contrary to her wishes or punish the children, because if the woman feels offended, she will either beat the husband or leave him. Then, if the wife leaves the house, all the children follow her, knowing no other father than the next husband their mother may take.

They have no laws whatsoever. Individual choice governs the actions of each one. Transgressions are punished by war, if they are of the crowd; by hatred, if they are of the individual. Nevertheless, any custom long in use has the force of law. They do not have many wives nor do they marry relatives, if one can call marriage what were better called concubinage, for lack of perpetuity; for they may separate and take another husband or wife at any trifling quarrel. However, if a man leaves his wife, it costs him a great deal, for he loses his property and his children. But women can do this at no cost, and they do it often out of jealousy, because if they suspect some unfaithfulness, they can punish them in various ways. Sometimes the aggrieved woman summons the other women of the village. Wearing hats and carrying lances they all march to the adulterer's house. If he has crops growing, they destroy them; then they threaten to run him through with their lances. Finally they throw him out of his house. At other times, the offended wife punishes her husband by leaving him. Then her relatives gather at his house, and they carry off everything of value, not even leaving a spear or a mat to sleep on. They leave no more than the shell of the house and sometimes they destroy even that, pulling it all down. If a woman is untrue to her husband, the latter may kill her lover, but the adulteress suffers no penalty.

Their beliefs, like their government, are full of errors and blindness. They were persuaded that they were the only people in the world and that there was no other land than theirs. But after they had seen our ships passing and those of the Dutch, they put aside this error and were persuaded that there were many other lands and people. From this they fell into the contrary error, incorporating into their traditions the belief

*Their Religion and Government*

that all other lands and all other men and everything else sprung from one land, the island of Guam. The island was at first a man and afterwards a stone from which issued all mankind, and from there they spread to Spain and everywhere. They add that as the people went away from the country of their origin, they forgot their mother tongue, and that people of other nations now know no language at all, but jabber like lunatics; they don't understand one another, they don't know what they are saying. They contend that all other people than themselves are ignorant, because their language makes no sense. They affirm that our ships, by sailing through their lands, brought rats, flies, mosquitoes, and all their diseases. And they prove their statements about diseases: after the ships have been in their islands, they have colds and other illnesses. But the reason is their greed for iron and other trifles, so that as long as the ships are in port, they never leave the shore, either day or night, in the sun or in inclement weather. They are continually shouting, so that they return home hoarse and with other ailments.

Regarding the creation of the world, they say that *Puntán* (who must have been the first man) was cast up by a storm in these islands. He was a very ingenious man who lived many years in some imaginary spaces that must have existed before earth and sky were made. This good man was about to die, when he took pity on mankind who would be left without land in which to live and to provide them sustenance. He called his sister, who like him had been born without father or mother. He made known to her the benefit he intended to confer on mankind and gave her all his powers, so that when he died, she could create from his breast and back the sky and earth; from his eyes the sun and moon; a rainbow from his eyebrows. And in this way she would arrange everything else, not without some correspondence of the lesser world to the greater, such as the poets make everyday. If only this had remained symbolic and had not turned into scripture and gospel! This they sing in some poor verses, which they know by heart. Yet with all this, there is no one who renders *Puntán* or his sister any worship or visible ceremony, invocation, or petition, whereby they might seem to recognize in them any divinity. These and other old tales and deeds of their ancestors they tell and sing at their feasts, and those who boast of being experts bet on who can sing the most verses.

They recognize the immortality of the soul and speak of hell and paradise, to which men go for no other merit or demerit than that of whether they died a natural or a violent death. Those who die of violence, they say, go to the inferno they call *zazarraguan,* or the house of *Chayfi,* who is the devil who has a forge in which he heats them like iron, and hammers them continually. Those who die a natural death go to another place beneath the earth, which is their paradise, where there are bananas, coconuts, sugar cane, and other fruits of the earth. There is not found among them either sect or shadow of religion, nor priests of any kind. There are only some imposters who set themselves up as prophets, called *macanas,* who promise health, water, fish, and similar benefits by invoking those dead persons whose skulls they keep in their houses

*Book Three, Chapter 2*

without other altar, niche, or adornment than some little baskets where they are left about the house, and where they are forgotten until the time comes when the *macanas* want to ask for some favor. But recently, as I believe, because of a Chinese idolater who was cast ashore in a storm, of whom we will speak later, some of them are showing reverence for the bones and skulls of the dead, whom they paint on the bark of trees and blocks of wood. The *macanas*, like all the *bonzos*, or priests, of India, look out for their own interests, from whatever the living give them, not for the profit of the living. They do this by invoking the dead, from whom the *macanas* and practically everyone else recognize there is nothing to be gained. But if they invoke the dead honestly, it is not to obtain favors, but rather to placate them so they will do no harm. For the devil, in order to maintain this respect and slavish fear, is accustomed to appear to them in the forms of their parents and ancestors to frighten and mistreat them. This is the most the devil is able to accomplish among these poor *Marianos*. There are no temples or sacrifices, no idols or profession of any sect whatsoever, a thing that will facilitate the introduction of the Faith. It is, after all, easier to introduce a religion where there is none, than to cast one out in order to introduce another. With all this, the *Marianos* have certain superstitions, especially when they are fishing, at which time they observe silence and great abstinence, either from fear of, or to flatter the *anites*, which are the souls of their grandparents, so they will not punish them by keeping the fish away or by frightening them in their dreams, of which they are very credulous. Some, when a man is about to die, place a basket at his head, as if inviting him to remain in the house in the little basket, instead of the body he is leaving. Also, he would thus have a place to rest when he returns from the other world to pay them a visit. Others, after annointing a corpse with fragrant oil, carry it about to the homes of relatives, in order that the soul may remain in whichever house it chooses, or that it may, when it returns to visit them, find refuge in the house of its choice. Their demonstration of grief at funerals are very singular, with many tears, fasting, and a great sounding of shells. The lamentations usually continue for six, eight, or more days, according to the affection or obligations they have toward the deceased. They spend these days singing sad songs and having funeral meals around the tumulus that they raise over the grave or near it, decorated with flowers, palms, shells and other objects that they value. The mother of the deceased cuts off a lock of his hair as a memento of her grief and counts the days after his death by tying a knot each night in a cord she wears around her neck.

These expressions of grief are much more intense at the death of a noble (a *chamorri*) or of a well-known matron. In addition to the ordinary rites, they decorate the streets with garlands of palms; they erect triumphal arches and other funeral structures; they destroy coconut trees; burn houses; break up their boats and hang the torn sails in front of their houses as a sign of grief. They add more verses to their songs (no less tasteful than emotional, which to the rudest hearts would convey a feeling of sorrow) with such expressions as "From now on life will be a burden, lacking the one who was the life of all, lacking the sun of nobility, the moon that illuminated them in the night of their ignorance; the star of all good fortune; the valor of all battles; the honor of his line, of his village and of his land." And in this manner, until far into the night, the praise continues in honor of the dead man, whose sepulchre is crowned with oars, as the sign of a great fisherman, or with lances, the sign of a brave warrior, or with both, if he was both warrior and fisherman.

In such great blindness the islanders had lived through many centuries, when Divine Providence, whose secrets are open to our adoration and closed to our understanding, especially in the great question of the predestination and vocation of nations, calls the peoples to his Church, like the laborers to his vineyard, some in the early morning, others at the hour of terce, others at sext, others at none, and others at the eleventh hour, at the time preordained by his Wisdom from all eternity; and yet the last cannot complain that they are not the first.[123] For God gives to all men the light of reason, so that guided by this light they become capable of greater splendor. Determined then to lead to the regions of life those who lay in the shadow of death, he sent to them the Venerable Father Diego Luis de San Vitores to carry to them the first news of the glory and the kingdom of Christ, adorning him for this apostolate with the graces and virtues that we have seen in the course of this history and will see further on even more.

---

[123] Matt. 20:1-16.

# CHAPTER III

*The Venerable Father Diego Luis de San Vitores's First
Entry into the Mariana Islands and the Premonition of Evil*

We entered the islands with the explorers and left the others [on the ship] to turn our eyes to this new land. But now we will join the explorers as they return to Father San Vitores, who awaits them impatiently on the ship.

As the Venerable Father Diego Luis de Medina and Father Pedro de Casanova jumped ashore, conducted by a noble, a group of Gentiles armed with lances came out to meet them, until little by little the beach was filled with armed men. The secular companions feared that the barbarians might kill the fathers, but the latter, who had come in a spirit of charity, which expels all fear, encouraged them to continue on, and soon they realized that it was friendliness and welcome and not preparation for war, as they had thought.

The fathers embraced the *Marianos* and the latter, not to be outdone, kissed the new arrivals. They brought them to the leading noble of the town of Agadña, who was in a hut much decorated with palm mats, accompanied with other *Indios*. They kissed his hand and passed theirs over the breast of the chieftain. They then explained their embassy and the occasion of their coming, which was to teach them the law of the true God and the road to heaven. Quipuha answered that they were very welcome and that for a long time he had hoped they would come to his country.[124]

This hospitable reception was attributed to a visit that the Blessed Virgin made to these islanders, appearing on the island of Tinian, which for this reason Father San Vitores named Buenavista Mariana. It happened in the village of Chiro (Chelo), which means "brother," and is now called San Vicente Ferrer. Father San Vitores says the memory of this apparition is still kept fresh on the island of Tinian.

The Blessed Virgin appeared in Chiro in the year 1638 to an *Indio* named Taga and urged him to be baptized and to help the Spaniards who had been cast ashore that year in these islands. The *Indio* was baptized by the hand of Marcos Fernández, one of the survivors of the shipwreck, who gave him Corcuera as a family name, which his descendants bear even to this day. It was the name of the governor of the Philippines at the time.

The Christian *Indio* arranged with his brother that the Spaniards might sail to the Philippines and bring back someone to preach the gospel. Other Spaniards from the ship remained in the Marianas. Thus we may call Mary the First Apostle of the Mariana Islands not only for

---

[124]There were two Quipuhas. The first and the elder, was the one who was referred to as the last of the great Chamorro chieftans. It was he who received and entertained Father San Vitores and his party, aided in the construction of the first church, and when he died, was buried under its altar. Another Quipuha, a nephew of the chief, will appear later in the story. (M.H.) See Book 3, chap. 5:188; Book 5, chap. 8:399.

His First Entry into the Mariana Islands and the Premonition of Evil

the overall influence she has in the conversion of the Gentiles, she who alone exterminates heresies in the whole world, but especially because it was she who urged the *Indio* to receive baptism and call the preachers. Though they did not come at that time, the fact that these islands did call them prepared their minds to receive them when Mary sent her preacher and apostle to continue the work she herself had begun.

The two fathers made Quipuha the present of some iron hoops and a hat, which pleased him very much. When the *Indios* understood that the fathers were to remain in their islands, they were glad, except for the chief of one of the mountain villages. He came down complaining about Quipuha because he had admitted strangers to the land. But on learning that they were *padres*, he said that it was well that they had come, and that he wanted them to come to his village; and the other nobles said the same.

The fathers asked permission of Quipuha to remain that night in his village. He gave it with great pleasure and kept them in his own house. He gave them something to drink before they retired to their beds, which were spacious and clean.

That night they set up a cross on the beach in a village called *De Los Martires*, because of a promise they had made during the voyage to call the first village they entered by the name of the saint on whose day they could first see the islands. It was the Feast of the Holy Martyrs Vitus, Modestus, and Crescentia, the fifteenth day of June.[125] The fathers, on their knees, reverenced the cross, and the *Marianos* imitated them. With the standard of our Redemption raised as a sign of victory over the powers of hell, they consecrated to Jesus the islands of Mary.

Scarcely had the day dawned on Sunday, June 17, when they returned to the ship and told of the good will and hospitality with which they had been received and entertained. Shortly afterwards they were followed by some of the leading chiefs, who thanked the Venerable Father for his coming. They asked the captain of the ship to leave the fathers here, who would show them the road to heaven.

Who can say what consolation this gave Father San Vitores, an embassy sent not so much by the *Marianos* as by Mary herself, who spoke through the mouths of those islanders, ignorant as they were of how much they were asking and even desiring? He could not restrain his joy, giving thanks to God and his Mother for such singular mercies. Like another Jacob, those seven difficult years appeared to him very short indeed, spent in hardships and difficulties, contradictions and fatigue, journeys by land and sea, short, indeed, because of the great love and possession of his Rachel.[126]

The *Marianos* in turn expressed great joy. They carried the fathers on their shoulders and gave them gifts of the fruits of their land, poor things, but of great value for the spirit in which they were given.

---

[125]*Pueblo de los Martyres.* It is impossible to say exactly what location was given this name. It is known, however, that Father San Vitores disembarked on the beach near Agaña. It is possible that their landing was thus dedicated. In all the history of Father San Vitores's work, this name does not appear again. (M.H.)

[126]Gen. 29:20.

They held a welcoming celebration with singing and dancing, and to make up for their lack of clothing, they came covered with branches of banana trees and palms. Soon, Mass was said on the beach with an altar improvised from materials at hand, offering to [God] the Father the sacrifice of his Son, in order that the devil might be banished from those islands. The Servant of God permitted that the Gentiles assisted at the Mass, but separate from the Christians, and they admired the holy ceremonies.

When news reached Mexico of the friendly manner in which the *Marianos* had received Father San Vitores, his Sodality of Saint Francis Xavier expressed a profound joy. They held a great *fiesta* and a father of the Society preached the sermon. The archbishop was present at the Mass, and in the afternoon, the viceroy and the vicereine and, indeed, the whole city came to the *fiesta*. There was a procession of the most Blessed Sacrament, which was exposed throughout the day, and a *Te Deum* was sung with great solemnity and the rejoicing was universal. They recognized in these happy beginnings the great harvest of souls that the apostolic father was to send to heaven.

The resentment of hell, in view of the war they had declared against the kingdom that Satan had peacefully possessed for so many centuries, was evident. That this was not mere conjecture, Satan proved at this time in Spain. Two Jesuit fathers were giving a mission in Fuente de Cantos, a village in Extremadura, when a possessed person was brought to them to be exorcised. The priests prepared themselves with fasting, prayer, and other pious deeds to encounter the devil, who was especially rebellious. They performed the exorcisms, and the demon answered, "Don't exert yourselves. For all your efforts you will not expel me." They repeated the exorcism. The demon repeated the same words, adding once, "If it were Father San Vitores, he would drive me out, but you won't do it so quickly." They asked him if he knew Father San Vitores and he answered, "Yes, very well!" Asked a second time if he knew where the father was, he asked for time to answer, and after a brief pause he said, "He has now entered some islands very far from here where he wages cruel war against us." The priests pursued their battle until they dispossessed the father of lies from the body that he occupied. A year and a half later they learned that he had spoken the truth, or that God had made him speak, when the news came to Spain of his arrival in the Marianas and of the success he had begun to enjoy.

There was, indeed, good reason for the resentment of the demon. In his first sermon, he informed the *Marianos* of the reason for his coming, which was to bring them to heaven. For this it was necessary to believe in the divine mysteries, keep the Commandments, which are the Law of God, and be baptized. Fifteen hundred adults were converted to our holy Faith. Because it was necessary to delay their baptism until they were instructed, they offered their children, twenty-three of whom were baptized the first day, the rest on another day, because on this day the ship had to sail. The parents were disconsolate and in tears at the postponement of their children's baptism, though their grief, of course, was a

*His First Entry into the Mariana Islands and the Premonition of Evil*

consolation to the father. Since they all wanted to learn to make the sign of the cross and the fathers were busy teaching them, they had no time to write letters to the Philippines.

On that same day the chiefs began to compete as to which one would bring the fathers to his village. From the island of Zarpana, or Santa Ana, they arrived that day to ask them to come with them. So that to satisfy all of them, the fathers had to promise to split up and visit all the villages of the island.

A sad thought stabbed the heart of the Venerable Father, worthy of his apostolic zeal, when he began to gather the harvest with full hands and saw all those regions white and ripe for the harvest[127] and the many souls who had been senselessly left to be lost in hell, when they might so easily have found the road to heaven. Thus he writes to the provincial of the Philippines and then adds, that as a compensation for past losses, the Lord and his Holy Mother would now hasten to bring the poor islanders to the waters of baptism, in which all wished to be washed clean.

The ship departed for the Philippines, and Father San Vitores proceded with the baptism of the children and the instruction of the adults. The baptism of these was to be delayed until after the harvest of children, whose mothers competed for first place for their little ones.

Not content with those of Agadña, which was the first village he entered, he went out with one companion—and with no other protection than the picture of Christ and of the Blessed Virgin and his breviary—in search of children and adults (who were dying throughout the other villages of the islands) to gather the harvest that Christ had been keeping for him.

The Servant of God had made frequent prayers and hard penance in the port of Cavite, to the end that God might spare the lives of all the dying *Marianos*, and especially the children, until he might arrive in the islands, and they could receive the water of holy baptism. Now he garnered the fruit of this supplication, for he and his companions baptized many children and many old people, whose lives, it appeared, had been miraculously preserved. After receiving baptism, as though they were waiting for nothing else, they took flight for heaven. At this point, I record a particular case, although it happened later. The Venerable Father was in Cavite on August 7, 1667, saying Mass and praying earnestly for the above-mentioned intentions. At the same time a girl was born on the island of Agrigan. An *aniti*, or demon, appeared to her father and threatened to kill his daughter. He begged the demon not to kill her, but to kill him. He related the apparition to his wife, and two days later she found him dead in his bed. Now, Father Luis de Morales arrived on this island at the beginning of December, in 1668. When he landed they called him to baptize the girl, who was seriously ill. She received the waters of baptism and died in the arms of her mother. It was from her mother that we learned the story of the apparition of the demon and the time of the birth of her daughter.

---

[127] John 4:35.

*Book Three, Chapter 3*

Father San Vitores had visited several villages of the island when he was called back to Agadña, since the nobles made it a point of honor that he live in their village. After all, the superior of all the fathers should live in the principal village. Since he could not make them see reason, he was forced to yield to violence, in order to avoid public disturbances, which were feared and had even begun. It was a harsh mortification to his zeal, which was too vast for one island and sought to encompass all the others. But to be caged in one small village!

But what the devil planned in order to block the spread of the Faith, the Lord used as a means to establish it more solidly. He made Agadña the stronghold for Christianity in the islands, with a church and a house of the Society of Jesus. The Venerable Father, adoring the Divine Providence, which makes use of human means for the high ends of his glory, sacrificed his will to that of God. He wrote to one of his companions: "I confess to Your Reverence that, although my example may be of little value, I am not a prisoner here without consolation, obeying the divine disposition of affairs as if it were the most glorious of missions." And later, "In whatever place, and especially in these beginnings, there is much to do and much to suffer for the love of Christ." And this Apostle of the Marianas could have added what the Apostle of the Gentiles said when he was a prisoner, because in this prison his lips were not sealed from preaching and teaching, nor his hands from working and baptizing, but rather in those two months of detention he did the work of years.[128]

---

[128]Acts 28:30-31.

# CHAPTER IV

*How He Began the Church and Residence in Agadña,
and the Method He Used to Catechize the Infidels*

The island of Guam is the principal one of the Marianas and has 180 settlements. The chief village is Agadña, which is located on the coast in the northern part of the island. This village, because of its location near the sea, its relatively large size among small settlements, its role as capital of all the other villages, and much more for having been the first to receive the two ambassadors sent by Father Diego Luis, and a village where he was then so well received, because of all this, it deserved to be head of all Christianity in the Marianas. Here, the first church and house of the Society were built on land donated by Chief Quipuha, who had received them with such graciousness.

Father San Vitores named the village San Ignacio de Agadña, dedicating it to his holy father and patriarch. The church was begun and was built of the tree called *maría* (*palo maría; daog*) as a house for Mary, to whom he had already dedicated all the temples he would build in the Marianas. The house and residence of the Society was begun, and was to be and has been the mother of all those built in those islands, an *alcazar* of the Faith, the spiritual armory of the heralds of the gospel, from which they would go forth, fortified by the strictest observance, to do battle against the enemy of souls, who had usurped from Christ so many thousands in these islands. That this might truly happen, he initiated in that house such a level of religious perfection as he might find in any *colegio* of Europe, harmonizing the exercises on the inside with the ministries on the outside and the care for their own spiritual progress with concern for the salvation of others. Father San Vitores made himself an example that they might follow (but with giant steps) in the work for the salvation of souls.

Here, I would sketch a portrait of his life, which others might copy who wish to be perfect religious of the Society of Jesus and true apostles of Jesus Christ. In prayer, in which he spent all the time his other duties permitted, and in penance, always greater than his strength, he planned with God the work that he and the other missionaries would have to do. His food (if that is the word for it) was that of the ancient anchorites of the desert; his habitation, a cabin poorly roofed with palm leaves; his bed, the earth or a board. He gave away as an alms the mosquito net, which others of necessity use here against the plague of mosquitoes. In its place, he made for himself an oven of mats (as one of his companions called it) in whose burning tide he passed the time he allotted for rest. I shall not speak of his hairshirts and disciplines, because the former was a garment he never took off, and the latter he inflicted upon himself nightly to the point of bleeding, without slackening in their rigor nor in his work in spite of many days of high fever, which he suffered on two occasions. And the abundant harvest he gathered in a short time showed clearly that his penance and prayers bore fruit. He took as his own the humblest tasks in the house, doing them all with humility and charity. He only appeared the superior in his virtues, not in authority or in giving orders.

That in which he principally set an example was in charity and zeal for the salvation of souls. During the time he was building the physical church, with even greater care he was forming the spiritual one out of the living souls of the faithful. He catechized the adults all day long, repeating and singing the doctrine until his voice was hoarse.

It would be pleasing to anyone at all and very useful to those engaged in a similar ministry to know the charming and effective way in which he explained the divine mysteries to a people so rude and so barbarous.

He hung about his neck two pictures, one of the Santo Cristo de Burgos (the one in Cabre) and the other of the Virgin with the Child in her arms. He began by asking the *Marianos* why man is of upright stature with eyes that look towards the heavens, while the beasts are not thus. They found no answer, but liked his. The beasts are created to live on the earth, and man to rise to heaven. He showed them, in general, the treasures and joys they have in heaven, greater than all that could be told or imagined. He asked them how one could ascend to heaven that was so high; which was the way? Then he showed them the Child Jesus in the arms of his Mother, and said that the Child was the Lord of Heaven; he had come down to earth to teach men the road to heaven, and he himself had sent him (San Vitores) to their land to instruct them.

He explained to them, as well as he could, how in the womb of that Virgin, God became man, to suffer and die for man. Then he would bring up other examples to explain the birth and mysteries of the life of Christ, our Lord, so that they might form some concept of them and might remember them better. Here, he told them of the beauty, the integrity, the power, and the sanctity of the Virgin Mary, mother of that God-man, and advocate of men. He strove to imprint in their minds a lofty concept and love of that sovereign queen, since, as he used to say, in the infancy of the Faith, God wishes that the tender infant Christians should be raised on the milk of devotion to the Blessed Mother.

Afterwards, he explained the mystery of the Redemption, the Passion and Death of our Lord Jesus Christ, showing the picture of the Santo Cristo de Burgos and sometimes other pictures as well of different phases of the Passion, praising the love of God towards men, which caused the Lord to suffer and die in order to satisfy for our sins and save us from the pains of hell. And especially the love he had for the *Marianos* in sending them preachers from far-off lands to point out the road of salvation. And since the picture of the Santo Cristo de Burgos showed his father (*don* Jerónimo) kneeling in worship, he taught them and urged them to adore Christ. In explaining the Mystery of the Redemption, he emphasized the gravity of sin; how great an offense it is when man dares to offend God who is his Creator and Redeemer. It is he who sustains us and grants us so many blessings; and it is he who can cast us into hell; so he would exhort them to flee from sin, which had been the cause of the delay in receiving the light of the gospel; and even now they would not deserve to receive it, a pure gift of his infinite mercy.

With the example of the sun, which is one and shines upon the land and the sea, the mountains and the valleys, the Spaniards and the *Marianos*, and all the other nations, he proved that God is one and should be adored by the *Marianos*, the Spaniards, and all the peoples of the world. In an attempt to adapt his words to their understanding, he said that even as the rays of the sun came from the direction of Castille and of Rome, where the Holy Father resides, so the light of Faith comes from the same direction. They should be more anxious to receive the light of faith than the rays of the sun, since the latter illuminates the earth, while the former shows the way to heaven and keeps us from stumbling on the road.

He taught them that in God there are three Persons: the Father, the Son, and the Holy Spirit, and by means of examples suited to their simplicity, resemblances that God had imprinted in this created world, he formed images of this profound and ineffable Mystery.

He told them of the excellence of baptism, how it takes away original sin and all other sins and makes the soul more beautiful than the sun, and that this sacrament is the first door into the kingdom of heaven, and that those who do not enter by it go down to hell, where in company with the demons, they suffer fire and innumerable torments. When they heard this, they all asked for baptism with cries and tears in order to enter heaven and free themselves from hell. They seemed to see right in front of them hell with open mouth ready to swallow them.

The nobles urged their nobility as first claim to immediate baptism. But the Venerable Father informed them that they must first know the Christian doctrine and told them to make haste to learn it, stimulating with this hope the desire to hasten to the catechism. Here he proposed to them the obligations of a Christian and the Ten Commandments, which he called ten steps to heaven.

Not the least stimulating to bring them to the doctrine were the gifts and the kindness that he brought to them, as the father himself writes: "Because of their eagerness to get to the biscuits and bits of jewelry, they came very early in crowds, men and women, children and old people, to say the prayers and learn the Mysteries of the Faith." And for this reason, he was so liberal with the *Marianos* that he gave them whatever came into his hands, sacrificing the very food of his mouth. If it had not been for the need of his companions, he would not have left in the house a bit of food or any small article he could give to his *Marianos*.

If for any reason he had nothing to give them, or they were simply negligent in coming for instruction, he used other means of attracting them, sometimes highly original. As the *Marianos* were naturally fond of singing, dancing, and buffonery, he took advantage of their fondness of amusement, and like another David before the ark of the

*Book Three, Chapter 4*

covenant,[129] he made himself, so to speak, another *jongleur de Dieu*, to become another Paul, who made himself all things for all men, to gain all for Christ.[130] And so, when he saw a group of *Marianos*, he would gather them in a circle about him and begin to dance about and sing in their language, clapping his hands:

> "Joy, joy, joy!
> Good joy, Jesus and Mary,
> Our joy, Jesus and Mary,
> Amen, amen, Mary and Joseph."[131]

He would repeat the last words, beating out the rhythm with his hands, singing all the while and dancing as they joined in happily, "Oh, how good are Jesus, Mary, and Joseph, and how good is the Great Padre, how happy, how amusing!"

When he had them in a good humor, he seized the opportunity to explain the Mysteries and the Commandments, exhorting them to believe them and observe them, and their answer to all this was, "How good is all this that the Great Padre says." When the instruction was over, he would end up with the same dance as before, so that they would be happy till the end. Other people may admire Father San Vitores for his great miracles; as for me, I admire him for the great zeal which made him do things so contrary to his nature, modesty, and seriousness: he played the madman, when he was most sane; and he played the buffoon, though he was so serious and religious.

For the children, he started a school of reading and prayer, a measure employed by other apostolic men that has produced the greatest fruit for new Christian communities. From these tender plants, watered with the teachings of heaven, fruitful trees will grow that will enrich the nation with good examples. For this reason, he applied himself at once with great care to the teaching of the children, as if he had no other thing to do. He began to teach them the alphabet saying "Jesu Christo, María! A B C" with such grace and love that the children did not want anyone else to give them lessons. He was never seen without them, as it seemed he was with the angels when he was with the children. He repeated many times the words of Christ: *Sinite parvulos venire ad me, talium est enim regnum caelorum*, "Let the little children come unto me, for such is the Kingdom of Heaven."[132]

Those beginning to talk, he had pronounce the sweet names of Jesus and Mary, and when they repeated them in their stammering way, he could not contain himself for joy and said with deep emotion, "Blessed be God, my Angel, you know more than Alexander the Great, more than Aristotle, who never knew how to say as much as you. May God keep you! You are more fortunate than the Roman emperors. You call

---

[129]2 Sam. 6:14.
[130]1 Cor. 9:22.
[131]The Spanish tranlation is *Alegria, alegria, alegria, buena, buena, Jesús Maria. Nuestra alegria, Jesús y Maria. Amén, amén, Jesús, Maria, y José.*
[132]Matt. 19:14.

upon and you know Jesus, whom they never knew. Ah! What happiness! Blessed be God!"

He was so happy to see Jesus invoked and adored by those tender little ones, that for this alone, he considered well worthwhile all his labors and the dangers he had experienced in order to arrive at these islands.

# CHAPTER V

*He Distributes His Companions throughout the Islands,*
*and the Baptism of Adults Begins*

The other members of the Society were not idle while Father San Vitores worked so apostolically. They could not be, in view of his burning zeal, which was enough to inflame even the most lukewarm and still more those who were so fervent.

From the beginning he put them to work in Agadña and other settlements, not waiting until they should know the language well, telling them not to worry, since God and the Blessed Virgin would give them words and courage in time of need. And one of his companions confesses that often they experienced the fulfillment of the promise of the Servant of God.

He also gave them an explanation of the Creed and the Commandments that he had prepared in the Mariana language, in order that they might read it to the people.

He was obliged to remain in Agadña and could not go to the other islands as he wished, but remained with Father Bustillos, who was still a scholastic, sending the Venerable Father Luis de Medina to visit the villages of the island of Guam. He sent Father Pedro de Casanova to Zarpana; Father Tomás de Cardeñoso to Tinian with Father Luis de Morales. And although the devil placed many difficulties in their way in all the villages they entered, it appeared that Father San Vitores was with them in spirit, although he was forced to remain in Agadña. They were all able to accomplish much good, although at the cost of many hardships.

Father Casanova was well received in Zarpana, the island which had first asked for missionaries. There, he baptized more than three hundred children within a few days and prepared a great number of adults for baptism.

On Tinian, they received Father Tomás de Cardeñoso and Father Luis de Morales with enthusiasm. They had been waiting for them for a long time, they said, because the memory of the apparition of the Blessed Virgin was still fresh in their minds. Within two hours of the fathers' arrival they had baptized twenty-five children and later baptized many more and catechized both children and adults. I shall not speak here of Father Luis de Medina, to whom God granted such an abundant harvest on Guam, that within three months, more than three thousand were baptized by his hand. At this place I will not mention the many wonders that he worked.

It was not strange that the religious of the Society made such a great harvest, when so many of their secular companions performed work worthy of ministers of the gospel. They were co-workers with the fathers in the apostolic ministry, and God approved their zeal by giving some of them, eventually, the crown of martyrdom. In order that their own lives

## He Distributes His Companions throughout the Islands, and the Baptism of Adults Begins

might assist and not hinder the work of conversion, the Servant of God insisted that all live in a truly Christian manner, that their works be not contrary to the word they preached. They took, on his advice, a firm resolution not to taste wine, nor to draw off tuba, which is the liquor of the coconut palm that they use as an intoxicant in the Philippines. The Venerable Father begged that none be sent to the Marianas who did not feel strong enough to do without wine, for by introducing drunkenness in these islands more harm than good would be done.

He instructed them with great care in the methods of baptizing and teaching the catechism, and those whom he judged most capable and dependable, he sent to the villages where ministers were scarce and the work plentiful, as it always was in the beginning. And they realized that the results they obtained were due largely to the prayers of the Venerable Father, which followed them everywhere. In this manner Father San Vitores preached and made conversions on the island of Guam and on other islands by means of his companions, both religious and secular, while he himself was like a prisoner in Agadña, where he now began baptizing adults.

Before he was a month on the islands, he had many adults of all ages and conditions ready for baptism, but the devil, who is very astute, placed a difficulty in his way, which was the pride of the nobles, to delay the baptism of the common people.

They had heard so much in praise of this sacrament that they did not wish to permit the plebeians to be baptized nor even to hear the Christian doctrine, saying that so noble a sacrament should be reserved for nobles, and that a law so fine as the one that the Great Father set forth was not for the common people. Thus the Venerable Father and his companions suffered some disrespect and some danger from the *chamorris* (nobles) for their defense of the plebeians.

It was necessary for Father San Vitores to declare that in the matter of salvation there is no difference between nobles and plebeians, for God is no respecter of persons,[133] and even as he created all men and created for all men the same elements, the same sun and the same heaven, so also did he die for all and desires to save all and has given them the same Mysteries to believe, the same Commandments to keep, and the same sacraments to receive. Therefore, one cannot cast out those whom God admits, but must admit them with the same graciousness. Otherwise we lose true nobility for a false and illusory one. Rather, they should make a point of having the plebeians believe what they themselves believed, for it was to their honor to have all beneath them accept the beliefs of the nobles so that no one should be exempt from the precepts that to them were obligations.

If they did not wish to be equalled in anything by the common people, he said, they should try to outdo them in their observance of the Commandments and in the practice of their Christian obligations. That difference would be laudable, whereas what they were claiming was rather the daughter of envy than of true nobility. And when all his

---

[133] Acts 10:34.

Book Three, Chapter 5

reasoning was insufficient to cope with the foolish pride of the nobles or the fear of the plebeians, who were afraid of displeasing their leaders, Father San Vitores refused to baptize even one noble until they promised not to oppose the conversion and baptism of the plebeians. He said they simply lacked the charity and humility that were necesary to receive the great sacrament.

The first adult to be baptized was Quipuha, the chief noble of Agadña, God thus repaying him for his kindness and hospitality to the fathers at the time of their arrival. The ceremony of baptism was effected with great solemnity with a view to impressing those who witness it.

He was named Juan, in honor of Saint John the Baptist, patron saint of that island. He was also the first to be buried in the church, since he had given the ground on which the first church was built. Thus was overcome the resistence of the people toward burying their dead in any but the old manner, which was to inter the deceased under certain houses that they call "great ones." It is said that after his death he appeared to his son and told him that he was in heaven, a matter that confirmed in the Faith many of the new Christians and encouraged the catechumens.

The baptism of *don* Juan Quipuha, for so he was called after he became a Christian, was followed by that of other nobles of Agadña and many of the plebeians, the nobles no longer objecting, but rather exhorting the common people.

Before baptizing the adults, the Venerable Father tried to banish from their hearts and their homes all superstitions and every shadow of idolatry, not without great opposition. He made them bury the skulls and bones of their ancestors, and he burned the images that they had made of wood and had even carved on trees. There was one man who threatened the Servant of God and a Spaniard named Diego Bazán who was with him. The native came toward them brandishing a lance as if he would kill them, but Diego Bazán, who was engaged in destroying images under the direction of Father San Vitores, did not desist. They merely smiled at the threats of the native. Other *Marianos*, who were looking on, laughed also, for not all of them venerated the skulls of their ancestors and cared less when the fathers told them that their souls were burning in hell.

Father Lorenzo Bustillos met with similar trouble when he took figures and idols out of a house. The people confessed that they had been taught to venerate them by a Chinese named Choco. One of the figures had three heads on its shoulders, an invention of Lucifer himself, who never ceases to desire the same worship as God most high, Three in One. Yet providence benefits from it in that it is not so difficult for them to believe in the Holy Trinity.

With the grace of holy baptism and the words of the Servant of God, the new Christians acquired a horror of sin, and if one, through weakness, broke a commandment of the Law of God, he became greatly afflicted and said, "Father, I have sinned. What remedy can I take to be healed of my guilt, since you say I cannot be baptized again?" He answered that they had already been told that the remedy was the sacrament of

188

*He Distributes His Companions throughout the Islands, and the Baptism of Adults Begins*

penance. He explained to them the inviolable secrecy of the confessional. They then became accustomed to confession, and it was necessary for at least one father always to be in the church, as they came in such great numbers to be relieved of the weight of their faults. Before entering the church, they went first to one of the secular members of the mission group and begged him to give them a rigorous discipline with the cord that they wore about their necks, in order that their sins might be forgiven. And if the seculars tried to excuse themselves from administering punishment by explaining that confession would bring about the desired pardon, they still refused to go away until they were whipped, saying that they preferred to pay for their sins in this life and not in another. Thus it was that within a short time of the establishment of Christianity among these people, they appeared to be fervent Christians.

In consideration of Christian decency, Father San Vitores dressed in the materials he had brought from Mexico all those he clothed with Christianity in baptism. Although it is said that God multiplies in quantity that which is badly needed, there began to be a shortage of clothing. Seeing the lack of garments for the crowds that arrived daily for baptism, he ordered a quantity of shirts and skirts made of palm matting.

The *Marianos* refused to wear them, partly for the absurd appearance of the garments, and also because of their own custom of going unclad. The Venerable Father, in order by his own example to remove their objection to the garments, dressed himself in one of them and walked up and down before a large group of people, at first causing laughter at his disguise, but later bringing tears to their eyes to see their "Apostle Paul" wearing the costume of Paul, the first hermit, as if the latter were preaching in their village and the former had retired to do penance in the desert.

In this livery of heaven, he afterwards went to all the missions and his example was followed by his companions of the Society of Jesus, which as it has no religious habit but zeal for the glory of God and the salvation of souls, took on in these islands the one given by the love of God and neighbor.

# CHAPTER VI

*The Persecution that an Idolatrous Chinese Instigates Against the Faith and How the Servant of God Converts Him*

It would be a miracle if the Faith were ever established in any region without persecutions and hardships. Ever since the foundation of the Church, thorns, stones, and men have encumbered its path, in order that the grain of wheat might not take root, or grow and multiply a hundred to one, because of the frosts and winds with which the enemy of souls assails it.

That same enemy had been unable to deter the burning zeal of Father San Vitores in Manila or in Mexico, nor even in the Mariana Islands, with the many difficulties that were raised against him and the numerous artifices that were contrived to try to fetter the extension of the gospel. He had tried to prevent baptism by the pride of the nobles. Now he raised against the Church a more dangerous persecution in the person of a *Sangley*, an idolatrous Chinese called Choco, who arrived in these islands[134] twenty years before the fathers, cast ashore in a storm as he was sailing from Manila to Terrenate (Ternate) in a sampan.[135]

The island of Guam had received him well, taking to its breast this serpent, who soon began to spew the venom of idolatry over the land, until that time free from such contagion. He now began to obscure the light of truth, which began to dawn so happily over these islands.

And it was by a special providence (as the Venerable Father notes) that they did not disembark in the southern end of the island, as they had intended to do in a conference aboard ship, because at that point there was a good harbor [Umatac]. But they landed on the north, whither God carried them, contrary to their own decision, because on the southern side lived Choco, in the village of Paa. He would have blocked their first baptisms, with much harm to the Faith and great danger to the ministers.

But as soon as the *Sangley* knew that the fathers had arrived on the island of Guam and were baptizing many, he began to circulate a report that the fathers were people despised and loathed by the Spaniards, and for this reason they had been banished to Guam; that they were killing those they baptized, especially children; and if one who was especially strong was able to resist that poisoned water, it would at least cause him to have dropsy, declaring he had seen it thus in Manila. Actually, some children did die a short while after being baptized, because they were already in a dying condition, or because God, as he is accustomed to do in new conversions, wished to harvest the young fruits of a

---

[134]*Sangley:* a Chinese residing in the Philippines for business purposes.
[135]Ternate: island in the Moluccas, Indonesia; also the principal town of Ternate.

190

*An Idolatrous Chinese and How the Servant of God Converts Him*

land till then barren. And so Choco saw his opportunity to make the people witnesses to the truth of what he told them.

It is not easy to say how great a change he made in these islanders, accustomed to fear only death, by the rumors that the sower of darnel spread throughout Guam and the other islands.

Those who formerly called the fathers to their villages and would not allow them to leave, using a thousand strategems for this purpose, even hiding the paths with branches to make them return to the same village they had left, these villagers now came out to meet the fathers with spears in their hands. They denied them the *rimai*,[136] the food customarily offered to travelers, calling them murderers and threatening to kill them if they remained in the village. What was most disheartening to the fathers was the fact that mothers hid their children or fled with them into the hills, so that they could not baptize them, and when they were sick or dying, they hid them with even greater care.

It is true that God consoled the fathers with the baptism of some new Christians who, overcomning their fear, received the sacrament, and answered those who tried to alarm them: "What is there to fear from such a good law, which they preach to us, which is to honor our parents, not to steal, not to kill, etc.? And how could they wish to kill us, when they teach us not to kill?" There were fathers who in spite of the mothers' fears, and mothers, with an even greater victory, in spite of the fears of the fathers, bravely gave over their children to the waters of baptism. And there was no lack of children who fled their carnal fathers, moved by a spirit greater than their bodies, and came running to their spiritual fathers to be baptized.

*Don* Tomás Bungi, a noble of the village of Agadña, two days after his baptism, went very late one night to call Father San Vitores to his house to baptize his two-months old son, whose mother had not wished to bring her child to the church. Frightened by the words of Choco, she believed that the water of baptism might harm the child who was already ill. Father San Vitores found the child at the point of death, but the mother still resisted. On the insistence of her husband, she gave the child to the priest, who baptized it. That same night it died. In the morning *don* Tomás sought the Venerable Father to tell him of the child's death. He was sad but resigned to the will of God. He returned home so happy at what the father told him about the joy of the child in heaven, that he brought another son, eight years old, asking the father to keep him in the school with the others who were being brought up there in order that he might better learn the Christian doctrine and teach it to others.

Other marvels were observed, many brought about by the lay missionaries sent out by the father. Going through the island in search of children, Captain *don* Juan de Santa Cruz met a pagan woman in a delicate and perilous condition. He said prayers over her and she soon gave birth successfully and *don* Juan baptized the infant, who appeared to be dying. Then the mother told *don* Juan that she could hear the *anites*

---

[136]*Rimai*, now *lemai*, breadfruit.

crying out, but not so close to her as on some former occasions. The captain answered that the reason the demons were complaining was that a newborn child had just been baptized there, and that if she wanted to banish them forever, she need only make the sign of the cross upon herself and repeat a prayer that he would give her, which was a brief invocation of the Holy Trinity and of our Lord Jesus Christ, and a declaration of the principal mysteries of the Catholic Faith, which had been composed in the native language by Father San Vitores, and which all catechumens were made to learn. The woman made the sign of the cross and repeated the prayer, promising to be baptized with her husband and all their household, and that they would go to Agadña to have this accomplished. Then the woman said the *anites* were gone and that she no longer heard them.

Notwithstanding these victories, Father San Vitores, seeing the cruel war and great harm brought by Satan by means of Choco, resolved to disarm the enemy by converting Choco himself to Christianity, for his own baptism would give the lie to what he had broadcast about that sacrament.

Father San Vitores prepared for the battle with many prayers and penances, praying that God would be of inestimable benefit to many other souls. He took for his patrons, besides the Blessed Virgin, Saint Ignatius and Saint Francis Xavier, who were the patrons of all his undertakings, the *Mariano* children who died in the grace of baptism.

He determined to set out at once for Paa,[137] where Choco lived, but difficulties arose at once to delay his plans. He had set August 16, 1668 for his departure, but that evening Father Luis de Morales arrived from Saipan with a severe wound in his leg, which he had received from a lance on August 14, while actually administering baptism. Shortly afterward, the Venerable Father Luis de Medina came in with his face badly inflamed as the result of wounds he had received about the head and face in the village of Nisichan, or Saint Francis Xavier, on the island of Guam. Father San Vitores received them both with his usual kindness and remained with them that night. On the following morning, August 17, he said to them, "My fathers, I had intended today to attempt the conversion of our friend Choco, and it is well that I go at once, for although the devil has contrived to have you both wounded, and thus to delay me with my duty to you, my brothers, he shall not come off the winner, however astute he may be, for I am going now. Remain with God and commend this affair to him."

He left the wounded men in the charge of Father Lorenzo Bustillos, for the other fathers were all away on various missions. By the will of God and the prayers of the Venerable Father, they soon recovered, and when Father San Vitores returned to Agadña a month later, Father Luis de Medina had already been out to visit all the villages and Father Luis de Morales was waiting to accompany him on a tour of the other islands.

---

[137]Paa was near Merizo, a distance of some twenty miles from Agaña. There is a small stretch of beach between Merizo and Inarajan that is even nowadays called Paa by the local residents. That is no doubt the site of the village name and the home of the Chinese, Choco, who had been cast ashore in the Marianas by a shipwreck. (M.H.)

He had a boat made ready for a trip to Paa, a very unusual thing, because when he visited the villages he never cared to go by water but only by land, to do all the damage he could to the devil, as he said, by seeking out newborn infants to baptize, sick and dying to console, and children and adults to instruct as he went along, never failing to improve an opportunity to benefit some soul. But now, he understood that he had received advice from heaven that it would be well to arrive that day in Paa, and this he could not do by land, since it was a journey of three days. By water he could get there that day, and he did, early.

He entered the village singing the Act of Contrition with its sentences, and the explanation of Christian doctrine, which he had composed in the Mariana language. And as this call went forth, it seemed a signal for all the people deceived by Choco to gather against the Servant of God. But they all came out of their houses to hear him, forgetting their former hostility. Indeed, many believed and brought their children to be baptized.

Since his principal intention was to convert Choco, he went in search of him, and in the presence of all the village, began to argue with him. It was easy to answer his reasoning, but his unreason was a problem.

The dispute lasted three days, during which time the Venerable Father was able to convince Choco of his errors, proving by reason and experience how the sacrament of baptism does not remove life from the body, and teaching him at the same time how it causes the life of the soul. He dispelled all his calumnies and deceits to the extent of obliging him to confess publicly that all he had said against the fathers and against the Law of Christ was false, and that nobody could be saved without holy baptism. He begged for baptism and seemed to mean it.

The Servant of God decided to baptize him on the Feast of Saint Bernard, August 20, 1668. Everything was in readiness and the people of the whole district assembled, through curiosity, to witness the solemn act. The common enemy was irritated at seeing himself outdone by Father San Vitores and deprived of the best person he had with whom to persecute the Faith. And so he sought to avenge this insult to his pride and upset the plans for the baptism and by one blow deprive Father San Vitores of two of his four Filipino companions and perhaps of his life as well.

When Father San Vitores was at the point of performing the rite, as he took up the holy oils, the devil entered two Filipinos who accompanied him, and like fanatics or infernal furies, they began to make horrible faces and to shout nonsense and absurdities, to the horror of the *Marianos* who could not understand their language and who thought they must be crying out against the sacrament of baptism.

One of them, who was called Bautista, fled to the mountains and could not be caught. The other drew his knife and started to attack the Servant of God, as if to kill him. *Don* Juan de Santa Cruz came to the aid of the Venerable Father, who calmly faced his attacker with a smile, saying, "What are you doing, my son?" At these words, the Filipino turned on *don* Juan de Santa Cruz and stabbed him three times in the arm.

*Book Three, Chapter 6*

Father San Vitores, seeing the excited state of the *Marianos*, said to them, smiling as if he were making fun of the devil, that those lads had not done that deed of themselves: the devil, the enemy of man, had possessed them and had spoken through their mouths and worked through their hands. The things they had seen had only been done to alarm them and cause them to refuse baptism and thus be consigned to hell.

With these words they were quieted, and Choco was baptized and was called Ignacio, and many followed his example. They were no longer afraid of the waters of life, which they had formerly believed to be the waters of death.

An apparition, which occurred in Sunharon, on the island of Buenavista Mariana (Tinian), on August 17, the same day that Father San Vitores began his argument with Choco, makes one think that this victory of Father San Vitores was owing to the intercession of the Blessed Virgin and the prayers of the *Mariano* children recently baptized and at that time in heaven. Father San Vitores refers to the apparition in this manner: "We usually pay no attention to the apparitions of which the *Indios* tell, although this does show their attachment to the things of our holy Faith."

Some are visions of *anites* and of evil spirits, who try even against their will to possess the poor Christian natives with the same fears and mistreatment from which they have been freed by means of holy baptism and the holy cross, and the holy names of Jesus and Mary and Saint Ignatius and Saint Francis Xavier written on the crosses that they place in their houses with very good effect. Sometimes they mention good spirits and the Blessed Virgin, such as we hear from the mouth of an *Indio* called Ignacio Ipaga, a native of the village of Sunharon, which is called *de la Inmaculada Concepción*, on the island of Buenavista. Although the station of the person to which it happened does not lend my credence to the story, other circumstances give it more verisimilitude and pertinence.

Dreaming, or perhaps awake (as he says), the Blessed Virgin appeared to him on the night of August 17, three days after Father Luis de Morales was wounded in Saipan, complaining with her own voice (which the *Indio* says he heard) of the wickedness of Saipan. The form in which she appeared (he says) was the same as the image of Our Lady of Guadalupe, in Mexico, which he had seen in an oratory in the residence of the fathers, opposite his own house. Only, he said, instead of having the hands together as in the image of the Immaculate Conception, she was holding two children as if she were nursing them at her sacred breast, and besides there were eight larger children, who with a leash of eight strands led a dog to the feet of the Virgin, in spite of its resistence and barking. All this by no means detracts from her maternal works, nor from the past victories of the Blessed Virgin, renewed in our day in these her islands, through the innocent children baptized and instructed in our holy Faith, not withstanding the barking of the infernal Cerberus and his minister Choco, who was then still an idolater, even when he went about free and victorious in wounding Father Luis de Morales in

Saipan and in achieving the death of two lay missionaries in the sea near Tinian.[138] Nevertheless, he was securely bound by the command of the Blessed Virgin and the prayers of the *Mariano* children who were in heaven or the school of Christian doctrine. Be that as it may, the fact is that the idolater Choco (the origin of the persecution) had at last given up and begged for the holy baptism for himself, which he formerly impugned in others.

---

[138]Cf. Book 3, chap. 7:198. Sergeant Lorenzo Castellanos, Spanish; Gabriel de la Cruz, a Tagalog servant of the sergeant. These were the first deaths for the conversion of these islands. (M.H.)

# CHAPTER VII

### The State of the Church in the Marianas
### After the Victory Over Choco

Although Choco's influence over the natives declined somewhat after his apparent conversion to the religion of the fathers and the number of baptisms continued to increase, it was still hard to overcome the prejudices of the people, and the rich harvest reaped by Father San Vitores and his companions cost them much sweat, fatigue, danger, wounds, and even death.

And even today (1681) there remain echoes of that pernicious voice, even though with less effect, yet always with some harm, for continuous persecutions have been born of the first one. Choco became again what he was before, because he had not received baptism with Christian sincerity, as some believed of his sudden change, which they attributed to the natural inconstancy of the *Sangleys*, as I am inclined to believe. But in any case, by his baptism, or pretended baptism, he served the cause of the Faith in others, by condemning now what he had received and by receiving what he had condemned.

Before leaving Paa, Father San Vitores sent *don* Juan de Santa Cruz to Agadña to recover from the wounds he had received at the time of Choco's baptism. The *Indio* who had wounded him he had taken to Agadña as a prisoner, not to receive punishment, but for fear that as a fugitive he would be lost.

There remained one cause for concern, which was the loss of Bautista, who had fled to the mountains and did not return. He was relieved of his worry, however, by Christ, who revealed to him the hiding place of the man several days after leaving Paa. He sent in search of the fugitive an *Indio* named Torres, whom the fathers had sent from Agadña to help carry the articles needed for Mass, because the other, called Pedro Jiménez, who was with the father, was not able to carry much because of his great age.

At that time, Father San Vitores wrote a message to the fathers in Agadña, saying: "I had a kind of dream about Bautista, in which I saw the poor man in danger of being lost, if we do not send someone to look for him. As soon as Torres came, I sent him to Paa, where, in my dream, it seemed he was. We will talk about this again in Agadña, when I get there."

He never cared to give the details of this vision, although he was often asked about it by his companions, but it is known that he told Torres that he would find Bautista in the company of Choco, in grave danger of perversion, because of the fact that Choco had returned to his old ways. The fugitive Bautista thought he would find safety in the house of the apostate. It was no small pity on the part of God that he revealed to his servant the hiding place of this poor lad who had worked in so praise-worthy a manner since the beginning of the mission and continued later to do so. Father San Vitores prudently gave him other work to do, and instead of having him accompany the fathers on their journeys, he employed him in the house in Agadña as a carpenter, which office he understood very well.

Father San Vitores, before returning to Agadña to gain the fruits of victory (over Choco) and in order not to arrive empty-handed, although he had in Paa harvested spiritual fruits, decided to visit the other villages on the way. He performed hundreds of baptisms, miraculous cures, and many other miracles, which the Lord worked through the hands of his chosen Apostle of the Marianas, in confirmation of his holy Faith, as Father Lorenzo Bustillos testifies, without further specifying the works of this time. Even his lay companion, Pedro Giménez, was absent many times on necessary errands, and so no one observed the miracles and Father San Vitores, in his humility, hid his miraculous works in order to avoid praise.

At this time, Lorenzo Bustillos, who was passing through another part of the island, witnessed an occurrence of which he writes and for which he gives all credit to the one who sent him. He testified to this for the *Processus*. When he arrived at the village that formerly was called Tarisay (Talisay) and now San Januario, the women and children fled to the hills and the men came out to meet him with lances, telling him to go away at once from that place, because he was a killer and God was likewise a killer, an evil one.

Father Bustillos replied, "How can I be a killer. Neither I nor my companion (a lay missionary) carry arms." The *Indios* answered, "With the water of God," as they called the baptismal water.

Then Father Bustillos took a small gourd of water that he carried in his belt, as did all the missionaries on the advice of Father San Vitores, in order to baptize children on the road or who might be found where there was no water. He drank some of it, of what they took for deadly poison. And when they were surprised that it did no harm, he told them that God was good. He did not want their death, but rather their life; the water of God does not take life from the body, but does give it to the soul. He told them that Choco had retracted his statements and had been baptized in order to testify in word and deed that what he had published against holy baptism was false. On hearing these words, the barbarians were quieted, and he read the explanation of Christian doctrine that Father San Vitores had written. As they heard, the *Indios* gradually laid aside their lances, listening with attention to what he said. They ended by praising God and the Mother of God and the fathers, who had come to their land from such a distant country to teach them the road to heaven.

They offered him food, and he answered that he needed no other food and drink than the salvation of their souls and the souls of their children; then they brought him three children who had been hidden in the village, in order that he might baptize them. They promised that at another time they would themselves be baptized, as would those children with whom their mothers had fled to the hills.

197

Father Bustillos baptized them and experienced the importance of certain instructions that Father San Vitores gave to all the missionaries: "In the villages where there is resistence, try to baptize at least one child. That way, you will leave imprinted on that village the very grace of God for the future teaching and baptizing of the others." And thus it was in San Januario that the baptism of those three little angels opened the door for others.

A few days later the villagers heard that the missionary was coming again to visit them. Now, instead of the lances with which they met him the first time, they came out with small gifts to offer him, and the greatest was the gift of the mothers who brought their children to be baptized. They were so happy that they begged him to remain in the village, promising to build a house and a church, but he was at that time unable to accept their offer for lack of ministers.

Two other fathers, who were traveling over the island of Tinian, were at this time in a precarious situation. The influence exerted by Choco was still very great on the other islands, although it had ceased to be of so much importance on Guam. Besides, five days after Father was wounded (August 14), the natives had killed at sea, near this island, Sergeant Lorenzo Castellanos, who, as an able mariner, had accompanied Father Morales on the journey from Guam, and also a servant of the sergeant, a Tagalog named Gabriel de la Cruz. The influence of Choco must have been the cause of these deaths, says Father San Vitores, since the same people had also wounded Father Morales. At any rate Gabriel de la Cruz certainly died innocent of the blame that they imported to Sergeant Castellanos.

The natives were in a state of unrest and took up arms, some to escape punishment because they feared the foreigners, others to punish the crime for which they blamed one person. Hence, the two missionaries, in their plight, wrote to Father San Vitores, explaining their trouble and the danger in which they found themselves and the whole Christian community on the island. They asked if he could hasten to their rescue at once with his prudence and authority, and put out the fire of rebellion that every day burned brighter.

The Servant of God knew, by the light of heaven, how astute was the enemy, who by that means wished to rob him of the advantage he then enjoyed on the island of Guam. He wrote them a letter that began with the words of the Psalm 125: *Euntes ibant et flebant, mittentes semina sua,*[139] in which he consoled and cheered them, predicting that they would suffer no harm but would have much success. He promised that he would go to see them as soon as he returned from the journey on which he was then engaged.

With the letter and the consolation of some baptisms they secured, they were so encouraged that they wrote to the Venerable Father in these words from the same Psalm: *Venientes autem venient cum exaltatione, portantes manipulos suos.*[140]

---

[139] Ps. 126:6. They went forth weeping , sowing their seed.
[140] Ibid. But back they came exaulting, bearing the harvested sheaves.

Thus it was with those two missionaries and thus it was with all who were sent by the father. If they went afflicted and weeping to sow the evangelical seed in suffering and distress, from each difficult undertaking, they returned joyful, their hands full of grain and also thorns, which appeared as roses to them and as such caused additional rejoicing, thorns suffered as they were for the love of Christ and the souls that he redeemed with his Blood.

About this, the Venerable Father says: "Although the poor seed sowed on Guam by Choco will produce a goodly crop of hard work for the missionaries, if no souls are lost, they will consider their time well employed, recognizing it as a means of Divine Providence for rooting the Faith still more firmly, in spite of these persecutions, which are not as harmful to the Faith sometimes as our lukewarm attitude might be if the persecutions did not exist. Against such an attitude we ask the fervent prayers of the devout and the zeal of new workers who will bring to perfection the labor begun in these lands."

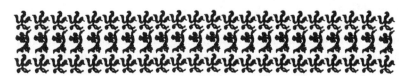

# CHAPTER VIII

*The Servant of God Goes to the Island of Tinian and the
Neighboring Ones; How He Dresses and Conducts Himself
When Visiting the Villages*

Having returned to Agadña after a trip around the island, Father San Vitores wished to carry out his promise to visit the island of Tinian.

His companions tried to dissuade him, each one offering to go in his stead. They urged him to consider how great was the risk to which he exposed his person in practically throwing himself on the lances of the islanders, already dyed with the blood of a priest whom they had wounded and of two lay companions whom they had killed. They begged that he allow someone to go before him as a scout, to reconnoiter the paths, investigate the dangers, someone whose death, if such should occur, would not have such serious consequences for the Church in the Marianas as would the death of Father San Vitores. If one of the others were killed, it would simply mean the life of one missionary. But if he were killed, it would mean the destruction of the entire mission, since without the head, the body would remain lifeless and unable to move.

They urged him to think first of that newborn Christian community, which would die at its very birth if he were killed; his zeal should not thwart the success of his own zeal, which reached out to the welfare of all these islands and the extension of the Faith and of the kingdom of Christ. They said that he always counseled them to avoid death whenever they could do so licitly, because they did not belong to themselves but to the souls for whose conversion God had sent them to these lands. They begged him to do by example what he counseled by words and not to be in such haste to gain the crown of martyrdom, which would be his sooner or later, after he had won over many islands.

To these and other counsels, the holy man replied in words that showed how little he cared for himself and how much he cared for others. He said he could go more safely than any other; he merited less than any the good fortune of dying for Christ; in case he died, he would be less missed, and his blood shed in such a good cause would do more good for Christianity than his life, so poorly employed. And when his companions would not accept his reasons and continued to insist that he abandon his plans for the journey, he said to them with firmness: "Do not be disturbed, my fathers, that I am to be the first to go. If they strike me with their lances, I shall happily await other blows, and yet others, for the love of God."

He left in Agadña the Venerable Father Luis de Medina that he might work in the principal residence and administer the sacraments, and he ordered Father Bustillos to visit all the villages of the island, to teach and baptize all he might encounter, giving him very detailed instructions in what he was to do.

He embarked with Father Morales for the islands of the north on October 20 of this year 1668. When they arrived on Tinian and Saipan, the natives were surprised to see more fathers coming to their land, when they were expecting the departure of those who were already there, on account of the dangers with which they were continually surrounded. When these new fathers approached them with forgiveness and peace from God, they said in great surprise and some terror, *Mauri si Dios! Mauri si Dios!*, which means, "How good God is!"

The Venerable Father and his companions were able to do much by their good example, so that several enemy villages made peace among themselves, and for the time being, the danger of war was averted.

From the island of Saipan, where Father San Vitores remained for a time, eager for a wound such as that suffered by Father Luis de Morales, he sent the latter to look for other islands, which he did happily. Within six months he discovered six islands: Anatajan, Sarigan, Guguan, Alamagan, Pagon (Pagan) and Agrigan, baptizing on all of them a great number of children and adults.

Father San Vitores traveled over the whole island of Saipan, and there was not a single village, either on the beach or in the hills, that he did not visit, with as many baptisms as the steps he took and as many dangers as baptisms.

A knowledge of his costume and mode of travel on this and other islands will surely give much pleasure to readers as well as some counsel to his imitators.

His cassock, which he invented in Agadña, was a sack woven of palm leaves. To this he added a hat with a brim and a cap of the same material and shoes, or sandals. Since these wore out so quickly, although the material for them was available everywhere, he mostly went barefoot, walking on the harsh grasses and weeds with bleeding feet. He thus enriched the soil in order that it might return him a hundred to one the harvest that he sought and so desired. At other times it was necessary to go unshod, because of the many small streams and swamps through which he had to pass.

In the linings of his cassock, or sack, which hung down to his breast, he had two bags that served him as a valise, where he carried all the articles needed for the journey: a breviary, a *Contemptus Mundi*,[141] the rules, the letters of Saint Francis Xavier, the holy oils, a small bottle of ink, paper for baptismal certificates, his disciplines and instruments of penance, a few bright stones and trifles of which the *Marianos* were very fond, and which he gave out as prizes to accompany his teachings.

Around his neck he wore a rosary of our Lady, as if it were a chain of great price and a picture of Christ crucified.

In his hand he had a long staff with a cross at its head. This, with a handkerchief or similar object, served as the standard or banner at the catechism meetings.

---

[141]*Contemptus Mundi* (instrument of penance).

*Book Three, Chapter 8*

As he was very nearsighted and as the roads are for the most part rough and tortuous, in order not to get lost but to remain on the trails used by the fathers, he tied a cord to his belt and had one of his companions go ahead, leading him by the cord. When it was necessary to go speedily to a village to baptize someone who was dying or help someone in trouble, he went ahead of everyone, running or, as it seemed to them, flying in the arms of the angels. And if he had to climb a steep hill, as often happens in the Marianas, the companion would go up first and Father San Vitores would follow, guided by the knotted cord tied to his waist, very often in grave danger of falling off a cliff or even into the sea.

Upon setting out, besides reciting the *Itinerarium*[142] and other prayers, he chose a patron saint for the mission, to the place he was about to visit, which was usually the saint of the day. He observed as far as possible the daily order of our *colegios*, and if his companion was a Jesuit, he formed a "portable *colegio*", of which his companion was the father rector and himself the subject.

In the country, when he was not in prayer, he chanted the Christian doctrine in the Mariana language to attract those he met on the way and others who might be hidden in the deep thickets or were walking through mountain and valley.

Entering a village, even though he knew it to be of the most hostile, he hoisted his banner and went through the streets singing couplets of his own invention as invitations to hear the Christian doctrine. If there was a cross in the village, he went at once to pray there and then went through all the houses in the village, omitting none, baptizing and confessing those in need, explaining everywhere the Christian doctrine and singing prayers that he had composed in verses in their language to ask God for temporal blessings and spiritual ones as well for each house and village, especially, that they be freed from fear of the *anite*, or demon.

After he had visited all the houses in the village, he built a portable church or shrine which looked very much like the Crib of Bethlehem, in which God, newly born in that land, entered willingly because of the welcome accorded him by the poor islanders. In this temple, which he would dedicate to the saint of the day on which he entered the village, he offered Mass. Day and night, hither came the children and others of the vicinity to hear the doctrine. As long as he remained in the village he never ceased teaching them what they needed for salvation.

The children, who were as wax in his hands, learned readily and were devoted to the Great Father for the little presents he gave them. Whatever gifts he left in the village were for them. They followed him about in groups from one village to another to compete in the recitation of the doctrine with the children of the next village.

The one who was cleverest in the doctrine he made captain of all the others, and gave him his arms and banner, which was the cross.

And with this squadron of *Mariano* infantry, weak in the eyes of men, but as formidable to demons as it was agreeable to the angels, he

---

[142]Prayer for the journey.

laid siege to the villages, God drawing his praises from the mouths of children to confound his enemies.

And although he might arrive at a village exhausted from the heat and fatigue, he took care first that his companions rested while he made ready to baptize and preach. When haste was not necessary, he celebrated baptisms with all possible solemnity, in order to gain more veneration for that sacrament. If he had ample time for the visit, he also performed the *Acto de Contrición* in the form in which it was composed by the Venerable Father Jerónimo López, which he had translated into the language of the Marianas.

As evidence of the great harvest of souls that God gave him on this island (Saipan), it is enough to recount what happened in Sogua.

This village had been seriously affected by the calumnies circulated by Choco and threatened wounds and death to any preachers of baptism that might come that way. Father San Vitores went into the village full of confidence. In his first talk he told them the reason for his visit. He then explained the Christian doctrine to them and the importance of holy baptism. They were so moved that they all cried out: "And they told us to kill the fathers! Why? Because they teach us to live better? What do they seek in our land where there is no iron or clothing, which they have in abundance in their own country? And why should they wish to kill us with the water of God? This is good water that washes the soul and there is no need to flee from it." There was hardly a child or adult who was not baptized on that very day, which was the Feast of Saint Charles Borromeo, November 4. Truly, they did not need much exhortation or human teaching, says the Servant of God, taught as they evidently were by the Holy Spirit and filled with noble resolution and good will. He called the village San Carlos, according to his custom, since it was on that day that the great conversion was made. And in the same manner and with equal success, he visited the islands of Tinian and Agrigan.

Although he was usually well received in the villages and was given presents of bananas, coconuts, and other fruits of the land, as they do for important guests, which the Venerable Father accepted in order not to displease the people, and which he kept to be used as premiums in his teaching; nevertheless, in many places he was badly received by the villagers and treated as an enemy who came to take the lives of their children. Sometimes, while preaching, he saw the lances being aimed to run him through.

But from these and other dangers God protected him by a special providence, preserving his life that he might give life to those who wished to give him death. Besides, the Lord gave him power in his preaching, with certain miraculous results, of which we know only those that his humility was unable to conceal.

At Fumhon, a village on the island of Saipan, Father San Vitores found a woman who gave evidence of being possessed by a devil, and the whole village seemed to be so possessed, says the father himself, because of the extreme obstinacy of that village, in which the devil, not content with the voice of Choco, had possessed the people themselves, to the end that no adult would hear of holy baptism.

The Servant of God pitied the affliction of the woman and even more the obstinacy of all the village. He performed the ordinary rites of exorcism and other actions that the Lord inspired him to do, such as applying relics, saying prayers to the Virgin, to Saint Joseph (the patron saint of the island) and to Saint Ignatius and Saint Francis Xavier, and the woman was freed of the evil spirit and the village of its stubbornness, so that it listened to and accepted the teaching of heaven.

In Opian, a village of the same island of Saipan, he baptized a paralytic woman who was deprived of the use of all her limbs and suffered also from a burning fever. With no other medicine than the water of God, he left her perfectly well. Thus he offered ample proof that it was not a deadly poison but a medicine to restore health.

On the island of Agrigan, he found a woman in the throes of a difficult parturition, quite unable to give birth. He applied to her some letters of Saint Ignatius and tied a picture of that saint to her right hand, saying a prayer and promising to give the name of the saint to the child about to be born. Very soon a little girl was born and he named her Ignacia.

He spent somewhat more than three months on the tour of Tinian, Saipan, and Agrigan. He established a residence on Tinian and left one father in charge and returned to Guam by way of Zarpana (Rota) on the eve of Epiphany, January 5, 1669.

They arrived late at night and were unable to go ashore because of the dangerous reefs and high seas and thus were compelled to pass an unpleasant, dangerous night at sea.

Father Casanova, who was then on the island [of Rota] and who writes of it, heard a joyous ringing of bells and hastened out from his hut to ask of his companions what it could be, since there was only one small bell there, the one that was used to call the people to instruction.

They answered that they, too, had heard bells ringing, but that the sound had ceased when he came out of doors, and no one knew what it could be.

They passed the night discussing it, until in the early morning Father San Vitores came into the village. They learned the hour at which he had landed on the island and knowing that it was just then that they had heard the bells, they knew that it was a festal salvo from heaven, greeting his safe return.

# CHAPTER IX

*He Establishes a Seminary for Boys on the Island of Guam,*
*and He Dedicates the Church in Agadña*

On his return to Agadña [about the middle of January], Father San Vitores was received by the Venerable Father Luis de Medina and Father Lorenzo Bustillos as if he were an angel from heaven. He, too, had great satisfaction in seeing how conditions here had improved during his absence. He began to build a *colegio*, or seminary,[143] that he had been planning for a long time for selected *Mariano* boys, to be named Colegio de San Juan de Letrán, with a rector or preceptor who would be elected by vote of the boys each week and with rules suited to the climate and to the age and capacity of the seminarians.

They served in the church with strict punctuality and order. They went out morning and afternoon with a bell to call the children of the town to the doctrine, and they made up a choir for the church, in which they sang twice daily.

On Saturdays they decorated an image of the Virgin with flowers and trinkets and sang praises; in the afternoon they had confessions. Their time was as well planned, says Father Casanova, as in the seminaries of Spain.

The brightest boys, the most advanced in Christian doctrine and customs, accompanied the fathers on their journeys from one village to another, serving as interpreters and teaching catechism. Father San Vitores applied himself with singular care to the instruction of these boys. It seemed to him that they would be the leaven by means of which the whole mass of those islands would be raised, through their words and their good example. And if he had been able to do nothing more than maintain these boys apart from their former manner of living, he would have judged it worthwhile. He ordered that in other residences similar schools be established, the better to help all the islands.[144]

From the beginning, even though the boys had been badly brought up, after receiving the instruction the fathers gave them, they turned out very well and were of great assistence. Of this I shall give only one example.

This boy was twelve or thirteen years old. He was the son of a noble. One day he went out fishing with his father in a small boat, bearing the banner of the holy cross, as he was accustomed to.

The father saw a fish that the natives like very much called *guatafe*,[145] and without stopping to think, he was carried away by the

---

[143]All the earliest constructions of the Spaniards were of wood or thatch. In 1676 the first *momposteria* (uncut stone set in mortar) construction was undertaken, and this was the fabrication of a large and substantial church. (M.H.)

[144]In 1675 all the residences on the island of Guam established schools, erecting separate buildings in which to house native boys and girls. These schools are mentioned as having been located in Agaña, Ayrran, Orote, and Ritidian. (M.H.)

[145]*Guatafe*, in modern Chamorro *gatafe*. In some parts of Guam it is pronounced *tagafe* (*Lutianus bohar*; family *Lutianidae*, red snapper. (M.H.)

*Book Three, Chapter 9*

old custom and began to invoke his *anites*, to gain their help in catching the fish.

The boy was distressed at this, and weeping, said, "Father, don't call to these enemies. You won't catch anything." The father answered, "What can I say?" "Invoke Jesus and Mary and you will catch the fish." He did so, and he had scarcely uttered these sweet names when he caught the fish. Then he came running to our house with his son, singing praises to Jesus and Mary, and telling what had happened to himself and his son and asking pardon for his thoughtlessness.

Father San Vitores wished to establish this seminary on a permanent basis. In a memorial to Her Majesty, with the deepest feeling, he recommended the foundation of the school as the highest priority for the new Christian community. In the following passage he gives his reasons:

> May it please Your Majesty to found a seminary on the island of Guam for the good instruction of the boys of this land, orphans by nature or by the customs of this nation, by which they are in all things without any education or control from their parents. Their barbarity will give way more easily to the introduction of our correction and training in such houses as the seminary. Thus we will oppose our holy and royal seminary to those that the devil has founded in these islands for the *urritaos (hulitaos)*, or unmarried men, who live with girls in public houses, with no other regulation than that which the devil or their own appetites may dictate, with the liberty of their age.
>
> For this seminary in Agadña, until there are established others in other islands, only boys of the greatest ability, best disposition, and application to the Christian doctrine will be chosen. They can serve later as teachers for the others, and the best ones can eventually be ordained as priests, since the *Marianos* do not have the vice of drunkenness, which has made it impossible for the natives of other places to receive holy orders.
>
> The Apostle of the Indies, Saint Francis Xavier, placed his greatest hope for the fruit of the gospel in the children, whose instruction and education he recommended beyond anything else to his companions, because Christianity, if it is introduced during childhood, increases with age, and they will be good Christians when they are men and old men if they were Christians since childhood.
>
> The same Saint Francis Xavier applied to the governor of eastern India (for the instruction and rearing of Malabar children) for four thousand *pardaos* that were assigned to the *chapin* (slipper money) of the queen, *doña* Catalina of Portugal, from the tribute of the *Pesquería* (Fishery Coast). He then wrote to the queen, requesting that she consider the money well employed, giving this reason: "Because these children, sons and grandsons of Gentiles, are, *Señora*, the best *slippers* with which Your Highness could most surely enter heaven."

*A Seminary on the Island of Guam, and He Dedicates the Church in Agadña*

And we can say of this boys' seminary, whose establishment we hope for from royal generosity and the piety of Her Majesty, the Queen, that these Christian boys, sons and grandsons of infidels and barbarians, will be the best guard for the king, our Lord, and this house will be the best castle and fortress in all his provinces.

He then adds:

And if there were means, it would be very desirable to establish also a seminary for girls, into which we could take them before the devil catches them for the *urritaos*, or public houses, where they live, as I have stated, young men with the young unmarried girls, whom they choose and take from one place to another with the infamous consent of their parents who allow it for the pay they receive.

The queen, *nuestra señora doña* Mariana de Austria, whom God keep, by a decree of April 18, 1673 [one year exactly after the martyrdom of Father San Vitores], through her great piety and zeal, granted the request of Father San Vitores, ordering the *señor Marqués* de Mancera, Viceroy of Mexico, to send three thousand pesos every year from the Royal Treasury for the foundation of the seminary for boys, as long as it was located on its own land; and she ordered the same viceroy to communicate with Father San Vitores concerning whatever would be necessary, according to his letter, for the foundation of a seminary for girls.

And in the decree that she sent to Father San Vitores, advising him of her decision, she wrote: "Also, I give you my thanks for the zeal and care with which you conduct these matters; and I charge you that, in my name, you thank your companions, encouraging them to continue, for it is a useful work, both in the spiritual sphere, which is its principal purpose, and in the temporal also, and you will keep me informed of the state of the seminaries, as occasion offers."

The seminary for boys today [1681] is in very good condition on the island of Guam, in its material edifice and much more in the spiritual, according to what Father Lorenzo Bustillos wrote, who had it in charge, in his letter of June 1679. They have a house of three spacious rooms, with a Chapel of Nuestra Señora de Guadalupe de Mexico. The older students live apart from the younger and newer ones. Father Bustillos says that the older students are so well rooted in the Faith and in Christian customs that they would even have the advantage of some Europeans. And the employment of their time is such that they appear more like religious novices than secular students, brought up though they are in the greatest freedom imaginable, owing no obedience to their own parents.

Father San Vitores hastened the construction of a church in Agadña, and it was completed within a few days after his return from his visit to the other islands. It was dedicated on the Feast of the Purification, February 2, 1669, to the *Dulcísimo Nombre de María y de la Santísima Familia Mariana.*

*Book Three, Chapter 9*

It was built, as he said, of the tree they called *maría*, and its own name consecrated it to our Lady of these islands.

Innumerable people flocked to the dedication, not only from Guam but from the other islands, marvelling at the holy ceremonies that the Servant of God prepared and explained in order to gain greater respect for that sacred place.

He added many original inventions to make the *fiesta* more pleasant and understandable. But what was most worth seeing for those who knew how to appreciate it, was the argument between Father San Vitores and Father Luis de Medina over which one was to dedicate the church. Each one insisted that the other was the one who should exercise the office on that day, each one giving excuses for declining the honor. And this showed that both were worthy of it. The outcome was no other than that of their rivalry to be the first martyr, so that Father San Vitores had only the role of acolyte, as he had later in the dedication of other churches that were built in the Marianas, not wishing to accept any place other than the most humble.

People came from everywhere to this temple, many to ask assistance for their needs, since God wished to consecrate it and make it more venerable by miracles.

A man and his wife came from the village of Fuuña,[146] on the island of Zarpana (Rota), with a boy eight months old who suffered from dropsy. They brought him to the church in Agadña, hoping to find there the health they sought for their son. The child had not been baptized. When Father San Vitores questioned them about it, they answered "yes", fearing that baptism would kill it or at least augment his ailment, for they had not yet forgotten the voice of Choco. They admitted that they had not been baptized, and after learning some catechism, they received baptism, but as they refused it for their child, they delayed his recovery, because when Father San Vitores applied certain relics and recited a gospel over him, he remained as sick as before, the life of his body being continued by Providence, in order that he might receive the life of the soul.

The couple returned to their home disconsolate, for the child's condition became worse day by day. At last the parents realized that his failure to recover was due to the fact that he had not been baptized. The parents brought him a second time to the church in Agadña, confessing their fault to the Venerable Father. He baptized the child and by means of the sacrament God gave him perfect health; and thus, when Father San Vitores passed through their village some days later, they thanked him for the life and health of their son. The father told them to give thanks to God, who had given them that great grace in order that they and all the others might lose their fear of baptism.

Father San Vitores recalled the fathers who were on the other islands, leaving only one to attend to the needs of the people. He wished to consult with them about the means for the advancement of the mis-

---

[146]Fuuña appears to have been a favorite name with the *Marianos*, since there was a village called Fuuña on Rota, another on Guam, south of Umatac Bay near Fouha Point to the north of Fouha Bay. Father López's map of Guam shows also a small island in the vicinity of Orote Point, also called Fuuña.

*A Seminary on the Island of Guam, and He Dedicates the Church in Agadña*

sion in these islands and to plan the celebration of their first Holy Week in the new Church of the Marianas, in order that the occasion might be celebrated as it was in the ancient churches, as Father San Vitores said, with the repository, the *pasos*, the processions, the disciplines even to blood, and the confessions of the neophytes even of less than a year. And there was not lacking the good music of the Blessed Virgin, as we may call the boys of the school, who with their pure voices and various modes and tones, now sad, now happy, singing the prayers of the Christian doctrine, and with singular grace, the *Ave Maria*, accompanied the processions and *fiestas* and made them all so agreeable to those poor people. The Church in the Marianas, through the zeal and ability of its apostle, had advanced and grown to such an extent that, although it was not yet one year old, it appeared old and well established in the order and regularity of its life.

The most remarkable thing was the increasing number of those who were baptized and of the catechumens, for the fathers, in a conference during which they reported on all their labors, found that within eight months, there were more than thirteen thousand Christians and more than twenty thousand catechumens. The Venerable Father offered this news to the queen, *doña* Mariana de Austria, in these words, which show the religious zeal of the queen, to whom he wrote on April 25, 1669, saying: "As the first fruits of this *Tierra Mariana*, we offer Your Majesty not diamonds, perfumes, pearls, or gold, nor other riches of that nature, of which we have not even a trace here, but only the utter poverty of these islands, already known to the Dutch, who have searched them many times and have given them up as worthless, a poverty that has prevented there being anything that would attract the enemies of our holy Faith. We offer, I say, what Your Majesty is always seeking and redeeming at great expense to the Royal Treasury, and I refer to the souls redeemed by the Precious Blood of our Savior. By his grace and the help of your royal piety, the Blessed Virgin has in this one year, in spite of the vigorous complaints of Satan and the perverse voice of Choco against baptism, gained more than thirteen thousand *Marianos* who were baptized in these eleven islands and more than twenty thousand catechumens. But those who most signally form a special part of this triumph and serve as a guard for the king (whom God save!) are the hundred or more infants who, recently baptized, have flown to heaven and, there, with the angels, form a bodyguard for His Majesty, for now there are all these little angels in heaven who would have been lost forever, if we had delayed one year longer in coming."

I must not fail to say that Christ repaid this abundant harvest of souls with a superabundance of divine pity, for although these poor *Marianos*, as he says, do not need to see many miracles in order to accept our Faith, Christ saw fit to work at least a few.

Father San Vitores contrived to conceal those marvels that were worked through him, but told freely of those that happened to the other ministers, though not mentioning their names. It has seemed right to me to mention here, in his own words, two that throw light on the events

209

that took place in the earliest days of the mission and were due in part to his merit.

The first was in the village of Muchon, called Saint Francis Xavier, on the island of Santa Ana, or Zarpana (Rota), where a man called Francisco Nufa, after a long and distressing illness of which twice he almost died, was restored to health on the application of a medal of the holy Apostle of the Indies.

The second and most notable was in the village of Fuuña, on the same island, where the residence is named for Saint Francis Xavier. A child of three months lay for six hours, stiff as a board, and already annointed, which here is the same as being placed in his shroud, and was given up for dead, when the father saw him. This child had been previously concealed in order that the father could not kill him with baptism. The father took him in his hands and offered him to the Blessed Virgin, in honor of whose Immaculate Conception he had celebrated Mass on the previous Saturday.

He decided to call the child Francis Xavier because that day, December 1, was the former vigil of the Feast of Saint Francis Xavier, which he always celebrated by a fast. And so he tried to say the prayer of the Mass of the Feast of Saint Francis, *Deus, qui Indiarum gentes, etc.*, but three times he was unable to do so. Always, the first half of the prayer for the Feast of Saint Ignatius came to his lips, and he would conclude it with the second half of the prayer for the Feast of Saint Francis. Finally, in the presence of almost all the villagers, the child returned to life, the first signs being a flutter of the heart and a slight movement of the hand on that side. Seeing this, the father immediately baptized him conditionally. But the signs of life disappeared, and again the father repeated the same prayers. At last the child moved, his breath and color returned, and he opened his eyes to find all the witnesses joyful at his tears, so profoundly moved were they by what they had seen. The father reproved the parents for their lack of faith. Now the child was given unconditional baptism, and the people, seeing this, had much greater belief in this sacrament, which they had heretofore detested in all those villages. The child lived ten days, and on December 10, the octave of the Feast of Saint Francis Xavier, he passed from this temporal life to the eternal.

The following occurrence, as related by Father Lorenzo Bustillos in a letter to Father Juan Guillén, cannot but be attributed to Father San Vitores and deserves admiration for having been done by his signature. Father Luis de Morales, on the island of Agrigan, came across a child about a year old who had refused milk for a day and was gasping out its life. The first thing that occurred to the father, in order that the Lord might prolong its life until he could baptize it, was to apply to the infant a letter of Father San Vitores. This he did, and the child revived at once, was fed, and lived till the following day, when, after receiving holy baptism, he departed for heaven.

At this time, a rumor was heard on Guam that Father Morales had been killed with four of his companions while visiting the island of Gani. While all believed it to be true, Father San Vitores, coming one morning from his prayers, told the others not to be disconsolate. He assured them that "one of the house" had revealed (and it was himself who had experienced the revelation) that Father Morales was at that moment on his way to Guam after discovering six islands and baptizing more than four thousand *Marianos*.

# CHAPTER X

*Father San Vitores Visits the Islands Already Discovered and Discovers Those of Assonson and Maug; the Beginning of the War on Tinian*

Father Luis de Morales returned from the voyage in which he discovered six islands [to the north] but was unable to go farther because of inclement weather and the small size of the craft in which he sailed. Father San Vitores had information from heaven, at a time when he was in an elevated state or as it were outside himself, that there were two islands still farther on that ought to be discovered.

He assigned his companions to their places in the islands already discovered (first instructing them in what they were to do) and set out alone from the island of Guam, in the beginning of July 1669.

Prior to Father San Vitores's arrival on Tinian, Father Casanova, at night, on the Feast of Saint Peter, June 29, heard either in a dream or half asleep, the soft music of distant voices. He believed it to be no more than an illusion, but on the following morning he saw Father San Vitores on the beach. He knew then that it was more than a dream and that heaven had been celebrating his safe arrival on Tinian, just as it had celebrated with the ringing of bells his arrival on Zarpana (Rota) on a former occasion.

Passing on to the island of Saipan, or San José, he was sentenced to death by the villages various times in their town meetings, because he continued to go about baptizing and teaching the Law of God, and they had never lost their fear of the water of God, which they had learned from Choco.

They entrusted the execution to a certain noble who possessed considerable authority on the island. He, in turn, entrusted the execution of Father San Vitores to a noble from another village as a favor to the latter noble. This person wished to know if the Great Father was such a miracle worker as they said. So he asked him why he had come to his land. The father answered that it was to lead them to heaven. The man went on asking many curious questions, showing a great desire that some miracle be performed in his presence.

But the Servant of God, seeing him play so well the role of Herod, resolved to imitate the example of Jesus and not answer a word to any of his questions.[147]

When the proud barbarian saw that he would not answer, he reviled him as an insane and senseless man and sent him back to the first noble in the hands of the *urritaos*, the young fellows at loose ends, from whom he suffered insults and mockeries. They were ordered to tell the first noble that this man was a simple fool, crack-brained, and nearly

---

[147] Luke 23:8-11.

blind, who went from island to island and village to village teaching lies and absurdities, singing couplets with children and others as foolish as himself who gathered about him. He said he had not wanted to kill him, satisfied just to mock him so as not to deprive them of the entertainment they could get out of that crazy man. So those people were content not to kill him, but they teased him, whistled at him, scorned him, and tormented him by word and act.

But in spite of all this mockery, in those same villages he gathered a copious harvest of baptisms, not only of children but also of adults who, scorning the mockeries of the rest, listened with pleasure to the Christian doctrine and heard it with esteem. This, the Venerable Father told various times later to Father Bustillos, finding comfort and joy in the fact that, without meriting it, he had enjoyed the good fortune of seeing himself likened to Jesus Christ when he was taken from Herod to Pilate and treated as insane.

He continued his voyage through the other islands with similar results: no less suffering and dangers to himself than souls for God. And the dangers of the sea were no less formidable than those of land, for it was not the best season for navigation in those islands, the sea being rough, the roughest in all the south, hard sailing for even large vessels, as the galleons *Concepción* and *Margarita* had learned when they paid for their temerity by being wrecked. The boats, or canoes, of these islanders, even for a smooth sea, are dangerous enough and look more like things cast up from a shipwreck than any kind of craft in which to sail.

They are made of one or two boards tied together with cords, with no shelter from rain or sun, in which the poor sailor goes as if he were clinging to a log, says a companion of Father San Vitores, and one cannot move from one place to another, but must sit, soaked continually by sea water and often also by rain, which at this season is frequent or continuous.

The greatest happiness that one may dare to hope for, not being a fish like these natives, is to escape with his life, for death is always before him, the imminence of it not permitting him to eat or sleep, and when dire necessity makes him take some sustenance, the fare is nothing more than a few roots, which together with seasickness serve rather to purge the stomach by vomiting than to succor his needs.

In this type of boat, in continued danger, or rather experience of death, the Apostle of the Marianas sailed with only two lay companions. They felt safe, because they were in his company, and because he was carrying the light of the gospel to those who lived in darkness.

Having passed the islands then discovered, he arrived at the island called Assonson, which with slight change and for a good reason, he called Asunción, because he had arrived there on August 15, the Feast of the Assumption of Our Lady.

He then went on to Maug, where he arrived on August 17, and because it was the octave of Saint Lawrence, he called it San Lorenzo.

He converted and baptized the natives of these two islands, who had not yet heard of the light that had come to the other islands nearby;

nor had they heard of Choco. Because of this Father San Vitores was able, without hindrance and favored by the grace of the Holy Spirit that brought him hither, to baptize them all, or nearly all.

Being unable to proceed further in those fragile boats, he left on the last two islands, his two lay assistants, well instructed, in order that they might baptize in case of necessity, to help to a good death, and to care for the church that was built there. He returned to the island of San Juan (Guam), visiting others on the way. Arriving at the island of San Joaquín (Anatajan), he sent a lay companion called Lorenzo to baptize in a remote village, while he carried on his work in other parts. And the good Christian, Lorenzo, found the crown of martyrdom, as we may piously believe, while seeking those to baptize, because, as he was just about to administer baptism to a little girl, some natives who had a few days before lost a newly baptized child and had been influenced by the talk of Choco, accused the catechist of being a killer of children and murdered him with such horrible cruelty that not content with repeatedly wounding him, they tore out his eyes and threw him into a filthy ditch.

This fortunate Lorenzo, a Malabar, was one of those who remained here in 1638 after the wreck of the *Concepción*, since God willed that he be lost in these islands that he might find the glory of martyrdom. When the fathers arrived here, he joined them, serving as a catechist and an interpreter, like them, exposing himself to continual danger of death, to gain souls for God, and, therefore, he deserved to attain before them the crown desired by all.

As soon as Father San Vitores heard of the death of Lorenzo, he was happy for the latter's good fortune, though sad at the thought of how much he would miss him. He asked some natives to lead him to the place where Lorenzo had been killed, so that he could baptize the little girl. They said she was ill, and at the same time he could baptize any other newborn children.

But the *Marianos* said to him, "Where are you going, Great Father? For that very baptism they have killed your companion." He answered, "Let us go. Even that does not matter." He was so insistent that the *Indios* had to give way and take him there, leading him by a cord over the rough country.

But pitying him for the risk he was facing, they led him out of the village, and after a few turns about the hills, Father San Vitores found that he was again in the place from which he had started, instead of that village whither he had wished to go. He expressed disappointment over having lost an opportunity in which he had hoped to win souls, and perhaps the death, or rather the life, that Lorenzo had found there.

A few hours after they killed Lorenzo the Malabar, a horrible explosion was heard on the island of San Joaquín (Anatajan) and a dense, burning mass fell into the sea, which, says Father San Vitores, was not lightning. The islanders were so frightened, because they had never seen such a thing, that they ran to Father San Vitores to beg his forgiveness for the murder of Lorenzo. They firmly believed that the soul of Lorenzo had flown to the Philippines to demand vengeance of the governor, or that God had informed the governor through the prayers of Father San Vitores, and the governor had sent his artillery against them.

This explosion spread a heavy cloud of smoke towards the island of Buenavista (Tinian), where the Venerable Father Luis de Medina was in grave danger from a civil war that had broken out among the islanders, and also towards San José (Saipan), where later Father Medina was martyred.

Father San Vitores saw a great mystery in this phenomenon, saying that God was thus calling his soldiers to arms, to make them fight manfully against the devil, who walked about so freely in those islands. He also stated later that, that comet had foretold the present danger and future martyrdom of Father Medina. He added that Father Medina was saying Mass and was elevating the Host when the thunderous noise occurred, and that Father Casanova heard the noise distinctly, although he was forty leagues distant at the time.

Father San Vitores knew, and it was believed, by divine revelation, that a civil war was brewing in Tinian, as he knew the difficulties that threatened Christianity and the dangerous situation of Father Medina and his companion, Father Casanova. He set out, therefore, at once from Anatajan for the island of Tinian to try to effect a remedy. For a long time he had foreseen this war, for when he was visiting Saipan and was looking for the head of a statue of the Blessed Virgin in a certain house, where he had heard it would be found, in place of the head he found a small piece of artillery and had it sent to Tinian with other military supplies. This was more than a month before the war began, and at the time, there were no signs of it.

The reason for this war was, on the part of the enemy of man, the dislike for our holy Faith, which, because it is the law of peace, is badly received among warlike people. On the part of the *Tinianos*, the cause of it was their arrogance and pride, in which they exceed all the other islands.

I do not know what differences there may have been between the nobles of Marpo and Sungharon, the chief villages of the island, but as often happens, personal quarrels between leaders become public hostilities, and civil wars turn village against village. They lay waste the fields, kill many nobles, until all the island is involved and every village allied with one side or another.

From a single spark a sudden flame flared and soon the whole island was enflamed. As souls already burning with hatred quickly kindle to anger for any reason, and as many on both sides were deceived by Choco, so the fathers, who came as mediators, were seen only as enemies and were threatened with death. And so the fathers found themselves in grave danger.

When Father San Vitores arrived on Tinian, there were two armies in the field, just going into battle. He took a cross in his hand and with great spirit and confidence went out between the opposing armies and began to exhort them to peace with reasons, promises, and threats. But as anger is as deaf as it is blind, they turned on him and began to pelt

*Book Three, Chapter 10*

him with stones. But a great marvel occurred, to which there are as many witnesses as soldiers in both armies. All the stones that touched the Servant of God or the cross that he carried in his hand, disintegrated and immediately fell to earth, as if they were no more than flour. The stones, as we have said in another place, are as hard as jasper or alabaster, and the natives throw them as skillfully as if they were thrown from a battering ram. Father San Vitores used to say to his companions, in order to allay their fears and increase their confidence in God, "I do not know what manner of stones these could be, but when they touched me, they fell apart like flour."

The natives of these islands were harder than stones and did not soften on hearing the words of the Servant of God, not even after seeing that miracle, which they themselves afterwards told about with awe.

When Father San Vitores realized that peaceful methods would not stop the war, and he had tried such means, he decided to turn to the methods of war in order to obtain peace, which was so necessary to Christianity. Thus, leaving the fathers well instructed in what they were to do in his absence, to delay, if they could not stop the riots, he returned to Guam, where he arrived on the Feast of Saint Eugene, Archibishop of Toledo and Martyr, November 15, 1669.

Arriving at the residence in Agadña, he found Father Luis de Morales and Father Bustillos discussing with their lay companions how far he must have traveled on his voyage through the islands and where he might be at the moment. Some said he must be on the third or fourth island, other thought he might have gone even farther.

When he entered, and they saw him, they were alarmed, for they believed he must have had some misfortune that had obliged him to return ahead of time.

And when he told them that he had visited all ten islands and had discovered two new ones, baptizing everywhere many children and adults and administering the sacraments to those who were able to receive them, describing each island as if he had remained there for some time, they could not believe their ears and were astonished. For, as Father Bustillos says, it naturally seemed impossible to them that even with the help of angels he could have completed so long a voyage in such a short time. He took only three months to complete a journey for which the natives, accustomed as they are to these waters, require a whole year, in order to avoid sailing in bad weather.

Father asked them for the necessary articles with which to celebrate Mass. He said that for lack of hosts he had been unable to celebrate it on the two previous days. His companions reminded him that it was already four o'clock in the afternoon.[148] He lifted his eyes to heaven and offered his frustrated desires to the Lord, and said, "May it be through the love of God that he receive my good intention." They begged him to break his fast, late as it was, and gave him a little cooked rice, which was the best they had there to offer. But when he tasted it, as was his custom, he said, "How good this is! It is a pity to eat it," and he gave it to a child

---

[148] He had been fasting from food and drink since before midnight and he could offer Mass after twelve noon.

in the catechism class. And not wishing to take any other food nor rest after his long, tiresome voyage, he went at once about the task of preparing for the pacification of the island of Tinian and had a long fervent talk with his lay companions about the importance of this undertaking.

# CHAPTER XI

*The Pacification of the Island of Tinian and
Some Miraculous Happenings*

Father San Vitores published, in Agadña, the jubilee granted to those about to fight the infidels.[149] He heard the confessions of his lay assistants who were about to go on this expedition, and for a week he preached to them fervently, praising the glory that such a war would bring them, a war in which they sought not captives or spoils, neither gold nor silver, but only the glory of God and the conquest of souls, liberating them from the slavery and tyranny of the devil. He told them how great would be their merit in pacifying those who by means of war blocked the spread of the gospel. By their own hands, they would open a way for those feet that bring the gospel of peace.

And he added: "Do not be afraid because you are few and the enemy many, because the Lord of Hosts marches under our banners, or rather his banners. A few men with God are a multitude, while the many without God are as nothing. I assure you that the barbarians, without natural courage, without the military arts, and almost without arms, are nothing even though they crowd the field. The Spaniards, with their natural spirit, with their generosity, and with their military cleverness, are never weak, although they are no more than ten. When the Lord wishes to give them victory, he gives a greater victory to a few than to many. If there were many, they would attribute their success to themselves, but when they are few in number, they recognize God in their victory. It is impossible to count the victories that God has given the few over the many or has given to one man or one woman over a whole army. It is enough to remember in Scripture the Maccabees, or Gideon, Deborah, David, Judith, and if we pass over from divine to human histories, from the distant to things close at hand, how many triumphs do you suppose were realized in Spain and in the Indies by a few Spaniards against the great armies of the Mohammedans and the Gentiles?

"Fear not then, *Ejército Mariano* (*Mariano* Army), bearing with you God and Mary, who is the *Bellona* of the Christians, the *Señora* of battles and the Mother of victories. Fear not, then, for you shall carry peace with you. You have the favor of that angel, who with the celestial army attended the nativity of Christ to sing, 'Glory to God in the highest, and on earth peace to men of good will.' "

His lay companions were aroused by the words of Father San Vitores, their zeal and enthusiasm so stirred, that, as Father Bustillos writes, they could scarcely wait for the hour of departure to bring peace to their enemies and to give their lives, if necessary, for this cause, be-

---

[149]The jubilee: the indulgences granted by the *Bulla Cruciata*, a papal bull, to crusaders going to war against the infidel.

*The Pacification of the Island of Tinian and Some Miraculous Happenings*

lieving, as they did, that victory was already assured, whether by winning the fight or by dying for the glory of God.

With everything in readiness, the fleet left Guam about November 25, 1669. It consisted of three or four canoes and ten soldiers, who believed themselves as strong as ten thousand, because they had in their company Father San Vitores. All of the soldiers were Filipinos, with the exception of one man named Juan de Santiago, who was a *Viscaino*, and the captain of them all, *don* Juan de Santa Cruz.

A friendly wind carried them to Tinian and, on disembarking, Father San Vitores learned that the two armies were ready to attack. With the cross in his hand, he rushed out between the two camps, exhorting them to peace, threatening them with punishment, if they refused to lay down their arms and become reconciled.

Those of Marpo replied, as they had done before, throwing stones at him, but God repeated the miracle and those that touched Father San Vitores or the cross fell disintegrated as before.

Seeing that it was useless to plead peace against their warlike stubbornness, he called *don* Juan de Santa Cruz and ordered him to set up camp in exactly the same place where he had tried to exhort them to peace and to dig his trenches and set up fortifications according to the nature of the land, and he gave them such other orders as were necessary to achieve peace without bloodshed, which was what he desired.

From this location (which he occupied in order to impede the encounter of the two armies) with the small troop of soldiers with three muskets and one field piece, he tried to control the two armies in which there were thousands of *Tinianos*.[150]

*Don* Juan de Santa Cruz sent a message to the two camps stating that he did not come to make war, but peace, not against them but in their favor, not for the benefit of Sungharon or Marpo but for all, to keep them from foolishly destroying each other and making enemies of friends and relatives. And if they did not pay attention to these arguments for their own good, they should not be surprised if the Spaniards, their best friends, became enemies and spoke through the mouths of their muskets and artillery to those who refused to hear the voice of friendship.

The barbarians would not listen to the first messengers, since they were so many and the Spaniards so few. But because they have a great fear of firearms, they did not dare to start a battle as planned or to attack our soldiers in the open, although they tried to catch our soldiers off guard, especially at night, and take their weapons away.

At the same time Father San Vitores and Father Medina, fired by their holy zeal, took each the side of one army. Father San Vitores chose the side of the inhabitants of Sungharon; Father Medina that of Marpo. Each went through the camp he had chosen. They were threatened with lances and stones. They told the people how much peace would benefit them and how harmful war was, as they themselves could see in the destruction of their fields and villages, the death of their relatives.

---

[150]Thousands of *Tinianos*? Most of the Spanish soldiers seem to have been Philippine boys between twelve and fifteen years old.

*Book Three, Chapter 11*

They told the opposing armies that they could now arrange peace without appearing cowardly or showing fear of the enemy, since everyone would know that peace had been brought about through their regard for the Spaniards, who had come as mediators; that it would be better to make peace through their own free will than from necessity, as they would do if the firearms of the Spaniards were turned on them, and they would have no means of resistence.

At last the islanders, overcome by the combination of reason and fear, tried to reconcile their differences, and those of Marpo sent an embassy to those of Sungharon, bearing a shell as a sign of peace and friendship. But the devil, that sower of darnel, inspired someone from Sungharon, we know not whom, to plant sharp points in the path on which the embassy from Marpo had to return. And, as in all nations, even the most barbarous, it is customary to respect the rights of ambassadors and others who try to make peace, the villagers of Marpo were sorely offended and called the people of Sungharon cowards and traitors who made war against those who came in the cause of peace and assured their safety only to wound and harm them.

With this, the war began again and with greater danger to the fathers than before, because now they were looked upon as mediators in a peace that was a deception. But because the fathers again used every means towards another reconciliation, they were able to hold back, but not to quench, the flames of war.

Father San Vitores saw that it would be impossible to pacify the natives of Marpo for some time, angry as they were with just cause. While waiting for time to cool their anger, he sent Father Luis de Medina to visit Saipan, while he remained in Tinian, hoping to soften the anger of the villagers of Marpo and prepare them for a peaceful settlement of the war. When Father Medina returned from Saipan, they began as before, and with the same zeal, to plead for peace until it was at last achieved, by favor of the Blessed Virgin, Saint Ignatius, and Saint Francis Xavier, whom they had taken as patrons of their undertaking. This was effected on the same day that the Feast of Our Lady of Peace was celebrated in the Archdiocese of Toledo [January 24, 1670]. And it was a great satisfaction to men and no less for the angels, the performance of a public ceremony of such great devotion.

That is to say that the armies met again in a suitable place, but this time in a religious procession, not for battle. Father Medina led those for Marpo with the standard of the Blessed Virgin, Saint Ignatius, and Saint Francis Xavier. After him, the children followed who were receiving instruction in Christian doctrine, and after them the youths and older nobles of the village, each with a small gift of fruit or rice. Last of all, they carried a great shell, which is the principal sign of friendship, which only a few days before had come into their hands on one of the rare turtles that are found in these waters. It was believed that the turtle was like the dove of peace, for it was caught at the time when peace was being arranged, but when they lacked the shell that was customarily used at such a time.

The *fiesta* that followed was dedicated to María Santísima, and the shell was placed at the feet of her picture in the Church of Guadalupe, on the island of Tinian, otherwise called Buenavista Mariana.

What most pleased the fathers was that all the reconciled passed in the procession, repeating after Father Medina the Act of Contrition with a great show of feeling.

Father San Vitores, leading the natives of Sungharon, advanced to meet them. He carried the cross that had been damaged by the stones that the villagers had thrown on a former day. They now fell on their knees before it, beating their breasts and repeating the Act of Contrition, saying they were sorry for having injured the *babao,* or standard, of God. To make amends to the holy cross in the very place where they had insulted it, they called the field "the field of Santa Cruz," and afterwards built there the Chapel of Our Lady of Peace, in order that the chapel might become a fortification, protecting the peace won there between the two warring bands on January 24, 1670. And although the natives of Marpo had only one large shell, while those of Sungharon brought several, they were all satisfied, because the men of Marpo had, in all humility, offered their shell to the Virgin.

They promised one another that on their land they would build a church and dedicate it to the Blessed Virgin, and Father Luis de Medina helped to cut the wood for the church of Marpo before he left for the island of Saipan, on January 27, 1670. He was in haste to return to Saipan for the baptism of many children, or perhaps he was urged in that direction by God, to reward him for all his labors by the crown that awaited him on that island.

A few days after arriving on Saipan (and having visited several of those villages that were most in need) with a companion whose name was Hipólito de la Cruz, in search of children to baptize, they both found the crown of martyrdom on January 21, 1671,[151] as we shall say more in detail in our brief biography of Father Medina,[152] whose eulogy we defer reluctantly since he was the first of the Society of Jesus to merit the martyr's palm [in the Marianas], the Marianas he had watered with his sweat and blood, being himself totally *Mariano* in the purity of his life, in his devotion, and in his zeal to gain souls for Jesus.

There is no doubt that Father San Vitores had a revelation from heaven as to what awaited his fortunate companion, because in the days preceding Father Medina's death, Father San Vitores seemed to be preparing him for martyrdom, showing him in what it consisted and praising its excellence, asking if he might share in his labors and work, and advising him to say the prayer composed by Father Charles Spinola to obtain the grace of martyrdom.[153] Father Medina said it every day, asking God for this grace, through the merit of Father San Vitores. The latter, when he heard of his death, sent some lay assistants to look for his body, which he received on the beach on Tinian with a *Te Deum.* He

---

[151] The date in the text is a misprint. It should read 1670, for as clearly stated elsewhere, Father Medina left Saipan in January 1670, and a few days later was killed with his companion and assistant Hipólito de la Cruz. (M.H.)

[152] See Book 5, chapter 5.

[153] Blessed Charles Spinola, S.J., martyr in Japan.

venerated it as he would a true martyr of Christ, with expressions of the deepest feeling, commending himself to him in his prayers, and never ceasing in his praise of his beloved companion. Nor was Father San Vitores without his own martyrdom, the cares, the weariness, the hardships, and the risks, that nurtured the desire to die for Christ and to quiet the holy envy that he had for his companion when he thought of his happy death. For two months after the barbarians had been quieted, with their usual capriciousness, they were back in a fighting mood, when the villagers of one side killed one of the other crowd, and these burnt a village as a form of vengeance, so far were they from the path of our Chapel of Our Lady of Peace.

Father San Vitores now saw that all Christianity was in grave danger, and that particularly his little *Escuadrón Mariano*, which was the bodyguard of the Faith in all the Marianas, was now in grave peril. The people of Marpo wished to destroy it by every possible means. By night, the men of Marpo tried all manner of attack on the village of Sungharon, hoping to burn the village and our residence as well. They posted their sentinels and animated the populace, promising them a happy outcome.

Knowing though he did, that the people of Marpo were determined to kill him, Father San Vitores went among them, walking from one village to another, trying to calm them with his counsel, taking no notice of the burning sun, the rains, storms, and thousands of other discomforts, without food, drink, or sleep.

These hardships, together with the severe penances he practiced in order that God might grant peace, brought on a fever from which he was nearly prostrated, but through which he continued walking and laboring for nine days. Nor did he discontinue his penance, until at last his weak body could no longer follow the desires of his spirit, and he fell on the hard earth, which, with no more than a straw mat, served as his bed in a poor cabin to which he was carried by the natives who accompanied him.

From this place, which was far from the fort of the Spaniards, he aided his soldiers, because although his body was absent, he was with them in spirit and saw all that happened in the camp.

He knew through divine revelation that the men of Marpo were approaching our trenches, hoping to take our men off guard and seize their arms. He wrote to *don* Juan de Santa Cruz, and having no one at hand to send, he tied the paper to the collar of his little dog, telling him to carry it to *don* Juan. The obedient messenger set out at once and, after running several leagues, arrived at the camp of the *Mariano* army and went at once to *don* Juan who, seeing the paper, opened it and understood the treachery of the enemy. Because they were about to put their plan into action, he fired the field piece and two muskets, giving them only a light charge, because his object was to frighten them rather than kill them. But the shots did not go into the air as they had done at other times[154] because it was necessary that they know that our arms were not just thunder, but also lightning as they now knew. One was killed and

---

[154]Father San Vitores had ordered the soldiers to fire into the air lest they hurt the *Marianos*.

*The Pacification of the Island of Tinian and Some Miraculous Happenings*

another, the prime mover in the war, was wounded, and was finished off by a Pampango boy of little more than twelve years, named Andrés de la Cruz. Others were attacked with much courage by another little Spaniard, called Diego Bazán, a native of Mexico. Captain *don* Juan de la Cruz encouraged them all to action.[155]

The enemy forces were so prostrated and so disheartened by the thunder of our arms and the few losses in their ranks that they had neither hands with which to fight nor feet on which to flee. If our men were not likewise men of peace, they could have made that day a great slaughter.

Father San Vitores wrote later:

> God was pleased with this first demonstration, which is the just punishment of the enemy by those *guirragos*, for thus in this land they call our Spaniards and other foreigners or men from beyond the sea. The natives of this and other islands were afraid of our arms, and they were surprised that they were much more than noise, and that infractions against the Law of God and the good customs that we taught them did not go unpunished. But when they ceased hostilities among themselves, they lost most of this fear, because when the natives of Marpo joined with the enemies of Sungharon, where the church and house of our companions are located, the rumor was circulated that all the *guirragos* had gone. (Some of our companions were absent for four days, by reason of a journey to Saipan, as we shall see later.) But before they arrived at our village, they heard the sound of our bugle, and realizing that not all the *guirragos* had gone but that two or three still were there, as well as one *pequi* (*pake*, musket), for this is the name they give to firearms, they retired at once and returned to their villages, not daring to attack ours, because of the said fear. What would it be like if we had on each island, even if not in each village, men and arms competent to introduce such a healthy fear, with justice and government as necessary here as elsewhere, as much to prevent barbarous wars, as well as incest and other abominable sins that exist in the most ancient and civilized Christian communities if they lack, at any time, the fear of justice and force to restrain and punish wrongdoers.
>
> The fact that this fortunate demonstration of our arms was thus delayed and did not take place sooner appears to have been a special and loving providence of our Lord, whom it pleased that there should never be lacking to this Mariana mission, in its beginnings, the glory of those first missions that His Divine Majesty founded on his holy apostles, with no more arms or escort than sheep among wolves, and gave them the opportunity to shed their blood for the Faith. So also, the Lord has willed that these new evangelical fields be irrigated by the blood of martyrs, as the most flourishing churches in all Christendom have been fertilized.

---

[155]Diego Bazán. See Book 3, chap. 16:247 ss.

*Book Three, Chapter 11*

And he arranged also that he who had most distinguished himself in the service of the Blessed Virgin in the first battle, which was a truly Marian victory, should soon receive the reward of his labors. This batttle was a battle of peace for these poor people, as it meant war against the princes of darkness, the thieves and tyrants of these islands.

Soon after Father San Vitores dispatched the dog with the message for *don* Juan de la Cruz, *don* Francisco de Mendoza, an interpreter, arrived at his hut from one of the villages, where he had learned the plans of the men of Marpo. He came to speak in secret with Father San Vitores and found him in a strange ecstatic state, lying on his bed, which was suspended in mid-air three feet from the ground, surrounded by a great splendor, which the eyes of *don* Francisco could not suffer. He ran out, frightened and filled with reverential awe.

He entered the hut after a long interval and found the father enveloped in rapture, his face glowing like a flame. *Don* Francisco told him of the danger to our men and of the enemies' plans, and Father San Vitores answered, "Calm yourself, *don* Francisco, we have already won by the help of the Blessed Virgin, Saint Francis Xavier, and Father Marcello Mastrilli." God had shown him, from afar, the victory that our soldiers were to win; Saint Francis Xavier, it is believed, revealing it to him, as in years past God revealed to the holy Apostle of the Indies the victory that the Portuguese won over the Azenos.

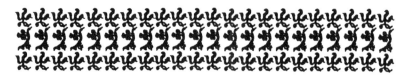

# CHAPTER XII

*He Returns to the Island of Guam and
Sets Admirable Examples*

While in the state of ecstasy before mentioned, Father San Vitores saw many things that were to occur in the future: that he was not to die of the disease from which he constantly suffered; that *don* Juan de Santa Cruz would fall ill, but would soon recover; that he himself would be a martyr on the island of San Juan (Guam).

Thus, knowledge was the answer to the affectionate pleas that they had heard him make to the Blessed Virgin Mary, as he lay in his miserable hut. At that moment he believed that his life was drawing to an end, and he feared that he would die without shedding his blood for the Lord. He said to the Queen of Angels, who fortunately was present to him, "This is not our plan. This is not what you promised me, most Holy Virgin." Words that show that the Mother of God had promised previously that he would give his life for her Son. This was now confirmed as she showed him the place of his future martyrdom.

Because of this, he made all haste in returning to the island of Guam, which he looked upon now with a special affection as the scene of his final battle and victory, for he was to overtake the devil and death itself, dying for the Faith he preached. And after he arrived again on Guam, he did not wish to leave it again to visit other islands and went to Zarpana for two months for the reason that I shall soon explain.

Leaving Tinian pacified, he returned to Guam in May 1670. And as one who knew that there remained to him but little time, he hastened to tread the path of perfection, giving examples of virtue and particularly of charity and mortification in order to better merit the promised crown.

One of the fathers returned to the residence in Agadña very ill. For his own mortification and that of others, he was covered with open sores, from which there ran continually a filthy and ill-smelling humor, which offended the sight as well as the olfactory sense. And although there was another whose duty it was to act as nurse, Father San Vitores took that office upon himself during every moment that he was free from his duties of instructing children and adults.

It occurred that when the sick man's shirt was changed, it was so repugnant that the other attendant would not touch it, even though he was a good and charitable man. But the Venerable Father, wanting to overcome in himself all repugnance, took the shirt, and going to another room, put it on secretly, though there was no concealing that mortification.

When he returned to the sickroom, the patient begged Father San Vitores to lay his hands on him, hoping, and with good reason, that he could restore health to the sick as Christ did. The Venerable Father replied, confused and embarrassed, "My hands, of themselves, are worth

*Book Three, Chapter 12*

nothing, unless, because they are the Superior's hands, they possess some virtue of those of Christ." He laid his hands on the sick man, and to dissimulate his part in the miracle, he applied a signature of Venerable Father Luis de Medina to the patient, bidding him have great confidence, and immediately his health was restored.

He realized how important it was that the Faith strike deep roots here, because soon would come the time of storms and persecutions. He walked up and down Agadña every day, teaching the ignorant, strengthening the weak ones, and inviting all to hear the sermon he preached in the church every morning with great fervor and spirit.

At the end of the sermon, he reminded them of the religion lesson he gave each evening when the people returned from the fields, terminating the service with the rosary and the Litany of Our Lady and the Act of Contrition.

God wished also to convince these islanders by means of miracles, in order that they might realize the emptiness of the superstition in which they had been brought up and the truth and excellence of the religion that the Venerable Father taught them.

During the month of June of this year (1670), there was a great drought, and all the crops were on the point of destruction. The suffering *Marianos*, still attached to their old customs, turned to the *macanas* and asked them to invoke the *anites* by means of the skulls "of the rain", as they call those, that dedicated to the devil, are thought to produce rain. They keep them in their houses and through them pray for rain. They call this *maran anuchan*, which means "a miraculous thing for rain," a name they also apply to the skulls.

Father San Vitores heard of this and went in haste to the place where the people had gathered, and taking in his hand the crucifix that he always carried, he fell to his knees and intoned a devout supplication that he had composed in verse in the language of the *Marianos*, a prayer for water and all the spiritual and temporal benefits that might be desired.

Soon all the natives knelt, repeating what the father was chanting. Then he gave them a fervent talk, berating them for their inconstancy and infidelity, exhorting them to repentance, warning them not to invoke the *anites*, or demons, who could give them neither water nor anything else and could only carry them to hell to suffer every sort of misery. Let them turn to the Creator of heaven and earth, who because he had made them to his image and likeness, would take pity on them in their need and would attend quickly to their petitions, if they themselves did not prevent it by their faults.

The *Marianos* were remorseful and begged God for pardon, and Father San Vitores promised that it would rain on the following day (it was then six o'clock in the evening) if they gave him their word to attend Mass on the next morning and to pray to our Lord in the Blessed Sacrament for rain. They all promised and said, "God is good. He will make the heavens rain."

That night the Venerable Father prayed fervently and the following morning at daybreak it began to rain heavily. The *Marianos* ran

226

## He Returns to the Island of Guam and Sets Admirable Examples

to the church, surprised and happy, praising God, who through the efforts of the Great Father, had given them rain. And those who at that time were only catechumens begged for baptism.

Because of the illness of the missionary father on the island of Rota, and because of some trouble among the nobles of that island, it was necessary for Father San Vitores to pay a visit there in January 1671.

He visited all the villages on Rota and accomplished a prodigious amount of work. He had many times to slide down steep hillsides, often in danger of plunging headlong. Hunger and thirst, weariness,and danger were his inseparable companions, but the harvest was as great as the hardship, since he made peace between the chiefs and added a great number of children and adults to the flock of the Church.

A serious problem awaited him on his return to Guam. Some of his lay companions, who had formerly helped in the cultivation of the vineyard of the Lord, desirous of freedom, had fled to certain apostate villages. (These people had risen against the Spaniards in his absence.)

He regretted the loss of his soldiers, and much more that they were losing their souls and could cause the loss of others. He offered prayers and penances and asked the other fathers to do likewise. Then he sought a messenger and wrote letters full of affection to persuade them to return to the camp of Jesus Christ, whose soldiers they were, and not to cast a stain upon their honor and conscience. Now they could erase by tears of penance what later they must pay for in eternal fire. They should remember how long they had served the Faith and should not seek to lose it, and not to increase the number of the infidels and scandalize those Christians to whom they themselves had once been an example. He wrote that human weakness was not unknown to him and that he could forgive them; nor were they shut out from the love of God, who would receive them with all compassion if they came back repentant.

Believing in the kindness of Father San Vitores, the men returned to his side, sorry for what they had done. He received them with open arms and embraced them with joy, like that of the angels in heaven, for their repentance.[156]

But in order that his gentleness might not cause them to think too lightly of their offense, he bared his back and began to scourge himself with a discipline made of steel disks, until he was bathed in his own blood, until they, confused and repentant, took it from his hands. But he said to them, "My sons, among ourselves we have to satisfy God for this sin. You will go to confession and repent in your hearts, but I will suffer the punishment and the penance."

And knowing that idleness was the occasion for their errors, he placed them as apprentices to other soldiers who had responsible offices, to the end that their work might keep their thoughts well occupied and away from vice. He tried also, in that nation devoid of the arts, to teach them by example and experience the useful necessary duties of their country.

---

[156]Luke 15:7.

The Venerable Father celebrated Lent of this year (1671) with even greater devotion and solemnity than before, for now the Faith was becoming well established, while the piety of the new Christians had increased. After Lent he went to visit certain villages of this island in which difficulties had begun to manifest themselves, as we shall later explain.

Returning to Agadña, he began to prepare his account of all that had taken place in the two preceding years. Our father general had ordered this, in order that news of the copious harvest already reaped might call more workmen to that vineyard of the Lord, and in order that those who were giving alms for this work of God might be consoled, seeing it well in hand.

The ship *Nuestra Señora del Buen Socorro* arrived on June 9, 1671, and brought to this mission the succor of which it stood in great need, that is, soldiers, who were sent by Her Majesty, through the providence of the Lord, who saw how greatly they would soon be needed. It also brought spiritual consolation, because His Holiness Clement IX sent a brief to the Servant of God, in which he gave him and all the Christian community his paternal blessing, praising his zeal and that of his companions, urging them to continue as they had begun.

Also, to increase the devotion of the neophytes, he sent a large box of blessed crosses, medals, and *Agnus Deis*, with many privileges and indulgences. All these the apostolic father received with great veneration and consolation, knowing that his labors were approved by the Supreme Pastor, hoping that with this blessing the harvest of the gospel would continue to grow, which the Lord had blessed with a generous hand, so that there were already more than 30,000 baptized persons.

# CHAPTER XIII

*New Companions Arrive to Join Father San Vitores,*
*and How He Sends Three Marianos to Manila*

The ship *Buen Socorro* [June 9, 1671] brought four new fathers to Guam. They were Father Francisco Ezquerra,[157] who was later privileged to shed his blood for Christ; Father Francisco Solano;[158] Father Alonzo López;[159] and Father Diego de Noriega.[160] The two former came here from the Philippines by way of Mexico, where they were joined by the others. And although four ministers came, the mission was only increased by one, since the other three relieved Father Pedro de Casanova,[161] Father Luis de Morales,[162] and Father Lorenzo Bustillos,[163] who went on the same ship to the Philippines, in accordance with an order from the father provincial of the Philippines and with the willing consent of Father San Vitores, who had promised them when they came to the Marianas that they would remain only until others came to relieve them.

It is impossible to say how sad those three fathers were at leaving their beloved Father San Vitores, as well as the children whom they had brought into the world of the gospel, and at leaving those islands where they had hoped to gain the crown of martyrdom that others had obtained here. Nor can one imagine the grief of Father San Vitores, who sacrificed his love to obedience and his zeal to that zeal itself, sending away those companions whom he sorely needed, in order that they might be even more apt as a result of the studies that awaited them.

With these three fathers he also sent three *Marianos* to Manila—I do not know whether as three examples of the harvest in the Promised Land or as the Three Kings—to adore the Lord in an old established

---

[157]Francisco Ezquerra, S.J., was born in Manila in 1644 and was member of a distinguished family. His uncle, Domingo Ezquerra, S.J., was provincial of the Jesuits in the Philippine Province when Father San Vitores left for the Mission of the Marianas. He had a brother who was also a member of the Society, Juan Ezquerra, S.J. His father was General *don* Juan Ezquerra, who held numerous posts of importance under the Spanish Crown. (M.H.)

[158]Francisco Solano, S.J., was born in Jarandilla, Spain, and received his education in the Jesuit *colegio* of Oropesa. He arrived in the Marianas on June 9, 1671. After the death of Father San Vitores, he served as superior of the mission. (M.H.) He died on June 13, 1672 of tuberculosis, which was already very advanced when he sailed from Mexico to the Marianas.

[159]Very little information is available about Alonso López, S.J. He served the mission in the northern islands of the Marianas and drew the first reliable map of these islands. This map, together with certain writings of Father Luis de Morales served as the book published in France in 1752 with the title: *Les Isles Marianes Sur Les Cartes du P. Alonzo López*, by J. N. Bellin, French hydrographic engineer.

[160]Diego de Noriega, S.J. This missionary arrived in Guam very ill of tuberculosis. His superiors sent him to Guam, hoping the climate would benefit his health, but he declined rapidly and died in Agaña, January 13, 1672. (M.H.)

[161]Pedro de Casanova, S.J., was born in Vélez el Blanco, Spain, on August 26, 1641. He entered the Society in 1658 and came to the Marianas ten years later with Father San Vitores. He was the first missionary to Rota. When, in 1694, he was en route to Madrid to assume his newly assigned duties as *Procurador de la Provincia en Madrid y Roma*, he was lost in the wreck of the Galleon *San José*.(M.H.)

[162]Luis de Morales, S.J., was born in Tordesillas, Spain, in 1641. He entered the Society in 1658 and after some years of study in Salamanca, he went to Mexico where he met Father San Vitores and joined his group of missionaries, who were preparing to embark for the Marianas. He labored in these islands for three years, after which in obedience to orders from the provincial in Manila, he went to Spain, then returned again to Manila, where, while serving as rector in the Jesuit College in that city, he died on June 14, 1716. (M.H.)

[163]Lorenzo Bustillos, S.J., was born in Burgos on August 18, 1642. He entered the Society in 1664. He arrived in Guam in 1668 and was several times rector of the College of San Juan de Letrán in Agaña. It is said that he applied himself vigorously to the study of the Chamorro language, and that he attained proficiency in its use, and that through the elegance of his speech, he was able to persuade the islanders to accept Christianity. (M.H.)

Christian community. There, they might see the grandeur of the temples, the majesty of the divine cult, and the life of good Christians, and they might return to Guam, telling what they had seen to those who believed their land to be the first in the world because of their ignorance of other countries.

The three *Marianos*, baptized a short time before by Father San Vitores, were nobles who were held in high esteem, heirs to important lands, with which they live in as much content and vanity as do the titled ones and grandees of Spain with their honors and riches.

Their names after baptism were *don* Ignacio Osi, *don* Pedro Guirán, and *don* Matías Yay. And now, we shall follow their progress, leaving Father San Vitores in the Marianas, working and suffering for the glory of God and the good of souls.

They sailed from Guam on July 13, 1671, in the galleon *Nuestra Señora del Buen Socorro*, and after some delays and the ordinary accidents of navigation, they arrived at Manila, July 31, 1671, the Feast of our Father Saint Ignatius.

They were cared for in our *colegio* with more love than magnificence, although to them even the simplest things seemed magnificent, because of the poverty to which they were accustomed in their own country. They visited the governor, who received them with hospitality and with honors appropriate to what they believed themselves to be.

What was notable about the visit was their lack of self-consciousness, for they went about with no more concern than if they were among their own people, and with a certain air of magnanimity and courtesy that bespoke nobility in spite of their barbarity. No less admirable was the zeal with which, on their own initiative, they affectionately complained to the governor that he did not send soldiers to control lawless people who stand in the way of people who desire to receive the Law of God. They added that for this lack of control certain barbarous men had taken the lives of a holy father and of six companions of his, which could not have happened if there has been anyone to fear.

The governor treated them kindly, praising their zeal and assuring them that his desires were the same as their own, and that he would take measures that the Faith might be extended to all the islands without any dangers to the fathers.

During the time these men were in Manila, they visited the churches, admiring their construction, decoration, and riches. They were even more impressed by the vestments and solemnity with which the Divine Offices were celebrated, and by the devotion with which the older Christians received the sacraments in our church (one tried to keep them apart from people who would scandalize them). But even more did the old Christians admire the devotion of these new ones, who, only a short time before, did not even know there is a God, but now confessed and received Communion with great reverence and humility, showing in their outward demeanor a great devotion to the Faith.

They remained more than an hour on their knees in front of the high altar before confession, which they made with many tears and, after Communion, remained another hour giving thanks, quite immobile and forgetting all else, so recollected that they would not turn their heads for any noise or accident that might occur.

They liked to watch the baptism of children, their minds dwelling on the beauty that those souls received by means of that sacrament, as they had been told by Father San Vitores. But what attracted them most and moved them most deeply were the processions and *pasos* of the Passion of Christ that they witnessed during Holy Week.

They burst into tears at the sight of the sad and devout mysteries, and they said with sighs that Christ must have much love for all men, suffering so much for them. They said it was a great pity there were so few fathers in their land to teach the people these things that now they are witnessing, that they too might know and adore a God to whom they owed so much and could go to see in heaven and not fall like blind men into hell, where they could burn with devils in perpetual fire. Withal, in all their acts and words, in their exterior appearance and their inward consciousness, they showed that they had been well instructed and baptized by Father San Vitores, whom they praised wherever they went, assuming that everyone knew him, and whoever said he did not seemed to them to be exaggerating.

*Don* Matías was so pleased with the quiet manner of life in Manila that he determined not to return to his own land, where people lived barbarously. *Don* Ignacio and *don* Pedro would also have remained with him had not the fathers, in order to prevent frustration of their original plans, persuaded the two to return to the Marianas to help the ministers in the conversion of the natives, passing on to others the light they had received, in order not to be misers of the riches and compassion of the Lord.

*Don* Ignacio and *don* Pedro sailed aboard the galleon *San Telmo* in the year 1672 with Father Juan de Landa, who was on his way to Rome as procurator of the Province of the Philippines. When the ship was forced by contrary winds to return to Manila, they reembarked in 1673 on the *Buen Socorro*. Twenty leagues out from Manila, there being no wind, the ship anchored near an island and *don* Ignacio went ashore. Meanwhile the wind began to blow and the ship put out to sea leaving *don* Ignacio. He returned to Manila in a small boat, taking a month for the voyage. And it was a providence of the Lord, who wished to save his life, for Father Juan de Landa and *don* Pedro Guirán were lost off the coast of New Spain in terrible weather. *Don* Pedro ended his embassy in a happier manner, as we may hope, since God rewarded his zealous desire to bring new light to his country by showing him the eternal brightness of heaven.

The two *Marianos* who remained in Manila, *don* Ignacio and *don* Matías, sailed, at last, from Cavite on June 5, 1674, with Father Lorenzo Bustillos, who had brought them to Manila and now, having completed his studies, was returning to the Marianas. Seventy leagues out from

Manila they met the *Buen Socorro*, then returning to Manila, and from it they learned of the death of Father Landa and *don* Pedro Guirán, who was the brother of *don* Matias.

Father Bustillos was sad at receiving this news, and when the two *Marianos* heard of it, they went to him and said these words, "Father, what can we do but have patience, even though Pedro has died? And as God has willed it thus, we shall console ourselves with his will, with which we are content, because we believe that Pedro's death has pleased God, who is our Father and Lord and knows better than we what is best for us, and for this we should give thanks, for it is a sign that he remembers us. And we should pray that if perhaps Pedro is in purgatory, he be relieved of suffering and taken to heaven soon. And thus, my Father," added *don* Matías, "I do not mourn that my brother has died, for it was the will of God and we all must die. What worries me is whether there was anyone present to hear his confession and give him Communion and the sacrament of the sick, because Father Landa died first."

To this Father Bustillos answered that no doubt there was someone present to give the last sacraments, for there were some Franciscan fathers on board and some of other orders. With this the two *Marianos* were consoled. In three years they had acquired the true sentiments of Christians of long standing.

They arrived at Acapulco on January 13, 1675, and in Mexico City on January 31. Three leagues from the latter city, Father Vidal came out to meet them. He was then procurator in Mexico for the Mariana Islands. He came out in a coach, which they called "ship of the land" and praised the ingenuity of the one who had invented it. They were received in our *colegio* as the first fruits of Mariana Christianity and as sent by Father San Vitores, and for both reasons they were for our people and for others the objects of much esteem and affection.

In Mexico, the *Marianos* admired, and with greater reason, those things that had attracted their attention in Manila, the wealth and grandeur of the city, the great edifices, and the temples, wondering how they and their people could once have believed that there was no other land than Guam and no other city than Agadña.

On the second day they went to visit Archbishop-Viceroy *don fray* Payo de Rivera. Kneeling before him, they asked of him the same favor they had requested of the governor of the Philippines, saying that as they were vassals of the king, they wished His Excellency might send to Guam a captain or other officer with soldiers, who would form a military government, or *presidio*, as they had seen in Manila, to punish the cruel, godless men who had taken the lives of the preachers of the holy Law (they already knew of the death of Father San Vitores), as a guard and defense of good Christians, as a source of fear and deterence to evil men who neither wish to become Christians themselves nor will allow others to do so.

The archbishop was deeply touched by their plea, and embracing them, promised in the name of the king that he would do as they asked.

In a similar manner they were received by the *señores oidores* (judges), who asked them many questions about their country and Father San Vitores, to which they responded praising the holiness and charity of the Great Father.

Many times, they said, looking in wonder at the houses that the Society of Jesus has in Mexico: "Truly the order of the Society of Jesus has had pity, charity, and compassion for our souls. Leaving the comfort of their own houses, they have come to our land to suffer such hardships, even to give their lives at the hands of a mad and barbarous people in order to give them eternal life, baptizing them, and sending them to heaven. We owe much to the fathers of the Society and especially to our holy Father San Vitores for having been the cause of our salvation and of this mercy shown us."

The fathers wanted to send one of the *Marianos* to Madrid to present him to the king as the first gold of the only kind that was to be found in the Marianas. But it seemed to be better service to God if both of them returned to the Marianas, since people there were saying they had been killed by the Spaniards, since their absence was so long. It seemed better to send them back to preach to their own people, who they said were senseless and stupid and condemned to eternal fire for not having believed those things about God and his Mother.

The day they left Mexico City for Acapulco, they went to confession and received Communion. They spent more than two hours hearing Mass and making a thanksgiving and praying for a good voyage.

The fathers gave them many garments of silk and other materials, in order that they might set out for their own country feeling that they could give a more convincing account of the charity and love that the Spaniards had for them. They promised to return to Mexico when they had given an account to their own people concerning the wonders of the Christian world that they had seen. In this manner they went to Acapulco, where we shall leave them, for we have no other news about them.

We shall return to Father San Vitores and to the month of June 1671, in which we left him in the Marianas at the time that four fathers had arrived from Mexico and three others went on from Guam to the Philippines.

# CHAPTER XIV

*The Origin of the Great War on Guam,*
*and How it is Prophesied in Mexico by the Beads of Sweat*
*on a Statue of Saint Francis Xavier*

Father San Vitores first prepared his new companions for their new life by the spiritual exercises of our father, Saint Ignatius, and then assigned them to the several islands. He sent Father Francisco Ezquerra to accompany Father Tomás Cardeñoso, and Father Francisco Solano went with Father Alonso López. He gave them interpreters because they did not know the language. And because Father Diego de Noriega was ill, he kept him in Agadña.

But soon it was necessary to recall everyone to the residence in Agadña, and he sent in all haste for Father Ezquerra and Father Cardeñoso, who were already embarked, by reason of the cruel war that the common enemy of man had started in retaliation for the battle Father San Vitores had fought against him and of whose great labors he was well aware. At this time a statue of Saint Francis Xavier in Mexico City foretold it by the sweat on its face and other marvels, as the *Processus* in Mexico records on the evidence of eyewitnesses.

It happened in the month of March of this year, 1671, in the Colegio Real de San Ildefonso, in the City of Mexico, a *colegio* of the Society of Jesus. Two of the students named Pedro Vidarte and Maximiliano Pio entered the chapel to say their prayers. They looked up at the painting of Saint Francis Xavier that was on the high altar among other pictures of saints, and they noticed that the face of the holy apostle was sending out flames as if it were on fire. They came closer, saw that it was sweating, changing its warm colors into a heavy pallor. Surprised, they called Father José Vidal, who was the rector of the *colegio*. The sound of their discussion brought all the other students and a teacher of theirs, Father Prudencio Mesa, who swore by his honor as a priest, that for several days, while saying Mass, he saw the sweat on the picture, but he did not examine it, thinking it was bits of silver or tinsel sticking to the picture.

Father Mesa put on a surplice and wiped the face with some cotton, and everyone watched carefully to see if that "sweat" could have arisen from the humidity, but they could find no natural cause for it, since all the surrounding pictures were perfectly dry. This sweating continued for several days, and the face retained its extreme pallor, which differed so markedly from the natural color of the hands. For greater veneration, this miraculous picture was moved to our Colegio de San Pedro y San Pablo, to the patronal chapel, and copies of the picture were made by persons devoted to the apostle. Because they could find no natural cause for the sweating, there was a persistent belief that Father

# The Origin of the Great War on Guam

San Vitores was suffering some exceptional hardships in the Marianas, and that this caused a show of emotion in the lifeless image of the holy Apostle of the Indies, whose living image Father San Vitores was. And they were not mistaken, because, at that very time, the disturbances began, the first stage of war on Guam, the worst the Christian community and the fathers suffered in those islands, unless the miracle was also a premonition of the blessed martyrdom that happened a year later. We shall now tell of the beginning and reasons for that war.

Certain villages of the island of Guam were uneasy, and there was unrest because of the natural inconstancy of the islanders, who change just for the sake of change and because their shoulders, unaccustomed to the weight of law or reason, felt the yoke of Christ too heavy, although it is light and easy for those who love him.

The *macanas* helped to agitate and increase the tempest, angry as they were, because Father San Vitores had deprived them of the authority and veneration they had formerly enjoyed, revealing the futility of invoking the *anites*, as they called them.

The *macanas* threatened the people with drought and sterility in the fields and in the sea, sicknesses, and every type of evil and misfortune, if they did not throw the strangers out of their country.

More than any other, there was a highly respected noble of the village of Agadña, called Hurao, who, because of their respect for him, wielded a powerful influence in favor of the *macanas*.

And although Father San Vitores knew the evil Hurao and his followers had caused at the time that the *Buen Socorro* was at Guam, the father sought to quiet the agitators through fear of the Spaniards who were on board the ship.

He forgave them, and because, with their guilty consciences, they were reluctant to go on board the ship, he accompanied them for their protection, and had the general of the ship give them presents and treat them with kindness instead of punishing them as they deserved. Hurao was especially well treated and was given twice as many gifts as the others, in the hope of overcoming evil with good and of placing under obligation to Christian charity those who were Christians in name only.

But the result was that Hurao and his companions became even more insolent than before, as cowards are accustomed to do when treated with benevolence, and they again broke the peace more dangerously than ever on the occasion that I will now narrate.

Father San Vitores had sent a boy named Joseph Peralta, of the village of Los Angeles,[164] to cut a quantity of crosses to be placed in the houses of the new Christians. He set out on July 23 to cut wood from which to make them, and some *Indios* who lay in ambush, out of greed—not to attribute it to some higher motive—for a knife he had and a machete, fell on him and killed him, wounding him eighteen times.

He was somewhat to blame for his own death, in that he had gone out without a companion, contrary to the general order of Father San Vitores, who had told them never to leave the house alone, and in

---

[164]Puebla de los Angeles, Mexico, now Puebla.

235

that he had that wretched knife and a machete, provoking the greed of the *Indios* who highly prize that weapon. But because his error was born of simplicity and not malice, and because he had gone to confession on the previous day, God, who had prepared him for death, took him in the laudable employment of the service of the cross, after much service to the Faith during the three years he had assisted the ministers of the gospel. These assurances of his salvation were a great consolation to his companions, even in the lamentable occurence of his death.

The treachery of the murderers and the sorry sight of the dead body caused a just grief in the other soldiers, but they did not wish to punish the crime by military measures. Civil justice, they thought, might avoid further disturbance. Hence, by order of the sergeant major, *don* Juan de Santiago,[165] several people of Agadña (where the murder occurred) were arrested, together with others from more distant parts who seemed to be involved. And although the Spaniards proceeded justly and freed without punishment those who proved innocent, the barbarians were so greatly offended by justice, to which they were strangers, that they behaved as if they would rather be killed without trial than be arrested and examined.

The people of Agadña then began to reclaim their former liberty and impunity for crimes, which the foreigners had tried to take away from them, calling those men tyrants who tried to prevent their tyranny. It was no use to try to explain to them the great benefits of justice, which would protect their lives, guard their property, make their homes safe, and bring them peace, relieving them of the need of war, involving many for the punishment of the one individual, in which the innocent suffer for the guilty, while the winners are more insolent than ever and ready to do further harm.

The barbarians could not understand these arguments, preferring the evil to which they were accustomed to the good that they rejected, believing it to be intolerable slavery to submit to any law whatsoever.

The death of a noble named Guafac in the mountains made matters worse. He was killed by a Spaniard, while going with a group of soldiers to seize an accomplice in the murder of young Peralta. This noble and some of his neighbors attacked the soldiers and tried to protect the culprit. One of the Spaniards accidentally killed Guafac. The result of this affair was that 2,000 people from Agadña and surrounding settlements joined to oppose the Spaniards. The rest of the islanders remained neutral, unable to help our men for fear of their own people, nor their compatriots for fear of the Spaniards or for love of the fathers.

We should not fail to mention our gratitude to a good *Indio* called Ayhi, whose baptismal name was Antonio, out of respect for *don* Antonio Nieto, who brought the fathers to these islands and was godfather to a son of his who went to heaven before he was two years old. His father fell a little short of going with him. One day he was reproving a *macana* for the diabolical impiety with which he invoked the *anites*,

---

[165]This is evidently a misprint in the Spanish text. The sergeant major (*sargento mayor*) at this time (1671) was *don* Juan de Santa Cruz. *Don* Juan de Santiago did not arrive on Guam until May 1672. (M.H.)

when the sorcerer turned on him and seized his throat, tearing it with his nails and leaving him with the scars of the *macana's* impiety, which are now the signs of the Faith and Christianity of the good Antonio. He avoided all signs of friendship with the Spaniards, the better to help them without doing harm to himself.

Through him the Spaniards learned the plan of their enemies, which was to do away with the fathers and the other Spaniards, once and for all, and free their land of the foreigners who were trying to give them laws and deprive them of their liberty.

It would have been very easy to execute this design if the fathers had been scattered among the missions as they had once been. But Divine Providence willed that they were all in Agadña, with the exception of one father and a few companions. There had been no time to bring them back. Thus they were able to help one another, and thus was saved the *Escuadrón Mariano* (*Mariano* Corps), religious and lay, that preached and defended the Faith in these islands.

# CHAPTER XV

*The War of the Marianos and the Victory of the Spaniards
Due to the Prayers of the Servant of God*

The Spaniards had been in these islands three years (1668-1671), during which time they had sufficient experience of the infidelity and treachery of the islanders. Yet they had not erected any castle or fort to defend themselves against their violence. This they suffered in order to show more clearly that our law is one of peace, and that they had not come to their land to make war, although they showed no fear of it.

But now, seeing two thousand men in campaign with arms, it was necessary for our men to make some kind of fortification, which the barbarians gave them time to do as they spent much time sending messages and embassies, assembling their friends for the war.

The Spaniards surrounded the church and residence with a stockade of trees and branches. On the side toward the sea, on a point overlooking the beach, a tower was raised, which Father San Vitores named *Castillo de Santa María y Santiago*. He placed in it—to serve as *castellana* and guard of the castle—a picture of the Immaculate Conception that had been blessed by the archbishop and which he had brought from Manila.

On the side toward the mountain, another tower was built and was called *Castillo de San Francisco Xavier*, where the gun was placed that remained from the shipwreck that had cast Choco on these shores, the man who was the origin of all these wars and persecutions.

The soldiers, of whom there were thirty-one, were assigned to their posts. There were twelve Spaniards among them and nineteen Filipinos, some with bows and arrows, others with firearms. The greatest precaution was the confession and Communion with which Father San Vitores armed them all, encouraging them to be brave in a good cause. No one could fail to have God on his side who fought for his glory, and to one who has God, the whole world of men and devils is as nothing.

A consultation was held to discuss the best manner to proceed, and it appeared best for the soldiers to seize Hurao, the chief mover of the war, to make the barbarians fear them, showing at the same time that they had no fear of the barbarians, for threatened with a war, they began by taking prisoners, and above all, to take one who would cause the enemy to sue for peace.

The plan was put into execution, although it did not work out as simply as was expected, for the *Marianos* were more astute in their treachery than their barbarous condition would seem to promise. As soon as Hurao was taken prisoner, half the population of Agadña, who were his relatives and dependents, pretended repentance, hoping thus to save Hurao from his merited punishment and to assure the safety of those in prison. But at the same time that they were pretending to want peace, they were sending messengers among the people, inciting them to war and urging them to rid the country of the Spaniards.

Their deception was not known at once, and as Father San Vitores had come as an angel of peace, he exhorted the leader of the Spanish soldiers, *don* Juan de Santa Cruz, to try every peaceful means of settlement with the natives, although they no longer deserved that consideration. Meanwhile, the soldiers, being military men, thought it better to win peace by their arms than by their prayers and to keep the barbarians in the dark about our desire for peace, since that would only make them more insolent and rash.

But Father San Vitores said, "The honor of a Christian is the honor of Christ. The soldier's honor and all else must be sacrificed to that." He added that rather than pay attention to what the barbarians said, they should observe the advice of the angels and the Lord of the Angels and of men of reason and judgment in Europe, so that merely to win one "point of honor" they should not permit the loss of so many souls. He told them that honor was never lost when it was given up for God, but that to lose it in a just cause was to win it, and whosoever risked his own for the greater glory would be doubly repaid by the Lord.

The Spanish soldiers were convinced by the reasoning and authority of Father San Vitores and overcame themselves, behaving as if overcome by the barbarians. They asked for peace, and according to the custom of the country, sent emissaries with food and tortoise shells. These they sent in such quantity as would have served the natives for ten such occasions, thus demonstrating that they esteemed peace and kindness far more than earthy goods or anything else. But they did not release Hurao.

But the barbarians, who could not understand this Christian philosophy, accepted the gifts and attributed the entire ceremony to cowardice. This they celebrated in their *romances*, although their joy was short-lived, because what happened next made them change their satires to lamentations. Now they met Father San Vitores with stones and lances, but what particularly grieved him was that as he stood there with crucifix in hand, inviting them to peace, they threw stones at the crucifix in his hand.[166]

The cause of the Spaniards thus justified, God took their side for his own, favoring them with miraculous providences, giving courage to the very few soldiers who stood against the large army of barbarians, all of which was owing to the prayers of Father San Vitores and the Sacrifice of the Mass that he offered daily.

On the eleventh of September, 1671, the barbarians made their first attack, throwing more than two thousand men against our trenches in an attempt to take the house and church. The thirty-one soldiers fought with such remarkable valor that they repulsed the enemy and sent them running in retreat. The Servant of God went out, crucifix in hand, rebuking them in words of a father for their inconstancy, but they answered with insults and stones.

---

[166]The *Marianos* used slings and smooth almond-shaped stones that could be thrown with great force and accuracy.

The assaults continued for eight days. Day and night they threw stones with such violence that some of them went through the roofs of the church and residence. As there were so few men, it was necessary for the fathers to take their posts as sentinels while the soldiers slept. Father San Vitores chose the second watch, which was from eleven at night until four in the morning, making rounds of the camp, to the great admiration of those who saw him walk serenely among the stones that fell in a constant shower and over obstacles with which the ground was littered, never falling. His own sleep was reduced to an hour.

When the *Marianos* saw that they came out of those attacks with some loss, they realized that they needed a defense against the firearms. So they made some shields like platforms, a new invention of the apostate Choco. With these they could protect themselves at a distance, which enabled them to throw stones, lances, and fire balls.

They also dug earthworks to protect themselves from the sallies of our soldiers, who were not content to fight within their fortifications. But the barbarians, seeing that the Spaniards destroyed their work, took counsel with their *macanas* and commended their trenches to the devil in an explicit pact, placing in them the skulls of their deceased. With the new confidence they gained from the happy promises of the *macanas*, they drew near our fortifications, protected by their shields from our musket balls. Of our artillery they had little fear, knowing from experience that it was used only to frighten them, not to kill, since Father San Vitores forbade strong measures, even when they were sorely needed.

Our soldiers were not discouraged at seeing the enemy so courageous. Rather, they, too, were revived, telling one another that they would rather die fighting for the glory of God than submit to any faction. And in order to place the power of the angels against that of the demons, they made, on the advice of Father San Vitores, a vow to the leader of the heavenly host, Saint Michael, on September 28, the eve of his feast, promising that for an entire year they would daily recite an Our Father and a Hail Mary every evening, that they would offer Mass at the end of the war, and that they would dedicate to his name the first castle or fort that should be constructed in these islands by the king.

Soon they began to feel how favorable to them was the glorious archangel. On September 30, at dawn, they saw in the thatched roof of our church a lance on fire. It had been thrown by the enemy the night before without being noticed by our fathers or the soldiers. The fire had consumed part of the shank of the lance but had not touched even one straw of the roof. The same thing happened with more than fifty stones wrapped in flaming materials that were thrown and were later found on the same roof. All these favors and many more Father San Vitores attributed to Saint Michael, but no one can deny the following one.

The enemy had started a fire nearby, hoping to destroy our church. The fire, which could not be put out, was rapidly approaching our buildings when the soldiers invoked the holy archangel, and one of the fathers said, in the language of the *Marianos*, "Saint Michael. Rain!" And at that very moment out of a clear sky rain fell, quenching the fire

*The War of the Marianos and the Victory of the Spaniards*

and freeing our church from danger. It was not Father San Vitores who invoked Saint Michael, as someone mistakenly said. But there is no mistake in attributing this occurrence and other marvels of this war to the merits and prayers of the Venerable Father. So believe all his companions, lay and religious, who feared no harm when he was near, believing they had God with them when they had his servant.

On the eighth of September, God, as Father San Vitores said, taking a hand in the war, took out of his storehouse and armory the winds and tempests, firing his artillery not only to frighten but also to punish those, who spurning every offer, still despised peace.

In short, a typhoon, which the *Marianos* call *baguio*, or *pahgo*, of the most furious sort that had ever been seen in these islands, blowing from every point of the compass, passed in a brief time over the island and caused damage that could not be repaired for many years. Almost all the houses in Agadña were in ruins, as well as in the other villages of the island. The most serious damage occurred to the property of those who had been instigators of the war, as they themselves knew at the time and have since admitted.

Breadfuit trees were uprooted, as were palms and other plants upon which the people lived, leaving them at once without property, shelter, and food.

The Lord did not spare his own house, whether to show his ire against those barbarians who did not respect it or to try the patience of Father San Vitores. One of the *macanas*, whose house was in no way damaged, boasted that he was more powerful than our God, since the wind had demolished the church but had not been able to overthrow his house.

But even in the ruin of the church, God showed that it was truly his house that he had destroyed in order to build a new one with greater strength and glory. For besides having warned Father San Vitores, in order that he might have time before the building fell to save various valuables that might be destroyed, he caused the roof to fall so gently that the principal beam gradually rested on the shoulders of the statue of Saint Francis Xavier, so that it leaned a bit forward and served (with all due reverence) as the Atlas of the house of God. Other boards fell on this beam in such wise that it formed a shelter under which the crucifix and a painting of the Blessed Virgin and another of our father, Saint Ignatius, were found safe.

In this small chapel, formed by the ruins, Father San Vitores celebrated Mass every day until the end of the war, and because of this, the devil tried in vain to destroy it by fire or by the stones that the barbarians continued to throw, one of which fell with great force near the head of Father San Vitores while he was saying Mass.

With the same care the Lord destroyed our house, which was his also, as there were two sick men in it when it collapsed, besides a child, Father San Vitores, and Hurao. No one was injured.

The house of Hurao did not receive so much consideration. Our soldiers had wanted to destroy it, because it constituted a danger to ours. It was higher than our house and so located that harm could be done. But Father San Vitores would not permit this, so as not to further irritate his friends and supporters. But now the typhoon left of it nothing more than a heap of stone and wood. The fathers and Spaniards experienced the same paternal providence in all things. The towers and castles, though they leaned a bit out of reverence for the justice of God, did not fall, and the statue of the Immaculate Conception is still standing, and even the artillery is still in place, ready to fire. The stockade fell but will easily rise.

I fear I must omit many wonderful things that occurred in all this general havoc. But most wonderful of all was the serenity of the Servant of God amid all the dangers: all the destruction from heaven and earth; from the elements as well as the barbarians; from the wind and the sea that swelled the river till it even flooded the church; and finally from the burning lances and stones that fell continually. He always showed such a cheerful face, a companion said, you would not think disaster was all around him.

When our enemies saw that our house and church had fallen, as well as the stockade—our main defense—embittered by the punishments that should have taught them peace, they assembled more fighters than ever. Now certain of victory, they made what they thought was a final assault, with loud cries, stones, lances, and fire, and what most distressed Father San Vitores, with blasphemy against God and his Law.

But our men repulsed the attack with equal spirit and success, without receiving even one wound, but with a cost to the enemy of many wounded and some dead. For this reason they came the following day to ask for peace, bringing two friends of Hurao, making his liberty the only condition.

The commander of the Spanish soldiers did not wish to show any inclination to an agreement, nor to make peace with any conditions whatsoever. That would only rekindle their arrogance. But the Servant of God looked upon them as sons and not as enemies. Although he knew their fickleness, he persuaded the captain to accept their offer of peace to show the natives the only reason they (the Spaniards) had taken up arms and to show them more clearly that the Law of God was the law of peace and not of war. He said that even if the barbarians changed, God does not change, and that he would help them in the future as he had helped them in the past and would do so all the more powerfully, as they had sacrificed their rights for his greater glory.

The prisoner had scarcely been released, however, when the friends and supporters of Hurao, who had not dared to take up arms for fear that the Spaniards would give him his well deserved punishment, now renewed the war in league with those already in arms. This time they attacked with greater fury from all sides and did not relax their attack, night or day, for thirteen days. They drew back from time to time as they suffered losses but returned with new spirit to the fray.

Finally, on October 20 (1671), the enemy hurled himself at our enclosure. Our men made a sally with such courage that in the shortest

*The War of the Marianos and the Victory of the Spaniards*

interval they put the enemy to flight, destroyed the earthworks, cast the skulls on the ground, and trampled on them.

That terrified them to such a degree that on that very afternoon, they came with great humility to beg forgiveness, peace, and mercy. The mediator was Quipuha, one of the major nobles of Agadña, a relative of the Quipuha who had received the fathers on their arrival.

The Spaniards agreed to peace with certain conditions that were agreeable to the barbarians. They were required to attend Mass and Christian doctrine on all Sundays and feast days, and they had to send their children to learn the Law of God and other things of similar piety.

With this the war was brought to a close, after a duration of forty days. The pride and disdain of the barbarians had now changed to fear and reverence. They had learned that the desire and the search for peace did not mean fear of fighting a war, but rather the desire to avoid it on the part of those who had brought them the law of peace from so far across the sea.

For God, this war brought praise and glory, Father San Vitores said. For people were saying, both on this island and elsewhere where the story was told, that God was worthy to be acknowledged, feared, and loved as our Sovereign Lord of Heaven and Earth. He is at once the powerful and the loving protector of those who trust in him. Never had men suffered such destruction of their houses and fields as they did in this war they had waged against God. Well might one see that their demons were powerless and that God is the Lord of the elements, which he wields as arms of justice to wound and punish whom he wishes, and he had certainly used them in this war against the evil-doers. They now said that their *macanas* were imposters who promised things they could not give. They spoke of other matters in which their eyes had been opened and praised the Great Father who had shown himself to be their real father.

In all the discussions during the war, the Lord approved the dictates of his servant, though often contrary to the principles of warfare. He blessed the blind obedience of the soldiers who listened to the father as the Hebrews listened to the oracles of the Ark of the Covenant.[167] God favored his own, so that the forty days were a continuous miracle or chain of miracles.

Because of their frequent assaults the barbarians always came off the losers. Two thousand men were overcome and scattered by thirty-one soldiers of whom not one was lost. A Filipino was the only one of our men who was wounded. On the Feast of Saints Cosmas and Damián (September 26) he was struck by three lances from ambush when he went out to hunt for food. Although he was mortally wounded, he recovered in a few days through the prayers of the Servant of God and was able again to serve in the war. *Don* Antonio Alexalde, who served as general of artillery and was in the tower of Saint Francis Xavier, was struck in the chest by a stone. The violent blow left him unconscious and it was feared he would not live long enough to receive Extreme Unction.

---

[167] Exod. 25:10; Judg. 20:27.

But Father San Vitores invoked Saint Francis Xavier and Santa Teresa, whose feast day it was (October 15), and within twenty-four hours he was fighting again with the others.

# CHAPTER XVI

*The Last Missions of the Servant of God and the
Death of Several Lay Companions*

Now that peace was arranged, on October 21, 1671, the charitable fire that burned in the breast of Father San Vitores could no longer suffer the imprisonment that had detained him forty days because of the war. He remained only six or eight days in Agadña to assign various tasks to his companions. Then he left to visit the villages of the island, rejecting the fears and warnings of the others. They urged him not to trust so easily those enemies who had been reconciled through fear. Surely he must know the treachery of the barbarians who concealed war behind a mask of peace.

To these and other arguments, he responded with the urgent need to restore what the devil had destroyed and that of the multitude of children who awaited the grace of baptism. He had no fear of death, he said, in so good a cause, but rather would meet it, whenever it came, with open arms. And this he demonstrated on the first mission journey, because he went with another priest and two laymen, entirely unarmed, as was his custom. He received word that in the village of Chuchugu,[168] called Chochogo (famous for its treachery and violence and that believed itself safe from punishment because of its inaccessibility), there was a child who had not been baptized, and he wished to go there. The native guide told him that it would be better for him to go alone, because the villagers were afraid of Spaniards, even when the latter were unarmed, and would therefore meet him armed and dangerous. He ordered his companions to proceed with the journey through the villages along the beach. He went up the mountain alone, climbing with much difficulty. He entered the village, a true apostle, as a sheep among wolves. He was looking for one child, but found eight whom he baptized that day, with such consolation in his soul as could not be described.

The Servant of God and his companions made various apostolic journeys throughout the island of Guam. Then he sent the Venerable Father Francisco Ezquerra to the island of Santa Ana (Rota) and Father Alonso López he sent to the three islands of Santo Angel (Aguigan), Buenavista Mariana (Tinian), and San José (Saipan), which he had not been able to visit since the death of Father Luis de Medina.

The two fathers embarked together, meaning to separate later when twelve boats would set sail for the various islands. Father Ezquerra, because of his confidence in Father San Vitores, begged him to bless his boat. Very soon they reaped the benefit of this blessing. The sea rose in mountainous waves from the force of the wind and all the boats were lost except that one in which the fathers traveled. That one went ashore at

---

[168]Churchugu is northest of Agaña, in the valley called La Cañada; today called Chochogo.

## Book Three, Chapter 16

the village of Matidpan, on the same island of Rota. There, while waiting for the sea to calm, they calmed the spirits of the natives, no less aroused than the sea by the past war and the evil reports of the enemies of the Faith. What success Father Francisco Ezquerra had on the island of Santa Ana through the miraculous providence of the Lord, we leave to be described later.

Father Alonso López accomplished no less on the islands that were in his charge, as may be read in one of his letters to Father San Vitores, in which he gives an account of all that he has done, according to the instructions he was given.

Among other accomplishments of great service to God, he founded in the village of Sungharon, on the island of Buenavista, a seminary similar to the one in Agadña, where he gathered many children of ability. In the same letter he speaks of many baptisms of children and of those times when his life was threatened, first by the sea and again by the barbarians, in whom there yet survived a belief in the warnings of Choco that the fathers would kill the children with the waters of baptism.

The same day on which Father San Vitores dispatched the two fathers to their missions, November 17, 1671, he set out again to visit all the villages of Guam.[169] And although he knew that in one village the natives had formed a plot to take his life, he neither fled nor retired until necessity caused his return to Agadña to celebrate Christmas. He had learned from experience that the solemn celebration of these feasts was an effective exhortation for these barbarians, who were ruled more by their eyes than by their ears.

He arrived at the residence on December 18, the Feast of the Expectation of Our Lady. Since he saw the fervor, spirit, and zeal with which Father Francisco Solano, whom he had left there, attended to all the ministries, he judged that he was not needed. So he began the spiritual exercises of Saint Ignatius. To this end, he retired to a little shelter made of palm leaves that was so small that he could hardly get into it, and where he would have suffocated from the heat if he hadn't stepped outside occasionally to get a breath of fresh air. The severity of his fasts, disciplines, and chains, clearly showed that he was preparing himself for the martyrdom that he saw close at hand.

After he completed the exercises, he celebrated Christmas with the greatest possible solemnity in the new church, which had been built in Agadña from the remains of the former structure. He then resumed his circuit of the villages of the island in his happy search for children, until he was again obliged to return to the residence because of the illness of Father Diego de Noriega. This father was anxious to have Father San Vitores at his bedside. From his hands he gave his spirit into those of the Lord on January 13, 1672.

We have scarcely any important information concerning this father. However, I find a written example of his obedience, at least enough to show the greatness of his religious virtues. Although he had tubercu-

---

[169] These settlements, which García calls *pueblos*, were undoubtedly very small, if forty be assigned to a single small church.

*The Last Missions of the Servant of God and the Death of Several Lay Companions*

losis, his superiors sent him to these islands for lack of others to send, hoping also that the change of climate would improve his condition. His illness was one that required the best of care, which was not to be found here, yet he sacrificed himself with blind obedience and generous heart to the mission. Daily his condition grew worse, while he was an example of all the virtues to the *Marianos*, especially of patience and conformity to the will of God, preaching by his works when he could no longer preach by his words. He enjoyed a happy death, full of consolation and confidence, to which the assistance of Father San Vitores contributed not a little. The sick man accepted this as one of the greatest benefits he had received from the Lord.

After the ceremony of burial, Father San Vitores went out again to the villages. He wanted to improve the religious administration of this island, which he loved best of all the islands, since it was to be the island of his martyrdom. Above all he wished to have several places where Mass could be celebrated with more decorum. Hence, he determined to erect four churches in localities where they would be within easy reach of the natives and to assign forty villages to each church.

Father Francisco Ezquerra returned from the island of Zarpana and was sent to Merizo, where he built a beautiful church, although the material was the wood and leaves of the coconut and other palm trees. Two other lay assistants were at this time constructing another church at Pagat. The Venerable Father took for himself the village of Nisichan, for it was in the most difficult and dangerous location but there were many children there. These, with the help of the Christian doctrine, consoled him for the rudeness of adults and their reluctance to hear the word of God. From this village he went out to visit his Christians who lived in the vicinity, returning occasionally for a brief period to the Residencia de San Ignacio in Agadña.

Peace had lasted five months, not without hardship and hazard, when the prelude to Father San Vitores martyrdom took place in that of some of his lay helpers, the first of whom was Diego Bazán. Father Francisco Solano sent this lad to carry a letter to Father San Vitores, in which he gave the information that Father Tomás de Cardeñoso had arrived from the fifth island.[170] He had been selected to go to Pigpug to build a church there.

Quipuha, the noble of whom I have previously spoken, knew about the journey that Diego Bazán was about to make. Quipuha, although supposedly a Christian, was not Christian in his way of life. He had in his house and as a public scandal, a married woman, as if she were his own wife. Father San Vitores admonished him on different occasions, now with flattery, now with the threat [of hell], but he in his blind passion answered that he would rather go to hell than leave the woman.

For this reason Quipuha hated Father San Vitores and his companions, as if they were prosecutors and judges who wished to put a brake on his appetites. Now that he heard that Diego Bazán was on his way across the island, he went with the woman to Chuchugu, a village

---

[170]The fifth island, presumably Saipan. Cf. Book 3, chap. 1:165.

## Book Three, Chapter 16

not far from the road, and urged the men of that village to kill the boy. Two of them volunteered and set out for the road where they met him and engaged him in a friendly conversation. When they saw he was off his guard, one of them gave it to him with a machete and the other stabbed him with a lance and left him there dead. This was on March 31, 1672. They had no other cause for the murder than the admonitions of Father San Vitores and the fact that Diego Bazán, who was a friend of Quipuha, sometimes expressed his regret at the loss of the latter's soul. They threw his body in a pit.

Death for such a good cause merits special remembrance. Diego Bazán was a native of Mexico, of good character and appearance. His parents were of humble estate. Their greatest honor lay in having such a son. He was fourteen years old when Father San Vitores came to Mexico, en route to the Marianas, and he called Diego to the mission in a singular manner.

He met him one day at the gate that they call Portal de las Flores, in the Plaza Mayor, of Mexico City. Looking at him attentively and affectionately, he said, "Son, do you want to come with me to be a martyr?" The lad answered, "Yes," and at once the father took him as his companion, with the consent of his parents, and he kept him at his side, instructing him in all the virtues necessary to form a missionary soldier. And this he was in the Marianas. He not only showed courage in the wars on Tinian and Guam, and on all occasions, defending the cause of the Faith, but he also showed apostolic zeal, accompanying the fathers on their missions and going out on mission visits alone. Father San Vitores sent him, knowing the boy's virtue and good example, and thus entrusting him with many undertakings for the glory of God. This true soldier of Jesus Christ suffered with great constancy and joy all manner of affronts, blows, and mockery, showing more valor in this victory over himself than over the enemy.

It is clear that he understood and prized the riches of the cross and the glory of suffering insults in the name of Christ. Four years of exemplary and zealous life gained him a happy death surely precious in the eyes of the Lord,[171] which he suffered for the cause of chastity or the Faith, or, as I believe, for both together.

The same night that the men of Chuchugu killed Diego Bazán, they were planning to burn one of the sentry boxes of our soldiers. They could have done so quite safely, because we had only nine men here. The rest were scattered in various villages and there was no sentinel. But the Lord did not grant them this triumph, which they would have counted a great victory. A dog smelled them and began barking. Two soldiers came up, who were going the rounds, to find out the cause. They spotted the enemy and fired an arquebus in the air; the natives fled, left their incendiary equipment, and hurled three lances, which were found next day stuck in palm trees.

In the morning Father Solano sent Nicolás de Figueroa and Damián Bernal to Father San Vitores to inform him of this occurrence.

---

[171] Pss. 116:15.

*The Last Missions of the Servant of God and the Death of Several Lay Companions*

On their arrival, they learned that Diego Bazán had not arrived, and they were now certain of his death, which had been reported by a boy of the land.

From these beginnings the Venerable Father recognized the danger that threatened them all. His first concern was for the welfare of the Christian community, but he was also happy at his destiny, which he saw so near. He ordered the two messengers back to the residence, and he sent out orders in all directions to assemble all the fathers and soldiers in Agadña, while he alone would remain in the danger zone.

Nicolás and Damián were joined by another Spaniard, Manuel Rangel, who was going that afternoon, because it was a Friday of Lent, to a discipline in the church of Agadña.

The three arrived at a place near where they had murdered Bazán, when a crowd of more than twenty *Indios* from Chuchugo and Mapaz rushed out of ambush. They killed Rangel, who was unarmed. Nicolás and Damián, who had shields, defended themselves vigorously and killed the noble of the village of Chuchugu, who was at the head of the party, and to frighten their enemies, they chopped him in pieces with their cutlasses.

Their activity had the desired effect, since the rest fled in terror. Nicolás de Figueroa had his thigh pierced by a lance, and Damián Bernal had a small scratch from a lance that almost missed his ear.

On their return the two became lost in the hills. Nicolás came out at the village of Ipao, where he was killed, notwithstanding the demonstrations of friendship with which he was received. An *Indio* embraced him, as was the native custom, then threw him over the cliff, when he was slaughtered with lances. Damián came out at the village of Funhon (Tumhon), where a friendly native asked him to let him look at his cutlass.

He had scarcely handed it over, when the native split his head with it.

It would seem that the Lord had saved their lives from the ambush and had separated them in order that they might die alone and defenseless, although in a just cause. They would thus prove all the better that the cause for which they were murdered was certainly the same that sought the death of the ministers of the gospel. They, after all, were assistants of these ministers, protecting the lives of those who gave eternal life to so many by baptism and even baptizing them themselves when it was needed.

The glory of Damián was all the greater to have died on the same day and in the same place as Father San Vitores, just a few hours after his martyrdom.

Father San Vitores had with him five lay helpers for building the church. He sent them to Agadña, and one of them called Manuel de Nagua, rashly separated himself from the others and found himself in the village of Guay, where he was thrown hundreds of feet down from a high cliff.

249

The four others, afraid of being killed on the road, retreated to the village of Nisihan,[172] whence, amid continual dangers and threats, with the help and the courage of certain faithful Christians, they survived that day. During the night, one of these Christians guided them to the village of Pagat, where they were hidden for two weeks in some caves, formations in the cliffs, until finally they were brought secretly in a boat by some friendly *Indios* to Agadña. Father Francisco Ezquerra, having completed the church in Merizo, had set out on a mission journey through his villages. Although he had not received the order sent by the Servant of God, Divine Providence guided him safely back to Agadña, protecting his life in order that he might give it later, after performing greater service. Heaven was now content to take the life of the Venerable Father San Vitores—to give him the crown he had deserved.

---

[172] Nisichan was on the east coast, approximately at the present location of the University of Guam.

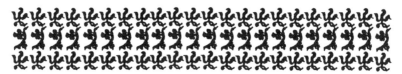

# CHAPTER XVII

## Father San Vitores's Glorious Death for Christ

At this time God wished to reward the apostolic zeal of his great servant and give him the long-promised crown, a crown that he had earned by labors in the face of danger, labors performed for the greater glory, and now God led him on towards death by those means that should be told, for they were precious in the sight of the Lord.

A certain *Indio*, a Visayan, who had been cast upon these shores after the wreck of the *Concepción* in 1638 and who Father San Vitores had brought back to Guam as an interpreter, had fled from the company of the father.

In the beginning he had served the mission laudably. But later he became tired of the hard, laborious life, and desirous of liberty, he ran away and went to live the unrestricted life of the *Indios*. Father San Vitores's heart was deeply wounded at the loss of this sheep. And now the time was drawing near when he should go to give an account of his flock to the Supreme Pastor. In order, then, to be able to say to Christ, as Christ had said to his Father: "Of those you have given me, I have not lost one,"[173] he went out in search of the last one in the caves and rocky hillsides, meaning at the same time to baptize the children of the mountains.

He left Nisichan on the first day of April 1672. On the way he received news of the death of Diego Bazán. He gave his lay assistants the order that we have mentioned, that they all retire to the Residence of Saint Ignatius, in Agadña, saying that he meant to remain alone in the hills with the one Visayan as his companion. The name of the latter was Pedro Chalangsor, who well merited to share his martyrdom.

Night overtook the two in one of the villages along their way, and in the very early morning they headed for Tumhon, a league and a half from Agadña. They arrived here at seven in the morning, when Father San Vitores learned of a newborn baby girl. He went at once to the house of the father, whose name was Matapang, and begged him to bring out his daughter for him to baptize. He asked him at the same time if there was any other woman there who had recently delivered.

Matapang was a Christian, instructed in religion and baptized by Father San Vitores himself. Also, he had received many favors from the father. Among others, he had once been badly wounded in the arm by a lance thrown by another native, and Father San Vitores drew out the bone tip, and through his care, perhaps even more through his prayers, the man was cured of that poisonous wound. But forgetting God and the kindnesses received, the ungrateful *Indio* said, "Go ahead, imposter, go into my house and baptize a skull there." And adding other insults, he threatened him with death. To this the charitable father replied, "Well, you are baptized, so let me baptize your daughter and

---

[173]John 18:9.

251

*Book Three, Chapter 17*

then kill me. I will gladly give up the life of my body, that she may gain the life of her soul."

Then, in order to give the barbarian time to calm his anger, Father San Vitores gathered a group of children and began to teach them the Christian doctrine, calling Matapang to come and listen. But he answered, "I don't want to learn. I'm fed up and angry at God." The father quietly continued the catechism lesson. Then Matapang tried to persuade another *Indio*, a pagan, who had come to where the children were, to kill the father. Hirao resisted. He said he had no reason to kill the father, because the father was a good man who harmed no one, but did good to all. He was the one who had brought about peace, and they had received many other favors as well. When Hirao saw that Matapang persisted in his purpose, he said, "Don't forget that the Great Father freed you from death. Don't repay that great favor so evilly." Then Matapang called him a coward and said that if Hirao didn't dare kill the father, he would do it himself, because he was a real man and a brave one, and he needed no one to help him.

Hirao, not wishing to be thought a coward, consented, and Matapang, glad to have an accomplice, went to get their three lances, giving Father San Vitores time to baptize his daughter, which he did. The barbarian was angered still more because of this. He first attacked Father San Vitores' companion, throwing lances at him, which he managed to dodge. He could easily have avoided death if he had simply fled, but he did not wish to leave Father San Vitores alone and helpless, preferring to die at his side, as a good soldier of Christ. And thus, after he had avoided many thrown lances, one at last struck him, and Hirao, running up with a cutlass, gave him the crown of martyrdom with a deep wound to the head. Fortunate boy! How well rewarded were his four years of service performed with such fidelity for God in the missions, accompanying the ministers of the gospel. He deserved to die for the Faith in company with the first apostle of these islands and as the precursor in heaven of his martyrdom.

Father San Vitores, happy over the fate of his companion and preparing himself for a similar end, took in his hand the ivory crucifix, a little less than half a yard in length, which he always wore hanging from his neck, and began to preach to them, saying that God was the one and absolute Lord of all, and that he only was to be venerated in all the land of Guam, and other words that the barbarians scorned. Seeing them approach and knowing that they were about to kill him, he wished to imitate the meekness and charity of his Lord when he died. He spoke in the Mariana language, "May God have mercy on you, Matapang!" Whereupon Hirao struck him with a cutlass, wounding his head, which dropped forward on his neck, while Matapang ran him through the chest with a lance. His spirit, released from the prison of his body, flew to heaven, on the Saturday, a week before Palm Sunday, April 2, 1672. On that day, twenty years before, he had received the order of deacon and the power to preach the gospel, which now he preached better than ever with the voice of his blood.

*Father San Vitores's Glorious Death for Christ*

Hoping to enrich themselves with his poor garments, his executioners stripped the venerable martyr of the garments that are precious indeed to one who knows how to appreciate them. They found the virginal body girdled by three sharp iron belts, at which they marvelled. They had heard that Christians performed penance for their sins and they knew that the father was good and had no sins. So they said, in wonder, that the father did as Christ had done for the sins of others, of the islanders themselves.

Matapang removed a small crucifix that Father San Vitores wore at his throat, and laying it on a stone, chopped it to bits. He broke the other one also, cursing it as he worked, saying, "This is what the *Castillas* venerate as noble Lord and Chief." No one doubted that Christ was the motive in his having followed and attacked the Servant of God, and that Christ wished to suffer in his image, when his servant suffered in his body. Matapang took the ivory crucifix that Father San Vitores had held in his hand, and believing it to be valuable, kept it to dispose of it advantageously. He later sold it for thirty bags of rice, lest he fail to play the part of Judas up to the hilt.

The cruelty and impiety of the parricides was not yet satisfied by the death of Father San Vitores. They brought fire and threw it on the pools of blood to consume it. They took the two bodies, that of Father San Vitores and his companion, and dragged them to the beach. They tied heavy stones to the feet, placed them in a light boat, and took them out to sea, where they threw them overboard. But a strange thing happened. The body of Father San Vitores, having sunk, came twice to the surface, and the hands seized the outrigger of the canoe, which the natives use here to counterbalance the sail.

Matapang, who was alarmed, twice loosened the hands with a stick, but the body rose a third time and grasped at the stern of the small craft, where Matapang was stationed. By now he was so frightened and aghast that he did not know what to do. He wanted to throw himself into the sea, believing that the father was going to climb into the boat. At last he got back his nerve and struck one heavy blow at the head with one of the oars. Then he quickly rowed away from the scene, leaving that sacred body buried in the sea, to the perpetual grief of those whom he left behind. Now they had not even the company of his venerable relics, unless the Lord determines, as we may hope, to let the sea restore this treasure, which it guards, to appease the envy that the earth now has for the sea and to give the precious body the veneration it deserves for having been the repository of that blessed soul.

Thus he died, if one can call death that glorious martyrdom, and thus he began to live in heaven, whom the whole earth could not hold, at the age of forty-five years, thirty-two of which were passed in religion, twelve of them in the Indies, the final four in the Ladrones. He rose to glory with three crowns, martyr, doctor, and virgin: virgin, in imitation of the purity of Mary, doctor of his people, martyr in his islands, which he called Marianas, to oblige the Queen of Heaven to look upon them as her own, and to make them look upon Mary as their Queen.

## Book Three, Chapter 17

In this land, ignorant of the holy gospel throughout many centuries, he opened a great door through which the Church might receive many souls; he left thirteen islands brightened by the light of the gospel; some fifty thousand souls baptized by him and his companions, and many thousand catechumens who hoped to be washed by the waters of baptism; eight churches erected; three seminaries for children; and at last, he showered the earth with his own blood, to fertilize that which had given him such a great harvest in return for his labor and hardships. This is not to mention the many sinners he converted, pagans, Moros, heretics, or the works of piety and religion that he left in Spain, Mexico, and the Philippines that are beyond counting, for wherever he went, whether to remain or merely in passing, he left signs of the charity that demonstrated the apostolic zeal that inspired his heart.

The skies of the Marianas, which had for some time been serene, became enraged after the death of the Servant of God. There were tempests, the worst that had been seen in those islands; and on the island of Guam, in the place where they killed him, there was a great deal of lightning, which terrorized and horrified the natives, who saw this as a sign of God's anger. They said that heaven made war against the earth and fired the artillery of its anger against the murderers of the Venerable Martyr and against the island where the execrable cruelty had been committed.

Captain *don* Damián de Esplana erected a chapel on the spot where Father San Vitores was martyred. He also planted a cross in the place where his blood was burned, which is in front of the chapel. He did this because he had promised it when he was cured of an illness by the intercession of Father San Vitores. This chapel and holy place was visited by Father Bustillos, who writes of it, and by other fathers of the Society of Jesus who arrived in the Marianas on June 4, 1675, aboard the *San Telmo*. They kissed and reverenced the holy ground and gave thanks to God for permitting them to see that fortunate soil where the first apostle of these islands shed his blood.

When news of Father San Vitores' death reached Manila, there was a great celebration, with the ringing of bells and general rejoicing, Faith overcoming natural grief, for the knowledge of his glory dried the tears of those who loved him. The *colegio* of the Society of Jesus went to the cathedral to sing a *Te Deum*; and later, on the third of October 1676, the feast of Saint Francis Borgia, in their own church, they celebrated a thanksgiving to the Lord for the triumph of so illustrious a son of that very religious province, which had brought him forth to a life of martyrdom and sent him forth to the land where he received the crown.[174] All other demonstrations, however, were exceeded, of course, by that in the capital, Madrid, at our Colegio Imperial, where he was called miraculously to the Society by Christ and his Mother; where his martyrdom was prophesied and promised to his mother by Saint Ignatius; where he was born into the religious life, overcoming insuperable difficulties by astonishing providences; where he was called to the Indies by Saint

---

[174]Presumably the Jesus church in Manila.

*Father San Vitores's Glorious Death for Christ*

Francis Xavier and Marcello Mastrilli; whence he set forth finally for his coveted mission and promised martyrdom, from this *colegio*, which was so many times the mother of this admirable man.

On the eleventh day of June, 1674, a Mass in honor of Saint Ignatius was offered in our church in Madrid, celebrating the happy death of Father San Vitores. The festivities began on the previous night with a display of fireworks and the ringing of bells. For the Mass, our capacious church was filled to overflowing by the members of religious orders, grandees, academics, ministers, cavaliers, various nobles, and all manner of people who were invited to attend the solemn Mass. The sermon was preached by Father Pedro Francisco Esquex, the famous preacher to His Majesty. And although with his discreet eloquence, he was high in his praise of the martyr, he fell short in his eulogy of virtues far greater than his praise.

The most remarkable circumstance of the celebration was the presence of the martyr's father, *don* Jerónimo San Vitores, although in concealment, lest his grief disturb the ceremony. He attended the memorial of the death of his son with tears of joy; he accepted congratulations for the killing of his beloved son; he received the blessings of everyone, who called him fortunate in being the father of a martyr. And in a sense, he, too, was a martyr in the shedding of the blood he had given his son. To all the blessings and congratulations, the old man only replied with his eyes, his lips stilled by quiet joy, and a heart that thanked the Lord for an honor beyond his deserving.

And in order that his portrait may not be lost to us as we have lost his body, this must suffice: Father San Vitores was of medium height. His skin was very white and his hair was a light chestnut color. He had a wide forehead, bright blue eyes, red cheeks, a long and somewhat curved nose, and bright red lips, though somewhat thin. His aquiline face had a rather grave and majestic beauty. But the changes in climate, exposure to all weathers, the hardships he suffered, and the penances he performed had changed him so much in the Philippines and much more in the Marianas, that those who had known him well could hardly recognize him. A friend who met him in Mexico on the occasion of his second visit, failed to recognize him because of his burned and discolored complexion. In the Marianas, Father Bustillos said he looked like a living skeleton, no more than skin and bones. If those portraits that were made of him before he left Spain were compared with one that was sent here after his death, showing how he looked in the Marianas, one could not reconcile the two as being the same individual.

Of the gifts of his soul, we have already spoken and that required a finer brush and finer colors to paint the picture. He had a very keen mind, a good memory, excellent judgment, even in childhood, was sanguine and coleric from the point of view of the humors, which made the victory of his mortification all the greater, since he became so calm and gentle with everyone that art might be taken for nature. For the rest, he was liberal, compassionate, magnanimous, capable of great enterprises, an example of how the Creator could crown the gifts of nature by those of grace. Indeed, they constituted a person complete in virtues and gifts, as we shall see in the following book.

# BOOK IV

*Of the Life and Martyrdom of the
Venerable Father Diego Luis de San Vitores,
of the Society of Jesus, First Apostle of the
Mariana Islands*

Fig. 5. Before the devastation wrought by World War II, in Saipan, this picture of Father San Vitores hung in the Catholic church at Garapan. It depicts the martyrdom of the priest, crucifix in hand, as he is struck by Hirao's cutlass and pierced by Matapang's lance. (See page 252).

In translation, the Spanish caption states: Father Diego Luis de San Vitores, a native of Burgos, an angelic and guiltless man. Miraculously called to the Society of Jesus while at the *colegio*, in Madrid, and to the conversion of the Gentiles. God favored him with exceptional virtues and grace. He was the first apostle of the Mariana Islands, where he and his companions suffered great hardships and converted thousands of souls, preaching with a holy crucifix. He was killed by [foes who thrust] a lance through his chest and severed his head with a cutlass.

# CHAPTER I

*Father San Vitores's Reputation for Sanctity*
*Among His Own and Among Strangers*

If Saint Jerome says that blessed is one whose life is saintly and noble, so that not even by way of calumny can anyone devise anything against the greatness of his merit, then Father San Vitores was indeed fortunate and blessed, for no one could accuse him of the least defect. Nor do I find in any of the letters and family papers anything that could be a complaint against the Servant of God. Rather, all praised fully his blameless life, his admirable virtues, and rare perfection. Such was also the praise of Saint Judith, whose virtue was famous everywhere and nothing evil was ever spoken against her.[175] Nor can I easily describe the high concept and great esteem that both strangers and those close to him had of his holiness.

I begin and I could also end with a testimony of our father, Saint Ignatius. He appeared to the mother of Father San Vitores, when she tried to remove her son from the Society of Jesus, and told her to leave her son there, because he wanted him to be in his house and become a saint. These words tell us what he was to be, and now we may read what he actually was.

From the same words we may infer what the boy was then and what he would be, since Saint Ignatius wished to have him in his house. But if we are to use such testimonies, how much better is Mary's calling him with clear voice to the Society of her Son and her Son's calling him to his Society with such extraordinary signs. But if we remember what his confessor told us of the virtues of his boyhood, greater than his age and size might lead us to expect, virtues that were equal to those of the great saints whom God chooses from the time of their birth for an eminent perfection, we will not wonder that the heavenly inhabitants yearned to possess this boy. So did their king, who coveted in him the treasures he had placed and would still place in him.

To come down from heaven and the celestial ones to us mortals, His Holiness Pope Clement IX, in a special brief addressed to the Servant of God, thanked him, as we have seen,[176] for his labors and his zeal for the propagation of the gospel. He sent him his apostolic blessing and a quantity of indulgence medals to distribute among the new Christian communities he had founded. King Philip IV, now in glory, in the last year of his reign, moved by the esteem he had for his zeal and his holiness, ordered by royal *cédula* that the governor of the Philippines provide him with a vessel with all the necessary provisions so that he could sail to the Ladrones Islands, notwithstanding all the obstacles to this mission. And the queen, our lady, *doña* Mariana of Austria, always had the same

---

[175]Jth. 8:8.
[176]See Book 3, chap. 12:228.

*Book Four, Chapter 1*

esteem for the Servant of God, approving whatever projects he had and granting all his requests. In dispatches, which highly honored him, she commended to his prudence and zeal the spiritual and political governance of the Mariana Islands. Her Majesty valued as relics of great worth some pictures and fragments of others that were sent to her by Father San Vitores.

That great servant of God, Cardinal Sandoval, Archbishop of Toledo, always showed special appreciation for this Venerable Father. He revered him as a truly apostolic man chosen by God for the salvation of souls. With great trust in his merits, he took advantage of Father San Vitores' labors for the good of his own flock and entrusted to him enterprises in the service of God, which neither he nor others had been able to manage successfully, in spite of their authority and diligence. The illustrious *don* Miguel Poblete, Archbishop of Manila, whom he called, for his zeal, another Cardinal Sandoval, held him in the same esteem. This most zealous prelate, in a letter to *don* Jerónimo San Vitores, after greatly praising his son, says that he has kept for himself a letter that Father San Vitores had asked the archbishop to forward to him, because he esteemed and revered it because it was handwritten by the Servant of God.

Their Excellencies the *Marqueses* de Mancera, Viceroy and Vicereine of Mexico, showed their esteem when he passed through en route to the Marianas. They gave him every assistance, especially for his voyage to the Philippines. The *señora marquesa* venerated him as a saint from heaven. The *marqués*, writing to his father, *don* Jerónimo San Vitores, about the consolation that he and his whole family received when they met Father San Vitores in Mexico, adds: "I assure Your Lordship, without any flattery, that I see in him the living image of Saint Francis Xavier. Your Lordship should hold yourself most fortunate, for our Lord has given you such a son, and I am full of consolation for the promise he made of keeping this household in his prayers."

I do not wish to delay on particular testimonies, even if they be of great authority, for the veneration that strangers had of him was so general that there was no one who did not think him a holy man. This is the reputation he had in the University of Alcalá, both as a student and a professor there, among teachers and professors, religious and laity. Even the most disorderly students, on seeing him, began to behave and used to say, "That priest will be a martyr." One of our fathers who dealt with him all the time that he lectured there on philosophy, observed him carefully to see if his life was in accordance with his reputation. Afterwards he wrote that the high opinion that people had of Father San Vitores was incomparably less than the reality of his angelical life, of his observance of the rules of the Society, and zeal for the salvation of his neighbor. The same opinion was held in all places where he had been, whether in passing or to stay.

Concerning the veneration that he received in Mexico during his second stay in that city and later in the Marianas, I will transcribe here the statement of Father Casanova, who was fortunate to be his companion in both places:

*Father San Vitores's Reputation for Sanctity Among His Own and Among Strangers*

Because of the great reputation as a saint that he left in that city because of the fervent *Actos de Contrición* that he introduced there, as well as his other apostolic work, the admiration they showed whenever they met him passes belief. When the holy man went along the street, craftsmen stopped work to watch him, others went out to kiss his hands, and still others came to that city only to know him. All desired to have some article belonging to this Venerable Father as a precious relic, often using the stratagem of asking for his signature, so that they could remember to commend his missions to the Lord. A very distinguished gentleman took a thread from his cloak, since he could not obtain a memorial of him of greater quality, and was delighted to have it. A religious of our Society kept for a long time, among relics of other saints, a part of his signature. Even those of his household tried to get hold of something by the same means mentioned above. An admirer of the holy priest exchanged his hat for that of the holy father when he arrived in Mexico, on the pretext that it was so torn and colorless as to be below his dignity.[177] They tried hard to get hold of his old and mended shoes as a souvenir of the holy man. And because they forced him to accept new ones, he gave in, lest he disappoint his donor, and also so he could later give them away to some poor man. All had such a high notion of his extraordinary virtue and sanctity that there was one who received his letters on his knees, and he kept them with such deep feeling that he would not allow the least part of one to fall to the floor. A cassock that had belonged to Father San Vitores was given to a companion of his, so that he could wear it in the missions, and it was as if he had put on, with it, the wings and the spirit of a missionary. And remembering that that cassock had belonged to the Venerable Father, it seemed that he was filled not only with motives of devotion but with an eagerness to imitate his holy examples. His other companions who lived with him in the missions had the same esteem for his precious belongings. With extraordinary affection they preserved the least object that he had possessed. Which is much to say, since constant contact with him did not at all diminish their high esteem.

Thus far Father Casanova.

I have already mentioned the esteem that his brother Jesuits had for him. These were domestic and constant witnesses, bound to see any faults not easy to contradict. Yet their reverence for him was so great that those who dealt with him considered themselves fortunate and regarded as relics whatever precious thing they got from him. From the time he taught in Alcalá, whenever he was given a haircut, the barber used to sweep the floor beforehand, so that his hair would not be

---

[177]Cf. Book 2, chap. 16:155.

## Book Four, Chapter 1

mixed with that of others, and he distributed it as if it were that of a canonized saint. And what is more, the handkerchiefs with which he wiped his forehead, notwithstanding the care they had for cleanliness, were kept as relics, so much were they coveted by many. Particularly outstanding in this piety was Father Juan Gabriel Guillén, who, thanks to the great familiarity he had with the Servant of God, took him for a heavenly being, more like an angel than a man. Lest I be repetitious, I do not include here what is said by others of the Society, especially by his companions in the Marianas, who could not pronounce his name without praise. They called him a second Xavier, another Paul, a herald of the Law of God, a most valiant captain and a most wise doctor of the Mariana Church, angelic promoter of peace, most brilliant of the Christians in the Marianas, noble martyr, most pure virgin, and many other similar titles. A father who had known him in Mexico was not far from the truth when he called him the saint of this age, meaning that he was a miracle of God's grace in his Church for the proof of his power and the proof of his mercy.

Even the barbarians in Mindoro held him as a man more than human. They claimed they saw in him something they failed to see in other men. And in the Marianas the islanders called him Great Father, in spite of the effort of his humility to discourage the use of this title of honor, which he claimed he did not deserve; they also said that he was like Christ, who, although free from sin, suffered for those of others.

Father Bustillos brought Father San Vitores's cassock to Mexico to send it on to Madrid. It was the cassock in which he had suffered martyrdom, and which was later kept as a most priceless treasure by the Duchess of Aveyro, a great benefactress of the Mariana Islands.[178] But he had to give a piece of it to the Mariana islanders he had brought along, because they begged for it so insistently. This fragment they placed in a reliquary and wore it around their neck. When people in Mexico asked them what they were wearing, they answered with deep feeling, "Clothing of our saint and Great Father San Vitores, who baptized us." These words filled the Mexicans with emotion. They kissed the relic and placed it on their eyes and their head and said, "Oh, how blessed you are to have been baptized by a saint! You do not know the gift you have in being baptized by Father San Vitores." They continued with other praises, with which the *Marianos* joined in, raising their eyes to heaven, "Oh, holy Father San Vitores! How great was the name and the reputation you left on earth with your charity, your virtue, and your sanctity! We beg you, our Great Father, to intercede for us with God, our Lord, since you will be more appreciated in heaven than you were on earth. May he make all our nation good Christians, that they may go to heaven and praise him and enjoy him forever!"

All those who anywhere heard of the fame of this servant of God commend themselves to him with great confidence. But why won-

---

[178]The cassock was presented to the Bishop of Agaña, the Most Reverend Felixberto C. Flores, on May 18, 1970, and remains in Agaña. Cf. Note on page 199 of Alberto Risco, *The Apostle of the Marianas*, Agaña, 1970.

der that people pray to him who believe that he is in heaven, when, while he was still here on earth, people sailing to the Philippines commended themselves to him, after he had made the trip to the Marianas?

# CHAPTER II

*The Greatness of His Sanctity and His Perfection*

Such was the reputation that Father San Vitores achieved. I wish now to speak of the deeds and virtues for which he so fully deserved that fame. In this I am like the Queen of Sheba when she heard of the wisdom of Solomon. What they told her was not half so wonderful as what she herself witnessed.[179] So, too, after I heard so many praise the sanctity and perfection of this apostolic man, when I take a closer view of his works, his virtues, and his perfection, I feel that they have expressed much less than what I am seeing myself, and I am forced to address the Venerable Father in these words: "Blessed are the disciples and companions who had personal contacts with you, listened to your words, and witnessed your example. They will also be blessed who will see your works in this mirror and will know how to reproduce them in themselves."

God chose Father San Vitores as a vessel of election to make his name known to new nations and new peoples and to be the guide and leader of those who would proclaim that name to nations where it had never been heard. And so God endowed him generously with all those gifts and graces that were proper for such a superior vocation and with all the virtues in a heroic degree. Among these are the virtues that pertain directly to God and are called the theological virtues. By these, man offers in sacrifice to the Creator the most pleasing victim, blindfolded by faith, bound by hope, and inflamed by charity. Accompanying charity are the moral virtues, some infused and some acquired, as powers or instruments for performing all the good works with which man may go forward to his ultimate end. Saint Thomas, after Saint Gregory and Saint Ambrose, groups them under four headings called cardinal virtues, since they are, as it were, the hinges [Latin, *cardines*] of moral philosophy on which the rational and Christian life turns.[180] They are also called the principal virtues, because they embrace all the others (and so are like the four elements of the material world) that make up the whole of moral perfection. They regulate the four faculties of the soul that are capable of virtue or vice. They are the following: *prudence,* which enlightens the understanding, so that it in turn illuminates the will regarding what it should decide; *justice,* which prescribes laws to the will, so that it pays to Caesar what is due to Caesar, and to God what is owed to God; *fortitude,* which is the bridle and the spur of the irascible faculty in the sensitive part of the soul, and so makes it run or stop according to the norm of reason; *temperance,* which controls the desires of the concupiscible part, so that it may not stretch out a hand to forbidden fruit and be like another Eve, the cause of the downfall of man.

---

[179]1 Kings 10:1-13.
[180]Cardinal virtues, *Summa Theologiae, Iª IIae 56-61.*

*The Greatness of His Sanctity and His Perfection*

These four virtues are rightly compared to the four rivers of paradise, because the soul, through which they flow, is a garden planted, as it were, by God, always to be green and beautiful, full of flowers and fruit.[181]

To start with the innocence of Father San Vitores, which is the first part of sanctity and the best throne of the virtues, presiding from what others say, I content myself with the testimony that the Servant of God gave about himself, which speaks affirming his highest praise when he meant the greatest contempt. His companions used to hear him repeat often that he was the greatest sinner born of women. They retorted once, "How can Your Reverence say that, when we know that never in your life did you commit a serious, not even a deliberate venial sin?" To this he answered with great confusion, not being able to deny the truth or show himself ungrateful to the one who granted him such an extraordinary favor, "Even for that reason I am the worst man in the world. Because of those many favors and mercies that the good Lord and his holy Mother have granted me, I am not as worthy as I should be of such great favors. If God had given them to another man, even if he were a great sinner, he would be more grateful to God and his holy Mother." For all that, I don't deny that Father San Vitores committed the venial sins to which the human frailty of the greatest saints is subject. For Scripture says that there is no man who is without sin, and he who says he has no sin is a liar, and that the just man falls seven times a day.[182] Nor does his sanctity contradict these texts, in view of the small faults that are committed without full attention by all persons.

Father San Vitores acknowledged those faults in himself, and with great care he tried to cleanse himself of them, purifying himself more and more through the sacrament of penance, going to confession two or three times a day, when a priest was available, once in the morning, again at night, and also at noon. And if in the morning after having confessed, a half hour passed before he said Mass, he returned to the confessional, and if after that the same period of time elapsed, he went to confession a third time. Besides his love of purity, his hunger and thirst for justice and his insatiable desire for an increase in grace moved him to this great care. Hence, when a companion asked him why he went to confession so often, he answered, "Does not my angel know that whenever we approach the sacrament of penance, even after having confessed and renewed our sorrow, we receive more grace, as many graces as the times we confess? Why then should we miss this grace or receive Communion or say Mass without it, since it is of greater value than all the treasures of this world?" He also used to say that an act of virtue with which to attain even one additional degree of grace was better than to revive the dead. With this frame of mind, he used to repeat the words of Christ: "What does it profit a man, if he gain the whole world, to the loss of his own soul?"[183] And he used to add: "A loss of the soul is a loss of grace, and a loss of grace is a failure to gain all that we can gain of it, if we neglect to carry out any good work that we could possibly do." In order

---

[181]Gen. 2:10.

[182]1 John 1:10; Prov. 24:16.

[183]Matt. 16:26; Mark 8:36; Luke 9:25.

*Book Four, Chapter 2*

not to suffer this loss, he never wasted a minute of time, and at all times he tried with the exercise of the virtues to progress toward the highest sanctity. He used to fulfill with the greatest exactness the particular examination, noting down his progress every day, morning and evening, comparing the evening examination with the morning, yesterday with today, one week with another, and one month with another, to see if he advanced or stepped back on the road to perfection. He had the highest regard for this practice recommended by our father, Saint Ignatius. Consequently, he engaged a companion of his to remind him morning and evening to note down the examination score. This he did so that the companion would remember to note down his own examination. He himself never forgot, even in the midst of the most pressing activities.

He not only did as much work as he could, but he did it with the greatest perfection he could, and with the highest motivation he could. He sought the highest motive and as many good motives for each act in order to give his actions the highest perfection.

For this purpose, in his childhood and youth, he chose as his model Blessed Aloysius Gonzaga. When he began his ministry he chose Saint Francis Xavier and our father, Saint Ignatius. Or rather I should say that after the example of Saint Ignatius, he took for models all the saints whose lives he read. He looked at these as in a mirror in order to copy some perfection. For as Father Lorenzo Bustillos certifies (and he heard others confirm it), this servant of God tried to imitate all the saints in all their virtues, especially those saints who excelled in devotion to the Blessed Virgin and in zeal for the salvation of souls. He also states that he did not read anything in the lives of the saints or of other holy men that he did not notice in Father San Vitores during the three years that he was his companion.

However, in order to appreciate the greatness of the sanctity of this Servant of God, it is enough to know that he is a second Xavier. This name is given him by all those who dealt with and conversed with him, and no other eulogy is more often repeated in the *Processus* and letters. Expressing my own mind, I do not find in all our annals one who was more like Saint Francis Xavier than this admirable man. And it seems that God has consoled us, who have not deserved to see the great Apostle of the Indies, by giving us a living portrait of him in Father San Vitores, even as he consoled the world that did not know Paul by giving it Saint Francis Xavier. Since the portrait always loses something of the original, so does the copy of the portrait. That is why I do not try to make Father San Vitores equal to Saint Francis Xavier or Saint Francis Xavier equal to Saint Paul. Still, no one can deny that, as the second apostle of the Gentiles was similar to the first in his virtues and graces, the third was similar to the second in the same perfection and privileges.

From the time he dedicated himself heart and soul to the good of souls, he said, "In all my actions and judgments I try to be totally Xavier." He continually asked this from the holy apostle. His devotion was constant; every day he read a chapter of his life or a part of his letters or instructions. And he did this so perfectly that a companion of his stated that he did not differ in any way in his actions from those of the holy apostle, guiding himself by those that he found in his apostolic life, and that as he read the life of Saint Francis Xavier it seemed that he read the life of Father San Vitores. If we wished to compare the portrait with the original, feature by feature, we would have to match the actions of the one with those of the other and so repeat the same things twice. Hence, I will content myself with recounting for our edification the more outstanding examples of Father San Vitores, so that anyone who is curious to see the similarity may compare them with those of the great Apostle of the Indies.

# CHAPTER III

### *His Faith, Hope, and Charity*

In order that the divine faith, which is the foundation of the whole spiritual edifice, may be perfect, three conditions are required: firmness of the heart in believing what God says; profession with the lips of what one believes; and the active implementation of what is professed. The firmness proves that it is true faith; the profession that it is faith worthy of praise; and the action that it is a living faith. The voice of the blood, shed in defense of the truth, showed openly with what firmness Father Diego Luis believed the divine mysteries. How glorious was his profession of faith, the words he uttered at his death testified so well, as he proclaimed the faith for which he died. Already before this, the zeal with which he had taught the divine mysteries in a Christian land, proclaimed his faith as clearly as the fourteen thousand leagues he journeyed over land and sea to make it known to the Gentiles. He was not content with professing the faith himself, unless all men professed it, and he would gladly have taught them all. His works gave life to his faith. This is shown by his ardent charity, never idle, and always active in the love and service of God and in drawing all men to God's love and service. And all his virtues proclaim it as they reveal the greatness of his faith, just as the height of a magnificent building proves the depth of its foundation.

Corresponding to his faith was his hope, which was built upon his faith, raising its arms to heaven to win from God the eternal treasures. With what certitude did this Servant of God hope for his salvation and perfection, the crown of martyrdom, and many other extraordinary favors and graces. Although with his humility he judged himself unworthy of it all, he fixed his eyes upon the goodness and kindness of the Lord, so that very often he repeated: "Oh, how good a God we have! He is better than we ever thought!" This hope was the source of his contempt of any ambition to be important and exalted in the world. A career of honors was something promised him by the high rank of his family and his own natural gifts. For him they were but shackles that he broke when he entered the Society of Jesus. Moved by this hope, he left Spain, his father, his brothers, relatives, and friends, so that he could sail to the Indies, to live among barbarians and die at their hands, overcoming difficulties, hardships, and perils, insurmountable by strength less than his hope. He expected such great benefits and happiness not only for himself but also for others, even if they did not know God or had forgotten him or were drowned in wickedness. Strengthened by prayer for their conversion, he infused courage and comfort in the greatest sinners, telling them: "How much greater than our sins is the divine mercy, and how much God wishes, not the death of the sinner but that he be converted and live eternally.[184] He will pardon them as he did the Magdalene, the Good Thief, the Samaritan woman, and other great sinners. It is the same God who pardoned them and his mercy has not diminished, nor has it been used up by the pardon of so many." And with these words, full of his own confidence, he inspired the greatest sinners, bringing so many to penance and not a few to perfection.

His hope never wavered and was always undaunted at the sight of opposition. Rather, as they say of the palm tree, which grows even higher as it grows heavier, his trust increased with the difficulties. He himself used to say: "The more difficult in the eyes of men was the business of God's glory, the greater hope he had in the same Lord, and the greater courage he had in serving it." This is seen clearly in the enterprise of the Mariana Islands, when in the face of so many obstacles and difficulties and impossibilities, for so they seemed to men of the greatest zeal, nothing dismayed or stopped him. Indeed his superiors, as we have seen,[185] ordered him not to mention this enterprise when speaking with the governor of the Philippines (so much did they fear a hostile reaction on his part) but to change the subject if it came up. It was then that he declared with greater certainty that his entry into the Marianas was assured and without any doubt. He based the certainty that he had in the most difficult enterprises on these words of the angel to Mary: "For nothing is impossible with God."[186] It seemed to him that the more obstacles men placed against the works of his service, the more insistent was God to show his power in carrying them out. The intercession of the Mother of God expelled all fear he might have from his humility and sense of unworthiness. Her intercession was the harbor of good hope to which he fled in all his desperate moments and difficulties. As one of his companions said, there was nothing that he did not hope to obtain through the intercession of the Blessed Virgin Mary.

The virtue of charity, which is the queen of all virtues, was the queen of those that shone in this Servant of God. Supreme in itself, the love of God inspired the acts of all the other virtues, causing all to be motivated by the greater glory of God, after the example of our father, Saint Ignatius. In the Marianas this was the subject matter of his particular examination: not to do or say anything that was not inspired by this motive. He loved God with all his heart, with all his soul, and with all his strength, for he harbored in his heart no other love. God was the sole object of his memory, his understanding, and his will. He never forgot his favors, always discussed his greatness, and loved his perfections. He employed all his strength in serving him whom he loved, never omitting whatever he could do for his Lord. Whatever he did for the Lord, to whom infinite service is due, always seemed to him little and of no account.

There was not room enough inside his heart for the fire of love, and it swelled out in words or burning flames, as he said: "Oh, sweet Jesus of my soul! Oh, good Jesus! Jesus, my good Jesus! How good is the God we have! How good a Lord he is! Oh, Jesus of my soul, my life, my

[184]Ezek. 33:11.
[185]See Book 2, chap. 14:145.
[186]Luke 1:37.

heart!" Father Lorenzo Bustillos says that it seemed so ordinary to him and as natural as breathing to repeat the names of Jesus and Mary and these loving ejaculations. Since he never ceased even when he was with companions, be they religious or lay persons, he used to say with great bashfulness and humility, "Pardon me, if I err. I can't help it. I'm such a sinner!" He uttered these words accompanied with sighs and tears, sometimes with great sweetness out of his love for Jesus, at other times with great sorrow because of the offenses committed by men. Not a few times it seemed that he could not control himself and that he would burst if he did not pour forth these sentiments and sighs. The same Father Bustillos says that we cannot explain with our words the ardor of his, and that his burning heart seemed to melt with the fire of the love of God expressed in those loving sentiments that he so ceaselessly repeated. In all those who heard him he inspired the love of God, heating and burning the most frigid souls with the fire that burst forth from his mouth. And he caused his companions to acquire the habit of repeating the name of Jesus. His lips, so accustomed to pronounce the most sweet names of Jesus and Mary, did not cease even in his sleep to repeat these names; and so during his sleep he was frequently heard exclaiming: "My Jesus, God of my soul; no, Lord of my soul; most holy Mother of my soul; no, my dear Lady."

This seraphic man knew no other language but that of the love of God. In conversations and letters, whenever he ran short of words, he continued with expressions of his love of God, moving from whatever subject matter he was dealing with to that of love. He always ended his letters with the love of God, to which he exhorted his correspondents, and prayed for it for himself, for those to whom he was writing, and for all others. Very often he began with the subject of love, continued, and ended with it. He wrote a letter to his father from Cádiz, which he began before they set sail and continued after. He began it with these words: "The Holy Spirit, whose feast day we await, will send us favorable winds and will lead us where it pleases him that we should arrive. May he kindle in us, in you, and in the whole world the fire, which during this holy season he poured out on the apostles and disciples, so that they might set the whole world on fire with his divine love, with the tongues of fire, and with their hearts aflame with love." And later he continues, "I am consoled, even humanly speaking, when I earnestly consider your excellency along with my brothers and the little angels, some asking blessings and others giving them, all of them so pleasing in their innocence to the heavenly Father, who force him to have mercy on sinners and convert them to his divine love, and to give the light of his gospel to those who are in the darkness of death, and to make of his ministers men according to his heart, and to enkindle them in such a way that they may inflame the whole world in the love and homage of him who created all men and died for them and sent to all his divine Spirit. Oh, may such a great gift not be wasted!" And he ends the letter: "May the Holy Spirit favor us with good winds, so that we may set sail and arrive at the port that his most holy goodness has prepared for us. May he inflame you and all others with his love. May he lead us to the port of happiness together with many others who may know him and may praise him for all eternity." A good proof of how much he tried to spread this love is his diligence in trying to establish everywhere the *Acto de Contrición*. He refers to something that may seem to be of little account, but that is precisely a great manifestation of this love that he wished to enkindle. In the letters to his parents he used to request that they recite for him an Act of Contrition. It seems to be only a request for prayers, but it was really meant to inflame their hearts with the fire of the love of God. Out of this love and the yearning to enkindle it, there arose in him the grief and pain for any offense that he committed against our Lord. His heart used to be broken whenever he heard a blasphemy against God or against his Mother. It seemed as if he must die of pain. He would speak with Christ as if he saw him present, crucified or scourged, and he would repeat with deep tenderness and affection, "Oh, sweet Jesus, oh, good Lord and good Lady!" When in his sermons he exhorted the faithful to the love of God and said that no one should offend such a good Lord, his face used to flush and it seemed that it was all aflame with the love of God. Soon after arriving in the Marianas he contracted a burning fever that lasted more than nine days. One of his companions believed that it was due to his love of God and to the pain caused by the obstacles to the preaching and spread of the faith placed by the devil through his instrument Choco. The same thing may be believed regarding the fever and sun stroke that he had later on the island of Tinian. No doubt this was caused, aside from the effort to establish peace among the inhabitants of that island, by the pain he felt because the war made an end to the spread of the gospel. When they asked him if he was sick, to disguise his maladies he used to answer, "I am sick with love for God, because I have so little of it." But with more reason could he say, like the spouse, that he was sick with love because he had so much of it.[187]

As the fire tends to rise upward toward its own sphere, this heavenly man desired to go up to heaven, as to his own place, to be united with, to embrace his Lord forever. And with a sigh he used to add, "How many holy men, many that we have known, are already in heaven, and we are in this valley of tears, in this world. Oh good God and holy Mother, when will the happy day come when we will see you in heaven?" While waiting for that day, his greatest consolation was to see our Lord, even though hidden, in the Blessed Sacrament and to embrace him in Holy Communion. That is why he never failed to say Mass whenever he could, whether on land or at sea. Very often he had to wait till noon to have the opportunity of saying Mass.[188] At other times he walked many miles on foot and moved from island to island to arrive at a place where Mass was to be said. He felt real suffering when he could not say Mass or receive Holy Communion because of the lack of hosts or other difficulties in the missions. When ill, he received Communion every day. In one sickness in Alcalá, according to a father who assisted him, he could not

---

[187] Sg (Song) 2:5.
[188] Thus he would have to fast from food and drink from midnight on.

be persuaded to take medicine or rinse his mouth after midnight, so that he could receive Communion in the morning. Such was the case on all the days of his illness. Every day he made many visits to the Blessed Sacrament and spent long hours there, contemplating the goodness shown by our Lord in his sovereign gift. In the end he had no greater consolation in this long exile than to speak with God in prayer, to serve him by the conversion of souls, and to suffer much for His love. We will deal with all these points in their proper places, dwelling everywhere on his love, since, as the iron penetrated by the fire looks like the fire itself, so all the actions of this Servant of God, penetrated by this fire, appear to be sheer acts of the love of God.

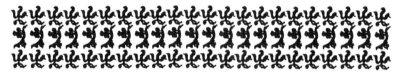

# CHAPTER IV

*His Charity Toward His Neighbor*

The love of God bids us love our neighbor for the love of God. And so Christ calls it a second commandment similar to the first. That is why after we have described how he fulfilled the first commandment to love God, we should describe how he observed the second commandment, to love our neighbor for the love of God. This charity obliges us to love our parents, relatives, friends, benefactors, enemies, the faithful, the pagans, and all men, beginning with the concern for their souls and then with concern for their bodies. How much more noble is that part of man whose true home is heaven than that which was fashioned from earth. This Servant of God, then, loved all men with well ordered charity.

He loved his parents and relatives with the love he was taught not by flesh and blood, but by the heavenly Father, joining together those extremes of hatred that Christ commands in several places of the gospel. He loved them in what is related to the service of God and not in what is contrary to it. Thus, he first left them for the sake of the vocation to which God called him; and then in order to go to the Indies where God wanted him. When he was about to set sail for the Indies, no one was able to persuade him, even though his father begged him to see his brother, the viscount, who was then in Jaén, since it was only a short detour, and if he lost this occasion, he could never again see him in this life. Father Blas de Mura, who was his companion at this time, writes in a letter to Father Guillén that he tried with many arguments to have him make this trip and thus please his father. But he answered that he would only go if he were told to by his superiors, because he was completely detached from all his relatives and was without any love based only on flesh and blood. So it was necessary for him to be ordered by his superiors; then he gave in to the will of God. Although he was detached from his relatives he never forgot them; rather, they were the first in his prayers and his sacrifices. He wished them all spiritual and even temporal welfare, but in the manner in which he explains in a letter to his father from Cádiz: "I will never forget to commend to our Lord even the temporal affairs of my brother, in the sense that you wish; which is that we should pray for them to His Divine Majesty, only that they may be in accordance with Holy Providence, that all be for his greater glory, the greater good of his soul, and that of yourself, and all your household. And I have no doubt that such will be the case in whatever happens, in view of the goodness of him who wanted us to ask with this confidence, and who on his part procured for us the merits that cannot be found in us." In another letter, written from the Philippines, he writes that the farther away he is from his brothers, nephews, and cousins for the love of God, the closer he holds them in that same love and in his humble prayers. He made his father a companion in his missions, reporting to him on his journeys, his labors, his successes, and he asks him to cooperate by carrying out his errands and sending alms for all his apostolic enterprises. He thus attributed to him in great measure the conversion of souls. In his letters he considers him two or three times his father, one for the existence he gave him, then because he permitted him to enter the Society of Jesus, and thirdly because he let him be assigned to the Indies. Thus his father showed that he loved him more after he offered him in sacrifice to God. Finally, he does not spare any occasion in his letters to exhort him respectfully, as well as his brother and sisters and relatives to love the Lord and serve him in all sincerity.

I do not know if I will be able to describe his love for the whole Society, for those who were his fathers and brothers in Christ. There was nothing he commended to his father as more important than the affairs of the Society, begging him to regard them as his own. He loved those who had been his spiritual fathers more than if they had been his earthly parents, and each one of the Society was for him more than a brother. He remembered particularly the Province of Toledo as a mother who gave him birth in Christ and nourished him with the milk of virtue, and deprived itself of him for the sake of the Indies, for the good of that pagan world, as he tells Father Guillén in the following words: "I will never forget the fathers and brothers of that province, never more mine than it is now (just as we call that other gentleman two times father, ever since he gave his good consent). For whenever I am freed from dangers, when I am successful in anything or at least do not spoil what others accomplish with the help of divine grace, I owe it all to my good mother and holy province, which brought me up, and I trust will not forget me in her holy prayers and sacrifices, especially in the prayers of those who know how very much I need them, that I may not disgrace with my behavior the name of my good fathers and brothers." It is a source of consolation to read in his letters how he remembers in particular all those who have sent him tokens of their remembrance of him. In one letter he sent from the Marianas he recalls eighty by their names, and in general he sends messages to all the scholastics and novices. To some individuals of his province he recommends some particular towns in the Mariana Islands, that they ask God for their conversion and perseverance in the Faith, and that they have special influence in the success that he attributed to the prayers of all.

If this was the love he had for all his brothers in Christ, what must have been his love for those who in the Marianas and in other missions helped him in the conversion of souls? Among them he includes the lay persons who accompanied him in his ministries as assistants in the work of God. In matters spiritual and of heavier responsibility all found rest in him, particularly when he knew his companion was tired or reluctant to do something. Then, as if he were not aware of it, he would do it himself with pleasure. If someone objected to his doing it, he adduced such reasons for the convenience of it, that he convinced him that only he should do it. In his travels he carried in those two bags that he had made of coconut leaves, provision of things that his companions might need, even needle and thread. For this purpose, he picked up off the floor articles of this sort, and whenever someone needed it, he gave it to him with much love. He had some clothing stored in the mission station, not for himself, but for his companion, in case he should get wet. As for himself, he covered himself with some matting while his clothing dried. He would recall that he was superior, only when caring for his companions, taking advantage of this authority to order them to accept what was better in the matter of food, dress, or quarters, when they, as was to be expected, were reluctant to accept them. He was wont to give his bed or straw mat to the native or layman who accompanied him, with the pretext that he was tired or needed it more, while he spent the night seated on a bench for the brief time he slept, spending the rest of the night on his knees in prayer.

When some companion, whether a layman or religious, was ill, no mother could care for her son more devotedly than he cared for the sick man. He remained at his bedside during the daytime and left only when it was necessary. At night, he stayed with him, dispensing with his own repose, and if the sick man complained of pain, he immediately placed his hands on the afflicted part, so that with this contact the patient felt relieved. The sick men themselves wondered at this care. It was the effect of the love with which he carried out this ministry of the sick, wishing that he could remove all pain and anguish and assume them himself. All the natives were benefited by this love and service. Thus when he went out to visit the sick of one town, those of the other town whom he failed to visit felt it very much, since they claimed that they felt relieved by the mere sight of the Great Father. But this charity, which followed him to the Marianas, had accompanied him all his life everywhere, in the cities, on the roads, and on board ship. It could not desert him, nor could he desert the sick, for his greatest consolation was to comfort the afflicted, and his greatest repose was to help the needy. When some lay companion, tempted by the devil, desired to go free and fled to the pagans, he could not rest day or night until he found him, searching for him in the mountains and valleys, with great peril for his life, until he found the lost sheep. In order that the fathers, who were distributed among the islands, might not be deprived of the consolation of sacramental confession, he would expose himself many times to the danger of drowning. Once a father complained that Father San Vitores went to the island where he was at a most risky time, when it was more reasonable that he himself should come to Father San Vitores. But he answered, "If anyone should be in danger, it is better that it should be myself, for I will be less missed."

Of the affectionate relationship he had with his friends, suffice it to say, as we read in the testimony for canonization, each of those who dealt familiarly with this servant of God thought that he was his best friend. And since his friendship was based on God, it suffered no changes, nor did he feel any anxiety or distance from him. This is shown by a letter he wrote from Manila to Father Juan Gabriel Guillén, who was his closest friend. I quote this letter so that we may learn from his own words how our friendships should be. "In this year of 1664, although the ship arrived from New Spain, there was no mail from Castille. But this lack assures us that there is nothing lacking in the sacrifice we made to God when we parted for his love. But above all, we are consoled that our principal means of communication is not across distant lands and seas but through the one undivided, immortal third party, in whom even the dead are alive and the absent do not depart, and who with the most loving care that he has for his own, saves us from the worry that something may have happened or might happen to those whom we love solely in the hearts of Jesus Christ and the Virgin Mary."

Regarding his love for his enemies (although I could report many examples, since all his life he cared for those who did him wrong, conquering with good deeds the evil done, in accordance with the counsel of the apostle),[189] I content myself with the love he showed by his death, imitating the love of Christ, praying for mercy for his assassins. But why do I distinguish between enemies and friends, acquaintances and strangers? His charity, like that of the apostle, reached all as if they were his own, making himself all to all to win them all.[190] He treated them all as friends to make them friends of God, embracing with his apostolic love the whole world, Spaniards, civilized natives, barbarians, Moors, Jews, heretics, and pagans, wishing that all might know, love, and serve their Creator and Redeemer. And he treated all with such exquisite courtesy that they could not part from him, according to Father Lorenzo Bustillos, because in dealing with him they felt consoled, relieved of their afflictions and hardships. The same Father Bustillos admits about himself, that when he went to confession to the Servant of God, he felt sorry that the confession ended, and he would like to be continually confessing to him because of the consolation he felt in his soul. The greatest sinners, kneeling at his feet, lost all shame and embarrassment for the sins they had to confess. The children of the Marianas wanted no other for their teacher, and although the Venerable Father used to scold them so that they would not be too attached to him and refuse to attend another teacher's class, they went back to his with the same affection saying, "*Padre Maagas* (Great Father), teach us for the love of God."

This yearning to be of service to all made him walk so many miles, sail through so many seas, expose himself to so many dangers, dangers in rivers where he nearly drowned; dangers from thieves (as they formerly named the *Marianos*); dangers from their country or religion, since he did not lack persecution from the Christians themselves; dangers from the pagans, who often threatened him with their spears; dangers in the city and dangers in the wilderness and dangers in the sea; dangers from false brothers, since the natives who accompanied him tried to wound him and were the cause of so many risks; in labors and weariness, walking mostly barefoot, on sharp stones and thorny places that made him shed so much blood; in many vigils, in hunger and thirst,

---

[189] Rom. 12:21.
[190] I Cor. 9:22.

*His Charity Toward His Neighbor*

in many fasts; in cold and nakedness, passing many days and nights, now on land, now on sea, exposed to the rigors of the weather; besides the continual solicitude for the churches that were under his care, being ill with those who are ill, and burning with those who suffer scandal, lacking nothing in the catalog of the apostle's hardships, even unto stoning and shipwreck, since this follower of Paul, no less in hardships than in zeal, was stoned many times, especially when he was stoned twice on the island of Tinian and their stones melted on reaching him. Many times he suffered shipwreck, day and night, on wild and stormy seas, looking on death in the waves to give life to the pagans.[191]

Many years back he had made a vow to spend all his life in the salvation of souls. And so as far as obedience would allow, he added the ministry of popular missions to the other positions he held in the Society. He was not content with the knowledge that all the ministries and occupations in the Society are directed to the salvation of souls and work together as parts of one body engaged in an apostolic task. He would rather give himself directly, right now, to their conversion and salvation. Hence, during the day he was busy teaching, catechizing, baptizing, hearing confessions, preaching, and in other ministries. At night when he could not be with other people, he spent the time in prayer, asking God for their conversion, and in writing letters and memorials to the king, ministers, and superiors, begging them to see that the gospel be preached. He also gave himself to composing books and devotional tracts for the promotion of all manner of piety and devotion. He regretted that any instant of time was lost, even if it were not employed for the salvation of souls, and this with such scrupulosity, that when he had to write something, he had the chair ready for his secretary lest time were lost in having to look for it. And if the secretary asked Father San Vitores to sit down (seeing him standing there), he felt it very much, saying the time was wasted in polite addresses.

He would not stop nor slacken in his priestly work for being ill. Father Lorenzo Bustillos emphasizes this regarding the first sickness he had on Guam. When Father San Vitores set out with Father Morales to visit the other islands, he left Father Bustillos with Father Luis de Medina on Guam with instructions about what he had to do during his absence. When Father Bustillos said in reply, "How can I take care of all those things that you are telling me to do?" he revealed to him his sickness in order to encourage him, and said, saying, "Listen, Little Angel, we are capable of more things than we think with the grace of God. I never thought I could get through these last nine days with the continual fevers I have endured, busy with all that you have seen, and the fever even still continues." Father Bustillos, who reports this, exclaims: "Oh, the wonderful power of God! How much this tireless man accomplished in nine days oppressed with fever, never relenting in his work, with nothing to eat but our ordinary roots and herbs boiled in water without salt. And yet he seemed to work with more energy on those days, because he had each day divided into periods for catechizing, baptizing, finding and studying

---

[191] 2 Cor.11:23-28.

*Book Four, Chapter 4*

new words, in dictating and teaching methods of composition and the use of vocabulary, and finally in all the other domestic occupations, seeing to the welfare of all and watching until midnight in the porter's lodge, so that the others might all get their rest." This is what Father Bustillos tells about the sickness on Guam. In that on Tinian, which was more serious, he followed the same routine, not ceasing after serious sunstroke from his journeys on foot, his work, his prayer, his fasting, and his penances, in order to establish peace and friendship among those warring islanders, until his weak body collapsed and fell to the ground, unable to keep up with the energy and quickness of his spirit.

There was no means that he would not make use of for the good of souls: sermons, conferences, conversations, letters, emissaries, promises, threats, catechetical sessions, the spiritual exercises of Saint Ignatius, and countless others. But the first means was to approach God in prayer for the conversion of those to whom he had to preach. Every day he repeated many times the prayer that Saint Francis Xavier composed for the conversion of the infidels, which begins: "Eternal God." I will place it at the end of this book, translated unto Spanish for anyone who may wish to recite it every day and thus help in any possible way towards the good of souls, as the Servant of God desired and requested.[192] He saw to it that it was recited by all his companions, not only the religious but also by the laymen of the community, every night after supper after the litanies and rosary of our lady. He used to say it with great tenderness and fervor during his travels and at the end of the canonical hours, as well as at other times during the day.

He would visit the islands many times by himself, going about incessantly from one place to another. As often as possible he went by land in order to inflict all the damage possible on the devil, teaching and baptizing all those he met. He instructed his lay helpers in the manner of catechizing, baptizing, and helping the dying, so that they could exercise these ministries in cases of necessity and make up for the lack of ministers. He taught the children, so that he might, with these first letters, lead them to a pious life. For this reason he founded the Seminary of San Juan Letrán in Agadña, and he ordered that others be established in the other islands. He translated into the Mariana language the Christian doctrine and the Act of Contrition. So that the natives might discard their prayers to the *anites*, he composed in verse in their language a very devout prayer to God. The *Marianos* were fond of singing, so he made a song of the sweet names of Jesus, Mary, and Joseph. And since they were such natural dancers, he danced and sang with them to make the Christian doctrine attractive to them. How many obstacles and contradictions he had to overcome everywhere he stayed in order to establish the *Acto de Contrición* along the streets. In the Philippines he introduced the custom that on Sundays, feast days, and Saturdays, the choirs, and there were good ones in each town, instead of the usual hymns, should sing the *saetillas* on the Four Last Things, on the gravity of sin, and on the Passion of Christ, and these he composed in the language of the country.

---

[192] See Appendix.

He used to write letters and reports to Europe about the fruits he harvested in the Indies, and he begged those in Europe to write to the Indies, because of the encouragement that each would receive from the knowledge of the work of the others in the service of God and the good of souls. Hence, when he answered Father Guillén, who had sent him news about his mission and *Actos de Contrición*, he told him how profitable such news was to them. He adds, "Let not Your Reverence stop writing about this matter, for one letter of this type bears as much, even more fruit than many spiritual conferences and costs less than a sermon. Not without reason did our holy apostle Xavier desire that news of this kind be sent everywhere." I omit the other means of which Father San Vitores availed himself, which can be verified in the account of his life. Hence, I need not repeat all here. Suffice it to say that he had no other thought or discourse day and night than to promote the glory of God and the good of souls.

From this zeal sprang the joy he felt when he learned of the conversion of sinners and the spiritual progress of souls. One evening at supper in Mexico City, after performing the *Acto de Contrición*, he exclaimed joyfully: "Oh, how tasty the supper is after performing the *Acto de Contrición*." Once in the same city he asked an acquaintance of his to buy him a book by *padre fray* Luis de Granada. He found a well-used copy in a bookstore and brought it to the Venerable Father. He was afraid the father would be displeased with it for being in such poor condition and so expensive. But the Servant of God, on seeing the book, said, "I'm glad that it is so spoiled, because it is a sign that it has served its purpose, and perhaps some persons have derived much profit from reading it." When in the Mariana Islands he heard the children repeating the names of Jesus and Mary, he was overwhelmed with satisfaction and clapped his hands with pleasure, bursting out in the joyful sentiments we have mentioned above.

The source of this zeal was the supreme value the souls had for him. He used to say that there was no need of a reward for the conversion of souls other than the conversion itself and that for the salvation of only one soul all the hardships of this life, no matter how great they may be should be regarded as well employed. Consequently, when he went about in his missions and fell into rivers and mud holes and shed blood because of thorny bushes that cut into feet and hands, he would remark laughingly to Father Bustillos, as this father himself reports, "If we find a child to baptize, it will be a nice reward for us." The Servant of God used also to say that if in crossing from one island to another the boat were to break up in the middle of the sea and there were not enough boards for the safety of all, and someone were to say that he was in the state of mortal sin and did not have any contrition and necessary disposition to make his confession, he would give up his own board to save that man's life and thus give him time to dispose himself for salvation. Yes, he would allow himself to drown, happy to die for the salvation of that soul. This was not much for one to say who affirmed in all truth, "We must undergo a thousand deaths in order to see that a soul gains the grace of God."

## Book Four, Chapter 4

With such a great desire to die for Christ, he even repeated many times that there was no death so glorious that he did not regard it as less than winning one soul for God. He used to say to his companions, "What you should try for is to gain many souls for heaven, without worrying about martyrdom, for that is something God grants to those who deserve it." We would never end if we were to relate all that he did and suffered for the salvation of souls. And all that seemed to be so little to him, and it was if we compare it with what he was anxious to do. For after having converted all the Mariana Islands, he intended to go to Japan and to the *Tierra Austral*, the unknown land to the south, which is regarded as the fifth part of the world. And all this was small sphere for his zeal, since he wanted to enkindle the whole world in the love of God.

He was not content with his own missionary work; he tried to make missionaries of as many as he could. He particularly prayed that all Jesuits should be missionaries, joining this ministry to whatever others were assigned to them by obedience, provided it was compatible with the fulfillment of their obligations. If they excused themselves for lack of time, he begged them to at least go out on one mission. If they answered that they didn't have talent for preaching or lacked practice, he said they should explain religious doctrine and include a pious story. He had others conduct the *Acto de Contrición*. Those he found with talent for the missions, he brought with him to instill in them the love of it. He set them all on fire with the zeal that burned in his own heart; especially in the Marianas, it seemed that he infused his own spirit in all who accompanied him or were sent by him to convert the pagans. To those who were successful in the work of conversion, he showed his gratitude, as if they had done a favor to him, and he praised them in his letters to Europe, for it seemed to him that all those who were employed in such a fruitful ministry were worthy of all praise.

# CHAPTER V

### *His Admirable Prudence*

The virtue of prudence, which is the guide of all the other virtues and the measure of all actions and the rule for all success, was, according to his companions, admirable in this Servant of God. Before he reached maturity, his prudence was mature, inborn rather than learned, supernatural rather than human. At the age of twelve, his mother used to send him to discuss the most important affairs of their house with the first ministers and with the *conde duque*, and he conversed with him with such wisdom and discretion that the *conde duque* would listen to him for a long time with admiration.[193] With the years and experience his prudence increased, and much more with the light that God gave him for the success of all his decisions, especially after God made him an apostle and teacher of new peoples. For God illumined him in a special way as a man who was to enlighten others. It may be said that he was endowed eminently with all those kinds of prudence pointed out by Saint Thomas Aquinas, such as the personal, which they call solitary, to govern his own actions; the economic, to rule his house and the school of the Marianas; the civil or political, to direct the republic of the Marianas; the legislative, to make laws and rules for the guidance of many for their salvation and perfection; and even the military, to direct an army.[194] For God gave all these charges to him. True, that as his prudence was supernatural, he did not always conform to human rules, but guided himself by higher principles. The results themselves showed that they were divinely guided, though they seemed to human eyes, less wise.

Whenever he could, he consulted prudent, wise, and holy men, especially his superiors, knowing that for the religious, the voice of the superior is the oracle of the propitiatory, one who is supported by him who is seated above the cherubin.[195] When he was superior he used to consult his subjects and even the lay persons in areas where they were competent, seeking success through humility. But since he could find it only in God, he did not decide anything important until light came from above. In the matters that pertained to the glory of God and the salvation of souls, which seemed to be easier or required more prompt action, he used to visit the Blessed Sacrament and have his companions visit the Blessed Sacrament, saying an Our Father and a Hail Mary there to beg light from our Lord through our Lady. Then he decided what was to be done. The more difficult affairs he commended for some days to God and his Mother and had his companions do the same in all their prayers and masses. Then there was a pause, during which he sought to know the will of God, and then he said, "This we should do because it is pleasing to God and the Blessed Virgin." After all these efforts, he sometimes

---

[193]Cf. Book I, chap. 5:23, n. 22.
[194]The five different kinds of Prudence.
[195]Exod. 25:10, 16. The propitiatory or throne of mercy was to rest upon or cover the ark of the covenant.

told his companions to commend it further to God. And then when they least expected it, he would call them, and after visiting the Blessed Sacrament, he would decide what was most for the glory of God. One of his companions describes this manner of making decisions in detail and states that he never decided anything, no matter how small it might be, without consulting our Lord through prayer. To this same companion he gave a method for the solution of doubtful cases when there was no superior to consult nor anyone to ask for advice. He said they should first say an Our Father and a Hail Mary silently; then they should ask God for light to know what should be done in that case through the intercession of the Blessed Virgin and all the saints.

I will not delay in relating examples and adduce particular cases of his prudence, since all the actions of his life were such, always done for the greater glory of God and the salvation of souls. About his prudence in the governance of his subjects, one of them, Father Casanova, used to say that he built the house of Saint Ignatius in Agadña in the form of a residence with such effective order of the domestic activities and such a good arrangement of the ministries that it seemed that he had been engaged in that occupation for a long time without any other office to attend to. He treated his subjects with an effective gentleness and a gentle effectiveness so that they advanced in personal perfection as well as in zeal for their neighbors' salvation, and this more by his example than by his words. Yet, these, too, were such that they obtained what he wished, by impressing in their hearts a deep appreciation of God's grace and of the souls that Jesus Christ purchased at the price of his blood. Thus he led them to yearn for God's grace for themselves and for the salvation of souls. Then he measured the strength of each one and assigned him to the occupation most suited to his capacity and talents. He wished that all would walk in the joy of the Lord, since sadness is such an obstacle in the exercise of God's service. He used to tell his companions that the ministers of the gospel should use every licit means of planting the faith and the grace of God in mission country. He strongly urged them to protect themselves from the danger of death, as much as was possible and licit. Otherwise the harm to the new Church of Christ in the loss of many souls of children recently baptized and of dying adults still unbaptized, was greater than the usefulness of any kind of death no matter how glorious. Because, he added, in the villages where such deaths occur, since they are enemies of the Christians, they would let no missionary enter for fear of the punishment that such crimes deserve. He also added that the lay companions and their equipment were not sufficient as a guard and escort for the clergy. It was better to go with the fewest companions possible, and that for three reasons: that there would be a smaller loss of personnel if death should occur; that they would be more assured that they suffered for God alone; that they would learn to place their trust in God alone and not in the protection of men. He used to add that all the missionaries should always see death close at hand, lest it surprise them suddenly, should it happen. One of our men confessed to him that he had feared death on one occasion. And he said to

*His Admirable Prudence*

him, inflamed with the love of God, "Are you afraid of that? Let no one hear about it. I would be glad if they would catch up with me and take my life because of God, since on account of that many would come from Europe to this mission eager to die for Christ." These words were so forceful that never again did that priest have that fear. On the contrary he encountered continuous dangers for the glory of God, desirous to meet death as his reward.

Although the means he made use of to lead the *Marianos* to God, of which we have already spoken, were ordinarily gentle and courteous, and for this they loved and revered him, calling him "Great Father" and "Good Father", he could be strict and stern when the occasion demanded. Once when one of the missionary companions of the Servant of God was teaching Christian doctrine in the church, a leading pagan noble, who was partial to Choco, approached the catechumens. The missionary asked him, as he did the others, who was God, and he answered that it was Puntan. He repeated the question many times and always received the same answer. Father San Vitores stood there watching, and as he knew the ancient error of the *Marianos*, he stood in the middle of the church and asked him with great gentleness, who was God. When the answer was as before, that it was Puntan, he scolded him severely and expelled him from the church, saying that he who uttered such blasphemies did not deserve to be in the church where the Lord had his altar and tabernacle. And turning to the other *Marianos*, he asked them one by one who was God. When they answered as good Catholics, he told them, "My children, always confess the truth and now do it aloud." The Christians and the catechumens did just that, confessing and praising in unison the true God, Jesus Christ, our Redeemer and Savior. This severity bore its fruit among the Christians and catechumens. But it was most fruitful for the noble himself, who came back the following day begging pardon for his fault and that they would teach him the doctrine of the God in whom he believed and whom he adored. The Venerable Father embraced him with great love and admitted him into the number of catechumens to be instructed and baptized.

The nomothetic or legislative prudence he revealed in the rules that he gave to the Sodality of Saint Francis Xavier in Mexico City. Through these rules he taught persons of all conditions the means to save their souls and as far as they could to help save others. He also revealed it in the rules that he gave to the Seminary of San Juan Letrán on the island of Guam.

Testimony to his military prudence lies in the victories that they won under his direction, where a few Christian soldiers defeated many thousands of barbarians, though this was due especially to his prayers. These victories were won first on the island of Tinian and afterward on the island of Guam. And in regard to the war in Guam, what seemed to be imprudent was found to be an act of great prudence, surpassing human counsels and a glory of the Law of God.[196] The Venerable Father wrote an account of it in which he magnifies the power and wisdom of

---

[196] See Book 3, chapter 15.

the Lord, which turned discredit into honor and ignominy into glory. He also praises the bravery of the Spanish soldiers who conquered themselves in a matter most difficult, that of honor, and thus merited to be honored by him, for whom they sacrificed their own.

We could call apostolic prudence the kind he exercised in the conversion of pagans, following a very wise method to facilitate the acceptance of the great mysteries.

It would take a long time to report the sayings and opinions of this most prudent man, and it would be necessary to copy here a great part of his letters and instructions. However, I will not omit a certain part of a letter he writes to his father. Thus, I will show how he reproaches those who travel to the Indies in search of human gain and encourages those who seek only the glory of God. May his words be an inspiration to both! He says: "I do not wish to omit here what consoled me upon seeing certain aspects of the Indies and the discussion we had regarding them. The question was should my brother come in some high office to the Indies. You made the decision that he should not come. If anyone is in doubt, this is the advice we should give him for his greater good. Anyone who does not come purely for the good of souls or for the evident will of God, makes a clear mistake if he comes even in the highest positions and offices. The reason is perfectly evident: the expenses of the voyages and of sustenance in these lands where money is of so little value are so great, that either a man should resolve to return even poorer than he came, assuming that he returns alive and with honor, or else he deliberately risks his salvation and his honor in this life by making use of dishonest means to gain some wealth. And the temptation to use such means is so great, seeing that otherwise, the whole purpose of their coming is frustrated. And their purpose is ordinarily to increase their wealth, and that is why they expose themselves to so many risks, to so many hardships and dangers at sea, to changes of climate and food, and to greater dangers from the natives and the conditions under which they have to deal with them. And all this is in addition to the risk that the families have to take of being infected by the many vices that abound more in these lands than elsewhere. I say this in the hope that it may some day help someone who depends on you for advice. May God withhold from those whom we wish well, the offices they undertake to enrich themselves where it is most difficult to acquire wealth without the loss of honor and of their souls." Thus far Father San Vitores, very much in agreement with the verdict of Saint Francis Xavier, as in all his other ideas, for in the reading of all his letters and instructions he had assimilated the prudence of the saintly apostle.

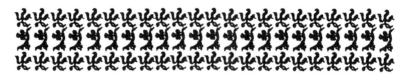

# CHAPTER VI

### *His Justice in Regard to God*

We do not speak here of the general justice, or righteousness, by which we call all the saints just, in the sense that they conform to the rule of life. This justice includes the observance of all the commandments, the fulfillment of all the obligations, and the possession of all the virtues. We are here speaking of that particular justice, a most noble virtue, which has its tribunal or throne between heaven and earth; in its hand, a golden scale with its pointer always in the center. It gives to each one his due, to God, to the angels, and to men, being fair to all. As we deal in this chapter with justice in regard to God, which is also called the virtue of religion, we reserve for the next chapter the justice Father San Vitores observed towards men.

How just or how religious toward God was this? His servant was shown by his dedication, his prayer, his praises of God, his sacrifices and his vows, and all those acts by which honor and worship are offered to the Creator, and which are due to him as the first principle, in himself and in his saints. His devotion was most perfect, for ever since he reached the age of reason, he consecrated himself to God, beginning so early to know him and to love him. At that tender age, his sole pleasure was to repeat his prayers, to erect make-shift altars, to serve Mass, and to perform similar acts of piety. These were flowers and fruits that together pointed to his future sanctity and already implied it. At the age of twelve and a half he consecrated himself totally to the Lord in the Society of Jesus, so that he would not belong to the world or to himself, but entirely to God, committing himself with the three vows of poverty, chastity, and obedience.

From his first years, God began to deal with him as with another Samuel, speaking to his heart, for he saw him so simple, pure, and humble.[197] From that same age the child delighted to converse with God. From these beginnings, without realizing what he was doing, he spent long hours in contemplation of the divine mysteries and the greatness of God and his Mother, with such enlightenment, feeling and discernment, that he disregarded the things of this earth and esteemed those of heaven. He loved to dwell on these heavenly thoughts with such pleasure and sweetness that being satiated with them, it meant nothing to him to be left three or four hours alone without his meals, freezing in the cold of winter.[198] As he said, he was not short of things to entertain him or of good things to think of. After he chose Father Ramírez as his confessor and his spiritual guide, he followed his direction as well as the "additions"[199] and other counsels that our Father Saint Ignatius gives for mental prayer, and so advanced marvelously in this holy exercise.

[197] 1 Samuel, chapter 3.
[198] Cf. Book 1, chap. 2:9.
[199] Special directions to assist the exercitant at various stages of the spiritual exercises of Saint Ignatius.

After he entered the Society of Jesus, during his novitiate, his studies and his professorship, he gave to prayer all the hours permitted by obedience. He even hungered for this prayer and did not leave off or slacken in it even when God tried him with dryness and distractions. Then he used his own natural mental powers to persevere in all the usual spiritual exercises, just as he did in times of greater devotion. As is usual in the Society, a scholastic in the *colegio* of Alcalá was assigned to visit the rooms during the times of mental prayer. All the days of the week he found Father San Vitores in his room on his knees, close to the light, reading in the book of meditations of Father Villacastín. Later, in a friendly conversation with him, he expressed his surprise at his need of that help to meditate. His reply was, "Sometimes God wishes that we learn the lesson after the manner of a child who reads the syllables with the help of a pointer; thus I read and meditate on the matter and points of the meditation in that book, since God wishes then that we fulfill his will, whatever other methods we may have in our memories." The more ordinary matter of his meditation was the Passion of Christ, for which he had a warm devotion and a great compassion. Father Bustillos says that when he recalled some torment suffered by Christ, he was overwhelmed with sorrow and it seemed that he would die of grief. In the missions he gave more time to prayer, as if he were more in need of the divine help for himself and for the souls of others. We have said that on the island of Mindoro he spent the nights in prayer and in the open. Father San Vitores himself confessed that, in the Mariana Islands, God had granted him a notable facility in prayer.

It would be better to say that Father San Vitores never stopped praying day or night, except for the little rest he gave himself, which used to last two or three hours, for he always had God present, like our guardian angels, who do not lose sight of the heavenly Father, even though they are among men, teaching them and leading them to heaven. That is how it was with him when he was teaching and catechizing the pagans. He used to ask Father Lorenzo Bustillos whether, when he explained Christian doctrine to the *Indios*, he had his attention fixed on God and on the Blessed Virgin, meditating and contemplating the mysteries he was teaching. He used to say that in those mysteries we have copious material for meditation. When he was not occupied in these exercises, he was wont to raise his heart to God unceasingly, moving continuously the wings of his breast to come closer to God, not unlike the seraphs of Isaiah.[200] Such could be the ejaculatory prayers that he repeated continually. These flights gave him relief in all his ailments and rest in all his labors. In a severe illness that he had in Alcalá, he used to ask sometimes that those who assisted him leave him alone for some rest. When they left his room, they would delay at the door and listen, and they would hear his loving colloquies with Christ, with his Mother, with our father, Saint Ignatius, and with Saint Francis Xavier and other saints for whom he had great devotion. And when they came back two or three hours later and asked him if he had rested, he used to answer that he had

---

[200] Isa. 6:2.

## His Justice in Regard to God

enjoyed a great period of relief. He used to make the spiritual exercises of Saint Ignatius many times and wished his companions to do the same, even in the midst of such glorious occupations as they had in the Marianas. He did not believe that they were wasting time needed for the conversion of souls, just as the soldier does not waste his time when he arms himself in preparation for battle. Not long before his death, he retired, as we have said, to the residence of Nisichan, where he spent more time in contemplative prayer to prepare himself for the crown of martyrdom.

He always recited the Divine Office on his knees, considering himself to be in the presence of our father, Saint Ignatius, and Saint Francis Xavier, so that they might teach him and help him to praise God. And he recited each psalm, verse, and words with such attention, humility and tenderness, as if he saw with his eyes the Lord with whom he spoke, pondering the words and arousing his affections, as befitted each prayer. He said the rosary and other prayers with the same feeling. Only in the Mass was his devotion greater, and it was shared by those who were present. When he reached the Our Father, with his eyes fixed on the Host, he was deeply moved by each word, which he uttered with such spiritual vehemence that he seemed to wish to force our sacramental Lord to grant him what was asked for in that petition, especially when he said, "Hallowed be thy name." He was fired with desires and yearning that the name of God be known, praised, and adored by all men. Since this is the best prayer, he repeated it often during the day, with the same devotion, reminding Christ, our Lord, of the promise he had made that his Father would grant whatever was asked for in his name, especially to make known that name among by those who were ignorant of it.

Concerning the efficacy of his prayer, suffice it to say that he candidly stated as a child that he had never asked anything of the Blessed Virgin that was not fully granted to him. Witnesses, too, of this are the miracles he obtained with his prayer, and the many conversions of great sinners that were granted through his prayers and tears. Finally, he sought for help in prayer in every undertaking, and the successful issue always showed that he had been heard by that Lord, who has his eyes on the just and his ears attentive to their prayers. He could not keep hidden from others the favors that God granted him in his contemplation, carefully though he tried to keep them to himself. Thus, Father Casanova relates that in different missions, in the mountains of the Philippines and perhaps in the Marianas, while he was at prayer, they saw him suspended in the air; as we have said, Captain *don* Juan de Mendoza found him in that position on the island of Tinian, surrounded by a brilliant splendor.[201] We have reported in other places many other favors and celestial visitations, which we consequently do not include here.

He revered all things sacred with profound humility; he tried to give the pagans a great esteem for them. For this reason, he celebrated Mass and performed baptisms with all solemnity and with the singing of the Mariana children as often as he could. He celebrated the liturgical offices and processions of Holy Week with like solemnity. When he conse-

---

[201] See Book 3, chap.11:224.

crated churches he assisted as the altar server, so that the pagans might understand that in the house of God there is no service that is not a great honor. Whenever he passed in front of an altar, he made a profound reverence, striking his breast as if he were a publican not worthy of raising his eyes to heaven because of the multitude and greatness of his sins. I pass over, at this point, his observance of the vows of poverty, chastity, and obedience with which he consecrated himself to God in the religious life, as well as by other vows he made at his profession, since I have later to speak of these virtues. It is enough to say now that he was always faithful to God in all his promises, fulfilling them even beyond what he promised, although it always seemed to him that he was not fulfilling the obligations imposed on him by so high a vocation as the Society of Jesus.

Passing now to the devotion to the saints, which belongs secondarily to the virtue of religion, how can we describe the love and devotion he had for the Blessed Virgin? One of his companions writes that it was very great; and truly I cannot see how it could be any greater. Since his childhood, he loved the Virgin as a mother, and he had recourse to her in all his afflictions and needs with the trust of a son. And the Virgin treated him as such. Through the years he grew in this devotion, trying to serve in every way his beloved mother. In this lovable Queen, lay his confidence in prayer; she was the object of his conversations, the subject matter of his writings, for only in Mary, through Mary, or for Mary did he know what to do, what to say, or what to think. If he begged anything from God, it had to be through his Mother. He knew not how to praise the Lord, without including the praise of our Lady. Whenever he invoked the name of Jesus, his prayer to Mary followed. He frequently showed his tenderness toward the Virgin, repeating with emotion and sighs, "Oh, my Mother! Oh, Mother of my soul! What a good Mother you are, my Lady! Oh, most Holy Virgin, ah, Lady of my soul! Most Holy Mother!" Then he felt most tenderly moved toward Jesus, to return again to Mary, moving around this circle of Jesus and Mary, into which entered Joseph as spouse and putative father. "Oh, blissful circle, symbol of the eternity that is assured us by such good intercessors!" At other times while conversing with other persons, he would say, "Oh, what a good Lady we have!" And he would continue with the praises of the Virgin, inflaming his hearers with her love.

He used to say the rosary of our Lady with special devotion, and when he was sick, he would ask someone to help him pray. His companion would pray on his knees and he would lie in his bed in the most reverent posture permitted by his sickness, so as not to let a single day pass without his tribute to the Queen of heaven and of earth. In his travels, he used to say the rosary with the mule guide and with the other travelers. He did not abandon his custom even in the company of high dignitaries with whom he traveled. He introduced it with such good grace that all were edified and joined him in his devotion. He always carried the rosary around his neck like a golden chain, a badge of his free slavery and of the glorious servitude he professed toward the Mother of God. He would quote in this respect the words of Ecclesiasticus: "Put your feet into her fetters, and your neck into her collar ....Then her fetters will become for you a strong protection and the foundation of your virtue, and her collar will be your crown of glory."[202] To Mary's honor, after the glory of God, he consecrated all his works and enterprises. He dedicated the eight churches he built in the Marianas to her, and all those that were to be erected in these islands he had already consecrated to the memory of her feasts under the titles of her principal images venerated throughout the world. He named these islands themselves the Marianas, thus consecrating them all to the Virgin, although to honor other saints and patrons of his devotion, he gave to some islands and towns the names of other saints, among whom the principal ones were those related to the same Virgin: Saint Joseph, Saint Joachim, Saint Anne, and Saint John the Baptist. He used to remark that he owed much to all the saints of the Virgin's holy family, because of their great help when he entered the Marianas. He owed a special debt to Saint John the Baptist, who, as precursor of the Law of Christ, had cooperated towards the preaching of the gospel by inspiring King Philip IV to sign the royal decree on the day of his glorious nativity (June 24, 1165). Through his intercession then, and by so disposing, how many thousands of souls were born to new life during the happy reign of our lady, the queen, *doña* Mariana of Austria!

Not content with loving and serving his Lady and Mother, he tried, since she was not loved and served by all men, to kindle in those with whom he dealt this most useful devotion. What did he not do in Alcalá, when he was prefect of the Sodality of Our Lady, in order to extend her veneration and enkindle her love among the students, so that he earned the glorious title of "Our Lady's page?" And what did he not try to accomplish in other places? When he gave conferences on the Marian devotion, which was quite frequently, he uttered no other words but those that were inflamed with that ardent fire that burned in his heart and that he tried to set blazing in those of his hearers. He would speak of the graces, the exalted perfection and prerogatives of our divine Mother, as one who had pondered and frequently meditated on them, and he extolled her piety and liberality as one who had experienced them.

He wished that those already brought up as Christians would nourish themselves with the holy bread of this devotion and that the new Christians would be raised on this milk, and he used to state that it was God's pleasure that those newly born into the Faith should be fed with the milk of devotion to his Mother. That is why, when he taught Christian doctrine to the neophytes, he always explained the Hail Mary to them, telling them who she was and what sort of person was the Mother of this Creator and Redeemer, so that they might love and serve her as mistress and mother. He also tried to spread her devotion by his writings. In addition to other loose papers, which he had written on this matter and translated into other languages, he published the book, titled *Voto de la Inmaculada Concepción, de Diego Alonzo Maluenda, Esclavo de la*

---

[202]See Book 2, chap. 17:158; Book 4, chap. 6:287.

*Purísima Concepción.*[203] In this book, besides exalting the many perfections of the most Holy Virgin, he intended that the order of Saint John of Jerusalem and Malta should vow to defend the Immaculate Conception of our Blessed Lady. For this reason he dedicated it to the Grand Prior, *don* Juan of Austria. He was exceptionally devoted to this mystery, which he had sworn to defend ever since he was a sodalist in this royal *colegio.* On the voyage that he made from Manila to Acapulco, he persuaded all those on board ship to take the oath of defending the Immaculate Conception. He said a special prayer for the definition of this mystery by the Holy Father. As we have said, it was for this purpose that he helped so much in the composition of Father Juan Eusebio's book, *De Perpetuo Obiecto Festi Conceptionis.*[204]

In the last analysis, Father San Vitores was *Mariano* by reason of his devotion to Mary, as well as by reason of the favors Mary granted him. It was Mary who called him to the Society of her son, and he served her as much as he could in the Society. Mary made him the Apostle of the Ladrone Islands; she saw to it that the royal decree was expedited and through the guardian angel informed him of its arrival, while he, on his part, made the islands Marianas (Mary's islands) and he made her their apostle, converting the pagans by her pictures. In Mindoro, he had experienced wonderful conversions of the pagans by sending them an image of our Lady, accompanied by a message in the name of the Mother of the Lord of Heaven. Since then he adopted the custom, which he mentioned in a certain letter, of sending messages to the pagans through the Blessed Virgin. I will not mention the Virgin's favors, which are believed to have been very frequent, since he took great care to conceal them. Although individually he kept them secret, he could not hide the fact that they were many, especially in Manila during the seven years when he begged to be sent to the mission of the Marianas, and in Acapulco, when he was preparing for the voyage to those islands.

He dealt familiarly with his guardian angel. Many times at night while alone in his room, he was heard conversing with another who answered him, and they believed it was his guardian angel, for no other person was there with him. He revealed this familiarity to Father Lorenzo Bustillos at a time when he was teaching him some devotions. When Father Bustillos asked him who had taught him those things, he replied that it was a certain personage, and then he added, "Believe me, my brother the holy guardian angel, if we behave as we should, does great things with us." What he wrote to his father from Cádiz, when he was about to set sail for the Indies, may be a confirmation of this. After thanking some friends of his father for showing him so much kindness, he adds: "If men do this, what will the guardian angels do? These holy angels are messengers even at sea; and since there is often no one else to carry letters and to assist you, do not hesitate to let me know what you wish through your guardian angel, asking him to tell me what you would want to tell me personally, and with more confidence of success than if

---

[203]Madrid, 1665. Note the use of his mother's name.
[204]Juan Eusebio Nieremberg y Otín, S.J. (1595-1658), one of the more important spiritual writers of the time.

*His Justice in Regard to God*

you told me directly. And you may tell him at other times to assist me when our good Lord may deign to send me labors to accomplish, and he will also do it better than our friends here on earth who have assisted us, however great their help has been."

He enjoined the same thing to other persons, that they tell their angel what they wished to tell him. When it was necessary to rush to the aid of souls over inaccessible paths, although he was almost blind and was weakened by hardships and penances, he ran with such swiftness that his companions, who were healthy and robust, could not follow him. They left no doubt that it was the holy angels who were carrying him. Father Lorenzo Bustillos narrates that in the Marianas he used to walk through places full of matted thickets, mud, and swampy holes, and up pointed, rocky crags. Through all of these, even those who were light of foot and sharp-eyed had need to use their hands so as not to fall. When others wondered how Father San Vitores could go through all these places, the lay companion who used to go with him remarked: "Father, when Father Rector used to come to these places, the angels would carry him through the air. For without realizing it, I found myself left behind as he sped through these rocky places. I could not understand how, nor could I see his feet touch the ground, so lightly did he move." Father Bustillos witnessed this same lightness of step on the island of Guam and on Santa Ana where he accompanied him. So, he concluded that it was no great matter that he could visit in three months the islands for which others needed a year. It was the holy angels who guided him and saved him whenever he found himself in the greatest difficulties.

He loved our father, Saint Ignatius, as a father, and as a father who had chosen him as a son, a son he desired to have in his house as a saint and a martyr. And so it was by imitating the virtues of Saint Ignatius and by referring all his own works to the greater glory of God that he strove to enhance his patron's honor and veneration as much as possible. That is why, as we have said, in Alcalá, he procured that due veneration be given to the room where the saint used to live when he served the sick in the hospital of Altozana, which he himself used to visit often.[205] And in the Marianas he gave the name of the holy patriarch to the first town and first residence of the Society. The saint was the patron of all his enterprises; for all of them he sought his favor, after that of the Blessed Virgin, for he knew well that all the works of the Society must be the work of the Lord through its father and patriarch. During the day he frequently commended himself to the saint, especially after Mass and the Divine Office or any one of the canonical hours. If he recited the hours separately, immediately following the prayer *Sacrosanctae et individuae* he used to add, on his knees, after the Divine Office, a very devout prayer to our father, Saint Ignatius, which begins: *Te ergo, Pater animae meae, summeque mihi venerande.*[206] It is a quotation from a letter that Saint Francis Xavier addressed to his father and master. He used to recite it with such affection and devotion as if he saw the holy father present and

---

[205] See Book 1, chap. 9:50.
[206] To you, O Father of my soul, I owe the highest reverence.

*Book Four, Chapter 6*

conversing with him. And how greatly was he favored by the holy father. Surely as much as that son deserved and as the saint in his kindness knew how to do, even for those who did not deserve it. On one occasion, Father Bustillos, on entering the sacristy of the church of Agadña, saw Father San Vitores standing above the table of the sacristy, as if in ecstasy, with his right ear pressed to the mouth of an image of Saint Ignatius that was there, and moving his hands as though resisting that suspension. He says he did not notice the location of the feet. We do not know what Saint Ignatius said to him in that rapture, because when Father Bustillos asked him what that was, he answered it was a fainting spell in which he almost lost his senses. But it is clear that it was the swoon and delight enjoyed by the spouse when she asked to be comforted with flowers and apples.[207] Perhaps the holy patriarch was instructing his son in view of the governance of that Mariana mission.

I am at a loss how to describe the devotion he had to Saint Francis Xavier, of whom we said he was the living image.[208] Suffice to say at this point, he was not only another Xavier through imitation, but also through love, the love of friend for friend. And it is no wonder that having taken that saintly apostle as his model and keeping him always as his ideal, studying his virtues and contemplating his perfections, he should grow ever more in the love of the one loved by God and man, one who cannot be known without being loved. The favors that Saint Francis granted him when he appeared with Father Marcello and restored him to health so he could go to the Indies, convert many souls, and obtain the martyrdom that the saintly apostle yearned for so much, increased his love all the more.[209] Aside from other favors, in all that he accomplished for souls in the Marianas, he acknowledged a debt to the Apostle of the Indies. I say nothing of his devotion to Blessed Aloysius Gonzaga, because of whom he added the name of Luis to that of Diego when he entered the Society. I say nothing of his devotion to Saint Francis Borgia, from whom he received the favors that he mentions in his letter to the general; or of his devotion to Father Marcello, who was his special patron together with Saint Francis Xavier; and lastly of his devotion to all the saints of the Society, through whose intercession he hoped to obtain great favors from our Lord.

He loved the great patriarch Saint Dominic de Guzmán, recognizing that he owed him his life and paying him much veneration, especially on his feast day.[210] He was very devoted to Saint Stephen, as the first martyr of the Church and to Saint Lawrence, whom he used to call a messenger to Mary for some of her servants. In this regard, no doubt, he spoke not without experience. His devotion to Saint Teresa was no less, because of the great zeal she had for the salvation of souls. We should never end, were we to recount all the acts of devotion he had for the angels and the saints. We may gather this from what he felt compelled to dictate to Father Bustillos. In order to satisfy his devotion to all

---

[207]Sg (Song) 2:5.
[208]See Book 4, chap. 2:266.
[209]See Book 1, chap. 11:61.
[210]Cf. Book 1, chap. 1:6.

the blessed and take advantage of the intercession of all of them, he distributed them in choirs among the days of the week, so that they would be his special patrons on a particular day, and they would obtain from God for himself and for others the virtues in which they most excelled. And from each choir he chose more especially as intercessors some saints whom he named. Perhaps at the end I should place this devotion together with others, so that those who wish may profit by them, since they were the devotions of a great Servant of God.

I will not omit here the devotion and compassion he had for the souls in purgatory, for whom he offered masses, prayers, and penances, and tried to have others do the same. He availed himself of their aid to obtain from God the difficult things that he desired, promising them to offer masses; and then he would experience their favor. On one occasion in the Mariana Islands, he wished to baptize three children whose mothers had hidden them and taken them to another town so that they would not be baptized. He offered some masses for the souls in purgatory so that they might help in finding them. On the following day, when he was looking for them in a certain town, three women came out to meet him on the way; they had with them their children and they told him, "Father, we bring them to you, the children you are looking for. We have taken them from their mothers, so that you may baptize them." Although they spoke the language of the country, they were not of the country, for they were of much whiter complexion than the women of those islands; so that they seem to have been souls of purgatory, who, desirous of his prayers, came to bring him the children he wanted.

# CHAPTER VII

*His Justice in Regard to Other Persons*

Justice in regard to other people includes piety towards one's parents and relatives, respect for our elders, obedience to our superiors, gratitude toward benefactors, sincerity towards all, punishment of crimes, friendship, liberality, and habitual temperance. And this incomparable man possessed them all. As regards his parents, aside from the love of which I have spoken, he had the utmost respect for them, recognizing God in them, God whom they represented. This is seen in his letters, in which he always addresses his father with great humility, acknowledging himself his debtor in all things, in his being, in his upbringing, even in the fruit that God derived from his labors in the Indies, attributing it all to his prayers and concern.

He shows the same respect and humility towards his uncle, the bishop. He had great regard in his letters for his brother and sisters and other relatives, although in his remembrance of them he turned their thoughts to God, joining some lesson and exhortation to the errands he sent them. While he was under his parents' authority, he never gave them any reason for the least complaint; and although his mother was not very affectionate towards him, he showed her the same affection he would have shown if he were her favorite child. When God called him to the religious life, he tried in every possible way to gain the consent of his father and mother and of his uncle, so that even in a matter so just and so holy, in which his parents did not have complete authority, he would not go against their will. In the end he obtained from the Lord that he change the decision of those who were most opposed. And in this way, His Divine Majesty granted this consolation to the one who so sincerely desired to serve him and give him glory.

The obedience and reverence that he professed towards all his spiritual directors, towards his superiors, and all other persons endowed with dignity and authority was extraordinary. He never forgot in the Indies those who had been his confessors. He would write to them with great humility, acknowledging the indebtedness he had to them and recalling their memory in his letters to his father. Whenever he spoke in his conversations or letters about prelates or superior persons, it was with great reverence. And if perhaps it was necessary to mention scandals or sins that required correction, he never blamed the superior, rather he excused him and tried to remedy the fault. When he visited dignitaries with whom he had to discuss matters pertaining to the divine service, he entered with lowered eyes, saying, "Praised be the Blessed Sacrament," and on approaching the person he bent his knee, he kissed his hand with great humility and no less edification of those who were watching him. I add here what he did and felt in regard to courtesy, according to one of his letters to his father from Seville on the way to Cádiz. He says: "We will kiss the hand of the Lord Viceroy in the port, on handing him your letter, as well as the hand of the Duke of Medina, who also told Father Vello he wanted to see me. Since these matters do not impede our principal purpose, but can be of help to those whom we should lead to their salvation and to the divine service, if only by giving them the booklet of the cases of confession and a picture of the Santo Cristo, the superiors think I should not omit them, especially in view of your considered opinion, which for me is of such great value. And incidentally, because these things have to do with civility, my answer to what you have hinted at regarding what is done there, is, that although these things may not seem to relate so immediately to the divine service, they surely please him, just as do the other things, like eating and dressing and others that have to do with the preservation of this life and the decency of one's position. And so, whenever you judge them suitable for these ends, and conducive to the success of the affairs that you handle for the good of your children and your house, they are most licit and are embellished besides by the motive that you have in all things, saying, "I do this because God is pleased that we take care of these matters." They will all turn out to be works for the true love of God, which is the best thing we can desire and is what we all have to do even in caring for the needs of our poor bodies, such as eating, etc."

His obedience to his superiors had the three conditions required for a perfect obedience; it was blind, prompt, and unswerving: blind, because it did not consider who the superior was, whether he was wise or ignorant, but that he was taking God's place. Neither did he examine the reasons for their command. It was enough for him that it was the superior's command, as long as it was not a sinful one, in order to understand it to be the will of God. It was prompt, because without delay he carried out what was commanded him; nor was an explicit mandate necessary for him, it was enough that it was suggested by his superiors. It was unswerving, because there was no difficulty that would make him hesitate to follow his superior's orders. A good proof of his obedience is, that although his desire to be sent to the missions of the Indies was so ardent, he proposed it to his superiors with great indifference, as we saw in the letter he wrote to our father general. And this indifference is in conformity with the conviction that we find in his letter where he advises those who have a vocation to the missions or to the Indies that they submit their desire to the superior with great indifference, understanding that for the religious there are no better Indies than those of obedience, and that in the Indies, he will find consolation who places it in doing the will of God through obedience. He calls obedience the surest rule of the will of God and the safe way of the religious. He adds other praises in accordance with what our Father Ignatius says about this virtue, which he recommended so much to the Society. In order that he would not miss the merit of obedience in the Mariana Islands where he was the superior of all the missionaries, as we reported before, when traveling with another religious of the Society, even if he were only a scholastic, as Father Bustillos was then (and he narrates this), he appointed his companion as superior, and he ordered that other companions, lay or religious, obey him in everything as their superior. He himself was the first to obey him and consulted him on what he was to do, and he gave him an account of his conscience, just as any humble novice would do to his novice master. The same account of conscience he used to give to his confessor, because he said that the account of conscience was one of the most important means for the religious to overcome temptations and to advance in virtue. We may add here his perfect observance of all the rules of the Society, which in themselves do not oblige under pain of sin and are only manifestations of the will of God and of the order. He observed them with such exactness that never did anyone notice the least violation of them, a thing admired by anyone acquainted with the meticulousness, perfection, and difficulty of our rules. In Alcalá those who accompanied him when he left the house noticed that when he found himself in a predicament where he would seem forced to violate one or other of our rules or which called for what the world would call a matter of policy or prudence, the Servant of God showed such discretion that, without failing in courtesy, he complied with their observance, giving satisfaction to the layman and edification and a lesson to his companions on the smooth and discreet observance of the rules.

He showed exquisite gratitude to anyone who did him even the slightest favor. Not satisfied with gratitude expressed in words and prayer, which was his greatest payment, he begged his father, as we read frequently in his letters, to help him pay what he owed, favoring his creditor with whatever he could, for he had no one else in this life on whom to rely for the satisfaction of all his obligations. He could not do or say enough to thank those who helped him in his enterprises for the service of God and the good of souls. In a letter of the year 1662, he writes to his father concerning the *Condes* de Baños, who had so generously supported his voyage to the Philippines: "At last our Lord has disposed that I should be indebted to this noble couple for the fulfillment of my desires, and that just as I owed to my mother my admission to the Society, and to you my coming from Spain, to these I owe the arrival at this last stage of my journey. May the Divine Majesty grant that I know how to repay them by being grateful, at least with the efficacy of my prayers, for the great indebtedness I have to Their Excellencies."

I say nothing of his truthfulness, for even as a child, never was a lie found in his mouth. Nor of his affability, with which he made himself lovable to all. Nor of his generosity, which he possessed in the most heroic degree, for he despised all the wealth of this earth in order to gain that of heaven and to imitate his Redeemer. In the Society, his generosity was shown by the pleasure with which he distributed all the gifts he received among the sick and to persons who deserved well of the order, keeping nothing for himself. As superior, he was liberal to his subjects, wishing that they lack nothing that was permitted by our profession. And although this liberality was most generous, it always seemed to him to fall short of what the servants of God deserved. And so when he was minister in Oropesa and sent some fathers to the villa house for recreation, he ordered the brother who was to care for them to treat them very well, remarking pleasantly: "The Church sets aside one day a year to celebrate a solemn fiesta for all the saints and so make up for what was slighted on any one saint's day; so I want to make up today for all my neglect during the year."

I have spoken in another place of the friendship and warm relations with his friends. We have also seen that he knew how to punish when necessary, although his punishing was full of mercy, not that of a judge, but of a father. In a word, Father San Vitores had all the virtues that made him not only just, but loving and compassionate, never injuring anyone by insult, gossip, or uncharitable judgment, but doing to everyone all the good of which he was capable.

# CHAPTER VIII

## *His Invincible Fortitude*

Fortitude is a noble virtue and the virtue of the noble hearted. It shone splendidly in this great man in the victory over his passions, his disdain for danger, in the endurance of hardships, in the magnitude of his undertakings, and in the unswerving perseverance in all his resolutions.

He conquered himself by continual mortification in such a way that he could say with the apostle, as he did so many times: "I live, no, not I, but Christ lives in me,"[211] because his life was the life of Christ crucified. The unpleasant traits left by Adam of old could not be seen in him. He seemed to be rather dead than mortified and to have no passions save those under tight control. Although by nature he was of a choleric temperament, as was revealed in his undeliberate acts, he was calm and peaceful with everyone, so that what was an effort looked like pure nature. When he was a novice in the school of perfection, he developed a scruple as to whether in some manner he cooperated in the fault of those whose cutting remarks he received with pleasure. But later he overcame this scruple and formed the principle that he later expressed in Mexico. There were some persons who treated another harshly, though he bore it with much humility and patience; however, this person was concerned that his patience was an occasion for the others to treat him more harshly each day. He reported the matter to Father San Vitores and said that he intended henceforth to show his anger. The Venerable Father answered, "Don't do such a thing. If you do not overcome the others with your humility, you will overcome yourself, and that will be a great victory."

He never trusted past victories, and that is why he always was victorious. He kept strict watch over his senses lest the enemy enter through these doors and windows of the soul. To keep far from what was illicit, he denied his senses even what was permitted, not allowing himself any pleasure, so that he could give it all to God and displease the devil. I content myself with one example out of the many I could bring. And if anyone should consider it a trifle, let him consider that mortification in insignificant matters is usually more difficult than in more serious ones. For the more licit what is offered, the more is the privation. And so it follows that he who is faithful in lesser matters will likewise be so in greater ones. His superiors in Mexico had ordered him to join in a festal celebration in the palace of the viceroy, and this at the request of the viceroy and the vicereine. To obey was a mortification for the father. But in all the festivities he did not raise his eyes once and could give no account of anything that took place there. With such perfect mortification he enjoyed that peace that those who are slaves of their appetites

---

[211]Gal. 2:20.

*His Invincible Fortitude*

can not enjoy, no matter how much they may claim to have peace, peace that can hardly be found here on earth, since it dwells very close to heaven. No winds could ruffle the peaceful sea of his soul, where reigned only the Spirit that hovered over the waters from the beginning of the world.[212] Nothing disturbed the peace of his soul: neither adverse events nor prosperous ones could raise a storm in that sea, neither persecution nor applause nor the scorn of men; always he was the same, without change in a changing world, since his life was rooted in God who is unchanging, since he wanted nothing but God's will.

A good proof of this is the bravery with which he encountered dangers for the glory of God and the good of souls. Death could not turn him back when he faced it, armed as it was with the reefs and tempests of the sea, with swords, lances, and stones on land, and everywhere with terror, threats, and betrayal. Who would fail to admire him entering alone and unarmed, except with his courage, into the mountains of Santa Inés and Maralaya, the islands of Mindoro and the Marianas, among outlaws who took him for a spy, among idolaters who hated the Spanish and Christian name, among barbarians, strangers to law and reason? Who would not fear, watching him on Tinian, standing fearless between two weaponed armies, facing spears and stones hurled at him; or on Guam, stepping out to meet the enemies who were besieging him and attacking him with stones and fire-tipped spears; and departing for Paa, where his mortal enemy, the enemy of Christ, the Chinese idolater was awaiting him; then walking to the village where they had just massacred most cruelly Lorenzo, the Malabar; taking upon himself the dangers that were almost as many as the steps he took? But all this is no wonder to one who knows the yearning he had to die for Christ. And yet in another way he showed even greater fortitude: in controlling his desires, giving up the risks, when it was better to avoid them for the greater glory of God and the good of souls; for he esteemed this more than the palm and crown of martyrdom.

All this implies his patience amid hardships. In his illnesses, he never complained, either against the malady or those who were assisting him, or at the lack of anything he needed. When he was offended or disregarded, he remained silent or reacted with great modesty and peace of soul, which his words revealed even more than his silence. But surely this was nothing to one who rejoiced at insults and hardships. His hardships were great throughout his life: those of all twelve years in the Indies were enormous, but the last four, in the Marianas, were the worst, but always greater still was the joy of suffering them for Christ. Consequently, in all his labors and fatigues, he repeated with inexplicable happiness: "Let it all be for the love of God. How little it is, compared with what the good Lord deserves, with what he suffered. How much more we should desire, O, my good Lord, to suffer for love of you!" Father Bustillos says his desire to suffer for his beloved was such that he would not accept in his journeys the help of the holy angels or the consolations of heaven, and with his heart aflame he would cry, as another Xavier, "Enough,

---

[212] Gen.1:2.

*Book Four, Chapter 8*

enough, my good Jesus!" Indeed, suffering in this life was for him a crown of glory and he found it painful to feel pleasure, since his God and Lord had found this world a place of suffering. He wrote from Mexico to a father of this province, a friend of his: "Father, we have already journeyed over a thousand leagues without our Lord entrusting to this blind man either the sufferings or the maladies of sea or land or the hardships of climate endured by the braver men of our mission. I do not know what our Lord wants of me with such worldly softness and comfort, if Your Reverence with your holy sacrifices and prayers does not obtain for me henceforth some hardships that are for the glory of God and the good of souls." Of the same kind was his complaint in other letters regarding the labors that God was not sending him, whereby he considered himself less favored, since he was less afflicted by what his love would desire.

The breadth of his undertakings proclaimed the greatness of his spirit. They embodied his dreams for the greater glory of God, and God's glory was the soul of all of them. Never content with mediocrity, he reached for the heights. Yet in seeking the greater service of his Lord, he did not neglect the little things. Such love neglected no detail. His zeal was not enough for Spain or America; nor would it be enough for the whole world, because he wanted to convert the whole world to Christ, and even then he would not be satisfied. In Spain he begged for assignment to the Indies, and in the Indies he was concerned for the missions in Spain. This is seen in the letters he wrote to Father Juan Gabriel Guillén, recommending to him the conversion of souls,[213] as well as in the letters that he wrote to his father and to other individuals, commending to them the care of some mission. He had hardly arrived in the Philippines, when he begged the governor there as well as the court in Madrid (through letters) to advance the conversion of those islands and that of the Marianas as well, as we have seen so many times. This great man showed in all things his generosity, as much in what he was actually doing as in what he desired to do. It pleased him more to give than to receive, never flattering the powerful, keeping a holy liberty when prudent courage demanded it and a discreet resignation when his zeal required it. He never asked anything for himself and he was not embarrassed when begging for those in need, both for the good of those for whom he begged and the greater good of those who gave. He showed all the signs given by Aristotle, by which we recognize the magnanimous man.[214]

And what was his perseverance in all that he undertook? He never neglected his customary spiritual exercises; he never gave up what he had once begun, no matter what difficulty might arise. This is shown by the persistence with which he insisted on entering the Society, contrary to the will of his parents, and with which he solicited his assignment to

---

[213] Succeeding Jerónimo López was an uncommon pair of preachers, who worked together as a team from 1665 to 1672 and had no rival in Spain in the art of conducting a home mission, Gabriel Guillén and Tirso González. Willaim V. Bangert, S.J., *Historia de la Compañía de Jesús en la Asistencia de España*, Madrid, 1902-1925, 7 vols, vol.5, pp.94-95.

[214] Nicomachean Ethics 1124 b 9-1125 a 16.

the Indies against the opposition of his father and others who desired to keep him in Spain, as well as by the diligence with which he sought entrance to the Mariana Islands against the opposition of so many who opposed it. And finally, it is shown by the firmness with which he always strove for the good and the best, until he obtained the crown of martyrdom, which can be won only by fortitude, and by the crown of glory, which is given only through perseverance.

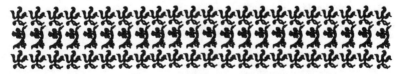

# CHAPTER IX

### *His Rare Temperance*

The temperance of this Servant of God was more to be admired than imitated, because with his fasting, he not only overcame the pleasures of the flesh but almost destroyed it by the penance and harsh treatment that went on increasing with the years until in the Marianas he was nothing but skin and bone. We have spoken in its proper place of the penance he practiced while still a child.[215] We need not repeat his continuous fasts, vigils, and other rigorous practices that were beyond his strength and age. Of his use of the discipline and chain, his confessor has left a written account, stating that they were proper to a most austere religious. After he entered the Society, both as a novice and a scholastic, his austerities had to be checked by rules of prudence, although the inadvertence of a superior caused him to go beyond reasonable limits, satisfied that he did not trespass those of holy obedience. Regarding the time when he was a teacher in Alcalá, those who dealt with him more familiarly claim that he often fasted on bread and water, and he always managed to spoil the taste of what he ate by mixing in something unpleasant. Most of the year he slept in his clothes and his bed was more like a rack than a bed, because under a thin mattress he placed books and other things in such a way that they gave him more torment than rest. They say that he always wore hairshirts and chains, and besides the continual private disciplines, he took many public ones in the refectory along with the other mortifications and humiliations of our order. When he went out to give missions in the outskirts of Alcalá, if he was given a bed, he begged his companion to use it, and even if he refused, he ordered him to do so, while he lay down on a platform or chest to rest for the short time that he slept.

After he finally was working in the missions, he gave himself completely to penance, as if he had to make reparation to God for the faults of the sinners whom he wanted to convert. As we saw, it was the barbarians themselves who said: "The Great Father was like Christ, who being sinless himself, did penance for the atonement of others' sins." In the Marianas he never tasted biscuit, meat, wine, or any other delicacy, and obliged himself by a vow never to take chocolate, reserving for the sick a little of what he had been given in Mexico. He did not want to eat fish, which was rather scarce there, excusing himself, because he said his teeth were bad, and at other times because it was a delicacy there, since it was scarce and consequently not according to the rule, which says: "The food, clothing, and bedding must be something proper to the poor."[216] He always deprived himself even of the coconut water, on the score that it was something tasteful. His ordinary food was roots

---

[215]See Book 1, chap. 2:8.
[216]*Summary of the Constitutios of the Society of Jesus*, no. 25.

*His Rare Temperance*

dug from the ground and their poorly cooked leaves, and perhaps as a delicacy, a little grated coconut. To those who wondered at seeing him eat wretched coarse food, he was wont to reply that the good grace of the Blessed Virgin cooked it with such flavor that he did not miss the food of Spain. This was not a mere pretext invented by him, but that his food was a delicacy and a favor often granted him by his Lady and most Holy Mother is seen in the following instance. When he fell sick on Tinian with that burning fever, not having any sustenance but some rotten and repugnant roots, which the barbarians themselves threw away, since they could not eat them and the mere sight of them caused them nausea and retching, he ate them as a healthy man eats the greatest delicacy, and the more rotten they were, the more he liked them, saying what he said at other times, that the grace of the Blessed Virgin seasoned them all. In the missions he spent many days without eating at all, saying, "The body and blood of Christ was enough sustenance for the day."

Of his bed and sleep he says elsewhere that the latter lasted two or three hours and that the former was the hard ground covered with a mat or some badly arranged wood. If in the residence his companions gave him a mattress, he made it so lumpy by placing sticks and stones under it that it was more uncomfortable than the ground. Because of the humidity and heat of the islands and because of his continuous work, his whole body used to be bathed in sweat, so that his cassock was soaked through. Yet in spite of this, there was no way of making him change his shirt for one or two months, since he remarked: "This luxury is a delight for the ass. That's all he needs!" On the first days of his arrival in the Marianas, he wore shoes that were without soles, after the example of our father, Saint Ignatius, and to disguise them he used to mend the uppers and thus kept the secret, until finally they tried to take them away from him and give him others. But he kept them carefully, saying that they were worth all the riches of Peru. It was well said, since they had hidden in them a mine of mortification. Later he made shoes out of palm leaves, which made him walk almost the whole year bare-footed, because thanks to his hasty walk, they got torn off and he was quite careless in finding a replacement. This was the cause of his always walking with wounded and bloody feet, thanks to the sharp stones and thorny plants. Blood also flowed from his hands on many occasions, since he had to use them to keep from falling from the cliffs.

Yet none of these and many other hardships he encountered on his journeys on land and sea seemed any reason to discard his ordinary disciplines and chains. Rather, when he once asked a companion whether in his mission work he put on the chain, the companion was surprised and answered in the negative, because more than enough chain was to walk over mud holes, cliffs, rocky thickets, and hillsides so wild that one stepped on the sharp grass that cut one's feet and bathed them in blood. At this the Venerable Father replied even more surprised: "It is possible that one does not wear the chain. But there is no great virtue in the suffering and hardships of these trails and you find them without much effort. But in order that God may grant us success in our journeys and mission it is good that we should add on our part some mortification." He used to wear a loose shirt, or tunic, woven of rasping herbs to which was attached a sharp pointed cross. It was something horrible to see and there were a thousand other inventions of small chains that he fastened around his arms and legs together with instruments of continuous martyrdom. One of his companions took a liking to one of these chains of the Servant of God, which had very sharp points. Moved by his pleas, Father San Vitores lent it to him. He wore it for an hour and then returned it, saying that he could not stand it, because when he was teaching catechism to the children, they leaned against him and made the points penetrate his flesh in an intolerable torture. The saintly man recovered his chain, remarking graciously with a smile that for that very reason he should wear it since it was such a good help to the children on that occasion. The disciplines with which he afflicted himself were made of thistles and steel wheels with which he scourged himself every night, even in times of sickness. In his first sickness in the Marianas he did not give up this penance. Hence, Father Bustillos asked him with a loving reproach, "Why is it that in your fever you are taking such rigorous disciplines? Do you want to leave the neophytes without a father when they have such a need of you and leave the islands without your help and teaching?" To this he smilingly replied, "Do not interfere in this matter. The more rigorous and continuous the disciplines, the more health they bring me, no matter what the sickness." In fine, such was his rigor, that according to all, before suffering martyrdom, he was already a martyr, since he was himself the tyrant and executioner, and the more rigorous since he was himself the victim.

His religious poverty was not inferior to his penance. After he renounced all things for Christ and entered religion, he desired and strove always to be the poorest of all, choosing for himself the worst and the least of necessary things. No entreaties could make him accept a precious or exceptional thing, even if it were a devotional object. He even wanted his breviary to be of the poorest kind. He was in need of an overcoat and the superior had a new one made for him. But he was so uncomfortable with it that he begged that it be taken back, which eventually was done, and in its place, to his great satisfaction, he was given an old one. The cassock that he brought with him to the Marianas was so old that it had changed from black to blue. As we have said, in the islands he wore interior and exterior garments of woven matting, and he even patched this clothing to add poverty to poverty. He wrote his notes on scraps of paper and old letters, and in Alcalá he used them in sending petitions to his father, so as not to waste white paper. And many have remarked, to show the details of his poverty, that he wrote in small and tightly lined letters, so as to use less paper. Without the explicit permission of his superior, he would not dispose of anything, and he was so scrupulous about this that when a person asked him for a half sheet of paper, he left his room without saying anything and asked his superior for permission to give it to him.

*His Rare Temperance*

We will speak later of his chastity, which this angelic Servant of God kept in the highest degree. Of his meekness, we have admired so many examples in the course of his life. We have seen him silent when insulted, offering peace to those who made war on him, and repaying wrongs with kindness.[217]

We will deal now with his humility, the companion of meekness and one of his principal virtues. Though he was so pure and saintly, he thought himself the worst sinner in the world, a mystery we always admire in the greatest saints, one that they alone understand and those who are not saints do not. Perhaps it is because they consider what they would be but for the grace of God, or perhaps when comparing what they have received with what they have repaid, they reckon this as little or nothing. Father San Vitores fled from the praise that acclaimed his work. When he taught philosophy at Alcalá, he never offered his opinion. All his good works and the favors received from God, which could bring him praise, he kept hidden. It is for this reason that we do not know the revelations he received, the many miracles he performed, and even the exact number of pagans he baptized, because he frequently went alone, with no witnesses who could report them. And if they asked him about them, he replied with all seriousness, so they would not insist on the question, "How can God do anything for me, the worst person in the world?" If they tried some scheme to make him reveal some of the favors he had received from God, he would see into their plans and say nothing, telling them nothing, excepting when it was for the glory of God; then, after the example of the apostle, he would make known the secrets of the Lord out of love for that same Lord. It is worth noting that when he revealed to Father General, in that letter that we printed in the first book,[218] the favors God gave him in view of his being sent to the Indies, he omits those that were granted by Christ and his Mother to prepare his entrance into the Society, because the information about these wonderful favors did not seem to be needed to obtain the permission he was asking, and he did not wish to go beyond the limits of the necessary. The miracles that could be hidden, he disguised through the application of some medal or holy card of the Blessed Virgin or Saint Ignatius or Saint Francis Xavier or some relic of the Venerable Father Luis de Medina, so that they would be attributed to the intercession of the saints and not to his merits.

For his acts of virtue, he offered the pretext of their convenience, saying that eating little helped him to walk faster, that the disciplines were good for his health and similar excuses. In his letters he would call himself the bad blindman or a bad servant, or in those to his father, a bad son. The "N" that he used to add to his signature means *nequam* (good-for-nothing), as Father Casanova explains, since he took himself for the most perverse and wicked man in the world. Not only did he despise himself, but he desired to be despised by others. And so he listened and bore with pleasure and delight the taunting and mockery of the

---

[217] See Book 3, chap. 10:212; Book 4, chap. 8:298.
[218] See Book 1, chapter 11.

## Book Four, Chapter 9

barbarians, particularly when that Mariana noble treated him as a simple and foolish man, a fact that we mentioned in its place.[219]

All his actions and words bore witness to this concept of himself and this desire. In the linguistic conferences he used to have with his companions, although he was their master, he used to listen to them as if he were a pupil desirous to learn. When his companions explained the doctrine or commented on it, he remained standing or sitting with the children on a stair or on a floor, listening to them with great attention. He used to ask one father, who was very young, to give him conferences and to teach him about the spiritual life. He used to listen to him with great attention, obeying him as any novice might obey a man experienced in the way of perfection. He used to ask his companions to admonish him regarding his faults, because he was so blind that he could not be aware of them. In order to be faithful to his own holy custom and that of our order, he used to serve at table in our residence, even though there were only one or two at table. And he used to kiss their feet in the presence of the neophytes and catechumens. He also washed the feet of his companions, both religious and laymen, Spaniards and natives, to the amazement of the *Marianos*, who regard such actions as shameful, but who began to view them with respect and veneration, since the Great Father was performing them, and all the more when he told them that Jesus Christ had done the same thing on the night of his Passion. For Father San Vitores there was no better, no more honorable office than the most humble one. That is why he took the office of porter while the others were taking their siesta. He performed it with such strictness that he stationed himself at the door to read, so that the children would not enter and disturb his companions. At the dedication of the churches he would take the part of the altar boy. And what I most admire is that when they all gathered to celebrate the Holy Week ceremonies, although he was so devoted to the Blessed Sacrament and never failed to say Mass and receive Communion on any day that he could, such was his humility that he did not wish to preside at any of the offices of Holy Week; rather, he had a priest companion perform them, thus depriving himself of Communion on Good Friday, so as not to deprive himself of that humiliation, since he considered himself unworthy to preside as superior in the offices of those holy days.

---

[219]See Book 3, chap. 10:212.

# CHAPTER X

*With What Excellence the Gifts of the Holy Spirit
Were Found in the Venerable Father San Vitores*

Together with the theological virtues, the Holy Spirit infuses in the just the seven gifts that, according to Isaiah, rested on Christ.[220] They are *wisdom, understanding, knowledge, counsel, fortitude, piety,* and *fear of the Lord.* These are given to a soul like sails to a ship, so it may easily move with the winds of the Holy Spirit, just as the virtues are like the oars with which the soul tries to sail towards the port of happiness, always with the help of the divine grace. In order to describe how excellently these gifts were found in the Venerable Father, I shall start with the less perfect and ascend towards the more perfect ones, so that through his obedience and docility, we may realize how well he ran and climbed as though step after step to the height of perfection.

He was so innocent that he never committed a single mortal sin and he always lived with the most perfect care to avoid all venial sins, and yet he trembled at God's judgments, since he never held himself safe, avoiding the least occasion of sin. He knew that the greatest safety in this life is not to consider oneself safe, and that only he who fears God does not have to fear. This fear was the cause of his repeating so many times: "Better to burst than to sin; rather die a thousand deaths than offend such a good God. Thanks be to God that we are not in hell!" And other similar ejaculations, since he thought himself deserving of greater penalties and hardships than those he was suffering.

From this fear of God was born the supreme reverence he felt in the presence of God, since he felt himself unworthy to appear before the eyes of God. When he passed before the altar where the Blessed Sacrament was reserved, he struck his breast with such deep sighs, as if he were the publican in the gospel.[221] This fear, however, was a filial fear, one so full of confidence that he fled from sin, not so much because of the punishment as because of the offense to so good a God, to a Father worthy of reverence and love.

The Holy Spirit had kept his servant far from all sin by the gift of *Fear.* And he joined him to his will so intimately by the gift of *Piety* that no consideration, difficulty, or danger was ever able to keep him away from what he knew to be the divine pleasure, manifested to him by the law, precept, rule or simple insinuation of his superiors, setting aside every personal advantage and convenience (as though the greater service of God were not our greatest advantage and convenience). He would gladly dispense even with martyrdom in order to do the will of God in the baptism of one child. That's why he emphasized so much in his letters the fulfillment of God's will, declaring to the religious that

---

[220] Isa. 11:2.
[221] Luke 18:13.

*Book Four, Chapter 10*

their perfection does not consist in doing the more perfect thing but in doing what God wants them to do, for this will be the more perfect thing for them.

Father San Vitores with his keen determination, continuous study, and the grace of God had acquired a great knowledge of philosophy and of theology, scholastic, expository,[222] and moral, as well as of church history and other areas of learning. And God illumined him with the gift of *Knowledge* so that he could make use of all this learning for the good of his soul and that of all the people he instructed and dealt with. He never studied just to know, which is foolish curiosity, nor to be esteemed, which is foolish vanity, but to improve himself and his neighbor, which is the reason why our father, Saint Ignatius, wants his sons to study. When he was a student in Alcalá, in order not to neglect any of the major subjects required by obedience, he spent his holidays learning more about Scripture, the holy fathers, and history. Later on he used this in sermons and in books, especially in the *Epitome* that he wrote about the Apostle of the Indies, which with other writings resulted in great advantage for the Christian Church.[223] Finally, on every occasion he turned his knowledge of letters, human and divine, to the glory of the Lord, and although he was a brilliant philosopher and theologian and possessed a mastery of other sciences as well, he could say with Saint Paul that he knew nothing but Christ and Christ crucified, because he believed that he, unless he employed what he knew for the glory of God, he knew nothing.

With the gift of *Fortitude*, the Holy Spirit strengthened him to overcome the world, the demon, and the flesh: the flesh in all its passions, the devil in all his temptations, and the world in all its contradictions. In all his battles, he came out the victor, so that no enemy could pride himself on having triumphed, not even once, over this brave soldier of Jesus Christ. Already we have given abundant testimony to this truth when we spoke of the virtue of fortitude. Let us now recall only that one victory, difficult as it was glorious, that he won over the flatteries and coaxing of the woman who tried to catch him in the net of lust.[224]

His *Counsel* is highly praised in the *Processus*, as one of the most striking gifts that he received from the Lord to guide his own actions and those of others, so that I need not add anything to what I said when speaking about his prudence.

With the Spirit's gift of *Understanding*, God illumined that of his servant, that he might comprehend the divine mysteries, seeing into the depths of the love, the power, and the wisdom that shine forth in them, and he recognized the divine perfections in the human things themselves that he saw and heard. Heaven and earth, Creator and crea-

---

[222] Exegetic, biblical?

[223] *Apóstol de las Nuevas Gentes*, México 1661, 1661, 164 pp.; in addition to various pamphlets and tracts he also wrote *Memoriale al Serenissimo Señor Don Juan de Austria...en rason de la grande conveniencia del voto de la Inmaculada Concepción...scrivolos Diego Alonso de Maluenda*, Madrid,1655; *Fórmula del Acto de Contrición* in Spanish, Tagalog, and in *lingua Mariana*; *Arte y Vocabulario de la Lingua de las islas Marianas*; various prayer books in Tagalog; and probably (with Jerónimo López, S.J.) *Casos Raros de la Confesión*, México 1660. He seems to have enlarged a much smaller work of this name in several editions. It was published without the author's name in Mexico, but it bore the name of Cristóbal de Vega in Spain. Cf. Book 1, chap. 8:45; Book 2, chap.1:87.

[224] Cf. Book 1, chap. 7:40-41.

tures, all served him as a book and as matter for the highest contemplation, as we see in his letters, where frequently he points out the lessons of events and draws from all of them some teaching for the edification of his spirit and that of others. From the profound penetration he had of the divine mysteries arose the excellence with which he explained them, finding reasonable arguments for them and discovering new insights into what the Lord did and suffered for us. Remarkable also was the intuition he had while explaining them, as if he saw with his own eyes what God has hidden from us under a curtain of obscurity.

Together with the gift of understanding, with which he penetrated into the most hidden mysteries and eternal truths, God gave him the gift of *Wisdom*, with which he savored with delight spiritual and heavenly things, so that nothing but God pleased him. Of nothing did he speak but of the riches of heaven. Hence, he had no desire to know of worldly events, unless they served the good of souls and the prevention of sin. All his comfort was to know what was happening in the missions, that the Faith was spreading, that the Lord was being served and revered by all. This was the news he wanted to hear and this was the subject of his letters. Thus, in the first letter that he writes to his father from Mexico, he remarks how consoled he is to see the Faith planted in that land, to see such magnificent temples and so much else. Then he adds: "Concerning the information that we have received about the Christian Church and the missions that await us in the Philippines, Brother Francisco Solano will give you a better account, including the report with all circumstances of our voyage. I cannot but be delighted at what is repeated about the hope, which our good Lord gives of the harvest in the mission of Japan, and of the sparks of faith that still live in that empire, and especially that the emperor was sending an ambassador to the City of Manila, asking for fathers and ministers of the gospel." He writes the same from the Philippines with the same joy and enthusiasm.

# CHAPTER XI

### Of the Graces Gratis Datae With Which
### God Adorned His Great Servant

After the virtues and gifts granted by God to the Venerable Father San Vitores, I must now treat of the graces that are specifically called *gratis datae*. These the Lord usually gives to his apostolic servants for the benefit of those who receive their instruction and preaching. The apostle Paul, in his first letter to the Corinthians, reduces these graces to nine, and they are: *words of wisdom, words of knowledge, faith, graces of healing, the working of miracles, prophecy, discernment of spirits, the gift of tongues, and the interpretation of words.*[225] And although ordinarily the Holy Spirit gives only one of these graces to one person and another to another, as he pleases, he sometimes joins many or all of them for those he chooses as preachers of new nations, as he did with the sacred apostles and with Saint Francis Xavier and also, it seems, with Father Diego Luis de San Vitores, the first doctor and apostle of the Marianas.

The first two graces, which are *words of wisdom and words of knowledge*, are for explaining, respectively, what regards customs and what regards mysteries. We have already seen sufficiently in this history how excellently the Servant of God possessed them, since he explained the most profound mysteries with such clarity that he made them clear and acceptable even to these blind barbarians, whose eyes were not lifted beyond the things of this earth. And he explained the commandments of God in such a manner that they appeared to be just and holy to those who had no law or religion. All claimed in unison: "Oh, how good is this that the Great Father tells us. And we had been told we should kill him who teaches us not to kill." The many thousands of Gentiles whom he converted to the Faith are witnesses to the power of his words, of this gift of God. One day, in Mexico, he uttered with great feeling these few words: "The salvation of those infants of the Marianas." At this a priest was moved to beg for the mission of the Marianas, a grace that he obtained, with great good for those islands.

The gift of *Faith*, of which the apostle speaks here, is also called "confidence" and is, as it were, the mother of miracles, the faith that moves mountains.[226] Only someone who did not know the marvels he performed and the assurance with which he began the most difficult undertakings for the glory of God, could fail to see the supreme degree to which Father San Vitores possessed this gift. Here, I will report only a few of the Lord's providential acts, which were, at once, an effect and a reward of the confidence of his servant.

---

[225] I Cor. 12:8.
[226] Matt. 21:12; Mark 11:23; I Cor. 13:2.

*Of the Graces Gratis Datae With Which God Adorned His Great Servant*

Father Bustillos says that it happened many times in the Marianas that Father San Vitores distributed all the food in the house to the natives, in order to attract them to classes of Christian doctrine. He left nothing for his companions. But as soon as he had finished distributing his portion of the food to each *Mariano,* four or six *Marianos* would enter the house loaded with food in greater abundance and of better quality than what had been distributed. Father San Vitores used to say that this better quality was due to the fact that it had been seasoned by the hands and grace of the Blessed Virgin.

We find a further proof of this faith in what is related in the annals of Mexico. Father San Vitores wrote a letter from the Marianas to *bachiller* Cristóbal Javier Vidal, whom we have praised elsewhere.[227] In that letter the father said that he should trust in God and should not hesitate to beg alms to buy the things that he was listing separately, and that in the first tight situation in which he found himself short of money, he should beg alms for the love of God from the first one he met in the streets. *Bachiller* Vidal did just that. As he was going along the street with *bachiller* Juan de Gárate, a priest who testified to this, he was concerned that he would lack money for the things Father San Vitores had requested. Suddenly, they saw a man whom they judged to be a stranger since they did not recognize him. In appearance he seemed wealthy, so Cristóbal Vidal approached him and asked him for an alms so he could send some articles for divine worship to the Mariana Islands where Father San Vitores was preaching. Without asking any questions, the man answered: "You have solved a problem for me, since I have three hundred pesos to be applied to any pious work I choose and I don't know which one. You may have them, sir, and apply them to that good work, and upon receiving your receipt, I will give them to you tomorrow." This he did and the two priests gave praise to God who so promptly rewarded the trust of his servant; and they praised, too, the one so far away, who had foreseen the help to his *Marianos* through such extraordinary means.

We have already given enough proofs of the *grace of healing* the sick in Mexico, the Philippines, Mindoro, and the Marianas. We need not repeat them here. He tried to hide these cures, as we have said, by applying relics of other holy persons, so that it would not appear that God granted the cures through the imposition of his hands. Yet precious objects associated with him gave him away. They revealed that it was he who restored health to the sick and publicized how efficacious is the gift of healing, as though in the case of a contagious disease, the disease would cling to his clothing or personal object, while health would attach itself to the sick. To the cases of healing already mentioned in the course of this history, I wish to add only two, which Father Bustillos reports in a letter from the Marianas to Father Juan Gabriel Guillén. He was sent by the Servant of God to a mission station where one night he found two sick persons at the door of death. He applied to them an object that Father San Vitores used (he does not say what it was) as well as a letter

---

[227] Cf. Book 2, chap. 2:93-94.

and a signature of his. Upon his return next morning, he found them in good health, without any sign of the malignant fevers that had gripped them in a death agony. He saw one of the dying persons set out that morning and walk four leagues, and he said happily in his own language, "How good God is, who restored my health with the clothing, letter, and signature of the Great Father."

Next there is the *power of working miracles*, that is, the greater miracles, namely those that affect the soul or which are beyond the ordinary. I am not speaking here of the marvelous conversions he obtained, many of which he reports in the book, *Casos Raros de la Confesión*, although he does not claim them as his, and other singular conversions we have already narrated. But what shall we say of the other special and extraordinary miracles that he performed?

The *Marianos* used to call him *macana*, which means miracle worker, after they saw the spears and stones they threw in the Tinian war break up on contact with him. It seems, too, that he had power over the waters, because the sea and the winds obeyed him. Father Bustillos, in the letter mentioned above, writes that many times it happened that on leaving one island for another, with contrary winds and furious, stormy seas, he calmed them instantly with only one blessing. And he says that this happened whenever he wanted and whenever he was asked by his companions. And he did this graciously and with charm to disguise the great power the Lord had given him over his creatures. One day he left one island for another accompanied by four or five canoes. All, except his own, were lost.

Not to repeat particular cases, in general the continual success of his travels by sea, without the sickness or deaths that commonly occur on sea voyages, was commonly held as a miracle.

I will pass over the wonders he worked on the Island of Mindoro. But I do not know whether I should add here the miracles God performed in Father San Vitores's own body. The health that God gave him in such a variety of climates, in spite of such great hardships and labors, could not but be more than natural, since he was so delicate and sickly. For this, he repeatedly gave thanks to God in his letters, acknowledging it as a singular favor. Just recently arrived in New Spain, he wrote to his father: "Through God's goodness and the mercy of the Blessed Virgin, I find myself with the same health, without any relapse since my last sickness in Madrid, in which the Divine Goodness finally disposed us for this mission. It seems rather that my strength grows greater every day, at least greater than that of my companions who are stronger than I. While they have suffered more illness, what with all the hardships of the road, I certainly have not suffered the least sickness or hardship. It must be that God is treating me as the weaker in virtue." He says the same things when writing from the Philippines to Father Juan Gabriel Guillén. He assures him that he had not suffered even a headache in such a long time, on such journeys, in such climates. Later, he lost his health and strength on account of his exhausting work and the hardships he had to undergo, principally in the Marianas. But Father Bustillos testifies that at

*Of the Graces Gratis Datae With Which God Adorned His Great Servant*

times, although he was ill and his face was like that of a corpse, he still set out on his mission journeys. And yet, though exposed to the tropical sun, to hunger and thirst and wearing weariness, walking barefoot and laboring night and day, he returned stronger and more robust than when he left. I do not mention that lightness of step, more like that of a bird or an angel, with which he walked so many times in Mindoro and the Marianas. But who would not call it a wonder in a sick man, so weakened by labors and penances, unless it was a singular favor of the angels who bore him up in their hands lest he stumble, so that he might perform the office of an angel for those who stumble and fall in the road to perdition. His many apparitions, while still alive, either by the bilocation of his body or by being carried by an angel wherever need or charity required him to be, are phenomena admired in the greatest saints.

When Brother Marcos de la Cruz, who had accompanied Father San Vitores in Mindoro, as we have said, was grievously sick in the Kingdom of Siao, the Venerable Father appeared to him in the company of another venerable person, whom he did not recognize. He spoke to him and comforted him for a little while and then disappeared, leaving him happy and cured of his sickness. On another occasion, when the same brother was sailing in the *San Diego* from Manila to Nueva España in 1669, a hurricane struck them in the gulf, so terrible that they all saw themselves in the jaws of death; with the force of the winds, the galleon was upset and turned on its side in the waters where it remained for three hours quite out of the control of the frightened seamen. Then Brother Marcos saw Father San Vitores (who was then in the Marianas) close to the mizzen mast with his hands raised to heaven, praying to God that the men of the galleon might not perish. Instantly, the galleon righted itself as the half of the ship emerged from the water where it was submerged. All believed that this was a miracle, but only Brother Marcos knew at that moment that it was Father San Vitores to whose prayers they owed that heavenly favor.

We have already told that in Manila and Mindoro he was neither splashed with mud or soaked by water during the season of the great rains, while his companions were so affected.[228] And this happened many times, as Father Bustillos writes, in the Marianas, as he walked the roads and sailed the sea in those unroofed boats, swept by every passing wave, besides being exposed to continual rains. Once when his companions were soaking wet they were surprised to see that he was quite dry. They asked him why he did not get wet. He answered with a noticeable shrug of the shoulders, "We have a good God."

*Prophecy*, strictly speaking, refers to all future things. Yet in the widest sense it extends to all unknown things, past, present, and to come. God granted this admirable gift in all its extent to Father San Vitores. From childhood the spirit of prophecy was noticed in him. When his entry into the Society was opposed by his father, he told him that he knew that he would change his mind. When the opposition to his vocation was at its strongest, he told his confessor that on the following day he

---

[228] Cf. Book 2, chap. 14:147.

would be received into the Society. When his confessor asked him how he knew it, since all the signs were to the contrary, he answered that he had been told by one who used to let him know other things that fitted him well. With these words he revealed how often God spoke to his pure and simple heart. Leaving aside the mysterious dream that he had while a novice, that he would go straight to heaven and other prophecies that have been referred to, I will add some that have not yet been mentioned.[229]

To Father Baltazar de Mansilla, who sailed to the Philippines along with the Servant of God and desired to accompany him when he went to the Marianas, he revealed that he would be of greater help by not going to the Marianas rather than by going there. And that is what happened. After ten or twelve years, Father Mansilla went to Mexico to be procurator of the Mariana Mission, where he begged and still begs for all its needs. When sailing from Mexico to the Marianas in the *San Diego*, Father San Vitores often said to a citizen of Manila, named Nicolás Fernández, who was voyaging as clerk of the ship, "I wonder if on your arrival in Manila, you will find your wife in the other life." And it happened just as the Servant of God had said, even though his prophecy was disguised in the form of a doubt, thus revealing the news sufficiently to Nicolás Fernández, so that he would not be taken by surprise by it upon his arrival. On June 13, 1669, *don* Manuel de León arrived in the Marianas on his way to be governor of the Philippines. More than four months previously, many times the Servant of God had unwittingly told that a new governor was arriving, although when he realized what he had said, he tried to correct the statement in some way so they would not think him a prophet. In the year 1670, he knew that no ship would pass by enroute to the Philippines, and he clearly let his companions know about it. Father Pedro de Casanova was forewarned by him some days before about some difficulties he would encounter. He also revealed that Father Tomás Cardeñoso, whom his companions thought had died on another island, would return to the Saint Ignatius Residence. Returning from Antipolo to Manila, which is some ten or twelve leagues distant, Father San Vitores informed one of the most respected fathers of the Philippine Province about events that had recently occurred in that residence, with details that could not possibly be known then. The same thing happened with others of the Society. Not even the thoughts and desires that are a privileged secret of the human heart, did God conceal from his servant. In the port of Acapulco, he revealed to a Spaniard the feelings and thoughts of his mind. Father Bustillos says, "To us who were fortunate to be his companions in the Marianas, with his usual shrug, at different times he revealed something that took place in our souls and was known only to us. And this he did to console and teach us and for our greater encouragement to work in that vineyard of the Lord." And he states that in making his confession to the Servant of God, it happened to him several times that even before he spoke, that the Venerable Father told him all that he intended to confess; and he adds that his other companions can declare the same thing.

---

[229]Cf. Book 1, chap. 7:37.

*Of the Graces Gratis Datae With Which God Adorned His Great Servant*

Leaving aside other prophecies, I will narrate a very well-known one, or many included in one, which show at the same time the power of his prayer and the degree of his merits. *Don* Diego Salcedo, who was governor of the Philippines at the time Father San Vitores was preparing his voyage to the Marianas, asked him two or three times to obtain from God by his prayers that he might have his purgatory in this life, since he feared so much the pains to be endured in the next. The Servant of God made no reply until the very day of his departure. *Don* Diego Salcedo with tears in his eyes, repeated the request he had made. The Venerable Father, as a farewell to him and a reward for all that he had done for his mission, asked him, "Is Your Excellency ready to suffer in your body, in your property, and in your honor what God may decide in your regard?" When the governor answered affirmatively, saying that this was what he desired, the Servant of God took him by the hand and with a countenance shining like burning coals said, "Courage, because Your Excellency had much to suffer, and with this you will have bid farewell to the kind offices you have performed towards our preparation for the voyage to the Marianas in the *San Diego*." And so, the Venerable Father departed for New Spain and immediately (and these are the words of a witness of the whole cruel process) *don* Diego was assailed by every sort of misfortune, danger of death, and false witness such that he was arrested by the ministers of the Holy Tribunal of the Inquisition. He was worn out with being dragged from one place to another, loaded with chains, and cruel imprisonment, and the sequestration of his property, of which he lost a great deal. Three days before they arrested him, he received a letter of Father San Vitores from the Mariana Islands in which he gave him an account of his voyage and arrival. The father told him to have courage and remember his words. God sent him this last strengthening before the blow fell. The governor was arrested in Manila and treated like the worst criminal in the commonwealth. Then they transferred him from prison to a ship and he was taken to New Spain. God, who tries but does not abandon his own, wished to give him his reward and an end to his sufferings. So on the fifth of October, God sent him a warning. That night he seemed to see in a dream Saint Brigid, to whom he was very devoted, and Father San Vitores. They consoled him in his hardships and said that, if he survived the twenty-fourth of that month, he would not die soon. The event proved that the dream was not a vain one, but a notice and a premonition of heaven, because he died on October 24, 1670, with great conformity to the will of God and profound resignation, recognizing that all those hardships were a special favor of God, and that God, through the prayers of his servant, had commuted the terrible pains of purgatory into those others, which, for all their severity, were much lighter than those suffered in the other life. In gratitude for this favor, he left in his last will ten thousand pesos for the Mariana Islands. Soon after his death, his innocence was established and his brothers possess official testimony to the fact from the Holy General Inquisition. It is no secret that the person who was responsible for the unjust imprisonment came to New Spain and died in the same situation as *don* Diego. Father San

Vitores was in the Marianas at the time when these events took place. Knowing them by divine revelation, he wrote to the Inquisitor General through his father, in defense of *don* Diego Salcedo, refuting one by one the charges against him, a testimony that helped much toward a favorable outcome. After the year 1671, he received a letter in the Marianas about all that had happened. He read this letter with great consolation and joy, not being able to disguise the fact that he knew it all beforehand, and even before this, had often informed his companions of these events. Having read the letter he said, "A good gentleman! He had his purgatory in this life and without passing through more purgatory he went straight to heaven." I end with what is emphasized in the sworn *Processus*, that *don* Diego Salcedo appointed four executors for his will, but Father San Vitores wrote only to the last, who was called *don* Jerónimo Pardo de Lagos, accountant of the higher tribunal of accounts of Mexico, enjoining him to take care of the property of *don* Diego Salcedo and of the alms that he left to the Marianas. He could not naturally know that the will was going to be in the hands only of this last one because of the absence and inability of the others.

This admirable man possessed in an eminent degree the discernment of spirits, so necessary to those who are to be the teachers and guides of many, so that they may know in themselves and in others if the thoughts and desires came from the Holy Spirit or from the bad one, from nature or from grace. We can see this in his letters and instructions, of which I have some in my possession, particularly one instruction that he gave to one of his companions on how to distinguish the gifts that are from God from those that are not. But since this is so spiritual and beyond the common ability to understand, I will not include it here, although it is an excellent one. I hope that it will one day be published along with his letters and papers, to the advantage of all.

The *gift of tongues* was not wanting in this preacher of the new peoples. We have shown how in Taytay he learned the Tagalog language in a very short time with great perfection, something that all considered to be a miracle.[230] In Mindoro he spoke at least six languages, as he himself divulges without meaning to in the reports on that mission. Father Bustillos, besides repeating that Father San Vitores spoke all the languages in Mindoro, says in a letter to Father Guillén that God had given him a special gift of tongues, by which he understood and spoke all the languages of the Philippines. He had a perfect knowledge of the language of the Marianas, composing in it a grammar, a vocabulary, and a catechism. Even before arriving in the islands, during his voyage from the Philippines to Mexico, he used to correct the natives whom he took along as interpreters of that language, becoming the teacher of his teachers and teaching what he himself had not studied. On the same voyage, as we have said, he knew the languages of all the nationalities that were sailing on that ship. Father San Vitores not only knew the Mariana language with the perfection we have mentioned but, in a way, he communicated this gift to others, for the Lord granted to his companions, at the begin-

---

[230]Cf. Book 2, chap. 4:98-99.

*Of the Graces Gratis Datae With Which God Adorned His Great Servant*

ning of the mission, when they had not yet learned the language, that they should not lack for words in time of need, as the Venerable Father had promised them, trusting in the promise of Christ to his disciples that in that hour it would be given to them to speak.[231]

I come now to the last grace, which is the *interpretation of words*, and it consists either in explaining the obscure mysteries of the Sacred Scriptures or in translating an unknown language into one that is known. This gift was recognized in the Servant of God in both its forms. He explained with great accuracy and penetration the texts of Sacred Scripture, as we see in the books that he wrote. He translated from one language to another the mysteries of our Faith, so that we could say that he was a translator of himself, because he translated into the *Mariano* language papers on Christian doctrine and various devotions that he had written in Tagalog, so that he could do good in all languages and that God might be praised and glorified in all.

---

[231]Matt. 10:19; Mark 13:11.

# CHAPTER XII

*How Father San Vitores Was Endowed With the*
*Three Halos of Martyr, Doctor, and Virgin*

God withheld no gift in favoring his servant. He was not content with granting him his graces; he also gave him the glories that he is wont to distribute among other saints, adorning him, humanly speaking, with the three halos of *martyr, doctor,* and *virgin.* These are three gifts of accidental glory with which God honors those who have fought valiantly against the world, the flesh, and the devil. Although I have already given this praise to Father San Vitores, here I will establish the basis for such high praise and show the very perfection of his singular prerogatives.

This extraordinary man was an illustrious *martyr* of Christ, who gave his life for the Faith he was preaching and gave it in the act of preaching, his breast pierced with a lance and his head wounded with a sword. We have already told the circumstances of his martyrdom.[232] Now I will point out how far in advance God revealed that he was going to be a martyr, so that he could be one all his life long, dying each day with the offering and the desire or rather the impatience he felt at the deferment of the death he was to suffer or rather enjoy one day. Nor should we fail to note how Saint Francis Xavier, accompanied by Father Marcello Mastrilli, had cured him of a serious illness so that he should sail to America [sic] where he was to suffer martyrdom.[233] Saint Francis Xavier made him another martyr, a living martyr, a spectacle to the world, a singular prodigy, no matter how often we may say so. But although nothing was wanting in the martyrdom of the Servant of God, neither in perfection nor splendor, in view of the prodigies that later took place when his body was thrown into the sea, still all his sufferings were not enough for the desire he had to suffer for Christ, such as to be roasted alive like Saint Lawrence, or flayed like Saint Bartholomew, or to have his body cut in pieces, because all these sufferings seemed to him few or light, or rather sweet when suffered for Christ. And so when in our refectory they read in the martyrology of the most terrible torments of the martyrs, he would be full of joy, savoring the accounts, as it were, and would say, "Oh, how good, how beautiful." He was all the more delighted as the pains were more atrocious and would beg the Lord to allow him to suffer even greater torments for his love.

This enlightened man was an excellent *doctor,* a doctor of old and new nations, a doctor who by word and deed made himself great in the kingdom of heaven. He practiced what he taught and he taught what he practiced. He taught the doctrine of heaven to innumerable

---

[232]See Book 3, chapter 17.
[233]Cf. Book 1, chap. 11:60.

*How He Was Endowed With the Three Halos of Martyr, Doctor, and Virgin*

souls, whether Christians, pagans, heretics, or Moors. He taught with words and with books, with letters, instructions, sermons, and familiar conversations. He taught by himself and through his disciples and companions, whether they were religious, laymen, old Christians or neophytes. He instructed them all and taught so that they would teach others, sharing his light and fervor with all he could reach, so that there would be more who would spread the light and the fire. He did all that was necessary for the new Church that he founded, to the extent that it had in him an exemplar of all the virtues. Therefore, he deserves the praise given by the Prophet Daniel to the doctors when he said: "The learned will shine as bright as stars forever";[234] and what Christ said about the Baptist: "He was a lamp, alight, and shining."[235]

This admirable man was a *virgin* all his life. Never did he consent by word or deed or thought to anything that might stain his purity. From childhood he was called Holy Angel, and he looked like one in his purity, more angelic than human. I nowhere read that he ever had conflicts or rebellions of the flesh. Speaking only of the time in the Marianas, among naked people, Father Bustillos says that he did not feel any temptations of the flesh, which naturally all would feel. But he did not lack as a young religious of the Society the same temptation as Joseph of which we spoke in the proper place.[236] This temptation he overcame by fleeing, like that chaste patriarch. If he was spared other more interior conflicts, battles more than worldly and domestic, battles of the flesh against the spirit, aside from the fact that it was a privilege of heaven rather than of earth, he merited it and preserved it. For the penance that he practiced was great, even from childhood. Always he kept perfect guard over his senses, closing his eyes and ears to all objects, which, once they penetrate the soul, are difficult to reject. It was for this reason, that having used eyeglasses all his life because of his poor vision, which was much worse during the last years of his life,[237] he gave them up as soon as he landed in the Marianas among those naked people, preferring to stumble on stones than on objects that, if they did not stain, would at least offend his modesty. I have to attribute in great measure to his prayers and merits the privilege that God gave to his companions in the Society, of which he wrote in his report for the year 1669: "This people does not have any clothing, though they want it and ask for it constantly. We have found from experience that through the mercy of the Lord their nakedness does not disturb us in the ministry of the gospel any more than if we were preaching to well-dressed people. However, for the sake of due decency, we wish that the persons whom this report may reach, would help us with available clothing, especially such as can serve as some kind of shirt or light tunic, no matter what the color, so that this poor people may be dressed, or rather, our Lord Jesus Christ, who is naked in them." For this reason he distributed among these poor naked people all the

[234] Dan. 13:3.
[235] John 5:35.
[236] See Book 1, chap. 7:38.
[237] Matt. 25:36-43.

clothing he could, even the curtains in the church. He said that the principal purpose for which they have been collected as alms was to dress those poor *Marianos*, not to adorn the churches and altars, and that the Lord was more pleased if we used them to dress his children than to decorate his house.

# CHAPTER XIII

*Miracles and Apparitions of the Venerable Father*
*San Vitores after His Martyrdom*

After his death God honored his servant with certain favors granted through his intercession. He helped some persons who commended themselves to him, and thus he showed that even in the great glory he enjoys in heaven, he has compassion on mortals in the miseries they suffer. He began by the promise he made to his father at his departure for the Indies, that he would assist him at his death. I came to know this through the oral and written testimony of the *Marqués* de la Rambla, son of *don* Jerónimo and brother of Diego Luis. I pass over certain circumstances that later were spread abroad by ill-informed persons. When *don* Jerónimo fell grievously ill, on the night before his death, he ordered two maids who were assisting him—one of them called María de la Concepción and the other María de Hervas—to leave him alone. They got up to make the sick man believe that they were leaving. They closed the door but remained hidden in the chamber. Then they heard *don* Jerónimo San Vitores speaking these words: "My son Diego, I was sure that on this occasion you would not fail me. For this I am most grateful to you." This he repeated three times, shedding tears of consolation, a fact that left no doubt in the minds of the maids, that since the sick man was of sound mind and judgment, that Father San Vitores was present there, consoling and fortifying his father for his death. This took place on the following morning at seven o'clock with great peace and tranquility, after he had asked the maids to bring him the crucifix. They said that he died with it, and holding it in his hands, he surrendered his soul into the hands of the Lord on Friday, December 20, of the year 1675, at the age of eighty. A fortunate father, to have received from God such a son, and all the more fortunate since he gave his son to God; and even more fortunate that his son was taken by God for a most fruitful absence and a precious death, so that he could come to assist him in his own death and show him the way to eternal beatitude.

I could add much more about the zeal, integrity, and justice of this gentleman, minister, and model of ministers. His was a deep piety and a generous willingness to assist the needy in body and soul, and in this, he worked hand in hand with his son. Praise enough to say that he was worthy to be the father of such a noble son, one who became a martyr, a second Xavier, and the Lord's chosen vessel of election. No less worthy of notice is another apparition in the Philippines, in fulfillment of another promise and prophecy of the Servant of God, a mark of the gratitude with which he richly rewarded small favors. Brother Mateo de Cuenca had sailed for the Philippines together with Father San Vitores. He became his secretary and the witness of many of the matters that have been mentioned in this history. I know not on what occasion, but it must have been when the father noticed that he was worried about his perseverance that Father San Vitores predicted that he would die in the Society and that he would assist him at his death. After some years, Mateo de Cuenca was dismissed from the Society in the Province of the Philippines and obtained the benefice of the district of Ahun. But he did not enjoy it for long, because the kind and just Lord, wishing to punish him with mercy, sent him a serious illness, which kept him from leaving the house and doing as he pleased. Conscious of his illness and of his need to go to confession, and not wishing to leave the town where he was, he sent twice for the nearest confessor, signifying to him his need and danger. Twice the confessor excused himself. God permitted this for the greater good of the sick man. The natives of his town, moved by their piety more than by their native wit, shipped their pastor to the town of Iloilo, which was under the ministry of the Society of Jesus. But a storm arose with contrary winds, which were extraordinary at that time of the year. It was as if it were the work of the common enemy of mankind, to oppose, though in vain, the saving wind of the Holy Spirit, which was bringing that soul back to the harbor of salvation. The sick man was deeply troubled that he could not reach Iloilo. He pressed to his lips a relic of Father San Vitores and began to call upon him in his fear and anxiety, begging him to ask our Lord not to let him die without confession. The Venerable Father appeared to him. Although he spoke no word to him, the very sight of him comforted him, dispelling all fears of being lost, and giving him a certain hope of reaching the desired port and of receiving the sacraments. His trust was not in vain, because the wind changed its course and he arrived at Iloilo. There, he reported what has been narrated here to Father Pedro Vello, of the Society of Jesus, who was in charge of the mission and knew of the promise that Father San Vitores had made to the sick man. Mateo de Cuenca had kept the same love and veneration for the Society that he had before, and if he heard anything against her, he would publicly declare that he had been expelled because of his faults, and because he would not follow the regular observance of that religious order. He held it to be a holy one, not tolerating those who wished to live as they pleased, not observing the rule. He asked Father Pedro Vello with remarkable insistence to receive him back into the Society, for he felt he was going to die. Father Vello would not dare to receive him back. He wrote to Father Provincial in Manila, but because an answer was slow in coming and the sickness was getting worse, and much more because of the sadness of the sick man, Father Vello presumed the permission of the provincial because of the promise previously made to the sick man. Moreover, he assumed that the provincial had received his letter, but above all, he felt supernaturally inspired and was impelled, as he swore later, by a force that he could not resist. He received him back into the Society with indescribable consolation of the sick man. When he saw himself vested with the Jesuit cassock he felt he was dressed with a robe of immortality. He made a general confession and begged pardon of all those present for the bad example he had given and died having received the last sacraments on April 27, 1677.

*Miracles and Apparitions of the Venerable Father San Vitores after His Martyrdom*

Not very different is what happened to another religious of the Philippine Province. He had helped the Venerable Father in some matters, and the Venerable Father asked him how he could pay him back for the service he had given him. His reply was that he wished him to obtain for him his perseverance in the Society. He was at that time doubtful about his perseverance and Father San Vitores promised to pray to the Lord for it, and he consoled him by his assurance that he would die in the Society. That is what happened; for before he could fail in his vocation, God sent him a sickness in which, having received all the sacraments and thanking God for not expelling him from his house, he died on the same date and almost on the same hour when Father San Vitores died a martyr in the Marianas, as it was verified later. The good death and perseverance of this religious, whom Father San Vitores rewarded with a great favor for a small service, was attributed to the merits and intercession of the venerable martyr.

I pass over other favors that diverse persons obtained in their different needs. Father José Vidal, of the Province of Mexico, whom Father San Vitores designated as the procurator of the Mariana Islands when he set sail for them, felt most distressed because he had borrowed a quantity of pesos from different persons in order to send some necessary things to the Mariana Islands, and when the time came for payment, he did not know how he could pay that debt. He had recourse to Father San Vitores and asked him for help in the emergency in which he was involved because of him, and asked him to provide the amount needed to pay the debts incurred for his sake. Suddenly, at that very moment, a young man knocked on the door of his room and offered, on the part of his master, the amount in pesos that he urgently needed to liquidate his debt. And this same thing happened to him a second time almost under the same circumstances. These two cases are reported in the *Notices from Mexico*. Although it is not explicitly stated that they happened after the death of the Venerable Father, it seems that was the case. And yet it would not diminish the wonder of it, but rather increases it, in a way, if the Servant of God were still alive in the Mariana Islands when the said father commended himself to him and sought a remedy for his situation.

There was a certain distinguished lady in Madrid who was related to the Venerable Father. She was in great distress because of dire need and other serious problems. She had no idea where to look for help, so she turned to a portrait of the venerable martyr that she had in her house, and weeping bitterly, she said to him: "My saintly Father, if you were in this world and saw me in these dreadful difficulties, you would surely come to my help. But since you are in heaven and see them, you are better able to remedy them." At the very moment she offered this prayer, which was at nightfall, a young man appeared at her door and delivered to the person who went to open it two hundred reals, without saying who sent them, though they asked him. All he said was that the person who sent them would be happy if they were two thousand ducats.

When this same woman was down with malarial fever and had received Viaticum, on the fourteenth day, *don* Jerónimo San Vitores came to see her. When he asked her how she was, she answered, "Lord, how I wish to die!" To this *don* Jerónimo replied, "Be quiet. If I could speak, perhaps I could assure you, on the part of a good relative, that you will not die of this sickness." It was eleven o'clock in the morning and that night after ten o'clock, as the sickness grew worse and her suffering more intense, one of her sons came and said to her, "Mother, commend yourself to Father San Vitores and say one Our Father and one Hail Mary, and send him a message by your guardian angel." The mother answered that she could not pray unless he helped her. The son brought a portrait of the Venerable Father and placed it above her head, and together they said the Our Father and the Hail Mary. A little later the sick woman fell asleep, and within the hour, she awakened in such copious sweat that she was cured of the fever and free of the sickness. A daughter of this woman told me of these cases and later put them in writing for me. And she testified under oath before God and the crucifix that she was eyewitness of both cases.

Sister Isabel del Espíritu Santo, a nun of the most pious Convent of the Magdalene, in Alcalá, a long-time devotee of Father San Vitores, writes in a letter of December 13, 1674, that she applied to herself a picture of the Servant of God and was freed of the pain of gout that tormented her cruelly. She also writes that another religious of the same convent, *sor* María de San Bonaventura, was struck in the eye with an iron rod, which caused severe bleeding. She applied a picture of the father to the injured part and immediately both the bleeding and the pain ceased, though this is so delicate and sensitive an organ. Another religious, this one of the Convent of Villa Mayor de Los Montes, of the order of Saint Bernard, under the jurisdiction of Las Huelgas of Burgos, used to suffer attacks of intestinal pain that lasted for days at a time. She had a great devotion to Father San Vitores, since she had heard in Burgos reports current there of his holiness and martyrdom, and because she had read a short account of his virtues and miracles. This account circulated widely. It was a collection of articles to be submitted as official testimonies to His Eminence Cardinal Aragón. Then, on the eve of the Feast of Saint Dominic [hence on August third] her illness gave her such serious pain for twenty hours that it occurred to her to appeal to Father San Vitores, which she did in all sincerity and confidence. This religious sister, in a letter of August 1675, said that she was instantly freed of that pain and she adds that in view of the circumstances with which it began, it was not likely to last any shorter time than it had at Christmas, when it lasted thirty days without a moment's relief day or night.

Father Francisco de Herrera, of our Society, who was a resident of the *colegio* of Badajoz, a learned and prudent man, had been a pupil of Father San Vitores. In certain notes written in his own hand, which he sent me containing accounts of prophecies, virtues, and miracles, he tells me that on one occasion, when suffering great pain in his throat, he applied a relic of Father San Vitores and the pain disappeared immediately. He experienced this many times. "I also prayed to him," he says, "in times of interior trials and have enjoyed grand relief." He adds a case in which he had personal experience. A resident of Badajoz, called Beatriz de Cascos, was near death. She had received Viaticum and Extreme Unction and had been despaired of by the physicians. Father de Herrera was called to help her to a good death. He brought with him the relic of the Venerable Father and applied it to the sick woman, encouraging her to pray to Father San Vitores and to trust that she would recover her health through his intercession. The dying woman did that, and soon the result was evident. From that moment she felt a notable improvement. She escaped both the danger of death and the sickness itself. The physician, *Don* Jacinto Lobato, physician-in-chief of the Army of Estremadura, well-known for his abilities and learning, who had assisted her, stated to the said Father Francisco de Herrera, that it appeared miraculous, as much because the improvement was instantaneous, since her pulse had improved beyond the range of danger to the patient, while it had previously been non-existent.

Father Pedro de Montes, of the Society of Jesus, was rector of the residence of Silang, in the Philippine Islands. He stated under oath that he had been grievously ill and felt that he was going to die. He prayed to Father San Vitores before his picture, making a vow that he would beg to be sent to the Marianas. He then felt noticeable improvement and recovered perfect health. Father Bartolomé Vesco (Besco), also a religious of the Philippine Province who sailed to the Mariana Islands, affirmed that on different occasions, being plagued with many grave afflictions, he prayed to God through the intercession of the Venerable Father San Vitores, so that both on land and sea he experienced many favors and graces, as well as spiritual and temporal consolations.

I conclude with what happened to *don* Antonio Saravia, who in the year 1680 was enroute as governor to the Mariana Islands, more because of his zeal for the conversion of those islanders than because of any ambition for the post. He fell sick of dysentery in Mexico and it was bringing him rapidly to his death. He called to Father Baltazar de Mansilla, procurator of the Marianas, and said, "Your Reverence told me that you have a portrait of the saintly Father San Vitores. Bring it to me. I wish to commend myself to him." Father Mansilla brought the portrait. When the sick man saw it, he was filled with confidence and asked for his recovery so that he could continue his voyage to the Marianas, offering himself to serve him in them as far as his strength could reach. Father San Vitores listened mercifully to the prayers of his Mariana governor. At the instant the portrait entered his room, his sickness, which all the remedies had failed to cure, disappeared without any trace whatsoever, and in a few days the sick man recovered perfect health. And so he made the voyage to the Marianas, eager to serve our Lord there, who had given him his health and life to that end through the intercession of the first apostle and doctor of those nations.

I have no doubt that Father San Vitores will grant many favors to those who sincerely commend themselves to him, asking for help in their sicknesses, a remedy for their needs and consolation in all their afflictions, because already since his death, he has granted so many favors to those who prayed to him, even as he did in this life for those who sought his aid, because his charity and his power before the Lord have increased in heaven where everything is brought to perfection. Considering his heroic virtues and rare gifts, and considering that the Lord honors those who honor him and glorifies both in heaven and earth those who have promoted his glory, I trust that some day holy mother Church will venerate him who expanded the boundaries of God's kingdom on earth among peoples to whom the Gospel was as yet unknown. Indeed, I hope that Christian piety will see, raised to the altars, the one who built for the true God so many churches and altars. Oh, may the time be shortened for the arrival of such a joyous day for the glory of God, who is admirable in his saints; for the honor of his Church, which crowns itself with such sons; for the good of Christianity in the Indies, which will be encouraged by such patrons; for the honor of Spain, which can take pride in such heroes; and for the credit of the whole world, which produced this good and noble man, proving that the land that produces such fruits is far from sterile. May the Society of Jesus rejoice to be the mother that brought up in Christ this new apostle of new nations, this new Xavier, in whom heaven and earth glory, as well as Spain, America, and God himself, who manifested in him and through him his power and his mercy.

# BOOK V

*Of the Life and Martyrdom of the Venerable Father Diego Luis de San Vitores, of the Society of Jesus, First Apostle of the Mariana Islands*

Fig. 6. The Reigning Queen *doña* Mariana of Austria. This picture, taken from an old lithograph of unknown origin, shows the young Mariana dressed in garments appropriate to her widowed state. Her parents were the Hapsburg Emperor Fernando III and his Spanish-born wife, the Hapsburg princess María Ana. Widowed at age thirty-one, Mariana was the queen regent from 1665 to 1675. During her regency, Father Diego Luis de San Vitores established the mission and first Spanish settlement in the Mariana Islands. She was supportive of the Jesuit efforts and designated an annual subsidy of 3,000 pesos for the support of their school in Agaña, the Colegio de San Juan de Letrán. In recognition of the Holy Mother and the generosity of the queen regent, Father San Vitores named the islands Las Islas Marianas.

I f Sacred Scripture states that good sons are the crown of their parents, then great indeed will be the crown of the Venerable Father San Vitores,[238] a crown of the virtues and precious death of his spiritual sons and disciples. They followed in his footsteps in the enterprise of the Mariana Islands and, with their example and teaching, converted to the Lord many thousands of souls during the lifetime of the Servant of God. After his death, his spirit not only doubled but multiplied within those, who no longer his companions, were the worthy successors of his apostolic zeal. To those who came later and were inspired by the fire of his charity, to these, too, he bequeathed the spirit that still flames in those islands. We will begin with the life and martyrdom of the Venerable Father Luis de Medina, his closest companion and the principal imitator of his holiness. Preceding Father San Vitores in death, he was the first of the Jesuits who gave their lives for the Faith that they preached and spread throughout those islands, a hundredfold harvest worthy of that good earth.

[238] Prov. 17:6

Fig. 7. Map of the Island of Guam, by Alonso López, S.J. (See Figure 4). Note locations marked with a cross atop a small circle, designating churches; small circles alone marked the locations of missions, or *visitas*, served by an itinerant priest.

# CHAPTER I

*The Birth and Manners of the Venerable Father*
*Luis de Medina Before He Enters the Society of Jesus*

Father Luis de Medina was born in the City of Málaga, on February 3, 1637. He was baptized on the twenty-first of the same month. His parents were honorable, and they were virtuous, especially the mother. People still remember her devotion to the Blessed Virgin. Her parents were Francisco de Medina and *doña* María Peral, natives of the same city. We might even say that his mother was the Blessed Virgin, because, from the womb of his mother, this Lady began to favor him as a son and to preserve him to be an apostle of the Marianas. From the time he arrived at the age of reason, the child loved the Queen of Angels so much that he had more recourse to her than to his own parents, as will be seen by some events that we will report and by some accounts in his own handwriting. We will quote them in his own words so that we may know better the devotion he had for this Lady and the protection he found in her. In one of these writings, he speaks of the first favor he received from her, even before he could know her: "Millions of times may you be praised, blessed, and glorified, O most Blessed Virgin Mary, my most Holy Mother, for this first favor that you granted me within the womb of my mother. During the last days of the nine months, on February 2, the Feast of the Purification, the pains began, and you, most loving Mother, with your protection rescued me from death, so that I was born the next day with a reminder of this great gift of life, a token lest I should forget. For I was born lame in one foot and stuttering. Would that my steps and my tongue were always employed in praising you and thanking you for this grace." These are his words. They show us how God gave him defective feet and a stuttering tongue, him whom he had chosen to run over new lands and to preach his gospel, even as he is wont to do with great saints and prophets, so that we may see how God chooses weak instruments to do great things and the humble in this world to confound the strong.[239]

From childhood he gave signs of what he was later going to be. He quickly learned reading and writing as well as the Christian doctrine, which he enjoyed repeating, and he was a model to the other children in the school. After a few years he began to study grammar in the Society's school in Málaga. Those who came to know and deal with him testify that he studied hard and was most exemplary in all the classes, as well in his personal habits and in the reception of the sacraments. In this he surpassed all the students of his time, because he used to receive Communion on all the Sundays and feast days of the year. He was most devoted to our Blessed Lady.

---

[239] 1 Cor. 1:27.

As to the games and amusements of his age, he was so withdrawn from them that not only on class days, but even more on feast days and short vacations, he did not leave our church and *colegio*, not even to go to the homes of his relatives. When he did they were surprised to see him, though they desired to see him and complained about his strange behavior.

Because of his well-known good judgment and competence, on one occasion he substituted for his teacher, Father Cristóbal de Aguilar, in his class for upper-level students, because Father Aguilar was absent, making the spiritual exercises of Saint Ignatius, in accordance with the custom of our Society. Later because of some little prank, Father Aguilar showed a slight sign of displeasure, and the boy Luis had such a scruple about the displeasure he had caused his teacher that in the school's lobby in the presence of many, he fell on his knees and kissed his hand and begged his pardon, as though he had committed a serious offense, a matter of great edification to those who saw or heard of it.

Aside from this, we know about his boyhood and youth from what he wrote in his notebooks (or confessions, or praises of the Blessed Virgin). They deserve all these names. In these writings there are so many vows and devotions that it is a matter of wonder to see in such young years, so much care for his soul, so much solicitude to avoid faults and practice acts of virtue. One perceives how God was reserving him to be his martyr, guiding his steps and leading him through the straight paths of perfection. In a certain memorandum he says: "Most worthy Mother of our Lord Jesus Christ, may you be a thousand times glorified for having saved me in the world from various dangers and snares that the devil made ready for me, so that I might violate the vow of chastity that I made. In particular, you saved me from a very insidious snare, in which you manifested your great compassion, giving me an early warning of the trap and enlightening my heart about the danger and giving me grace so that I might not fall into it." Much is contained in these words, which signify that with God's grace he obtained those victories over the devil and the flesh, victories that are most noteworthy in the story of Joseph, the Viceroy of Egypt, and in other great saints.[240] Surely these victories are the most difficult to obtain, since in them the man is his own enemy, which he must conquer, so that if he wishes to overcome himself, in order to be the victor, he refuses to conquer himself, lest he be vanquished.

In honor of the Blessed Virgin, he practiced many devotions to which he committed himself by vow, as we know from his own words. In a memorandum, he professed himself a slave of the Blessed Virgin, which profession he expressed in the common form in which it is usually printed, with the addition of many vows worded in the most tender manner. He says: "I vow to keep perpetually my virginity and chastity, binding myself irrevocably all the days of my life." And further down: "I also offer myself and vow, O most Holy Mother, to go to confession and communion on all your feast days, all nine of them, and on all other feast days that the

---

[240]Gen. 39: 6 ss.

*The Venerable Father Luis de Medina Before He Enters the Society of Jesus*

Supreme Pontiff may declare. I also vow to say all the days of my life the rosary of the Virgin Mary, my Mother and Lady; also in memory of the twelve stars that are the twelve most excellent prerogatives that your Son my Lord Jesus Christ gave to you, I vow to say twelve Hail Marys and one Our Father and three Credos to the most Holy Trinity for having crowned you with a crown of twelve stars." Later, speaking to Christ, he says:

My Lord Jesus, as God, Father of the most Holy Virgin Mary, my Mother, and as man, Son of this Sovereign Queen of the Angels, in reverence to you and gratitude for the honor that your Divine Majesty showed to this Lady by taking her as your Mother and for having filled this sovereign princess, my Mother, with so many graces that she has and enjoys in heaven, desiring to serve and to please your Divine Majesty and your most Holy Mother as well as mine, I, your humble servant, promise under vow to your Divine Majesty to go to confession and receive Communion on all the days of your feasts, which are thirteen in number, and on all the other feasts that the Supreme Pontiff should establish. I also promise to say six Our Fathers and six Hail Marys in honor of your most holy Passion and Death and in memory of the most Blessed Sacrament, of which I am the lowly slave.

And turning to the Eternal Father he says:

Omnipotent and eternal God, Father of my Lord Jesus Christ and of the most glorious Virgin, my Queen and my Mother, I beseech your Divine Majesty to receive kindly into your hands this humble offering and sacrifice that I have made to your most Holy Son, my Lord Jesus Christ, and to your most Holy Daughter, the Blessed Virgin, my Mother and the spouse of the Holy Spirit, in an odor of sweetness; and I beg that you give me the grace to fulfill these vows that I have made and to be the son, though all unworthy of the Sovereign Queen of the Angels, Mary most Holy, and that I may receive from you the grace to praise her all the days of my life, and that I may glorify her through the merits of the Passion and Death of your most Holy Son, my Lord Jesus Christ. In testimony thereto, I have signed this with my name, written in the blood of my heart on August 15, feast of the most glorious Assumption of my most Holy Mother in the year 1654.

Then follows in letters the color of blood the signature "Luis de Medina."

What fire was this that burned in the heart of this youth, from which emerged such flames? What was his love for Christ and Mary that he should speak with such loving, burning words to them and with them, obliging himself by vow in so many ways in order to serve and honor them? I do not seem to see in these papers letters written in ink but

*Book Five, Chapter 1*

characters of fire that can melt the most frozen hearts of his readers. This is why I so often quote his words, not venturing to substitute my own lest they lose their power, and the readers be deprived of the fruit they may derive from them. Also, in this I imitate Father San Vitores, the author of his first biography,[241] almost all of which was made up of the writings of this Servant of God, forming a chain of his words that they might better set out the beauty of his works.

The life of one who so frequently approached the sacraments and gave himself to such devotions could not but be a most holy one. Father Melchor de Valencia, his confessor, who was his spiritual director for a long time and who received his general confession before he entered the Society, testified and testifies today that he had never lost the grace received in baptism.

He pronounced the above vows at the age of sixteen, an age in which other youths follow freely the path of vice. He is thus a great example to youth and a reproach to those who think that to expect virtue at such an age is to ask for snow in August and flowers in December.

It is no wonder that such a lover of Mother Mary should be favored by that sovereign queen, who favors even those who do not serve her. Our Luis was eager to enter the Society and explained that he would be better able to serve God and his Mother in it. The vocation was so firm and constant that his confessor proposed to him certain difficulties in order to test him. He overcame them all, so that so far from slackening his ardor, it grew more inflamed with each day, so that he could not doubt that his vocation was from God. At this time, he fell ill and was deeply distressed, fearing that it would prevent or at least delay his entrance into the Society, and so for consolation he fled to his ever-constant refuge. He begged the Blessed Virgin that she restore him to health if it would be for her service. God granted this on the Feast of Our Lady of the Snows.[242] God thus rewarded his fervor, because without regard for his sickness, he got up from bed in order to go to confession and receive Communion, in compliance with the vow he had made. Through his devotion to the Blessed Virgin and his perseverance, the many difficulties raised against his entrance into the Society were overcome, as much regarding his poor health as the defects of his feet and speech, since many judged that these were real impediments to the ministries of the Society. At last, these obstacles were bypassed by the solution offered by Father Francisco Franco, Visitator and Vice Provincial of Andalucia, who was undoubtedly inspired by God when he said, "Let us accept him to become a saint." These words show clearly what was his way of life, since even when they doubted whether he could take part in the ministries of the Society, they received him, moved by the hope that in it he would be a saint.

After he received permission to enter the Society, the devil placed many obstacles in his way, for he guessed how he would serve God in it.

---

[241]Chapter I, note 3:In *Archivo General de la Nación*, México, 1273, vol. 650, f. 25-32. *Inquisición*, there is a list of books purchased by Francisco Rodríquez Lupercio, bookseller in the City of Mexico in 1681, including in the list: *P. Diego Luis de San Vitores, Vida de P. Luis Medina, en Sevilla.*
[242]August 5.

But he vanquished the devil in all his trials through the grace of God and the help of the Blessed Virgin, as he wrote in his memoirs. Addressing our Blessed Lady, he exclaimed:

> May you be praised a million times by the heavenly spirits, because you saved me in a temptation that was an obstacle to my entering the Society. For it happened that after Father Provincial had accepted me for the Society on March 25, the Feast of the Annunciation, I returned to my home that night depressed, since in spite of having obtained what I desired, I was tormented by thoughts from the devil against entering the Society. My sadness was so great that my parents noticed it and understood the cause. Since they did not wish me to enter the Society, they seized this opportunity to persuade me not to enter, offering many reasons. But in my great distress I turned to an image of our Lady, knelt down and began to say the rosary, begging for her consolation and that she free me from that sadness. The Blessed Virgin deigned to save me from that temptation and when I finished the rosary, I was filled with much joy and new desires to enter the Society.

# CHAPTER II

*His Entrance Into the Society and His Life*
*in It Until He Departs for the Indies*

Father Luis de Medina entered the Society of Jesus in Seville, on April 3, 1656. If he led such a devout and careful life as a layman, we may well imagine how fervent he would be as a novice. He devoted himself to prayer, meditation, and the reading of pious books and the practice of other spiritual exercises. He was given to penance and mortification, which, rather than encouragement, needed restraint. He was most humble and delighted in the practice of servile works. He was most obedient, not showing any self-will and subjecting himself in every way to the will of the superiors whom he venerated as an image of Christ. He took pains especially in showing his devotion to our Lady. This devotion increased daily, and he searched assiduously for new ways of pleasing her and new services to offer her, so that he neither thought nor spoke of anything else.

To the ordinary exercises continuously practiced in our novitiate, which are many and of great perfection, he added several devotions that clearly showed his fervor and love of Jesus and Mary. These practices he proposed to keep up after his novitiate. I report them here for anyone who might want to imitate them.

Each day upon arising from my bed I have to salute our Lady, and then I have to visit the Blessed Sacrament, as well as the Blessed Virgin and pray for grace from her; I will ask the same grace at the beginning of the daily meditation. On leaving my room, I am to ask her blessing, saying *Iube, Domina, benedicere.*[243] Whenever I see her image, I must say, *Eia ergo, advocata nostra, illos tuos misericordes oculos ad nos converte.*[244] When I visit the Blessed Sacrament I must say: *Gratias agimus tibi, Domine, quoniam Matrem tuam Dominam meam elegisti. Ora pro me Sancta Dei Genitrix ut dignus servus tuus, filius tuus, efficiar promissionibus Christi.*[245] Whenever I hear her most holy name I must remove my cap and make a profound reverence in my heart. And finally, whatever I shall do in my whole life must be for the honor and glory of the most Blessed Virgin, my Mother and my Lady; and whatever I may be asked by anyone in the name of this sovereign Lady, I will do it or grant it, provided it is not illicit. Whenever I hear the clock strike the hour, I shall say: *Maria, Mater gratiae. Mater misericordiae,*[246] and wish her

---

[243]Please, Lady, a blessing.

[244]Turn, then, most gracious advocate, your eyes of mercy toward us.

[245]We give you thanks, Lord, because you have chosen your Mother to be my Lady. Pray for me, Holy Mother of God, that I, your son, your servant, may become worthy of the promises of Christ.

[246]Mary, Mother of grace, Mother of mercy.

*His Entrance Into the Society and His Life in It Until He Departs for the Indies*

as many blessings as there are strokes of the clock." "What I have to do every day out of reverence to my Lord Jesus Christ and the most Holy Virgin Mary, his Mother, as well as mine and my Lady. In general, each day of the week I have to offer her all my works: on Monday, I shall offer her all my works out of reverence for her most pure Conception and Purification; on Tuesday, it will be out of reverence for her most holy Nativity; on Wednesday, it will be out of reverence for her most holy Name and Presentation; on Thursday, out of reverence for her most holy Annunciation; on Friday, out of reverence for her most holy Visitation; on Saturday, out of reverence for her most holy Name and Expectation; on Sunday, out of reverence for her most holy Death and glorious Assumption and Coronation. In the visits I should make every day to our Lady, I must say the antiphons and prayers that correspond to the mystery of that day. On Saturdays and Wednesdays, I must make nine visits to the most Blessed Virgin, my Mother, and six visits on the other days. And on Saturdays and Wednesdays, I must say the Office of the Most Holy Name of Mary, and on the remaining days that of her most pure Conception. On Saturdays, I must fast, and on Saturdays and Wednesdays, I must take the discipline and the chain. I will take part in the public discipline on Saturdays, and on the remaining days, I will take the chain on one day and the discipline on the other. On Communion days, I will take the chain and the discipline.

The offices and devotions, of which he makes mention in his paper, he carried with him written in a small book that was found at his death, with clear signs of frequent use. For each month he had the following devotions:

In the months in which some feast of the Blessed Virgin occurs, generally in all the months, I must prepare myself for eight days, but for the feasts of the Incarnation, the Nativity, the Immaculate Conception and the Assumption, my preparation will be for fifteen days, taking the discipline and wearing the chain on each of these days. And on the eve, I will fast with what is given to the community and on the day itself and on the eve I will say the Little Office of Our Lady. These two things I will do under vow, and on these days I will perform some acts of humility and charity out of reverence for the feast.

Then he adds what he has to do in honor of our Lord Jesus Christ in the following words:

Out of reverence for our Lord Jesus Christ, every day upon rising, I must go to visit the Blessed Sacrament, which I will also do when retiring. I will do the same in honor of the most Blessed

*Book Five, Chapter 2*

Virgin. Every Sunday and Thursday, I must make eight visits, and six on the remaining days; and on Thursdays and Sundays, I will say the Office of the Most Blessed Sacrament; also, I will receive Communion every day. And every thing that I do on the feasts of the Blessed Virgin, I shall also do on the Feasts of Our Lord Jesus Christ. On the feast of his Nativity, of his Resurrection, and of his Ascension, and on that of Corpus Christi, I must prepare myself by doing the same things I mentioned for the feasts of our Lady, my most Holy Mother. On Fridays, I will fast and take the discipline in reverence for the Passion and Death of my Lord Jesus Christ. In the daily examination of conscience, I shall demand an account of all this. And to oblige myself even more in this, I will sign my name, on the third of May, the Feast of the Holy Cross, 1658. Luis de Medina.

His method of saying the rosary, or *corona*, of our Lady is very devout and deserves to be known and imitated by all. He writes:

On the method of saying the *corona* of my most Holy Mother, the Virgin Mary, Queen of the Angels: The first decade I shall offer to the Nativity of our Lady, asking for love of God, and that she obtain for me the grace to serve her and that I may say this rosary with devotion, and that I may have the patience to bear all the sufferings that the Lord may send me. At the end of the first decade I shall say the "Glory be to the Father," etc. I will also say: "Most Holy Virgin, may the whole Blessed Trinity bless you ten thousand million times and may your most Holy Son, in the name of the Three Persons, grant you ten thousand million blessings and even more. I will offer the second decade to her most holy name and Presentation in the Temple, begging for the grace to be obedient and to fulfill the rules, even the smallest of them. And in the end I will say: "Most Holy Virgin, may all the nine choirs of angels bless you twenty thousand million times, and in the name of all of them may Saint Gabriel bless you twenty thousand million times and more." I will offer the third decade to the most holy Conception and Purification, and I shall ask her for the grace of chastity and modesty in all my senses, saying: "Most Holy Virgin, may all the prophets, patriarchs, and Saint John the Baptist, and your most holy spouse Saint Joseph, in the name of all, bless you thirty thousand million times and even more." I will offer the fourth decade to the Annunciation of the angel Saint Gabriel to our Lady while she was praying. I will beg of her the gift of prayer and of the presence of God. I will pray: "Most Holy Virgin, may the holy apostles and evangelists, Saint Peter and Saint John, in the name of all, bless you forty thousand million times and even more." I will offer the fifth decade to the Visitation of my most Holy Mother to Saint Elizabeth, imploring her to grant me the virtue of humility and

*His Entrance Into the Society and His Life in It Until He Departs for the Indies*

charity toward my brothers: "Most Holy Virgin, may the holy virgins and martyrs, and Saint Catherine of Siena and your mother, Saint Anne, bless you five hundred thousand million times and even more." I shall offer the sixth decade to her most holy Death, to her most holy Assumption and to the Coronation of this Royal Princess, begging her to obtain for me from her most Holy Son perseverance in her holy house and a good death, as well as the grace to preserve my chastity; and then I will say: "Most Holy Virgin, may all the saints, martyrs, and confessors and my father, Saint Ignatius, in the name of all, and Saint Jerome bless you sixty thousand million times and more.

Having described his method of saying the rosary on the rosary beads, which he must have recited more and more, as one may infer from the length of time he spent with the rosary in his hands, even during his many occupations in the Mariana Mission, he adds:

And on Monday, I have to say the rosary for the Conception of our Lady; and on Tuesday, out of reverence for the Incarnation of the Son of God in her womb; and on Thursday, out of reverence for the Blessed Sacrament; and on Friday, in reverence for the Passion and Death of our Lord Jesus Christ; and on Saturday, out of reverence for her most holy Death, Assumption, and Coronation." And he expresses the offerings in this manner: "O most Holy Virgin, my Lady and my Mother! I offer you these ten Hail Marys and one Our Father in reverence for your most holy Conception and Purification. And I beg you, through your Immaculate Conception that you obtain for me from your most Holy Son the grace to keep my vow of chastity, as well as the modesty of all my senses, and the grace that I may be able to say this rosary with great devotion," etc. He continues in this manner the offering of the other decades, expressing the most tender feelings towards his Lady and Mother, asking of her various virtues according to the mystery for which he is offering the ten Hail Marys.

With what care he avoided any fault, no matter how small it might be, and kept our rules, detailed though they are, we can see sufficiently well in his notebooks, where he says: "My soul, be resolved to die a thousand times rather than commit a deliberate venial sin no matter how small it might be. Rather die a thousand times than violate a rule, no matter how minor it might be. My soul, let me rather lose my health and die an instant death rather than commit the slightest offense against God."

So that this resolution might be more firm and all his works more pleasing to God and to Mary, he adds: "On the first day of the week, which is Monday, I must make my meditation with great care and examine in it whether I keep well the rules and how I can keep them better, and whether I observe my order of

*Book Five, Chapter 2*

time, etc. And each month, on the day of the jubilee, I must read the rules and examine myself whether I keep them. Before beginning each work, no matter how insignificant, I shall pay homage to the Blessed Virgin; and before I begin to eat after the graces I must say one Hail Mary and then *Benedicta sit, O individua Trinitas, per infinita saecula saeculorum.*[247] May your will be done on earth as it is in heaven. Our Father, etc.

In another place he said,

Every day of my life I shall say in honor of the most Holy Trinity, three Hail Marys to the Virgin Mary, my most Holy Mother, in order to obtain their patronage at the hour of my death. And I shall offer them thus: "Most Holy Virgin, my Lady and my Mother, I offer you the first Hail Mary in honor of the Eternal Father and of the Divine Omnipotence, so that as he deigned to raise you, my Mother, to the throne of such high majesty, so that after God you might be the most powerful in heaven and on earth, even so may you assist me, most sovereign Lady, and comfort me in that dangerous hour of death. I offer you the second Hail Mary in honor of your Son and of the Divine Wisdom, so that as he endowed you, my Lady and Mother, with the highest wisdom and divine knowledge more than the rest of the saints, so that you might enjoy more the vision of the Blessed Trinity and might surpass all the rest as a most brilliant sun, so also may you deign to illumine me as with the light of faith, hope, and charity, and of true knowledge, in order that I might not be deceived at the hour of my death. I offer you the third Hail Mary, O most Holy Mother, in honor of the Holy Spirit and the infinite charity and love of God, so that as he filled you with tenderness and love, in order that after God you might be the most lovable person in the world, so also you may favor me, most kind Lady and Mother, and you may console me with your presence at the hour of my death, granting to my soul the sweetness and love of God and making that bitter step more easy. And I beg you, my Mother, that in this hour you may carry my soul in your most holy hands, to present it to your Holy Son.

Who will not be filled with wonder to see so many spiritual exercises, so many devotions, so many vows, and a day so well shared with God, Mary, and all the saints? He seemed not to live on earth or deal with humans, nor have time to do so, since all the year round, all the months, all the weeks, all the days, and all the hours he was engrossed in heavenly things, consecrating each of them with some special exercise of devotion. Above all, who is not amazed to see the affection, so tender and loving, that he had for Mary most Holy, always calling her his most Holy

---

[247] Blessed be the Holy and undivided Trinity for endless ages. Amen.

*His Entrance Into the Society and His Life in It Until He Departs for the Indies*

Mother? This name never ceased to be on his lips as if he savored it by repetition, for he repeated it so many times, in season and out of season, in his notebooks, if one may repeat unseasonably a name that fills the mouth with sweetness and the heart with tenderness and joy. From this devotion alone who could not conclude that he had arrived at a height of perfection, even in his first years, for as our father, Saint Ignatius, used to say: "Mary is the gate of grace; and so he who enters through Mary, gains much grace from God and is lifted to perfection and sanctity."

In such fervor Brother Luis advanced in his novitiate, but when he left it, his devotions and spiritual exercises were not left behind in the novitiate, as happens to those who begin to build a house and fail to finish it, to the laughter of the on-lookers, as Christ said.[248] These devotional practices accompanied him in his studies and afterwards from the time of his priesthood till his fortunate and happy death. Rather, he kept on fortifying these resolutions and vows, together with new ones that he made; he was so far from forgetting the previous ones. Signed with his name and dated February 2, 1662, is a long manuscript of his. It was the sixth year since his entrance into the Society. To the vows that we have already mentioned he adds the vow of fasting every Saturday in honor of the Blessed Virgin, with the proviso of being able to commute it to something equivalent in times of sickness or other impediment that might occur. He would also say the Little Office of Our Lady on those Saturdays and during the fifteen days from the Expectation of the Virgin to the Feast of the Circumcision, as well as on January 24, on which the Descent of Our Lady is celebrated in the archdiocese of Toledo, although it was not celebrated in the diocese where he was living. After the vow of receiving Communion on the feast days of our Lady and of our Lord, which he had already made, he added that of fasting on the vigils of all the feasts of our Lady and of the thirteen feasts of our Lord. To all this, he added the vow of fasting (with the same proviso mentioned above) on the vigils of the feast of Saint Joseph, Saint Joachim, Saint Anne, and of all the holy apostles and evangelists and of the saints of our Society, Saint Ignatius, Saint Francis Xavier, Saint Francis Borgia, Blessed Aloysius Gonzaga, Blessed Stanislaus Kostka, and the three martyrs of Japan, Saint Paul Miki, Saint James Kisai, and Saint John Soan of Goto; also on the eve of the feast days of Saint Bernard, Saint Thomas Aquinas, Saint Bonaventure, Saint Ildefonsus, Saint Lawrence, Saints Fabian and Sebastian, Saint Catherine of Siena, Saint Catherine Virgin and Martyr, and of Saint Elizabeth, the cousin, he says, "of my most holy Mother." He makes the same vow of fasting on the eve of the feasts of the holy angels Saint Michael, Saint Gabriel, and of Saint Raphael, whose feast was celebrated in Córdoba on May 18, and of the Guardian Angel. With the days of fasting by vow and devotion added to those of the Church, he spent the greater part of the year fasting. In honor of the Apostle of the Indies, Saint Francis Xavier, he had another special vow of visiting his altar five times a day, wherever there was an altar, and if there was none, then some image of his, from the eve until the octave day of his feast,

---

[248]Luke 14:28-30.

reciting on each visit two Our Fathers, two Hail Marys, his antiphon, and prayer, and during the year he would do this once every day.

He says that he makes all these vows to show his gratitude for the favor he asks and hopes to obtain through the intercession of the Blessed Virgin and of the above-mentioned saints, the favor that is, of having a ready tongue to preach the gospel in the whole world. In this, it is noteworthy that he was already thanking for what he had not yet obtained, such was his trust in the Blessed Virgin that she would not deny anything he asked of her.

He was yearning so much for this because of his concern for the salvation of souls; but we have to admire how he tempered these desires with indifference and conformity to the will of God and of the Blessed Virgin. And so he says in a most devout prayer in which he begs the Virgin for this favor: "Most holy Virgin Mary, Mother of our Lord Jesus Christ and mine! For the love that you had, O my most Holy Mother, for your most Holy Son when you cared for him as a child and carried him in your arms, as well as the love you have for him now in heaven, I beg you to give a little ease to my tongue that I may speak well and a drop of milk to my lips to free them from their muteness and that they may better serve to praise you, my Holy Mother, and better serve the Society. Hence, I put it all in your hands and ask of you whatever you may see as best for your service. I beg that in all this, not my will be done but yours, most Blessed Virgin, my Mother, so that if it be for the salvation of my soul, you would give me a good tongue, but if not, I do not want it."

The Queen of Angels granted his prayer so fully, that as a scholastic, in ordinary conversations he had his speech impediment, and he could not sit for his general oral examinations in Córdoba, although he was among the best, if not the best in his class. Still, when he gave lectures on Christian doctrine, as was the custom of our scholastics, he did not have the least impediment nor the least hesitation in speaking, as those affirm who knew him in his province.

His companions write that after he went to the Mariana Islands, he obtained the grace to preach the holy gospel to such a degree of perfection, that although in ordinary conversations he may have had some difficulty with his tongue, in his sermons and in the singing of the Christian doctrine, he preached and talked with ease, as if he never had had such an impediment. The father himself acknowledged it, and he thanked God and the Blessed Virgin for it by observing perfectly his vows and devotion and employing his tongue continuously in the praises of God and Mary and for the good of his neighbors.

The vows with which he prayed for this favor have caused us to mention it ahead of time, before we have reported on his studies. We will discuss them now. Brother Luis studied philosophy in the college of Córdoba. When he finished, surpassing all his classmates, he made one year of theology in the same college. He completed the year at the college in Granada, where he had both his first and his general oral examinations, because he was so advanced in the subject matter, although he still had that impediment in speech that had kept him from the examinations in Córdoba. It appears that this scholastic talent of Brother Luis had a supernatural dimension. In his first year of Arts, on the Feast of the Purification of Our Lady, he felt discouraged, because it seemed to him that he was not improving in his studies and that he did not understand the notes of his teacher. He felt that he would be useless for the Society. So he appealed to the Queen of the Angels, in whom he placed all his hopes. On his knees, with great tenderness and affection, he begged her most earnestly to come to his rescue and to obtain from her Son the talent necessary to be an apt instrument for his order. On that same day, he received Communion with great devotion. After he made his thanksgiving full of consolation, he went to Father Francisco Guillaude, who was prefect of higher studies at Córdoba. Falling on his knees, he told him that the Blessed Virgin was sending him to him so that he would place himself in his hands to be guided in everything by what he would tell him. The father admired the holy simplicity of Brother Luis, which is what he called it, and promised to help him in everything, as much in his studies as in his spiritual life. From then on Father Guillaude began to repeat the lectures with him and to counsel him well, and it was a wonderful thing how from then on, Brother Luis began to understand the written lectures of his teacher and to surpass all his classmates. When Father Guillaude narrated this, he implied, though not quite openly, that the Blessed Virgin had appeared to Brother Luis and had ordered him to place himself in his hands. We can surely believe everything that has to do with his devotion to Mary and even more the compassion of this Lady and Mother.

The important thing is that he was advancing every day in the religious virtues. All those who knew him in Granada and Córdoba noticed what a good example he gave, how humble he was, most recollected and most studious; how he avoided amusements and found his pleasure in books and spiritual exercises. They particularly noticed the great devotion he had to our Lady; this could not escape notice. He was so constant in this that even on the day of his general examinations in Granada, in spite of the fatigue of the day and legitimate occupation, he could not take time to rest, no matter how much they begged him, until he had recited the Little Office of the Blessed Virgin, as was his custom.

He was a good Latin poet. At the time when our scholastics of that province composed verses in honor of the birth of Christ our Lord and our father, Saint Ignatius, he expressed in verses no less devout than elegant his tender and fervent love for Christ and Mary and for our father, Saint Ignatius.

Although the zeal for the salvation of souls with which God inflamed his soul was great, and he already desired to preach the gospel throughout the world, still, in his first eight years in the Society, he did not volunteer for the mission of the Indies, leaving the matter to the common providence of the superiors and contenting himself with being ready to go wherever obedience would send him. He would satisfy himself with the occasions offered him by God to teach Christian doctrine, to give conferences and take advantage of other opportunities that always occurred. The Lord disposed thus that at this time he should fit himself for such a high and difficult work while engaged in exercises of literature and virtue. But when he reached the age and the course of higher studies, he could no longer contain the zeal in his soul and wrote to Father General of the Society asking for this mission, having made the following vow, which was found among his writings:

O omnipotent and everlasting God, I, Luis de Medina, although most unworthy to present myself before your most holy presence, am moved by the desire to serve you more faithfully and to undergo more labors and sufferings for your Divine Majesty, and because of the great love I have for you, O my God, and to make reparation for my sins, I vow to your Divine Majesty in the presence of the whole heavenly court and in the presence of the most Holy Virgin, my Mother, to go to the Indies or wherever Father General of the Society may choose to send me. I must write to him to send me to those parts where there is greater need of laborers, if it should be for the greater glory and honor of God our Lord; under these conditions, however, that if it should seem to His Paternity that it is for the greater honor and glory of God and that it is more suitable for me, in order to please God better and for the salvation of my soul that I remain in Spain, should such be the command of His Paternity, I will most readily remain here, that being the will of God. That this is the truth, I have affixed here my name, on the Feast of the Assumption of Our Lady in the year 1664. Luis de Medina.

We should notice, for our admiration and imitation, with what indifference and detachment of will he behaves in all his vows and petitions, avoiding the satisfaction of his own desires, good as they are, but ever seeking in all the greater glory of God, as a true son of our father, Saint Ignatius.

Father Luis was ordained priest while the permission from Rome to go to the Indies was on its way. As each day seemed to be a continual delay, he kept up the fervor of his zeal by working for the good of his neighbor, in so far as obedience gave him scope. He was sent to the *colegio* at Montilla to teach grammar and to be minister of the house. He performed these offices to the satisfaction of the community and all others. Not satisfied with this, he gave himself with great fervor to the other ministries of the Society, such as hearing confessions, preaching sermons and conferences, and explaining Christian doctrine. To the spiritual charity toward souls, he added the corporal charity to bodies seeking alms to help those in need. He begged in person along the streets together with other devout persons who accompanied him, attracted by his example. His diligence in these works of mercy was so great that the whole city admired it, was edified by it, and hailed him as a saint.

While he was in this *colegio* of Montilla, news came to him that his mother was dying in Málaga and that she desired that he proceed

*His Entrance Into the Society and His Life in It Until He Departs for the Indies*

immediately to that city, that she might have the consolation of seeing her religious son at her bedside at the hour of her death. He went to the rector of the college with the letter and the request of his mother, so that he might decide what he thought was most fitting. The rector's opinion was that he should give this well-merited consolation to his mother and gave him permission to depart for Málaga the next day. Father Luis retired that night to the choir loft of our church to commend to God the health of his mother and he beheld her coffin being carried along the center aisle of the church. He went at once to Father Rector to give him an account of what he had seen, saying that now it wasn't necessary to go to Málaga because his mother was dead. But the rector insisted that he should go, saying that this was all imagination and no vision. But Father Luis assured him that he had seen it and so the journey was not necessary now. Soon, it was proved that at the same hour of the same night on which he had seen his mother dead in the church in Montilla, at that same hour she had died in Málaga.

Father Luis was yearning for his Indies and was already imagining himself preaching in those parts and winning many souls for God. But when he turned his eyes to the difficulties in the way of permission, he felt as one awakening from a dream with hands now empty that had been filled with gold and silver. He controlled his anxiety by renewing his vow, especially at Mass, for which he prepared himself with various devotions that he had written down, some inspired by his own love and zeal, others written by saints and of common use, although always some praises or sparks from the fire of his love for Mary and his zeal for souls were added. And in the formula of the mementos and the offering of the Mass, which many use, after these words, *Ad laudem et, gloriam nominis tui et in honorem Domini nostri Jesu Christi et Sacratissimae Virginis Mariae,*[249] he added this clause, *Et Maiestatem tuam humiliter exoro ut mihi concedas pergere in Indos, si hoc est secundum voluntatem tuam et ad maiorem gloriam tuam et utilitatem animae meae; spiritum Societatis, et tuam gratiam, et perseverantiam in bonis operibus mihi concedere digneris.*[250]

Although the Lord did not immediately satisfy his desire, his purpose was that with this delay, the longing of Father Luis would increase and with it the merit of such a singular favor. However, long before this, the Lord had given him signs that he had chosen him for the Indies. While he was still a scholastic in the college of Córdoba, the Venerable Father Diego Luis de San Vitores passed through that college on the way to the Philippines from Spain. At the sight of him, Brother Luis felt moved especially to ask for these missions, and it seemed to him that there, inside his heart, he heard the voice that was telling him: "You are to go with this man." At the moment he did not understand the mysterious voice, because Father San Vitores left for the Indies, while he had as yet no permission for this mission. Later the prophecy was verified, for

---

[249]To the praise and glory of your name, in honor of our Lord, Jesus Christ, and of the Blessed Virgin Mary.

[250]And I humbly beg Your Majesty, that you grant me to journey to the Indies, if that is according to your will, to your greater glory, and to the benefit of my soul; deign to grant me the spirit of the Society, and your grace, and perseverence in good works.

in Mexico he joined Father San Vitores en route to the Marianas. The father himself related this to his companions who went with him from Spain to the Indies. It was from them that we learned it, although Father Luis intended to write it in the Marianas among his memoirs along with other sentiments and similar events, partly old and partly new, that savored much of the supernatural. They were due to a very familiar communication of the Lord with this his faithful servant, as well as to interior revelations of the angels and saints, especially of the Blessed Virgin, together with frequent inspirations or impulses concerning absent or future things, all of them ordained to the glory of our Lord and the good of souls. Father San Vitores judged that, in view of the scarcity of ministers and time, it would be for the greater glory of God to employ the time he would spend writing it in teaching the *Marianos*. Hence, he told him to give it up. The humble father cut off the thread of thought that he was engaged in writing. Thus his obedience deprived us of a rich treasure of wonder and edification that we would have possessed in these writings, though the time was well employed as an example to us of obedience and humility.

# CHAPTER III

### *Father Luis Departs for the Indies;*
### *What He Does on the Voyage*

While he was in Montilla, busy with the tasks we have mentioned, there arrived the permission from our father general to go to the Indies in fulfillment of his vows. The letter contained strict orders to his superiors, that without objections or appeals they should immediately send Father Luis to the mission of the Philippines, even though they should feel the loss of such a fervent and edifying subject, since God, to whose voice men are bound to listen, was calling him. I cannot sufficiently describe the pleasure with which Father Luis received this letter, but I can well surmise it from the longing he had for it. But this joy of his soon vanished, because the immediate superiors of his province, although they had opposed him before, not wanting to deprive themselves of a subject of such great edification and zeal, now, even after such an explicit mandate of Father General, were resisting him and wished to make representations to His Paternity, since they could not decide to give up what they loved and esteemed so much. Consequently, Father Luis, having committed the matter into the hands of the Lord, wrote to Father Cristóbal Pérez, who was then the provincial of the Province of Andalucia, the following letter:

Pax Christi!

Father Provincial, I find myself beset by many scruples, because Your Reverence does not confirm the permission given me by Father General to go to the Philippines. So that I may be spared these scruples and Your Reverence may be well informed and so may decide what should be for the greater honor of God, I shall declare to Your Reverence the motives that move me for going to the Philippines. A year before entering the Society I had a very serious illness, in which I was even more afflicted by not being able to enter the Society than by the sickness itself. In this time of distress, on the Feast of Our Lady of the Snows,[251] I knelt before a picture of the Blessed Virgin and implored her to obtain from her Son the health I needed to enter the Society and go to the Indies that I might preach the gospel to the *Indios*. From that day, to the wonder of the doctors, I have enjoyed the health that permitted me to enter the Society. After I entered the novitiate, God our Lord gave me intense and efficacious desires to go to the Indies. And in order to know better, if it was the will of God, I proposed to go to the Indies if upon finishing my studies, God our Lord should keep these desires in my heart. These desires, then, have grown every day and now, five years

---

[251] August 5.

*Book Five, Chapter 3*

later, on the Feast of Saint Francis Xavier, I felt such a great desire for the Indies that it forced me to make a vow to the saint and another to the Blessed Virgin, so that they would obtain from His Divine Majesty that he reveal his divine will or else free me from these desires of going to the Indies, if it were not his will. For three years, I kept on asking the same favor of God our Lord, doing many penances for the same purpose. At the end of these years, on the Feast of our father, Saint Ignatius, while making my thanksgiving after Communion and asking God through the intercession of the saint to make his will known to me, I heard in my heart a voice by which our father, Saint Ignatius declared to me that I should make a vow to go to the Indies on finishing my studies, for this was the will of God. But I still could not decide to do it. Then on the Feast of Our Lady of the Snows, I begged the same grace from the Blessed Virgin while making my thanksgiving after Communion. What happened now I cannot explain. What I can say is that I heard within me these words as coming from this most powerful Lady: "Son, make a vow to go to the Indies because that is the will of my most Holy Son, since it was for this purpose that he restored you to health on this day through my intercession." Although I was not yet determined to do so, I kept on doing many penances, commending it all to God, until on the Feast of the Assumption of Our Lady, because of the many spiritual consolations that filled my soul, I felt almost morally impelled, wherefore, I made the vow of going to the Indies on terminating my studies. And from that time until now, I feel such desire to fulfill this vow that my greatest pleasure is to imagine myself already among the natives of the Indies. I have written to Your Reverence at such length, because I judge that it is my obligation to do so, so that Your Reverence informed of the motives that move me to go to the Indies, may decide what would be for the greater glory of God, our Lord. And if Your Reverence, notwithstanding my declaration, should not let me comply with this permission granted by our father general, may Your Reverence know that on the Day of Judgment, when God our Lord should ask an account of what I have said here, the reply I shall give to His Divine Majesty will have to be what Your Reverence would give to this letter, and with this intention, Your Reverence should sign it, so that I may remain in this province without scruples. I am writing this to your four consultors as well; and so Your Reverence will do me the favor of consulting them a second time, so that having been well informed they may decide what would be for the greater honor of God. May he keep Your Reverence for many years. Montilla, April 27, 1666. Your Reverence's servant, Luis de Medina.

When the provincial and the consultors read this letter of Venerable Father Luis de Medina, in which, with such truth and sincerity, he

*Father Luis Departs for the Indies; What He Does on the Voyage*

reports the manifestations of God's will that he go to the Indies, from which they understood that he had been chosen for great works for God's service and glory, they hesitated to resist the clearly expressed will of our Lord. The provincial confirmed the permission, keeping, then, the letter as the token of a zealous missionary and now as the relic of a glorious martyr. Note how the letter of this Servant of God gives us a portrait of Father Diego Luis de San Vitores himself in his vocation to the Indies.

Having obtained the permission, Father Luis de Medina departed for Seville, when the galleons of the year 1667 were about to sail. During his stay in this city, he continued with his usual acts of charity, visiting, consoling, and serving the sick in the hospitals and those who were in prison. He helped the needy, heard confessions, and carried out other ministries with his companions to whom he gave the benefit of his singular example, leading them all in the works of the divine service, so much so, that, at the time when the mission was about to sail, since the procurator general who was in charge of them had to remain in Spain for the needs of the Philippine Province, he appointed Father Luis as superior of the rest because of the many qualities of virtue and prudence that he recognized in him. In this, without realizing it, the procurator was serving Divine Providence, which by means no less smooth than efficacious was providing for the entrance of Father Luis into the Mariana Islands.

He embarked with his companions on July 19, 1667. The example he gave to the passengers was impressive, and so was the zeal with which he tried to help them. He found the sea very rough and he suffered several ailments that he bore with great patience. Besides this, there was some unpleasantness caused by the unfairness of the voyagers, but in revenge he did them all the good that he could. He used to gather the people to hear the Christian doctrine and the homilies he preached with such fervor. No matter how weak he was, whenever he rang the bell for these holy exercises, it seemed that he got rid of his infirmities or forgot them, as if he had never had them. He read in public the indulgences for the missions and the teaching of Christian doctrine with much advantage to all on shipboard. Very few or no one neglected to do their part in order to gain these indulgences; all were present at the conferences, which lasted for eight days; on the last day, which was the Feast of the Assumption of Our Lady, they received Holy Communion. On this last day a devout and solemn procession was held with a statue of the Blessed Virgin. The governor, together with the armed contingent of the galleon, took part in the procession. Rounds of artillery and musketry were fired, as well as other celebrations in honor of the Queen of Angels, whose devotion Father Luis inspired in all. He fed and cared for the sick, and he served them with great humility and charity. For long stretches at a time he stayed with them under the hatches not minding his sea sickness and illness. With kind words he consoled the afflicted. He tried to prevent gossip, oaths, blasphemies, and other offenses against God, our Lord. He took special care that all should go to confession, especially those he saw in greater need; he gave the poor small gifts. To win their souls, he sought to win their good will.

*Book Five, Chapter 3*

He best showed his spirit, zeal, and apostolic charity when a rumor circulated that ships were close by, enemies both of Spain and of our Faith, because he rejoiced at the hope of shedding his blood for Christ and our holy Faith. He encouraged his companions and exhorted them with great fervor to give their lives for the Lord in the following words:

> My brothers, death suffered for Christ menaces us. Let us rejoice in the Lord, because we shall be fortunate if we find in the sea what we are looking for in port, if instead of arriving in the Indies we arrive in heaven. He who remains in the sea for having entered the port of heaven does not suffer shipwreck. I know well that we do not deserve to die for him who first died for us. But if God, moved by his mercy and goodness, wishes to grant us this grace, what should we do, but offer our necks to the knife and open our breast for the spear or the swords to enter and release our soul that waits for the port to be opened for it, in order to fly to heaven and embrace its Lord and see its Lady and loving Mother? Who will fear such a glorious death, a death that is better than a thousand lives? A death that is the beginning of immortality? O, let death arrive, which comes with long steps to those who desire it and hope to meet it with open hearts! O, let it come full of crowns and palms to be the laurel of victory for those who shall conquer by being overcome by it and by dying will triumph over its horrors. What do you say, my brothers? It will not be long in coming. Do you wish that we look for it ourselves, if it does not come? Let most Holy Mary be our patroness and advocate, my Lady and Mother. I say my Lady and Mother and the Mother of all those who invoke her and wish to be her children. Under her patronage there is nothing to fear, and from her we may hope for everything, the palm, the crown, death, immortality, and life eternal.

He also told them that he had left his province in search of martyrdom, and he was in search of this wealth in the Indies, and he advised them to prepare to merit and receive this grace from the Lord with penances, prayers, and devotions to the Blessed Virgin, whose litanies he repeated three or four times together with his companions. In this and in other exercises, he spent the greater part of the night until the rumor died out, to his great disappointment, but not without fruit for all those who prepared themselves for martyrdom through confession and other good works. For if the desire for death was not realized, the desire for death was not wanting, nor did this desire fail to receive its well deserved reward.

Father Luis arrived in New Spain, and as a respite from the hardships of the voyage, God offered him ample opportunities to employ his fervor while awaiting a ship for the Philippines. Bishop Diego Osorio, of Puebla de los Angeles, wished that the fathers of our Society would

*Father Luis Departs for the Indies; What He Does on the Voyage*

give missions in the city and other places of his jurisdiction. Father Luis immediately offered himself for this mission to the great edification of the fathers of the Province of Mexico. He went to that mission, labored hard and gathered abundant fruit in confessions, with many extraordinary happenings, so many that none are detailed, such as the removal of many scandals and preventing serious sins, so that the good odor of his virtues and the example of his fervent life was felt everywhere.

While he was so well occupied, he was summoned to Mexico by the news that the ship for the Philippines had arrived. And since he was informed at the same time that Father San Vitores would be on board en route to the Ladrones Islands, his countenance was changed, according to one father who helped him in the mission, for he remembered, as he admitted later, the words he heard in Córdoba, when they said: "With this one you are to go."[252] It seemed that God wished to carry out the promise made to him, of landing with Father San Vitores in these islands. This hope gave him extraordinary joy. But he was worried that our Jesuits, with holy zeal, would not allow him to leave them, since he was their superior until he discharged them in Manila. But God, who had chosen him to be an apostle of the Marianas, settled everything easily through the same means that seemed to be an obstacle to him. Father Luis de San Vitores had orders from Father Domingo Ezquerra, Philippine provincial, to take with him two priests of those who would arrive from Spain, provided their election was agreed upon by the father who was their superior. Since Father Luis de Medina was the superior, it was easy to come to an agreement with Father Luis de San Vitores that they go together to the Marianas. Then what began as an election became a necessity, because other companions also remained with this mission, as we said in the life of Father San Vitores, by virtue of the requirements made in the name of His Majesty that they should remain in the islands because of the great need they had there of ministers of the gospel.

In Mexico, Father Luis began his work as a missionary of the Marianas by helping Father San Vitores in the procurement of things needed for the mission. When the time for the departure arrived, Father Luis first went to the chapel of the Sodality of Saint Francis Xavier to ask for the blessing of the holy apostle and for graces for the mission of the Marianas, and for this he offered the Holy Sacrifice of the Mass. Then he left for Acapulco, and in this port, he helped Father San Vitores give a mission, giving talks and instruction in Christian doctrine, all with notable fervor, emotion, and fruit. He gave a special mission to those who were confined to the fortress, seeing their need for grace, providing alms for their needs. He did not forget to visit the sick in the hospital and to perform for them acts of humility and charity. He noticed that sometimes the sanctuary lamp of the church of that port was without light because of its great poverty. He felt this very much because of the great devotion he had for the Blessed Sacrament. He begged and obtained that the sanctuary lamp be endowed, so that it could always be lighted

---

[252]Book 1, chap. 13:76.

and the Blessed Sacrament be cared for with proper decency. From Acapulco to the Marianas he continued his customary exercises, inspiring all with his words and even more with his deeds, and promoting the spiritual and temporal means for a successful entry to the Marianas.

# CHAPTER IV

*The Achievements of the Venerable Luis de Medina in the Mariana Islands and the Hardships He Suffered*

We narrated in the life of Father San Vitores the events of the arrival in the Marianas and the qualities of those islands; how the first ones to land in them were Father Luis de Medina and Father Pedro de Casanova, who were another Joshua and Caleb, explorers of the Promised Land.[253] Now we will report on the achievement in the islands of this apostolic man. The achievement was very great and it seems as if, since God was going to give him only a short time to labor in the vineyard, he gave him the energy and grace to accomplish in one hour what other laborers accomplish in one day.

Father Luis had made a happy beginning of the great number of baptisms, that he would eventually make during those few days in the first village of the island of San Juan. He decided to go around to the other villages of the islands, offering himself to what was the most difficult part of the mission work, the journeys. Although these were most painful for all the missionaries because of the roughness and wildness of the roads, for him they were much more so because of the lameness of his feet. But though he could walk only with difficulty on those crippled feet, he flew with the wings of his zeal in search of souls, principally of the children. The hunt for them gave him so much pleasure and consolation, because he knew that theirs is the kingdom of heaven. He had much to overcome in order to pass from one village to another. The devil, fashioned by the greed of the natives or their love of the father, who gave them little gifts, shackles that he found difficult to break in order to get out of any town he entered. The devil would tell him there was no further road by land, and he would not let him have a boat to go by sea. Sometimes he would make the roads invisible and at other times he would cause the guide to return to the same town that he had left or to go to another where he had no intention of going. Of these obstacles, he narrates many cases in his letters, recognizing in some the stratagem of the enemy of souls, so that he would not baptize some children, whom later, through heavenly providence, he would find.

Father Luis conquered all these difficulties and other greater ones. He went around the island with such success, that having visited it three times in three months, he baptized three thousand of the *Marianos*, between adults and children, of whom some went flying to heaven, having waited only that baptism should open to them its doors. And often God disposed in his singular providence, that contrary to what had been planned, he should go to some place where there was great need of his presence. Once, he returned from a mission quite shaken by the bad

---

[253]Numbers, chapter 13.

353

roads and the waters of land and sea, which caused a great swelling in his face. Father San Vitores left him at the residence with Father Luis de Morales, who had come from Saipan, wounded by the barbarians with a stroke of a lance. Father Luis could not stand the rest given him, and after eight days he got up one morning with great haste, saying to his companions, "What has gotten into my head is not good and I cannot free myself of it. I must go at once to Apurguan (which was a place nearby) even if there be no Mass tomorrow for our community (it was the Feast of Saint Bartholomew), because of an extreme necessity that is awaiting me there, and it urges me more and more." He left the house with the intention of going around the island without stopping after attending to that urgent call. He arrived at the village and found what he writes in one of his notebooks: "The thought that struck me, for which I left the house, was partly realized when I arrived in Apurguan and baptized the chief of that place. Then in another town I was informed the chief of Apurguan had been pierced with a lance. I went immediately to that town and found out that he had received three wounds, of which one was very dangerous. I anointed him and heard his confession and then returned to the place I had come from." In other letters he tells of other acts of Divine Providence. In one written from Paa, he says, "Thanks be to God and to his Holy Mother, my mission is proceeding with great success. Many have been baptized, and I already have one María in heaven, who will pray to God for us and for his *Marianos*. It seems that the Blessed Virgin had preserved her health so that she might be baptized. This was a six-year old girl who was very ill and emaciated. I baptized her on Sunday and she died on Monday. I will relate another wonderful event when I get back to Agadña. Thanks be to God and to his Holy Mother to whom everything is really due. And Your Reverence should also give thanks to the Blessed Virgin for what she has done for this mission. I am staying in Paa where I have been very well treated by these people, etc." I do not know what this wonderful thing is that he promises to report verbally to his superior. He did not fulfill this promise, at least for us, leaving us in suspense, dissatisfied and in admiration.

That God might grant him these achievements, Father Luis offered prayers, fasts, and penances, which he increased when the infidels resisted conversion. He had gone three times to the town of Nisichan of the island of Guam. He always found them rebellious and stubborn. All he got from them were insults, bad treatment, and two rather dangerous wounds caused by the beatings. One wound was on his forehead, and the other, as he describes it, was a big one, between the eyes and the nose. It tore a vein, with much effusion of blood. But on the Feast of Saint Francis Xavier [December 3], he felt strongly moved to insist on its conversion, hoping that God would soften their hearts through the intercession of the Blessed Virgin and the Apostle of the Indies. He placed it with great love in the hands of the Queen of the Angels, through the holy apostle, and he offered to name the town after Saint Francis Xavier, if it should surrender. He asked for special prayers from his companions and he organized a set of public prayers said on all the eight days after the

Saint's feast, with varied devotions and penances. The latter were such that he took at least three disciplines a day, using a rather rough and slender iron chain; and there were nights when he took the three disciplines, which were heard by the companion who was with him in the residence, who was awakened by the noise. Although he tried to hide these austerities by retiring to a hidden place among the trees, the companion found him by chance, holding the rough instrument and bathed in blood. The octave of the Feast of Saint Francis Xavier arrived, and having offered his Mass for this special intention, he went off with great trust. Upon arriving at the village of Nisichan, when he began his homily, suddenly the natives were so moved that they all asked for holy baptism and to be taught and catechized by the father. They were baptized on the octave of the Feast of the Immaculate Conception of Our Lady [December 15] and, with great satisfaction, he returned joyfully to the residence full of gratitude to the Blessed Virgin and Saint Francis Xavier, after whom he named the town, as he had promised. Father Luis used to say that there were two things that had moved him strongly to hope for the conversion of this town and to insist on it. One was that his third visit to Nisichan was occasioned by losing the way to another town where he was going to establish a mission. It seemed that God was leading him by the hand to that village, so that he would insist on its conversion. The other was that from the beginning, he was treated worse in that village than in any other and was grievously wounded there, and so he wanted to pay them back this favor, for such, he held their insults and wounds, by procuring in all earnestness their salvation.

In order to uproot once and for all the superstitions of these *Marianos*, when he baptized them, he used to take away their idols or the figures of their ancestors to which they give some veneration, and he used to burn them, so that through the light of these bonfires they would see better the truth of our holy Faith. He put to the fire a good-sized mound of these idols on his first visit to the island of Guam. This he did in the presence of the holy cross on the feast day of its triumph, on July 16, 1668. Moved by this victory, obtained by the cross against the devil, he named the village, previously called Pigpug, The Triumph of the Cross. He had them bury the skulls of their ancestors, which was his condition for dealing with them as God's people. He asked them to build churches and he assisted them in building the church in Agadña with his diligence and with his own hands. On the Feast of the Purification of our Lady, February 2, 1669, this church was dedicated, as we said, to her most holy name and her Holy Family. To decide who should preside at the ceremony of the dedication, lots were cast between him and Father San Vitores, because he was so humble that though it was a service to the Virgin his Mother, it was at the same time a personal honor that he would not accept, no matter how insistently they asked him to do so, until the lot cast decided the pious rivalry: it fell on the one whom the Blessed Virgin wanted to serve her in this ceremony.

Thanks to his zeal, the Christian traditions and ceremonies of solemn masses, processions, sermons, offices of Holy Week, and other festivities of the year took root on the island of Guam, according to the ability of the villages to absorb them. To accomplish this, he made use of all the attractive means possible in order to have the *Marianos* love our holy Faith. That they would more readily go to Mass and Christian doctrine, he gave them some small gifts, which attracted not only the faithful of the village of Agadña but also those of the surrounding villages. For the feast of Christmas he built an altar of the Nativity and almost all the towns of the island came to view it. For them to view it, he imposed the condition that they recite the Creed, the Commandments, the Act of Contrition, and other prayers. The father himself testifies that he reaped a great harvest from the altar of the Nativity.

Later, when the chief, Quipuha, who had received them on the island, died, the father had to overcome many difficulties in order to bury him in church. He went to his house, sounding a trumpet and bearing the standard of Saint Ignatius and Saint Francis Xavier. He performed ceremonies of the vigil of the burial and he sang Mass and he had the prayers and masses customarily offered for a Jesuit offered for him. Though at first quite opposed to the burial, the people of Agadña were so pleased that they asked whether, when they died, they would be buried in the same manner.

At a meeting that he had with the other fathers, Father San Vitores decided that they should be distributed among the islands to the north, in order to bring to all the light of the gospel. Father Luis, for whose zeal the island of Guam was too small, offered himself to go to any island or nation that might be assigned to him, even though it might be the most arduous. In this partition, three islands were assigned to Father Luis: Aguigan, Tinian, and Saipan, which were certainly the most perilous and difficult. But he accepted them with special pleasure, moved by a special impulse and light given to him by the Lord, that in one of these islands, what he came to seek was awaiting him: the crown of martyrdom, as he informed his superior.

Having left on Guam more than three thousand baptized souls, he departed for the islands assigned to him, visiting on the way the whole island of Zarpana, where he baptized all the children who had been born since the last visit of Father Pedro de Casanova, who were thirty-four in number. On the three islands of his mission he administered many baptisms, principally on that of Saipan, where on his first visit he baptized six hundred and seven, including both children and adults.

But this caused him much fatigue and many risks. For since the Fall, the laborer does not harvest his bread until he has watered the field with the sweat of his brow. So also, the preachers of the gospel do not see the fruit of their preaching except at the cost of much labor and fatigue. Except that in the first case, the labor is a curse, but in the second, it is a blessing of the preacher, since the greater the labor, the greater will be the reward.

It is not easy to describe the hardships this worker of God suffered in cultivating the fields in the Marianas, the perils to which he exposed himself, the times when he saw himself threatened with death,

*The Achievements of the Venerable Luis de Medina in the Mariana Islands*

yet all the time experiencing continuously the protection the Lord had for his faithful servant. In general, it may be said that on land and sea, along the trails and in the villages, hardships and dangers that followed him came not only from the barbarian infidels but also from those who were already Christians. But Divine Providence was always with him, guarding him, defending him from all risks, leading him through such perilous steps to the crown of martyrdom, reserved for the time established by him from all eternity.

Without ceasing, without any respite, he walked many trails, for in three months he visited three times the whole island of Guam. From here, he passed to that of Santa Ana, which, as we have said, he visited in its entirety. Then he covered the islands of Tinian, Saipan, and Aguiguan. And the Venerable Father was not content to visit a town once; he returned many times to baptize children who had been born since he left, to help the sick, and to repair whatever damage had been done. On all those trails he went on foot, whether through arduous mountains covered with sharp stones, through muddy swamps or thorny trails. And he walked barefoot or ill-shod. The fathers had brought from Spain some leather soles, which at the beginning they tied to their feet with strings. But the *Marianos* begged for them so they could walk without pain on trails covered with sharp rocks and without hurting themselves with the thorns scattered along the paths by their enemies. So they gave them away. Father Luis used for his feet some sheets of palm leaves, which were the shoes formerly used by the *Marianos* or by those who did not get the leather soles. The good father took more account of his neighbor's danger and hardship than of his own. We may easily imagine the hardships and labors he suffered on these journeys. He also endured many perils in the rivers. On one occasion, they forced him to leave one village, lest he disturb them in their *atotas*, that is to say, in their silence, which they keep at the time of fishing and is required by the *anites*, or the devils. On another occasion, someone offered to help him by carrying him on his shoulders across a pole that served as a bridge over the river. On reaching the middle of the bridge, he pretended to fall off the pole and together with the father, he fell off into the middle of the river, from which he saved him, because he only wished to tease him and annoy him. But the father got off soaking wet, and while he was drying his clothes, he had nothing to cover him but a mat or straw cape peculiar to the island, which the fathers wear along the roads in place of the clerical cape, since they do not wear that extra layer of clothing. The *Marianos* go naked, and when they see someone with more clothing than they think necessary, they ask for it, and since those mats are rough local products, they neither like them nor ask for them.

He had much to suffer in regard to food and drink. His fervor added other mortifications to what one usually finds in foreign lands. Having been brought up in Spain, Spanish food was congenial to him. When he arrived in the Marianas, he contented himself with the little supplied by that land, not only after the provisions were exhausted, which the kindness of His Majesty, the king, and the liberality of some devout persons had supplied, but even before that, when he sallied forth to visit the villages, he did not take anything with him, only his trust in the providence of God, who is not wanting to those who serve him. In the beginning he used to find some hospitality and kindness in the villages. After a little more than a month, when the words of the idolater whom we mentioned above, began to circulate, everything became scarce, and this was the source of much hardship for Father Luis. But even when the kindness is greater, how much the missionaries will suffer in a land where there is no bread or wine or meat, where fish is given only as a rare treat to a guest, and that seldom, and rice even more seldom! So that the ordinary food of Father Medina on his missions, and that in small quantities, consisted of some roots that had neither flavor nor taste, the fruit of the *rimai*, which lasts three months, and some squash of Castille, which is found there and is cooked in water, as well as its shoots, which the natives do not eat but leave for missionary fathers, who regard the gift as coming from Providence, since it is edible by both sick and well. In some places, the missionary's food is reduced to a little grated coconut, with which Father Luis was so content that even while staying in the residence, the grated coconut was enough for him with some roots, though even they were not to be had at times. Father Medina was so satisfied with this limited and coarse menu that he used to say that he would not run out of food anymore, because the coconut and the roots are found everywhere, although in some parts they are very scarce. And he said he did not miss any of the Spanish food, because even the sweets, the preserves, *manjar blanco*, marzipan, and other delicacies were to be found in the fruits of the trees of the Marianas, principally in the *rimai*, in which he found all the flavors of manna,[254] and in all of Spain, he said, there was no lemonade or other drink as fresh and hearty as the water of the green coconut, and this, without any danger of a headache or other harm to body or spirit.

Thus, God knows how to give relish and flavor to the coarsest of foods on behalf of those who abstain from delicacies for love of him. And he causes the manna to rain from heaven for those who truly serve him. With such nourishment, the Lord gave Father Luis very good health in these islands, without any need of medicines or special dishes, which even in Spain, he needed because of his poor health.

Although Father Luis found so much pleasure in these labors and hardships and in the scarcity of necessary things, still he used to say that efforts should indeed be made to procure all the help and the means to make the missions more bearable for the missionaries in the future, since God wants us to make provision in this regard and not ask for miracles or other extraordinary means. However, he held that he and all his companions should give thanks to God for having brought them to these islands at a time when they were so short of human means and so full of hardships, lightened only by the help of divine grace.

The one who caused Father Luis most difficulty and danger through his pernicious attacks on baptism and his accusations against

---

[254]Exod. 16:31; Num. 11:7.

the father was the Chinese idolater. Of Father Luis in particular, he used to say that he was depraved and of low breed, that he ate snakes and fish from the river, of which they have a horror. These were insults that were very much the same as those the *bonzos* used against Saint Francis Xavier. This calumny regarding the fish was occasioned by the fact that the fathers of the Society used to catch some fish from the river that runs close to Agadña, the site of their principal residence, in order to make up for the lack of other needed foods. But Father Luis saw later that the *Marianos* were scandalized by this. Hence, he decided to abstain from this nourishment, imitating the example of Saint Francis Xavier, who, when he went to Japan, resolved not to eat meat or fish because of the criticism of the *bonzos*. But Father Luis and the other companions learned that the reason of the Apostle of the Indies for not eating meat or fish was lest the *bonzos* be scandalized at his lack of abstinence, which they make much of and regard as a virtue; whereas the objection of the idolaters and the *Marianos*, as they found out, arose from their superstition of not touching the fish of the rivers, just like the Jews and the Moros regarding pork.[255] They, therefore, followed the contrary practice of eating fish when they found them, although not so often anymore. And it is suspected that the devil, since he saw that through this means he was not gaining ground but was losing it, had removed them from the river.

Because of the clamor of Choco against baptism, the *Marianos* began to regard Father Luis as an enemy who came to fill their houses and their islands with death, who burned their idols, buried the skulls of their ancestors, and criticized the superstitions and laws that the *anitis* had imposed on them: that they should not eat fish from the river or certain fish from the sea; that they should keep silent while fishing and not utter a single word; that no one should enter the house of one who was fishing, not even his wife and children; and other matters of this sort, about which Father Luis had many encounters with them. So much so, that several times they tried to spear him because he would not be silent, nor would he cease to recite the Christian doctrine in places where the *anitis* had forbidden any dialogue. But his greatest risks came from the administration of holy baptism. Besides the two wounds inflicted on him once again in the town of Nisichan (or San Francisco), one of the *Marianos* threatened him with a lance if he baptized a certain child. At other times he was stoned, ill-treated, insulted, and abused, while he rejoiced at suffering something for Christ.

But above all, the perils he underwent on the island of Tinian in order to stop the war that had broken out there, were innumerable. They were in every way similar to those suffered by Father San Vitores, of which we have spoken in their place.[256] I only add that after the peace was declared, war broke out again between the natives of Sungaron and Marpo after Father Medina had gone to visit the island of Saipan. Now his charity could not rest, since he knew how troubled were its children, the remedy for whom depended on peace on Tinian, or at least on his

---

[255]Were the rivers polluted, at least in certain places?

[256]Book 3, chapters 10 and 11.

## Book Five, Chapter 4

second intervention. If he did not win the peace, at least he meant to administer baptism to the children who might have need of it. God was moving him to this journey because of the great advantage to be gained by it. And so, in a letter he wrote from Opian, a town of Saipan, he said that it seemed to him that the Blessed Virgin wanted him to go to Marpo, and that he felt moved to go there. Thinking more about it he adds: "The thought occurred to me of *Quaerite primum regnum Dei et iustitiam eius.*[257] I understand from this, that I should go first to Marpo in search for the kingdom of heaven for the children."

He reveals even more his charity and zeal and his scorn for dangers in a letter he wrote from Arrayao, a village of the same island of Saipan. To understand this, we have to remember what we said, that in order to settle the differences between the factions, one of the fathers pretended to be more attached to one band and the other to the other, so that each faction would be more assured of its protector and believe him more and agree to use the means proposed to them for their own advantage. This would lead them, out of respect for the father who was favoring them, to restrain themselves from attacking the opposite faction, so that though they seemed for a time not to be united, they might still be united by the bonds of peace. And so Father Luis de San Vitores pretended to be in favor of the faction from Sungaron and Father Luis de Medina of that of Marpo, so that some of Marpo were inviting him to their territory, although there was little reason to trust such inconstant and cruel barbarians. Father Luis de Medina then reports in his letter:

> God our Lord and his most Holy Mother are notably disposed that I go to Marpo, so that I am almost convinced that I am obliged under these circumstances to go for the following reason: If Saint Francis Xavier judged that he was obliged to go to the Maurican region because there were so many Christians there, although he knew that they killed people who went there, what would have happened if they had invited the saint and promised him security and good treatment if he went? Is there any doubt that he would have felt a greater obligation to go? Well, the fact is that they are inviting me to go to Marpo and promising me not only security, but that they would treat me well. And they say that I could live in Marpo and Father Superior in Sungaron.
>
> Consequently, I will have a greater obligation to go and attend to the extreme necessity of those children, all the more when no one but myself can go, because they say that I am good and Father Superior is bad, and because of all the advantages that will result from my going. And what moves me more is that Your Reverence is inclined that I go, so that I am persuaded that Your Reverence will order me to go, with the pretext that I am going there, having fled (from Sungaron) saying that I do not want to be in Sungaron, and that I am going

---

[257]Seek ye first the Kingdom of God and his justice.

*The Achievements of the Venerable Luis de Medina in the Mariana Islands*

there to save them from destruction, and that Father Superior does not want the *pequi* (muskets) to leave, but that those of Sungaron[258] prefer that I stay with them, for I will defend them, for they are my friends and brothers. To better accomplish this, I'm going unaccompanied, since my companions are afraid and dare not go, and in going alone, I am safer since I have God and his Holy Mother to defend me. If His Divine Majesty should permit that they take my life, may his will be done, for that will be the greatest joy I can have in this life, etc.

How inventive is charity! How many different forms it takes, making itself all things to all in order to gain them all![259]

Father Luis then, went into the territory of Marpo with greater risk than when he went there the first time. Even greater and more just was the resentment of these people because of the barbs sown in the ground by their enemies, as well as because of the broken agreements, and the scorn of the mutual understanding they had made at the insistence of Father Luis. God willed to reward at once his zeal and trust with the baptism of many children, with the attendance of the adults at the classes of Christian doctrine, and the burial of the skulls of their ancestors, and, lastly, with the peace that cost him added difficulty, because, although he was summoned by some in Marpo and the first villages received him well, others of the same faction, when he visited them to baptize their children, tried to spear him, treating him as an enemy and stoning him. In the end, thanks to his perseverance and prudence and the intercession of the Blessed Virgin and of our father, Saint Ignatius, and of Saint Francis Xavier, through whose standard he brought peace to these villages, he led them to thank God and his Holy Mother and celebrated the peace, as we related in the life of Father San Vitores. Then, after he had helped to cut the wood for the new church in Marpo, he returned to the island of Saipan to receive the crown of martyrdom as a reward for his hardships suffered in this war and peace-making.

But before we come to the time of his death, it is fair that we speak of his labors and the dangers he suffered at sea, which were not less than those he suffered on land. Along with the continuous stomach pains that he suffered and for which he deserved so much from the Lord, the perils were continuous, arising from the storms and tempests that abound in those seas, and even more from the fragility of those boats he sailed on; besides, they were so uncomfortable for being open to the rain, the winds, the heat of the sun, and all the rough changes of the weather. Yet all of that, he said, was submerged in the immense sea of the mercy of the Lord and the pity of the Virgin Mary. In one letter, he reports a terrible hurricane that he went through and the manner in which God saved him from it through the intercession of the most Holy Virgin, not without some supernatural circumstances. He tells his Superior:

---

[258] Those of Marpo?
[259] 1 Cor. 9:22.

Your Reverence has already three more risen from the dead (he speaks of three companions whom the Lord saved from great dangers), because I believe we now begin to live again. The reason is because yesterday, since Pedro and the other companions from Rota saw such good weather, without much ado we set sail toward Rota. But then a north wind met us, so rough that it did not allow us to enter, but was carrying us instead to Manila, and because of the danger, at ten o'clock at night we folded the sails. But the movement of the sea and the waves was so great that we feared that we were going to drown and saw our good Peter deeply distressed. I told them to make their confessions and I prepared to die. We all commended ourselves to God and to his most Holy Mother, the Mother of the afflicted, whom we revered as our advocate, and we made a vow to fast on two days, once in honor of the Blessed Virgin and the other in honor of her blessed mother, Saint Anne, so that her most holy daughter would help us; and the two others made a vow to receive Communion on one day in honor of the Blessed Virgin, and I made a vow to say six masses, three in honor of Her Majesty and the other three in honor of our lady Saint Anne, and I threw into the sea my holy relics, and our offering was not in vain, because the Blessed Virgin, ever ready to help those who invoke her in similar dangers, favored us also. The way it happened I did not tell. Suffice it to say that, thanks to Her Majesty, we did not drown and we were saved from all that danger. I write this to Your Reverence, so that you and all may give due thanks to the Blessed Virgin and offer one Mass to Her Majesty in my name, since I cannot say it. I shall only say that this night, I remembered the children, who baptized by me, were already in heaven and I prayed to them. As soon as I did this, I heard clearly and distinctly words external to me, as of a girl very close to me. With a very friendly voice she was saying these words, "I am here always." And again, I heard *Pare* (*Padre*). At other times I seemed to hear a child crying. But the truth is that it was not a dream, because I was not about to sleep then. If it was not a dream, it could be a mere fancy of mine. As soon as it dawned, we realized that we were going towards Manila, already well beyond Rota, and not being able to sail there, I thought of Guam. But at noon, we arrived at Aputon, where we stayed, waiting for a wind. May God and his most Holy Mother give it to us, and I earnestly beg Your Reverence, the fathers and the notary apostolic to commend me to the Lord, that my sins may not be the cause of these storms and these delays.

After his signature there follows: "I have been much consoled this afternoon, and I regard my suffering at sea as well borne, because in search of some child to baptize, I baptized one of twenty days, very thin and very sick, whose mother had died six days before. And we may well

*The Achievements of the Venerable Luis de Medina in the Mariana Islands*

believe that the boy will go to heaven, and it could well be the one whom I heard crying and calling me *Pare*. Thanks be to God for such providence of his." In regard to the manner in which the Queen of Angels saved him from this danger, he speaks in mysterious terms and indicates some singular favor, although his humility kept silent about it. But we may presume any favor for one who so loved and served the Queen of the Angels.

In another account that he wrote five days later in a village on the island of Guam, where our Lord was delaying his trip, which was to the island of Santa Ana for the good of the souls there, he adds this incident, a continuation of the event mentioned above: "Last night a little girl whom I had baptized died here. And on that same night, another of four months died, and it can be that it was she who helped us on that night, because I had baptized her." Having arrived on the island of Santa Ana, he writes the following, which is also related to what has been said, in which he declares the desire he had to die for Christ. "Who could guess that having debarked at Aputon after the storm, something good would have resulted from it. Because there was a man here in Aputon who told me that he would hurl a spear at me, because in Aputon I had killed a child with baptismal water. That is that child of twenty days I baptized then, in Aputon. May God our Lord be glorified in all and his most Holy Mother, who through that means brought that child to heaven. This little angel from the Marianas prays to God and his most Holy Mother for Your Reverence and for all, that we may be his companions in heaven."

With a similar providence, though in a different manner, God saved him in the sea from another danger that was threatening him on land. The same father recounts it in a letter in which he gives an account of the baptisms and events in one of the missions on the island of Guam. There, in a village called by the natives Inapsan and by us Our Lady of Good Counsel, he had baptized, among others, a child of already-Christian parents and, with some of those difficulties that generally go with all baptisms after the campaign by the Chinese idolater, he says:

> On the following day in the morning (which was the eve of the Nativity of Our Lady), I departed for Tarragui and I stayed to eat in one of the houses that are on the outskirts of the place to baptize some people. Three *Marianos* who were present at the baptism of the child went there, and they learned from us when we were going to Tarragui, and two of them went there, and one remained to go with us. But God our Lord, who did not wish me to die on this occasion, disposed that a very small boat should arrive there from Ritiyan that was going to Tarragui. A man and his wife were sailing in that boat, a couple whom I had baptized. And learning that I was there and that I was going to Tarragui, they told me they would take me along and that they did not want *cuati* (any pay) and I accepted, quite careless about what was waiting for me on land. Since the boat was small and in order that there might be room for me and all that I was

carrying, the woman went on foot with Andrés and Nicholás, and the man who was left behind also went with them, but when he saw that he would not succeed in his attempt, he stayed behind. I, meanwhile, was traveling with all my baggage [by sea]. Midway, in a thick forest that was there, the two *Marianos* of whom I spoke came out, meeting Andrés and Nicolás. Seeing that I was not going along with them, they were dumbfounded, and without asking about anything else, they asked about me. Upon learning that I was traveling by sea, they then tried to kill Nicolás and Andrés. But these ran away so fast that they could not reach them, and so they let them go; besides, the woman who was with them stopped them. Thanks be to God that we all arrived safely in Tarragui in this boat that God had provided. Father, this is what happened and I did not deserve to be a martyr. May the will of God be done, which is the best.

At this time and at many other times, God saved Father Medina from death, not to deny him the crown of martyrdom but to prepare him better for it by so many dangers. These were deepening in him the desire for the palm of martyrdom, which had eluded his hands so many times, just as he grasped at it.

# CHAPTER V

*Father Luis de Medina's Death for Christ With His Companion Hipólito de la Cruz, and the Discovery of Their Blessed Remains*

It seems that the Lord gave Father Luis de Medina some prophetic knowledge of the martyrdom that he was to suffer. His companions who lived with him more than suspected this, because in a conversation he had with Father Pedro de Casanova some few days before his death, concerning these missions, he said to him with heart-felt emotion, "Father, it is difficult to convince ourselves that these missions will not cost the blood of martyrs." At any rate, he came in search of it in the Indies, and the closer he came to martyrdom, the more he yearned for it and hoped to attain it. To this end he said a very devout prayer composed by the celebrated martyr Father Charles Spinola of our Society. In it he asks for the crown of martyrdom. His companions noted some other details, which rather incline one to suspect this. But I omit these because they are not very persuasive. But I must recall that light that fell upon the sea between the islands of San Joaquín and San José, which, according to Father San Vitores, signified the martyrdom of Father Luis de Medina, which took place in the following way:

After the island of Tinian, which was his mission, had been pacified by Father Luis in the manner that we have seen, on January 27 he sailed to Saipan, which was also under his charge and which he had not been able to visit in its entirety, because he had been prevented by the war. Upon returning to Saipan he decided to visit the villages that he had not visited for a longer time, since this delay had been more dangerous for the eternal life of the infants. These villages to which they were going were the most dangerous, since they were the most opposed to the Christian way of life and had shown the most resistance to holy baptism, since even those who had been baptized refused it for their children, because the words of the Chinese had made the greatest impression on these villages and on this island, his wife and the members of her family being natives of it. Father Luis did not pay much attention to this, in order not to lose the right already acquired by the Church to continue the baptism of the children after that of the parents, as well as the natural right of children (whose life might be in danger) to be assisted with the only means for their salvation, in spite of the cruel kindness of their parents. He continued with his usual persistence in searching for the children and baptizing them. In this he met with even more contradictions than ever, because the devil, the ancient assassin of souls, then revived the pernicious preaching of the idolater.

Ever since the entrance of Father Luis into Saipan, some islanders, deceived and incited by the devil, persisted in following him, without ever ceasing to insult him and to harass him by word and deed, all of which the Servant of God bore with much patience. To his two lay companions, who used to go with him, he recommended that same patience, so that while they carried arms with which to defend themselves and the father, they made no demonstrations with them anywhere on the road. The Servant of God did not want them to defend him with any other arms than those of patience. But with this, the barbarians became more daring, and they called them *ababas*, that is, fools who do not know how to defend themselves.

The first village they visited was called Raurau. Here, he looked for a male child whom they had hidden. Although he was not able to find it, he found himself being stoned for his search, and he bore this with much patience for the love of God. In Tatafu, another village of this island, he administered many baptisms and taught Christian doctrine, and this greatly pleased the inhabitants. But when he left it, in other villages where he went, they taunted him as a child-killer and as the eater of children of Mount Sugrian. When he went in search of the children in this village, they told him the mothers had taken them down to the sea. But when the father went in search of them, some barbarians followed him and threw him down the hill, shouting insults at him. On reaching the shore of Tipo, where it seemed that the children of Sugrian were, he saw a child born just a few days before and asked to be allowed to baptize it. Then many barbarians who had been following him from the mountains and those on the shore were upset and rioted, saying that the father had come to kill their children and that it was a lie to say that baptism was necessary to enter heaven, and that our God was evil and a liar. The father, in order to stop these blasphemies, said that he wanted to baptize that child, since no one can enter heaven without baptism given us by the Blood of Christ, as God taught us. Still, since the parents were opposed, he would not baptize the child, and they would have to endure the anger of God, etc. Since it seemed to him that the child was not ill at all, he postponed the baptism for a better occasion, although with more hurt for not baptizing it, as he said to his companions, than for all the affronts and insults and hardships that he could suffer. These barbarians were not satisfied by the postponement. The mere possibility of the child's baptism hurt them. They began to get together and to conspire more openly against the father. They would have then and there carried out their evil intent, as they had threatened to do, were they not so close to the village of Raurau, whose inhabitants were not so perverted, or better disguised their feelings. They came out to meet him and invited the father to spend the night in their village. But the Servant of God noticed that the chief, who had offered him hospitality, had some figures on his shirt, which were put on at burials out of superstition or for help from their deceased, which smacked of idolatry. The father reproved him, saying that he would not accept his hospitality unless he first removed all those figures. The hosts were much offended by this, saying that those figures were their gods, a new name in that land, since previously they did not give that name to their *anitis* until the Chinese idolater convinced some to accept it. But since the father resisted in his zealous exhortation, the host removed the figures so that the father would not leave his house. Although the father seemingly found a good reception in this town, and later on the neighbors washed their hands of any guilt and declared themselves innocent of the death of Father Luis, it is well proven that some agreed to commit such a great crime and were accomplices in his death, which took place the following day.

Father Luis left Raurau, which is located on the beach, and went on with his mission in the villages still to be visited in the mountains. After a few steps his two companions noticed that they were being followed by some *urritaos*, or unmarried youths, who are the ordinary assassins and authors of atrocities in the villages. As they went farther, they realized that these youths were trying to intercept them, crossing several trails and coming closer to them. Then they began to assail the father and his companions with a great battery of blasphemies against God and insults against the father, calling him child-killer. In spite of this, the father continued his search for children to give them the true life, until he arrived at the village of Cao. Here, he went from house to house looking for children, with every intentions of visiting them all, notwithstanding the insults and the threats, in order that no child who was in danger of death might be without help, although his companions, seeing the turmoil of the people, were urging him to stop, for the moment, the visit to the remaining houses.

At this, the father heard the cries of children in a house. His zeal could not help but go there to baptize anyone who seemed by his cries to be asking for it. He insisted on entering the house, and suddenly he and his companions found themselves surrounded by more than thirty men with their spears. These they hurled at the Venerable Father, shouting at the same time their usual blasphemies and insults against God and against Father Luis. They called him fool and child-killer and other such names. The Venerable Father was wounded by the first spear thrown, which stuck in the middle of his back. He did not fall, nor did he faint. Rather, with the spear fixed in his body, he retained his usual serenity and measured steps in search of children, even as a deer wounded by an arrow and thirsting keeps on in search of the streams of water. Not a word did he say as he moved ahead but "Jesus, Jesus, Jesus, Mary", and he beat his breast until struck by a continual rain of spears, he fell to the ground. Then he got up and twice stood as erect as he could. He began to pray, holding a cross to his breast, a cross on which was carved an image of the crucified Christ and another of the Blessed Virgin, together with various relics. He held this cross in his hands after those sacrilegious assassins had taken away from him another cross that topped a staff, in accordance with the custom of the missionaries. The natives call this *babao Dios* (image of God) in contrast to other images which they place in their houses and boats as a reminder of their *anias*, or superstitions, as well as of their employments, deeds, and acts of bravery. The killers gave vent to their anger and fury at the cross, which they tore from the blessed father. Breaking it in pieces, they threw it away into a field, thus expressing their contempt for our God and the father. At the sight of such sacrilegious deeds, the father remained constant, fearless, and unperturbed in his tender colloquies with the crucified Christ and with the Blessed Virgin, his Mother. He prayed to God with such love and such a strong voice that the barbarians were frightened, fearing, as they said, that God would come at his cries to avenge his death. But the disciple of Christ, with an indescribable meekness, in imitation of that of his master, addressed them with great love and gentle words. He calmed them and exhorted them, as they themselves confessed, to repent of their sin and return to God whom they had offended, that he might pardon them, since he for his part forgave them with all his heart.

His actions and his words aroused great admiration in some of those barbarians and in others on the island who learned about them. They conceived such respect and veneration for the Venerable Father that they called him in their language *macana*, which means "marvelous," for having risen from death, as they said, in order to tell them those things. They must have considered the father's standing erect after falling mortally wounded as a resurrection. As Father Luis continued to address the crucifix, one of those barbarians was infuriated at his continuing to speak and endure so much. He struck him in the neck with another lance and with this wound he died on January 29, 1670, at the age of thirty-three, so that in this too, this privileged son of Mary might be like Christ. Those who seek this sovereign Queen find life; and he who looked for her with such care, with so many gifts of his love, found death, but a death better than life, even better than a thousand lives, a death that was the door to eternal life, a death that was precious in the eyes of the Lord, who merited for him that precious crown that God places on the head of those who lose their lives for love of him.

One of the companions of the Venerable Father Luis de Medina, Hipólito de la Cruz by name, a native of the Visayas, was pierced with a lance along with him and shared his crown, just as he had been the principal companion of his labors and fatigues in the war and in the peace on Tinian. With singular care and devotion to our Lady of Guadalupe, he had assisted in her church of Buenavista Mariana, with so much benefit to the *Marianos*. He instructed them, gave them good example, and skillfully played the harp, all in honor of the Queen of the Angels. With the harmony and sweetness of his music he attracted them to attend divine worship and other services, and Mary rewarded him with the crown of martyrdom.

The father had another companion called Agustín de la Cruz. The Lord preserved his life that he might bring the news, as he did, to Buenavista Mariana, and in order that he might testify to the above-mentioned circumstances up to the point when Father Luis fell wounded, though he was not present after it. But the whole event has been confirmed by more than twenty witnesses who were examined on the island of Tinian, as well as by the confession of the assassins themselves or of their confidants. There is also common knowledge of the case on the island of Saipan, where it was widely reported. Lastly, the principal witnesses were examined a second time on the island of Saipan by Captain *don* Juan de Santa Cruz, commander of the soldiers in the Marianas. Their testimony confirmed the account. Many other witnesses, who were again examined, ratified the story. All of them agreed that the natives of Cao, instigated and accompanied by some of Sugrian and of Raurau, assassinated Father Luis de Medina, because of the visits he made to their villages to preach the Word of God, and because they claimed that our God is a bad one and our Law a lie, and because the baptism of the infants caused their deaths. Those of Cao had special hatred of baptism. Consequently, they met with those of Sugiran to commit this crime. They had been recently incited by the devil on the occasion of a baptism administered by Father Luis on the previous afternoon. Their neighbors of Raurau, who also helped them, unanimously testify that those of Cao and Sugrian are bad people, most notably opposed to the customs and teaching of the Law of God, and that they had heard them say that the fathers are bad persons and child-killers, and that their teaching is a lie. The one who gave the sign to attack, who incited the others, was heard to utter many blasphemies against God and insults against the ministers of the gospel; and the other spear-throwers did the same. The immediate occasion for this crime was the peace and calm with which the father, even confronted by their agitation and evil disposition, went around the town in search of children to baptize, without fear and without desisting from preaching the gospel, even if the majority was following and accompanying the *urritaos*. For this persistence and calm in the discharge of his office, they called him *ababa*, a fool, together with other insults and blasphemies. What also led to the death of the apostolic father was the exhortation he gave to some to bury the skulls of their parents and not keep them as a remedy for their needs. For this reason also they called our God an evil one and a liar because he would not give that veneration to the dead. And they called the fathers evil men, because they objected and forbade them to show that veneration.

After the happy death of Father Luis de Medina, the other ministers of the gospel and lay companions were saddened at being deprived of his holy body, and because the body itself was deprived of due veneration, since it was in the hands of those barbarians. Fearing that they would make lances out of his leg bones in order to kill the other fathers, Captain *don* Juan de Santa Cruz resolved to enter the island of Saipan a second time in search of the relics of the martyrs, sparing no effort to find them, no matter what the cost. Consequently he went back to the island with nine other companions on Thursday, April 29, almost three months after the death of the two martyrs. He landed in Opian, also called Asunción, a village of friendly people. On the following day he went to Raurau. From Raurau some friends of the Cao people notified them that our captain and some soldiers were en route to their village in search of the bodies of Father Luis and his companion. They advised them that the only way to placate the captain was to anticipate his request by bringing the bodies of the martyrs that he was seeking. Thus the men from Cao did. They brought the bodies of the father and his blessed companion Hipólito as far as a hill, which they did not dare to pass, fearful of some severe punishment. Then our captain, having been advised by a chief from Raurau (the one who gave this advice to the Cao people) went on to receive the sacred bodies. This was done with demonstrations of joy for the glory of the martyrs and for the finding of their remains. They welcomed them with lanterns, which they had already prepared, with the sound of a trumpet and the singing of the Christian doctrine in the language of the land. At the same time the guilty ones acknowledged their guilt and their sorrow, whether or not this repentance was sincere or out of fear for the arms of our soldiers.

They then surrendered themselves as prisoners of the captain without daring to resist and stated, that from the time they learned that he was to come for the bodies (which was fifteen days earlier, when he landed on the island to make the first investigation and demand for the holy body) they had not been able to rest, seeing, not only when half asleep but wide awake, so many *guirragos*, or men from abroad, some dressed just like the fathers and some like the captain and his companions who were coming to their village and causing them so much fear, unless we say, rather, that it was fear that made them see these figures and phantasms.

The captain pacified them, saying that because of what they had done and the reverence for the holy body that they were bringing, he would not punish them then and there as their guilt deserved, nor would he burn their village, although it was necessary to go there and set up the *babaos Dios*, or standard of the holy cross over the grave where the body of the Venerable Father had been. He verified the body of Father Luis and realized that a great part of it was missing, which they had failed to bring since that part was not entirely decomposed. He then believed that it was even more necessary to go to the village. It was already late and they told him that he could not arrive in time to do anything on that day. So he left it all for the following morning, which was Saturday, April 26. He was accompanied by a noble of Cao (an innocent man, according to what they were saying), the others having left earlier with two other nobles of Raurau to bring some refreshment, it seemed. He went up the mountain and arrived first at the place where the blessed Father Luis fell and gave his soul to God. He planted a cross there and afterwards three other crosses, one where Hipólito de la Cruz gave up his soul, and one at each of the graves where the holy bodies had been buried. He also recovered the missing remains of the body of the Venerable Father Luis. These arrived accompanied by those who had taken part there, about thirty in number, among them the principal assassin who had hurled the first spear. This one had fled at the first sight of our soldiers in Raurau, soldiers whom he actually met on the occasion of the baptism of a child who had been born a few days before. The natives no longer dared to resist the baptism. Even his own father brought the water for one of the soldiers to baptize it. Thus the blood of Father Luis began to bear fruit in that land by making the baptisms easier to administer.

The captain arrested the principal killer, named Payo, and another of the more responsible ones, named Daon, whom he recognized and picked out from the rest, rather than punish them all.

These he placed under guard until the time for setting sail. They resisted, but threatened by a musket, they entered the boat. The group of those from Cao and Raurau did not dare resist, although they were close to one hundred and fifty men, while the captain stood at the edge of the sea with only nine men. Our men had two boats, in one of which they placed the prisoners, guarded by two musketeers. The captain with the bodies of the martyrs sailed on the other, which was named *Santa María de Guadalupe*. The boats, after a safe and short trip, landed at the village of Sungaron, with its church of our Lady of Guadalupe de Buenavista Mariana, on Sunday, April 27. Here Father San Vitores welcomed the body of Father Luis with the singing of the *Te Deum* and other demonstrations of veneration for a true martyr of Christ, for he esteemed him as such. With the arrival of this blessed body, what varied feelings fought for the heart of the Venerable Father: sadness, joy, hope, envy? Sadness, because he missed his dear companion; joy, for the glory that was his; hope, for winning a similar fortune some day; and holy envy, for he had gone ahead of him. I dare not state which; let him ponder it, who would know. He shed tears without daring to decide if they were of pain or of joy. But if they were of pain, it was more because he remained alive than because his companion was dead, for he knew that death had taken his life to crown it with immortality. I wonder at and praise God for the singular providence in saving his body from the hands of the barbarians, so that it could be honored by the Christians. There were so many occurrences that seemed miraculous. Word had gone around that the people of Cao and Raurau had decided to resist and join battle with the *guirragos*, if they came to their land. Those of Opian declared that it was impossible to bring the body of Father Luis because of the great danger of going to the mountain for it, where they themselves did not dare to go for the bodies of their chiefs, when someone killed one. In spite of this, ten men alone landed on an island full of their enemies to inform themselves of their crimes and recover from them the body of one whom they had killed, instilling fear in all, examining the suspected ones, arresting those who were guilty, removing from the island the murderers, and returning prosperously to their own island, rich with the treasure of the bodies of two martyrs; and all this without bloodying a sword or firing a musket but only with the terror with which God filled those barbarians, conquering them with imagined armies who opened the way for a tiny squadron of our soldiers who recovered the bodies from the barbarians, in much the same way the explorers of the Promised Land brought back the great cluster of grapes from among the man-eating giants.[260]

On Friday, April 25, the day on which the people of Cao brought the remains of the body of Father Luis to Captain *don* Juan de Santa Cruz, Father San Vitores organized public prayers for the success of this trip, including the stopover in *Our Lady of Guadalupe*. And on Saturday,

---

[260] Num. 13:23 and 32.

the 26, when the remainder of the body of the Venerable Martyr Father Luis was found, in the same church, a Mass was sung in honor of our Lady by the royal chorale of the Mariana children, for the same intention, and the Queen of Angels disposed that all should come off as desired in honor of her faithful servant, glorious martyr, and faithful son.

One of the special signs of the Lord's providence in this voyage of Father San Vitores was to obtain an immediate verification and human certitude concerning the martyrdom of Father Luis de Medina. In the first place, Captain *don* Juan de Santa Cruz had already made a second investigation with positive results. He is the captain of these islands and at the same time *fiscal mayor* (fiscal procurator) of the bishop of the Most Holy Name of Jesus and of the City of Cebu, to which diocese these islands belong. As such, he was appointed and sent particularly for this investigation, by virtue of the common privilege of these missions that are committed to the fathers of the Society by its superiors. He was also delegated to them by special authority of His Excellency, *fray* Juan López, bishop of the said diocese. This bishop had sent the fathers with the same authority that he would give to a vicar general, which authority was exercised on this occasion by Father Pedro de Casanova, the missionary in charge of Buenavista Mariana, together with Father Luis de San Vitores, the superior of the mission.

In addition to the first investigation and the second one of the said captain and *fiscal mayor*, another one was made verbally with the murderer himself, Payo, and his accomplice Daon. This was done in the presence of Father Luis de San Vitores, superior of the whole mission, and Father Pedro de Casanova, who was juridically delegated by the bishop, with the same interpreter who had acted as such in the investigation made by Captain de Santa Cruz. This interpreter was called Pedro Jiménez. One may add to his linguistic knowledge that of the fathers, obtained by two years' study and practice of it. It was made clear immediately to all by the confession of the murderer himself, Payo, to which his accomplice Daon agreed, that Father Luis de Medina died pierced by a lance, in the village of Cao, at the instigation, they said, of the people of Raurau, who told them to kill him, because he was spreading illnesses with the water that he poured on the children, and that those of Raurau were also incited by the people of Sugrian, because he had baptized that very afternoon a child of Sugrian on the shore of Tipo, where they had also wanted to kill him. And it was true that the Cao people hated him as much as those of Sugrian and Raurau only because he looked for children to baptize, and because he wished to do away with prayers to the *aniti* and other customs of theirs. In this way, it was clearly proven through the statements of many witnesses, many times repeated, that the death of Father Luis de Medina was the result of his teaching of the Law of God, and of his objection to the barbarian customs and superstitions, but it was principally the result of baptizing the children. All this evidence of martyrdom is only a matter of human conviction. May God grant that it be certified by the Holy See, so that we may venerate on our altars this fortunate martyr as the first fruits of the blood of Jesus Christ offered by

*Father Luis de Medina's Death for Christ With His Companion Hipólito de la Cruz*

the Mariana Islands and that these may boast of giving martyrs to the Church, so that it may be said of the Church of the Marianas what Saint Ireneus affirms: "The Church in every place, out of its love for God, sends martyrs to the Father in every age."[261] I trust that Mary most Holy will one day honor her martyr, so that we may see his martyr's crown with eyes of divine Faith, which we now see only in our human way.

The relics of Venerable Father Luis de Medina were brought by Father San Vitores from the island of Buenavista to that of Guam, where he celebrated the glory of the martyr with a sung Mass of thanksgiving to the Lord, for the honor granted to his servant, with a homily in praise of him. Then followed a salvo of arquebuses and the ringing of church bells. The remains were placed in a casket bearing his name and were buried under the high altar of Saint Ignatius of Agadña. It seems that God sent the sacred body to that village for the protection of Christianity against the war that was soon to break out on that island.

---

[261] Irenaeus, *Contra Haereses*, chap. 33 (not 34), no.9 Migne, P.G. VII,1078A.

# CHAPTER VI

*The Virtues and Miracles of Father Luis de Medina*

The devotion and love of Mary most Holy were for Father Luis de Medina the source of all his happiness, as it is for all those who are truly devoted to her. From this virtue sprang all his other virtues. With this virtue, mercy was born, as it was for Job, and it grew every day in him.[262] For this reason we will treat first of this virtue and then of the others. But who could speak of it more worthily than the father himself, whose words contain such tenderness as would inflame the coldest hearts with love for Mary most Holy. Let him who will read once again the devotions we mentioned at the beginning, using his own words and the paragraphs of his letters that are quoted in his life, and in all, he will read his great devotion and most tender feelings toward this Lady. In Mary, he placed all his trust; through Mary, he begged of God all the things he desired; and through Mary, he expected the fulfillment of his desires. He had Mary for his Mother, a title he used so frequently that he seemed to know no other. The name of Mary was sweeter to his lips than honey and the honeycomb, and the memory of her was all the joy of his heart. The books he ordinarily read were about the Blessed Virgin. The conversations he loved best were about the praises of this Lady, so that his eyes, his ears, and his language were dedicated to the praise of Mary most Holy. To speak of his eyes, his ears, and his tongue is little enough. The hands, the feet of this apostle, his memory, his understanding, his will, his body, and his soul were all at the service of this sovereign Queen. His thoughts, his words, his deeds, his sufferings were all for the honor and glory of Mary, in accordance with the promise he made, which is recorded in his writings. For this purpose, each day he offered her his works in reverence for her manifold perfections. The glories of Mary most Holy gave him the most profound joy, and he thanked God every day for the graces and blessings he had bestowed on her. And though he blessed her in so many ways, this was never enough, and so he prayed the Father, the Son, and the Holy Spirit to bless her, and he asked all the angels and saints of heaven to give her thousands of blessings. In honor of Mary, he went to confession and Communion on all her feasts; he fasted on the eve of all of them and on every Saturday of the year; on these and other days, he took the discipline and wore the chain. He said in her honor a variety of prayers and offices; he made her many visits, having special devotions for each month, for each week, for each day, and for each hour.[263] All of these I mentioned at the beginning and I will not repeat them here. He dedicated to Mary most Holy the churches he built in the Marianas. For the construction of the church on Tinian, which he named after Our Lady of Guadalupe, he was the first to wield the

[262]Job 29:11-20.
[263]See Book 5, chapter 2.

tools on the job, since it seemed to him a glorious thing to hold any office, so long as it was for the service of Mary. Above all, he tried to imitate her in all the virtues, particularly that of purity, so that he made a vow of perpetual virginity, living with great care, lest he lose this most precious gem consecrated to the Queen of the Angels, winning for its sake many dangerous battles through the intercession of the same Virgin. But he was not content to be alone in this devotion. By all means possible he tried to have others share it. Witnesses to this are his companions on both ocean voyages and in the Marianas. When he preached or taught the Christian doctrine, he earnestly exhorted all to practice this devotion. Even when he gave prizes to the children, he insisted on the condition that they have great devotion to the Blessed Virgin. To this same end, he sang her litany with the children of his residence and village every evening before her image, and he included other devotions that he composed in their language. His many occupations and dangers could not prevent such salutary devotion; rather, he used to say the greater the risks the greater the need for the shield of prayer.

The Queen of Angels does not remain in debt to anyone. Rather, all her devotees are indebted to her, and so she favored generously her most devoted son, Father Luis. He attributes to the Queen of Angels the fact that he did not die at birth, when his mother received a heavy blow, on the Feast of the Purification of Our Lady. She cured him of one sickness, which was proving an obstacle to his entrance to the Society. Then she smoothed out other difficulties in regard to his admission, and once he was granted approval, she removed the temptations to sadness that the devil provoked when he was about to enter. And she spoke to him, as is believed, enlightening his mind for success in his studies. Then she helped him with his speech whenever he had to preach the holy gospel. And what is more, when he was still a layman, she freed him from the many snares set by the devil against his virginity, inspiring him in time of danger so that he could escape them. His entrance into the Mariana Islands was made easier for him by the Blessed Virgin as he sang her litanies, and there as well as on the voyage there, she freed him from many dangers of death on land and on the sea. The copious harvest he made in the Marianas in such a short time was due to the favor of the Blessed Virgin, to whom he had recourse through prayer and penance. The conversion of the village of Nisichan, which was rebellious and obstinate in refusing to be baptized, was a favor of this Lady; and it was through a novena that he made to the Blessed Virgin, in addition to prayers and mortifications, that he won the peace, so difficult and perilous, for Tinian. During those days, his companion, Father Pedro de Casanova, noticed that in the celebration of the Mass, particularly during the Mementos, when he raised his eyes to the picture of the Blessed Virgin, it seemed that he was lifted up. And during those days, he could not speak of anything but the favors that the Virgin grants her devotees, and he found both repose and fervor from reading the book on her patronage. Conversing with his companion on this matter, Father Luis began to speak these words, "Father, the most Holy Virgin!" And here he

*Book Five, Chapter 6*

stopped for a long time, while the great affection and sweetness that he felt at the memory of the Queen of the Angels would not allow him to proceed further. If it were not that his humility stopped him, he surely would have told of some great favor he had received from her. No doubt these favors were many more than those already mentioned, although we regretfully lack knowledge of all of them, since he was prevented by obedience from recording his feelings and the graces received from God and his Mother.

Of his devotion to the Blessed Sacrament, to the angels, and to the saints, much has been recorded in the writings that were mentioned at the beginning.[264] What I should point out here is his perserverance in carrying out his devotions. It was such that though they were many and required much time, for no occupation whatsoever would he leave them undone, not even on the day when he had his comprehensive examination in theology. When, as a scholastic, he was present with the other scholastics during some recreation and the time came for one of his devotions, he left them and retired to perform it; and if he could not leave the place where they were, he would retire to a corner to perform his devotion, without regard for what the less fervent might say.

As we said, from his devotion to Mary there flowed all the other virtues in which he tried to imitate the Blessed Virgin. He excelled in the virtue of humility, as we can see in the remarkable examples he gave of his virtue. When he was a scholastic studying in the college of Granada, he served an old father, a teacher there, in the most humble services in his room, and although he knew that some noticed it and attributed it to human motives of self-interest, he never gave up this service, nor did he interrupt it, no matter what opposition or gossip it occasioned. He bore with good grace the mortification for the sake of the Lord, for whom he was engaged in that work of mortification and charity. When he was about to embark for the Indies, while on his way to Seville and San Lucas with his companions, as superior of the group, he ordered a coadjutor brother to do a certain thing. Since the brother resisted with some obstinacy, Father Luis knelt at his feet, kissed them, and asked him with great humility to do what he asked. I could relate similar actions in which he made the same demonstrations, when he suspected that he had offended one of his companions. When he was superior, there was another superior who used to treat him arrogantly. One of his companions became indignant that he should be treated worse than anyone else, but Father Luis just laughed it off and said it didn't matter.

When he entered the Marianas and visited Quipuha, the chief who received him in his village, he knelt down and kissed his feet, which left the barbarian quite astonished. He never refused any service, no matter how lowly it might seem, if it led to the good of souls. At the funeral of this chief, he sounded the trumpet, an instrument he used to use for the more solemn ceremonies. A lay companion had been asked to do it, but had refused, as being beneath his dignity. With this same dignity, he concealed as much as he could his virtues and gifts, and he

---

[264]Ibid.

showed pleasure, when with actions or words, others drew attention to his natural defects, and he himself invited them to do so in order to be humiliated and despised by all.

He clearly showed his patience in the weaknesses and ailments that he suffered in his frequent voyages and journeys in the Marianas. These, he bore with joy, and all the more in the continual dangers and hardships that ever surrounded him. Here are some examples, chosen from those that never were written down. On one occasion, he called the children to listen to Christian doctrine. They were annoyed at being taken away from their games. They began throwing sticks and stones at him, which Father Luis calmly endured, without any exasperation at them. On another occasion, while he was with Father Pedro de Casanova, a youngster came up behind him, seized him by his cassock and his neck and threw him to the ground. Father Casanova scolded the youngster for his action and for his disrespect. But Father Luis stopped him, "Pay no attention. They don't realize what they are doing. They are only boys." He sincerely forgave those who insulted and maltreated him, inviting them himself to be his friends and doing them more favors than the insults they had inflicted on him. One of the reasons why he insisted on the conversion of the town of Nisichan, as we have said, was the fact that they had ill-treated him and wounded him in this village. In a memorandum he writes how he behaved toward the man who wounded him there: "The one who hurt me most lived in this place and so he did not want to come for fear of the harm I might do to him. I sent someone to summon him with Iaipiru (his host) and when he came I embraced him; and to give an example to this new Christian land, I said that I was forgiving him in the presence of the whole town that had come together to see what I was doing. In their language, I told them how good our Lord Jesus Christ was who taught us what I had done, and that they should also do the same. That seemed good to them, and he was quite happy. Then I heard his confession, for he had already been baptized a few days before." His conduct was the same toward others who had ill-treated him or planned to kill him. But it was a small matter for one who desired to suffer so much for Christ and die for him that he should love and be grateful to those who caused him to suffer. He laments in one letter that having been threatened with a spear, he did not deserve to be a martyr. In another letter he reports that a good thing was about to happen to him, because a certain barbarian told him that he was going to strike him with a lance. He was wounded twice and he writes: "I was most happy to see my blood flow for teaching the Faith." In other letters, he speaks of the longing he had for suffering or dying and of his disappointment at having missed an opportunity for doing so.

Although his desire to suffer and die for Christ was so intense, yet his obedience was so great that he fled from the death that threatened and followed him, because the superior, who was aware of his desires, in order to preserve his life longer for the good of that Christian community, ordered him to evade as far as was licit the occasions of meeting death. His reaction to this order may be seen in this sentence from one of his letters: "May Your Reverence be assured that if I do not see myself obliged under pain of sin to defend the Faith, I will not place myself in danger of losing my life, etc." And that is how he acted at times. On one occasion he ran, fleeing from one who was following him with a lance to kill him. But he was fleeing with the desire that he be overtaken. He tripped and fell and he thought that he now had what he was seeking. But God prevented his death by means of a woman who detained the aggressor. But who ever saw such a thing? To desire the death from which he was fleeing, and to flee the death that he desired? To die in the act of obedience is a great thing, but it seems as fine a gesture and an even more difficult thing to not die for the sake of obedience, while longing for it, as though Father Luis, while fleeing from death, turned his head to see if it was arriving and chided its laziness, saying, "Why did you stop running? Why are you defeated by a man without legs? For others you have wings, for me alone you run with fetters on your legs, if you run at all? I cannot wait for you. Make haste and overtake me. See, I trip and fall. Here you have me prisoner, unable to escape. But what ill-fortune is mine! Your running ceases, or someone holds you back from seizing me, and me from seizing what I so desire."

Thus did Father Luis obey in a matter so difficult and strange as fleeing from the crown of martyrdom, and thus you may judge his obedience in all the rest. He proposed to our father general his desire for the Indies with the resignation and indifference that we saw in his vow.[265] In the Indies, he could not do anything except under the direction of obedience to his superior, in whom he always saw God himself; nor did he ever fail in it, no matter how difficult it was for him. When he was on the island of Guam, his superior ordered him to assist every Sunday in the principal village, which was Agadña, and although to obey and not miss any Sunday, it was necessary to walk many leagues on his crippled feet, he writes: "I have carried out the order Your Reverence gave me; hence I have not failed so far, nor will I fail, except for one Sunday, when it was impossible to get to Agadña, etc." An explicit command was not necessary for him to obey; it was enough to know the inclination of the superior. In sum, all his life he took great care to obey his parents, confessors, and superiors with great humility.

His mortification, arising from that desire to suffer, was extraordinary. We have seen the many fasts imposed on himself, by vow or devotion, all his life, as recorded in his writings. From the time of his voyage to the Marianas, he began to give greater examples of this virtue, and in the Marianas, even greater ones. The *Marquesa* de Mancera, Vicereine of Mexico, presented the fathers, when they sailed for the Marianas, with a quantity of chocolate for the voyage and for their new life in the islands, where it seemed necessary, at least until they became accustomed to the food of that land. All the fathers resolved to abstain from it, reserving it for their lay companions. Father Luis made a special vow not to take it, although his poor health seemed to need it. On arriving in the Marianas, he resolved not to eat any of the biscuits, of which

---

[265] Id. 344.

some quantity was left over from the voyage. Moved by his example, the fathers and their lay companions decided to do the same thing. They reserved them for the *Marianos*, seeing how much they liked them, and used them as bait to attract the *Marianos* to Christian doctrine. Ordinarily his food consisted of herbs and roots; if sometimes they gave him fish, he gave it away to the children attending the Christian doctrine. At other times he gave it to a companion, with the excuse that it did him no good. At a time when food was scarce, he was sent a small quantity of fish, but he distributed it immediately among the people in the village where he was. He also distributed among the children a small quantity of sugar and a small barrel of preserves that those of the ship sent him as alms. Thus he deprived himself of a treat, which for him was a necessity because of his ailments and even to make up for lack of other food. For his necessary sleep, he lay down fully dressed on some mats made of leaves that the natives weave from palm leaves. He never missed having a bed, blankets, mattress, or sheets. He used to wonder at the restful sleep he enjoyed, fully dressed, lying on the hard ground, whereas in Spain, undressed and lying in a good bed, he spent so many sleepless nights.

Concerning his hidden penances, disciplines, chains, and fasting even from the foods we have mentioned, it is enough to say that Father San Vitores, whom he informed of them according to the rule, found himself obliged to moderate his austerity and ordered him to abstain from much of what he was doing, lest he shorten a life so necessary where missionaries were so few. In this, he gave as great an example of obedience in what he gave up as of constancy in what was allowed, without excusing himself for lack of time or place, for he needed to retire among the trees for his penances. In lieu of other examples, we will simply mention two, though these are rather extraordinary.

In those islands the mosquitoes abound in such quantities and are such a nuisance that one cannot write or do anything without constantly raising the hand to drive them away, especially from the face. But Father Luis, with his hands and face covered with mosquitoes, sat calm and undisturbed at his work, as if he did not feel them, so much so that his companions, admiring him for such mortification, asked him how he could bear those little beasts, so importunate and maddening. He answered, "I do not mind them," as if to say, "I don't feel them sting." With these equivocal words, he disguised his mortification. He also suffered an ailment that can best be explained in his own words: "Brother Bustillo and I are well. We have only the one thing we had missed, one of the pleasures of living on this island and which at times causes us to suffer. May God reward the brother who first infected me with it when he returned from his mission." This ailment, so sickening and painful lasted a year and a half. In all this time, he refrained from taking the natural remedy, which he normally would take, to the great admiration of his companions who had the same difficulty, and who could admire but not imitate such constant mortification. To his external mortification, he joined the interior one of controlling his passions, to such a degree that when he landed in the Marianas, he seemed to be of somewhat harsh disposition, but afterwards he tended toward the contrary extreme, treating those barbarians with as much gentleness as if he were the father of each one, thanks to the mortification with which he controlled himself on repeated occasions as well as during the interruptions in teaching children who have no experience of discipline.

Mortification without prayer cannot last, just as prayer cannot without mortification. They noticed how he was much more given to prayer in his years in the Marianas. For more quiet in prayer, he used to retire to the wooded hills, enjoying there the consolations earned by his fervor. In our residence, he used to spend at times the greater part of the night and much of the day in prayer. He deprived himself of many hours of sleep, to give them to prayer. Whenever he could he prayed before the Blessed Sacrament in the chapel or in the church of our Lady, because of his great devotion to that sovereign Sacrament and to the Queen of the Angels. I refer here to his mental prayer, for we have seen in his writings so much evidence of his vocal prayer. We do not know how many favors he received from God and Mary in his prayer, although we believe that they were many. Praying in Montilla, he saw his mother at that same hour in Málaga, as we have reported.[266] Regarding other supernatural experiences and prophetic lights, we are without evidence because of the obedience of Father Luis, who omitted writing them down, in obedience to his superior. We have already expressed our regret at the loss of this consoling reading. How powerful before God and his Mother was his prayer that it is seen in the many favors that he obtained through prayer for himself and for others, a fact we have recounted elsewhere.

Concerning his poverty of bed and board, we have already seen that he had less than the poor and the beggars. Personal treasures he had none, and he was content to possess just what sustained life and covered his nakedness, as the great apostle says of himself and all apostolic men.[267] His cassock was the poorest, and instead of the cape, he wore an outer covering of palm matting, and he used to say jokingly that the outer garment of this land was better than the Spanish cape because it had a thousand uses: it was a burnoose, a cape, a cassock for a quick change in case of need, a bed sheet for sleeping, a pillow, etc.

The hat that he made of the same woven palm was, he said, better than a beaver hat, and even his *biretta* and shoes were made of the same palm leaves, from which he fashioned sandals that served as shoes. Clothing that was not absolutely necessary, he gave away to the *Marianos*, just as he gave away the soles that he brought from Spain, and that he needed so badly to walk over the sharp stones and the barbs that the natives used to scatter on the trails. And he was so satisfied with these privations that he gave thanks to God for bringing him to the Marianas at a time when there was nothing there but souls to save.

We have said enough about his zeal for souls and his love for God and neighbor. All that he did, all that he suffered, all was to spread

---

[266] Id. 345.
[267] 1 Tim. 6:8.

*The Virtues and Miracles of Father Luis de Medina*

the Faith and the glory of our Lord Jesus Christ and to lead to heaven those whom his Lord had redeemed, even at the cost of shedding his own blood and giving his life for it. This love made the trails easy for his feet, the dangers a matter for contempt, the hardships sweet to bear, and death itself a thing to be desired. Because of this love, he served the sick in hospitals, consoled prisoners, and begged alms for the needy, as we saw in Montilla, Seville, Mexico, and Acapulco. This same charity toward the sick, he continued in the Marianas, assisting them, and serving them with great love, showing his compassion for their suffering like a loving mother, and encouraging them to bear with patience the hardships God sent them. If they were wounded, he brought them bandages; he helped them with the medicines he could find and other things necessary for the health of the body and much more with the sacraments for the salvation of their souls. Some of the sick gave him much to suffer, because they were impatient with the pain of their wounds, and they would not allow remedies to be applied to them, either medical or spiritual. He suffered as much from their relatives and others who assisted them. They turned against the father, as if he came to kill the sick and not to bring them health. Further proof of this great charity were the fasts, disciplines and chains, and prayers that he offered for the conversion of sinners. The journeys by land and sea in search of children and adults to baptize, the endless task of preaching and of teaching Christian doctrine, effects of his ardent zeal, so ardent that neither in health nor in sickness did it allow him to rest; he was ever occupied in this ministry. This letter that he wrote to his superior is worth a thousand others. He had received the two wounds in Nisichan, of which we have already spoken, and one of them was quite dangerous. It bled all that day and he could not stop it. He says: "In the afternoon I came to Saipan and I was well received by all, and they showed great sorrow that I should be in such a condition. But in spite of the devil, though I felt so ill, yesterday afternoon I baptized here many children and adults, as many as thirty-two. Today, God willing, I must do the same, although my eyes are swollen, as well as part of my face, so that the devil may not have his own way. I have been cared for here with medicines and I am not any worse, although I had a little fever last night and I did not sleep." Following the signature he adds: "I already have one hundred and thirty Christians, in spite of the many obstacles placed by the devil." And in another report he says: "I was doubting whether to go there (to the residence). But having learned that God, our Lord, does not want me to go (because of what the superior had written) I shall not go, but will attend to my cure here, because, though I am in this condition, no time is lost, since yesterday I baptized and explained the catechism to forty-four adults and some children. Now I will do the same, although I do it with much hardship, since my sight is not well and my headache is rather intense."

In short, he distinguished himself in all virtues, especially during the last two years of his life, which he spent in the Marianas. Although he was always very devout and observant, as we have seen, on entering these islands, he suddenly changed into another man, to such an extent that those who knew him before could not recognize him later. That is what those who dealt with him in the Marianas state with admiration. Before he came to the islands, externally he led the common life in the Society (which is of no little perfection, if one follows the practices of the community). He would interrupt the rigor of the observance of the rules with the relaxations permitted by the order, when he judged that he had need of them. But from the time he entered the Marianas, all looked upon him as a saint, because overcoming all fears and hesitations and rejecting them for what was truly necessary, he gave up all those relaxations and deprived himself even of those that even the most observant religious allowed themselves to relax. He began the most austere life, rigorous, and of the highest perfection. He delighted in dealing more with God than with men, unless it was for the good of their souls. Work became his rest and the fulfillment of the will of God his food and drink. He carried the cross of Christ and mortified himself in all things possible, ever trying to please God and the Blessed Virgin in all things. With the thought of them he seasoned all his actions. In this manner the Lord prepared him to be a most able missionary in these islands and to merit the crown of martyrdom. With this the Lord would crown those virtues with which he had adorned him.

God enhanced the reputation of Father Luis de Medina with some miracles that he worked through him. When Father Luis was visiting the village of Pigpuc, on the island of Guam, he saw a woman who was totally deaf. She was over a hundred years of age. Her relatives had hidden her many times when Father Luis visited the village, so that he would not baptize her. But now God, who had preserved her so that she might gain eternal happiness, saw to it that she was found by Father Luis, who applied to her ears a relic of the wood of the cross, in order that the portals of the Faith might be opened to her. Simultaneously he said the prayer of the spouse of our Lady, Saint Joseph, whose feast it was that day. The holy cross, which shuts the doors of hell through the intercession of Saint Joseph, opened the ears of that woman. She soon heard whatever Father Luis asked her for her instruction. Then she asked for baptism, which she received willingly, and then she heard everything that those of her house asked her, to the astonishment of those who knew that previously she was completely deaf.

In Tarrifac, a village of the same island, he found another woman who was very ill, a woman who had lost her speech five years before. She was unconscious and could not ask for and receive baptism, which previously she had obstinately refused, persuaded by the words of the Chinese idolater. Father Luis took pity on her for the loss of her soul. He cried out in his heart to God, said the prayer to the sweet name of Mary, to which he had a special devotion, and then to the Apostle of the Indies, Saint Francis Xavier. At the same time he applied to the patient a relic of the same apostle. A marvelous thing! Instantly she showed signs of consciousness. With a clear voice she asked twice for baptism and responded to the questions of the instruction. She was baptized and her speech lasted all that afternoon, but the following morning she was

The Virtues and Miracles of Father Luis de Medina

without it, as before. How many miracles can be counted in this one miracle? The greatest of all is that she, who was so obstinate in resisting baptism, found herself so changed that she herself asked for it twice, having repented of all her sins. And yet, if we were to count all his miracles, the count would be too long, so many were the obstinate sinners whom he converted by his prayers and words, among which the most extraordinary miracle was the conversion of the village of Nisichan, which we have reported elsewhere.[268]

Another marvelous thing took place on the island of Santa Ana, which Father Luis himself relates to his superior for the glory of Saint Anne. I shall record it in his own words for the glory of that saint. He says:

That my Lady Saint Anne may be glorified I will relate to Your Reverence a miracle that she performed last night. The daughter of our host came here shedding tears because her mother, our host, was dying in another house. I went there immediately. She was speechless and unconscious and appeared to be dead, although she understood something and so gave signs of contrition, and I absolved her. I also applied to her my relic of the cross, with the intention of also applying the relic of Saint Anne. But the first prayer that occurred to me was that of our holy Father Saint Ignatius, mixed with that of Saint Francis Xavier. When I realized this I applied the relic of this saint, but with no effect. I then said the prayer to Saint Anne, and as soon as I pronounced the last words, *eius patrociniis adiuvemur* (that we may be helped by her intercession) she got up and regained her speech, and holding in her hands the relics said, *"Mauri si Dios* (God is good) for I am well now." And she came with me and is very well. May the Lord be glorified who has deigned to glorify his grandmother.

I pass over the miraculous providence with which God saved him from death on many occasions, some of which I have mentioned, but they are so many that his companions excuse themselves from relating them, saying that his missions were one continuous line of singular manifestations of God's providence. Nor do I repeat here the miracles with which the Blessed Virgin restored him from sickness and from his defective speech, and the others that I have already narrated.

After the martyrdom of the Venerable Father Luis de Medina, a companion of his who was ill, asked Father San Vitores, as we related in his life, to touch him with his hands. Father San Vitores did so, leaving him at the same time a signature and some writing of Father Luis de Medina, saying he should apply it to himself and should sprinkle the area of the sickness with holy water. Also he should pray to the Venerable Martyr and have great trust in God and the Blessed Virgin. If he did that he would recover his health. And he did. Whenever Father San Vitores found a signature or other writing of Venerable Father

---

[268]Book 5. chap. 4:355.

383

## Book Five, Chapter 6

Medina, he would kiss it with much tenderness and affection, admitting that every day his devotion to the angelic Father de Medina grew more fervent.

This Venerable Father was of average height, his color rather dark. His face was long and, in Spain, rather full, but in the Marianas, it grew thin from the hardships and penances. His forehead was narrow, his eyes black and small, his nose well proportioned, his hair and beard black and thick. He was slow in speech and limped with his right leg. But in this body with its imperfections there lodged a soul that had none. He was by nature suave and was easily attracted to whatever was good. He was joyful and jovial with all, without being a burden for anyone. He was ever-constant in bearing hardships. He was exceptionally talented and diligent in study. He had an excellent background in literature and philosophy. With even greater diligence, in the way of perfection, he acquired a great capital of all the virtues, which in the Marianas, he copied from Father San Vitores, trying, as one companion asserted, not only to carry out his commands and counsels but to imitate his example with the greatest care.

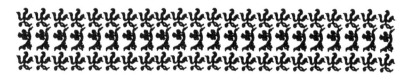

# CHAPTER VII

*The State of the Christian Community in the Mariana
Islands After the Martyrdom of Father San Vitores, and the
Death of Several Spanish Soldiers for a Good Cause*

The events between the death of Venerable Father Luis de Medina and that of Father San Vitores two years later are related in Book III, Chapter XI, and following. At this point we return to the state in which we left the islands on April 2, 1672, at the death of their father, teacher, apostle, and superior of the Society of Jesus, who had propagated that Christian community. He was succeeded as superior of the mission by Father Francisco Solano, an old disciple of Father San Vitores in his zeal for souls, and he needed all of it at the time when he took the mission in charge. The island of Guam was then divided into two factions. The villages of the southern part were friendly towards the fathers and the Spaniards, not to defend them, but merely to tolerate them, while those of the north were declared enemies. Thus the fathers could go about with relative security in only one part of the island, but it was not safe for them to go very far from Agadña for fear of their enemies, who not only went to all parts of the island but could easily make enemies of other natives whom the fathers believed to be friendly.

Seeing matters in this critical state, God wished to send succor for the missionaries in the form of manpower and supplies, for by this time they were greatly in need, and because of the death of so many lay helpers, there were few soldiers left.

The galleon *San Diego* arrived on May 2, one month after the death of Father San Vitores. This was the ship that had brought him to the islands and was commanded by Admiral Diego Coello. Although it was anchored at San Antonio de Umatag, the fathers were not aware of its arrival, since the natives purposely hid the news from them, fearing that because of their murders and other crimes this ship had come to bring them some type of punishment. And although the fathers, foreseeing the arrival, had given several letters to the natives with instructions to deliver them on board whenever a ship arrived, meaning thus to advise those on board of the death of Father San Vitores and of the precarious situation in which the whole Christian community then found itself, the letters were not delivered, even though the natives went on board the ship.

At last Father Solano was informed of the arrival of the vessel by Antonio de Ayhi, of whose loyalty we have already spoken.[269] The father set out for Umatac to visit the ship (although he was still very ill with tuberculosis) in a small boat, which fortunately had been cast up here on the shore just a few days before. He found the ship encircled by

---

[269]Book 3, chap. 14:236.

native boats, but they all fled at the sight of him, fearing the news that he must give to the Spaniards.

It is not easy to describe the sadness on board the ship when they learned of the death of Father San Vitores. Admiral Leandro Coello was especially touched, as was Captain Antonio Nieto, for they had both known him well. They mourned the loss to the Marianas and to all the *Indias Orientales* and were consoled only by the cause of his death, so deserving of envy, and by the assurance that from his place in heaven he could help those he loved and favored on earth. How many things they said about his virtues and miracles! In their zeal for the propagation of the Faith and to restrain the attacks of the barbarians who were preventing it, they gave much assistance, even leaving their firearms. They put ashore some soldiers, not ordering any of them to remain, but there were many who asked to, from a desire to punish the murderers of Father San Vitores and cooperate in the harvest that this land, watered by the blood of many martyrs, now promised. The ship, having taken on water at the port of San Antonio (Umatag) sailed on May 7, 1672, taking advantage of the good weather, for the Philippines.

Then the fathers tried to establish their former custom of visiting the villages and missions of the southern part of the island. But two misadventures occurred in this area due to the excess zeal or impatience of our soldiers, and these gave rise to new and greater disturbances.

On the eleventh of May, one of our soldiers encountered two natives who had been leaders in the war of Guam. It happened that one of these was Hurao, who had tried to exterminate the fathers and the Spaniards. The sight of him reminded the Spaniard of the past war, and he ran Hurao through with his sword, leaving him dead, and would have done the same with the other, Agao, if the latter had not availed himself of the swiftness of his feet. Another encounter that took place the same day was even more unfortunate, when two of our soldiers saw two natives, a man and a woman, natives of the island of San Joseph ( Saipan), fleeing from them as was the custom of these people, who have a natural fear of firearms. One of the soldiers, perhaps believing them to be fleeing from justice, discharged an arquebus, killing the woman and wounding the man, who held the woman in his arms.

The missionary fathers deeply regretted this excess fervor on the part of the new soldiers, who for lack of experience and to make themselves feared, placed the whole Christian community in jeopardy, since the natives now retired from their own villages to others more distant from Agadña. It was feared, and with reason, that all the island would rise against the Spaniards and the fathers, as against murderers, who, some with baptisms, as many alleged, and others with arms, had come to kill them and their children.

Father Solano called together all the men of the *presidio* and told them that while arms, used at a suitable time and place, were the defense of that Christian community, they could also prove its destruction if used unreasonably, for they would not only irritate the natives but would also incur the displeasure of the Lord, and without his favor, what could twenty or thirty men accomplish against thirty thousand? He said that until now they had been able to defend themselves only because the natives were afraid of their firearms. But if that fear were lost, it would be impossible for the Spaniards to resist the multitude. This fear might easily be dispelled and to their own misfortune, for the natives, throwing themselves only once against those arms, could seize them, and our defense would at once be converted to our harm. He charged them, especially, that in the villages in the southern part, which were the only ones in which the fathers could make their missionary visits, they abstain from all hostility, in order not to impede the only work that at that season could bear fruit or make enemies of those natives who appeared friendly. The soldiers approved of the discourse and promised to restrain themselves within the limits of justice and prudence.

Captain Juan de Santiago, who commanded the *Escuadrón Mariano*, tried to erect a fort in Agadña that might resist the fire, which the barbarians were able to throw so cleverly affixed to their lances and to stones, since he foresaw the possibility of another war. They decided to build it of earth, because stone would require much more time and they lacked tools. They began to haul clay to make adobes on May 13, with an escort of arquebusiers, for it was necessary to go some distance from the post to obtain it.

When the barbarians got word of this, they planned to wait in ambush on the appointed day, hiding in the underbrush and strewing the trail over which the Spaniards would travel with thorns, brush, and other impediments.

Inasmuch as the Spaniards advanced with care, they discovered the barbs and then the enemy, who began at once to shower them with stones and lances. Our men advanced, firing several shots from their arquebuses, whereupon the enemy turned their backs and fled. Nevertheless, the Spaniards gave up the undertaking, realizing that each load of earth would cost them a battle with the natives, into whose trap they could easily fall without warning.

When they realized that they would be unable to carry out their plan for the erection of a fort, the soldiers consulted among themselves and decided to go in search of the murderers of Father San Vitores and at the same time punish the villagers who had assisted them, for it is customary here, when any crime is committed by a villager, for the whole village to defend the delinquent against those who seek to punish him. It seemed to the captain and his soldiers that it was not well to leave unpunished an offense that might prove a bad example, or which might give the natives the audacity to commit other offenses against the fathers, whose lives were so necessary to the new Christian community, for in the loss of one father, they lost all those souls whom he would have saved by his preaching.

Believing this enterprise to be the work of God, Captain Juan de Santiago arranged his soldiers, of whom there were twenty-one, thirteen Spanish arquebusiers and eight Filipinos, four with cutlasses and bucklers and four with bows and arrows, leaving a few in Agadña for the

*Book Five, Chapter 7*

defense of the fathers. This *Escuadrón Mariano* left Agadña on May 17, after all had confessed and received Communion, taking the trail to Funhon at four o'clock in the morning. On the way they met a native, the nephew of Agao, the one who had escaped death in the encounter already referred to. They detained him and his wife so they could not get to Funhon ahead of the soldiers and give warning. The settlements through which they passed, although they were enemies and they were armed, made no effort to stop the Spaniards on the way, permitting them to pass unhindered in order to assail them from the rear and carry out their stratagem from a safe position.

On the hill near Funhon they found the *Indios* in ambush and realized that they must have been warned of the arrival of our men. The path was strewn with sharpened obstacles made of wood and of human bones. The barbarians threw stones and lances without being seen by our men. These, imploring the favor of the Queen of Angels, patron of these islands, and of Saint Michael, protector of their arms, went forward without delay until they reached Funhon, where they did not find Matapang, the principal murderer of Father San Vitores. However, they burned his house, and when the villagers tried to stop them, they burned a dozen others and several boats, a punishment the natives use against their enemies.

The Lord did not wish to kill the people of that village, but only to frighten them, because in spite of the many shots that the Spaniards fired, not one enemy was killed. Instead, when Sergeant José de Tapia, a Pampango, was running after a native, cutlass in hand and ready to strike a blow, he was stopped by some branches of a tree and fell to the ground, at which the native fled, leaving behind six lances so that he might run faster. This barbarian learned nothing from experience, for he was found three months later throwing lances at our men from ambush and was shot by one of our soldiers with an arquebus, was badly wounded, and died after a few days.

The Spaniards, having completed this undertaking without having received any harm from the lances of the barbarians, and because it was now midday, set out toward Agadña, and in the villages along the route that had been confederates of the village of Funhon for the defense of Matapang, they burned a number of houses without being hampered by the enemy, who followed after them and harassed them without trying to fight, which they were afraid to do. They wanted only to delay our men in order that they might overtake them at night, so that they could, with the help of darkness, execute some treachery. Matapang followed along close to the shore in a small boat, shouting encouragement to his friends. He arrived at a safe distance from our men, who were walking along the beach and called out, "I am Matapang. You have delayed long in coming." The soldiers answered him with ten or twelve musket balls, and in spite of their being good shots, not one wounded him. The fathers believed that Father San Vitores was guarding the life of the man who had murdered him until he should have time to repent and gain eternal life. But the barbarian persisted in his pride and pertinacity; at the moment

*The State of the Christian Community in the Mariana Islands*

when he was about to throw a lance at our men, he was stopped by a musket ball fired by a soldier named José López.

Just when our men thought they were out of danger, they encountered the worst of all, from which they could not have escaped were they not favored by the strong arm of the Lord. The enemy, which now consisted of nine confederated villages, had closed the road with tree trunks and brush, to oblige our men to go by way of the beach, which they had likewise planted with sharp points. The natives themselves were waiting on some high rocks near the road, from which point they could harass our men easily, but where our men could not reach them.

Captain Juan de Santiago, who moved in front of his men touching the ground with his lance (he had experience of the tricks of the barbarians) found the sharp points and guided his men into the sea, which now at high tide occupied part of the road. They waded in water up to their waists. More than half the soldiers had passed, when the enemy, hidden in the rocks and angry at seeing their plan frustrated, raised a loud outcry and began to throw lances and roll down stones from the cliff to the sea trying to crush the soldiers and kill them. At the same time, our men were attacked from the sea by natives in boats, who threw lances as if they had no fear of our arms. Those on land had a very superior place from which to attack; while those in the water were protected by their boats, which they steered with great ease as if they were round shields, and diving into the water, they laughed at our fire. The natives had thrown more than five hundred lances and had wounded two soldiers of the rear guard, whom Captain Juan de Santiago went back to aid. Another soldier was later wounded in the ankle, while the captain received a lance in his shoulder right to the bone. The natives were delighted with this success and began to celebrate their victory and make fun of the Spaniards, but soon their laughter was dissolved in tears, for a soldier named Lorenzo Berte, who had been struck by a stone, shot a ball with such dexterity that he hit a native who thrust his head out of the water and killed him. Captain Juan de Santiago said to the enemy that his own wound, over which they were rejoicing, was nothing of importance and advised them to see if the death of their neighbor was not more worthy of notice. Placing his wounded men in the center of the group of soldiers, himself remaining as rear guard, he managed to pass in good order along the shore, from time to time frightening, if not wounding, the enemy, who were alarmed, and with reason, by the valor of our soldiers, comparable to similar deeds that Spaniards have done in America and Asia. The natives retired, not daring to engage in land warfare with those men who in the water had shown themselves so valiant.

The soldiers arrived in Agadña, giving thanks to God for having liberated them from grave danger. And truly it appeared to be a miraculous providence of the Lord that even one escaped with his life, for the *Marianos* are exceedingly dexterous in throwing their lances and in making them fall like rain over our men, and on this occasion there were particular circumstances of note. A soldier named Martín de Uriza had the brim of his hat pinned to the crown but did not receive the slightest

*Book Five, Chapter 7*

injury. Later three more lances passed through the hat and did not harm the wearer. Several soldiers knew the experience of having lances pass through their clothing without being themselves in the least harmed. From this engagement four came out with wounds, of whom Captain Juan de Santiago recovered quickly. God wished to crown the labors of the other three, as we piously believe, in heaven, with a happy death in defense of justice, the Faith, and the ministers who preach it.

One of these men was Pedro Basijan, a native of the village of Salug, in the Visayas, who came to these islands with Father Francisco Solano (June 9, 1671) and fought in the war of Guam (September and October 1671), demonstrating at that time his bravery and zeal. On this latter occasion, he begged to go with the party to serve the Christian community in whatever manner he could, and after having shown much valor in that encounter in the water, was wounded in the heel by a thrown lance. The wound itself was not serious, for the lance was not of bone but of wood, but the convulsions that followed, probably caused by the wound having been wet, increased to the extent that the man died on May 26, 1672, having first received the last sacraments with great devotion.[270] God thus repaid with a death that was full of the beauties of eternal salvation his work done in this mission without thought of temporal returns.

Another who was wounded at this time by a lance that was driven through his leg was Juan Beltrán, of the Province of Cinaloa. They drew out the lance, which was made of a human bone. He seemed, after a few days, to have recovered, but as a small piece of bone had inadvertently been left in the flesh, he died on June 6, 1672, in the same manner as did the other soldier. He came to these islands when he was past fifty years old, with a desire to serve God and died in the hope of being with him for an eternity.

The third was José de Torres, who has been mentioned before in this book.[271] He was a native of Puebla de Los Angeles, a carpenter, in which capacity he served God and his Mother, making crosses and sawing wood for the construction of churches. He suffered intolerable agony from the wound received in this battle, the kind of suffering that is always caused by the poison from the human bones used as lance tips. But he bore his suffering with singular patience and conformity to the will of God, which is easy to believe, since he said that the Mother of Mercy consoled him in his last hours, making the devil flee when he tried to disturb him, and encouraging him to trust in the divine mercy, and on May 28, 1672, he died after receiving all the sacraments.

The Lord gained very good results from the punishment of these natives, who know no other rein but fear, because on the day following this skirmish, May 18, the natives from three villages in the southern part near Agadña, which were called Aniguag, Asan, and Tepungan, came to celebrate peace and friendship with the Spaniards, bringing them presents of rice and coconuts.

---

[270] Did they regard Agaña Bay as polluted? The population seems to have been dense in this area.

[271] Was this the *Indio* named Torres, mentioned in Book 3, chap. 7:196 (August 1668)? If so, was he an Amerindian?

*The State of the Christian Community in the Mariana Islands*

Their offer of friendship was accepted on three conditions: (1) that they send their children twice a week to Agadña to recite Christian doctrine; (2) that they destroy the public house occupied by the *urritaos* and unmarried girls; (3) that they attend Mass on all feast days. The first condition was easily fulfilled, since the children went to hear the doctrine because they were attracted by the beads and bright stones that the fathers gave them. But the second and third conditions they did not wish to meet, although they were repeatedly urged to do so. Although the fathers went out frequently to invite them to the Mass, there were few who attended.

The same day on which peace was concluded with these three villages, some of the enemy came secretly to the sentry house where the nephew of Agao was detained, who, as we saw, was made prisoner at the skirmish and was being held as a hostage for bargaining. They were heard by our soldiers and fled together with other villagers who awaited at some distance the results of their attempt to free the prisoner.

On this day Father Solano went out with some soldiers to cut coconuts for food. One of them was high up in the tree when a lance came flying at him, hurled by the enemy lurking in the brush. Our soldiers pursued them and came across others, who although not in ambush, were, none the less, enemies. Our soldiers could well have castigated them justly, but were restrained by Father Solano, who exemplifying the piety and charity he had learned from Father San Vitores, wished to try again, in spite of all his disappointments, to see if with kindness he could not tame these wild people. But hatred of the Faith had made them obstinate and they wished to banish it from their islands. For this reason they warned their children not to attend the doctrine, and on May 28, 1672, they tried to set fire to a church that was on the other side of the river, thrusting long poles with flaming ends into the thatched roof. They were surprised at this by the soldiers who fired a musket at them, whereupon they fled leaving in flames the roof made of palm leaves. But the Lord anticipated the danger to his house with a shower, which was soon repeated. And so on the following day, they found the long incendiary poles on the roof of the church consumed by fire and the roof itself unharmed. But later they removed the roof as a danger to the church and then moved the church inside the palisade that the soldiers had built for their defense, and there the fathers then built a better edifice, which they dedicated towards the end of June (1672) with a procession of the Blessed Sacrament, dances, and every kind of entertainment they could think of in order to give the natives a happy festival. The *fiesta* was attended by natives from various villages.

On the island of Tinian, or Buenavista Mariana, the Christian community was at equal risk, but came off more safely than Guam, no doubt because of the special favor of the Blessed Virgin, who had visited that island, so that it remained peculiarly her own. Father San Vitores had sent Father Alonso López to this island with four lay companions. It was this group that could not be reached when Father San Vitores sent word to all the missionaries to return for safety to Agadña. After the

391

death of Father San Vitores, several letters were sent to them, but not one arrived at its destination.

Father Alonso López was unaware of the situation of the Christian community on Guam, and so he sent four friendly natives there and they arrived safely. Father Solano quickly sent them back with news of what had taken place. The messengers delayed a long time on the return trip, I know not whether out of their own carelessness or through the cunning of the enemy, who seized this opportunity to incite the island of Tinian against the father and his companions. For some *Indios*, natives of Saipan (San José), returning from Guam to their own land, spread in Tinian a rumor that the Spaniards had seized the *Tinianos* who had carried the letters and had imprisoned them, killing one of their number.

The people of Sungaron, the village in which the messengers had lived, were aroused by the weeping of the wives and relatives of the men and went to complain to the father. He was able to calm them somewhat, refuting with sensible arguments the bad news that the natives themselves did not quite believe, since it circulated on poor authority. He assured them that they would soon see their friends and relatives.

He was assisted on this occasion by a chief named Cayza, who was always loyal to the fathers. He now persuaded the people of the village that the story of the men of Saipan was a lie. He had even before this demonstrated his loyalty, for he and other nobles had several times been approached with a suggestion that they kill Father López, but he said that he did not wish to do so nor to be ungrateful to one who had done him so many favors and who gave him what he needed. He added that his parents and grandparents had received the fathers on the island, and he had no desire to kill them; and since he was but a boy (he was 28 years old), he could not do what they would not have done.

Father López at once sent a Visayan, Francisco Maunahun by name, to bring back the Tinian messengers from Guam, and so convince the people that they were safe. This Francisco arrived on Guam on May 13 and soon returned with the men whom he met on the road, very happy, and proudly displaying all that the fathers had given them, shells, beads, and other articles. Thus was the false rumor dispelled and with it the danger to Father López and his companions, who could now proceed as before with their labors in the vineyard and with the harvest of baptisms and conversions.

A disturbance on the island of Santa Ana (Rota), near Guam, was in progress at this time. A confusing report had reached Agadña that the island of Santa Ana was in an unsettled state, and because of this Father de San Basilio, who was ready to sail for Tinian to assist Father López, was detained here. The Lord wished at that time to protect his life, which he would surely have lost if he had been on Santa Ana, as he would have been on his way to Tinian.

Father Solano charged Francisco Maunahun to put in at Santa Ana on his way to Tinian, and having procured accurate information there, to bring it to Guam. This zealous Christian did so and did more

*The State of the Christian Community in the Mariana Islands*

than was asked of him, since Father López had warned him not to stop at Santa Ana on his return journey to Guam because of the serious disturbances there. But judging the hearts of other men by his own, he was certain that these islanders could not be such ingrates as to kill him, for he had done them many favors during the years he had been in these islands.

But it did not turn out as he had expected, for after he had disembarked with a companion, a fellow Filipino, some natives of Guam who were at that time on Santa Ana, attacked his companion. They threw a rope around his neck and dragged him around and pierced him with lances. With a knife they stabbed Francisco Maunahun in the stomach and cast both bodies into the sea.

I do not call this a misfortune but rather a favor and grace of the Lord, this death that the enemies of Christianity meted out to these two Christians. The enemy wished to kill them because they were co-workers with those who worked for the extension of Christianity. These two Christians had assisted greatly in preaching the gospel and had administered holy baptism to many. They did not die unprepared, for before sailing from Tinian, they had confessed and received Communion, and for some time past had shown by their Christian lives that they were chosen for beatitude.

Francisco Maunahun was a native of the village of Indan, in the Philippines, and was one of the survivors of the shipwrecked galleon *Concepción*. He was living on Almagan when Father Luis de Morales arrived there, sent by Father San Vitores. When this man heard about the father, he went at once to find him and he soon joined with our fathers to help as much as he could in the apostolic ministry. He showed how deeply the Faith was rooted in his heart, since it still lived on during all those years amid a free-living population. He was, throughout four years, a faithful companion to the fathers, baptizing in their absence and teaching according to his abilities. During his last two years he was alone in the care of Agrigan and the church there, named for Saint Francis Xavier, and he attended to all the baptisms and Christian doctrine classes. He had returned to Guam (hoping to take some of the fathers back to the island) when he met the reward of his labors and zeal in that death that he met at the hands of the barbarians, in the form described on June 5, 1672.

His companion, whose name I have not found, was a Filipino who had been in the islands about three years. He came here with the desire to help the *Marianos*, which he did at the price of much suffering and danger. He accompanied the fathers many times on their mission journeys and spent two years in the islands of Gani (to which the fathers could not come) where he married and whence he brought his wife that she might not offend God, God to whom he offered so many souls, opening the doors of heaven to the children by means of baptism and instructing adults in the path to heaven, until the barbarians opened it for him, giving him a fortunate death in the company of Francisco Maunahun. After his death, his wife returned to her own country.

The often-repeated blows that were menacing the whole Christian community of these islands profoundly wounded the heart of Father Francisco Solano and were sufficient to hasten his death, which occurred on June 13, 1672, exactly one year after his arrival in the Marianas. But he labored in such a manner that by the vote of his companions he should be counted among those who accomplished most for the Christian community, because of the enterprises he was able to advance, even before he arrived here.

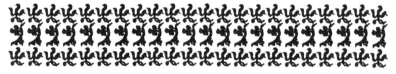

# CHAPTER VIII

### A Brief Account of the Virtues of
### Father Francisco Solano, Companion of Father San Vitores

Father Francisco Solano was born of distinguished parents in Jarandilla, in the diocese of Placencia. After he had learned his letters in Spain, he went to Rome together with Father Pedro González de Mendoza when the latter accompanied his nephew, His Excellency the Duke of Infantado, who was appointed ambassador to that government. In Rome he pursued literary studies, and through the favor of the ambassador, he obtained close to a thousand ducats in benefices, with which he returned to Spain, very well off, in the company of the same Father Pedro González and with hopes of gaining greater income and higher dignities. He studied philosophy in our Colegio de Oropesa, crowning it with a brilliant grand act, or public defense (*acto*). But soon he gave up those sources of income and all those hopes and ambitions in order to follow the penniless Jesus in his Society. I do not know but that his first disillusionment with this world came with a serious illness that befell him in Jarandilla at the time of his studies. There, he was visited by Father San Vitores, who at the time was minister of the *colegio*. He saw that Francisco was down-hearted at the thought of death, and so he encouraged him with the hope that he would not die of that illness. He said that they would be great friends, and in this it seems that the Venerable Father prophesied in his unassuming manner that Father Solano would enter the Society and sail for the Indies.

Be this as it may, he did ask later with great earnestness to enter the Society, and he was received in the Colegio Imperial on September first, 1657, at the age of twenty-two and a half. In accordance with that rejection of worldly ideals that brought him into the religious life, he advanced in it and was a most exemplary novice, so that the master of novices was constrained to mitigate his fervor with the rules of prudence, lest he ruin his health with penances and mortifications. From the novitiate in Madrid he went on to Alcalá to study theology, and through his association with Father San Vitores, who was in that *colegio*, he renewed his fervor. And since Father San Vitores was then planning to go to the Indies, he pleaded and insisted so much with God in prayer and penance and with his superiors, by revealing the longing the Lord gave him for the conversion of the infidels, that at last he succeeded in being one of those chosen out of the many who desired to go with the Venerable Father San Vitores, with whom he sailed to Mexico in 1660. He wrote a letter to *don* Jerónimo de San Vitores giving an account of the works of charity, humility, and zeal practiced by his son during this voyage. In these works he doubtless had a great part, serving the sick in the ship and teaching Christian Doctrine to the ignorant. His greatest desire, ever since he became a companion of Father San Vitores, was to imitate his apostolic spirit for the good of his own soul and that of others, as he later did in Mexico, in the Philippines, and the Marianas.

There was no greater testimony in his praise than the letters of Father San Vitores. In one, which he wrote from Mexico to Father Juan Gabriel Guillén, dated March 4, 1662, he mentions how well everything was going with all those who sailed with him from this Province of Toledo, and he adds: "Father Solano is confirming in a singular manner the hopes that he has always inspired of the great service he would give to our Lord in his vocation, in his studies, his observance of the rule, and his zeal for souls. It is in great measure due to him that the *Acto de Contrición* was established here. With his winning presentation he has attracted many to this holy exercise, etc." He even says more in one phrase, as we see in another letter to Father Guillén from Manila on July 2, 1664. He speaks of the great qualities those should possess who wish to sail to the Indies, and he remarks that those who are not endowed with the solid spirit of Saint Ignatius and Saint Francis Xavier, with their obedience, humility, and great purity, are harmful persons. As an example of those who should go, he mentions Father Solano, saying: "It would be a great help if many came over of the type of our Francisco Solano." In other letters he praises him constantly in every respect, and truly he lived up to this praise until his death.

Together with thirteen companions he was left behind in New Spain when Father San Vitores sailed for the Philippines in 1662. This happened because there was not enough room on the ship, and he deeply regretted the loss of Father San Vitores's amiable company. He eventually set sail at the beginning of March 1663. The voyage was most dangerous, as much on the sea as on land, where he traveled a hundred and fifty leagues after disembarking, partly on foot and partly riding on a cow that served as a horse, until he reached Manila. But all this hardship seemed light to him, because he bore it all for the love of Jesus Christ, to whom, as he remarks, he offered what he was suffering and what yet remained for him to suffer. But it all seemed even easier when he saw Father San Vitores, who went out to meet him at a *doctrina*, a mission that the Society has outside Manila. Father Solano exclaims that he cannot describe the joy he felt. In Manila, he completed the little that remained of his course in theology and learned the language. As much as he could, he assisted Father San Vitores in his ministries until, in February 1665, he was sent to the mission of the Visayas, on the island of Negros, which is one of the islands of the *Pintado*s, where he stayed for three years, generously serving our Lord, although I am not aware of the details of his work, which will be reported in the history of that province. From this mission, he was transferred to that of the *Substanos*, the people who live along the rivers, where their hamlets are situated. This mission is on the island of Mindanao and the natives are barbarians and ignorant. Here, he stayed for six months,with much pleasure, as he describes it, and it would be a pleasure for him, who gave all to our Lord, since it was a most difficult mission, the most remote from Manila. It would seem that God willed this to be a novitiate for him for the mission of the Marianas.

*A Brief Account of the Virtues of Father Francisco Solano*

The harvest of his labors in the Philippines was a great one, for great was his fervor and zeal for the conversion of souls. However, I am ignorant of particular details, except for those that he mentions in a letter written from Iloilo to *don* Jerónimo San Vitores in the following words: "Although I am not worthy of these apostolic enterprises, our Lord has been served by assigning me to this little mission in this year of 1667, ten leagues distant from the college where I reside. In this mission four Gentiles were converted to our holy Faith. According to the account they gave me of their age, each of them is almost a hundred years old, and although they have lived for sixty years among Christians, they have always been hard to convert. I sought them out in their fields and by reasoning and the grace of God, they most sincerely asked for the grace of baptism, which they received on the Sunday within the octave of the Assumption, to the great joy of my soul. And now in their decrepit age they are so encouraged that they made their way to Mass on the following Sunday to the place where I said it, and they have learned enough of the Christian doctrine."

From the time Father San Vitores began to offer himself for the mission of the Ladrones, Father Solano expressed strong desires to be his companion; and although he failed to make it on the first voyage, he tried with prayers, tears, and fervent observance to merit it from God. When he first made his request, Father San Vitores wrote to encourage him even more, but told him that he was not yet ripe for that mission, as he confessed of himself with humility in a letter to Father Guillén: "May God ripen me with his grace, for the day when new companions may be sent to the mission!" God granted his desire when he was brought back from Mindanao to be minister in Manila, and he volunteered again. Along with fulfilling his duties as minister, he used to handle with great care all the affairs of the Marianas. Likewise, with the help of the grammar of the Mariana language composed by Father San Vitores, which was sent to Manila, and the instruction by a native of the Marianas who came to Manila on the ship that left Father San Vitores in the Marianas (and to whom he had taught the Christian doctrine), he was learning that language. Meanwhile he kept urging the governor of Manila to send a ship to New Spain in the hope of sailing on it.

After repeated petitions, made with due indifference, he was granted the desired permission. Father Francisco Ezquerra, of whom we will speak in due time, was also granted permission to sail in a ship that was to depart for New Spain in the year 1670. And in order not to be a burden to the Philippine Province of the Society in this voyage and to be able to bring some help to the Mariana Islands, they went about from door to door asking for alms, repugnant though it was to Father Solano. They embarked about the month of July. I shall not tell of all the works of zeal and charity that they practiced on this voyage toward the sick and the other passengers, helping the former in all those humble services dictated by mercy and teaching to all the way to heaven. Suffice it to say that Father Solano was a true disciple of Father either by himself or with his companions. In everything he showed himself most fervent, suffering not a few hardships because of his zeal and bearing them with great patience. He even made use of the rations he received as ship's chaplain (without in any way diminishing the supply for his mission) to feed the beasts he was bringing along for it. He arrived in the Marianas on June 9 of this same year, together with Father Ezquerra and Father Diego Noriega, who was in the company of the mission of Father Andrés de Ledesma. They were received with great charity and joy by Father San Vitores. The joy of Father Solano was such that he shed tears, as he describes it, on seeing Father San Vitores, whose clothes were all patches and his cap made of palm leaves, but whose face was that of an angel.

Father Solano first made the spiritual exercises of our father, Saint Ignatius, and then, since he had a considerable knowledge of the language and an ardent desire to benefit the *Marianos*, he began at once on the island of Guam to work for the salvation of those barbarians, since among them, he encountered many recalcitrant individuals infected by the teachings of Choco. He combined gentleness and sternness, promises and threats; for this he incurred the hatred of many who desired to live in a freedom that could not bear the yoke of the Law of the Lord. Father San Vitores assigned him to the island of Santa Ana (Rota), which is close to Guam. But he was prevented from going there because of the disturbances and the war that broke out in that same year, 1671. He was principally responsible for establishing peace on the island of Guam, thanks to his bravery, zeal, and prudence, for Father Solano had a great heart and an ardent zeal that made him despise death and even yearn for it, for the sake of our holy religion. Consequently, he exposed himself to manifest danger of losing his life, whenever it was necessary for the glory of God and the good of the Christian community. This Christian courage was shown during the siege that our soldiers endured for forty days, for when eight of them sallied forth (the others were all too ill to move), he always accompanied them to hear their confessions in case any one of them should be wounded. He carried no other defense than a staff in his hands and a small round shield to fend off the lances of the enemy, and he showed such spirit on these occasions that the barbarians themselves admitted that, unarmed as he was, he put more fear in them than the soldiers with all their arms.

I say nothing of the other hardships that he bore in this siege, taking his turn at guard duty like the other religious, his share being considerably greater, since he watched even when it was not his turn. He slept very little, and this while exposed to the inclemency of the weather, in order to be alert for any attack of the enemy. This loss of sleep was no less due to his spirit of mortification, which led him to take on the worst and most laborious jobs for himself. On one occasion, his companions forced him to take a blanket, because he did not desire even that protection against the weather, but the natives, seeing the white color of the cover, began to throw stones at him. Without any show of impatience, he simply moved to another place for a little rest. Many were the hardships and dangers undergone by all the companions in the siege of Guam, but the dedication of Father Solano surpassed that of all the rest.

*A Brief Account of the Virtues of Father Francisco Solano*

The enemies of Christ bore a deadly hatred of Father Solano because of his zeal. They wounded him, not only with the sword of their tongues, ever sharpened against him, but they threatened him with their spears, desiring to kill him, and many a time they tried to do it. On one occasion some natives tried to ambush him. But he got wind of it and went another way and so saved himself from their treachery. When he was in a certain village together with Father San Vitores, a boy called Ambrosio informed him that the natives of that village had decided to kill him, and so by order of Father San Vitores, he left the village at eleven o'clock that night. This is the reason why the Venerable Father would not allow him to go to all the missions he wished to visit, namely to save that life, which was so needed by that new Church. This was a double mortification for his charity, which yearned to meet death for Christ and to bring Christ's life to the enemies of their Redeemer. Father San Vitores ordinarily kept him in the residence of Agadña, where besides teaching and administering the sacraments, he arranged to build a palisade, so that the Spaniards and the missionaries would have some defense against attacks of the barbarians, which are always to be feared, even when they show themselves most friendly. And to encourage the soldiers by his example, he himself carried poles and coconut trunks on his shoulders and acted as an ordinary laborer.

When Father San Vitores suffered martyrdom, Father Solano succeeded him as superior, much as he held himself unworthy of the office. At the first opportunity, a month after the death of Father San Vitores, he wrote to Father Provincial of the Philippines begging him to send another superior because of his inaptitude for governing those islands. But the zeal that he displayed during the short time he lived after the death of Father San Vitores, proved that after the death of the master, the most deeply regretted was that of the disciple of his teachings and virtues. Indeed, it seemed that our Lord wished to show that Father San Vitores still lived on in the person of Father Solano, as we see in an event that took place eight days after the martyrdom of the Venerable Father. We have spoken before of a native chief named Quipuha, who took to himself the wife of another native, with whom he lived in open concubinage, to the scandal of Christians and pagans.[272] Father Solano tried to separate him from this bad company, just as Father San Vitores had tried previously. But he answered as he had before, "I would rather go to hell than part with her." Father Solano told him with great sternness, "Think twice about what you are doing, for tomorrow you may die." Quipuha burst out laughing, but God who is not mocked, fulfilled the threat—or was it the prophecy of his servant? On the next day, while going to work with his mistress, without any sickness or accident, he fell dead in her presence, a thing that struck fear in those who already had some fear of God.

When the ship from the Philippines arrived, sick as he was, he boarded it and labored so tirelessly at the dispatch of letters and other affairs that he seemed about to die then and there. He returned to the

---

[272]See Book 3, chap. 16:247.

residence more afflicted by the troubles of the Christian community than by his illness. He fell on his bed, from which he repeatedly arose, his spirit making up for the weakness of his body, so that he might attend to the obligations of his office. During this short time, the events narrated in the preceding chapters took place. In his sickness he would not allow that anything be done for him that was not done for the healthy. So that he would eat meat, it was necessary that his companions obliged him to do so as a matter of conscience. He practiced all the virtues and wished so much to be released and to be with Christ that when he recovered somewhat, he said that he regretted that he had not died then,[273] since his affairs were so well in order, as he had carefully managed with the talents God had given him. And that is how he died, with great peace, without the anguish that is wont to come with death, on June 13, 1672, after receiving all the sacraments. His body, although quite exhausted, had such an air of holiness that it seemed alive and moved all who viewed it to tenderness and veneration.

  Among all the virtues of this Venerable Father, the one that shone brightest was the queen of all of them and all the more in a minister of the gospel: the love of God and of the souls redeemed with his blood. He frequently made acts of the love of God, and he spared no effort that men might know and love him. To this end he humbled himself, he prayed, he suffered insults, which were not few, he was vigilant, and took every means his zeal inspired him. He longed to die for Christ, but held himself unworthy of that honor and envied those who won such great good fortune, as we read so often in his intimate letters. However, although he did not die at the hands of the barbarians, his death deserves to be called martyrdom, for it was occasioned by the hardships and cares that he bore for the propagation of the Faith and by those that were brought about by the barbarians themselves who persecuted the Faith that he tried to spread. And since the enemies of Christ saw him as their enemy, he deserves to be accounted one of the greatest teachers and benefactors they ever had. Those who later followed him can take as a model the one whom Father San Vitores called the model missionary to the Indies. For this reason, as the good lamented his death, the wicked and the pagans rejoiced, thinking that it would be easy to pull down the edifice of Christianity in the Marianas, lacking the support of this column, but they soon felt the presence of another Father Solano or San Vitores in the person of the Venerable Father Francisco Ezquerra, who succeeded them in the office of superior, as we shall see in the following chapter.

---

[273] Phil. 1:23. He was still very ill with tuberculosis.

# CHAPTER IX

*Happenings in the Mariana Islands After the
Death of Father Francisco Solano*

Five days after the death of Father Solano, on June 13, 1672, the enemy, believing that now there was no one to resist them, began shouting, according to their custom, as a signal to begin a battle. Our soldiers paid no attention to their shouts but went out as usual to look for *rimai* for their food. The natives did not dare to attack them in the open field but hid in the trees and kept on shouting. The soldiers took offense at this and burned twelve houses. This demonstration inspired some fear among the natives, but these did not desist from their intent. The soldiers had freed the nephew of Agao in order that the natives might realize that they had come to their land not to make captives of them but to bring them the true liberty of the gospel. The natives supposed that this clemency was fear, gathered a crowd and often came to Agadña to yell and throw stones. But they never came within a musket shot, and when our men went out to face them, they turned and ran. I do not know whether it was fear or artifice, for on one of these occasions a soldier, called Matías Altamirano, moving out in front, fell into an ambush from which they threw six or eight lances, whereupon he coolly fired a shot with his musket and put them to flight, himself unscathed. He enjoyed a special providence of the Lord that His Divine Majesty had instilled such fear in the barbarians that they did not dare to engage the Spaniards who could not have overcome so great a throng.

In order to deserve these favors from God, the fathers made solemn supplications and held processions, reciting the litanies, and imploring the help of God and the saints. The soldiers cleared the land around our house to the distance of a musket shot to keep the enemy from finding cover and so coming too close to our house. The *Indios* felt this keenly, and in consequence, they built a wall and trench (*trinchera*) on the beach to block the way to their villages. The wall was made of coral and rocks from the sea, where it was protected by a rocky hillside, at a distance of an eighth of a league from Agadña.

Here they gathered, and at the approach of our soldiers, they began to throw rocks and lances among our soldiers, but by the grace of God, they did not hurt any of them, nor were our men injured by the barbs with which they sowed the paths over which our soldiers would pass. Occasionally, a few of the natives would approach our camp and call out blasphemies against God, showing on every occasion the cause of their hatred of the Spaniards, but as soon as they realized that their presence was known, they ran away faster than they had come.

Realizing that the islands were in danger of worse uprisings than they had as yet experienced, Father Francisco Ezquerra wrote to Father Alonso López on Tinian, advising him to return to Guam with his companions, to save their lives and augment the number of soldiers on Guam, who were now very few, for so many had met death at the hands of the barbarians. By the will of God the letter arrived safely, and it was no small favor, for the island of Santa Ana (Rota) was in rebellion and it was on the route of any boat sailing to Tinian. And it was an even greater providence that they found a boat that was sailing for Guam and which would not touch at Zarpana (Rota). Father López left the island of Tinian in the best possible order, to the end that all might be in readiness for any minister of the gospel who might come there, himself or another. His ministry was crowned with good results in baptisms and catechumens.

There was no lack of work and sacrifice for the fathers among the soldiers in the *residencia* in Agadña, for while the religious can only follow the path of love and of words to correct faults, this means does not serve for all. They preached fervent sermons to the soldiers every Sunday and tried to maintain the orderly and devoted congregations that Father San Vitores had formed, persuading them to frequent the confessional and Communion, urging them to perform the spiritual exercises of our father, Saint Ignatius, preparing them for death or martyrdom, which they might well fear or expect among so many enemies. Those who performed the spiritual exercises showed forth in their work the progress of their souls. They soon constructed a church and house, for since the typhoon of September 8, 1671, they had been in temporary quarters, and they surrounded the buildings with a stockade to protect them from invasion by the barbarians.

Not content with the work they were able to accomplish in Agadña, the fathers went out on various missionary journeys, covering more than half the island, part of which was more peaceful, although they were often in danger. They were deaf to the threats of those whom they knew to be enemies and even to the voices of the *Indios* who were friendly and who tried to warn them not to expose their lives to danger. And on these spiritual journeys they performed a great many baptisms in spite of the devil who always tried to revive the words of Choco.

One day as two of the fathers were leaving the village of Fuuña to go to the beach with several lay companions, some Christian natives advised them that certain settlements along the way had determined to kill them. They were not afraid but commended their undertaking to God, by the intercession of the Blessed Virgin. Trusting in this protection, they visited a third of the villages along the beach, gaining many children, who found in the waters of baptism the life of grace. This success they could attribute to the fact that they had gone out with better defense than at other times, for they had learned that the Faith, once introduced in the islands, needs some kind of escort that can defend it, without giving offense from those who try to banish it.

The fathers, seeing how far it was from Agadña to the usual anchorage of ships [San Antonio de Umatag], began to build a church in the village of Merizo, which is much nearer, under the patronage of Saint Dimas, the special devotion of Father Ezquerra, who attended to the building of the church with labor and care.

*Happenings in the Mariana Islands After the Death of Father Francisco Solano*

But realizing that there was also a dangerous distance to traverse in order for the Spaniards on the island to communicate with those on the ships, they decided that the village of Fuuña would be a better location, as it had many desirable features, both for receiving the ships and for spreading the Faith, and besides it was frequented by the *Indios* of the surrounding country.

Fuuña is celebrated among these natives, because they point out a rock there from which they believe that all men had their origin. It is near several harbors, and from one cape that points west northwest and which rises 36 to 48 feet above the sea, one can see at a great distance the ships that sail from Nueva España to the Philippines.[271] The sea bathes this cape, or cliff, on three sides, and hence it is inaccessible to enemies. The part that is continuous with the land can be easily guarded. It seems that nature or the Author of it foresaw this spot as a refuge for the Faith. And so they decided to build here a stronghold of the Christian religion, which is itself a temple of God.

When the fathers arrived at Fuuña they laid their plans before the natives of the place, who rejoiced that in their village there should be established a church and a residence. They gave the fathers the location they desired and helped them with the work of building, which was completed in a few months. The place was first cleared of all trees and underbrush. A house was erected, whose principal part served as a church, dedicated to Saint Joseph, the spouse of the Virgin Mary.

In this house and church two fathers and some lay companions served. They went out frequently on mission journeys to the villages in the mountains, baptizing many children and instructing the adults in the Law of God and Christian customs. They had no little difficulty in convincing the villagers and those of other parts so as to undeceive them in the matter of that stone, Fuuña, the reputed mother of all peoples, since it was difficult to make them believe anything that would detract from the fame of their village.

On May 22, 1673, the galleon *San Antonio*, which followed a course between this island of San Juan and that of Santa Ana (Rota), assisted by fair weather, arrived at the port of Agadña. There it remained the necessary length of time to leave the assistance, which the royal piety of the queen, Her Majesty Mariana of Austria, sent to these islands by virtue of her royal *cédulas*, surely the gift of a higher Providence at the moment when the Christian community stood in its greatest danger and need.

She decreed, by her royal *cédula* of October 10,1671, that at the expense of the royal funds, assistance be sent to the ministers of the gospel in these islands. In another of August 19, of the same year, she decreed that the churches be decorated at the expense of the Royal Treasury of Mexico, and that from Nueva España there be sent more workers for this new vineyard of the Lord, as she ordered in a third *cédula*, dated November 16, 1671. In yet another decree of the same date, she ordered that two hundred Pampangos be sent from the Philippines, in order that

---

[271] Fuuña. See Book 3, chap. 9, n.146. The rock is Lalas Rock at Chalan Anite Point.

403

the fruits of these labors might be harvested in greater safety, as Father San Vitores had requested.

She issued another *cédula*, also on November 16, ordering that there be constructed in Nueva España or the Philippines, a ship to be sent to the Marianas, in order that the fathers could sail more easily among the islands and even discover new ones, whither they could not now go in the light craft of the country. In obedience to this order, the most honorable *Marqués* de Mancera, *don* Antonio Sebastián de Toledo, Viceroy of Mexico, sent to Manila from the Royal Treasury three thousand pesos for the construction of the ship.

Furthermore, Her Majesty decreed that cost should not be considered for a mission of so much glory to God and the good of souls. The part that depended on the viceroy of Mexico was attended to at once. The portion that fell to the governor of the Philippines we hope will be accomplished to the extent that the Marianas need it.

Realizing the importance of this matter, Father Francisco Ezquerra, superior of the mission of the Marianas after the death of Father Solano, sent Father Gerard Bouwens to Manila on the *San Antonio*, the same ship that brought out the royal *cédulas*. He was to solicit the construction of the ship and ask for passage to Guam for the Pampangos.

This governor was the avowed enemy of the mission in the Marianas, and in spite of all the pleas of Father Gerard, telling him what a great service it would be for God and the king to execute this order, he wished neither to send the Pampangos nor construct a vessel. But as it was necessary to comply in appearance with the orders of Her Majesty, he ordered the chief master who builds ships in the Philippines to build a boat, giving the proportions of length and width. To this the master replied that he could not construct a vessel in the form prescribed, since it would drown anyone who tried to sail in it. But the order was repeated so many times that, at last, without further argument, he built it to these measurements.

He built it thus against his will and when the hulk was built, while it was still without planking, without masts, without rigging, without proper nails, and lacking other requirements, the governor ordered that it be put on board the *San Telmo*, in which Father Bustillos and Father Gerard were sailing, so that upon their return, they were to leave it in the Marianas and were to write to Her Majesty and the viceroy of Mexico how he had acted, namely that he had fulfilled the command of Her Majesty.

The two fathers, who well knew what had happened, informed the archbishop, who was also the viceroy, upon their arrival in Acapulco.

His Excellency ordered that the boat be put ashore. He also ordered, in the name of Her Majesty, the pilots, sailors, officers, and other competent persons to state under oath what they thought about the boat. They all swore that anyone who set sail in it would most surely be drowned because of the disproportion and other essential defects.

The captain of the galleon, because he was a creature of the governor of the Philippines, refused to let them examine the boat, having been ordered to leave it in the Marianas, near any of the islands they might pass. Some years before, all generals, admirals, and captains of ships had been ordered by the governor not to anchor in the Marianas or to visit the port of San Antonio or the island of San Juan (Guam).

This was the cause of increased insolence on the part of the barbarians, who could see the ships pass at a distance, not stopping and not evincing the least desire to punish their crimes and cruelties. Thus they lost their fear and killed more religious and laymen, as we will relate further on.

I shall not speak of the harm done by the governor, who, besides failing to send the Pampangos, also refused permission to several families who wished to come to Guam, families who would have been of great assistance to this Christian community.

It is no small advantage that history, which should do justice to all, has recorded this public scandal as a warning to others, although a better warning was the sudden death he suffered later. May God grant that by this temporal death, he may have atoned for all the harm he had done to the Christian community in the Marianas, so that all may know that above the powerful there is another more powerful, and over human tribunals there is the tribunal of God, where they judge the human judgments,and the judges are indicted, and where the powerful cannot resist the Supreme Judge.

Returning to the ship *San Antonio*: Among other useful things that the general, *don* Juan Durán Manfort, left in these islands was a horse, whose beauty and speed delighted the *Marianos*, for they had never seen such an animal. As soon as they heard of it, people came from all the other islands to see it and returned happy if they could take a few hairs from its mane to wear as an ornament.

The unmarried men, for some reason of their own, were accustomed to carry walking sticks, which they call *tuna* and which are curiously carved and colored with the root of a plant called *mangu*. At the head of this, they affix, through a hole, three streamers (half a yard in length and made from the soft bark of trees) with heavy threads in the form of tassels. In place of these threads, they now used the long hairs they had been fortunate enough to obtain from the horse. They brought the animal gifts of coconut to gain its friendship.

They praised the hardness of its teeth and the heat of its stomach, believing that it could masticate and digest iron, because it had a bit in its mouth. The arrival of the ship and the sight of the horse caused the enemy to retire inland. The fathers took occasion of this to send word to them to come and hear about the mysteries of the Faith, to put aside their fears and come with no fear of punishment.

A few began to come to church and it was hoped that others would follow, attracted by the kind treatment they had received. But seeing that the ship had gone to the Philippines after remaining here only three days without having administered any form of punishment, they realized that the Spaniards had no more strength than before. So

*Book Five, Chapter 9*

they went away without fear, saying that if the Spaniards tried to punish them, they would maintain their ancient liberty with a war.

Because of this, the fathers could not go far from Agadña, but they made as many mission visits as they could with conditions as they were; and God rewarded their zeal, giving them worthy fruits of their labors in the baptism of children and of adults who came to the church.

Matters ran more smoothly in the new residence of San José de Fuuña. Two fathers went out from that place on continual mission journeys to the villages along the shore and in the hills, with the result that they desired, for they baptized more than four hundred children and an increasing number of adults, rooting out the thorns that the common enemy of man had sown among the people in that period of persecutions and converting the territory again into a paradise, as it was in the time of Father San Vitores.

Children and adults hastened to hear the Christian doctrine, and in the mountains and along the beaches hymns were sung instead of the profane and fabulous native ballads. They now praised God, whose most perfect praise came from the mouths of innocent children.

These voices, which could well be heard in heaven, angered the infernal world against the ministers of the gospel, and it again tried to provoke the *Indios* to revolt. God permitted this in order that the roses might not be gathered without thorns, and that the desired harvest of souls should not be accomplished without hardship and danger. For after the fathers had been established four months in Fuuña, one after the other went out to visit the villages, in order that all might share the successes and the dangers that were increasing day by day, as the waves of the sea increase with the wind. They were informed by some Christian natives of the village of Pago that certain enemy *Indios* had prepared ambushes in several dangerous locations along their path. Thus it was necessary to return to Fuuña over rougher and poorly-defined paths and to suspend their plans for the time being.

Many times the fathers had appealed for peace, sending emissaries, but the natives only laughed at them. But on November 13, 1673, on the Feast of Blessed Stanislaus Kostka,[275] a young boy but a great saint of our Society, when peace was least suspected and most desired, the enemy came voluntarily to Agadña to ask for peace and submit to the Law of God. They offered their children for baptism in place of the *conchas*, by means of which peace was usually effected.

They were received with open arms and peace was agreed to on these conditions: that they be obedient to the precepts of God; that they bring their children to baptism, if they were not yet baptized; and that they go to church and attend Mass and religious instructions.

Many children and adults were baptized at this time, and those who had formerly been baptized were reconciled with the Church, receiving the other sacraments according to their need and capacity.

The missionaries, not content with the extension of the mission on Guam, which this new peace made possible, sent a father to the island

---

[275] Canonized in 1725, hence Blessed.

of Tinian, or Buenavista Mariana. But he could not make the voyage because contrary winds detained him for a month in the village of Ritiyan (Ritidyan) and other villages of Guam that he visited, baptizing more than fifty children and some adults, and administering the sacraments to the sick and dying and to others in need of them.

Thus, with the exception of a few enemy villages that have never accepted the Faith, all the island of Guam was visited during the year 1673, some villages several times: making new Christians, confirming those already of the Faith, uprooting vices, planting virtues, showing all the road to heaven by means of continual discussions, sermons, exhortations, gifts, caresses, and threats, trying by every means to attract the barbarians to the Faith and the Law of God, and to withdraw them from their former license and barbarous customs.

They were instructed in a pious custom, which was that when they met one of the fathers, in the place of the usual salutation, they said, "May the Blessed Sacrament of the Altar and the Immaculate Conception be praised." They frequently invoke the sweet names of Jesus and Mary on land and on the sea against the *aniti*, repeating their prayers with great devotion, erecting crosses, venerating images, especially those of Christ and his most Holy Mother, and showing the greatest reverence and devotion towards all sacred things. But most worthy of admiration has been the courage of certain Christian women, who in the midst of such unbridled liberty, have constantly resisted the pleas of those who sought them and have said, "God would be angry." Others, assaulted with violence, have cried out to be set free and have later complained of the aggressors to the fathers, begging their protection in order that they might not again find themselves in similar danger.

# CHAPTER X

### *The Happy Death of Father Francisco Ezquerra and Five Lay Companions*

The year 1673 was a happy year and a felicitous one because of the rich harvest of baptisms and corresponding fruits. But the following year, 1674, was a deadly one, from a human point of view, because of the many killings that covered it with blood. But to the eyes of faith it was a most glorious one and promised an abundant harvest, since "the blood of martyrs is the seed of Christians."[276]

All the religious had gathered on Christmas Day in the Residence of Saint Ignatius, in Agadña, in order to celebrate the birthday of Christ, our Lord, with greater solemnity and to discuss means for the progress of our mission. At the same time they were acquiring new inspiration and strength for work in the vineyard of the Lord during the restful days of the spiritual exercises of our father, Saint Ignatius. Their fruit was to be a spiritual renewal, according to the custom of our Society, in order to revitalize our neighbors by dealing and communicating with them. This holy activity was hardly over when Father Francisco Ezquerra's zeal could not bear any longer delay. He went to the Residence of San José de Fuuña, whence he went up to the villages of the mountain, since he knew that many children were recently born there and had to be baptized. He baptized up to two hundred and joyful at such a good hunt, he returned to the residence of Agadña to set things in order, as a good prelate and superior. Again, a few days later, he went to Fuuña, and tempted by his previous success, he went farther into the other villages of the mountain, though he knew he was risking his life. Yet his desire to give the life of grace to those who did not have it prevailed over everything. He spent thirteen days in these villages, instructing the adults, consoling the sick, administering the sacraments to those who needed them, and baptizing the recently-born. Over a hundred souls were added to the Church in so short a time by this Venerable Father; with such apostolic steps he was coming closer to the crown of martyrdom.

On the first of February, Father Ezquerra arrived at the village of Ati, which was on the shore of the sea. The port of San Antonio was there, where three years earlier he had disembarked when he arrived in these islands.[277] He spent the night there. On the following day, which was the Feast of the Purification of our Lady (February 2), in his desire to say Mass and give Holy Communion to the six lay companions whom he had brought along, he departed with them very early for the village of Fuuña, since he had not provided himself with the sacred vestments as he used to do on other mission journeys. He did not wish to burden his

---

[276]Tertullian, *Apologeticum*, chap. 50, no. 13: *Etiam plures efficimur,quotiens metimur a vobis. Semen est. Sanguis Christianorum*. We are found to be more numerous whenever you count us. The blood of Christians is a seed. *Corpus Christianorum*, vol.1, par. 1, Turnhout, Brepols, 1954.
[277]Umatac.

## The Happy Death of Father Francisco Ezquerra and Five Lay Companions

companions nor impede their way on such rough trails. They had hardly walked for one hour when they met four natives carrying a woman who had been for several days in extreme danger of death, caused by a difficult childbirth. She told him of the danger, and since she had been baptized, he heard her confession and administered the sacrament of Extreme Unction then and there. He always carried the holy oils and in any necessity or loss of consciousness would request permission to administer the sacrament. God rewarded him for his piety by giving him a precious death for such a Christian cause.

He was getting ready to administer the sacrament, when the natives began to resist his attempt, deceived by the long-standing teaching of Choco, who defamed the holy oils as well as baptism. He said that the anointing took the life of those who received it. It was easy to persuade the barbarians of this, because so many received this sacrament when they were dying. The Venerable Father insisted for a long time in his desire to administer the sacrament to the sick woman. Finally, the barbarians thrust him aside, left the woman on the ground, and began picking up stones and throwing them at him and his companions. They declared war on them for trying to kill with "oil of God," as they call the holy oils. When two of his companions had fled back to the town from which they came and the remaining four were returning little by little, Father Ezquerra kept on preaching to the barbarians, holding a crucifix in his hand and reprimanding them for the blasphemies, which, instigated by the devil, they were uttering against their Creator and Redeemer.

The natives realized that our men were few in number. Certain of victory, they called others to join them with spears and other arms and attacked them with barbarous rage and fury. Two of the companions, aware that they had no arms to defend themselves, fled in fear; but in their escape, one of them was struck by a lance that pierced his back. He threw himself into the water to escape by swimming. But they followed him and finished him off with thrusts of the lance.

This young man was called Sebastián de Ribera, a native of Manila. He had come to these islands in the year 1673. In that short time he had served the mission well, with great promptness and willingness, so that all the missionaries preferred to have him on their journeys. His example was a source of edification to all, and the Lord rewarded it with a holy death, for His Divine Majesty had provided that he carry no arms to defend himself nor did he permit that by fleeing should he lose what should be eagerly sought for.

When the barbarians had killed Sebastián de Ribera, they hunted for the other companion, whose name was Francisco González. But as they were pursuing this cruelty, he slipped into the mountain forest. Since they could not find him there, they set fire to several wooded areas in order to burn him to death or kill him, as he attempted to escape the fire. But God kept him safe for a while, because as they were looking for him, he dragged himself little by little through underbrush and high grass, until he was able to reach a point distant from the fire.

Venerable Father Ezquerra gained new courage on seeing death approaching so close, something he had desired all his life. He did not stop preaching the Law of God to those who hated it. Together with the two companions who were still with him, he moved away from the fire to the hill, and he threw into the fire the holy oils so that they would not be profaned by the hands of the barbarians. Now this man, who was so ready to meet God's judgment, a man whom the very shadow of sin filled with horror, prepared himself to die with acts of deepest devotion. He heard the confessions of his two companions, as appears from the account of the *Indios*, who said that the father and they were striking their breasts, and that the father was giving his blessing to his companions. This blessing was of course the absolution he was giving them and the fervent Acts of Contrition they were all making.

The barbarians were coming up the mountain, blaspheming against God. One of the companions remained at the summit, while the father, accompanied by the other, went down amidst the stones and spears hurled at them, to have them stop their blasphemies and to urge them to be converted to God, offering them pardon and peace. But they became more obstinate, as they kept on throwing stones and spears. The father's companion was wounded several times, and ultimately, with a foot wounded by a lance, his murder was deferred as he fell to the ground in agony. His name was *don* Luis de Vera Picazo, a native of the City of Manila and a member of a noble family. He had volunteered to remain in these missions at the time, it seems, when Father Ezquerra and his companions arrived in these islands. Here he labored tirelessly in the service of God for almost three years, amid continual dangers. He had been a companion of Venerable Father Diego Luis de San Vitores in the village of Nisichan, where he was staying when they killed the Venerable Father in Funhon (Tumon). He loved him tenderly, and for fifteen days his life was in continual danger, while he was hidden among some crags. He dared not return to the residence in Agadña, because all the trails were controlled by the enemy. This lasted until some good friendly natives took him to Agadña, God preserving his life so that he could lose it, or rather gain it, on a better occasion. And that he might merit such a fortunate death, a few days earlier, he cured him of a rather serious illness, during which he gave himself up to many salutary reflections on the vanity of this world, an ideal he embraced in these last days of his life. Then he died joyfully, pierced with many lances, encouraged the while by the Venerable Father Francisco Ezquerra, who remained at his side until he gave up his soul to his Creator.

While the Venerable Father was engaged in this work of mercy, one of those barbarians arrived and struck him on the arm and hand with a cutlass, on the hand that had saved so many souls from the captivity of Satan through holy baptism. The barbarian struck him so many times that the Venerable Father fell to the ground all bathed in his blood, invoking the sweet names of Jesus and Mary.

Others attacked him and inflicted wounds on his face and his head, screaming blasphemies against God, the sound of which tormented the soul of this lover of God. With streams of blood flowing down his face, head, and arms, he lost consciousness and appeared to be dead. So it seemed to those parricides who then began to strip off his clothes. Then, thanks to his virginal embarrassment, he recovered consciousness. He asked the barbarians to let him have at least a handkerchief to cover himself, since it was of no use to them. I do not know whether he obtained it. At least they were not able to withdraw from his hand, much as they tried to, a crucifix and an image of our Lady, which he held tightly. Christ crucified wished to remain with one who imitated him so well in his death, and Mary would not separate herself from such a favored son.

At this time the other two companions, who had returned to Ati from the main road, discovered the Venerable Father lying on the ground amid his dead companions. They tried to flee secretly to save their lives and seized the opportunity of a boat on the beach. They pushed off in it, but being without rudder or sail or even the experience of handling such boats, they upset the boat and fell into the water. The barbarians caught sight of them, left Father Ezquerra in his dreadful state, and with stones and spears finished off the men in the water and buried their bodies in the sea, leaving only the memory of them and that immortal.

One of them was called Pedro de Alejo, a native of Puebla de Los Angeles, in Nueva España.[278] He was a brave man, as he had proven on every occasion, but his solicitude and dedication to the missions was even greater, for he was a perennial companion to the fathers, who desired his company thanks to his charity, affability, and the good example that he gave to the Christians and Gentiles. He was the storekeeper, procurator, and cook, whenever the others took some rest from their labors. He found it so pleasant to serve the others and he did so with such good grace that there was no one whose goodwill he did not win. Not a few times he gave away his clothing to the natives in exchange for some sustenance for the religious and their companions. He bore so well the insults cast on him that he paid good for evil, showing greater affection towards those who tried his patience. With these virtues of a truly apostolic man he merited the fate mentioned above, having served the mission for almost two years. The other companion was Matías Altamirano, born in Guajaca. For almost two years he practiced the profession of physician in the Marianas, attending with great charity those who needed his assistance, dispensing with his rest to alleviate the sick. He was so dedicated to the missions and to the teaching of Christian doctrine that when he was accompanying some father he would anticipate his needs in caring for him and would question the *Indios* he met along the way. "How many persons are there in the Holy Trinity?" "How many Gods are there?" And he corrected them when they erred and he taught them what they did not know. He was more of a physician of souls than of bodies. With this, Matías merited the good fortune of dying in such a good cause.

While the killers were committing these murders, Father Ezquerra lay bathed in his blood, breathing fervent colloquies to Christ,

---

[278]The City of Puebla in Mexico.

naked on the cross, for whom he was dying naked, kissing the wounds of the crucifix that he held in his hands, remembering to call upon the loving mother of his Lord and hers, whose image he held that she might assist him in that hour. A youth of Fuuña happened to pass by, who had been instructed many times in the Faith by the blessed father. He looked at the Venerable Father with pity and gazed at him with loving eyes. That he might die preaching the gospel from that pulpit, the best he ever had, of his flowing blood, he asked him some questions about the Christian doctrine, which in other times he had taught him. Forgetting his own pain and mindful only of the pain that the native felt at his death, he said, "While living I was your father, and now in death I am still your father and always will be." He repeated these words, priding himself on being the father even of the ones who were taking his life. Another Christian *Indio* passed by and, halting in the presence of this pitiful sight, asked him, "Father, what is the cause of your death?" To this he replied, "Nothing but the desire to do good to you, to baptize your children, and to teach all the path to heaven." This native showed his indignation against the killers and wished to avenge his death. But the true disciple of Christ pacified him and said he should do no such thing, but that he should leave at once lest the killers come and do him some harm. And so he was alone again, speaking with Jesus and Mary, suffering the pain of his wounds and the burning sands of that shore, which were to his naked body like live coals adding new pain to his torments. At last the barbarians, having killed the two companions, returned and with renewed furor attacked the Servant of God and finished him off with repeated wounds, thus liberating the joyful spirit from that weak body, that he might receive the martyr's crown, which he had merited by an angelic life, as we have heard from the companions of the Venerable Father.

There still remained the companion of Father Ezquerra who was hidden on the hill. Their blood-lust up after five murders, the barbarians hunted him down and dispatched him with thrusts of their spears. His name was Marcos de Segura. He was born in Puebla de Los Angeles and he had come to the mission in 1673, where he served with his work and the example of his life. He was a nobly peaceful man, loved by all for the gracious courtesy with which he dealt with everyone, obedient to the ministers of the gospel, without restlessness or discord.

Finally, all the five who died together with Father Ezquerra were, in their zeal for the gospel, worthy companions of that illustrious martyr. They deserved to be such through the death that they suffered for the Faith, which they helped to spread in these islands, and for this reason were hated by the infidels and apostates who tried to expel Christ from these islands by assassinating the fathers and the Spaniards. The dead bodies of the six martyrs were thrown into the sea, lest buried on land they might infect it, as they said, with the oil of God. Thus the barbarians offered proof to the last act that all their cruel actions were caused by hatred for the sacrament of Extreme Unction and for the Faith that this sacrament brings with it.

The murderers' cruelty did not end here. As we said, Francisco González had evaded their hands. But that he might share in some way in the fate of his companions, his luck exposed him again to it. He had walked about two leagues through the thickets on the way to Fuuña. He thought he was finally close to it, and so he climbed down to the shore of the sea and arrived at the planted fields of a village called Pupuro. Here he met the enemies. One of them who had come in advance of the others, as if teasing him, asked him about Father Francisco Ezquerra. Pretending ignorance, he answered that he remained behind. But this dissimulation did not help him, because the barbarian, seeing that he was unarmed, struck at his head with a cutlass and hit him in the arm. Then he held him with one hand and rained blows on his head with the other and would have crushed his skull if the steel had been as hardened as the one who wielded it. As González lay at his feet, he thought him dead and dragged him through the grass, striking him in the face. As he saw no signs of life, he left him there and went off happily to join his people.

When the barbarian had departed, the wounded man took courage, and with an earnest prayer to our Lord, he rose to his feet and went back up the mountain. He made his way with infinite hardship, faint with the loss of blood that flowed from his wounds. When he arrived at Fuuña he was well received and cared for by the people of the village who were pious Christians, especially the chief who gave him something to eat and took him in his boat to the village of Agasan, where he entrusted him to another chief who in turn brought him to another village. In this way they took him from village to village until he was handed over to the most faithful *don* Antonio Ayihi, who took him to the residence of the fathers in Agadña. There he perfectly convalesced from his wounds. Thus God preserved his life, as it were miraculously, without depriving him of the merit of suffering for his cause, so that he might testify to the cause of the death of his companions and of the angelic Father Francisco Ezquerra, whose eulogy I shall include here, not as he fully deserves, but to the extent of the facts available to me, leaving to a better informed pen the complete account of his virtues.

# CHAPTER XI

*The Life of the Angelic Martyr, Francisco Ezquerra*

Father Francisco Ezquerra was born in the City of Manila of parents noble in ancestry, more noble still for their virtues and their charity toward the poor. And now they are newly ennobled with the blood shed for Christ and the virtues of their illustrious son and martyr of Jesus Christ. His father was General *don* Juan de Ezquerra, who had held honorable positions won by his superior merits. His mother, *doña* Lucía Sarmiento, was equal in nobility to her husband. Among other children she gave to the world, one would be a shining light in this world, Francisco Ezquerra, who was born towards the end of September 1644. Father Domingo Ezquerra, now deceased, was provincial of the Philippines, a man worthy of the highest praise. It was he who sent Father Diego Luis de San Vitores to the Marianas Mission. He was the paternal uncle of Father Francisco, whose brother, Father Juan Ezquerra, was also of our Society. Thus we may see by how many titles our Society is obliged to this most noble family. The whole Philippines owes much to it for having given it a wonderful martyr, and even more the Marianas, for having received such an apostolic man.

The child was baptized in the cathedral of Manila on October second. On this day, the Philippine Islands always celebrate the Feast of the Guardian Angels. He was devoted to them all his life, and to them, with the grace of baptism, he owed the purity of his life, which merited for him the epithet "angelic," given to him by those who came to know him and deal with him. His parents raised him in the fear of God. The deeds and words that he manifested during his childhood showed that God had chosen him for the fortune that awaited him, since even then he began to march with longer strides than his age dictated towards the crown of life-long sanctity. He learned his first letters without the pressure that the first years commonly require. Sufficient was his own inclination and the guidance of parents and teachers. This is seen in an incident, small in itself but notable in a child. The teacher had forbidden the boys to sit at a certain window in the school. One day he forgot or simply didn't notice and sat there with another boy. For this they were punished by a whipping they had been promised. His companion angrily invited him to go sit in the same place. But the obedient Francisco, who had undergone the punishment with patience, said he could go sit by himself, because he wanted to obey the teacher and not just be stubborn. In his tender years, he was inclined towards the Franciscan order, to serve our Lord in a rigorous and penitential life. But this inclination was without effect, because God kept him for the Society, to which in due time he brought him.

After finishing with proficiency his Latin studies and the course of human letters, in which he gave his classmates an example of modesty

414

*The Life of the Angelic Martyr, Francisco Ezquerra*

and devotion, at the age of fifteen he began his philosophical studies as a collegian in the Colegio de San Ioseph [sic], which was run by the Society. In his familiar converse with the religious he seemed to be a religious himself. He frequented the sacraments, and with repeated general confessions, he purified his soul more and more to make it more receptive to the lights and the grace of the Holy Spirit that called him to the Society. He begged for this grace insistently, despising whatever the world could give him because of his talents and gifts.

About the middle of January in 1660 he was admitted to the Society. In the novitiate he was in haste to build the edifice of evangelical perfection upon the foundation of humility that he loved so much. He also built upon the foundation of obedience, in which he did his best to excel. To exercise him in these two virtues the novice master used to send him around the city to sell unripe fruit at high prices. He went with much pleasure, because of the mortification that his patience could earn from cranky people who would insult him instead of paying the price. And so there was no lack of occasions for him to suffer, although once he met Archbishop *don* Miguel Poblete, who was edified by the novice and the Society, which thus exercises its novices, and he paid the high price for the fruit, esteeming it as a relic of religious mortification. Every Friday he usually carried on his shoulders through the streets the tray of food for the poor in the jail, and he distributed it with much courtesy, adding to the corporal food the spiritual sustenance of good counsels. They were satisfied and edified by this, because he told them, besides, some stories and exhorted them to make their confessions and to bear with patience the punishment of their faults. This exercise of charity, of such profit to his soul, he continued during all the time of his studies. He would go sometimes to the porter's lodge of Saint Francis to beg for his food, deriving consolation from appearing to be a beggar among beggars and by eating the remains of their food. Once the superior of the *convento*, who knew him and esteemed him as his person deserved, welcomed him and entertained him at dinner, a painful mortification for Father Francisco.

To prepare himself to be an apt minister of the gospel, during the time of his studies he joined the study of the humanities with that of the virtues, seeing to it that they both grew in fraternal company. He worked for the spiritual improvement of his lay classmates by example and counsels, edifying them with his modesty and composure on all occasions, using every occasion to spread the love of God and the hatred of sin. When he tutored them and explained the matter taught by their teachers, he mingled with the food of the understanding a measure of piety for the will. During the disputations, if some unpleasantness occurred in the heat of argument, he would yield his rights, preferring charity to reputation and peace to applause. This same charity was shown in his desire to please others, especially when he visited the sick of the house, whom he consoled and served with evident signs of love and compassion for their sufferings. Each month he was the first to come forward to wash the feet of the community, carrying out this service with pleasure, as acts of humility and charity, and he preferred the service that was less conspicuous and in which he slaved for others. For seven years he was in charge of the clock, and this gave him plenty of practice for patience and mortification, because the clock was generally out of order, and he had to run and reset it at all hours of the day and night. He slept ordinarily on the bare floor, and if he lay down on his bed, he would not remove his clothes, alleging that he wanted to accustom himself to life in the missions. It is clear that God was preparing him for the Marianas, where the missionaries, like the soldiers, sleep wherever night catches up with them. This desire for the missions was kindled brighter every day by his zeal for souls, which was growing greater every day.

During the season of Lent, every Sunday he used to go to the galleys to teach Christian doctrine to the galley slaves, who ordinarily were *Indios*, blacks, and mulattos who speak our Spanish language with so many mistakes and barbarisms that people who come from Spain cannot understand them. The zealous brother, in imitation of the Apostle of the Gentiles, became a barbarian among barbarians to be of benefit to them, speaking to the galley slaves in their jargon, purposely making grammatical mistakes to be understood by them, as the Apostle of the Indies did in another time in Goa.

About the month of June in 1669, he completed his studies and was ordained a priest. It seemed to him that this new state obliged him to a new perfection, and that the higher office demanded a higher sanctity, and so he began a new career of virtue with greater fervor. He prepared himself with exact care for his first Mass, and then every day before celebrating, as if it were his first Mass, he spent whole hours in examining and purifying his conscience, seeing the slightest faults as grave sins, a cycle aggravated by his scrupulous nature. After the third probation, obedience assigned him to teach grammar in our *colegio* in Manila, a task to which he gave himself willingly, because of the opportunity to lead the boys to a more virtuous life. On their education will depend the whole good of the country. But his personal inclination was for the missions of the *Indios*, where the most neglected and the richest crops were ripe for the harvest. He could learn there from Father Diego Luis de San Vitores, whom he had known well in Manila and had venerated as a new apostle. But he was especially attracted by the dangers and hardships that surely were waiting for him in that land as well as the hope of someday gaining the crown of martyrdom.

For these and other reasons God kept calling him to this mission, and so he strongly and insistently begged his superiors for it. And yet when permission was granted, it became an occasion for further scruples, as he began to think and to fear that with his insistence on the missions he had failed in obedience, that superiors had simply condescended to his strong desires and not freely conceded permission. From this there arose in him a dread that the Lord had abandoned him, as a man who had been guided by his own will rather than by the divine will. Was it thus that he entered upon an enterprise dangerous in the extreme for which he had neither virtue nor talents? Torn between the fear that assailed him on one side and the desires of converting the infidels that attracted him on the other, he had recourse to prayer. When he had placed his problem in God's hands, he determined to take back the requests he had made, to reveal the deficiencies that he found in himself for this enterprise and to place himself in the hands of superiors with complete indifference, so that the superior might decide what would be for the greater glory of God without regard for his inclination.

He wrote a letter to the provincial, from which I will quote some sentences in which he depicts his humble and obedient spirit with the colors proper to these virtues. They tell us what he did in this case, whereby he teaches us religious what we should do in similar cases. "I have no doubt whatsoever," he says, "that to depart even one iota from the will of the superior is a manifest error, a transgression against obedience and the will of God. This granted, I say that if my going to the Marianas is in any way contrary to the will and pleasure of obedience, or if somehow I made its will conform to mine, I beg Your Reverence by the wounds of Jesus Christ to revoke a thousand times my departure, for I neither wish nor desire in any way to violate in the least what may be the pleasure of obedience, so that Your Reverence should not be directed by my past petitions but rather forget them, as if I had never expressed them but had shown a simple indifference for any post. Thus I shall be freed from the scruple that sometimes worried me, whether or not I did wrong in asking. So I will go anywhere with complete assurance, putting myself in the hands of obedience, as a dead body or an old man's staff,[279] without expressing my will or desire for anything, but only indifference and more indifference, because to go according to my will was to err, all the more so that I am not fit for that position, etc."

Further down, after giving many reasons to prove that he is not fit for such a great task, he adds: "I feel that I am not for this post but only someone sent by obedience, into whose hands I place myself completely and for everything, so that Your Reverence may do with me and in me in accordance with your pleasure. And if it is the will of God, expressed by my superior, I will serve in the kitchen all the days of my life without expressing the least repugnance, nor shall I express it even if Your Reverence should cancel my assignment to the Marianas. Rather I will consider it a great good fortune for I shall know in this the declared will of God. Ever since Your Reverence appointed me, every day before Communion at Mass, holding the Lord in my unworthy hands, I beg him that if my assignment to the Marianas should not be for his glory and the good of my soul and of those poor people, that he should change the decision of Your Reverence and that everything should be canceled before it is carried out. And let not Your Reverence take into account that this has been made public, nor of the expenditure made by my parents, for I shall placate them, and I will bear willingly whatever mortification I may bear as a result of the publication. Should it not be the pleasure of Your Reverence that I go, I shall never say another word about it or make any claims. Only one thing will I have piercing my heart all the days of my life, and it is that my failure to go has been caused only by my sins, which

---

[279] "As a dead body or an old man's staff." *Constitutions of the Society of Jesus*, Part 4, chap.1, n.1.

*Book Five, Chapter 11*

I believe are the only things impeding what perhaps was the will of God; my demerits have given occasion for obstructing in me the works of God and with that, perhaps, my eternal salvation. May the Divine Majesty not permit it, for whose sake I decided to write this to Your Reverence, in accordance with your mandate given me, etc."

The result of this was that Father Provincial ordered him to go to the mission, realizing more clearly that the more he was stripped of his own will the more it was God's will that he should go. We cannot describe the satisfaction with which he received his mandate, assuring himself already of success in everything, since it was obedience that was sending him and he had forgotten his ineptitude, for he believed that the Lord, who was sending him, would make up for it. This consolation lasted until his death. Indeed, the religious cannot have it outside of obedience. Together with Father Francisco Solano he begged alms for his passage and freight expenses. In company with that father, he left Manila for the port of Lampago, bearing with joy the hardships of the journey, which he made barefooted. He used to say later that it had been a rehearsal for the missions of the Marianas. He embarked with Father Solano, as we mentioned in Chapter IX. On the way they underwent many dangers, including one of the worst storms ever seen in those seas. For the devil, fearful of the war that these two Franciscos would wage against him in the Marianas, tried to drown in the sea the hopes of those islands and the crowns that these two apostolic men were going to win. With an equally bitter storm of sadness and melancholy, the devil beset Father Francisco Ezquerra. But he fought back and overcame them with the light and grace of the Lord. He avenged himself on the enemy by laboring with all his strength to help the souls on board ship by his good example, fervent homilies, and holy conversations, seasoned with such courtesy and discretion that it was easy to deal with him and everyone loved him as an angel. He and Father Solano arrived in Acapulco on January 7, 1671. From there they traveled to Mexico, where they obtained abundant alms by begging in the streets. They returned to the port and set sail on March 19, the Feast of the Patriarch Saint Joseph, promising themselves that with such a patron and pilot they would enjoy the prosperous voyage, which indeed they had. Father Francisco Ezquerra resumed the same exercises and ministries as on the first voyage, studying moral theology and the Mariana language, which he had begun in Manila, studies so necessary for the infidels and the new Christians.

He made a happy landing in the Marianas on June 11 of the same year, at the same village of Ati where they later took his life out of hatred for the Faith. He was joyfully received by Father San Vitores who, in Manila, had known his fervor and solid virtue. Upon his arrival he made the spiritual exercises of our father, Saint Ignatius, and then, rested from his long voyage, he was assigned to the islands of Gani, which were the latest discovered in the north. He landed on the island of Rota, or Zarpana, and waited there for more than a month for good weather, in order to move on to Tinian, since the winds remained contrary to his

418

course. But he was not idle. He went around the island several times, seeking recently-born children to wash with the waters of baptism and for souls to teach the way to heaven. God granted him much for his zeal and no less for his mortification, for the labor was great and the suffering, too, from the rough and perilous trails and the coarseness and barbarism of the islanders. When he was about to embark for Tinian, he was recalled by Father San Vitores to Agadña, because of a persecution that the devil excited against the Faith. He obeyed promptly, amid clear dangers to his life on land and on the sea. During the forty days of the siege, his hardships and dangers were no different from those of the others, although for him the watching and guard duty were more fatiguing because he had such a great need for sleep. But his zeal and his charity kept him awake to the extent that many times he would not awaken his companion who was to succeed him in order to give him more rest and to take upon himself the greater hardship.

When the war on Guam was happily concluded in the manner described in its place,[280] Father San Vitores sent Father Ezquerra to visit the island of Santa Ana (Rota) and Father Alonso López to voyage to the remaining islands. They set sail on November 17, but forced by contrary winds, they disembarked at the village of Ritidyan. Here, while they were waiting for a more opportune time, they pacified the restless natives of that village. They made several excursions in that area, which resulted in the baptism of many children. Embarking again, they arrived at the island of Santa Ana on December 9. Father Ezquerra remained here, although many villages were restless and determined, according to report, to kill the fathers. But he went fearlessly about the island, baptizing many. He was advised that in a certain village there was a newborn child. He went in search of it, guided by a local boy. They could not find what they were looking for in that village, so the boy recommended that they return to their starting place. But his charity did not permit him to leave that child without the grace of baptism. He left his guide and had his guardian angel lead him. The angel, when he least expected it, placed two other boys in his hands, because he ended in a planted field where the *Indios* offered him their little sons for baptism. And so he felt that the hardships of the road were well repaid, and he thanked his angel for the lucky find, for losing his first guide and finding a better one.

Father San Vitores decided to build four churches on the island of Guam so that the Christian community there might be better administered and the Faith might take deeper root, assailed as it was by so many contrary winds. He summoned Father Ezquerra and told him to build a church in the village of Merizo, from which he could administer a third part of the island. Father Ezquerra set about building the church, which he placed under the patronage of Saint Dimas, the Good Thief, and in a few days it was well on the way to completion. But the construction was interrupted by the new persecution raised by the devil, when Father San Vitores was assassinated. From this town of Merizo he went continuously around the villages of his district, returning always with much fruit of his

---

[280]See Book 3, chap. 15:243.

419

labors. But the price was endless hardship, because it happened that when he arrived at the villages, he would find nothing to eat, after walking all day. He would spend the night without taking any nourishment and then on the next day would sally forth in search of souls, content with the food that Christ offered him, the children and adults instructed by and baptized by him. Eventually, forced by necessity, lest he die of hunger, he would courteously ask of the *Indios* of his mission station, "My son, give something to eat to your father and pastor." He was so careful not to give the *Indios* any cause for resentment that he would not take the food that the trees along the way offered without asking them for it. One of his companions, seeing his grave need, gave him a coconut, which he had taken from a tree at the roadside, visible to all. While he was eating, he saw some natives coming and he hid it, fearful that they might complain he had taken that coconut from their land.

The day before Father San Vitores suffered martyrdom, Father Ezquerra was with him and was only separated from him by his zeal for visiting the villages under his charge. This caused him much sorrow later on, because his bad luck and his many sins prevented him from dying at the side of his holy master and superior. He spent that same day in the residence in Agadña and by pure chance, or better, thanks to the providence of God, he delayed there. If he had returned that night to the village of Merizo, the prime movers of the persecution would have killed him. They had made their plans to do so. Because of the death of Father San Vitores and his lay companions [sic] he was forced to remain several days in Agadña and to suspend the work of the missions, a circumstance painful to this zealous man. And he kept making acts of conformity to the will of God, saying: "May the will of God be done." The suspension of the work to the Church for a whole month only fired his zeal all the more. For this, the narrow confines of Agadña gave too little scope, although he never ceased to serve his lay companions and the native Christians. Meanwhile, he continued his study of the native language, preparing himself to illuminate and inflame all the islands with the fire of the Holy Spirit. This delay lasted till the arrival of the galleon *San Diego.* Then the way began to open out again for the ministers of the gospel. But the joy of this hope was soon quenched by what was mortification for this humble man.

The time had come when God willed to reward the labors and virtues of Father Francisco Solano, superior of the mission, the successor of Father San Vitores. He saw that they would soon need a new head of that mission, so that the latter would carry it forward and augment it by his apostolic labors. He set his eyes on Father Ezquerra, whom he had come to know well. Now close to death, he gathered the fathers about him and named as his successor Father Ezquerra, and all approved of his choice. All but the one chosen, who tried hard to escape this position, one that he thought beyond his ability and merits. It is hard to imagine his grief at this appointment, the tears he shed and the appeals to be spared. Suffice it to say that Father Solano, at whose feet he fell begging release, revoked the appointment lest he sadden that humble servant of

*The Life of the Angelic Martyr, Francisco Ezquerra*

God. But when Father Solano died, he had to accept the burden laid on him by his companions. It was the will of God, as he saw, and he shouldered the heavy cross he could not refuse. Only one thing was a consolation to him. It was that as superior he could visit the mission without ceasing and could take upon himself the most difficult tasks, without anyone else's control. And that was what he did, because until the day of his martyrdom, he went about in ceaseless movement, not sparing any labor or risk in order to gain souls for God. I make no mention of the prudence he showed in his government, prudence that came to him in so few years and so little experience.[281] It was as if he had governed for many years. But it was a wisdom he had learned in the school of Father San Vitores in imitation of this master.

He was most moderate in his decisions. Before making any of them he asked for the advice of his companions and weighed the evidence on either side and commended the success to God. Then he chose what he judged to be for the greater glory of God without being affected by any human respect, although not a few times he submitted to another's opinion, persuaded that it was the wiser. His equal treatment of all was evident to all, without any taint of passion or inclination to one side more than to the other. He tried to please all as much as possible and he delighted more in serving than in commanding. During his brief tenure as superior the mission progressed: he finished the church and the residence in Agadña; he rebuilt the church of San José in Fuuña; and many missions were carried out, as many as the state of affairs allowed. Father Ezquerra was the principal missionary. With his hands he planted seeds that would yield a harvest in time to come, and he spared no effort to build up the Christian community both spiritually and materially.

All the virtues shone forth in this Servant of God. He had a deep reverential fear of the Divine Majesty, and he hated even the shadow of sin. He did no ill and spoke no evil in regard to anyone. When he could not speak well of his neighbor he kept silent, and if he must mention a fault he found excuses at least for the intention, if not for the deed. His religious observance was most exact, careful of the smallest details, in order to be faithful in little things as well as in the great. In the Marianas, he sought to be a living portrait of Father San Vitores and he succeeded. Father Lorenzo Bustillos remarks that his life was angelic, an example to all, a life filled with affection for the barbarians, whom he cordially loved. With the same love and tenderness he loved Father San Vitores, deeply impressed as he was by the latter's virtues, his humility, patience, meekness, spirit of mortification, and penance, his continual prayer, fervor, and spirit, and all the other virtues. Thus far, Father Bustillos, who praises in few words what would demand a much larger discourse.

The love he had for the *Marianos* was stronger than that of a father and more tender than that of a mother. Witness to this is the affection and pleasure with which he assisted them in their sufferings and needs, procuring them both human and divine remedies, never avoiding any risk or effort to do them good. He used to say that there were no

---

[281] He was twenty-seven years old, had been a priest for three years, and had spent only one year on Guam.

*Book Five, Chapter 11*

better pleasures for him than to suffer hardships for his poor *Marianos* in order to advance their salvation and to serve their need. One of them was sent to jail for his turbulent conduct. The Venerable Father went to the kitchen and prepared some food and brought it to him, bringing, too, the comfort of kind words and gestures. Such was his fear of being separated from those he loved so much that when the fathers of the Marianas wanted him to go to Manila on business for the mission, since they thought that no one else could do better than he in the dispatch of this affair, he pleaded so hard to remain that they yielded and sent someone else. But never was this love more evident than at his death, when he forgot his sufferings and the malice of those who inflicted them, and began to console the *Indios* who stared at him with anger and told him that he was the father of them all and ever would be.

His love of God is amply proven by his love for his neighbor, if we wanted further proof than the constancy with which he shed his blood for the Lord in a long martyrdom.

Who can adequately describe his humility, a virtue so conspicuous in him? His works, his words, his very thoughts bore witness to this. He saw himself as the servant of all and useless withal. He spoke modestly of himself and performed the humblest services with pleasure and the loftier ones with repugnance. He took delight in prayer, which is the nurse of the other virtues, feeding them at her breasts. In his prayer, he felt the assaults of the devil trying to disturb it, but he turned the devil's arrows against him, by humbling himself with those very temptations. The patience with which he bore both the hardships that abound in this mission and the scruples that tormented his soul, were admired by all his brothers. Thus, in spite of so many interior and exterior thorns, he always showed a spirit of joy and peace.

Only the position of superior brought him pain, and he used to say that, but for that, nothing could cause him fatigue.

He was ever a lover of penance, never content with the hardships of the mission, surely enough for any penitential spirit. But he added rigorous disciplines and the use of the penitential chain and the continual shortage of adequate food, difficult enough for one brought up in another land. He found ways of fasting even more and his rest after a day of weariness and hardship was on the hard ground, where he took a brief repose at night.

To that exterior penance he joined the interior mortification of his passions, which he had so subdued that he seemed not a child of Adam, but an angel *sans* flesh and blood. This was seen in his detachment from his relatives, worthy though they were of all esteem because of their virtue and noble blood. He never used to visit them, so that once his superiors ordered him to go to his home. There his sister, who had not seen him for three years, showed such extreme surprise, that his companion asked her to moderate it; and when he had to dispose of his share of the family inheritance, forgetting his own people, he left it to the *colegio* of Manila for the relief of the many needs that it suffered. In this he also showed the love he had for his order.

But he appeared all the more angelic in his virginal purity, which he ever preserved like a lily hedged in by the thorns of penance and the guard of his senses. He never looked a woman in the face. He avoided their company unless it was necessary for him to speak with one of them. Such was his reserve and circumspection that he fixed his eyes on the ground and his heart on God, and so edified them and did good to their souls, even more by his modesty than by his words. The Virgin of virgins was the guardian of one so pure. In order to preserve that purity, Mary, whom he loved most tenderly and bound by faithful service to be his helper and protector, and to profess himself a slave to one whom he loved as a son, he wrote a declaration of servitude in two distinct documents, signing it with his blood on the Feast of her Purification, with most tender and loving words, desiring to shed all his blood for her honor and that of her most Holy Son. And it is evident that the Virgin accepted this sacrifice, for he merited to shed his blood some years later on this same Feast of the Purification, February 2, 1674. Mary was with him in those last moments, as was shown by the fact that those murderers could not wrest from his hands her image or that of Jesus Christ. In those last moments, his joy was in his tender colloquies with his Mother and her Son, as his soul sped forth from so many wounds into their hands to receive the crown of martyrdom in the thirtieth year of his age—a brief career to win so precious a crown. But it was a career whose virtues swiftly reached a goal not attained by other apostolic men in a century. As a beginning of the favors that we hope the Lord will grant through the intercession of his servant and martyr, we will report in the next chapter how by the mere contact of his cassock, he restored to health the only horse they had in the islands.

# CHAPTER XII

*Several Uprisings of the Natives Are Quieted and the State of the Christian Community Is Improved After the Martyrdom of Father Ezquerra*

When the Marianas lost that zealous and fervent missionary, Father Ezquerra, who died in Fuuña on February 2, 1674, it was evident that he continued to help the Christian community from his place in heaven, joining his prayers to those that were offered for these islands by others who had passed on to glory.

The uprising that brought about the death of Father Ezquerra and his companions forced the recall of the father who was en route to Tinian.[282]

But while the work in Buenavista was temporarily delayed, the improvement that was seen on Guam among the lay companions and the new Christians was notable, thanks to the pious exercises of Lent and through the efficacy of the sermons, the good example and the *Actos de Contrición*, as proved by the reception of the sacraments, the general confessions, and the disciplines even to blood.

When Lent had passed, the fathers made some mission visits with good results, always hoping that a ship would arrive with the material things they needed so much for the furtherance of their spiritual activities.

The galleon *Nuestra Señora del Buen Socorro* arrived to pay a visit to the island of San Juan on June 16, 1674. The captain had intended to anchor at San Ignacio de Agadña, but a strong wind carried the ship out to sea, and it was impossible to launch more than one small boat with men and supplies.[283] The ship went on to the Philippines, whipped by the winds, carrying, besides supplies for the missions, three fathers who just came to these islands, as well as Father Peter Coemans, the superior of the Marianas, who had gone on board to welcome the new fathers and to remove the provisions.[284]

It is easy to understand the disappointment of the fathers of the Marianas when they saw their badly needed provisions carried away and their superior as well. But soon the Lord consoled them, hastening as he always does with divine help when they were most destitute of human aid for the growth of the new Christian community. To this the courage and zeal of Captain *don* Damián de Esplana contributed much. He had come ashore in a small boat and could not return to the ship and thus remained in the Marianas.

His experience and ability were well known to the Fathers by reason of the trust placed in him by *don* Diego de Salcedo and *don*

---

[282]Father Alonzo López, S.J. See Book 3, chap. 16:246.

[283]García will continue to hint that the anchoring off Agaña instead of in the harbor of Umatac was a deliberate attempt to deprive the Marianas of missionaries and supplies.

[284]Peter Coemans, a Fleming, spelled his name Pedro Comano in the Spanish missions.

424

Manuel de León, former governors of the Philippines, who had commended the care of these islands to Father Diego Luis de San Vitores and his successors. By permission of His Majesty, who addressed all communications to the superior of the Marianas, he was named *sargento mayor* (sergeant major) in charge of the military and his first acts justified his appointment.

The sergeant recognized that the worst enemy of the soldiers is leisure. It leaves them open to every sort of vice and also surrenders them to the enemy. Hence, he put his small army to work cutting down trees in the vicinity of the fort, thus depriving the enemy of a good place for an ambush.

He believed that for the good of the Christian community it was necessary to give an example of punishment that would warn the barbarians, whom mildness only made more bold. He decided, therefore, to begin with one of the most powerful and criminal villages on the island of San Juan, one called Chuchugu. In order to justify what he was about to do, he first sent several embassies, inviting the natives to make peace and asking them only to discharge their obligations as Christians, which they had so often promised to do, and he urged them not to place obstacles in the path of the ministers of the gospel who traveled about the island to teach and baptize. The barbarians felt that this proposal was mere cowardice and became all the more arrogant. They refused to give a hearing to the ambassadors. Instead, they continued to impede in every way the progress of Christianity.

Seeing their rebelliousness, the sergeant resolved to seek out the enemy in a village near Chuchugu, where he believed the guiltiest ones were to be found. He commended the expedition to God and they offered seven masses in honor of Saint Joseph for a successful outcome. At the same time, they sought the help of the prince of the angels and patron of these islands, Saint Michael. Then, trusting more in divine than in human aid, he heartened his soldiers with the hope of victory, and at nightfall, set out on Friday, July 13, 1674, with thirty men. Arriving near the village, he ordered the *alférez, don* José de Tapia, a man of known courage, to lead the vanguard against the houses at the edge of the settlement, while he, at the same time and with the remaining soldiers, would attack the others. He forbade the soldiers to kill women or children, but only those men who resisted.

Our men attacked, divided in two parties, and the natives, after long resistance, which cost them several lives, fled. In the darkness of the night, one woman was killed. In her arms they found a baby boy with two wounds, whom Father Alonso López, chaplain of the troop, took in his arms. He offered the child to the Lord in baptism as the greatest prize of the victory. He called him Miguel María Ventura, in recognition of Saint Michael, our Lady, and of Saint Bonaventure, whose eve it was [July 13].

They carried the child to our residence in Agadña, where they treated his wounds and cared for him. He was a joy to them because of the signs he gave of becoming a grand Christian. Though he was not yet two years old, he had a natural bent for things of the Faith. If they asked him, "Where is God?" he pointed with his hand to heaven; he would strike his breast if he heard the words of the Act of Contrition; he would kiss with great reverence the holy pictures and the hands of the priests, distinguishing those who were not priests, making the sign of the cross, and performing all the acts of devotion they had taught him with the greatest docility.

Although the rebels were frightened, their conduct was by no means improved, and so the sergeant decided to attack the village of Chuchugu itself. They set out on July 26, and after overcoming many difficulties on the road, arrived at a narrow pass that is at the entrance of the village.

The enemy, who had espied our people, occupied three eminences, one of which faced the road while the other two overlooked the two sides. As the vanguard under *don* José de Tapia began to go up the hill, the enemy gave the signal to join battle by throwing a lance at the place where the sergeant major was standing with Father López. But it did no harm and this was taken as a special favor from God. A storm of lances followed the first, obliging *don* José de Tapia to stop and protect himself from the front with his shield and his back by a tree.

The vanguard was unable to go through the narrow pass because of the shower of lances that blocked their progress. They, therefore, discharged their muskets, to which the enemy replied with another volley of lances, so great in number that our men were in grave danger of perishing, without knowing which way to turn. In this desperate situation, Father López called upon Saint Michael, whose standard he carried, and the soldiers, on hearing the name of the prince of the heavenly host, took new courage, and confident of his patronage, climbed the mountain, disregarding the lances and the enemy. The latter, terrified by the courage of our men and afraid of their gunfire, left their posts and entrusted their salvation to their swift feet. From the mountain the Spaniards threw themselves upon the village and seized it without meeting with any resistance. They burned the village and broke up a large number of lances.

The victory cost our men no more than one slight wound, from which the soldier quickly recovered. Nor did the enemy suffer great losses, a further joy for the Christian soldiers, because only one died at that time, and through the diligence of Father López, who administered baptism, he gained the life of the soul before losing that of the body. Later another died of a wound he had received in the final skirmish.

At the time of the battle, the Blessed Sacrament was exposed in the church in Agadña and the fathers were kneeling in prayer before it, kept alert by the sounds of musketry in the distance. Masses were being said during the time of the battle that God would grant victory to the Spaniards. In a few hours they were back, happy at the victory and thanking God for the event.

The sergeant major suffered no small inconvenience on the way back. He took a short cut over unused trails, and they got into a swamp

*Uprisings of the Natives Are Quieted and the State of the Christian Community Improves*

from which his horse could not escape. He had to dismount and continued on foot, loaded with weapons. He had to struggle through the mud, a painful task since he was lame in one leg from an old wound he had received in the service of His Majesty. But the pain was eased by his desire to serve God and his king, a service both fitting and necessary for the spiritual and temporal government of these islands.

At this time (1674) the fathers set up two schools, or seminaries, inside the *presidio*, one for boys, dedicated to the Guardian Angel, the other for girls, dedicated to Saint Rose. The latter was a special devotion of *don* Damián, and it was hoped that through the example of this holy virgin these tender plants might bear the fruits of purity.[285] The fathers believed they could support both themselves and the seminaries with the provisions brought here by the ship. But their supplies fell so short of this goal that no matter how much they economized by fasting and careful management, there was never enough for all. So they had recourse to the kindness of the sergeant major, who solicited native foodstuffs from the *Indios* themselves, wherewith to feed their own children and relatives.

This *caballero*, who knew no leisure, whose diligence suffered no item of carelessness, enclosed the *presidio* once again, with two points of a diamond in the revetments. He moved the *castillo* to a better location, built a boat, and not content with supervising the workmen, he himself helped to set the posts that formed the new stockade. Since he lacked experienced workmen for the blacksmith shop, he took up the hammer and beat out the ironwork. He made nails for the boat, sweating at times so that his clothing was saturated. He was a help to all more by his example than by his hands, since the soldiers were ashamed to neglect what they saw their leader doing.

These works completed, he set out to reconnoiter the whole island. With a few men he went to the village of Fuuña and from there to Pupuro, a settlement whose people were accomplices in the death of Father Francisco Ezquerra. He put the natives to flight, for they dared not remain in the village. He burned their houses, and leaving for a better occasion the punishment of other guilty villages, returned to the *presidio*. The soldiers and four religious took a different route for the return journey, hoping to find children or adults to baptize. It was a weary painful march as they broke their way through fresh wild trails.

In the northern part of the island the villages were at war, one with the other, and each faction tried to attract the support of the sergeant, knowing that whichever side he favored would be assured of victory.

They sent messengers to him suggesting the advantages of an alliance, but he did not wish to favor one side or the other, for both were friendly to the Spaniards. He exhorted them all to peace, and Father Alonso López and Father Antonio María de San Basilio (who was acting rector during the absence of Father Coemans) sailed to that part of the island. They went without military escort to avoid arousing jealousy or suspicion on the part of either faction. They entrusted their safety entirely to the providence of God for whose love they undertook this duty. When

---

[285]Chuchugu. See Book 3, chap. 16, n. 168.

they finally reached the villages they began the hard labor of reconciling both sides. One of the fathers climbed a steep hill to talk to the natives, at the risk of falling off the cliff that he was climbing more with his hands than his feet. He spoke of the advantages of peace and the destruction of war, and after overcoming not a few difficulties accomplished what he desired.

Meanwhile, in the village of Ritidyan, a church was constructed and dedicated to Saint Francis Xavier. Soon the people began to come to it to be instructed and baptized and eventually to receive the other sacraments.

With this good example before them, the people of Tarragui permitted the fathers to construct a church in their village under the patronage of Saint Michael the Archangel.

With peace restored and new churches built, the ministers of the gospel began to feel new hopes. They went out again to the villages to teach the natives the way to heaven, especially the children, in whom, as in soft wax, the virtues of our Christian Faith and customs are so easily impressed.

Besides many hours of the day, they spent a great part of the night teaching. The children never became tired of singing the prayers, lauds that surely were a delight to the Lord, sung by such innocent voices. And in order that there might be no lack of hymns, the fathers wrote in verse some of the principal mysteries of our Faith. These couplets they sing on the road during the day, in their houses and villages at night, as the sweet names of Jesus and Mary resound on all sides, where but a few years earlier they had never been heard.

It is surprising, the ease with which these children learn the Christian doctrine, for in less than two months they know all the prayers and songs of the doctrine and such other truths of our Faith as they can understand. The adults also, though more slowly, learn the doctrine and the religious songs by which their old fables and songs are being supplanted.

The jealousy of one village toward another aids in the facility and speed with which they learn, for they like to enter into competition as to who understands the Christian doctrine best, challenging one another to these holy contests, which the fathers attend as judges. When one village visits another to hold a contest, the father of the residence arranges for them to go in a religious procession. The standard of the doctrine is at the head of the line, then the boys follow on one side and the girls on the other, lastly men and women in the same order. The boys and girls wear crowns of flowers or leaves on their heads and carry palms. They wear white clothes, which are the prizes given by the fathers to those who learn their lessons best. On the road they sing the prayers and songs with such modesty and composure that it appears to be a procession of angels.

When they arrive at the village where the contest is to be held, the father of that residence leads his people out to meet them in a similar procession, and in a suitable public place they have their contest of mysteries and prayers. When it is finished they receive their prizes, and after entertaining themselves for a while with games, they return happily to their villages, looking forward to another day of debate. Those who have not acquitted themselves well may try again. These and other pious inventions are employed by the fathers to facilitate the instruction of the poor islanders.

The missionaries desired that this instruction might be extended to all the island. Hence the sergeant tried to attract the enemy villages to peace, especially the village of Funhon (Tumon), where the Venerable Father San Vitores was martyred. Many other villages, he thought, would follow this one in good things as well as they had in bad. It seemed wise to follow the maxims of the Venerable Father San Vitores: that they ought to try every means of kindness before resorting to force and to make use of words before arms, although they saw the danger that these barbarians, as they had done before, would mistake kindness for cowardice.

And this occurred now. They paid no attention to the proposal of the sergeant, who had set out for Funhon on November 14. He found the village deserted, for all the natives had fled. He himself attacked a boat, following it for some distance in the sea. His horse swam until it overtook the boat. Raising his saber, he struck down the native who was sailing it, the man who years before had cruelly murdered Damián Bernal. He made prisoners of the other men in the boat, who tried to save themselves by jumping into the water. The dead native was quartered and hung between two poles as a warning to the others. He then set fire to the village and returned to the *presidio*.

After these successful expeditions he determined to pass on to the islands of the north to castigate certain delinquents and clear the way for the ministers of the gospel. But when he was just about to depart, he received news that the natives of the mountain together with those of Chuchugu and its confederates had determined to kill all the fathers who remained on the island after he had gone. These rumors and consequent fears were increased when they killed one of our friendly natives, for no other reason, it seemed, than that he was our friend.

The sergeant felt this keenly and set out on December 17 against the rebels of Chuchugu and Mapaz,[286] the two villages which he believed were involved in the murder. He made a sudden appearance and attacked some hamlets that had been built in the mountain country when the natives no longer dared to live in their former villages. *Don* José de Tapia killed one man and the others fled.

*Don* Damián wished to punish the other villages but desisted on the urgent pleas of some of the natives, since he hoped that these punishments would be enough to move the natives to peace. During those wars, aside from the hope of copious harvests in the future, the Lord garnered some immediate gains in the baptism of children by the ministry of Father Tomás de Cardeñoso, who accompanied the *Escuadrón Mariano*.

A long-desired peace followed this storm of uprisings and violence. The people of Chuchugu and Mapaz came to offer peace, which was concluded under conditions that were for their own good and the advancement of Christianity. The ambassadors returned content to their

---

[286]Mapaz, near Chuchugu.

## Book Five, Chapter 12

villages, telling of the kind treatment they had received from the sergeant. For the future, they showed themselves most loyal and ready to do all that was asked of them.

One should not fail to mention the fidelity of a native, a chief of the village of Agadña whose name was *don* Diego Aguarín, who was won over by the sergeant major and who spoke to the people of the other villages. He persuaded them by his personal authority and his reasons to make peace with the Spaniards. These, he said, meant them no harm, but only good, which was to show them the way to heaven. He said that they would never be able to have quiet and security as long as they looked upon the Spaniards as enemies. Though the Spaniards were few, their bravery was great and their arms irresistible.

A new church was built at Tepungan,[287] and in honor of the special devotion of the sergeant major, it was dedicated to Saint Rose, from whom he had received special favors.[288] More than three hundred persons attended the church, making notable progress in the doctrine. With this work, the year 1674 came to an end, a year bloody in its beginning, but happy at its close, so great was the harvest of baptisms and promise of abundance in the following year.

---

[287] Tepugnan, on the coast near Piti.
[288] Saint Rose of Lima (1586-1617) was beatified in 1668 and canonized in 1671.

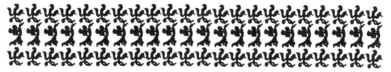

# CHAPTER XIII

*New Disturbances Are Quieted and Greater Progress
for the Faith Is Made; Several Miracles
That God Worked for His Soldiers*

The sergeant major had heard many things about the flourishing condition of the Christian community cultivated by the fathers in the villages of the northern part of Guam, San Miguel de Tarragui and Saint Francis Xavier de Ritidyan. So he set out for that area in the beginning of the year 1675, desiring to assist the missionaries in whatever way he could and to foster in the natives a greater sense of reverence for their teachers.

Consequently, when he arrived at Ritidyan he himself showed great regard and reverence for the fathers, and when he saw a large group of natives, he made a very earnest speech, exhorting them to have great respect for the fathers as ministers of God and teachers of the truth, who came to show them the way to salvation. He said, "Be warned. When you do wrong, the fathers can punish you and have you whipped, and you must submit to the punishment, because I, who am a captain, submit also. If I were bad, I would permit the fathers to punish me!" The words had much weight because of the natives' respect and fear of the sergeant.

*Don* Damián also tried to persuade the village of Sidia [in the western part of the island] to make peace with the Spaniards, although the people did not wish to do so and were very arrogant when it was suggested. He set out for that village on January 30. His arrival put the natives to flight and he burned the village. He continued that afternoon to Ati, and after throwing down a steep slope several natives who tried to impede his passage, he went down to the village and burned it and then returned to the hill top for the night.

The next morning many friendly *Indios* arrived captained by that ever loyal *don* Antonio de Ayhy. They had come to destroy the village of Sagua whose people were involved in the death of Father Ezquerra. When Ayhy reached the slope of the mountain where our men were, he said, "One captain is above and one below and that one is I." And all his followers said, "Captain, where you die, we too will die, because we are determined to follow you." Accompanied then by all these men the sergeant major moved forward. He treated kindly all the villages he passed, all who were friendly or at least not openly enemies. Arriving at Paa he recovered the crucifix that Father San Vitores embraced as he died. He received it to the sound of trumpets, venerated it with profound reverence, and had all the others reverence it. Exchanging then his role as captain for that of preacher, he set up the crucifix before all, telling the *Indios* that this Lord, crucified for love of us was truly God and Lord of all people. He moved them to tender

431

emotions, as they saw an action so devoutly Christian. He handed over the crucifix to Father Tomás Cardeñoso who had accompanied him here. On that day they went on to Hadian and recovered the cassock in which Father Francisco Ezquerra died, regarding it as the relic of an illustrious martyr.

The following day, which was Sunday, February 3, he went up the mountain in search of two enemy villages that were implicated in the death of Father Ezquerra. These villages were called Nagan and Hinca. He burned the first without meeting any resistance, since the natives had fled in fear. As he approached the second, he faced a troop of natives who attacked briefly and then fled.

While the soldiers were occupied in this way, the sergeant major went forward with two friendly *Indios* and a boy whom the fathers had reared, in pursuit of certain *Indios*. These had fled in such a way as to lead the sergeant away from his people and have him fall into an ambush that they had set up in a field of tall grass.

As soon as he was in position, they set fire to the grass on all sides and set up spears pointed in such a way that he could not pass through without great danger to himself and his horse.

Shutting his eyes to the smoke and fire that flared up in an instant, he spurred on and sped through the burning grass in pursuit of the natives who had flocked to a certain village. He searched the village, but they had taken refuge in the thick underbrush of the mountainside, frightened by such courage and determination and not daring to stand before one who had no fear of flames and had vanquished the strongest of the four elements.

The sergeant awaited the rest of his men, and when they arrived they noticed that the sergeant's horse had been wounded in the neck during the grass fire and that the sergeant, in the excitement of the chase, had not seen it. They extracted the lance tip with great difficulty, and with no delay, they set fire to the village of Hinca and moved on through other villages along the shore and in the hills, instilling fear wherever they went.

They came upon many rivers difficult to ford, but the natives were so loyal to him that they supported the horse with their backs and shoulders as they swam across the streams, for fear that the cold water would paralyze the wounded horse.

That night, which they spent in Nuninia, the horse refused to eat in spite of the weariness and pain of that day. The sergeant was extremely worried, because it would have been a great loss if it should die. He then took the cassock of Father Ezquerra, which he had recovered the day before, and looking towards heaven, he said, "Holy Father, you see that the reason for the horse's condition is our avenging your blood and subjecting these barbarians so they will be better persons. You know well how necessary is his life. He is the only one in these islands. I place here your cassock. Give him health."

He covered the wounded horse's neck with the cassock and at once, as the sergeant himself testifies, the horse began to eat with great

*New Disturbances Are Quieted and Greater Progress for the Faith Is Made*

appetite, and the next morning he set out with such vigor that he was able to reach the *presidio*, which was ten leagues from that place, and in a short time he was perfectly well.

This was not the only miracle with which the Lord favored this enterprise. One of the soldiers was at the point of death from a splinter of human bone from a lance tip in his foot. Though they opened the wound, they could not find the splinter. The sergeant had recourse to his patron, Saint Rose, and at his request a Mass in her honor was begun, when with no other treatment than opening the wound and exerting some pressure, the poisonous splinter started from the wound, even before they reached the first reading in the Mass.

The soldier was at once out of danger and all were filled with joy as they offered their thanks to God and to the saint through whose intercession they had received the favor.

But greater still were the miracles God wrought in the souls of the barbarians, changing their very hearts. Many children were brought to baptism by their parents, or were sought by the missionaries in their journeys through the villages and mountains, and increasing numbers of adults were coming to catechism, to Mass, and to confession in all the churches of the island.

More than 500 came to San Ignacio de Agadña, more than 300 to Santa Rosa de Tepugnan, more than 400 to San Francisco Javier de Ritidyan, more than 500 to San Miguel de Tarragui, and almost seven hundred to San José de Fuuña, so that the fathers were themselves obliged to tear down the old churches and build new and larger ones.

The missionary who served at the Residence of Saint Francis Xavier in Ritidyan built a school for boys, which he dedicated to Saint Michael the Archangel. There were twenty-two boys who went to church twice daily to learn the doctrine and recite their prayers. Thanks to their example, the adults, always more difficult and less diligent, obtained a greater knowledge of our holy Faith in a shorter time than was usually required for baptism.

The father was moved to establish this college by the great affection of the children of this village for the things of our holy Faith. In fact, when the father, at the end of one day's lesson, said that next day they would learn new material, they got up before sunrise, after praying till midnight, woke the father and said, "Father, teach us. Here we are, every one of us."

As a general thing, the children of all the villages show the same application to Christian doctrine. Indeed, the habit of repeating it throughout the day sometimes makes them say in their sleep, "Praised be the most Blessed Sacrament." They also have a genuine reverence for all sacred things and much respect for the fathers. If they meet one of them on the road, they accompany him to the church, singing the verses of the doctrine.

When they return from the fields laden with the roots that are their regular food, their first stopping place is the church where they place their load on the floor before they pray and then take it up after-

Book Five, Chapter 13

ward and carry it to their homes. God has shown by certain marvelous happenings how greatly he is pleased by this innocent devotion and devout innocence.

In the village of San Miguel de Tarragui, a boatload of natives was close to drowning, since their boat, already full of water, was beaten by powerful waves. Some children, seeing it from the beach, fell to their knees and prayed to God, begging him to save those poor people who were in obvious danger. This the Lord did, just as the children asked him, saving the boat and all aboard it.

One day some boys from the school at Ritidyan went fishing. Now, normally, the natives do not bring home many fish, because the sharks tear their nets. But the boys brought home very many fish without any damage to their nets. The father asked them for the reason, surprised as he was at the unusual event. They answered very joyfully that God had done it, because when they were fishing, they prayed, saying, "We ask you, our God, that you send us much fish and that the sharks may flee from us." And this was not the only time, because the Lord repeated the favor on other occasions, on account of the faith and the prayers of those boys.

Omitting mention of many special favors that God granted to the island for the credit of our Faith, I shall tell briefly of one example of the Lord's mercy, the result of the predestination of a poor native woman, as one may surely believe in regard to the divine clemency. One of the fathers had visited her many times in the village of Upi,[289] where she lay sick. He used to instruct her in the mysteries of our Faith. He put off baptizing her until she should be better instructed, because her illness did not seem to require haste. But the Lord who knows what we do not and disposes better than we understand, inspired the missionary to return one afternoon to visit her and baptize her, although her condition did not appear grave. This was later seen to have been a providential intervention of the Lord, since the following morning the woman was found dead, contrary to all expectations.

But the common enemy of man tried to oppose by every possible means this fortunate progress of our holy Faith. He appeared to the poor natives in various and horrible forms, revealing himself especially to the children of San Miguel de Tarragui. He revealed himself to them in the form of a frightful ghost. At first they were very much afraid, but the father taught them to display the cross at such times, so that they soon despised him, and at the sight of this weapon with which Christ vanquished the Prince of Darkness, these shades of the abyss disappeared. He appeared also to adults in yet more fearful guise, uttering horrible cries to frighten them. They ran to the fathers to beg crosses, so that by this means they might free themselves from this ferocious enemy.

The devil could not, unassisted, overcome the Christians who, armed with the cross, were not afraid of him. He, therefore, tried again to foment war and uproot the Law, which is totally for peace. He stirred up the villages to the westward through a certain chieftain of the village

---

[289] Upi, in the northeast corner of Guam.

*New Disturbances Are Quieted and Greater Progress for the Faith Is Made*

known as Tachuch.[290] Tachuch had tried at various times to kill the fathers and Spaniards, and now thought he could accomplish his wish by means of the signs of friendship and the kiss of peace. He had informed his people of the plan, together with the means and time for putting it into action.

The sergeant major learned of the scheme and went to the village of Tachuch and tried to win over this chieftain by kindness, hiding his awareness of the treachery. The same afternoon he went on to a village called Hahayadian, which was also concerned in the plot. He planned to pass the night there.

He left the village a little after midnight, taking a mountain road to avoid falling into an ambush. He knew that several were set up along the beach. He met a troop of natives. These provoked him to a fight, but he held off until they were in a clearing, and then he rushed at them on horseback, wounding their chief with a knife. Afterwards the man was killed by *don* José Tapia. The horse was mired in a swamp, which gave the natives a chance to flee.

Then our men returned to the beach, where the sergeant major managed to get his hands on Torrahi, the rebel chief. He was convicted of serious crimes and of being a menace to public security and a planner of future uprisings. The sergeant major had him shot as a warning to others. The soldiers then went to his village and burned his house, leaving all the others unharmed, as a sign that only the guilty would be punished, and the natives themselves confessed that this was well deserved.

With this act of justice all the island was warned and subdued, to the extent that the missionaries could safely visit the villages without escort and were well received everywhere. The Christian community was in the best state it had ever enjoyed; and to crown their felicity, the galleon *San Telmo* arrived on the fourth of June and dropped anchor in the harbor of this island of San Juan, a place formerly called Umatag, but now San Antonio.

General *don* Tomás Andaya, who was in command of the ship, gave the fathers a horse, knowing how useful it would be in these islands. He also gave them a quantity of nails, which was intended for that boat, which, as we have said elsewhere, was built for these islands.[291] In Acapulco they had pronounced it useless, being built contrary to all the rules of ship-building. This gentleman showed himself to be liberal and pious in all ways.

Father Bustillos and Father Gerard Bouwens arrived on this galleon.[292] Father Bouwens had spent the two previous years in the Philippines and Mexico attending to business for the mission and now returned to it as the new superior. He brought with him the most provisions that had entered these islands, and not the least important in the present crisis were twenty men, who by order of His Majesty were left in the Marianas.

---

[290] Tachuch, in the southwest corner of Guam, near Merizo.

[291] See Book 5, chap. 9:404.

[292] Gerard Bouwens, S.J. (1634-1712), a Fleming, was known in the Marianas as Gerardo Bouvens or Bovens.

*Book Five, Chapter 13*

With this excellent help, the affairs of the mission took a turn for the better. Schools for boys and girls were established in all the residences, in separate buildings. There was a notable improvement in these young people and in all the island, because their moral conduct proved to the adults that what these had judged impossible could be done, that people were able to preserve the chastity that the Law of Christ commands. Many of these children, some only seven years old, besides knowing how to assist at Mass, learned the Litany of Our Lady and many prayers. They learned to read and even learned some music, which the missionaries taught them so that they might eventually serve as sacristans and catechists and even assistants in the work of the gospel.

Not the least admirable fruit of these schools is the way these children try to imitate their teachers. There were some who saw the father fast during Lent and who fasted also. Knowing that the father took the discipline, they did too, and there was even one who wore a rough chain because he knew that the missionary father wore one.

They confess often and as well as if they were Christians of many years standing and men of judgment, since they have excellent qualities and are naturally good if they are not corrupted by vice and too much liberty.

They help with all their ability in the celebration of the principal *fiestas* of the year. They perform dances that are devout and well choreographed, representations of the divine mysteries that displace the pagan superstitions.

In Agadña they presented a dialog on the Passion and Resurrection of the Lord with as good grace as the most gifted children of Europe could have produced.[293]

In order that they may be well occupied for the improvement of these islands, they are taught to grow maize and cotton and other crops necessary for human life. The girls are taught to spin cotton and the boys to weave it. They apply themselves readily to this because they need textiles, which many now know how to cut and others to sew. Whatever is taught them, they learn easily.

Our common enemy, envious of the progress of this Christian community, tried by the most vicious means imaginable to destroy it. He chose as his instruments our own lay companions, who ought to have cooperated in its extension as they formerly did, but now some of them caused the Gentiles to blaspheme the name of God, while others tried to take the life of their commanding officer.

But the Lord, to whom those souls had cost so much, is ever compassionate, and he prevented a disastrous outcome by making the delinquency known, and so the culprits were punished according to their merits.

Matapang, the murderer of Father San Vitores, was also part of this. He returned to Guam from the island of Zarpana (Rota) to which he had fled. There, he met a Spaniard called Lorenzo Hernández de Puga, who with more spirit than prudence tried to seize him. He was unable to

---

[293] This was the age when Jesuit theater and ballet were an important influence in Europe.

do so, for the native was robust, although of advanced age, and Lorenzo was alone. Matapang escaped badly wounded and returned again to Zarpana. There, some of our soldiers hunted for him but could neither find him nor learn where he was hiding. But in order that their journey might not be fruitless, they employed their time removing two pieces of artillery from that island to Guam. Their work was interrupted by the news that some of the natives of the villages of Targua and Guegu had tried to kill a father who had journeyed with them to that island to look for children to baptize. He would have been killed had not a chief of the village of Tito prevented it.

    The soldiers set out to administer punishment. The enemy resisted by making a bulwark of their boats, which they filled with sand and by throwing spears at our men. But the soldiers, making light of this, threw themselves on the bulwarks and put the enemy to flight. They entered their villages and burned them and returned victorious to the island of Guam, bringing one piece of artillery that they had laboriously salvaged from the twenty-four feet of water in which it was sunk, leaving the companion piece for another time.[294]

---

[294] The artillery pieces may have been from the galleon *Santa Margarita* lost on Rota's northwest coast in 1601 en route ot Acapulco.

# CHAPTER XIV

*Brother Pedro Díaz and Two Lay Companions Die in Defense of Chastity; the Virtues of This Venerable Brother*

There was in the village of Ritidyan, as we have said, a residence of the Society named Saint Francis Xavier, with a school for boys, and another for girls under the patronage of Saint Sabina Martyr. Here they lived in great modesty through the vigilance of a Jesuit scholastic named Pedro Díaz, who at that time was assisting the father of the residence.

The Venerable Brother Díaz knew that there was a public house in the village where ten or twelve *urritaos*, unmarried youths, lived with only one woman. His zeal would not let him rest day or night, praying to God and considering means of stopping this scandal and offense to God. At last he was able to persuade the woman to leave the youths. He saw that she was repentant and desirous of living chastely, and so he took her into the girls' school where she might be safe. The devil, the enemy of all purity, could not stand having virtue so celestial flourish on this earth. He incited three of the *urritaos* to enter the girls' school to satisfy their insatiable lust.

They broke through the walls of the girls' house on the night of December 8, the Feast of the Immaculate Conception of Our Lady. The next day, when the Venerable Brother learned of the outrage of the *urritaos*, he went in search of the *urritaos* accompanied by an officer of the *presidio*, *don* Isidro León, a native of Seville. Burning with zeal for the honor of God, he reproved them for their boldness, setting before their eyes the enormous evil they had committed against God, promising that the divine justice would not leave it unpunished and that human justice as well would provide the punishment merited by their crimes.

The natives who were present there in great numbers, especially the *urritaos*, could not endure the strong words of the brother nor the idea that the fathers and the Spaniards had come to put an end to their sexual license and to impose laws against their wickedness. In their fury, they threw themselves upon the Venerable Brother and his companion *don* Isidro and finished them off with clubs and machetes, chopping their heads to bits with extreme cruelty and furor. Not even the tears of the chiefs, disgusted at their actions, could restrain the fury of the youths. Then, adding crime to crime, in order to show more clearly what was the cause and who were the authors of these killings, they attacked the residence and took the life of another Spaniard, a native of the City of Mexico named Nicolás de Espinosa. They sacked the church and the house, carried off the sacred ornaments and whatever else they found, and set fire to the church and the house and to the boys' and girls' schools and even to the body of Nicolás de Espinosa.

One must mention a marvel that happened to one of the sacrilegious murderers, which served to show the natives the respect they owed to sacred things. One of them picked up the chalice and felt it burning him, so that he immediately threw it away. When he looked at his hand he found it swollen and covered with drops of blood. Then another took it, perhaps with more reverence than the first, because he did not suffer the same punishment.

It would seem that God wished to illustrate with marvelous signs the death of the Venerable Brother and his two companions, who so jealously had helped the mission in spreading the gospel. This marvel was seen when the villagers of San Miguel de Tarragui, led by a young Visayan named Francisco Monsongsog, came to punish those of Ritidyan. They had burned the village and cut down the food- bearing trees and were waiting to see if they could get their hands on any of the killers. Some of these had fled to the jungle and others to the island of Rota, the refuge of criminals. Suddenly certain trustworthy persons saw on the site of the church three beautiful stars not far from the earth. These, they realized, were the souls of the Venerable Brother and his companions, whose shining had not been dimmed by death itself but only changed from earthly to heavenly light.

The Venerable Brother Pedro Díaz well deserved this happy fate for his many virtues and religious life. He was born in Talavera de la Reina of God-fearing parents who reared him in Christian habits, especially his mother, who often used to say, "My son, choose rather to die than offend the Majesty of God."

He studied Latin and philosophy in our Colegio de Oropesa and later studied law at the University of Salamanca, in the hope of a distinguished career in the world. But God, who wanted him for his service, touched his heart and called him to the Society. The most important influence was the sad death of a fellow student who was considered one of the most valiant in the university. Another student stabbed him as he drew his knife against his killer.

Brother Pedro was received into the Society in the Colegio de Oropesa on April 24, 1673. From there he went to the novitiate in Madrid, where I knew him during the three months that he was there. In that length of time he made more progress than others in the two years (of novitiate), running in haste the path of life that was to lead him to such a precious death. For Pedro, the novitiate was a true school of humility, patience, charity, mortification, penance, silence, obedience, and the exact observance of the rules, which is a continual practice of all the Christian virtues. He was so exact in conquering himself that once he burst into tears at the force he was exerting in overcoming the extreme repugnance he felt at kissing the feet of the poor people who came for alms to the door of our house. He was so scrupulous in obeying the orders of superiors, that once when the father rector sent him to visit *Don* Jerónimo San Vitores, a patron and benefactor of the Marianas, his novice companion said to him after the visit, "It would not be a bad idea now to go see some of the sights of Madrid, since you will soon be leaving for the

Indies." To this the mortified novice answered, "Brother, you, of course, can do as you please, and I will obey you, as senior here and in the place of the superior. But if you ask my opinion, I say we should return home, because Father Rector told us to visit *don* Jerónimo San Vitores, and he did not say to visit these things. Whether we see them or not matters little, since they are things that pass away. But to obey really matters."

While still a novice, he set out for the Marianas mission, and he continued his novitate en route with the same exact observance and punctuality as in the house with all the novices. Already he showed how solidly he was formed in virtue, since neither distractions along the roads nor the events of a long voyage diminished his fervor but rather were but a further occasion for a new and better practice of the virtues. And Satan gave him many occasions to practice patience by striving to prevent his voyage and so deprive the Marianas of the prospect of his harvest.

On the road to Seville, where he was to embark, there arose such a storm of thunder and lightning that it seemed the sky would be torn apart. A sudden shadow falling between the feet of his mule caused the beast to throw him to the ground. But it did not bother him. He piously pronounced the name of Jesus and offered that small hardship as a foretaste of the great ones that awaited him in the Marianas. In Córdoba, while he was going upstairs, a gentleman was coming down with an arquebus in his hand. He dropped it carelessly so that it struck Brother Pedro on the head and caused a large wound. He showed no impatience. He spoke not a word till he had recollected himself for a while and then burst out with these words, "May God be blessed forever. May this be to your greater honor and glory, my God!"

When he arrived in Seville, he never went out, they say, to see the many splendid sights of that city, because he had lost all affection for the visible in the love of the invisible and everlasting. On the road to Cádiz, he suffered patiently the antics of the servant boy. Annoyed by his all too free and easy way of speaking to the travelers, he simply occupied him with pious conversation to dam the flow of off-color language.

During the voyage, he showed his zeal for the good health of souls by the talks he gave, by order of obedience, to the blacks and people of the lower class. He gave the same good example all the time he spent in Nueva España awaiting his departure for the Philippines. Here, he joined academic studies to those of spiritual perfection. In Pedro one saw the fervent novice and the meticulous student, one in whom literature was no distraction to piety, and piety no bar to literature. He found time for everything, so that nothing escaped his grasp. He was precise in his daily schedule, circumspect in word and action, a lover of penance. Though he was of a lively disposition, humility made him a good listener of other men's words, careless of winning points in argument, more covetous of his own peace of soul than of the applause of others. What you noticed most was his prudence, the rule of his actions, the guide for those who sought his help. This was what people held in veneration when they dealt with him, yet it was so much less than the holiness and innocence of a life that left his confessors almost nothing to absolve.

The time came to sail from Mexico, and this second voyage was again a time of prayer and service. The long voyage brought him to the Marianas, and with enthusiastic zeal, still a novice, he entered on an apostolate dangerous and hard. His strong youthful body was hardly satisfied by the tasteless roots he gathered on his journeys, and if he found a fish, it was a small banquet. He almost always went about barefoot, walking up and down the rough steep hillsides. His consolation was the thought that he was imitating the Good Shepherd, who first had sought him over hills and valleys, and so, for love of him, Pedro sought out the lambs and sheep, the children and adults to teach and to baptize.

One of his greatest sufferings was from sunburn, which scorched his legs so badly that the burning did not subside for thirty hours and the pains were so intense that he said they were for him a living image of the flames of purgatory.

The sea, too, gave him something to suffer, soaking all his clothing so that his shirt dried onto his body while he had to sit for hours in a narrow boat, not half a yard wide. But his greatest sufferings came from the natives who repaid kindness with injuries and matched his enthusiastic love with insults, threats, and rocks.

But the Lord rewarded his servant with the consolation of suffering for the love of Jesus and for the good of the souls redeemed by his Passion. Other favors too, through Pedro, came to the islanders. While he was on a mission journey on Guam and was staying a few days in Pagat in the house of a native, it happened that the latter went out fishing with all the rest of the village. But he caught a great many fish while the others caught just one or none at all. The native realized that the Lord had done him this favor out of regard for the guest in his house. He said to Brother Pedro, "Because you are in my house and because the word of the Lord is with you, I have caught so much fish."

The same thing happened in other villages in which he stayed. He thanked God for these favors. With them he paid back the poor natives for the hospitality they had shown him, and with them he persuaded the natives of the truth of the doctrine that he taught.

Brother Pedro Díaz was in charge of the building of a house and a church in Merizo as well as of the instruction of the natives. One night in that village he heard some children crying. And yet, but a few minutes before, they had been joyfully singing their prayers. He ran to investigate the causes and found that one little boy was crying more than the others, because his mother had gone up into the mountain with a rope to hang herself. The brother went into the woods to look for the woman, but found no trace of her. Heart-broken, he returned home, earnestly begging our Lord to free her from that danger. The Lord was not deaf to his prayers, for the woman returned next day safe and sound, saying that God had freed her from that peril because Pedro had called out to him.

About this time he destroyed a skull, the kind they use in the worship of the devil. Some nights later, he was awakened from sleep by the cries of a native, who was running up and down outside our house.

## Book Five, Chapter 14

The brother and a father went out to investigate the cause. They heard the *Indio* saying over and over as he ran up and down, *Ari mangaronsie*, which means, "The skulls are wicked." They went up to him, and at the suggestion of Brother Pedro, the father made the sign of the cross. The man became quiet and the next morning the brother asked him the cause of his excitement. He said, "Father, Pedro should realize that the soul in hell of that skull that you smashed was the one that tormented me last night, following me wherever I ran. But as soon as he made the sign of the cross, that horrible apparition disappeared, and now I remain at peace."

The fathers who had passed on to heaven by way of martyrdom came to the aid of this Venerable Brother in banishing the superstitions of the natives. The vision seen by one Apuro, of the village of Ritidyan, is an example of this. One night Brother Pedro and a companion went to his house and found him cringing and panting with fear. Seeing them, he recovered somewhat and said, "Help me, fathers. Two horrible squadrons of devils are walking here, one in the shape of Spanish people, and they told me that they are going to kill me because I teach our ancient poetry. They frighten me, because they give out a terrible fire. It is not like our fire here, clean and bright, but dirty and foul smelling. Only one thing gives me courage, the three people who stand here so full of dignity, dressed in the habit of the Society and surrounded by shining light. The brother touched him with a relic of our father, Saint Ignatius, and he said he felt a wonderful force, and he said that those three persons had knelt down and had prayed to the Lord that those hellish spirits would not abuse him. When the brothers bade him good night, leaving him relieved and at peace, the native saw the three heavenly persons join them. On a later day he asked them, "Is it possible that you fathers did not see those three venerable persons who joined you when you took leave of me? I certainly thought that you saw them and that they left conversing with you."

Who those persons may have been is not definitely known, but it is believed that they were the three martyrs of the Society in the Marianas, Fathers San Vitores, Medina, and Ezquerra, who came to assist the workers in the vineyard that they had cultivated in times past, unless we are to say that those three martyrs came in robes of glory to symbolize the glory that three others soon would win by a similar death: Brother Pedro Díaz very soon, then a month later Father Antonio María San Basilio, and in a few months Father Sebastián Monroy. Others will offer other explanations, but the fact that it happened was confirmed by the rare change that took place in the *Indio* Apuro. Not only did he take no part in the death of Brother Pedro Díaz and his two companions, which took place in his village, but he was the means of preventing the death of a father who was then in Ritidyan. He handed over a missal and a picture of Saint Francis Xavier, saying, "Father, I took these, not for myself but to bring them to you." Nor did he continue to teach his *meris*, the native ballad poetry, nor did he hide in the mountains. But he accompanied our men, showing much love for the things of our Faith. And he

442

even expressed a desire that there be constructed in his village a new church and house of the Society.

I must mention the marvelous vision in the village of Merizo, a tribute of honor to the Venerable Brother. Shortly before this time he had dedicated the church in that village to the Assumption of Our Lady. On the night of that glorious day, the brother happened to be away on mission in the neighboring area, when many persons saw a globe of light descending from on high. First it touched our house and then rested on the new temple, and then it rose little by little toward heaven until it was lost to view. No one understood the mystery at that time, and until today it remains mysterious. It provides material for pious speculation, since some think that Mary is that celestial light, who wished to show how pleased she was with the temple that her devoted son had consecrated to her, while others suspect that globe of light was a symbol of Brother Pedro Díaz himself, who by the favor of Mary would soon rise to heaven after he had been a light and a fire of love and learning for that island.

But since the death, or rather the martyrdom, of the blessed brother took place in Ritidyan, it is more likely that this good fortune was symbolized by a dream that a native had a few days before in that village—if, at least, one can give credit to dreams, especially those of *Indios*, who dream what they see and see what they dream. But in view of the time and the events and the oppositeness, none of which he could have invented, this one merits some credence. This native remained on guard at the house and the church in Ritidyan from which Brother Pedro Díaz and his companion set out for Agadña, whither they were summoned by his superior for a general consultation about ways and means to advance the work of the missions. This was when he had the dream. It seemed to him that he saw two Jesuits in the church, one celebrating Mass, the other assisting him. Each one's head was crowned with a brilliant halo, and all the temple was filled with flames of fire. Later events showed that the persons in the church, one offering Mass, the other assisting, were the Venerable Brother Pedro Díaz and the Venerable Father Antonio María de San Basilio who was killed by the barbarians one month after Brother Pedro's murder, and both were crowned, as we hope, with the glory of heaven because their deaths were precious in the eyes of the Lord, that of Brother Pedro for defending chastity and that of Father San Basilio for the sake of justice, and both because of the hatred of the barbarians for the Christian religion and for those who preached it.

I will conclude with the words of one who was a fellow novice of his, a companion in Madrid, on the voyage to the Marianas, and in the islands, which he wrote to me in a letter of May 25, 1676: "I cannot restrain my tears for the loss of a brother and companion who was in every way so suited for this mission by his zeal for the salvation of souls, for his prudence, discretion, profoundly religious character, and competence in the Mariana language, an ability that seemed almost miraculous, since in the little more than a year that he lived in this mission, he surpassed all of us who work here.[295] Like Saint John the Baptist, he was

---

[295] June 16-December 9, 1675.

killed in defense of chastity, his beloved Jesus repaying him with this glorious death for the heroic vow he made at an early age and kept all the days of his life. His great love of this virtue rested not only in himself, but he wished to communicate it to all others, avoiding failure with all his strength, never sparing hardship or fatigue, that the Divine Majesty be not offended, especially in this matter, which is so difficult a problem in the Marianas."

# CHAPTER XV

*The Very Religious Life of Father Antonio María
de San Basilio, Killed at the Hands of the Barbarians*

I will leave for the present the marvels that God wrought in order to confirm the islanders in the Faith and proceed to tell of the death of Father Antonio María de San Basilio, a death precious in the eyes of God, if not of men, which occurred on Friday, January 17, 1676. Second only to the founder of the mission, Father Diego Luis de San Vitores, he was nowise inferior in sanctity and zeal to any other who worked in this apostolic mission.

In praise of this notable missionary we shall say only that which one of his companions said of him, calling him "the angel of the Marianas, father of the Marianas, angel of peace of these islands, doctor of medicine to their bodies and to the health of their souls, a truly apostolic man, aided by God with marvels, a seraphim being, burning with the love of God and man."

He was a Sicilian, native of the city of Catania. Of his lineage nothing is known. His humility saw to that. His was a life destined to great sanctity by the grace of God and the pursuit of religious perfection. God grant that another pen may give us the story of his childhood and youth, as a layman, and as a religious. He entered the Society in 1659, and in all his years as a Jesuit, he was a perfect pattern of the virtues, an ideal novice, an ideal scholastic, an ideal priest, and an ideal missionary, because at every stage, he was a lover of prayer and of the presence of God, the highest school of spirituality. From this familiar converse with God was born a modesty and exterior calm, an admirable peace and gentle courtesy that won the love and veneration of those who dealt with him, finding in him a true man of God.

When he was ordained priest, he decided that his new state required a new life, and that one who lifted up the Bread of Angels would live an angelic life, and he indeed seemed an angel the year that he spent in Spain at the Colegio de Alcalá, awaiting for place on a ship. I knew him there and admired his religious spirit. It was the same on his voyage to Nueva España and on the one to the Marianas. He was ever at the service of his companions, making their beds, if they permitted, and those of the sick on board. He consoled the sick with gentle words, acting as physician and surgeon, treating wounds, and administering remedies. This ministry he exercised even more in the Marianas, where for lack of doctors, he cared for bodies and souls. On the journey from Mexico City to Acapulco, they told him of a native who was at the point of death, with no one to administer the last sacraments. Typically, he broke off his journey and rushed to the place where the man was lying and gave him the comfort and the courage and the sacraments to meet death and the mercy of the Lord. The story would be a long one to tell of the examples of his virtues, which he left us in all the journeys of his life, especially in the Marianas, where they reached heroic proportions. But allow me to relate a few as an inspiration to us and for the glory of God, the source of all good.

Charity, the love of God and neighbor, the queen of all virtues, reigned in the heart of Father San Basilio, so that in every way he could serve his God and his neighbor, in whom he saw God's image. It was this love that drew him from Italy, over the roads and the oceans to the Mariana Islands, in hardships and dangers, and always in the joy of heart of one who suffered for his Lord, a joy that showed upon his face and brought an answering joy to others, however dark the melancholy of their hearts. So many have testified to his healing presence. His joy was greatest where the hardships were for the good of souls, especially in the Marianas, where no fruit was ever gathered without constant toil and danger on land and on the sea and mostly from the people.

In one of the wars between the native villages, he went back and forth from one to the other, climbing the cruel hillsides barefoot and with bleeding feet, if only he might bring them peace.

And to end these conflicts more quickly, he traveled not only by day but in the night, with only two friendly natives and a breviary in his hand and a cross that served as a staff, with no defense but his confidence in God, who guarded him from the dangers that met him at every step. God rewarded his labors for peace with a treaty that he won from both sides.

On one of his journeys on Guam to baptize and instruct the people, he came to a steep hillside, which he could only climb by using his hands, grasping rocks and thorny plants till his hands were bathed in blood. Yet even this was not enough to scale the height, and he fell from the cliff that overlooked the sea. A great wave carried him out, and in this desperate moment, he commended himself to God, when suddenly another wave swept him all the way to the shore. To those who watched, it was a wonder, but to Father Antonio it was the gift of a new life to spend in God's service.

As superior, he felt the hardships suffered by his men, suffering not only with his men, but from a certain Spaniard who persecuted him and his companions. His godless tongue attacked their apostolic works and even the person of this saintly man, because he tried to end a scandal the Spaniard had caused in the young Christian community.

To overcome the difficulties that surrounded him, he felt that he must first master those within himself. This led him to heroic acts such as we see in the lives of the great saints.[296] Often he cleansed the wounds of the sick with his own tongue. There was a native of the island of San Juan (Guam) who, besides being asthmatic, had a cancer of the leg. The Father took him on his back and carried him to a hut that he had built for him. There he waited upon the sick man with admirable devotion, feeding him with his own hands, making his bed, and serving him in every way. And because he was a doctor of the soul as well as of

[296] June 16, 1674.

*The Very Religious Life of Father Antonio Maria de San Basilio*

the body, he instructed the sick man and prepared him for death, and the man died in his arms with every sign of attaining eternal salvation.

To conquer his passions, he afflicted his body with rigorous penance, as if he had no other hardships to bear. He used to wear a cross with sharp points in addition to other types of chain. It was found after his death that he had three types of chain bound about his body. His disciplines were severe and he took them three times a day. His bed was a hard table, his food tasteless roots with a little rice on rare occasions and even more rarely, a bit of fish.

Humility was not the least of his virtues, as was evident especially when he was elected superior of the mission in the absence of Father Coemans, who was carried off to the Philippines in the galleon *Nuestra Señora del Buen Socorro* by a contrary wind. He made every effort to be excused from the charge, urging his incompetence and asking that they elect someone else, someone competent. When he could not change their minds, he did their will and was never more their subject than when he was their superior. When he gave an order he seemed rather to beg than command, saying, "I beg Your Reverence (or my Brother) if it were possible and you are not otherwise busy, to do me the kindness of doing this." He made up for giving them orders by being the servant of all, making the beds when they were coming from a journey, caring for them when they were ill, giving them as many comforts as the slender resources of those poor islands permitted, and taking for himself whatever was worse, whatever was more burdensome.

He took upon himself the care and instruction of the child whom our soldiers brought in wounded from the battle.[207]

His obedience was such as our father, Saint Ignatius, desired in his sons, yielding his own opinion, swift to carry out the command. Thus he used to say, when the superior summoned him to the residence and he was at a distance, "If only the Lord would give me wings to speed the execution of your orders!" He did not hear the word as a mere command but as the word of God.

In the matter of poverty, he was scrupulously careful in choosing the worst of anything. When someone once sent to his residence a chasuble and a frontal piece for his altar, which were somewhat attractive looking, he sent them back with the message, "It's too splendid, too valuable." Even in these matters he showed the spirit of poverty and humility.

No words of mine can better declare his love and devotion to our Lady than the letter he wrote to the sovereign Queen a few days before his death. I will quote it literally here without changing a thing, although it shows that Spanish was not his native language. In it, all may clearly read his devotion, humility, charity, and all the other virtues. It would seem from the text that he wrote it in his blood, or at least that he had shed blood from twenty-two wounds that he made in his body to multiply the mouths that would testify the love he had for his Mother and Queen. Thus he writes:

---

[207] See Book 5, chap. 12:425.

Letter to Mary most Holy, Queen of the universe, Empress of the heavens, Mother of God, and my Lady, I, the chief of all sinners and wicked people, write to you this memorial, that you may liberate me from the passions of my will and flesh, and that you may transfer me to perpetual union with Jesus and you. Most serene Queen, although I, the vilest of men, the slave of my passions, conscious of my vileness, poor in all the good things that the devil has robbed me of because of my ugly sins, son of wrath, target of all the pains of hell, deserving of all the pains and evils suffered in the abyss by the damned and the very devils, although so depressed by my faults, although rejected by all creatures, who would rend me in pieces if they could, in spite of all that, I do not cease to cherish hope, a very great hope in you, my only refuge and defense, since you have the heart of a mother, but with all confidence in all the promise of your titles, and prostrate at your feet, I beg that you deign to receive this letter, which requests that you give a hearing to my laments, which tell of my afflictions and desires to please the Triune God in his infinite mercy. I ask you to change my attitude and character, which are so disagreeable to your eyes and those of your most Holy Son, and because this tongue of mine is not enough to explain my desires, I have opened today twenty-two other mouths that they may tell of my need and longing, which is the desire and yearning to please you, and if in the least way, by thought, word, or deed, I should displease you, may I sooner quit this life that does such evil, and may I give this life for the love of your most Holy Son and my poor *Marianos*. I dare ask, too, a total abnegations of myself and a perfect conformity to all that your Son wishes for his greater glory.

I ask for an interior light that I may know myself and know your most Holy Son. Likewise a disgust and horror of every kind of sin, a love for the cross of Christ, a perfect zeal for the glory of God and the salvation of souls, a purity pleasing to you, and I offer you all of myself, body and soul, reserving nothing.

In view of all this, I have poured out my blood from those mouths to show my interior need and the love I have for you, desiring one day to pour out all of it for your honor and that of your most Holy Son. Ah, my Queen and Mother, show me your merciful heart and favor me now and at the hour of my death. At the end of it may I find you merciful and more than merciful to the life that I totally dedicate at your feet.

This loving mother repaid the tender love of this son with extraordinary favors, especially the one she granted in the *presidio* of Agadña. He was spending the night with one of the soldiers who was ill. This soldier was *don* Luis de Vera, one of those who died with Father Francisco Ezquerra. *Don* Luis saw Father San Basilio kneeling and a

*The Very Religious Life of Father Antonio María de San Basilio*

lady of venerable aspect who cast a light over him. The effect of this prayer and the heavenly visit was, that although the sick man was then dangerously ill, he was quickly restored to health by no other medicine than the prayer of the Venerable Father. To this prayer *don* Luis always attributed the health and the life that the Lord granted him that he might lose it for the holy Faith.

The Lord worked many wonders for this faithful servant, who healed many sick people by simply reciting the prayer of Saint Francis Xavier. But there was another marvel with which His Divine Majesty honored him. After a day on the road with ten lay companions, he was exhausted by travel and hunger and much more concerned for the needs of his companions than for his own. He asked an alms of a native. The latter gave him three vegetable roots called *suni*, all three of which would not have sufficed for even one person. The Venerable Father cleaned them off with a knife and bade his companions to eat them, although there was no more than a mouthful for each. But eleven of them ate their fill, and there were more left over, to the wonder of his companions, who never ceased to praise the One who multiplied the bread in the desert and now repeated the miracle by multiplying this rough food in the hands of his servant.

The Lord willed to reward such virtues and carried him to heaven in a death suffered for the love of his brothers. There was a serious shortage of food in the *presidio* for the fathers and the soldiers. In his concern for the others, he arranged with a native called Quinado, of the village of Upi, for a quantity of *nica*, a kind of root and one of the common foods of the country, and he paid him in advance.

The native was so slow in bringing the *nica*, that the father went up the mountain on Thursday, January 16, 1676, as he had done many times before without fear of these natives, since they were amongst the most tractable. He slept that night at Upi and on the following morning spoke to the native who brought out the *nica* with the help of his son.

The father noticed that it was of poor quality and said to him with his usual gentleness, "How is it that you are not keeping our agreement, but are giving me poor *nica*?" Quinado offered some excuses, which surprised the kindly father. He bent over to count the roots, and then the native moved by the devil, raised a club that he had in his hand and dealt him a heavy blow on the head, and then others, until he had split his skull. And his son assisted in that execrable crime. Some children, who had accompanied the father, said that after he was dead (but it was while he was dying), he rose to his feet and grasped a nearby palm tree, but fell again, dead. This was on January 17, 1676.

There remained on the palm tree traces of the blood of this Venerable Father, who died for charity, for justice, and for the Faith, which the native, raised without law or reason, hated, the Faith that they so often have tried to banish from these islands by killing its ministers.

Surely he gained the palm of martyrdom, this soul whose body died grasping at that palm tree as a symbol of that beatitude that he longed for and deserved by a life of hardship and danger.

*Book Five, Chapter 15*

These desires and hopes of dying for Christ are seen in a letter that he wrote from the Marianas to Father Diego de Valdés, who had been his rector in Alcalá at the time he was at that *colegio*. In this letter he tells of the many hardships he suffered in that mission as well as of the consolation God gave him when he suffered for his love. Hence, I have thought it well to quote it here. This then is the general tenor of it:

Pax Christi: God has granted me one of the greatest graces, which I never hoped to enjoy because of my sins, the grace to be in the Marianas Islands in 1672. And yet, though the spiritual comfort was great, it was much diminished by the death of Venerable Father Diego Luis de San Vitores. I had hoped to gain from him the knowledge and inspiration with which he inspired the fathers with whom Your Reverence has had dealings. May God be praised for his deep judgments, for if perhaps he deprived me of this as punishment for my sins, it reminds me of how much worse I deserved. Not for this do I give up hope, confident as I am that Father San Vitores will protect me and the other four from his place in heaven. By his intercession I hope to lose my life in these glorious hardships and labors. There are surely plenty of occasions for losing it, be it for lack of foodstuffs, which are usually roots, without bread, wine, or meat, or because of the traps and stratagems of the natives. They have a great craving for the articles we bring from Spain, such as glass beads, bells, knives, and tortoise shell, which they esteem as if they were gold, and because of this several lay companions of ours have been killed when the natives believed them to be carrying these trifles.

But if they had enough fear of our people, they would not dare to try these tricks but would listen to the doctrine and would attend church regularly. It is now difficult to require this for lack of sufficient forces, and the above articles serve as money with which we buy the food to sustain the men who serve as our military escort.

With all these cares, which are small in comparison to the happiness we enjoy in the Marianas, we live very contentedly. All the joy of life in other places cannot be compared to it.

To give you an idea of this, remember that this is an apostolic life *sine Faculo, et pera, et passim sine calceamentis*[298] partly because we do not have shoes, partly because if we do have them, they are made of palm, and it is necessary to walk without them in many muddy places and on the shore.

Our food is roots, which serve us as *antipasto*, main course, and dessert, without meat, bread, or wine. But as *non in solo pane vivit homo*,[299] it does not distress us, for the consolation

---

[298] Matt. 10:10; Luke 9:3. Without staff and purse and generally without shoes.
[299] Matt. 4:4; Luke 4:4. Man does not live by bread alone.

that God gives us in the missions is so great that I, for my part, hearing of it, tried for many years to come here.

Besides, our hearts overflow with joy when we go through these mountains hunting for children to baptize, and when we have passed most of a day without meeting with any, we finally find a group of them and pour upon them the grace of God.

I am especially happy because the natives, who are practiced in throwing lances in their wars, want my arms and legs, because they are long, in order to make lances out of my bones, since they are never made of other material than human bone; and they are so poisonous that one puncture causes death.

The language is not very difficult since they have few consonant clusters. The people are the same as they were described a few years ago by Father San Vitores.

There is no lack of grain here, Father, for the granaries of heaven. Even if it were only for the children, there is enough labor for a hundred laborers now. May God give us means to walk these lands and send to heaven these many poor people redeemed by the blood of Jesus Christ. May God gather us all in the homeland of the blessed. In these Mariana Islands, April 2, 1673. Your Reverence's servant in Christ, Antonio María de San Basilio.

The devotion of the villagers of Tarragui must not go unmentioned, beloved children as they were of the Venerable Father. Two years before, he had built a church named for Saint Michael. When they heard of the terrible crime, they went up the mountain, led by a Visayan boy, Francisco Monsogsog, a most faithful companion of Father Antonio in his labors. When they reached Upi, they began with shouts and war-cries to challenge their enemies, declaring them to be such as killers of the Servant of God. No one came out to oppose them, so they burnt the houses of the killer, and taking the body of Father Antonio, they carried it to Tarragui and buried it in the Church of San Miguel.

# CHAPTER XVI

*Miracles That God Worked in Honor of His Most
Holy Mother; Several Happenings at This Mission*

That which the devil tried to destroy by the death of two of the principal
ministers of the gospel, God restored by other means, working marvels
in confirmation of his holy Faith through the intercession of the Patron
and Queen of these islands.

On the island of San Juan, in a village toward the north called
Ayraan, there was a church and residence dedicated to Our Lady of
Guadalupe of Mexico.[300] Before her image was kept burning a lamp
made of wood, for lack of more precious material. By means of oil from
this lamp innumerable cures were effected by the sovereign Queen of
the Angels among the Spaniards and even more among the *Marianos*,
such as the reduction of swellings and the relief of intense pain. Even in
the method of cure the sovereign Queen has shown her benignity, for
when the natives fall ill they go to the father of the residence and say to
him, "Father, have me cured by Santa María." It often happens that the
father calls one of the children from the school, saying, "Go, child, and
anoint this sufferer with the oil from the lamp and ask the Blessed Virgin
to make him well." Then the Blessed Virgin, hearing the prayers of the
innocent children and knowing the faith of the sufferers, gives them
health, and they return to the father without being called and tell him
that Santa María has cured them.

The Blessed Virgin favors not only the sick but the well also,
answering their prayers, especially of those who go out fishing. These go
to the church before they go to the seashore, where they say with great
confidence in the Mother of God these words only, "Our Lady and Mother,
I am going fishing. Give me fish." And she gives them in great abundance, to the end that they may be confirmed and may grow in their
faith and in their devotion to Mary.

Among other fruits that were garnered at this period in the Christian community, the ministers of the gospel had the consolation of celebrating several marriages between their lay assistants and the women of
the country. This set an example for the natives to marry according to the
rites and ceremonies of the Church, and many did so. And there was hope
at this time that the work would be given a new impulse by the arrival on
Guam of new assistants. More missionaries and soldiers were on board a
ship that arrived on June 10, 1676, and came within sight of Guam with
the much needed supplies and men. But not all could be landed, since the
ship did not anchor at Umatag, because of the personal reasons of those
who looked more to their own interests than to those of the Christian
community and the service of God. The ship, which was the *San Antonio*

---

[300]Ayraan, on the northwest coast of Guam.

*Miracles That God Worked in Honor of His Most Holy Mother*

*de Padua,* landed five religious of the Society, four priests and one brother coadjutor, together with fourteen soldiers and two families, both of which were very useful to the new Christian community, one of them particularly as an example for the natives in the education of children, which is totally lacking in those islands. They were useful also for the skills that they employed with Christian charity for the good of all.

The fathers suffered a great inconvenience at this time in losing a commander for the troops, when *don* Damián de Esplana, who had commanded them for two years, embarked for the Philippines. But the general of the ship helped them out of this difficulty, and to him the mission has always been greatly in debt and would have been even more so if he were not accountable to the governor of the Philippines. But I may better say that God helped the mission, for the choice of a commander was his, if we observe the circumstances.

Captain *don* Francisco de Irisarry y Vivar arrived on that ship with no idea of remaining in the Marianas. In fact he had even persuaded a certain sergeant named Nicholás Rodríguez not to remain. But at one simple request from the general, God changed his heart and he accepted the office, thereby receiving the grateful thanks of the general. To further honor his readiness to serve God and king, the general gave him the title of Governor of the Mariana Islands.

The newly arrived missionaries were distributed among the residences, and all were well occupied in the work of baptism and marriages and in preaching the Christian doctrine to the newly made Christians and the more experienced ones as well. They succeeded in having the new governor make it obligatory for all baptized natives to attend church on Sundays and feast days and to send their sons and daughters not only to learn the things of our Faith but also to learn to perform certain offices and duties necessary to the formation of a Christian and political republic, banishing barbarism little by little from these people.

Through the care and efforts of the fathers and the governor, the schools for both boys and girls were soon filled, and the notable application of the children promised great advancement in these islands in matters both Christian and political.

Because of certain inevitable difficulties, the Feast of Corpus Christi was deferred until the first Sunday of August in 1676. At this time it was celebrated with all possible solemnity and display in the church of San Ignacio in Agadña. All the fathers came with the people of their villages and the pupils of their schools. When they arrived in Agadña, each village formed its own religious procession, carrying its banners and singing in Spanish the prayers and the *doctrina cristiana.* The procession formed by the children of Agadña went out to meet those of the other villages, and the two processions joined in one body. They then marched to the church singing the doctrine, and after praying there, they tried to find places to pass the night, such places as the charity and the poverty of the place could provide.

In this manner the people from all the villages met on the eve of the feast, for which they had already built triumphal arches and many altars, with the soldiers assisting in both tasks, competing to see which would turn out to best advantage.

Sunday morning, after the sermon and the solemn Mass, the general procession was formed. The standards of all the residences were carried at the head and were followed by two lines of children, boys on one side, girls on the other, all wearing such decorations and adornments as their particular residences could afford. They sang, as they proceeded, the Christian doctrine.

After the children came the chiefs of the villages. The governor, who was in the center of the procession, carried a rich royal standard and after him followed the members of the religious community. These, with a few musicians, sang the *Pange Lingua* as they walked along. After the monstrance, which was carried by the celebrant, followed the soldiers in all the panoply of war. At intervals they fired salvos from their muskets.

The surrounding fields were filled with native spectators, astonished at so much majesty and display. They fell on their knees and beat their breasts as the Blessed Sacrament passed.

When the procession arrived at the altars that had been constructed in various parts of the village, a hymn was sung, and the ceremonies that followed were carried out with as much propriety and perhaps with more devotion than in an old Christian community.

The feast continued throughout the afternoon with dialogs that were presented by the children, interspersed with several kinds of dances, such as the *pavane*, the *canario*, and the *tocotín*, which were worthy of similar tourneys in Spain, and the dexterity of the children in executing these dances was no less than their skill in the dialogs, recited in the Spanish language. I describe these small matters in order that the ability and capacity of these children may be understood, and to show how effective are our efforts to prepare these people to form a Christian and political republic in this land, once barbarous for lack of the Faith, of government, and of education.

The Feast of Corpus Christi was thus celebrated with a solemnity that made our religion not only venerable but acceptable and delightful to the barbarians. But when all had returned to their homes, it seemed to the governor that it was necessary to restrain the pride of certain villages and castigate the insolence of others, as well as to punish the murderers of the fathers and their companions. These murderers, urged on by the devil, never ceased to wage war against the Christian community, persuading many that the customs of the *guirragos* were evil and contrary to their own, inherited from their ancestors. They said they should not replace the customs of the islands with those of the Spaniards, nor should the liberty of their former life be exchanged for the austerity of the existence that the Spaniards tried to force upon them with their laws and punishments. It was urged that they do all possible harm to the fathers and Spaniards, to oblige them to leave their country in order that they themselves might once again live according to their desires and feelings.

*Miracles That God Worked in Honor of His Most Holy Mother*

The governor decided to begin with a village in the mountains, named Tarisay (Talisay),[301] whose inhabitants, believing themselves safe because of the inaccessibility of their village, bragged about their village and ridiculed the Spanish arms.

Having decided to teach them a lesson, the governor went out with his men towards evening and walked all night through the mountains. They stumbled and kept falling on the trackless hills. At daybreak they reached the village of Tarisay. They sounded the charge and, with a *Santiago,* fell upon the enemy, leaving five of them dead, while the rest, some badly wounded, escaped to the mountains. Afterwards they set fire to the house of the *urritaos,* or one might better say, to the house of ill-fame, desiring if they could, to quench one fire with another. Our people returned to the *presidio,* happy in their victory and carrying some spoils in the form of three children, precious pearls in the eyes of the Lord, a wise dealer, who had bought them with his own blood. They were brought to the residence and baptized, and one who was two years old departed soon for heaven, finding in the loss of his parents the sure means of predestination. Another, a bit younger, was well cared for and a third, about eight years old, entered the boys' school.

A short time after this battle, there were some weddings of Spaniards and of native men with Mariana girls who had been educated in the girls' schools. An interesting case was that of a marriage at the *residencia* of Orote. A native girl, following the example of one of her friends, resolved to be married in the church. She realized that if her parents or relatives heard of the plan, they would prevent it, because they wished to sell or rent her to one of the *urritaos.* She went secretly to the missionary and confided her secret to him. The village father at that time was Father Sebastián de Monroy. He brought up many difficulties and objections, but she had an answer for all, saying that if it were necessary, she would leave her parents and her village in order to live according to the Law of God. When the father saw so such resoluteness, so contrary to the natural inconstancy of the barbarians, he confirmed her in her resolution, and he immediately arranged a most solemn ceremony of marriage on a feast day, so that the natives, at the sight of the sacred rites and ceremonies of the Church, would recognize the difference from their own barbarous rites and the nullity of marriages that were merely temporary arrangements, as we have pointed out elsewhere.[302]

Just as the marriage ceremony was finished, and while the people were still in the church, the girl's father arrived to avenge the wrong that Father Monroy had done him in marrying his daughter to a Spaniard. The missionary knew that the father's anger was in reality caused by the foul custom of renting out their daughters to the *urritaos,* which was their best source of income and property. The priest tried to calm him by saying that he would not lose anything by the marriage of his daughter, because he would give him more than an *urritao* would give him. But

---

[301]Tarisay (Talisay) was inland from Agat, on the west side of Guam.
[302]See Book 3, chap. 2:172.

*Book Five, Chapter 16*

the barbarian was not quieted by the words of the father. Instead he tried to kill him and his companions, especially the one who had married his daughter. To this end he had gathered many natives from the surrounding villages with their lances and machetes. Then, feigning friendship, he approached our people and was on the point of striking the bridegroom with his machete, when the father saw his intention and prevented the knife from reaching its mark. Father Monroy, realizing the danger that confronted them, sent the newly married pair to the residence in Agadña for safety.

When they arrived they told the governor of the uprising in Orote, and he set out in all haste to quiet it. En route he lost one soldier, who became separated from the others for whatever reason. A native met him and with a great show of friendship led him to his village. When the soldier was off his guard, the native struck him down with a blow to the head and finished off the soldier with his own arms.

As soon as the governor arrived in Orote, he put down the riot and took the two guiltiest ones prisoners, one of whom was the father of the bride, and after a thorough examination and trial, ordered this one hanged, while he set the other free, as less guilty. For the execution, he ordered the people of the surrounding villages to assemble and explained to them the various crimes of the culprit, including participation in the martyrdom of Father Ezquerra.

Some of the priests who were most adept in the native language were charged with the duty of preparing him for a Christian death, but he was so stubborn that he refused to be baptized, although every possible means was taken for his conversion.

The *Mariano* children, angered with him for refusing baptism, attacked his dead body, pelting it with stones and sticks. They dragged the body to the beach, shouting, "Die, dog, die. You refused to be a Christian."

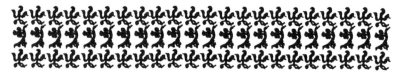

# CHAPTER XVII

*The Great Treachery of the Barbarians Against the Fathers and the Spaniards; the Precious Death of the Venerable Father Sebastián de Monroy and Seven Military Companions*

By their treachery alone or the many treacheries to which I refer, these islanders gave the lie to the reputation they had hitherto enjoyed in Spain because of first impressions.

The devil saw the war that the ministers of the gospel were waging, and he saw the grave danger of losing the domination he had usurped over these islands, since every day so many people were converted to the Faith. He resorted to the help of his best ministers, those who were murderers of the fathers and the Spaniards, and who could only find impunity for their crimes by finishing off all the foreigners, the only people who would punish them.

Hence, all the villages that had been implicated in the killing of Brother Pedro Díaz, Father San Basilio, and Father Diego Luis de San Vitores joined with the natives of Orote, Tarisay, and a few from Asan, of which the murderer of the above-mentioned soldier was a resident. This latter case was kept secret for a time, but it could not long remain unknown to the governor, who would take steps to punish it.

A noble of the village of Agadña, named Aguarín, joined the conspiracy. He was blind and he was one of Satan's best workers on the island. He made himself head of the alliance, not only of the disaffected natives of this island but also of Rota, in order to exterminate all our people. He began to complain against the fathers and the Spaniards, sowing the diabolical seeds of dissatisfaction among the peaceful natives.

First, he managed to draw to his side the most distant villages, who had, in his opinion, justifiable complaints, such as those of Tarisay, Orote, Fuuña, Sumay, and Agofan, whose residents were related to those who had been punished by the Spaniards. He gave many reasons why all the natives should unite and finish off, once and for all, all the *guirragos*.

"What are you doing, oh, brave islanders," he said, eloquent in his barbarity, "that you go on carelessly permitting this cruel enemy to live in this land, who has done you so much harm?

"Tell me all the harm we have suffered since they came to our islands? They have killed our children with the water of God and they hate with a mortal hate those of us who have been able to resist this poison, as we saw in Agadña, when the children stoned and dragged one of our friends, whom those tyrants had killed, calling him guilty for having defended his country and his liberty.

"They take our daughters from us to marry them, and we lose the price that the *urritaos* would have paid us. Many of our people have died, and soon they will kill all of us, if we do not immediately apply a remedy. And even if they spare our lives, what death is worse than the life we are forced to live, without pleasure, without liberty, being forced, as if we were slaves, to attend Mass and the doctrine, to go to church instead of spending our time fishing, weaving nets, or building boats? Where is the courage of your lances and stones with which you have so many times overcome the enemy? Do not fear these foreigners. They are few, while we are many. They are brave only because of our fear. I shall go ahead of you with my lance, which already has killed many, and I shall finish them all to restore the liberty which our fathers and our grandfathers enjoyed, and which we, because of our cowardice, have lost."

With these and similar arguments Aguarín was able to persuade the above-named villages and even others, promising them what he called liberty. They contrived to maintain strict secrecy, permitting the fathers and Spaniards to go about their usual affairs without showing ill feeling or in any way opposing them, awaiting the time when they should have an opportunity to carry out their design, which they began to execute on August 29, 1676. It was the eve of the Feast of Saint Rose, the patron of the residence in Tupungan. The people of the other residences began to congregate in Tupungan on this day to celebrate the Fiesta of Saint Rose, as was customary for the titular feast of each church. This seemed a good opportunity to the plotters to carry out their plan to kill all the foreigners. They sent some men to burn the residence at Ayraan, believing that as the personnel of the *presidio* were hurrying to the fire, the priests and a few soldiers would remain defenseless, helpless to resist the multitude prepared to attack Tupungan.

They set fire to the church at Ayraan at one o'clock at night. The entire structure was soon in flames, which spread to the school for boys and girls and the living quarters of the missionaries.

They did no more than set fire to the buildings and run, God willing it thus to save the life of a father, who, seeing the fire, had run into the church, with no thought of personal danger, to save the sacred images and vestments and the holy oils. With the help of some friendly natives from that village, who hastened to the scene on hearing the noise, the shouting, and ringing of bells, the sacred objects were saved. The buildings, however, were entirely destroyed.

The father sent word of this affair to the superior in Agadña, who in turn informed the governor. The latter set out at once to Ayraan with most of his men, to provide protection to the missionary. Meanwhile, the natives surrounding Tupungan were ready to attack the residence, only awaiting the signal of the plotters mingling with the crowd within the village. As they moved to the scene of action with lances and machetes, the death of the fathers seemed a foregone conclusion. But Providence intervened. The natives could have killed them all, ignorant as the Spaniards were of the plot, but they did not dare to begin till they had given some signs of mischief-making, and the fire was a clear danger signal. The soldiers became supicious, took their arms and joined the fathers at the residence. The latter were trying to quiet the natives and were asking them the reason for their restlessness. The natives, however, denied the imminence of an uprising, but the Spaniards knew from their manner that they were dissimulating.

When the governor arrived at Ayraan and saw the conflagration, although he was ignorant of its origin, he feared an insurrection and set out for Tupungan, where he arrived to find the fathers and soldiers in readiness for an attack by the natives.

When the natives saw the arrival of the governor, they pretended even more to be there only to celebrate the feast, and they answered readily all questions put to them, since they feared the governor.

Both the governor and the fathers were perplexed and did not know what course to follow in the existing situation, since in any case it was dangerous to take friends for enemies and enemies for friends. They let matters rest for the time being, not wishing to make a difficult situation worse, and believing that later developments would point out to them the course they ought to follow. The only decision they made was that Father Sebastián de Monroy should not return to his residence at Orote until all danger had passed.

When news of this decision reached the natives, they resumed their deceptions. They said that if Father Sebastián would not return with them to their village, that was only because he thought they were enemies, and in that case they would be frightened of the governor and his intentions. They refused to go, they said, without the father who taught them the Christian doctrine.

The fathers were moved by the pleas of the barbarians, and wishing not to neglect anything that would assure peace, they decided that Father Sebastián should return to Orote, and the governor assigned eight soldiers as his bodyguard, among whom was the lieutenant governor, Nicolás Rodríguez, who had orders to return at once to the residence in Agadña at the first sight of trouble among the natives, disregarding all pleas and paying no attention to any pretense of fear on their part.

An adequate guard was left at the residence in Tupungan, while the remaining missionaries and soldiers returned to Agadña with the governor.

The barbarians kept their treachery hidden for eight days longer, hoping the delay would further their ultimate success, and that they would be able to kill all the Spaniards in Orote. For this purpose they sent out word to all the allied settlements to gather on the morning of September 6,1676, which was Sunday, and they determined to stab the father that day while he was saying Mass.

But as our men were alert, always fearing some treachery, Father Monroy, by order to his superior, said the Mass very early, after which the soldiers, armed and in readiness, awaited the natives at the hour when they customarily arrived for the Mass and Christian doctrine.

Many more came that morning than usually attended or who belonged to that residence. They came armed with lances and machetes, but they had not the courage to declare their intentions, when they saw the Spaniards armed and waiting for them. They went into the church and prayed as if they had nothing else in prospect. Afterwards they retired, some to their homes and others to the woods, where they hid. Some who had children in the school had them ask the father for permission to go to the beach, as they did frequently. The father granted the request and both boys and girls went out to amuse themselves, whereupon the natives who were hidden in the woods seized them and took them to another village.

When the news of this reached Father Monroy, he showed his strong displeasure and protested strongly to the natives who were present. He told them he was going to Agadña with his people and would never return to Orote if they did not return the children to him.

A chief named Cheref, a thoroughly untrustworthy person whom the father did trust, tried to delay him, asking him not to go. "I'll see to it that the children come back," he said, while arranging for the *Indios* to arrive from the mountains. These natives, called *torotanos*, would become part of the force from the shore, and the whole multitude would do battle with the few Spaniards.

But Father Monroy, in obedience to orders from his superior, set out for Agadña with the eight soldiers. Cheref followed them, begging them not to go. They arrived at Sumay, where the father hoped to embark for Agadña but could find neither boat nor boatman, since all the natives in that village were united in the conspiracy.

Very soon they saw a great number of natives approaching, screaming and shouting in a barbarous manner, as was their custom in war. But this time they were shouting in glee. They knew that their prey was in their hands and could not escape.

The soldiers saw the immediate danger and prepared for battle with the enemies of Christ, but only after the father had given them absolution and prepared them for the death that seemed inevitable. One soldier, with a small native child (the only one that followed them), was sent to Agadña to carry word of what was taking place, so that they might send help.

He had no more than made his escape when the barbarians attacked our seven soldiers, who, in good order, began to fire their guns and resist the multitude of the enemy. The latter, seeing some of their people seriously wounded, did not dare to throw themselves into closer combat with our men but instead employed a stratagem of our false friend Cheref.

Cheref appeared among the natives and began to berate them for all they had done against the father and the Spaniards, who were friends of the natives. He even threw lances at them, saying that if they did not stop, he would be their enemy.

Father Monroy trusted Cheref, who dissembled so artfully that the missionary accepted his offer of a boat. He got into the boat with his seven soldiers and with Cheref steering. But Cheref, when he was well away from the shore, capsized the boat, a thing the natives are skilled in.

The eight men fell into the water, which was up to their chests and necks, wetting their powder and guns, the only things the barbarians feared. They plunged into the water. Naked and good swimmers, they

The last man to die was Father Monroy, who, with a small buckler, but without a weapon, defended himself from the stones and lances, while exhorting his companions to die for Christ as they had fought for him. At last a stone, which struck his arm, caused him to drop his buckler, whereupon a native struck him on the neck with a lance. The father asked him, "Why are you killing me?" And without awaiting an answer, the father thanked him, saying in the native language "*Si Dios maasi*," which means "God will repay you, and God will have mercy on you." Then they finished him off with blows from machetes and lances.

easily killed the eight men with lances, stones, and clubs. The traitor Cheref used a piece of an arquebus that a soldier had lost. The slaughter, however, was not accomplished without a struggle, for our soldiers, having lost their firearms, fought with sabers and machetes.

The last man to die was Father Monroy, who, with a small buckler, but without a weapon, defended himself from the stones and lances, while exhorting his companions to die for Christ as they had fought for him. At last a stone, which struck his arm, caused him to drop his buckler, whereupon a native struck him on the neck with a lance. The father asked him, "Why are you killing me?" And without awaiting an answer, the father thanked him, saying in the native language "*Si Dios maasi*," which means "God will repay you, and God will have mercy on you." Then they finished him off with blows from machetes and lances.

He was a truly apostolic man, ever zealous for the honor and glory of God and for the good of souls. He was a man of great humility, charity, and mortification, and of such a blameless life that he merited the fortunate death that was his through the barbarians' hatred of the Faith and especially of the sacrament of matrimony, by means of which he had tried to banish the licentious custom of concubinage, wherein lay the disgraceful commercialism of the barbarians.

The natives having won this victory, returned to Orote, where they burned the church, the residence, and the schools.

When Father Monroy's message reached Agadña, the governor embarked for Sumay with his men. He arrived off the shore at midnight, where he could hear the shouts of the natives, who now controlled the shore and the surrounding hills, where they were celebrating over the graves of the dead. The Spaniards thought best not to disembark till daylight, fearing an ambush.

Meanwhile, Agadña was in extreme danger with the *presidio* unmanned and all available men gone to quell the revolt in Sumay. The natives of *katan*[303] (the east), which is in the center of the island and faces the east, joined with those of other settlements near Agadña and retired into the forest, pretending to believe that they would receive the blame for past uprisings, which of course they deserved, since they were confederates of Aguarín. They fell on the town at midnight, meaning to burn the houses of the religious and their lay companions. They thought that during the confusion of the fire they would take the lives of all there. But they were overheard, and a few shots were fired in their direction from an arquebus and this caused them to retreat in haste, discouraged about their plan, which would easily have been carried out had not God confounded the designs of the barbarians in order to aid the Spaniards.

At dawn, September 7, 1676, the governor landed on the beach at Sumay and soon freed the surrounding country of natives.

The soldiers came upon two graves, which they uncovered and found that one body was that of the lieutenant governor. It was carried to the church at Tepungan for burial.

---

[303]*Katan*, the east.

The body of Father Sebastián de Monroy was never found.

Knowing now the treachery of the natives and realizing that their intention was to put an end to the Christian community, the governor ordered all the fathers in Tepungan to return to Agadña until conditions improved.

At one o'clock that day, when the fathers and soldiers in Agadña were very worried that the governor had suffered some disaster, since he was so late in returning, they saw a mass of natives coming from the direction of *katan*, armed with lances and machetes and carrying fish, a gift for the fathers, they said. The plan was, if the fish were accepted, to enter the stockade and behead them all, fathers and soldiers alike.

But they were suspected and chased away without a musket being fired, merely by the courage shown by missionaries and soldiers, or perhaps because God took away their courage.

When the enemy retired, the Spaniards saw the governor coming with his men and the fathers from Tupungan, who had suffered many dangers, although less than those of Agadña. There, God had many times protected the church and the house of the Society by a miraculous providence, through the intercession of the Blessed Virgin and of Father San Vitores and other martyrs of the Marianas, in order that the head, and as it were, the fountainhead of all that Christian community might not be destroyed.

# CHAPTER XVIII

## *A Brief Eulogy of the Venerable Father Sebastián de Monroy*

Father Gerard Bouwens, superior of the Mariana Islands, in a letter that he wrote concerning the death and the virtues of the Venerable Father Sebastián de Monroy, applies to him the words of the Book of Wisdom: *Consummatus in brevi, explevit tempora multa; placita enim erat Deo anima illius, propter hoc properavit educere illum de medio iniquitatum.*[304] And indeed his soul was very pleasing to God, and God wished to reward his merits quickly with immortal life, taking him out of the hardships and miseries of mortal life by a precious death. For in his twenty-eight years, four years of religious life, and a little more than two in the service of the Marianas, he lived many years of virtue and many ages of perfection, and won an eternity of glory, where we believe he lives with the aureole of a martyr.

Father Sebastián de Monroy was a native of Arahal, in Andalucia. He entered the Society at the novitiate of Seville with the special vocation of sailing to the Marianas. The Lord inspired his vocation by means of the missions preached in Seville by Father Juan Gabriel Guillén and Father Tirso González.[305] He informed Father Guillén of his desire. Father Guillén approved of it and helped him to enter the Society. He was received on June 23, 1672, being 24 years of age and a subdeacon.

He began his novitiate with great fervor. He enjoyed the humble tasks of a novice and desired to be humiliated. He never uttered a word of self-praise but rather repeated such things as were to his disadvantage, because he wished others to have a low opinion of him, but the contrary occurred. He was much given to penance and mortification, and since he desired no rest except on the cross, he put sharp stones in his bed so he would wake up before daylight and begin his prayer, the prayer he loved so well. One may say that he was persevering in prayer, in the words of the apostle, in every time and place,[306] because he walked ever in the presence of God and often broke out in tender words of prayer to Christ or Mary or one of his patron saints. His fellow novices observed and especially admired his victory over his natural affections, stripping himself of all that was flesh and blood to the extent that he even did not wish to write a letter to his parents, until, because ordered by obedience, he wrote a farewell letter when he set out for Cádiz en route to the Mariana missions. By way of answer, his father set out for Cádiz to prevent his leaving for the Indies. Supported by persons of considerable authority, his father petitioned the Jesuit superiors to with-

---

[304]Wisd. of Sol. 4:13. Being made perfect in a short time, he fulfilled a long career; for his soul was pleasing to God, and on account of this He hastened to lead him out of the midst of wickedness. A fitting text for one who had pronounced his first vows in the Society just two years before.

[305]See Book 1. chap. 9, n.49.

[306]Eph. 6:18; 1Thess. 5:17-18.

*Book Five, Chapter 18*

draw the assignment. They left the choice of going to the Indies or staying in Spain in the hands of Father Monroy. His father was pleased at this, feeling sure of victory. He took a room in our school there to have easier access to his son. He spoke to him, pressured him, and threatened him, sparing no appeal to love of flesh and blood. Father Sebastián listened to him quite calmly and calmly spoke a few telling words, at which his father changed his attitude and burst into tears of joy to see his son resolved upon an enterprise so much to the service of God. Indeed, if he were not bound by obligations to his wife and family, he said, he himself would go with him, so that he, too, might join in the conversion of the Gentiles.

Father Sebastián felt himself even more confirmed in his vocation, thanks to this victory that the Lord gave him. Note that he was still a Jesuit novice. Shortly before this he had been ordained a priest and now, deeply impressed by the dignity of the priesthood, he could not thank God enough for these great graces, and he proposed for the future to devote himself with greater care to all the demands of religious perfection. He must correspond to the dignity and the obligations that the Lord had laid upon his shoulders. If up till then he had been the servant of his fellow novices, from now on he must be the same to all his companions on the sea voyages and missions. On shipboard he served the sick with no regard for the disgusting aspects of the situation and the maladies, and he sought out the Negroes, cabin boy, and poorer people to teach them Christian doctrine. In the life of the Jesuit community on board, he chose the least comfortable accommodations and he did the same on land, from Vera Cruz to Mexico City, and on other journeys as well, choosing the worst mule, some nights sleeping on a table or platform so that none of his companions might be without a bed. From Mexico to Acapulco he ate the leavings of the others, and if they gave him some bananas, he would eat them with *cascaras* (skins) to make them unpalatable. He suffered the mosquitoes with admirable patience and never wished to use a parasol, as they do there for protection from the sun, which in those parts is intolerably hot. If the superior told him to take a parasol, he held it so that he got no protection, but only inconvenience. On the voyage to the Marianas he continued his practice of teaching Christian doctrine and caring for the sick. For them he used to beg sweets, biscuits, and whatever other little gifts he could obtain. And all the people with personal problems came to him for confession, because of his kind heart and the wise counsels that helped them bear their burdens with patience and conformity to God's will.

Who can tell the joy with which he finally looked upon his longed-for Marianas? To him it was as if he saw Paradise, an earthly one, or was it the heavenly Paradise, filled with the flowers and fruits that he would offer to the Lord, the souls who would know and adore him?

He arrived in the Marianas on June 16, 1674 on the ship *Buen Socorro* and placed himself in the hands of the superior with perfect detachment, that he might send him wherever he wished and employ him in any task he chose. After preparing by prayer and penance, he

*A Brief Eulogy of the Venerable Father Sebastián de Monroy*

pronounced his first vows in the Society of Jesus on June 24, 1674, the Feast of San Juan, in the Residence of Saint Ignatius, in Agadña.

He was immediately put in charge of the residence in Orote, which was just begun, so that with his hard work he might complete and improve the spiritual and physical structure of the station. It is hardly possible to realize what he put up with from the natives of that village, who were the most uncouth of the whole island. But with his courtesy and friendliness, he tamed those barbarians and completed a very pretty church, which he dedicated to the spouse of the Blessed Virgin.

Moreover, he built two schools, one for boys and one for girls, where the pupils were well cared for and carefully instructed. And it is a fact that his parishioners were the best instructed in matters of the Faith in all the Marianas. The children of his residence ordinarily won the prizes in the contests.

In this residence he continued to labor until his martyrdom, performing heroic deeds and practicing all the virtues.

Since humility is the foundation of sanctity, he strove since he first entered the Society to lay a deep foundation, in order that he might raise a lofty structure. Not to mention examples from earlier days, he, on a certain occasion, told his superior that he was going to make a vow to serve the people of the Marianas as their slave all the days of his life, if the superior would permit this; but even without the vow he served them as if he were their slave.

He foresaw the needs both of his companions and the natives, and with his own hands prepared the ground where the roots were grown on which they subsisted. He sewed and mended the clothing of the children and taught them to sew, to read, to speak Spanish, and to do many other useful things, serving them as nurse, teacher, father, and mother, so great was his humility and charity. He had a low opinion of himself and of his judgment, so that in meetings and conversations he was never stubborn, but accepted anyone's opinion rather than his own, supposing that other people understood better than he did.

Poverty was riches to Father Sebastián, so that he desired what others despised. His clothing was the poorest, but clean and befitting a religious. When he went on a mission, he went with feet and legs bare on the shore and in the mountains, wounding himself on the sticks and stones and spiny herbs. In his residence he did not have the precious objects, which the Sunamite provided for Elisha,[307] since he had neither bed, nor chair, nor table, nor candle. He slept on the ground on a palm-leaf mat, and when he had to eat some little food, he sat on the ground like the natives, unwilling that in his house their inescapable poverty should exceed his voluntary poverty. He was resolved never to ask for anything for himself, even in necessary matters, trusting that the providence of the Lord would not fail him. Poor as he was in his own life, he was very liberal toward the boys and girls in his charge. He took care that they did not lack for anything, and at the cost of his own work and sweat, he kept them well and decently dressed.

---

[307] 2 Kings 4:10.

His penances and mortification seemed more than human nature could bear. To the intolerable hardships of the mission he added chains and disciplines severely and frequently administered. He never stripped completely at night in the whole year, unless perhaps the need of cleanliness obliged him to change his shirt. And though one perspires so much in that country, he saw no reason to change a soaking wet shirt. He let the clothes dry on his body.

He never broke his fast till after noon, and then he only ate something the natives gave him as alms. He had so completely lost the sense of taste and was so adapted to native ways that he sometimes ate raw fish with them and rotten coconut swarming with worms, a thing that causes disgust and horror to people newly arrived in these islands. There was even a lack of drinking water and he had to search for it outside the village. But he found even greater mortification in the suffering from mosquitoes, which were a veritable plague in Orote, so intolerable that when soldiers were assigned to Orote, they thought it a punishment. He never seemed to notice the mosquito bites. When the soldiers asked him, "Padre Sebastián, how is it you don't feel the mosquitoes?" He answered, "They don't hurt me. They know me." And he put it well, because for him, they were a great source of merit.

His chastity was angelic, as the rule requires, and his modesty such as perfect chastity requires. When he passed by where there were women, he did not raise his glance from the ground, so that he might not see anything that might stain the purity of his conscience, which was so exceptional that his confessor claimed that he offered almost no matter for absolution. Before he came to these islands, his superior once sent him with a companion to visit a woman who was a benefactor of this mission. But he strongly urged the superior to send someone else. He said, "I will have to talk to the woman if I visit her, and I am no good at that. I'm too rude and tactless." He tried in that way to gloss over his modesty and to attribute his scrupulous caution to lack of tact.

He brought up the girls in the school with the strictest modesty, and when soldiers came to the residence, all the time they were there, he passed every night watching in prayer before the door of the school. Thus he not only protected their purity but moved the very soldiers to devotion and repentance. They said with admiration, "This father is a saint."

He was a true son of our father, Saint Ignatius, in his perfect obedience. He did not wait for a command from his superior. Even a slight suggestion of his wish set Father Sebastián to work on any task however difficult. Since he was alone in the residence with no superior present and without a large Jesuit community, which would require the punctual following of a fixed daily order, his love of virtue led him to work out a schedule, so that he might punctually observe the times for prayer, examination of conscience, spiritual reading, and the other traditional daily exercises. Only in the matter of food did he have to be reminded, and it often happened that he did not eat all day, because his companion did not call him until he finally remembered at night and called him to supper. His punctual obedience was born of his submission to the will of God, which he saw reflected in the will of the superior, and so he placed himself in the hands of the superior as he would in the hands of God.

This virtue was born of the love of God that burned in his breast continually. He fed the flame with prayer and the thought of what he owed the Lord, who had created and redeemed him and granted him such great favors. He used to prepare himself slowly and carefully for the celebration of Mass, which was his great delight amid so many labors and fatigues, and afterwards he made a long thanksgiving. He said the Divine Office on his knees at the prescribed hours with careful attention and a seemly pace. In the same spirit he said his rosary and other devotions to the Blessed Virgin, whom he loved most tenderly, and he spread these devotions among the barbarians, especially devotion to the rosary, which he hung about their necks as a protection from the devil. The fire of charity toward God and neighbor burned in his breast. All the hardships in the world, endured for Christ, would have seemed a little thing. He would have liked to carry the name of Christ to the whole world, that the whole world might know and love him. He grieved to see so many souls seated in the shadow of death, in the darkness of their ignorance and vice, who did not know or falsely conceived their Creator and Redeemer. Since he could not convert all the infidels and sinners, he spared no diligence and embraced every hardship and danger to rescue those who fell to his care. He roamed the mountains in search of children to baptize, adults to teach, and errors to banish. He had his two schools filled with boys and girls, and though he hardly had the means to feed them, with his trust in Divine Providence as his guide and a hunger to teach the doctrine, he sought out more children in the mountains and little valleys, where their parents raised them like little animals. He charmed them with his kind words and presents and carried them to the schools on his shoulders. Many times on these hunts for pupils, he was insulted and badly treated, but he rejoiced to be ill-treated for the love of Christ and for souls. At other times the barbarians, wild and angry, came to kill him. But finding him so serene and peaceful, and being well received by him, as if they were his beloved children, their indignation was soon calmed, and they went back to their homes astonished at such strength and holiness.

Such was the blameless life, the heroic virtues, the flaming zeal of the Venerable Father Sebastián de Monroy, which the Lord chose to crown with the precious death that was accorded him by the barbarians. As we have shown, they killed him through hatred of holy matrimony and a liking for the waywardness of their daughters, which brought them an income and a disgraceful business.

It would not be just not to mention the names of the companions of the Venerable Father Sebastián de Monroy, whom God granted a death for the truths and the virtues most needed by these islands: Father San Vitores and Father Medina for baptism, Father Ezquerra for Extreme Unction, Father San Basilio for justice, Brother Pedro Díaz for chastity,

*Book Five, Chapter 18*

and Father Monroy for the holy sacrament of matrimony. Doubtless, His Divine Majesty desired that these virtues, unknown in this land, might, when watered by the blood of martyrs, flower and bear copious fruits of life. But not only for matrimony and chastity did the Venerable Father die, but also, as is clear, for hatred of the Faith and the Christian religion, which those barbarians wished to banish from those islands, that they might shake off the sweet yoke of Christ, which was very heavy for their soft necks. This hatred of the Faith may be the reason for the earlier attempt to kill the Venerable Father when he was saying Mass and his companions as they assisted at it, though perhaps it was only for the greater facility at such a solemn moment.

It would be unjust not to mention the names of the companions of the Venerable Father Sebastián de Monroy, who wrote their names on the soil of Guam in their own blood, defending the Faith with their arms and their lives, and we believe that God has written their names in heaven in the splendor of glory.

They were called Nicolás Rodríguez de Caravajal, Juan de los Reyes, Alonso de Aguilar, Antonio Perea, José López, Antonio de Vera, and Santiago de Rutia.

Nicolás Rodríguez de Caravajal, who was an Asturian, arrived in these islands in this same year, on June 10, 1676, on board the galleon *San Antonio*, only three months before his death. He was left here by General *don* Antonio Nieto in the office of lieutenant governor, because of his bravery and other qualifications. He had served the king in Puerto Rico for ten years. He was en route to the Philippines as a sergeant, but was called by God to serve this mission and to die in it for the Faith on September 6, 1676. His captain and other friends were unable to persuade him not to remain in this mission, because God wanted him in it for the good fortune that awaited him, and which he earned by a good life. He was a good man, truthful and candid, a true Christian, and of great purity of conscience.

Juan de los Reyes, a Pampango, came to this mission with Father Diego Luis de San Vitores (June 15, 1668) on board the galleon *San Diego* and was his companion in the missions. From the beginning, the Venerable Father trusted greatly in his prudence, gentleness, and manner of procedure and gave him the rank of *alférez*. He valued his help in the conversion of the natives as much as if he were a religious of the Society. He was an example to others, a charitable person, who kept in his house supplies for the needs of the other soldiers.

Alonso de Aguilar, a Creole from Puebla de los Angeles, in Nueva España, served four years in this mission. [He arrived on the *San Diego*, May 2, 1672, one month after the death of Father San Vitores, accompanying the fathers most willingly.] He was modest and of good habits and a brave man who made himself feared by the natives. When he was a companion of Father Sebastián de Monroy, he often said to the superior of the mission, when he gave him clothing, shirts and other things, "Father, all this is for the *Indios*. They will kill me soon enough." And it seems that God gave him that idea in order to prepare him. Alonso kept this in mind and frequently went to confession and Communion, doing all he could for his soul's salvation.

José López, a Creole from Querétaro, in Nueva España, served two years in this mission. [He arrived in the Marianas on June 16, 1674, on board the *Nuestra Señora del Buen Socorro*.] He was a man of good disposition, an enemy of quarrels or dissensions among his companions.

Antonio Perea, a Creole from Cuernavaca, in Nueva España, served two years on this mission. He had arrived at the mission with José López in 1674. He was a very good barber and barber surgeon. He visited the sick with punctuality and charity and lived free of all criticism.

Antonio de Vera, a Creole from Cholula, in Nueva España, served this mission for two years. [He arrived at the same time as the two previously mentioned.] He was a good Christian who feared God, and when he went to Orote, he prepared himself by a good confession. He desired to live long and serve God and his king in these islands.

Santiago de Rutia, a Creole from Mexico City [had arrived three months earlier on the galleon *San Antonio de Padua*, on June 10, 1676]. He was a lad of twenty-two years, who gave hopes of great usefulness to the mission. He was the joy of the other soldiers, with no prejudices towards anyone, of good habits, which were brought to an untimely end.

# CHAPTER XIX

### New Wars of the Barbarians Against
### the Fathers and the Spaniards

The natives, encouraged by their recent victory, tried to finish what they had begun by exterminating the *guirragos* (Spaniards). Aguarín went from one village to another inciting them to continued rebellion, soliciting those who had not yet openly declared against the Spaniards, calling them his enemies and traitors to their country, if they refused to declare themselves enemies of the fathers and the Spaniards and refused to kill them. He assured his partisans of victory and promised them all the possessions of the Spaniards, saying to them proudly: "What do you fear, my friends, my flesh and blood? You need not come to blows with them. No, you can kill these enemies by hunger, by letting no one bring them *dago* or *nica*. What will they eat, if we deny them food? Let no enemy of our country remain in the land to which they brought too many customs opposed to ours. Why do we need their laws here? Without them our fathers lived; and we too shall live without them. Let us enjoy the liberty they enjoyed. So many (Spaniards) have already died, and lately we have killed the bravest ones. Now we will kill them all, and I alone will kill them, because my courage is enough for all. Yet I want you to follow me, that you may have a part in the victory, and in order that I may not have to call you my enemies, as I most certainly will, if you do not do as I say, I who seek only your honor and advantage."

All the month of September and half of October, Aguarín continued to visit village after village, giving a tortoise shell to all that joined him.

Certain villages at this time proved to be loyal and continued their friendship to the fathers and the Spaniards, paying no attention to the promises and threats of Aguarín. But the one among them all who best demonstrated his loyalty was *don* Antonio de Ayhi, who, besides preserving peace in his village, several times prevented the entrance of the enemy, even offering armed resistance when they tried to pass through his territory, thereby suffering great risk to his own life, not only at the hands of the enemy, who looked upon him as a friend of the foreigners, but even more from the people of his own village, because of the difficult situation in which he placed them by defending the Spaniards.

But when the fathers recognized the dangerous position in which *don* Antonio had placed himself, they persuaded him, but with some difficulty, to leave the village, and they urged him to tell the others to permit the enemy to pass through their land, in order not to antagonize them more; but they were not to join them or give them aid in any way, for the fathers did not want his people to incur guilt or to suffer the punishment that would surely fall later to all the enemies of the Spaniards.

The villagers followed the advice of Ayhi, who retired to Ayran, where with equal risk the natives preserved their friendship with the Spaniards, to the discomfort of Aguarín and his men, who threatened this village with severe punishment for being a traitor to the country.

But not even this kept *don* Antonio from helping the fathers and Spaniards or advising them frequently of the intentions of the enemy, supplying them with food himself or with the assistance of some of his friends in the mountains. From the beginning of the mission, God chose this good native to aid the Spaniards in time of need or peril, showing that he never leaves unaided those who serve him, supplying the remedy when danger threatens.

Profiting by the information brought in by *don* Antonio, the Spaniards fortified the *presidio*, moved the church to another location, and moved several houses that occupied the center of the enclosure. These were in a place, where, if during an assault, the stockade were scaled and the houses occupied by the barbarians, the latter would be in a position to do much harm to the *presidio*.

The stockade was renewed, for many of the posts had been rotted away by water, while the enclosure was cleared and several sentry stations were built at the intervals along the sides, from which the fort could be defended in several directions and would not suffer much damage from the enemy.

The latter, when they got news of the preparations in the Spanish camp, were discouraged from the assault they had planned to make at night with five hundred men. The Spaniards took new hope, seeing the fear on the part of the enemy. They even hoped they would attack so they might crush their arrogance.

Aguarín appeared with his army on October 15 (1676), in the afternoon. They took up a position at a distance too far for our guns to reach, and with barbarous yells, they began to throw stones with their sling shots.

When the governor saw that they did not mean to draw nearer, he decided to sally forth with a squadron of men, to show that he did not fear the multitude—a mob of more than fifteen hundred—and to do credit to their arms by making the enemy abandon their positions.

He went out with eighteeen arquebuses and began to shoot, forcing the greater number of the natives to flee. Only a few of the leaders remained, but when these were attacked, they fled also, leaving the place deserted.

The enemy returned on the following day, October 16, and on this occasion the governor, *don* Francisco de Yrrisarri, believed it would be better to remain within the stockade, waiting until the native army had come down from the mountain. There in the open field they would be better targets for the Spanish solders, whereas on the previous day they had been able to escape into the dense forest that served them as a shield. But the barbarians, seeing no one and hearing nothing, suspected a stratagem and retired coolly after throwing a few stones, which did no harm.

That night, however, they destroyed a field of corn that was the principal food supply of the fathers and soldiers. Some of the natives became so bold that they entered the stockade unseen by the Spaniards, and tearing down two timbers, gained entrance to a sentry station, from which point they threw a few lances. They could easily have killed the five soldiers who were sleeping inside, but it was the Lord's will that they did not see them, or that any of the lances should do any harm. This event, however, served to warn the Spaniards that in future it would be well for the sentinels to stay wide awake instead of sleeping, as had been their habit, and offering such opportunities to the barbarians.

Aguarín decided that he did not have enough men to overcome our forces. He, therefore, assembled more natives, with whom he returned after an absence of six days, and from his position on the hillside showered a tempest of stones on the *presidio*. A few soldiers went out to meet them and shot two arquebuses at the natives, who fled in great disorder.

Another day the governor sallied forth in the direction of *katan* (the east) to look for the enemy, and having prepared an ambush, he went on toward a village with his few soldiers. More than forty natives came out and the soldiers, feigning a retreat, drew the natives toward their ambush, where two who had been in the lead were killed, after which the others fled to the hills and the Spaniards were unable to overtake them, for it was already night.

They brought the head of one of the natives to the *presidio*, where they placed it on a pole as a warning of the punishment that the Spaniards would mete out for their crimes, if they persisted in them.

The barbarians were frightened and warned by the deaths of their companions. They suspended the war for a few days, but, meanwhile, they were able to prevent friendly natives from carrying food supplies to the Spaniards. And so the ministers of the gospel were thus compelled to pay the tribute of our first father, gaining their bread by the sweat of their brows, cultivating the land to be able to support themselves and consoling themselves with the thought of imitating in this way so many notable men of our Society, who in Ethiopia and other lands, farmed the land with their own hands, while they were cultivating the field of the Lord with their words.

When the time came when they would have harvested the corn, they found themselves with no food but a small amount of *nica* and *verdolagas* (purselane), which they ate with gratitude. As the amount of ground was small, they knew that God was multiplying the harvest, for every day they gathered enough for all and no one suffered, although the siege lasted six months.

There was no other means, except the providence of God, whereby so many people could have subsisted for such a long time, accustomed as they were to other foods, on *verdolagas* and *nica*, for the latter has no flavor and less nourishment than the *camotes* of Nueva España. Nor did anyone suffer the least illness. But at the end of October, a young man named Diego de Ayala, who had arrived during the year, died of tetanus. His burial took place on the day of the previously mentioned skirmish in the hills. His death was all the more regretted, in such a shortage of men. In such time of truce as the enemy permitted, the fathers applied themselves to the construction of a church of stone and mud, for until that time all the churches had been built of wood. The governor would not permit the fathers to do the actual building or to transport the stone, as they wished, but used soldiers for the labor. He determined also to construct a fort of the same materials, with a wall to protect the mission and put fear into the barbarians, who now began to believe that he was a great man, when they saw the structure of the church, which went forward rapidly. Yet they were never able to give up their own plans and their wicked provocations of the Spaniards.

On November 15, 1676, the Feast of the Patronage of Our Lady, God spared the life of one of the fathers who was almost strangled by the hands of an angry native, had not the hands of Mary, patroness of this mission, spared him.

The governor had gone out with his men on hearing that the enemy was approaching. He seized two natives and condemned them to death for their offenses. A father went to one of the sentry stations and exhorted him to die a Christian, since he was already baptized. The native appeared to be repentant but was only pretending, in order to seize a chance to kill the father, now that he could not escape or harm the Spaniards in any other way.

The father knelt to arrange a pallet on the floor where he meant to rest for a while. Whereupon the native fell upon him, seized him by the throat, and tried to strangle him and scratch out his eyes. The father was able to call out and was rescued by some soldiers nearby, but he was badly injured. They killed the native and exhibited his head in public as a warning to the enemy, who were then making preparation of new wars of arms and starvation.

With the arrival of the Feast of the Expectation of Our Lady (December 18, 1676), the enemy appeared and opened battle, this time from *luchan* (west). The governor went out with only twenty men, because the other twenty soldiers were lame or wounded and were forced to remain within the *presidio*. Still, he wounded five natives, of whom three later died in the villages. He caused them all to flee, leaving more than a hundred lances on the field of battle. He then returned to the *presidio*, since he was unable to pursue and overtake them nor rout them completely, because they hid themselves in the forest, in the mountains, and in the sea.

The barbarians were angry because they had been defeated in so many battles and because so many of their number had been killed or wounded. Yet they had not been able to wound even one of our men, while they were so many and we so few. So with the courage of desperation, they resolved to conquer or die. They summoned more men, calling themselves and the other natives cowards, saying: "How can we have so little courage that the foreigners can drive us out of our own homes? Let us conquer or die, and we will conquer, if we are not afraid to die. It is only our fear that makes them victorious. Let us not turn our backs to their arms, and then we will make them turn their backs to us. Let us fight for our women, our children, our lands, our liberty, and let us finish at one blow those who wish to deprive us of everything, and who are the cause of all our troubles."

The Spaniards at this time had recourse to heaven with sacrifices, prayers, and penances, with pleas and the frequent reception of the sacraments. The governor set a good example, for he was first at confession and Communion, as well as the sermons and discourses that the religious gave. They made many vows and novenas to the Blessed Virgin, Saint Michael, Saint Joseph, and Saint Francis Xavier, in the hope the Lord would have mercy on them, seeing they had such patrons. And indeed he did, in the greatest attempt and effort that the barbarians had yet made.

The enemy, having come to the town on January 7, 1677, retired the same day without giving battle. Four days later, January 11, they came with two armies, one on the sea, with over a hundred boats, the other on land, occupying all the beach and the hills back of the town. If our men went out from the *presidio*, as they had in the past, to meet the army in front, the others, hidden in the undergrowth behind, would attack the stockade and kill all within. There is no doubt that if they executed their design as agreed, their victory would have been assured, as would likewise our ruin.

But although the barbarians were able to carry out part of their plan, they could not carry it to completion, because the governor had already gone out with a squadron to a location opposite the native army on the beach, and when the natives from the hills began the attack on the stockade, they opened fire, and God gave the natives such fear of the firearms that they retreated, not daring to proceed. This helped the plans of the governor. He saw that they had to sally from the *presidio*. But this would leave the *presidio* in danger. So he ordered some crossbows (*ballestas*), loaded with arrows, to be placed at several points along the stockade, to frighten the natives. The field was sown with sharp sticks and bits of bone, over which the barbarians would have to walk if they approached the *presidio*, a stratagem that gave good results, since many were wounded in that way.

At this time the multitude of natives on the beach and in the boats began to throw stones and lances at the small company of Spaniards. The firearms were not effective, because when a shot was fired, some disappeared quickly under water, while others used their boats as shields. They soon approached for an attack. But all our men, with courage and steadfastness, still faced them without leaving their position. Finally, they achieved a victory by means of a small campaign piece, loaded with musket balls, with which they did much damage to the boats, and also by means of accurate gunfire, which killed two natives and wounded many, causing the enemy to flee, leaving the beach deserted.

*New Wars of the Barbarians Against the Fathers and the Spaniards*

The two armies returned on January 24 (1677) with a greater number of men, and this time they brought shields to protect them against the musket balls.

The governor ordered the scattering of splinters and bone fragments renewed on the side towards the mountain and had many more scattered in the water along the shore. He had a small flag planted midway between the two points, believing that some of the barbarians would want to capture it in order to gain some fame among their own people. He planned that when they did so, he would spray them with gunfire, which would leave them frightened and warned. He ordered the soldiers not to go outside and distributed them according to his plan, placing the larger number on the side of the flag, to support his stratagem.

The soldiers had prepared themselves that day for battle, going to confession and Communion and attending a solemn Mass in honor of Saint Michael the Archangel, on whose altar, as on the altars of the Blessed Virgin, lights were kept burning. As they took up arms and went to their posts, the captain encouraged them with the hope of victory, a hope based more on hope of help from the Prince of the Heavenly Militia than upon his own courage.

The countless number of the barbarians approached with twenty or thirty boats in the lead, whose occupants leapt into the water in their haste to seize the flag. When they arrived at the place where it was secured and as one was about to pull it down, the Spaniards began firing, critically wounding many. At the same moment our men began to shout *Victoria! Victoria! Victoria San Miguel! Victoria!*

The barbarians, hearing these cries, together with the noise of the firearms, and wounded by the splinters on the mountain and in the water, fled in terror, as if an army from heaven had descended upon them. And doubtless this fear was visited on them by the prince of the angels, to whom the soldiers accorded this victory, since he is the patron of Catholic arms, when they fight in defense of the Faith and to extend it in new worlds.

It was no small consolation to realize that this victory was gained on the day (January 25) that marked one hundred and twenty years since the discovery of the island, when possession was taken for the King of heaven and the king of earth with the celebration of the Holy Sacrifice of the Mass.

This long-continued succession of wars was followed by peace, or rather the cessation of war, for no capitulation or friendships were made. The barbarians merely retired in fear, and the Spaniards let the matter drop, reserving to themselves the right to punish those who deserved it when they were able.

They hastened the construction of the church, which was completed in time for Holy Week, which began on April 18, 1677. This edifice caused additional fear in the natives, since it was built with a solid flat roof that could be made to serve as a fortification. They were still more afraid when they saw houses built of the same material around the church, for these buildings would be safe from fire.

*Book Five, Chapter 19*

What alarmed the natives gave the Spaniards a greater sense of security and the hope of a brilliant future for the Christian community, which so many were trying to perpetuate here, marrying and building homes.

The natives at last solicited peace, but the governor made no haste in granting their request, knowing that if he made them wait for it, he could arrange it more to his advantage when he had stronger forces, for he had learned through experience, his own and other people's, that by fear alone could he maintain power over these barbarians.

In order to celebrate Holy Week with the greatest possible devotion, an eight days' mission was held in the new church, ending on Holy Thursday, April 15, and the fruit of these sermons and conferences was gained by means of the fervor and zeal of the ministers of the gospel. Especially effective was the *Acto de Contrición*, of which the *Marianos* are very fond. All the military made general confessions of their whole lives and the *Marianos* of their lives since baptism, receiving Communion with great devotion, imitated by the children who had been prepared for these sacraments.

The Holy Week ceremonies were celebrated with all the pomp that the poverty of the Marianas would permit. There were public penances on Good Friday, indulged in with such fervor that it was necessary to moderate their severity in order not to permit our soldiers to endanger their lives, which are so necessary to that Christian community.

There followed Easter, which was a very happy one because of the peace and harmony that existed among all the Spaniards in the absence of trouble from the *Marianos*. On the Sunday after Easter, April 25 (1677), the festival of the dedication of the new church was celebrated with a solemn Mass, a sermon, and dancing by the Mariana children.

It was dedicated to María Santísima in honor of her Sweet Name, and to all the Holy Family, to which the first church by Father San Vitores was dedicated, and although later the church was moved and improved in both location and material, the name was never changed. The same day a votive Mass was offered in honor of Saint Michael in gratitude for the recent victory.

Amid the continued risks that the Christian community ran of losing everything, the missionaries had one consolation and that was of seeing greater respect on the part of the barbarians for the name of God than they had formerly shown. Although they hated God's Law for the limitations it placed on their vices, no blasphemies were heard in these wars, whereas in earlier battles, these blasphemies were the common weapon by which they wounded the zealous hearts of the fathers. One of these barbarians, who had bragged in former battles with diabolical arrogance that he was God, has lately been one of the most faithful friends of the fathers and Spaniards and has risked his life many times for their cause. He had escaped one day from Aguarín and his men, who wanted to drown him. He came to our house and told of the occurrence and thanked God for freeing him from the enemy. He then asked to go to confession to thank God for such a great favor.

*New Wars of the Barbarians Against the Fathers and the Spaniards*

The constancy of many of the boys of the school in Agadña was admirable. They remained with the fathers and the Spaniards, assisting them in their work. The larger boys even fought against their countrymen. They would not be separated from their teachers and spiritual fathers, even in the face of the threats and promises of their carnal fathers, preferring to suffer affliction with the people of God, rather than to enjoy prohibited pleasures.

And yet, why should it be remarkable that they behaved thus, those who were accustomed to frequent the sacraments with much devotion, to examine their consciences on their knees every night, and to take the discipline as some of them did?

There were two in whom the light of constancy and devotion shone with special brightness. One of them, at the beginning of the uprising, had been compelled to go on an errand to another village. There, he encountered his whole family, friends and relatives, and all tried to persuade him not to return to the fathers. They tried every reasoning and threat, but they could not change his mind, and he condemned their intention of making war on the Spaniards and returned to Agadña, to the fathers who had believed that he would remain with his people.

The loyalty of the other was no less notable. His father had been killed in a skirmish and one of his brothers had been condemned to be beheaded in the *presidio*. The boy, naturally, was afflicted by the death of his brother and showed his grief. But he knew his brother's offenses, and he was convinced that the punishment was just and said that evil-doers, in this life or the next, must pay the penalty for their sins. This experience served also to make him a better Christian, frequently receiving the sacraments and fighting with valor for the Christians against the enemies of Christ.

And what am I to say of the native girls who were married to Spaniards and Filipinos, who lived contentedly in the *presidio* and were as fond of Christian ways as if they had been accustomed to them all their lives? They attended Mass every day and afterward returned to their family obligations, spending their days sewing, washing clothes, and doing other household tasks. Outside their devotions, they suffered the same risks, labors, and lack of necessities that all in the *presidio* experienced, nor did they complain or try to return to their people, which would have been an easy matter for them. Their constancy and affection for their husbands owed much to the grace of the sacrament of matrimony. All this is to be admired and valued in a land where marriage lasts only so long as the wife wishes it, and where by their own free will, without cause or occasion whatsoever, wives leave their husbands and marry others.

And yet in this matter, as in the case of other vices, there is an improvement because of the entrance of the Faith, for now the Gentiles are able to observe the customs of the Christians, and they can all hear and understand what the fathers preach about the perpetuity of matrimony and the ugliness of their vices.

Finally, there was noted in the recent wars the fidelity of many of the villages, loyal as they were to the fathers and the Spaniards, where such loyalty bore fruit for faith and religion.

# CHAPTER XX

### *Gains for the Christian Community*
### *With the Success of the Spanish Arms*

The letters and documents that were dispatched from the Marianas in 1678 never reached Spain, because the ship was lost that carried them. Thus it is that we lack first-hand information of the progress of Christianity in those islands from June 1677 until June 1678. We may, however, infer from later letters and official reports that the wars continued, but with less intensity, and the fruits of the new Christian community were harvested with increasing success.

But in order not to write by speculating, we shall leave the happenings of that year to be described later by anyone who may in time receive dependable information. We shall continue our narrative from June 18, 1678, when the galleon *San Telmo* arrived after a successful voyage and anchored in the port of Umatag, or San Antonio, as they had always desired in the past and had not done. This way we could land the supplies properly and not miss so much of them, as we had in past years.[308]

*Don* Juan de Vargas Hurtado came on that ship as the new governor of the Philippines, and since he was recently instructed by Her Majesty and possessed special mandates, he gave many orders for the preservation and extension of the Christian community here. Not content with this, he went ashore with the pilot, Leonardo Coello. He himself took soundings in the harbor, satisfying himself that it was a safe anchorage for the ships bound for the Philippines, as well as for the *patache* that the mission needed and he promised to send soon, a promise long frustrated in the past for the reasons and unreason of the enemies of this mission in the Philippines.

Among other favors that *don* Juan de Vargas granted the mission at this time was that of leaving thirty soldiers with a captain of his own choice, called *don* Juan Antonio de Salas, a native of Madrid, a man of military experience and great courage, to whom he gave the title of Governor of the Mariana Islands.

*Don* Juan de Vargas set sail for the Philippines after remaining three days at the port. The governor of the Marianas informed himself of the state of the Christian community and of the restraints and damage it had suffered from the rebels. Consequently, he decided that he must chastise them, if the road of the gospel was to be kept open. And so, on June 29, he set out with his men for Tannagi [sic], the most hostile of the villages, where many of the wrongdoers lived. Marching from two o'clock in the afternoon and almost all of the night, he could not get to Tannagi because the trails were impass-

---

[308]See Book 5, chap. 16:452 for the deliberate avoidance of Umatac harbor. Presumably there were advantages, politcal and commercial, in carrying off Marianas mission supplies to the Philippines.

479

able, and they turned to another village nearby called Apoto, where Aguarín lived.[309]

The soldiers ran a considerable risk from the traps the natives had made and concealed with false coverings of stones on the slope of a hill that the soldiers had to descend. If it had not been daylight, many of them would have perished, since they might only discover the danger when it was too late to save themselves. Two, in fact, were injured in a fall down the slope.

Before they arrived at the village, they were discovered by a native who was on the beach. With a horrible cry he warned his people to be on guard. The soldiers ran into the village hoping to take them unawares, and the natives fled, all except one companion of Aguarín, who was killed by the soldiers. The Spaniards sacked the village and set fire to the houses and then returned to Agadña, happy to have given such a good start to the new regime.

The destruction of a village so brave and so well fortified struck terror into the hearts of the natives. Many villages came to solicit peace, bringing great quantities of rice with which to provision the royal store-house, which was short of necessary supplies. Their request was granted with a warning of their obligation to attend Mass and Christian doctrine and to be instructed in matters of the Faith, since they were already Christians. Also they were warned not to harbor in their villages any murderers or enemies of the Spaniards and to obey the governor in all that he ordered.

The governor made a second sally against the enemy villages, taking as a guide a native who had been made a prisoner. He led the soldiers over the most dangerous paths, where they could easily have been wiped out by a few barbarians, a treachery for which he later paid with his life in the *presidio* as a warning to the others.

The first enemy village they entered was Tuparao (Tupalao), where they killed a native and took two children, whose parents abandoned them in the haste of their flight. They were taken to Agadña to be brought up and educated in the schools there. The soldiers set fire to the houses and passed on to Fuuña, also an enemy village.

A troop of natives came out to meet them, confident in the earthworks that they had made. They began to throw their lances with such enthusiasm and resolution that they split the shields of the soldiers, but by the gift of God, they hurt no one. On the contrary, our men attacked the barbarians with such valor that they captured the trench, killing some and wounding others who tried to escape by swimming in the sea. They put the others to flight, entered the village, sacked it, and burned it to the ground. They returned by way of Orote and Sumay, where they did the same, burning even the refuges that they had built on the hills. This accomplished, they returned well and happy to Agadña, recognizing all their success as coming from the hand of God.

As a result of these wars and because of the shortage of Spanish soldiers who could be sent out from the *presidio*, in some of the

---

[309]Apoto, in the northeast of Guam.

villages the natives began to build again the public houses, which the faith and zeal of the fathers had destroyed. The latter complained to the governor, and he set out with a company of soldiers, burned those houses and threatened the *Indios* with worse punishments, if they built them again.

The scandal caused by the true friend of the Spaniards and benefactor of Christianity, *don* Antonio de Ayhi, was no small matter. He had been married in church, but now he abandoned his legitimate wife and was living with another, and no one was able to persuade him to leave this woman either by pleas or threats. Nor was there any less difficulty from the wife's side. Seeing that she had been scorned, she thought it would be a disgrace to return to her husband. This matter was commended to God, and later one of the fathers spoke to *don* Antonio with such force and efficacy, proposing motives both divine and human, that at last he gave in, divine grace intervening, and he announced that he was ready to return to his wife, if she were willing.

The governor had her called in, and she agreed without serious objection, whereupon the two returned to their former life. In order to make certain, a house was built within the *presidio*, where they live with edification to all.

It is well known that the change in *don* Antonio was caused by the favor of the most high, because he bore with such patience, for the love of God, the mockery of the natives who called him a worthless man. This is shown by the answer he made to a father who asked him why he had allowed the *manceba* to take his property. "Father," he answered, "What need have I of property? I desire nothing but to follow the customs of God and to obey you who are my fathers. If that were not so, I might have hanged or stabbed myself. Their mockery of me for giving up the concubine is no small matter. But I am yours and all Spanish."

It is impossible to say how many were the good results of the resolution of *don* Antonio. Many concubinages were abandoned or converted into marriages. And if on this occasion *don* Antonio showed himself a Christian, he also showed himself a Spaniard, as did another native chief called Alonso Soon, who two years before had returned from Manila and Mexico. Why he had gone there I do not know.

These two Christians were of great importance for the Christian community. They were always ready to accompany the soldiers. They particularly distinguished themselves in the fight at Pigpug, of which we will soon speak. Ayihi served as a shield for the governor, and as he was dexterous in lance warfare, he averted the lances thrown at the governor. Soon did the same for the soldiers until his shield was at last split in pieces. The latter so distinguished himself in these encounters that he was a real affliction to the native wrongdoers, and they hated him more than if he were a foreigner. But they all respected him. When they heard someone say, "Soon says it," they obeyed and kept quiet.

The governor wished to pacify all the rebels. He sent seven times to call the natives of Agofan,[310] an enemy village, to discuss peace.

---

[310] Agofan, on the west side of Guam, near Apra Harbor.

Although they were a proud people, they answered coolly that they were afraid. He went to their homes to search them out.

He found the trails so strewn with sharp barbs that the soldiers had to remove them before they could proceed. At the entrance of the village the natives had formed a strong entrenchment of stone that blocked the passage. Behind it they had their sentry boxes, where sentinels were on duty all night. This was a fortification by means of which they could have defended themselves for a long time, if they had had the courage. But it was clear that fear had built it, because when the Spaniards captured it, not one person was found in the village.

Some were in the water, and on the persuasion of the fathers who accompanied the expedition, they presented themselves before the governor and were kindly and peacefully received by him. The houses of all those who had left the village were burned, but the houses of those who remained were spared. But this kind of treatment was not enough to reassure the natives, who still wished to escape, and a few days later they loaded their families and goods into their boats and left for all time, not only the village of Agofan but the island of Guam as well, moving to the island of Rota.

The boats were seen as they sailed past the north shore, but because of the lack of boats, our men have never been able to prevent contacts with the enemy by sea. Governor Juan de Salas was chagrined at seeing us thus ridiculed. His zeal and courage would not suffer the insult. He ordered a small boat prepared and got into it with five arquebusiers and two friendly natives and followed the enemy squadron. When the natives saw that the governor was trying to overtake them, they lightened their craft by throwing overboard some of their supplies. Only one boat was unable to keep up with the others. In this boat there were two native nobles and three children, with a cargo of supplies. The governor overtook it and seized it. He took the children to Agadña to be educated, while the men were held as prisoners until such time as the villagers should consent to return to their abandoned homes and our friendship. This affair made such an impression on the people that for a long while no enemy boats passed along that side of the island for fear of being seized by the governor.

Since these expeditions to the various villages were frequent, it was necessary to strengthen the *presidio*, whose stockade, being built of coconut trees, was now in bad condition. He renewed the whole structure and built it this time of the kind of trees that when planted in the earth, put out roots and perpetuate themselves. This saved the labor that had been required each year to renew it. Two new sentry stations were erected, and thus the parade ground was placed in good order.

At this season the governor learned that the villages of Sumay, Orote, and Tuparau,[311] which had been burned, had very large crops ready for harvest. He permitted a rumor to circulate that he was going to harvest the crops and so replenish the supplies in the royal storehouse; but his real design was to stage a surprise attack on the enemy.

---

[311] All on the west coast near Apra Harbor.

On September 27, 1678, he set out. Our men were seen when they arrived at the village of Fuuña,[312] and the enemy began to flee. The soldiers followed them, and although they did not overtake them, they burned the villages of Tayfac, Unian, and Pupuro.

The natives, seeing themselves so relentlessly pursued, were so discouraged and intimidated that all these villages and other distant and less guilty ones begged for peace, offering to obey readily the mandates of the governor. They were received in friendship, with the exception of known killers. They kept their promises by attending Mass and Christian doctrine on Sunday, even though many of them lived at a great distance from the churches.

There still remained some villages in the south that still enjoyed their liberty, some because of their remoteness from the *presidio*, others because nature itself had built fortifications around them. When these were summoned to appear before the governor, they had not done so, because they did not wish to recognize him.

The governor planned an expedition against the most arrogant among them, which were Picpuc and Tarufofo,[313] believing that when these villages were punished, the rest would submit voluntarily.

The natives, learning of his plans, armed themselves and prepared many ambushes along the trails, which were naturally the most difficult and dangerous ones on the island. Along these, they could effectively harass the soldiers, who would be unable to retaliate. With this in mind, our men sought a native as guide who was familiar with the country and who led them through another route for a great part of the way. But the most difficult part of all could not be avoided. This was a narrow mountain pass that was the only entrance to the village of Picpuc, and this the natives had blocked by a trench and embankment, which the natives defended from the mountain sides by a shower of stones and lances.

The soldiers began to climb up the narrow pass with courage— or was it recklessness?—and very soon found themselves in a quandary: they could neither advance nor retreat. Their arquebuses had not sufficient range to harm the enemy, while their shields were fast being smashed by the hail of stones and lances. They could do nothing but call for assistance from those who followed them. Two of these fell, badly wounded, as they hurried to the relief of their comrades.

The governor, seeing the extreme danger and realizing that his soldiers were afraid to advance, placed himself at the head of the party and began to climb the rough cliff-side with such great determination and audacity that a few men followed him and soon gained the height. They took the fortress of the enemy, who fled in all haste, depriving the governor of the opportunity to avenge the wounds of his men.

Nevertheless, he pursued them and burned the villages of Picpuc and Tarufofo (Talofofo) with all the goods contained therein, including more than twenty boats, much rice, and other foodstuffs.

---

[312]This Fuuña seems to have been on Orote Point.
[313]Villages in the southeastern part of Guam.

They destroyed the trench with which the natives had defended their village, and as they returned by way of that coast, all the other villages came out to meet them, offering presents and supplies for the soldiers, begging for peace, which was granted under the usual conditions advantageous to the Christian community.

These victories on the part of the Spaniards struck terror into all the islanders at the beginning of the year 1679, and the friendly natives no longer hesitated to declare themselves bitter enemies of the wrong-doers and rebels. They gave the governor very useful information, even offering to bring him the heads of the murderers.

On January 6, 1679, a chief named Ignacio Inete, accompanied by a group of his friends, encountered in the mountains a troop of enemy natives from Tarragui. He fought bravely and left three of the enemy in the field, stabbed to death. He immediately sent word to the governor, in order that the governor might send for the heads of the slain enemy and have them impaled as a public warning.

Very soon the villages that had been punished for their complicity in the death of Father Sebastián de Monroy, killed the murderer of Father Francisco Ezguerra and presented his head to the governor.

A friendly native also brought to the governor's notice the fact that the principal murderer of Father Monroy was then in the village of Merizo. The governor at once embarked for that place, accompanied by fifteen soldiers. They landed at Umatag and continued by land until they arrived at the place where the traitor was living. The latter, seeing the soldiers, tried to escape, but the governor killed him with one musket ball, which passed through his chest. He then ordered the man's head and the sacrilegious hand to be cut off and taken to Agadña.

Almost the whole island was now in a state of peace. It was thought advisable to make a tour of all the villages, to become acquainted with the people, to teach them, and baptize the children who during the three past years had not been able to receive the waters of baptism because of the wars, which had, in effect, made prisoners of the evangelical laborers.

Two fathers accompanied the governor into the hills. The latter wished to punish the villages along the route for having entered into hostilities against other villages. They had wished to burn their houses, because they had formed a friendship with the Spaniards and had submitted to the governor. But upon the death of the two nobles who had been the cause of all the trouble, the people were afraid.

The governor proceeded on this journey, which began at Umatag, and visited many villages on the southern side, where there were many gains for the Faith, for many children were baptized, while the adults were reinstructed in the mysteries of the Faith, until at last the approach of Lent (1679) caused them to return to Agadña.

A capture of greatest value was made at that time, all the more precious since all hope of attaining it had been presumed lost. This was a Filipino, who had come to the islands as an interpreter for the fathers and had passed over to the side of the infidels eight years before. He had

*Gains for the Christian Community With the Success of the Spanish Arms*

lived among them all this time as if he were not a Christian. But God, in his infinite mercy, placed him in our hands when he least wished it. He gave such evidence of repentance, however, that the fathers, the past forgotten, embraced him as if he were another prodigal son, and they took him to their house, where he lived as a true Christian.

As Lent began, a time that the fathers employed in instructing and preaching to the soldiers and the natives, they began the construction of two very necessary buildings, a church large enough for all the natives, with three aisles, since the older church was too small for the multitude that came to hear Mass and the doctrine, and also a fort and a royal storehouse, since the existing one was not strong enough. Both works were completed in a short time, and by the time the fort was finished, the villages of Inapsan, Ritidyan, and Tarragui, which had persisted in their rebellion, came and sued for peace. They feared the punishment that threatened and were in great need, because their contacts by land and sea had been cut off. They promised neither to protect in their villages any enemies of the Spaniards nor to defend murderers and wrongdoers.

They were received with much pleasure and were given to understand that the arms of His Majesty are not meant to do them harm but to oblige them not to shake off the gentle yoke of Christ that they had assumed by being baptized. Nor were they to hinder the fathers in their preaching, teaching, or baptizing those who wished to be baptized, for no one was obliged to be a Christian, and they were to be careful not to interfere with anyone who wished to become one.

With these fortunate results, which the Lord had accorded the Catholic arms, the prospects of the Christian community took on a more hopeful aspect. It was no longer threatened by the insolence of the barbarians. Now, not only the children but adults of all ages applied themselves diligently to things of the Faith and asked quite sincerely what they must do to be saved.

Every Sunday and on all feast days Christian doctrine was presented in this form: they all gathered in the church and began to chant the prayers of the catechism. When this was over, Mass was said, followed by Christian doctrine with all the brevity, clarity, and method that was necessary for them to derive the greatest benefit.

All the people could not come on time for the Mass, because many came from distant parts. Hence, all who came late gathered at midday and to them alone the Christian doctrine was explained. Besides, these days, the boys and the girls of the villages near the *presidio* came on Wednesdays and Saturdays to pray in the church and hear the catechism.

The *urritaos*, most indomitable people, came on Thursdays, and the fathers tried through the Christian doctrine to teach them a holy fear of God. All were instructed in their obligations, especially toward the married women of the *presidio*. Every afternoon, the latter prayed in church and one of the fathers gave them a talk, explaining how they were to conduct themselves towards God, their husbands, their children, their families, and towards strangers. Their excellent behavior helped greatly in influencing the neophytes to be married according to the rites of the Church. Seeing those women so diligent and so circumspect, the natives wished their own wives might be like them, and when they heard that this was a grace conferred by holy matrimony, they began to take a favorable view of the sacrament.

To impress in the hearts of these good wives and through them on all others (since women are always the most powerful instrument for good or ill) the devotion to the Blessed Virgin and all piety, they attended Mass every day, recited prayers every afternoon, and said the rosary in church on Saturday, forming two answering groups. They went to confession and Communion at least once a month to gain the plenary indulgence. And thus, the village and church of Agadña seemed like a new Christian people, and some old Christians could learn much from these new ones. And I must not fail to mention the good example that the soldiers have given this year, since every Sunday after Mass they hear a talk on the mysteries of the Faith, besides the sermons on the more solemn feasts. Every day at two in the afternoon they say the rosary in two answering groups in church, and on the first Sunday of the month, they prepare for the plenary indulgence by going to confession and Communion. During Lent they attended the sermons and in Holy Week did many penances.

The clergy were pleased by the care the new Christians showed in bringing news of sick people, in order that the Fathers might go to them and administer the sacraments. They carry some to the church to receive the sacraments, which shows the faith they have in supernatural things.

I must not neglect to tell of a very amusing case. A good native had frequently heard the fathers warn the people to inform them about the sick and infirm, in order that these might receive the sacraments. His son, one year and a half old, suffered an accident and his father took him in his arms and carried him in his arms to Agadña. They asked him where he had come from and what he wanted, and he answered, "I have brought Julianillo so the fathers can hear his confession and give him Viaticum, because he is dying." And as they were all amused, he was in some confusion, until they explained to him that these sacraments are not administered to infants such as Julianillo, who have not yet the use of reason.

The natives were even more careful to bring their children to be baptized, for their old fear that baptism killed babies had vanished. But it was even more astonishing to see them bring their deceased from places two or three leagues distant to bury them in consecrated ground, whereas they formerly esteemed the bodies of their dead so much that they would not be separated from them.

Also the vain custom or solemnity with which they celebrated the deeds of their departed has fallen into disuse. They formerly sang lugubrious songs around the arches and the adornments of the grave. But they now realize, because of the Faith, that their dead are fortunate and worthy of praise when they die in the Lord, and that others merit nether celebration nor praise, for they are in hell.

They are also improving in political matters, having greater veneration for the fathers and respect for the Spaniards, whose customs now seem good to them, especially the custom of wearing clothes. Their greatest concern is to find a petticoat or a pair of pants in which to appear at church, and anyone that does not have one borrows from another, for they are ashamed at their nakedness.

They now eat pork and are becoming fond of corn, although they do not make bread with it because they do not have the utensils with which to prepare or bake bread. They grow many watermelons and much tobacco, but they do not know how to prepare or roll the latter.

Of the school children there is nothing to say except that they are brought up like those of Europe. They are the best monitors of the customs of their own people, for they do not excuse their own parents when they are remiss in any matter of the Faith or the Law of God, their Christian zeal being stronger in them than carnal love.

# CHAPTER XXI

*New Gains of the Christian Community in the Marianas,
Following The Punishment of Several Rebels and
Malefactors*

While the affairs of Christianity in the Marianas were running smoothly, as we have heretofore stated, and gave promise of even a brighter future, the galleon *San Antonio* arrived. This was on June 17, 1679.

When the ship was first sighted to the north, some of the fathers set out to meet it in small native boats. They were anxious to obtain the supplies that they badly needed. But although the weather was good when they reached and boarded the ship, suddenly the wind rose from the south, which drove the galleon away from land. This was most distressing to the fathers who saw their supplies lost to them, as always happens because the ships do not anchor where they have been ordered. [Presumably in Umatag, where the governor of the Philippines had investigated and approved the anchorage.]

They loaded one of the ship's launches with as much of their goods as it would hold and set out for the shore. After they had made a considerable distance it began to rain and the wind increased. The clouds and rainfall caused them almost to lose sight of the ship. In spite of the serious need for supplies, they turned about and got to the galleon, offering the storm as a pretext, but the reason seems to lie elsewhere.

At the same time a boat came out from the mission and into this it was possible to load a large amount of supplies, together with Fathers Basilio de Rouxl, Tomás Vallejo, and Brother Baltasar Bonies, who had returned to serve on this mission. The same ship was bringing Father Francisco Salgado to the Philippines. He was procurator in Rome for the Province of the Philippines and a great friend of the mission in the Marianas. [He was enroute from Europe.]

These fathers, then, embarked in the small boat with a few soldiers who were also to remain in the Marianas. They spent that night and all the following day at sea, fearful of perishing, while trying to make a landing and hoping that fortune would at least carry them back to the ship or perhaps to the Philippines. But God, who looks with mercy on this mission, although he permits it to be lashed by waves no less than was that little boat, hastened with a remedy, at the time, of most dire necessity. At that moment they encountered the *alférez* Francisco Ruíz, an experienced sea-faring man, who was going in a large native boat to board the galleon, in order to sail to the Philippines. But seeing the fathers and their companions in such a desperate state, he left his own boat, and with the help of a breeze that the Lord sent and the labors of its occupants, the boat reached Agadña about nightfall. *Alferez* Ruíz had to remain in the Marianas all that year because of this.

The fathers from the mission who had boarded the galleon were in no less delicate a situation, because the ship was fast drifting away from the shore, and they had no boat in which to return to the island. Nor could they see any craft in the water. They were told that no boat could land then on that shore, that even those already making for shore would have to return to the ship. It seemed then that all would have to sail to Manila, leaving the mission in the Marianas with almost no staff.

But the Lord came to their rescue, sending some little native sailboats in which they embarked, taking with them some of the lighter articles, disregarding the other supplies in order to take care of the people.

At last, in spite of squalls and whirlwinds, they arrived late at night at Agadña, all except Father Tomás de Cardeñoso, whose small boat was carried by the wind very close to Rota. He was afraid to land here because this island is occupied by criminals and murderers. On the following day, almost exhausted by the labor, sleeplessness, hunger, and thirst, he arrived at Agadña, as the tempest changed to fair weather and all their cares into rejoicing.

For almost a year the island had been without war, although it had neither peace nor security. The missionaries could not yet safely leave the *presidio* without an escort. Many of the natives who had killed fathers and their companions or were prime movers in past wars were hidden in various districts, protected by their relatives or friends. Hence it was never safe to trust those who in the past had proved themselves faithless. For this reason the governor was determined to rid the country of these savages, so that the clergy might be able to walk about in safety.

Three native nobles of Tarragui had been held prisoner since long before the arrival of the galleon, because, although they had made peace with the Spaniards, they had permitted the prime mover in the war, Aguarín, to remain in their territory. The excuses they offered had indeed been accepted. The principal one was that they had no control of the people who had received him into their houses. And so he set them at liberty, but the governor still thought it wise to inspect that part of the island, accompanying the missionaries who wished to visit those villages that they had not been able to approach since the beginning of the uprisings.

The *Indios* did not know of the designs of the Spaniards, and so they fled to the mountains and caves, so that our men found very few people living in the villages. But when these were informed that the Spaniards had come for peace and not for war, many people began to come forward and to bring children for baptism, knowing that their children were their best peace offerings.

The people were not harmed, but the house of Aguarín, who had fled to the island of Santa Ana (Rota) was burned. Thus Spaniards refrained from placing any blame on the villagers for having sheltered him or for his flight. Thus they would be able to see that the Spaniards intended them no harm, but only good.

They looked for and found the bones of the Venerable Father Antonio María de San Basilio, and they carried them to the church in Agadña, except for the long bones of his arms and legs, which the barbarians had taken for their lances.

From Tarragui the party passed on to Inapsan, but as a warning preceded them, the natives left their village and were perched on a steep, rocky cliff, with as much of their goods as they were able to carry.

The captain searched all the houses and took everything that might be of use to the soldiers. He burned such lances as he found, along with the houses, and ordered that no one without his permission should abandon his village.

He went on to Ritidyan, where the villagers, in obedience to the decree that the governor had just made public, awaited the Spaniards and marched out singing the Christian doctrine. The fathers were glad to learn that the adults in this village still remembered so much that they had learned, and they rejoiced even more over the children whom they washed in the water of baptism.

While the soldiers were here, they saw a small boat approaching. They suspected what it actually proved to be, some malefactors who had fled and were now returning to the village to negotiate. The Spaniards concealed themselves on the shore. The three men in the boat proved to be three natives of Orote: two, Aguarín and Cheref, were prime movers in the war and in the death of Father Sebastián de Monroy; the third was an old man who had been host to the Venerable Father when peace flourished, but later became involved in the uprisings and took an important part in them as well as in the robbery of the church and residence in the village.

When they drew into the shore, the soldiers discharged their muskets, the sound of which was like thunder and lightning to those who did not expect it. The old man fell wounded into the sea, whereupon one of the natives who accompanied the Spaniards stabbed him in the eye with a lance. The other two fled and could not be overtaken.

They brought the old man up on land, and there was seen an example of the divine mercy that forgets our faults and remembers our good works and attends to the merits of God's servants. And so for the virtue of hospitality he had once extended to Father Sebastián de Monroy, God opened his eyes. He recognized that he had sinned and gave signs of repentance, and as he suffered the pains of death, he gained the life of grace and glory to which his soul took flight, just as he received baptism.

This happened on the seashore, almost on the very spot where they killed the Venerable Brother Pedro Díaz in defense of chastity, so that we can attribute to his blood and to the merits of Father Monroy the conversion of this *Indio*.

For some time past there had been some rebels in the village of Hanum, who, trusting in the inaccessibility of their location, disdained the mandates of the governor. The success they had enjoyed in the time of Sergeant Major Damián de Esplana had added audacity to their pride.

On that occasion, he tried to catch them unawares at night, but anticipating his stratagem with one of their own, they killed the man who was guiding the squadron and the soldiers withdrew.

Now the governor wished to humble their pride and arrogance, and on August 28, 1679, having traveled all night, he arrived at sunrise within sight of the village. His reputation had preceded him, and the *Indios*, who were posted as lookouts on the mountains, shouted warnings to their people of the danger and of our men's arrival.

The Spaniards realized that they were discovered and ran forward to invade the village by way of a ravine, hoping by swiftness to anticipate the organization of a defense by the *Indios*. But this they failed to do, and the natives, swarming above the slope, showered them with stones and lances.

The soldiers fought with spirit, on the defensive with their shields and on the offensive with their muskets, until the pass at last became so narrow that they could neither take aim at the enemy, who were hidden among the boulders, nor avoid the blows of the lances that caught them without cover and in close quarters.

At a time when neither courage nor fear could tell them which was the greater peril, to go forward or to go back, their spirits were fired with enthusiasm and they began to raise the cry, "Friends, if we die, let's die with honor! Their blood will pay for ours! Let's climb that rock to victory!" And with this, the bravest began to climb, encouraging the others by their example, even the friendly natives, and all climbed with such determination that the barbarians were frightened and discouraged and began to run headlong down the rocky slopes.

Now that our men occupied the ground, they began to wonder what they ought to do. The village was below them, defended by many natives, and they feared that if they attacked it, they in turn would be attacked by more barbarians who were in the hills, so that they might find themselves surrounded and the passes closed, leaving them no way out.

To avoid this trap, then, they divided the small squadron into four parts: one to occupy the eminence in order to observe the movements of the enemy and to hasten wherever they might later be needed; another group guarded the path and the narrow pass through the mountains; another was placed on the road to block the approach of any help that might be rushed to the enemy; while the largest group, which consisted of twenty men with a few friendly natives, attacked the village. The people there first threw a few lances at them, but soon fled to the sea to save themselves in their own boats. But this plan was useless, because the governor had forewarned the friendly natives of the neighboring village of Nisihan, who surrounded the village of Hanum with their boats. They did this with more than twenty boats, thus blocking every way of escape. As soon as they saw the Spaniards attack the village, they rowed to the shore and attacked the fleeing enemy, who encountered Scylla as they tried to avoid Charybdis, and unable to find any refuge, they threw themselves into the water or hid in caves, leaving their boats on the shore.

*Book Five, Chapter 21*

In this battle, the fiercest that had yet taken place in the Marianas, not one of our men was killed or wounded. A few of the enemy were killed and a few wounded. The houses, with everything that could not be used by the victors, were consumed in flames. Fifty boats that were taken as spoils of war were given to the friendly natives. Those they did not want were burned. The remaining booty was shared among the soldiers and the natives, except for the rice, which was kept for the general food supply and was taken by boat to Agadña.

While our men were enjoying a brief rest, two of the friendly natives, emboldened by victory, or perhaps coveting some booty, went on in advance of the others. And when they sat down to rest, the barbarians, who were hidden where they could see without being seen, threw lances at them, wounding one in the foot and the other in the side. They called out to the rest of the party, asking them to come to their aid. They ran up at once and scattered the enemy. But they could not extract the poisonous bone lance tip in the one man's side, and a few days later he died, giving his life for a good cause by becoming a soldier of the Faith and taking up arms for its extension and defense.

He was called Gregorio Ayirin, and had been among the first to be baptized when the fathers came to the islands, and he had lived a good Christian life. Now, having received the sacraments with demonstrations of true repentance, he died in the expectation of eternal salvation.

The victorious soldiers returned to Agadña, warning the inhabitants of all the villages through which they passed not to harbor the rebels until the latter had first made their peace with the Spaniards. And in this manner, the northern part of the island remained quiet.

During this year the diligence and courage of the islanders themselves served quite as well as the Spanish arms to rid the island of malefactors.

This was started by a woman who governed, insofar as the *Marianos* will suffer government, the district called Sydya, in the southern part of Guam, where they had killed the Venerable Father Francisco Ezguerra. This noble matron was devoted to Christianity and counseled her people, who were already tired of the constant unrest, to purchase peace and friendship from the Spaniards by means of the punishment of the delinquents.

Thus it was done. They delivered over to the governor some of the men who were guilty of the murder of Father Ezguerra. Some were taken alive; only the heads of the others were sent to Agadña. This served to quiet the country, and those natives were no longer fearful.

In Fuuña, some Spanish soldiers found two of the principal instigators of the war of Orote and the death of Father Monroy and his associates. They were taken as prisoners to Agadña, where the worst offender of the two paid for his crime with his life, while the other was set free, in order to give an example of justice and clemency.

I add here a tragicomic occurrence that shows the zeal of the natives in this hunt for wrongdoers. They caught a native who bore the

*New Gains of the Christian Community in the Marianas*

same name as one of the men they sought. The real criminal, a parricide, had fled the island, whereas the man they caught was innocent. The natives threw a rope around his neck, meaning to take his head to the governor. They left him for a moment, half strangled, and went for a knife with which to decapitate him. He began to recover, loosened the rope and was able to free himself. Fear of death gave him wings with which to flee from his pursuers. He presented himself before the governor, and with the aid of witnesses, established his innocence and the fact that he bore the name of the other man but not his guilt. One should not fail to mention the courage of Ignacio Ignete, a native noble, who was famous for his acts in favor of the Spaniards. A flagrant malefactor, without provocation, simply from a desire to shed blood, had treacherously killed a soldier of the *presidio*. He said that he knew perfectly well that some day he should have to die for his crime, but the Spaniards would pay well for it beforehand, since he intended to kill every soldier he could catch off guard.

Ignacio offered his services to the governor to search out and kill this wild beast who was threatening everyone with death. The governor agreed, and to give him some measure of authority, assigned a soldier to him. He set out with a group of companions to the place where they said the criminal was hiding, but when they got there, he had fled. Ignacio did find a man who could give him information and a boy whom he sent to the seminary in Agadña to be educated and instructed in the Christian manner.

As they started to search for the barbarian, some of the natives of the surrounding territory took up arms. Ignacio ran to them with his escort, and saw that they were merely bellowing in anger, complaining that prisons and jails, trials, judgments, and punishments for offences had been introduced into the country, which had never known of them before the arrival of the Spaniards. He said to them with great firmness: "Oh, either fight with me or obey the precepts of the Spaniards, because not by my will have I come to punish offenders. I came on their authority and I intend to defend their just cause with my blood and that of all my people. And I am certain that if I am beaten and killed by you, you will pay for it with your lives."

These words were pronounced with the authority of a man whose courage was known by all. Their arrogance melted away, and they said that they, too, would ally themselves with the Spaniards. Meanwhile, the man they were holding prisoner escaped, and the real culprit was not found. But Ignacio performed many other acts worthy of the Spanish courage he tried to imitate.

During all this time the missionaries never ceased their visits to the different parts of the island, with success worthy of their efforts, baptising children and adults who became Christians in their deeds as well as in profession and name.

But even after the whole island had been pacified, experience showed the Spaniards that they could not trust too far these barbarians, who were governed more by fear than by reason.

*Book Five, Chapter 21*

This was seen in the events of February 16, 1680, when the fathers completed a visit to settlements along the beach and started inland. They left the village of Pagat and climbed to the hill country around Macapaute. Meanwhile, they sent ahead some natives to advise the inhabitants of the vicinity that the fathers were coming to teach them. The villagers said they would welcome their arrival and would await them with anticipation.

Those were their words, but their acts belied them. When the fathers arrived in the vicinity on the following day, they sent ahead some natives of their escort to assure the people there of the goodwill with which they came. No answer came back, and the party, tired of waiting, went forward. Soon they saw armed natives running across the field, and the friendly natives advised the fathers to delay, saying there was an ambush in the valley.

Some of the companions of the fathers had already gone down the trail, where a very dangerous battle took place. The *Indios*, who were hidden, threw lances at our people, and these attacked courageously and wounded one of them with a lance and two with two musket balls each, after which the enemy fled abandoning the field. But the victory was not bloodless, for one of our companions was wounded in the leg. He was unable to follow them, and since to be separated from the group was unsafe, they all returned to the *presidio*. Although the governor went out to reconnoiter the area and punish the rebels for their perfidy, he did not find any who offered resistence or could be proved guilty.

On the opposite side of the island there was some disorder, because in the village of Hinca lived one of the killers of the Venerable Father Ezquerra, protected by his people from the friendly natives who on several occasions hunted him. The daring of Muta—that was his name— had so increased that he made war against the natives of the surrounding territory, although he came out the worse for it, because one of his confederates was killed by the other natives, who also burned many of their houses.

The governor, when he learned what had occurred, felt himself obliged to help those natives who had proved themselves loyal friends. He started for Hinca on March 29, 1680, and wishing to catch the enemy off guard, he spent the night at the edge of the village and attacked in the morning. However, he found no one there but women. He took away two women with small children in order that they might be baptized in the *presidio*, and also in the hope that by means of these hostages he could compel the children's fathers to make peace and come and establish friendly relations.

He passed through all the surrounding territory, burning the houses of the enemy, without encountering the least resistance, except for the village of Mapucun, where a native threw a spear at one of our natives, wounding him so severely that he died a few days later.

When the governor returned to the *presidio*, he was informed that the enemy had again taken up arms. He then set out again on April 11, 1680, and he had been on the road scarcely an hour when, on the beach, he met a boatload of natives who asked him to pause and receive a present that they had brought him.

This gift was the person of the prime mover in the recent uprisings, whom they had securely bound and whom the governor now sent to the *presidio* where he was later hanged, accepting his punishment with Christian fortitude, even exhorting his people to take warning and never dare commit offenses against the preachers of the Faith.

The governor continued to the place for which he had set out, but found that the enemy natives, already overcome and scattered by the loyal natives, had fled to their caverns.

The fathers, who had accompanied the governor on these journeys, sent the friendly natives here and there to bring in the children they might find to be baptized, and within two days they had baptized more than forty.

As a general rule, during all the battles and uprisings that were quelled during this year, Christ has won many souls because of the children who were baptized by those fathers who accompanied the soldiers, as well as those who became Christians by means of the visits that the fathers made for this reason over the greater part of the island.

But the greatest success was had in Agadña and its environs, where three *barrios*, or hamlets, have sprung up. To these, natives who lived in distant parts have lately moved, leaving their villages abandoned and even destroyed. This gave them a more stable home and the opportunity to attend Mass and Christian doctrine, which they do in the manner we have previously described: the married people, unmarried, and children being assigned to different days of the week, and all attending together on Sundays and feast days.

This year the reception of the sacraments has increased, as has the devotion to Holy Week and other feasts of the year, as well as the virtue of the children in the seminary and that of adults of advanced age, both men and women. These had formerly resisted the Divine Word, but they now take to their hearts the Law of God and listen attentively to the Fathers and what they teach. They not only receive well the Commandments of God but also the precepts of the Church, whose observance has influenced them noticeably.

In order that they may esteem highly the sacrament of penance, the fathers, not content with their receiving it once a year, have tried to have people receive the sacrament more often. Many have received Communion well prepared and instructed for their approach to that table. The number of marriages celebrated in church has increased, and some Christians have been punished severely for violating this obligation.

They may all be commended for the fact that, in spite of the poverty and limitations of the country, they dress decently.

I do not speak of the children who have died after being baptized, nor of the aged ones who recently baptized have exchanged this earthly life for life eternal, benefiting by the Precious Blood that was shed for them.

*Book Five, Chapter 21*

But all these things were flowers that became fruit during the following year, in which Christianity advanced rapidly with the foundation of new churches and villages.

# CHAPTER XXII

*Christianity in the Marianas Progresses Rapidly
With the Establishment of New Villages and Churches*

The galleon *Santa Rosa* arrived at the island of San Juan (Guam) on June 5, 1680, and although the fathers went out at once to obtain their supplies, of which they received the greater part, the remainder was carried on to the Philippines, for the reason that we have lamented on many other occasions. What was most regretted this year was the fact that the boat that *don* Juan de Vargas, Governor of the Philippines, sent to the mission was not delivered but passed by the islands.

General *don* Antonio Nieto, by order of the said governor, left here twenty Filipino soldiers, in addition to those sent from Nueva España, in order that the *presidio* might be better supplied with soldiers. But they had no officer, because *don* Antonio de Salas had left his post as governor, to which latter office General Antonio Nieto, on the advice of the missionaries at that time, assigned *don* José de Quiroga.

The superior of the mission in the Marianas at this time was Father Manuel de Solórzano, who succeeded to that position after the death of Father Bartolomé Besco, of whom I have no information by means of which I might eulogize him here. He was a religious man, very zealous for the glory of God and the good of souls, as he showed by his work in the missions in the Philippines and now recently in the Marianas, but the memory of his virtues lives on mainly in his Philippine Province.

It seemed to the new superior that it would be well to visit all the peaceful areas of the island in order to baptize all the children who had not yet received this sacrament. At the same time, the governor deemed it necessary to seek out the rebels and murderers, thus completing the pacification of the island of San Juan and ending all interference to the fathers on their missionary visits.

*Don* José de Quiroga set out, therefore, with his men and established his camp in the middle of the mountain called Machante. From there he sent out squadrons in every direction to look for rebels. Some were seized and their houses burned. The others were so frightened that they submitted to the governor. They asked for pardon and peace, which were granted on their promise of loyalty and the assurance that they would refrain from hampering the work of evangelization.

There were others who knew that the gravity of their offenses excluded them from all hope of pardon and were also aware that they would never be able to escape the diligent search of the governor. These people tried to ingratiate themselves by seeking out the principal authors of the tumults and delivering them over to the governor. One of those seized in this manner was a Christian *Indio*, Macazar, who had been in these islands since the wreck of the *Concepción* in 1638. He had lived as a man without religion, and the fathers had been unable, even from the beginning to influence him by counsel or exhortation to come and live among the Christians. In recent years he had become involved in the uprisings of the barbarians, until now, when he was facing death, God opened his eyes. He came to himself and realized that divine justice more than human justice had made him a prisoner, and weeping for his faults and asking to be reconciled with the Church, he at last merited eternal life, giving a clear demonstration of the divine clemency, which guards even the worst sinners in order that they may ask for mercy.

The news of what had been done on the island of San Juan alarmed the other islands. Thus it was that the cadaver of Matapang, the murderer of the Venerable Father San Vitores, was brought from Rota to Guam. They had placed him alive in the boat, but he died on the way from the wounds he had suffered from the lances of the men who seized him.

This example was followed by the people of Tarragui, who brought in the two killers of the Venerable Father Antonio María de San Basilio, one alive, the other dead. The former was soon executed, after having prepared himself for death in a Christian manner.

But the governor believed that the island of Guam could never enjoy complete peace if he also did not visit Rota, whither, as we have said, so many wrongdoers of Guam had fled. He notified the people of that island not to admit anyone from Guam and informed them that those who were already there would be treated as enemies. He paid a visit to Rota when the islanders least expected it, for the wind was unsuitable for sailing and it seemed impossible to make the voyage. He seized Aguarín, a prime mover in the past wars, as well as three other murderers of fathers or soldiers, all of whom paid for their transgressions with their lives.

He burned some villages in which the malefactors had been received and ordered more than one hundred and fifty fugitives returned to Guam, promising them complete security. He reconnoitered and subdued all the islands, accompanied by two fathers who baptized all the children who had been born since the beginning of the wars. He returned victorious to Agadña, where he immediately arranged for a festival of thanks to the Queen of the Angels for the happy outcome of his journey.

Now that the island of Guam was cleared of all disturbing elements and was pacified by punishment and fear, road building was begun. The dangerous passes and trials over steep cliffs were improved and made safer by the use of suitable tools. Not only the natives were employed in this labor but also the soldiers, on the example of their captain, who worked ceaselessly until roads were opened over which one could safely pass on foot or horseback.

After this, the location of villages received consideration. The most convenient locations were selected in which to assemble the natives in larger settlements. They were heretofore scattered in tiny villages or farming communities, some inaccessible, others too far from the center of administration. This plan was intended to facilitate the work of the fathers, a smaller number of whom would suffice if the people were not too widely dispersed.

In the eastern part of the island, on the shore facing north, the governor selected a location that is called Inapsan, which is spacious, pleasant, and abundant in trees for building purposes. It was surrounded by many hamlets, the inhabitants of which were made to move to the new town and build their houses there. But the river there did not have a good sand bar from which the men could launch their boats into the sea, a disadvantage to their fishing. Hence, a suitable channel was made by breaking through the coral reef, a task that the natives had judged impossible because of the breakers and the large rocks. But the undertaking was successful because of the constancy of the workers and their zeal for the glory of God. A large settlement was established, separated into two *barrios* that were about a mile apart. This division was an advantage both for fishing and farming.

At the same time all the settlements in the vicinity of Pago, which is two leagues distant from Agadña, were made to move in and establish homes in that village, which is in the part of the island that looks toward the south. Here they established a large settlement, no less agreeable than the other [Inapsan], for it is served by a large river that cuts the village in two, and which has a mouth suitable for launching boats. There are fields suitable for planting rice and vegetables, as well as an abundance of wood for the construction of houses, boats, and other things.

When the establishment of these villages was undertaken, fathers were sent to each to administer the sacraments and sustain the people with the bread of the Christian doctrine. And the natives, pleased to have the fathers in their midst, built a house for them in each place and a capacious church with three naves. The church in Pago was dedicated to the Virgin Mary, in honor of the Immaculate Conception. The church in Inapsan was dedicated to Saint Michael and the Heavenly Host.

The missionaries wished to establish another village on the southwest side of the island, near the port of Umatag, where the ships anchor that come from the Philippines. Their plan was at once put into execution by the governor and the soldiers, and in a short time a church was erected, which they dedicated to Saint Denis the Areopagite, a favorite devotion of the *Excelentsísima señora Duquesa* de Aveyro, to whose incomparable zeal and solicitude these islands owe not only their salvation but all their growth in matters both spiritual and temporal. A house for the fathers was also constructed. Because the location of the village was not spacious enough to admit all the people of the surrounding country, it was separated into two distinct parts, one of which was a quarter league distant from the other.

While the people were occupied in the construction of these buildings, an activity that brought so much joy and consolation to the fathers, there came, on November 11, 1680, a strong north wind that through the ensuring hours shifted to the east and became a furious typhoon that lasted throughout that day and the next, causing such destruction that not a single native house or wooden structure remained standing. Many fruit trees were uprooted and nearly half the boats on the island were dashed to pieces, and in the southern part, which was the last to be affected by the storm, the seas were so high that the people fled to the hills for safety, as if it were a day of judgment. It was worthy of notice that the *presidio* of Agadña and other royal buildings, which are in a location that is more exposed to the violence of the hurricane and the fury of the sea, received only very slight damage from the wind.

Throughout the island the roofs were blown off our houses and churches. Some houses of weak construction were completely destroyed, as were several plantings of corn.

God protected the governor and a good part of the troops from death, through no foresight of theirs. A short time before the typhoon they returned from an islet where they had been cutting wood for the Church of San Dionisio (in Umatag). If they had remained there two hours longer they would all have been swept into the sea, since the whole of the islet was covered and a portion of it was washed away by the furious beating of the waves, which carried off all the logs the men had cut.

The building of the church in Pago had progressed to the point where the upright posts and timbers were in place and the sleepers and other parts were in readiness. The storm tore out the rafters, broke the sleepers, and carried all the building material into a wood some distance away, a thing it would seem impossible for the sea to do so far inland.

Many circumstances suggest that the storm was not a natural phenomenon, but that it was caused by our common enemy, with the permission of the Lord. This was his ultimate effort against the Christian community, arming the elements against it, now that the humans had been disarmed, and tearing down the fortresses that the Faith possessed in these islands, namely the temples that were being built. But the demon ended up frustrated as usual, and God achieved his objectives, God who arrives at his goals so many times by roundabout ways, bringing Jonah to Nineveh by way of Tarsis. For the storm, by tearing down the houses of the natives, made it easier to gather them into the larger villages. The fathers at this time persuaded them that rather than repair their old homes, they should build new ones in the location assigned to them. And this they did, hastening to complete their houses, for they were otherwise without shelter.

With even greater haste, the churches were completed, and on December 8, 1680, to the joy of everyone, the church at Pago was dedicated.

On December 11, 1680, the church at Agat was begun. Many people from the north and west were assigned to this village. The church was dedicated to Saint Rose (of Lima).

Also a church was begun at Narajan (Inarajan), in which village many were assembled from the southern part of the island, as well as people from the settlements in the hills and on the beaches. This church was dedicated to Saint Joseph, spouse of the Virgin Mary.

In this manner and at the same time, all the island was occupied in building churches for God and houses for his ministers, who were greatly astonished at seeing so much activity on the part of people dedicated to leisure all their lives. Recently they had been enemies of the fathers, anxious to banish the church from the land and throw off the yoke of the Law of God, and now they were employed in constructing houses and temples where the Lord would be worshiped and where those men might dwell who taught his Law.

The governor, wishing to establish a political as well as a Christian government, assigned a captain to each village, with authority to rule in his name. The fathers designated individuals to act as *fiscales* in each church. This term *fiscal* is used in the missions of the Indies to indicate the ones whom Saint Francis Xavier called *canacapoles*, or *majordomos*, of the churches, whose duty it is to call the people to Mass and Christian doctrine; to inform the fathers when people were ill, in order that they may administer the sacraments; to keep an account of births; and to see that newborn infants are baptized. They also observe public morals in order that remedies may be applied when necessary, and, in short, they keep the missionaries informed about all that goes on for the benefit of the Christians and the growth of the Christian community. The *fiscales* perform their duties with great care.

There were more than a thousand baptisms this year (1680), including infants and adults.

I have not spoken of the temporal progress that has been made, although it is as important as the spiritual. The new regime has made rapid progress this year. Under it the children are learning many things that are necessary for human life. A special effort has been made to teach people to apply themselves to the cultivation of rice, maize, and those roots that they like, as well as cotton, which many know how to spin and weave, in order that they may have the means of feeding and clothing themselves. And when they are thus occupied in useful and decent pursuits, there will be no place for idleness, which is an old friend to the natives, but no friend to virtue, but a companion of vice.

Thus the affairs of the Christian community ran smoothly until the beginning of February 1681. When the church of San Miguel in Inapsan was completed a solemn dedication was planned in honor of that great patron of the islands, from whom, since the beginning, great favors had been received. On the third of that month, at midnight, someone set fire to the church in two places; who did it, we never learned. The wood was dry and it burned quickly, the fire spreading to the adjoining house of the fathers. They were not able to save anything, neither the images, the vestments, nor any articles at all, because when the fathers arrived on the scene, having been called by the natives at the first sight of the fire, the entire structure was enveloped in flames.

The natives felt this loss keenly, partly because their labor of many days had been destroyed in an hour, and partly because they feared that the father might suspect some treachery, and that he might not only abandon them but might even cause the governor to punish them. They begged the father not to leave them, since he knew them to be innocent. He promised to remain with them and sent a companion, a brother coadjutor, to Agadña to inform the superior of what had taken place. Even this was not enough to reassure the natives. I do not know if it was their natural timidity or a guilty conscience, but they took to their boats,

*Book Five, Chapter 22*

which stood on the shore. Not all of these were seaworthy and some of them sank. The others crossed to Rota, leaving the father alone with his house servants and with his regret at seeing his flock thus scattered, with almost no likelihood of their return.

As soon as the governor heard of this disaster he went to Inapsan, where he found the father with his few remaining companions. They all returned to Agadña to await the return of the natives to their old home. To this end the fathers sent messages urging them to return, telling them that they would be received as sons, and assuring them that the governor held nothing against them. If they had been guilty of setting the fire, the fathers said, they would also have tried to kill the fathers. But this they had neither done nor shown the least desire of doing.

In order that this untoward incident might not alarm the other natives and cause them to suspect that they were not trusted, since distrust is the mother of dishonesty, the fathers proceeded with the dedication of the church of San Dionisio, in Umatag, which was celebrated with due solemnity and rejoicing on February 15, 1681.

All the *Indios*, who were inclined to peace, regretted the burning of San Miguel Church and guarded their own churches with great care, especially the people of Pago, who posted sentinels at night around the church and the house of the father.

But this misfortune was soon followed by another distressing occurrence, which was caused, not by the natives, but by the Spanish soldiers of the *presidio*, and this caused harm to the whole Christian community.

One morning two Spaniards and three Filipinos took the boat in which the fathers usually went out to meet the galleons and receive their supplies and in which they made other short journeys. With no other supplies than a little water and three or four small baskets of vegetables, they set out for Manila, not considering the danger of the sea or the punishment that awaited them if they ever arrived in that port. Perhaps they thought they would find protection among some of the enemies of the mission of the Marianas. When their escape was known, they were still within sight of Guam, but they could not be overtaken by the natives who followed in their small boats.

But God, who knows how to obtain good from evil, gained from this flight a great benefit. The fact that this boat arrived at Manila after only five or six days, convinced those persons who believed it was impossible to sail that stretch of ocean between the Philippines and the Marianas. It was tried later, but in bad weather, by a small sloop [from the Philippines] that put into these islands in distress and afterwards, in good weather, attempted to return, we hope with more success, but we do not know the outcome.

The natives of Inapsan who had fled to Rota told the first messengers plainly that they would return. To the second message, asking the reason for the delay, they answered equivocally, and later showed plainly that they did not want to return. Finally, they joined with the *Rotanos* to resist the Spaniards if they decided to come to that island to subdue it.

*Christianity in the Marianas Progresses Rapidly With New Villages and Churches*

    The governor thought himself obliged to go there, and he set out on April 24, 1681, with some soldiers. They were met by the armed natives of Inapsan and Rota, but at the first attack by the Spaniards, they fled to the hills, leaving some of their number dead or wounded. The Spaniards burned the village in which the people of Inapsan lived and their boats as well. This was a lesson to open the eyes of those miserable *Indios*, so they would ask for peace and return to their former home. It is hoped that time and love will overcome the natural inconstancy of these natives, who through the mercy of the Lord are daily improving by the grace of baptism and Christian customs.

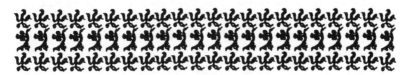

# CHAPTER XXIII

*The Present State of the Marianas Islands;*
*Success That Has Been Attained These Past Years and*
*What Is Hoped for in the Future*

The Faith was first planted in the Mariana Islands without the use of arms, in order that the people might know that it was a law of peace. The founder of the mission, the Venerable Father Diego Luis de San Vitores and his fervent companions, traveling over the islands without military escort, harvested the first fruits of a flourishing crop. But as the devil, the enemy of the happiness of souls, began to arm the barbarians against the ministers of the gospel, it became necessary, in order to preserve the work once begun and continue its progress, to resort to arms. In the same way, the priests in the time of Joshua, in order to throw down the walls of Jericho by the sound of trumpets, were protected by the army of Israel, so the ministers of Christ, the trumpets of the gospel, marched with an escort of soldiers, in order that the infidels and apostates might not silence the sound of the truth.[314] It has been necessary in this spiritual conquest, as experience has shown it is always necessary among barbarians, that our Spanish zeal carry in its right hand (the ecclesiastical hand) a plow and the seed of the gospel, and in the left (the secular) the sword and the lance, with which to prevent anyone from interfering with the work, until that time shall come when in the new lands the prophecy of Isaiah be accomplished for the law of grace, that they shall make plowshares of their lances and sickles of their swords, as we have seen in the case of the soldiers in this *presidio* who opened the hearts of the islanders with the plowshare of their teaching and reaped a harvest of souls with the sickle of the truth.[315]

Seeing the need of soldiers, the Venerable Father Diego Luis de San Vitores asked Her Majesty from the very beginning that two hundred Pampangos be sent here for the defense of the missionaries. Although the fathers were willing and even hopeful of giving their lives for Christ, the crown of martyrdom was very costly, because for every father who lost his life, many souls were lost who could have gained the life of grace, if he had been spared. For this reason the Venerable Father warned his companions to protect their own lives as far as they were able, and let God grant the crown of martyrdom to the one who deserved it; that though he himself desired martyrdom with all his heart, they still should not rush rashly into death and save their souls at the price of others losing theirs; that it was necessary for this land to be showered with the blood of martyrs, in order that the Church should reap her just harvest, but that it was not suitable that they should all die in that manner, for

---

[314] Joshua, chapter 6.
[315] Isa. 2:4.

## The Present State of the Marianas Islands

while some were needed to fertilize the soil, others would have to live to cultivate it and sow the seed.

In recent years we have felt all too keenly the lack of soldiers, because of the frequent uprisings, revolts, and snares. With these the barbarians have blocked the passage of the ministers on their journeys, sometimes obliging them to leave the other islands and gather on Guam, and even there they have at times had them surrounded so that they could not leave Agadña. This is the main reason why they have less success in recent years than in the earlier ones.

Nevertheless, the harvest of these twelve years has been worthy of a century. Fifty thousand Christians and many thousands of catechumens were left by the first apostle and founder, Father Diego Luis de San Vitores. Many hundreds of babies have been taken up to heaven immediately after their baptism. How many missionaries of the Society of Jesus have gained the crown of martyrdom, how many soldiers have died for Christ! And even in times of war and persecution the results have always been worthy of the labor, even though less than the zeal of the Fathers themselves. Many old superstitions have been uprooted; many thousands of baptisms accomplished; the frequent reception of the sacraments accomplished; public houses destroyed; marriages performed according to the rites of the church; and finally, there have been many examples of all the virtues, as I have frequently stated in this book, and which I now review briefly, to form them into a bouquet of beautiful flowers that will edify all the church with the fragrance of Christ, proving once again the fecundity of that great mother, who everywhere and in every age conceives and bears new children in holiness like their predecessors; and this for the consolation of older Christians who see today in a new land, a barbarous land, where a few years ago the name of Christ was not heard, where they did not know reason, law, or justice, a Christian society, with temples, religion, laws, and customs proper to Christianity, built upon the ruins of the errors, superstitions, and barbarism of the natives.

The veneration of the natives for the priests and ministers has increased notably, as their regard for the *macanas* has lessened. This fact contributed to the following occurrence: a certain *macana* had near his house a large stone. He persuaded the *Indios* to have respect for it in every way, and especially not to spit upon it, for if they did so, he told them, they would become insane. A missionary, who was passing that way, called a large number of the natives as witnesses. He then spat on the stone and called the soldiers who accompanied him to do likewise. Since they did not go mad, as the *Indios* there expected, the fathers told them to spit on it, too. By so doing they showed their scorn for the stone and the *macana*, and even admitted that they might formerly have been simple enough to believe him.

The same effect was attained by an investigation of the skulls that the *macanas* invoked, through which they promised rain and other benefits desired by the people. The result was that these and other instruments of superstition were reduced to ashes, including many lances tipped with human bones, to cure the natives of their impious practice of disinterring their dead in order to use their bones and of the cruel custom of using mortal weapons for whose poison there is no cure, if the bone remains in the flesh of the victim.

And the fruit of all this industry is felt when we see the natives more humane, more religious, more sincerely desirous of salvation, with more respect for the name of God, not shirking God's Law and heavy yoke, assisting devoutly at the Sacrifice of the Mass, celebrating the feasts with devotion, assisting attentively at Christian doctrine, attending to the fulfillment of their obligations, and making themselves more worthy of Holy Communion. This they desire and ask for, and it is given to all who are judged worthy to sit at the sacred table, to which the Lord calls the poor, the sick, the blind, and the lame, but which only those may approach who wear the wedding garment.[316]

Among all the people are visible signs of piety and devotion, especially in boys and girls up to eighteen years of age. They have built a chapel that they call Children's Chapel, to which nearly two hundred come daily to hear the Christian doctrine. And it is a joy to see that among these boys and girls there are many who are able to explain to others the essentials of the doctrine, such as who God is; how many persons there are in God; where he is; whom he rewards, and whom he punishes; what is mortal sin, venial sin, original sin; what is necessary to make a good confession and communion; and what would make a confession invalid. When asked what is the grace of God, they answer, "That which makes us friends of God, which frees us from hell and brings us to heaven, if we die in the grace of God." If one of the feasts of Christ or the Blessed Virgin is near, and the father says that it would be well to go to confession, they take the insinuation as a precept and prepare the evening before. Then they come to church very early in the morning and ask for a confessor. Nor is that the whole story. Not content to possess this treasure themselves, they try to share it with others. A boy will take the responsibility for four or five men and the girls for as many women and teach them the prayers and the mysteries of the Faith, helping the fathers to catechize in a brief time a whole village. If one of their adults does not come to hear the doctrine, the young person responsible for him reports it to the father. They also report as to who learns the doctrine well and who does not, and when the father examines these adults, he finds that the young people report truly, these young teachers. Thus they teach what they have just learned and the perfect praise of God is twofold, issuing from the mouths of these innocents, who praise the Lord and teach others to praise him.

The young people are the ones who are most careful to inform the missionaries about the sick of their village, so that they may administer the sacraments, and in the absence of the priests, they help them to a pious death by having them repeat acts of faith, hope, love and conformity to the will of God. This is a function that they have studied for such emergencies.

One day a father encountered a boy nine years old who, crucifix in hand, was helping a dying boy twelve years old by repeating the

---

[316]Matt. 22:11-13.

Act of Contrition. With no less zeal they inform the fathers of newborn infants so they may come and baptize them. In one case, a thirteen-year old girl summoned a father to come and baptize a newborn baby. She was returning ahead of the father, when she turned and saw that he was not hurrying. So she made signs from a distance, imitating the paroxysms of a dying person to tell him to come quickly, because the child he was to baptize was on the point of death. The father ran and brought the infant eternal life, because he baptized it as soon as he arrived and the baby died immediately.

What has most clearly shown the virtue of these young people is their chastity, something quite foreign to this region. One soldier, for instance, failed to conquer a young girl with promises and threats. So he insulted her by saying, "You're only an *India* anyway." But she answered, "I am an *India*, but a Christian *India*." Another girl, fifteen years old, when solicited by another soldier, bravely repulsed all his persuasions with the fear of God, whom she believed was present, and sent the soldier on his way saying, "Go on, get away from here. Don't you see that God is here?" They are constantly reminded to realize that God is present, so that they will not say or do anything unworthy of his divine eyes, and this consideration is a great help to avoid faults.

Other young girls of the same age, when offered gifts much esteemed by those people, have spurned them or simply hid themselves from the man, and one thirteen-year-old threw the gift her lustful suitor had sent her right in his face. A group of girls was returning from Christian doctrine when they met some Christians in name but hardly in practice, who solicited them. But all of them fled, crying out as they fled, "We are Christians, we are Christians." This sort of thing has happened so often that one solder said to a religious who was exhorting the old Christians not to scandalize the new ones and not to tear down with their evil lives what the word of God was building, "Does the father suppose that one word will make a conquest of one of those girls? Many days of warfare are not enough to overcome one of them."

The married *Indios* who live in the *presidio* offer just as edifying examples. One of them, whenever her husband had to go out to fight the enemy, had to win another war, a more dangerous one, against a man who tried by every means that mad love could dictate to break down her resistance. She resisted in a Christian manner, but to escape the danger inherent in such combats, she fled to the church and asked the father to find a remedy, because she did not wish to sin against either God or her husband. Another woman was solicited with gifts by a person whom a native woman would find it most difficult to resist, because she feared his position of authority. He had her brought to his house, called her to an empty room and expressed his desire. But she gave him no answer but to turn her back and leave him talking, as she exited the house in all haste, that poor native woman, that new Christian, imitating the conduct of the chaste Joseph.[317] These are the effects of holy matrimony, these and their subjection to their husbands, whom they recognize as their head and

---

[317]Genesis, chapter 39.

superior. And these are women raised in a land where the wife commands and the husband obeys. And this chastity they learn in the girls' school where they are brought up with special care. Many marry boys brought up in the boys' school, so that they are ready to live as married couples who are an example to the Christian community, living in peace and harmony and faithfulness and raising their children in the fear of the Lord. I shall not praise here the usefulness of the schools for boys and girls, of which I have already spoken. I shall merely add that one of the missionaries wrote to Her Majesty, praising the royal piety for their foundation. He called the children the novices of the Christian community, from whom the Faith hopes its greatest growth.

Nor will I speak of the *Marianos* of greater age, who have also given examples of their devotion, such as one who was almost martyred by a *macana*, and others who have died in wars against the infidels as soldiers of the Faith.

But if the harvest that has been gathered up to the present time through the grace of God is great, what remains to be gathered is in comparison far greater, that ultimate harvest of the blood shed by so many martyrs, not only to be gathered in the thirteen Mariana Islands, which their first apostle discovered and enlightened, but also in the innumerable islands that lie south of the island of San Juan. This island will be the doorway through which the light of the gospel will shine upon those new islands, as Father San Vitores always desired. Although we do not know exactly what is their number nor their size and population, it seems that all this is very great, according to the narration of certain *Indios* from there who in the year 1664 were blown from that southern mountain chain and landed on Lalaos [Palaos] and from there came to Siao.[318] A father of our Society questioned them about their country, its government, and religion, and they gave an account of more than fifty islands so full of people that they swarmed like ants. They said they had kings, but that must be only in name, because he does not make laws, and his subjects know no laws but their own appetites; that all his sovereignty was enclosed within a house that was long and built low, and that served him as a habitation and palace. They adore a divinity whom they call Loguiling, whom they say has three sons. One is in heaven, one embarked for an unknown locality, while a third is a great boat builder, who instructs men in that art. They give their deity a father and a mother and they say that he resembles them, perhaps. I say nothing of the hopes Father San Vitores entertained that the Faith would travel from these Mariana Islands to Japan, at the cost of much labor and expense, if this desire of all Christianity were ever realized.

In order to promote these hopes, which are also the wishes of God, who desires the salvation of all souls, and also of His Majesty, whose interest is in the service of God, Father Xaramillo, of our Society, and a missionary in the Marianas, wrote to the king, our lord, since His Majesty commanded that he do so, setting forth the means necessary for the conservation and extension of this Christian community. In this letter of

---

[318]Sian in Indonesia.

*The Present State of the Marianas Islands*

December 20, 1680, he also replies to various objections that are made against the Marianas, by persons who are moved, some by temporal interests and some by I know not what feelings. For the persecution that this mission suffered, when Father San Vitores first attempted its establishment, has not ceased. Winds and tempests are constantly raised against it by the enemy of souls and will be, until the Lord of the elements commands the waves and their pride to be calm, and the winds and the sea obey him.[319] Oh, may his fatherly care convert the gale into a fair following breeze and the opposition into zeal, in order that the fruits of heaven may be harvested in a land watered by the blood of its first apostle and many apostolic companions. May he send new laborers in regions where the harvest is great and the laborers are few, kindling in all the spirit of his great servant the Venerable Father Diego Luis de San Vitores. And may we, who cannot cooperate in any other way, may we assist the preachers of the gospel in the salvation of souls by our prayers, penances, and tears, so that those who are seated in the shadow of death may be reborn to the light of the Faith, in order that all men may know and praise and glorify Jesus Christ, our Savior and Redeemer, who with the Father and the Holy Spirit lives and reigns forever and ever. Amen.

**Laus Deo.**

---

[319]Mark 4:41.

# APPENDIX

### Prayer of Saint Francis Xavier

Eternal God, Creator of all things, remember that the souls of infidels have been created by You and formed to Your own image and likeness. Behold, O Lord, how in Your dishonor, hell is being filled with the same souls. Remember that Jesus Christ, Your only Son, suffered a most cruel death for their salvation. Do not permit, O Lord, I beseech You, that Your divine Son be any longer despised by infidels, but rather, being appeased by the prayers of Your saints and of the Church, the most holy Spouse of Your Son, deign to be mindful of Your mercy: and forgetting their idolatry and their infidelities, bring them all to know Him Whom You did send, Jesus Christ, Your son, our Lord, who is our health, life and resurrection, through Whom we have been saved and redeemed, to Whom may glory be given forever and ever. Amen.

# GLOSSARY

**Accidental glory:** A special gift additional to the basic happiness of heaven.

**Account of conscience:** A discussion of one's religious experience, generally with one's superior or spiritual advisor.

**Act; Public Act; Grand Act; *Acto*:** A ceremonial public examination. *See* Book 1, chap. 7, n. 4.

***Acto de Contrición*** (Spanish): *See* Book 1, chap. 7, n. 7.

**Additions:** Special directions to assist one in making the spiritual exercises of St. Ignatius.

***Agnus Dei*** **(Lamb of God):** A wax medal stamped with a relief of a traditional image of the Lamb in Revelations, Chapters 5 and following.

***Anites, anitis*** (Chamorro): Spirits or souls of the ancestors.

***Audiencia*** (Spanish): Tribunal, especially the tribunal with general jurisdiction over Mexico; also the Philippines.

***Bachiller*** (Spanish): Bachelor, one who has received the lowest degree in a university or theological seminary.

**Canonical hours:** The breviary.

***Castillas*:** A *Mariano* word meaning Spaniards.

***Cédula; cédula real*** (Spanish): A decree; a royal decree.

***Chapin*:** Literally a patten with a thick cork sole. Here, a certain sum of money given to the queen.

***Cilicio*** (Spanish): It may mean a hair shirt or a chain worn as a penance. García usually uses the word to mean "chain".

***Colegio*** (Spanish): A school combining primary and secondary levels.

***Contemptus Mundi*** (Latin): Contempt of the World.

***Corona*** (Spanish): Rosary, either the prayers or the chaplet of beads.

***Corregidor*** (Spanish): A royal magistrate with jurisdiction in all civil and criminal cases in a specified district.

***Dago*** (Chamorro) (*Dioscorea alata*): A plant with an edible root; also called *nica*.

***Daog*** (Chamorro) *(Calophyllum inophyllum)*: the tree called *maría* or *palo maría*; its wood.

**Discipline:** A whip used for self-inflicted scourging as a penance; the scourging itself.

***Donado*** (Spanish): A lay missionary serving as a volunteer, neither a priest or a Jesuit.

**Examination of conscience:** *See* particular examination.

***Fiscal, fiscales*** (Spanish): A layman or laymen who supervised religious observance of the natives; an attorney general.

**Four Last Things:** Death, Judgment, Heaven, and Hell.

**General:** The general superior of a religious order.

***Guirrago; guilagu*** (Chamorro): A Caucasian; a foreigner.

***Hermano*** (Spanish): Brother. García uses the title to mean:

  1. A Jesuit brother, *i.e.* a Jesuit with the vows of a Jesuit, but with no intention of becoming a priest.

  2. a Jesuit with the vows of a Jesuit, but (normally) in preparation for the priesthood.

  3. a volunteer working in the mission who is not a Jesuit.

**Holy day of obligation:** A day when attendance at Mass is obligatory.

## Glossary

***Itinerarium*** (Latin): A traditional prayer for travelers.

**Jubiliee:** A religious activity for which an indulgence is granted.

**League:** The Spanish *legua* was a little more than three miles.

***Manjar blanco*** (Spanish): A dish made of shredded chicken, rice flour, and milk.

***Merindad*** (Spanish): A district (including villages) under the jurisdiction and care of a city.

**Minister:** The second in command in a Jesuit community, in charge of the details of administration.

***Nica*** (Chamorro) (*Dioscorea esculena fasciculata*): A plant with an edible root , also called *dago*.

***Oidor; oidores*** (Spanish): One of the five chief magistrates, a judicial and legislative council, which, with the governor, governed New Spain.

***Palo maria; maria; daok*** (Chamorro) (*calophyllum inophyllum*): A type of tree; its wood.

***Pardao:*** A Portuguese coin.

**Particular examination:** A method of examining one's conscience prescribed in the book, *Spiritual Exercises of Saint Ignatius*, aimed at eliminating a particular fault or acquiring a particular virtue.

***Paso***: A statue or group of statues representing a scene from the Passion of Christ carried on a float in a Holy Week procession.

***Patache*** (Spanish): A small sailing ship, generally used as a tender.

***Pequi; pake*** (Chamorro): A small gun; a musket.

***Processus*** (Latin): The legal steps leading, if successful, to canonization.

**Professed house; *casa profesa*:** a Jesuit residence not attached to a school, expected to live on alms.

**Profession of four vows:** The final vows taken by priests of the Society some years after completion of studies for the priesthood.

***Rima, lemai*** (Chamorro): Breadfruit.

***Romance*** (Spanish): Ballad.

***Saetilla*** (Spanish): A short devotional verse; literally a small arrow, *saeta*.

***Sangley*** (Tagalog): A Chinese doing business in the Philippines.

***Santo Christo*** (Spanish): A crucifix.

**Scholastic:** one who has taken his vows as a Jesuit but is not yet a priest. García sometimes calls a scholastic *padre*, sometimes *hermano*.

**Sodality:** A religious organization for lay persons whose activities include prayers and social services.

**Third probation:** A period devoted to spiritual renewal lasting several months, which completes a Jesuit's formation.

**Venerable:** A title indicating the initial stage of the process of canonization. Used loosely by García of anyone whom he considered a martyr.

***Villa***: A residence outside the city, where Jesuits could spend their weekly day off or a longer holiday.

***Visita***: A mission station served by visiting priests who rested elsewhere.

# ACKNOWLEDGEMENTS

Among the books slated for discard at the Jesuit school in Manila was an aged vellum-covered volume that caught the young man's attention and sparked his curiosity because the words *Islas Marianas* were in the title. Since he was from Guam, one of the Mariana Islands, he quickly picked it up. When he returned to Guam after his studies, in the late 1920s or early '30s, Francisco Muña De la Cruz–*don* Paco– carried the book with him and eventually presented it to a friend, the late Reverend Monsignor Oscar L. Calvo.

*Don* Paco's copy of Father Francisco García's *La vida y martyrio del venerable Padre Diego Luis de Sanvitores, de la Compañía de Jesús, primer apóstol de las islas Marianas....* (*The Life and Martyrdom of the Venerable Father Diego Luis de Sanvitores, of the Society of Jesus, the First Apostle of the Mariana Islands...*) may not have been the first to reach the islands, but that particular book, an original 1683 publication, is known to have survived Guam's wars, earthquakes, and typhoons.

Father García's work is a compendium of five books, written in Spanish and running to more than five hundred pages. It is among the earliest religious and historical records of the people of the Mariana Islands and, as such, since Spanish is no longer commonly spoken or understood among them, the importance of translating it to English – today's *lingua franca* – was recognized some sixty-five years ago, if not earlier.

Many people have contributed to the preservation of the original book and to rendering it into English, and it is fitting to acknowledge their contributions.

When the Micronesian Area Research Center was established at the University of Guam in 1967, those associated with the Center recognized the need for an historical component that would address the long period of Spanish administration in the Mariana Islands. Thus MARC's Spanish Documents Collection came into being, and over time faculty members Sister Felicia Plaza, M.M.B., María Teresa del Valle, Marjorie G. Driver, Dale S. Miyagi, and Omaira Brunal-Perry have contributed to its growth.

MARC's first director, historian Paul Carano, encouraged research and acquisitions that focused on the importance of Father San Vitores and the Spanish presence in the Marianas. As a consequence, one of the Center's first undertakings was the transcription and translation of two hundred pages of microfilmed documents from Mexico's Archivo General de la Nación, historical documents concerning the establishment of the 1668 Jesuit mission in the Mariana Islands. The work, completed between March and September 1967 by Marjorie Driver, was published in MARC's Working Papers Series, Numbers 13 and 14.

In the fall of 1968, Sister Felicia Plaza, M.M.B., prepared a xerographic copy of the original García book – printed in old Spanish script – from the Agaña diocesan archival collection of Bishop Apollinaris

514

*Acknowledgements*

W. Baumgartner, OFM, Cap. Also that year, Sister Felicia obtained a copy of a typescript of the old book prepared by Sister Dolores Larrañaga, M.M.B., during her 1950-52, teaching assignment at the Mount Carmel School in Saipan.

Among materials collected at MARC during its early years were complete sets of the *Guam Recorder*, a monthly periodical published locally from March 1924 to November 1941. In 1935 Margaret Manlove Higgins, the wife of the commanding officer of Guam's Naval Hospital, arrived on Guam. Because of her interest in the island's people and her extensive knowledge of Spanish, she undertook the translation of the historically-based components of García's Books III and V, an endeavor in which she was assisted by Father Pastor de Arráyoz (1931-40), one of the local Spanish Capuchin priests. The translation entitled "The First History of Guam" was published serially in the *Guam Recorder* between September 1936 and July 1939.

In 1968 Marjorie Driver compiled the *Guam Recorder* selections, prefaced them with biographical data and an acknowledgment of Margaret Higgins's work, and prepared an annotated table of contents. Later, in 1985, the Nieves Flores Memorial Library, under the direction of Territorial Librarian Magdalena S. Taitano, assisted by Rose Atalig, Mildred Tai, and members of the Library's staff, re-printed the *Recorder* articles (selections from Books III and V) and published them in a single volume under the title of the original work, *The Life and Martyrdom of the Venerable Father Diego Luis de San Vitores*.

In 1969 Professor Driver prepared what was to prove a valuable tool for subsequent translators: a comparative index, line by line, chapter by chapter, of the translated and yet-to-be translated sections of García's five books.

In keeping with its focus on the importance of Father San Vitores's work and the growing interest in his beatification, in 1969, MARC contracted with a firm in Madrid for a translation of Alberto Risco's *En las islas de los Ladrones. El apóstol de las Marianas; Diego Luis de San Vitores...*, a biographical account of the martyred priest, published in Bilbao, in 1935. The translation entitled *On the Island of Thieves*, was completed and returned to MARC for publication in 1970. Unbeknown to MARC, another translation of the same book entitled *The Apostle of the Marianas*, had been prepared by Father Juan M.H. Ledesma, S.J., edited and published by Monsignor Oscar L. Calvo, Diocese of Agaña, in 1970. At Father Ledesma's request, Director Paul Carano agreed not to published the Center's translation. The unpublished manuscript may be consulted at MARC.

Through Sister Felicia Plaza's acquisitions' efforts at institutions overseas, a large number of documents pertaining to the San Vitores period soon accumulated in MARC's Spanish Documents Collection, and, as she was aware of the local efforts underway toward the beatification of the Jesuit missionary, she prepared – with the assistance of Albert L. Williams, the Center's librarian – a bibliography of the San Vitores materials held in MARC's collections. Her compilation was published in

*Acknowledgements*

1975 as *Sanvitores. Bibliografía de las materias existentes en el Microneisan Area Research Center,* MARC Bibliography Series No. 2.

In 1976, copies of the *Bibliografía* were presented to Bishop Felixberto C. Flores, D.D., to Father Juan M. H. Ledesma, S.J., and to others interested in the effort to beatify Father San Vitores. While Sister Felicia was in Madrid seeking materials for MARC's Spanish Documents Collection and because of her work on behalf of the beatification effort, she, Bishop Flores, and Father Ledesma were invited to an audience with Spain's king, Juan Carlos. On this occasion, a large oil painting depicting the martyrdom of Father San Vitores was presented to Bishop Flores on behalf of the Instituto de Cultura Hispánica. A photograph of the presentation is on display at MARC's Spanish Documents Collection and the painting is at the Basilica Museum.

In 1977 Emilie G. Johnston, the curator of MARC's Pacific Collection, compiled and published a series of articles from the *Guam Recorder* (New Series) under the title *Father San Vitores, His Life, Times, and Martyrdom.* The popular booklet, MARC Publication No.6, has been reprinted several times.

During her years at MARC (1968-77), Sister Felicia Plaza's untiring and very successful acquisitions trips to Micronesia and abroad earned her the nickname "The Vacuum Cleaner" among her colleagues. Her legacy also includes hundreds of index cards and innumerable pages of transcriptions and translations held in the Spanish Documents Collection. Among her translations are García's Books I and II, as well as Chapters 1, 2, 3, and 4 of Book III. In 1980, her translation of the Book III chapters was published as MARC Working Paper No. 22. Her work and Mrs. Higgins's form part of the present English translation.

Father Juan Ledesma, assisting the postulator for the cause for beatification of Father San Vitores, found Sister Felicia's *Bibliografía* useful in his research in Guam, Spain, and Rome as he prepared documentation for the volume *Beatificationis seu declarationis martyriis servi dei Didaci Aloishii de San Vitores. Positio...,* published in Rome, in 1981. In it there are numerous references to MARC's resources and credits to its faculty. In October 1982, the Spanish Documents Collection received a copy of this *Positio* autographed by Bishop Flores: "I hope this official *Positio Historica* on the beatification of the Venerable Father Diego Luis de San Vitores, S.J., proto-martyr of the Mariana Islands, becomes part of the precious collection of historical documents that MARC preserves for reference purposes." Father Juan M. Ledesma, S.J., added "For MARC with best wishes". A few years later, Father Ledesma prepared an English translation of the *Positio...,* entitled *The Cause of Beatification of the Venerable Diego Luis de San Vitores, Apostle of the Marianas.*

During the 1980s Sister María Teresa Arias, M.M.B., MARC's research associate in Madrid, located important information there and in Burgos concerning Father San Vitores for MARC's Spanish Documents Collection. Some of the materials had been published during his lifetime; some were materials pertinent to the training and daily activities of the

*Acknowledgements*

Jesuits of the period. Sister Arias also sent copies of materials published in Spain at the time of the beatification, including a set of photographs of the faithful who made the long trip to Rome to attend the beatification ceremonies at the Vatican, on October 6, 1985.

After the beatification of Father San Vitores in 1985, Father Ledesma labored for the next four years completing the English translation of García's volume. This included the untranslated chapters of Book III, all of book IV, and the untranslated chapters of Book V. When it was finished, Father Ledesma's assistants in Baguio, Flor and Teri, re-typed the translations of all five books, a typescript of some 912 pages. After it arrived at MARC in 1989, the script was bound in five separate volumes, in order to facilitate review and editing – and Marjorie Driver finished the comparative index she had begun twenty years earlier.

In 1992, Father James A. McDonough, S.J., of the University of Guam faculty, received a grant from the Guam Humanities Council to edit the compiled English translation of García's work, and Professor Driver, curator of the Spanish Documents Collection, gave him a set of the materials re-typed in Baguio by Father Ledesma's assistants in the late 1980s. The grant enabled Rosita Dueñas Tosco to prepare a computerized rendition of the manuscript, which after completion, was turned over to Father McDonough for editing and possible publication by the Guam Humanities Council.

In June 1999, at Father McDonough's request, and following unsuccessful attempts by the Guam Humanities Council and the University of Guam Press to publish his work, an agreement was reached between the University of Guam and the Guam Humanities Council that enabled MARC to publish Father McDonough' manuscript. On June 10, 1999, the Acting Executive Director of the Guam Humanities Council, Mark Skinner, presented "five floppy disks of the entire translation and the printed text as edited by Father James McDonough" to Professor Driver, of MARC's Spanish Documents Collection.

In the spring of 2000, Father Thomas B. McGrath, S.J., MARC's former publications editor, although retired from MARC and the University, began work as guest copy editor for Father McDonough's manuscript, but, unexpectedly, Father McGrath was soon re-assigned to a Jesuit mission in Africa.

Meanwhile, with copyediting yet to be done, Melissa G. Taitano, an off-island graduate student, was home for the summer of 2000, and at the time she was contracted by MARC to prepare the manuscript for formal publication. Her work was to include publication design and layout, image editing and development, as well as consultation with manuscript editors and printers. She continued her work on the project during the summer of 2001.

In the early fall of 2001, MARC's director, Dr. Hiro Kurashina, assembled a number of volunteers to ready a memorial copy of the complete English translation of Father Francisco García's *Life and Martyrdom of the Venerable Father Diego Luis de San Vitores* for presentation to His Excellency Archbishop Anthony S. Apuron, OFM

*Acknowledgements*

Cap., D.D., of the Diocese of Agaña, before the end of the year. The manuscript, sown by Magdalena de L.G. Castro with cover design and calligraphy by Ron Castro and encased in a beautiful ifil wood box carved by Robert Taitano, was presented to the Archbishop in commemoration of the 350th anniversary of the Ordination to the Priesthood of Blessed Diego Luis de San Vitores. Dr. Harold L. Allen, President of the University of Guam, made the presentation at the 9:30 Mass at the Cathedral-Basilica, on December 23, 2001.

Shortly thereafter, a copy of the commemorative manuscript was turned over to Marjorie G. Driver, of the Spanish Documents Collection, for final copyediting and publication. At long last, with the technical assistance of Mary M. Castro, the manuscript was completed for publication in early 2003.

As noted earlier many people have contributed their time, talent and interest to the preparation of this translation. Although there may be others, those known to have contributed in some way are the following:

**Translators**
> Margaret M. Higgins
> Sr. Felicia Plaza, M.M.B.
> Fr. Juan M.H.Ledesma, S.J.

**Editor**
> Fr. James A. McDonough, S.J.

**Copy Editors**
> Fr. Thomas B. McGrath, S.J.
> Marjorie G. Driver

**MARC Faculty and Staff (1967-2002)**
> Paul Carano, Director, 1967-76
> Marjorie G. Driver, 1967-
> Emilie G. Johnston, 1967-82
> Rosita Dueñas Tosco, 1967-91
> Sr. Felicia E. Plaza, M.M.B., 1968-77
> María Teresa del Valle, 1968-71
> Fr. Thomas B. McGrath, S.J., Editor, MARC Publications,
> 1968-73; 1977-95
> Albert L. Williams, 1973-89
> John P. Sablan, 1976-
> Hiro Kurashina, 1981-, Director, 1986-88; 1991-2003
> Rose P. Hatfield, 1984-2003
> LaVonne C. Guerrero-Meno, 1991-
> Omaira Brunal-Perry, 1992-
> Kenneth L. Carriveau, Editor, MARC Publications, 1995
> Dirk A. Ballendorf, 1979- Editor, MARC Publications, 1996-
> Thomas Iverson, 1998- Editor, MARC Publications, 2001-

**University of Guam, Presidents**
> Antonio C. Yamashita
> José T. Nededog
> Harold L. Allen

*Acknowledgements*

## Guam's religious community (1967-2002)
Bishop Apollinaris W. Baumgaratner, OFM, Cap., D.D.
Archbishop Felixberto C. Flores, D.D.
Archbishop Anthony S. Apuron, OFM Cap., D.D.
Msgr. Oscar L. Calvo
Fr. Thomas B. McGrath, S.J.
Fr. Juan M.H. Ledesma, S.J.
Fr. James A. McDonough, S.J.
Fr. Francis X. Hezel, S.J.
Fr. Daniel J. Mulhauser, S.J.
Sr. Felicia E. Plaza, M.M.B.
Sr. Dolores Larrañaga, M.M.B.
Sr. María Teresa Arias, M.M.B.

## Legislative Support
Senator Anthony C. Blaz, Twenty-Third Guam Legislature

## Photographs courtesy of
Sr. María Teresa Arias, M.M.B.
Lawrence Cunningham
Emilie G. Johnston
Hiro Kurashina

## Nieves Flores Memorial Library
Magdalena S. Taitano, Territorial Librarian
Rose Atalig
Mildred Tai

## Guam Humanities Council
George Boughton, Chair, 1989, 1999
Donald H. Rubinstein, Chair, 1996
Marilyn C. Salas, Chair, 1997
Omaira Brunal-Perry, Vice Chair, 1997, 1998, 1999
Joseph E. Quinata, Executive Director, 1997
Mark Skinner, Acting Executive Director, 1998-99
Jillette Leon Guerrero, Executive Director, 1999-

## UOG Press
Joyce M. Camacho, Dean, Graduate School and Research
Jane Jennison-Williams
Michael T. Hamerly

## Graphic Center
Brian Bell
Rick Biolchino

## Others
Francisco Muña de la Cruz
Melissa G. Taitano
Magdalena de Leon Guerrero Castro
Robert Taitano
Mary M. Castro
Ron J. Castro

# THE BOOK

Msgr. Oscar L. Calvo and Francisco Muña de la Cruz–*don* Paco de la Cruz.
From *Guam Tribune Weekender*, 2 December 1983, *Panorama* section.
"A Rare Book on Father Sanvitores" by Msgr. Oscar L. Calvo.

# THE TRANSLATORS

Margaret M. Higgins

Fr. Juan M.H. Ledesma, S.J.

Sister Felicia Plaza, M.M.B.
With King Juan Carlos, of Spain and
Bishop Felixberto Camacho Flores, of Guam

# PRINCIPAL EDITOR

Fr. James A. McDonough, S.J.

Fr. James A. McDonough, S.J. received a doctorate in Classical Philology from Harvard University (1953). He has published two critical editions of works by Gregory of Nyssa under the auspices of the Harvard Institute for Classical Studies in the Netherlands: *Inscriptiones Psalmorum* Brill, 1962 and *Contra Fatum* Brill 1987. There is a work in progress with Dr. Hedwig Hoerner of the Goethe University at Frankfurt-am-Main by Gregory of Nyssa entitled *De Opificio Hominis*.

He was a distinguished professor of languages and literature as well as an administrator at the University of Guam from 1969–1994 when he retired and shortly thereafter was given Emeritus status. Fr. McDonough returned to the classroom for special courses and completed his teaching career at the end of the semester in which he celebrated his 90th birthday in 2001. With a gift for languages he reads widely and confers an enthusiasm for learning. In addition he has been a Jesuit for over 70 years and brings his experience to bear on this work. Through his efforts this account of Jesuit missionary efforts in Guam and the Marianas written from first hand accounts by García is presented in translation for the first time in one complete edition.

# THE COMMEMORATIVE PRESENTATION

Presentation of commemorative volume of *The Life and Martyrdom of the Venerable Father Diego Luis de San Vitores...* December 23, 2001.

Front row left to right: Dr. Dirk A. Ballendorf; Fr. James A. McDonough, S.J.; Archbishop Anthony S. Apuron, of the Diocese of Agaña; Dr. Harold L. Allen, President, University of Guam; Back row left to right: Prof. Marjorie G. Driver; Mr. Rick Biolchino; Dr. Hiro Kurashina

# COPY EDITOR

Marjorie G. Driver

Photos: From the collection of the R.F. Taitano Micronesian Area Research Center

# INDEX

## A

Acapulco 90, 95, 138, 146, 151–153, 158–160, 234–236, 292, 316, 354–355, 383, 406, 420, 437, 452, 461, 481

*Acto de Contrición* 44, 52, 54–55, 59, 75, 79–80, 83–84, 88–89, 91, 96, 100, 107, 110, 112–113, 115, 117–118, 121, 129, 136, 167, 212, 279, 287–288, 308, 404, 505, 513

Aguarín, don Diego 430, 458–459, 463, 471–473, 479, 481, 491, 499

Alcalá 39, 42, 47, 49–54, 62, 64, 66, 73, 78, 84, 260, 276, 289, 305, 309, 311, 315, 322, 324–325, 332, 348, 419, 471, 475

Alexander VII, Pope 33, 45, 91, 184

Almanzor, Muhammad 4

Alonso Antolínez, Fernán 4–5

Alonso Maluenda, María. *See* San Vitores, María Alonso Maluenda de San Vitores

Alonso Maluenda, María. *See* San Vitores, María Alonso Maluenda de San Vitores

Aloysius Gonzaga, S.J., Saint. *See* Gonzaga

Ambrose, Saint 264

Andrade, S.J., Alonso 61, 64

*anites, aniti* 174, 179, 191–192, 194, 206, 236, 245, 247, 287, 359, 366, 372, 407, 512–513

Antolínez. *See* Antolínez. See Alsonso Antolínez, Fernán

Apóstol de las Indias y Nuevas Gentes 91

Arda 61–62, 64

Aristotle 184, 300

*auto-de-fe* 86

Aveyro, Duchess of 262, 499

Ayhi, don Antonio de 236, 385, 470–471, 481

## B

*babaos* Dios 370

Baños, Condes de 78, 95, 296

Baños, Condesa de 84

Bárcena, Ventura de 97

Basilio, S.J., Antonio María de 392, 442–443, 445–446, 448, 451, 457, 467, 488, 490, 498

Bazán, Diego 188, 223, 247–249, 251

Besco, S.J., Bartolomé 325, 497

Bonies, S.J., Brother Baltasar 488

Bouwens, S.J., Gerard 404, 435, 463

Bovens. *See* Bouwens, S.J., Gerard

Brigid, Saint 315

Bucao 114, 118

*Buen Socorro* (galleon). *See Nuestra Señora del Buen Socorro*

Bungahun 116, 121, 132, 135

Burley. *See* Buru

Buru 141

Bustillos, S.J., Lorenzo 144–146, 158, 186, 188, 192, 197–198, 200, 205, 207, 210, 213, 216, 218, 229, 240–241, 266, 268, 272, 275, 278, 284–286, 288, 294, 299–302, 305, 309, 312, 319, 321–324, 326, 332, 412, 430, 445

## C

Cardeñoso, S.J., Tomás de 148, 156, 158, 186, 234, 247, 314, 429, 432, 489

Casanova, S.J., Pedro de 158–160, 176, 186, 204–205, 212, 215, 229, 260–261, 282, 287, 305, 314, 353, 356, 365, 372, 375, 377

*Casos Raros de la Confesión* 45, 53–54, 87–88, 107, 308, 312

cassock 59, 147, 201, 261–262, 303–304, 322, 377, 380, 423, 432

*chamorri* 169, 174, 187

charity 5, 12, 40, 43, 48–49, 70, 79, 83, 100–104, 118–120, 124–125, 139, 142, 148, 158, 176, 182, 188, 225, 233, 235, 252, 254, 262, 264, 268–269, 273, 275–276, 313, 326, 329, 337, 339–340, 344, 349–351, 359, 361, 376, 381, 391, 395, 398–399, 411, 414–415, 419, 439, 446–447, 449, 453, 461, 465, 467, 469

charity and zeal 104, 182, 360, 397

Charles II of Spain 143

chastity 40, 248, 285, 288, 305, 332, 338–339, 436, 438, 443–444, 466–468, 490, 507–508

Cheref 460–461, 490

Chigi, Fabio. *See* Alexander VII, Pope

Chinese (Choco). *See* Choco

Chinese fleet against Manila 103

Choco 188, 190–199, 203–204, 208–209, 212, 214–215, 238, 240, 246, 271, 283, 359, 398, 402, 409

Clement IX, Pope 228, 259

Clement VII 94

Coemans, S.J., Peter 424, 427, 447

525

*Index*

Colegio Imperial 7, 10, 13, 18, 30, 62, 254, 399

Comano, S.J., Pedro. *See* Coemans, S.J., Peter

*Concepción* (galleon) 144, 160, 166, 171, 213–214, 251, 393, 497

contemplative prayer 287

costume of San Vitores 189, 201

Counsel, Gift of 307–308

Counsel, Our Lady of Good 13–14, 22, 31, 44, 80, 127, 363

Cruz, Hipólito de la 221, 365, 368, 370

Cruz, Marcos de la 99, 115, 133–134, 313

Cuenca, Mateo de 96, 132, 321–322

**D**

dance 170, 184, 278, 391, 436, 454

devil. *See* Bucao

Díaz, S.J., Pedro 438–439, 441–443, 457, 467, 490

discernment of spirits 310, 316

doctor 29, 50, 55, 60–61, 63, 88, 93, 155, 170, 253, 262, 310, 318–319, 325, 347, 445–446

Dominic de Guzmán, Saint 6, 292, 324

*donado. See* Cruz, Marcos de la

**E**

Esplana, Captain Damián de 254, 424, 453

Esplana, Captain Juan de. *See* Esplana, Captain Damián de

examination of conscience 47, 338, 466, 512

exorcism 178, 204

Ezquerra, S.J., Francisco 229, 234, 245–247, 250, 351, 397–398, 400–402, 404, 408–414, 418–421, 424, 427, 431–432, 442, 448, 456, 467, 492, 494

**F**

faith *(gratis datae)* 310

faith (virtue) 428

Farnese, Alessandro 4

fasting 8, 15, 19, 42, 174, 178, 216, 278, 302, 341, 379, 422, 427

fear of God 307, 399, 414, 485, 507

fevers 61–62, 128, 277, 312

fortitude (virtue of) 264, 298, 307–308

Francis Borgia, Saint 61–62, 66, 254, 292, 341

Francis Xavier, Saint. *See* Xavier, Saint Francis

**G**

galleon, none in 1670 314

Gonzaga, S.J., Saint Aloysius 3, 6, 8–9, 13, 15, 31, 39, 266, 292, 341

González, S.J., Tirso 76, 300, 463

Graces *"Gratis Datae"* 3, 95, 175, 264–266, 268, 289, 310, 318, 325, 333, 351, 374, 376, 450, 464

Guadalupe, Our Lady of 80, 194, 368, 374, 452

Guadalupe, Our Lady of (Church of) 207, 221, 371

Guadix 12, 75

Guillén, S.J., Juan Gabriel 47–48, 76, 84, 87, 104, 210, 262, 273–275, 279, 300, 311–312, 316, 396–397, 463

*guirragos* 223, 370–371, 454, 457, 470

**H**

Healing (grace of) 310–311

Holy Spirit (gifts of) 307, 310

Hope (virtue of) 101, 268

*hulitaos. See urritaos*

Hulk, the 404

Humility (virtue of) 188, 230, 305–306, 337–338, 346, 349, 376, 415, 421–422, 447, 461, 465

Hurao 235, 238–239, 241–242, 386

**I**

Ignatius of Loyola, Saint 6, 13, 15, 24–25, 28–29, 31, 33–34, 43, 46, 50–51, 59, 61–62, 66, 70, 72, 75, 85–86, 92–94, 112, 116, 129, 136, 140, 145–146, 148, 192, 194, 204, 210, 220, 230, 234, 241, 246, 251, 254–255, 259, 266, 269, 278, 282, 285–287, 291–292, 295, 303, 305, 308, 314, 332, 339, 341, 343–344, 348, 356, 361, 373, 383, 396, 398, 402, 408, 418, 442, 447, 465–466, 512–513

Ignete, Ignacio 493

Indies, greed, corruption 137, 152, 154, 218

Interpretation of Words (gift of) 310, 317

**J**

Joseph, Saint 42, 204, 289, 338, 341, 382, 403, 418, 425, 474, 500

Justice (virtue of) 264

**K**

Knowledge (gift of) 307–308, 310

**L**

Ladrone Islands 95–96, 99, 136–139, 141, 144–145, 148, 151–152, 157, 165, 171, 253, 259, 290, 351, 397

Lawrence, Saint 45, 213, 292, 318, 341

526

# Index

Legazpi, Muguel López de  137
Letrán, Seminary of San Juan  205, 229, 278, 283
López de Gomara, Francisco.  *See* Gomara, Francisco
López, S.J., Alonso  208, 229, 234, 245–246, 391–393, 401–402, 419, 424–427
López, S.J., Jerónimo  44, 53–54, 61–62, 85, 98, 111, 120, 203, 300, 308
Lorenzo the Malabar  214, 299
Loyola. *See* Ignatius of Loyola, Saint

## M

*macana*  173–174, 226, 235–237, 240–241, 243, 312, 368, 505, 508
Magellan, Ferdinand  167
Magnanimity (virtue of)  230
Mancera, Marqués and Marquesa de  151, 207, 260, 378, 404
Mangyan religion  119, 121, 123, 131
Mangyans  113, 116, 118, 121, 123–124, 126–134
Maralaya Mountains  110, 112, 299
*Margarita* (galleon)  213, 437
Mariana de Austria  23, 142, 160, 207, 209, 259, 289, 403
Mariana Islands  1, 81, 93, 113, 142, 158–160, 163, 165, 176, 190, 232, 257, 260, 262, 269, 274, 279–280, 286, 293, 295, 301, 311, 315, 323, 325, 327, 329, 342, 349, 353, 373, 375, 385, 397, 401, 446, 451, 453, 463, 479, 504, 508
Mariana Islands, the name  96
Marianos, religion  183, 188, 209, 226, 283, 355
Marianos, social and political institutions  168, 174, 176, 183, 206, 238, 276, 278
Marianos, visit to Philippines and Mexico  229, 231–233
marriage  5, 21, 77, 104, 106, 109, 113, 117, 120, 172, 452–453, 455–456, 479, 482, 497, 505
martyrdom  1, 5, 7, 22, 25, 42, 46, 58–59, 65, 69, 73, 76, 81, 87, 97, 99, 158, 163, 186, 200, 207, 214–215, 221–222, 225, 229, 235, 246–247, 249, 251–255, 257, 262, 268, 280, 287, 292, 299, 301, 304, 307, 318, 321, 324, 327, 329, 350, 356–357, 361, 364–365, 368, 372, 378, 382–383, 385, 399–400, 402, 408, 416, 420–424, 442–443, 449, 456, 465, 504–505
Mary, Blessed Virgin  9, 22–23, 31, 110, 165, 182, 225, 269, 276, 331, 333, 337–338, 342, 345, 361, 403, 499–500
Mastrilli de Sammarsan, S.J., Marcello  60, 95, 99, 145, 224, 255, 318
Matapang  251–253, 388, 436–437, 498
Maunahun, Francisco  392–393
*meris*  442
Mexico City  88, 94, 151, 154, 156, 159, 232–234, 248, 279, 283, 445, 464, 469
Mindoro  112–113, 123, 125, 131, 133–134, 136, 147, 262, 286, 290, 299, 311–313, 316
miracles  3, 39, 75, 92, 131, 134, 146, 197, 209, 287, 305, 312, 321, 358, 374, 382, 383, 433, 452
Monroy, S.J., Sebastián  442, 455–457, 459–464, 467–468, 484, 490, 492
Morales, S.J., Luis de  158, 160, 179, 186, 192, 194, 198, 201, 210–212, 216, 229, 277, 354, 393
Moros. *See* Muslims
mortification. *See* penance
Muñoz, Admiral Bartolomé  153, 157, 159
Muslims  106

## N

Naujan  113, 115–116, 120, 124, 127–128, 131, 133
nearsightedness  14, 29, 132, 202
Nicomachean Ethics  300
Nidhard, S.J., Johann Eberhard  142
Nieremberg y Otin, S.J., Juan Eusebio  45, 290
Nieto, Captain Antonio  149–150, 236, 386, 468, 497
Noriega, S.J., Diego de  229, 234, 246, 398
*Nuestra Señora del Buen Socorro* (galleon)  228–232, 235, 424, 447, 464, 469

## O

obedience  17, 20, 26, 31, 36, 39, 42, 54, 60, 64, 66, 69, 72, 74, 80, 96, 111, 145, 207, 229, 243, 246–247, 277, 280, 285–286, 288, 294–295, 302, 307–308, 343–344, 346, 376–380, 396, 404, 415–418, 439–440, 447, 460, 463, 466–467, 490
Olivares, Conde-duque de  23
Oropesa, Colegio de  43, 229, 296, 395, 439

## P

Palaos (Palau?)  508
Palma, S.J., Luis de la  20, 59, 165
Palo maría  166, 168, 181, 512–513

*Index*

Parma, Duke of. *See* Farnese
Paz, O.P., Juan de 104–105
penance 8, 15, 31, 47, 52, 88–89, 91,
    100, 103, 120, 139, 145, 154, 158,
    179, 181–182, 189, 192, 201, 222,
    227, 253, 255, 265, 269, 278, 291,
    293, 302, 304, 313, 319, 336, 348,
    350, 354–355, 375, 379, 384, 395,
    421–423, 439–440, 447, 463–464,
    466, 474, 476, 486, 495, 509, 512
Philip IV 23, 61, 140, 144, 259, 289
piety (gift of) 262, 277, 285, 307
Poblete (Archbishop of Manila) 140, 148,
    260, 415
poetry (native) 169, 442
Pola 116, 133
Portrait of San Vitores 74, 154–155, 255,
    266–267, 323–325, 349
poverty (religious) 230, 285, 288, 304,
    351, 380, 447, 453, 465
prophecy 3, 23, 25, 38, 76, 91, 97, 133,
    156, 310, 313–314, 321, 345, 399,
    504
prostitutes, rehabilitation of 77
prudence (virtue of) 104, 264, 281, 349
purgatory 31, 38, 52, 84, 142, 157, 232,
    293, 315–316, 441

**Q**

Quintanadueñas, S.J., Juan de 5
Quipuha 159, 176–177, 181, 188, 243,
    247–248, 356, 376, 399
Quipuha (don Juan) 188
Quiroga, José de 497

**R**

Rambla. *See* San Vitores, José
Ramírez, S.J., Diego 7, 15, 24–25, 33–34,
    59, 285
refuge for women 94
Rodríguez de Carvajal, Nicholás 453,
    459, 468
Rodríguez, S.J., Simón 140
Rose of Lima, Saint 427, 430, 433, 458,
    500
Rota 159, 165, 167, 204, 208, 212, 227,
    229, 245–246, 362, 392, 398, 402–
    403, 418–419, 436–437, 439, 457,
    482, 489, 498, 502–503
Rouxl, S.J., Basilio de 488
Ruíz, Francisco (Alférez) 488

**S**

Saint Bonaventure 341, 425
Saint Joseph 42, 204, 289, 338, 341,
    382, 403, 418, 425, 474, 500
Saint Michael 103, 155, 240–241, 341,
    388, 425–426, 428, 433, 451, 474–
    476, 499

Saint Paul's Earth 130–131, 135
Salamanca 76, 78, 229, 439
Salas, Juan Antonio 479, 497
Salgado, S.J., Francisco 488
*San Antonio de Padua* (galleon) 453, 469
San Antonio de Umatag (fort) 385–386,
    402, 435, 452, 479, 484, 488, 499
San Basilio, S.J., Antonio María de 427
*San Damián* (galleon) 95–97
*San Diego* (galleon) 145–146, 149, 313–
    315, 385, 420, 468
San Gil, parish of 6
*San Telmo* (galleon) 231, 254, 404, 435,
    479
San Vitores de la Portilla, Jerónimo 3–4,
    21, 31, 131, 148, 182, 255, 260,
    321, 323–324, 395, 397, 439, 440
San Vitores, Joseph 4
San Vitores, María Alonso Maluenda de
    3–5
San Vitores, Miguel de 5
San Vitores, O.S.B., Alonso de 4, 18
Sangley. *See* Choco
Santa Ana (island). *See* Rota
Santa Cruz, Captain Juan de 149, 191,
    193, 196, 219, 222, 225, 236, 239,
    369, 371–372
Santa Inés Mountains 110–111, 299
*Santa Rosa* (galleon) 497
Santiago, Captain Juan de 219, 236, 387,
    389–390
Sasanlago (Socanrago) 167
Sergeant Major. *See* Esplana, Captain
    Damián de
slaves 106, 116–117, 120–121, 123–126,
    157, 298, 416, 458
Sodality of Our Lady 10, 49, 289
Sodality of Saint Francis Xavier 39, 91,
    94, 154, 159, 178, 283, 351
Solano, S.J., Francisco 83, 95, 229, 234,
    246–248, 309, 385–386, 390–392,
    394–401, 404, 418, 420–421
Solórzano, S.J., Manuel de 497
Song 33, 271, 292
song 127, 170, 174, 278, 428, 486
Soon, Alonso 481
Soriano, Saint Dominic. *See* Dominic
    Guzman, Saint
Spinola, S.J., Charles 221, 365
Stephen, Saint 72, 292
Summa Theologiae 264

**T**

Tagalog language 98–100, 102, 106, 120,
    127, 129, 168, 308, 316–317
Tagalog people 113, 116–119, 126, 129,
    133, 149, 167, 198
Tapia, José 388, 425–426, 429, 435

*Index*

teacher. *See* doctor
teaching methods 278
temperance 264, 294, 302
Teresa of Avila, Saint 244, 292
Ternate 141, 190
Thomas Aquinas, Saint 281, 341
Tongues (gift of) 132, 149, 160, 310, 316
tuberculosis 229, 246, 385, 400

**U**
Ugarte, Ventura de 153
Umatag. *See* San Antonio de Umatag
Understanding (gift of) 307–309
*urritaos* 171, 206–207, 212, 367, 369,
 391, 438, 455, 457, 485

**V**
Vallejo, S.J., Tomás 488
Velas Latinas 165
Vidal, Cristóbal Javier 90, 93–94, 154,
 156, 232, 311
virtues (cardinal). *See* virtues (moral)
virtues (in general) 10, 13, 36, 39, 43,
 48, 92, 175, 182, 247, 259, 264–265,
 285, 292, 297, 305, 374, 381, 395,
 421, 438, 447
virtues (moral) 264
virtues (theological) 246, 248, 264, 307,
 343, 439
Visayan people 134, 251, 392
visions of the Blessed Virgin 145, 157,
 176, 186, 194, 343

**W**
War on Guam 234–235, 248
War on Tinian 212, 215, 248
wisdom (gift of) 307, 309
Words of Wisdom/of Knowledge (gift of)
 310
writings of San Vitores 288–289, 308, 331–
 332, 334, 344, 374, 376, 378, 380

**X**
Xavier, S.J., St., Francis 3, 13, 15, 31, 39,
 60–63, 65–70, 75, 79, 83–85, 91–
 95, 111–112, 114, 116, 118, 120–
 122, 124–125, 128–129, 133–135,
 140–142, 145–146, 151, 154, 156–
 157, 159, 178, 192, 194, 201, 204,
 206, 210, 220, 224, 234, 241, 243–
 244, 255, 260, 266–267, 278, 283–
 284, 286–287, 291–292, 305, 310,
 318, 341, 348, 351, 354–356, 359–
 361, 382–383, 393, 396, 428, 431,
 433, 438, 442, 449, 474, 501

**Z**
Zarpana. *See* Rota

Printed in the USA
CPSIA information can be obtained
at www.ICGtesting.com
JSHW081742031224
74705JS00004B/22